THE HOLLOW PARTIES

PRINCETON STUDIES IN AMERICAN POLITICS

Historical, International, and Comparative Perspectives

Paul Frymer, Suzanne Mettler, and Eric Schickler,
Series Editors

Ira Katznelson, Theda Skocpol, Martin Shefter,
Founding Series Editors

A list of titles in this series appears in the back of the book.

The Hollow Parties

THE MANY PASTS AND DISORDERED PRESENT OF AMERICAN PARTY POLITICS

DANIEL SCHLOZMAN

SAM ROSENFELD

PRINCETON UNIVERSITY PRESS

PRINCETON & OXFORD

Published by Princeton University Press
41 William Street, Princeton, New Jersey 08540
99 Banbury Road, Oxford OX2 6JX

press.princeton.edu

Library of Congress Cataloging-in-Publication Data

Names: Schlozman, Daniel, author. | Rosenfeld, Sam (Political scientist), author.
Title: The hollow parties : the many pasts and disordered present of American party politics / Daniel Schlozman and Sam Rosenfeld.
Description: Princeton : Princeton University Press, 2024. | Series: Princeton studies in American politics | Includes bibliographical references and index.
Identifiers: LCCN 2023034315 (print) | LCCN 2023034316 (ebook) | ISBN 9780691248554 (hardback) | ISBN 9780691248639 (ebook)
Subjects: LCSH: Political parties—United States—History. | Democratic Party (U.S.) | Republican Party (U.S. : 1854–) | Right and left (Political science)—United States. | Political culture—United States. | BISAC: POLITICAL SCIENCE / American Government / General | POLITICAL SCIENCE / History & Theory
Classification: LCC JK2261 .S3558 2024 (print) | LCC JK2261 (ebook) | DDC 324.27309—dc23/eng/20231113
LC record available at https://lccn.loc.gov/2023034315
LC ebook record available at https://lccn.loc.gov/2023034316

British Library Cataloging-in-Publication Data is available

Editorial: Bridget Flannery-McCoy, Alena Chekanov
Jacket: Karl Spurzem
Production: Erin Suydam
Publicity: James Schneider (US), Kathryn Stevens (UK)
Copyeditor: Jamie N. Thaman

Jacket Credit: American flag photograph by Noah Wulf / Wikimedia Commons

Printed in the United States of America

10 9 8 7 6 5 4 3 2 1

For our parents: Kay Lehman Schlozman, Stanley Schlozman,
Frances Hoffmann, and Richard Rosenfeld

TABLE OF CONTENTS

Illustrations are gathered after page 144.

THE HOLLOW PARTIES

1

The Problem of Hollow Parties

MAY 19, 1981: Richard Richards, chair of the Republican National Committee (RNC), sat alone at a table. It was a testy breakfast at the Capitol Hill Club. A who's who from the emergent New Right, whose myriad groups stood apart from the formal party, all avoided Richards: Terry Dolan of the National Conservative Political Action Committee, Paul Weyrich of the Committee for the Survival of a Free Congress, direct-mail impresario Richard Viguerie, Phyllis Schlafly of Eagle Forum and STOP ERA, Reed Larson of the National Right to Work Committee, Ed McAteer of Religious Roundtable, Tom Ellis of Jesse Helms's Congressional Club, and billionaire oilman and John Birch Society member Bunker Hunt. Richards, a conservative but tradition-minded political operative from Utah, had complained about the independent groups making mischief where the party did not want them. Their lavish advertising campaigns and repeated interventions in primaries usurped the traditional roles of the political party. The New Rightists were, he told them, like "loose cannonballs on the deck of a ship."[1]

Nonsense, responded John Lofton, editor of the Viguerie-owned *Conservative Digest*. If he attacked those fighting hardest for Ronald Reagan and his tax cuts, it was Richards himself who was the loose cannonball. The contretemps soon blew over, and no future formal party leader would follow Richards's example and again take independent groups to task. But it was a sign of the transformation sweeping American party politics, as the Right's loose cannonballs eventually came to dominate and define the Grand Old Party.

February 3, 2020: With all eyes on Iowa, the state Democratic Party offered up a kaleidoscope of party dysfunction. Following rules set down by the Democratic National Committee (DNC), the state's presidential nominating caucuses that year were set to be the most transparent on record. Iowans would gather in school gyms and cafeterias to debate their choices for a nominee, ascertain which candidates had met viability thresholds to elect county convention delegates, and reallocate supporters of candidates below the threshold. Precinct chairs would then use a smartphone app to submit three vote tallies: the number of supporters for each candidate both before and after reallocation, and, by a formula, the number of state delegate equivalents. That, at least, was the plan.

Then came reality. The cumbersome app, developed by a secretive start-up poetically named Shadow Inc., had not been properly debugged after last-minute modifications ordered by the DNC, and it soon broke down. Chairs who wanted to call the Iowa Democratic Party hotline to report results, as they had in caucuses past, failed to get through. Faced with catastrophe, the state party vanished, reporting no results until late the following afternoon, long after the candidates had departed for New Hampshire.[2]

Unable to implement the DNC's rules, the Iowa Democratic Party had failed to perform the basic task of election management. Enervation in the state party, of a piece with atrophied state and local party organizations throughout the country, had taken its toll. Meanwhile, para-organizations like Shadow that had emerged in the void left by formal parties faced distinct incentives and little accountability for grifting and incompetence. And in the days that followed the caucuses, the incompetence ironically fueled conspiracy theories that reached far beyond Iowa. The DNC, the theories alleged, was actually working all *too* competently to manipulate the process and deny the people's voice. Underneath all the recriminations was the caucus process itself, an artifact of the Democrats' 1970s-era party reforms. Their aim had been to take control from the bosses and give parties a new civic vitality. Inside the school gyms came signs of that civic vitality. But the breakdown that followed said something different.

The Richards breakfast and the Iowa debacle, four decades apart, tell two sides of the same story. Contemporary American parties are hollow parties. Hard shells, marked with the scars of interparty electoral conflict, cover disordered cores, devoid of concerted action and positive loyalties. Organizationally top-heavy and poorly rooted, the parties are dominated by satellite groups and command little respect in the eyes of voters and activists alike. Nobody, whether in the formal parties themselves or in the proliferating groups that swirl around them, has effectively brought political elites and the mass public together in positive common purpose.

Hollowness matters because parties matter. When vigorous and civically rooted parties link the governed with their government while schooling citizens in the unending give-and-take of political engagement, they give legitimacy to democratic rule. They bring blocs of voters together under a common banner, negotiating priorities among competing interests to construct agendas that resonate in the electorate. They render politics into ordered conflict, playing by the electoral rules of the game and gatekeeping against forces that might undermine such shared commitments. In each of these roles, competing parties at their best serve as stewards of democratic alternatives. When they falter, so does the political system.

Party hollowness has developed alongside polarization in linked but distinct processes. Paraparty groups like those that gave Dick Richards headaches in 1981 proved key instigators in both developments, as ideological warriors seeking simultaneously to tear down the power and prerogatives of the Republican Party and to make mercenary use of that very party. The two major parties now manifest hollowness asymmetrically, reflecting different pathologies in their approach to power—put bluntly, Democratic ineffectuality on one hand and Republican extremism on the other.

If ours are hollow parties, what might un-hollow parties look like? This book looks to the past for our yardstick. The long history of American party politics reveals no golden age but rather disparate fragments of a more vital organized politics to take to heart. Through the nineteenth century, parties rooted themselves deeply in everyday civic life. One of those parties stands out. Republicans in the party's first decades, from the 1850s through Reconstruction, pushed forward a party vision at its loftiest as they fought to save the Union and redeem the promise of American freedom. A century later, issue-oriented Democratic reformers mobilized partisan action for New Deal liberalism and civil rights. In those same years, cadres of practical-minded Republicans embodied a conservatism resistant to extremes and grounded in nuts-and-bolts organization. The past, in short, provides no model party to recover but offers suggestive models aplenty of American parties that succeeded where hollow parties fall short.

The coming chapters trace the path, stretching back to the Founding in the eighteenth century and running all the way forward, that has brought American political parties to their present state. But before our historical narrative begins in earnest, this chapter frames the problem of hollow parties and our approach to explaining it. We first define party hollowness and sketch its emergence since the 1970s. We then outline our wide-angle view of party. Finally, we end the chapter with a discussion of our perspective as scholars and as citizens in a troubled democracy.

Party Hollowness

Worry pervades the American political scene. The watchwords blaring from covers in bookstores and newsstands all tend toward doom: "dysfunction," "division," even "crisis" and "democratic backsliding." Yet political parties' specific contributions to our present discontents remain a subject of strikingly little consensus or clarity. Commentators peg parties alternatively as culprits in or casualties of toxic political conflict.[3] But whether as villains or victims, parties are nowhere accounted for as collective actors whose trajectories require explanation in their own right. Instead, they occupy a paradoxical status in descriptions of the polarized country's predicament: seemingly everywhere and nowhere, overbearing and enfeebled, all at once. This book untangles that paradox.

Party teams in both government and the mass public now define the politics of a polarized era, whose signal feature is dislike of political opponents that often rises to anger.[4] And as measured in sheer activity, from electioneering to advocacy to outreach, the actors in and around the parties *do* plenty—and, at least within circumscribed realms, have significant impact in doing it. But for all that activity, political parties neither set the terms for nor control the passions of our unruly politics.

Hollowness, we argue, is the condition that makes sense of these contradictory tendencies. Hollow parties are parties that, for all their array of activities, demonstrate fundamental incapacities in organizing democracy. This distinctive combination of *activity* and *incapacity* manifests itself across multiple dimensions. As a civic presence in an era of nationalized politics,[5] hollow parties are unrooted in communities and unfelt in ordinary people's day-to-day lives. Organizationally, they tilt toward national entities at the expense of state and local ones. Swarming networks of unattached paraparty groups, without popular accountability, overshadow formal party organizations at all levels. Finally, hollow parties lack legitimacy. The mass public and engaged political actors alike share neither positive loyalty to their allied party nor deference to the preferences of its leaders.

Today's parties are distinctive for the presence of so many figures entwined with and buzzing around but not organizationally part of formal party organizations themselves. We give this disorderly assortment surrounding each party a collective term that captures its amorphous and undirected quality: the party blob.[6] Fueled by the dual explosions of Second Gilded Age wealth and small-dollar online fundraising, the two party blobs now overshadow the formal parties. For many of these paraparty organizations, neither electoral success nor policy achievements serve as the front-and-center goal or metric of success and accountability. That leaves the core tasks of a political party—to corral allies and build electoral coalitions sufficient to take control of government and implement an agenda—paradoxically underserved. With outside groups dominating political life, the formal parties serve as punching bags for ideological activists and candidate operations more than as conscious stewards of a political enterprise.

The party blobs contain multitudes: single- and multi-issue ideological groups, many of them with paper members or no members at all; media figures, from talk-show hosts to online personalities, guided by profit and celebrity at least as much as by substantive or electoral goals; think tank policy wonks generating party programs by proxy; traditional Political Action Committees (PACs), run by interest groups and politicians, trading favors with their colleagues; nominally uncoordinated Super PACs and dark-money 501(c)s; billionaire megadonors with varied and often idiosyncratic agendas; and an ever-changing array of consultancies peddling technical services in electioneering, digital politics, and political finance in hopes of grabbing a share of all the money sloshing through the system. The defining feature of the party blob is precisely this amorphousness—a jumble of principals and incentives that contradict scholarly depictions of "party networks" seamlessly coordinating in the pursuit of shared goals.[7]

With the parties' incapacity to power purposive action and the party blobs' ascendance have come diminished expectations. Raise the bar for parties, and contemporary limits come into sharper relief. Back in 1987, the political scientist Kay Lawson took prescient note of what had already been lost: "The weaknesses of the parties in articulating and aggregating interests, recruiting and nominating their own candidates, and devising programs for which such candidates can in fact be held accountable are regarded as no longer worth mentioning: such functions are no longer what parties are all about."[8] Parties now find themselves hobbled in pursuit of all of the tasks on Lawson's list. As real political actors with particular claims and commitments—as opposed to mere abstract markers of identity—parties neither engender trust and loyalty from nor provide a source of meaning and belonging to most Americans. And the problem feeds on itself: the activity and incapacity that together characterize hollow parties render them particularly unsuited for conscious public conversation about parties and their place in public life.

How Hollowness Happened

We date the emergence of a hollow-party era to the demise of what scholars call the "New Deal order" by the late 1970s.[9] The historical accounts in ensuing chapters emphasize just how much was up for grabs, and how different party politics might have been, had the struggle come out differently during the critical juncture of the 1970s. Alternative political worlds for the parties, still possible at the eve of this "pivotal decade," became occluded in its wake.[10]

Two core processes worked in tandem to reshape American politics beginning in the 1970s: neoliberalism (to use an elusive but necessary organizing concept) and party polarization.[11] The postwar political economy had tied together steady growth, fixed exchange rates, active economic management focused on stimulating demand, and strong unions. Thanks to blows struck from both within and without, the arrangements that powered the New Deal order began to unravel rapidly in the late 1970s.[12] With time, as the neoliberal turn worked profound changes at all levels of party politics, the reentry of the South into two-party competition finally began to sort Democrats and Republicans into polarized teams. Even as this sorting drove a resurgence of partisan organizing and activism, however, the brittle and unrooted parties found they could not contain the conflictual politics that ensued.

New approaches to influencing policy and financing elections boxed in the parties just when they most needed to assert stewardship over their own destinies. The post-1970 "advocacy explosion" in Washington swelled the ranks of interest groups, think tanks, and lobbying shops.[13] A new system of campaign finance arose, suffused with cash but distinctly unhelpful for parties' efforts to shape and pursue agendas in power. The combination of the 1974 amendments to the Federal Election Campaign Act and the Supreme Court's decision two years later in *Buckley v. Valeo* constrained party fundraising while doing nothing to stem the rising costs of campaigns. A rising class of professional operatives plied their trade, typically inside the network of a single party, for some mix of candidates, party committees, PACs, and, as time went on, independent-expenditure groups.[14]

Initially, the formal parties' responses to this new environment seemed to revitalize them. The national party committees, with Republicans in the lead, ramped up funding, expanded staff, and reinvested national dollars into campaign support. With a label that suggests its very limits, scholars termed the model that emerged from these developments the "service party": parties would work primarily to provide campaign resources to, and broker interest-group support for, the candidate operations that now dominated electoral politics.[15] Even within those strictures, however, the formal parties' relative clout waned as outside groups, funded by both megadonors and armies of small-dollar givers, eventually overwhelmed traditional channels of political finance. In the wake of the 2010 Supreme Court decision in *Citizens United v. Federal Election Commission*, a tangled and often hard-to-trace multiplicity of pass-throughs, Super PACs, and dark money outfits have all showered money on campaigns and consultants. Candidate campaigns and outside groups together spent three times as much as national party organizations in 2020.[16] The money glut has only deepened the problems of party management that so characterize the era of hollowness.[17]

These changes have manifested in starkly different ways across the two parties. The Democrats' battered labor-liberal alliance, long the great champion of program and discipline in party politics, found itself adrift in the 1970s, while party actors began to regroup along different lines. Starting in the 1980s, they built up the national party's financial might and embraced paraparty lobbies and hangers-on but struggled to define an underlying party purpose. Some heralded a postindustrial future, while others unapologetically filled the party's coffers in the name of organizational revival. The coalitional and financial consequences continued to hold sway even as the party lurched haltingly leftward in the new century. On the other side, the political tendency that we term the Long New Right decisively captured the Republican Party during the same years in the 1970s. The right-wing brokers of the Long New Right treated parties as "no more than instruments" in a struggle for power.[18] Their triumph broke through the fetters that had long restrained political action. Unshackled, the Republican Party became a vehicle to fight its political enemies on any institutional ground it could find.

At the GOP's core was a plutocratic-populist bargain: an electoral politics of resentment would serve as handmaiden to a regressive policy agenda.[19] Politics-as-culture-war in turn fueled the growth of a media-advocacy complex that has at various times acted as principal rather than agent—and has at all times undermined party actors' ability to police boundaries against extremism. The Republican Party that emerged in its wake, desirous of power however it can be gotten, has retreated from the commitments that make parties central pillars of small-d democratic and small-r republican politics.[20] In short, since the seventies, a hollowed-out Democratic Party has been rendered listless by conflicting actors and a hollowed-out Republican Party pulled to radicalism by committed actors.

By rooting party hollowness's genesis in the political-economic developments of the 1970s and emphasizing the decisive role of the right in bringing it about, we treat as secondary what other scholars often depict as pivotal: namely, the end of traditional party organizations and the demise of old intraparty arrangements beginning a decade earlier in the 1960s. Following the disastrous 1968 convention, the Democrats' Commission on Party Structure and Delegate Selection, commonly known as the McGovern-Fraser Commission, unintentionally prompted the spread of state primaries to select presidential convention delegates. As political scientists have long noted, this shift undermined state and local party organizations that in the pre-reform system had benefited from control over their delegates.[21] It also left Democrats and Republicans rhetorically and politically ill-equipped to justify any special prerogatives for party actors in internal decision-making.

Critically, however, the McGovern-Fraser reformers' unrealized vision of open, activist-driven parties still operated within a venerable paradigm, ultimately tracing back to the rise of mass parties, which treated party forms as important and party contestation as a special category of conflict in the political system. This is precisely the paradigm from which the Long New Right made such a decisive break. Imagine a past that featured McGovern-Fraser but not the Long New Right. Such a scenario would have led to vastly different outcomes in later twentieth-century politics and beyond, not merely different rules for nomination. The counterfactual exercise helps to clarify the central point: in our actual past, hollow parties emerged from the world that the Long New Right made.

As our diagnosis looks rightward, its attention to the Republican Party gives our work particular urgency. The Trump era brought a torrent of scholarship on democratic crisis in America. One line of analysis emphasizes how polarized parties and fragmented Madisonian institutions together produce dysfunction and escalatory hardball.[22] Another looks to political behavior in the electorate and the toxic force of affective partisanship.[23] Still another has turned to America's troubled past for precedents and origin stories.[24] These inquiries inform ours, but none of them directly explain the parties' present incapacities. Indeed, even as many of the scholarly doomsayers have pointed the finger at the Republican Party, they have said less about exactly how the party took its present course.[25] By rooting present-day democratic discontents inside the history of American party politics, this book aims to meet that challenge. Hollow parties do not merely enfeeble governance, they endanger democracy.

Developments roiling American democracy resonate deeply with patterns abroad.[26] "Parties are failing," wrote the late Peter Mair, his eyes on western Europe, "because the zone of engagement—the traditional world of party democracy where citizens interacted with and felt a sense of attachment to their political leaders—is being evacuated."[27] In the distinct American institutional environment with a pure party duopoly, however, they take on a different cast.[28] Like other center-left parties in the rich democracies, Democrats have become increasingly dependent on votes from the college-educated middle class.[29] But polarized two-party politics renders Democratic hollowness distinct, as neither a continued march to the center nor inexorable electoral decline defines the party. For its part, like center-right parties elsewhere, the GOP has long mixed economic and noneconomic appeals. Now, its dominant figure echoes the rhetoric of right populists the world over, who stress the direct connection between leader and people.[30] In parallel with his counterparts abroad, Trump moved rightward on cultural and nationalist issues during the 2016 campaign, while sounding notes of a more welfare-chauvinist bent on economic issues, at least relative to Republican orthodoxy. But the uniquely polarized strategic environment in which Trump operated as president and party leader curbed those economic deviations.[31] The result has been a "plutopopulism" distinctive among global patterns, bringing together inside a single party enthusiasm to slash regulations and taxes, personalistic belief in a leader able to conjure up a people, and, above all, themes of cultural and ethnonational grievance.[32]

Party Projects

Even as we root the proximate rise of party hollowness in the 1970s, we delve much further back than that. When Americans argue about parties, they package and repackage ideas, practices, and institutional orientations that stretch back to the dawn of mass politics.[33] Parties have projects to wield state power on behalf of particular actors. Yet across history, very different social actors have sought to use parties for very different ends. Thus, we recognize in parties what Rogers Smith recognized in American political culture: no one true, transhistorical essence but rather a "complex pattern of apparently inconsistent combinations of . . . traditions."[34]

As a matter of definition, we follow E. E. Schattschneider: "A political party is an organized attempt to get control of the government."[35] Though many actors want influence in politics, only political parties formally contest elections whose winners then hold office.[36] But this essential truth explains only so much. The organizations that control parties' names and ballot access make up "the party" only in the most legalistic sense. What partisan actors "want" after taking their oaths has varied across American history. Some have empowered loyal partisans or grassroots activists, others have happily let the bosses rule, and still others have looked to a transformative leader. And so our approach rejects highly stylized theories of party.[37]

Cast a gaze across American history and consider the sheer scope of projects that collective political actors have pursued. The Jacksonians wanted spoils and a white man's republic. Progressives wanted energetic and capable administration. Postwar programmatic liberals wanted to fulfill the promise of the New Deal. The republic's greatest triumph—the destruction of slavery and building of a new, more equal country in the Civil War and Reconstruction—was quintessentially a party project of the Republicans. And with all these different projects have come varying organizational forms for partisans to realize their goals. More than enacting and administering policies or programs alone, parties design and attempt to realize projects that shape the material and symbolic distribution of "society's goodies."[38] They steer resources and prestige to favored claimants and rewrite the rules of the game to favor those claimants in future battles. Those regime questions of winners and losers are the real stakes in politics.[39]

Table 1.1 lists the distinct party formations that we explore, in greater or lesser detail, through the chapters to come, including the years when they were most significant in politics as well as two names of illustrative figures. Note that parties, even electorally successful ones, have not always made distinctive claims about the role and function of party politics. The Republican Party between the Gilded Age organizations and the Long New Right, electorally successful until Herbert Hoover and struggling thereafter, is a conspicuous case in point.[40]

As we follow the action across American political history, we examine party actors in differently constituted units, whether an entire major party (or the bulk of it), a minor party, or a party faction.[41] Party politics is politics done collectively, as individuals come together (or not) under a common banner. And so ours are all collective portraits.[42] Even as the depth of our treatments varies, these actors have all had projects for power that offered answers—however partial or inconsistent—to essential questions about the role and structure of the political party.[43] For those interested in looking under the hood at the building blocks of our framework, see appendix 1.

TABLE 1.1. Collective Party Actors

	Years	Emblematic figures
Jacksonians	1828–1854	Martin Van Buren, Andrew Jackson
Whigs	1840–1854	John Quincy Adams, Henry Clay
Free Labor Republicans	1854–1877	Abraham Lincoln, Thaddeus Stevens
Gilded Age Organizations	1877–1896	James Blaine, George Washington Plunkitt
Mugwumps	1872–1900	E. L. Godkin, Henry Adams
Populists	1874–1896	Charles Macune, Ignatius Donnelly
Socialist Party	1901–1919	Eugene Debs, Victor Berger
Progressives	1900–1916	Robert M. La Follette, Herbert Croly
Midcentury Pragmatists	1932–1968	Jim Farley, Richard J. Daley
Programmatic Liberals	1948–1968	Hubert Humphrey, Joseph L. Rauh Jr.
McGovern-Fraser	1968–1972	Donald Fraser, Anne Wexler
Long New Right	1952–1994	Jesse Helms, Paul Weyrich
Left Dissidents	2011–present	Bernie Sanders, Alexandria Ocasio-Cortez
Dem Institutionalists	1981–present	Nancy Pelosi, Joe Biden
Neoliberal Centrists	2001–present	Michael Bloomberg, Michael Porter
Reaganite GOP	1981–present	Mitch McConnell, Karl Rove
Right Populists	1992–present	Donald Trump, Pat Buchanan

Party Strands

Party actors combine and recombine approaches that recur and endure over time. Six ideal types, which we term "party strands," comprise the political traditions drawn from and in turn forged by successive party projects.[44] Each strand expresses distinct views of the role and function of the political party. Figure 1.1 shows our mapping of how party projects have cohered into what we term the accommodationist, anti-party, pro-capital, policy-reform, radical, and populist strands.

To connect our jargon: projects emerge at particular historical junctures, and strands convey their recurrent features. The most important party projects in American political history have no single manifestation in contemporary politics. Instead, divergent pieces of their legacies refract across the landscape. The free labor Republicans served as a vehicle of northern industry (pro-capital) and as a force that overthrew an

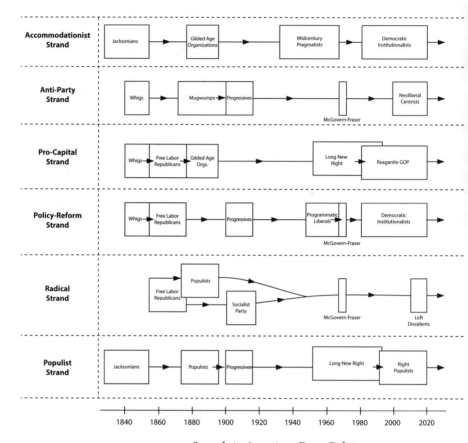

FIGURE 1.1. Strands in American Party Politics

entire economic order in the name of human freedom (radical). By the same token, the party-breaking Progressives have bequeathed a belief in the efficacy of technocratic government to solve public problems (policy-reform), a powerful executive that encourages adherents to look to the leader for political salvation (populist), and a plebiscitary tendency that liquidates party prerogatives (anti-party). A brief description of each strand helps to situate these pillars of our analysis.

Accommodationist strand: In the accommodationist strand, the art of government comes in the work of politics—and politics is a game of addition, not subtraction.[45] The goal, for ward heelers and party bosses alike, is to organize blocs of voters who can then divvy up the spoils of victory.[46] This is a politics not of inexorable conflict over first principles or of a search for a unitary public interest but of relentless dealmaking and jawboning, of favor traded for favor, of small courtesies remembered. Money for the party coffers can come from whatever source will pony up, with the expectation that contributions will not go unrewarded. Policy, then, is the by-product, not the driver, of accommodationist politics. Asked one evening in the early 1970s, late in the reign of Chicago mayor Richard J. Daley's political machine, about whether to give a donation to the Illinois Right to Life Committee, the legendary 25th Ward Democratic committeeman Vito Marzullo declined: "I don't want to get into any of those controversies. People for it and people against it."[47]

With group jostling against group, each with its own set of loyalties and enmities, the task of mediating among constituencies and balancing across claimants takes its own specialized skill. As accommodationists see it, the game ought to be played by political professionals who have learned on the job and risen through the ranks—not by dilettantes, amateurs, or theoreticians. Politics is its own sphere, organized by those who have walked the precinct and learned the rules. Though no form ever facilitated the accommodationist worldview so well as the regular party organization, the ethos has clung on even after the classic machines' eclipse.

Anti-party strand: For adherents to the anti-party strand, the partial commitments of party, and the low arts of party politicians, divide society and threaten the common good.[48] Such a view marks out the edges, as a political vision, of a skepticism toward political parties that runs deep in the American vein. Anti-partisanship cast a lengthy shadow over American political practice. Presidential candidates long stayed off the stump, leaving the campaign to party organizations; as late as 1932, when Franklin Roosevelt flew from Albany to Chicago to accept the Democratic nomination in person, it turned heads.[49]

The anti-party strand's adherents have shifted their targets of condemnation, from the very fact of party organization itself in the Early Republic to the mercenary corruption of Gilded Age machines to the extremist straitjackets and litmus tests of our polarized age. The Progressive Era marked an important turning point. In the anti-party tradition prior to the twentieth century, classical virtue served as liberty's necessary protector, and conniving majorities an omnipresent danger. After the Progressives, anti-party rhetoric would come to praise ordinary voters whose passions had formerly provoked fear. In the process, the strand's beau ideal shifted from the classically educated statesman to the market-oriented technocrat. Nevertheless, anti-party actors' core belief in enlightened leadership, and their apprehension about the baleful effects of party scheming, still endure. When parties take the patchwork quilt of society and make it the stuff of politics, the anti-party strand sees two conjoined perils—both an attack on individual conscience and a threat to social order.

Pro-capital strand: The pro-capital strand applies the logic of business to party politics. It offers only a thin conception of party. In contrast to accommodationism, politics for this strand is not an autonomous sphere of human life but simply another arena for capital to deploy in search of reward. When its exponents speak directly, their claims recast arguments for business's own pecuniary interests in terms of the common good.[50] But the tactical issues of party politics are epiphenomenal to the larger challenge: using the political system to secure advantage against those who seek to curb the power and influence of economic elites. Parties, thus, are instruments to be used or discarded as the situation requires. Formal parties themselves loomed larger in the Gilded Age than in the hollowed politics of recent decades. Substantive priorities come first.

The pro-capital strand emerges in the entente between business and right parties.[51] Its power waxes during the periods when political brokers can successfully bring together business sectors with strata that typically keep their distance—magnates and shopkeepers, financiers and industrialists—and then extend their reach into party politics.[52] If this happens, business moves beyond a search for stability and uses party as the lever to remake the state, while parties reach beyond the inevitable search for campaign funding to reshape themselves in business's service. In turn, the crucial question for the pro-capital strand comes in its willingness or unwillingness to make alliances, tacit or explicit, with exclusionary politics often represented by the populist strand.

Policy-reform strand: For the policy-reform strand, parties solve public problems. Diverse actors come together to overcome the barriers of a divided political system and achieve big things. The hybrid name reflects a dual emphasis, bringing together issues and good government. Parties serve as instruments to sweep away accumulated privilege and patronage and supplant them with well-crafted programs. Active and robust parties build an active and robust state. The policy-reform strand, which flourished among northern Democrats during the postwar heyday of the New Deal order, envisions a cross-class project powering a cohesive substantive agenda.

This strand offers a fervent brief for a particular, bounded view of parties' possibilities, rather than a defense of parties come what may. Reflecting the contradictory qualities in American liberalism, it takes from and builds on other views. It critiques accommodationism as too small, too myopic, in its workaday concerns, and generally too corrupt. It sees the anti-party strand as too aloof and too tethered to private solutions. Yet the politicians, activists, and intellectuals whose writings and actions make up the policy-reform strand owe a substantial debt to both of those traditions. From the accommodationists, they take a bedrock appreciation for parties themselves, as they bring interests and constituencies together under a common banner. From the anti-party strand, they take a suspicion of the boss and a commitment to expertise. And even as they share with the radical strand a desire to shake things up, they accept and work inside the system's limits.

Radical strand: For the radical strand, the political party serves as a lever to build an egalitarian society. Radicals want vast social transformation, and parties serve as a means to achieve that purpose. What sets the radicals apart is the sheer scale of their ambitions and the concomitant challenges they face when confronted with the daunting rules of the American electoral game.[53] Repeatedly, radicals searching for an electoral majority have foundered on different versions of the same problem: whatever their chosen strategy, they fail to bring together broad constituencies that bridge ethnic, racial, and religious divides to vanquish the powers of the existing social order.

Because the frustrations of electoralism feed on each other, exponents of radical party politics fight a two-front war. When radicals fail to deliver systemic change from a beachhead of concentrated support—a mayor here, a member of Congress there—they strengthen the arguments of both maximalists who want to make change through direct action rather than electoral politics, and pragmatists who want to focus on building majorities inside the system.[54] The radical party strand, then, is simultaneously an argument for the thoroughgoing reconstruction of state and society and an argument for party politics as the preeminent route to social change. In turn, the differences that distinguish the policy-reform and radical strands are of both degree and kind. The radical strand sets its sights on power—who wields it across society, and in whose interest—rather than on the mechanics of party or state action. So, too, the radical strand places greater emphasis on organizing oppressed groups themselves.[55]

Populist strand: Party politics, for the populist strand, cleaves the polity into "us" and "them," with only "us" as authentic members of the political community.[56] As the populist strand wields the language of republican liberty for those who fit inside its bounds, politics becomes a battle between "the people," invested with the requisites of civic membership, and everyone else, who are not.[57] In comparison with the other strands, the populist strand appears less as a cohesive approach to party politics than as a set of recurring tendencies and resonances. It roots itself less in the variegated terrain of civil society, as parties seek to assemble coalitions and mediate between elites and masses, than in the fundamental distinction between allies and enemies and the direct connection between leader and people.[58]

The populist strand has developed in combination with, and helps to shine an unforgiving light on, trends that cross the political landscape. It shares with the anti-party strand the same distaste for the connivances of the small party, but it celebrates the very transformative leader that the anti-party strand long feared as a demagogue who can prey on the mob. With its core support from members of the petty bourgeoisie, it often meshes with the pro-capital strand to make common cause against adversaries on the left. Finally, like the radical strand, it claims to speak on behalf of the plain people against malign elites who manipulate them.[59] But the records of the populist and radical strands diverge wildly when it comes to race—and the centrality of race to the American experience puts their worldviews in diametric opposition.

All six of these strands shine light on different dilemmas in party politics. The accommodationist strand foregrounds the omnipresent challenge of building coalitions. The policy-reform strand lingers on the connection between parties' appeals and the substantive workings of government. The pro-capital and radical strands point to ineluctable conflict rooted in political economy. And the anti-party and populist strands both cue questions about party and statesmanship.

One might also identify a reactionary lineage that connects ideas and practices across political eras. But such a politics—tethered to John C. Calhoun's doctrine of concurrent majority, overlapping at times with the populist strand, and rooted in the South—typically took the form not of us-versus-them party battles but of a flight from party altogether. Prior to the Long New Right's rise, southerners' commitment to regional power as they conducted what V. O. Key termed "the 'foreign relations' of the South with the rest of the nation" was less *anti*-party than *a*-party.[60] This explains why, from the Civil War era until the later twentieth century, ours is largely a northern saga.[61]

The critical 1970s link the historical trajectory of party strands to the emergent story of hollowness. Long-teetering traditional political organizations finally collapsed just as crises battered the New Deal political economy. Of these two linked developments, the latter is key. As the coming chapters argue repeatedly, a different balance of class power in a post–New Deal world would have led to different manifestations of party politics. Though the machines' hour had passed, if social forces had aligned differently, then accommodationism might have had fuel to sustain itself, both in a pragmatic and civically rooted politics of the center-right and in an organizationally dense politics of the center-left. The policy-reform strand would have been more willing to get its hands dirty in the political trenches rather than relying on expertise. And the pro-capital and populist strands that have strained the system to the breaking point would have faced far stronger headwinds pushing against their projects.

Instead, each strand now manifests its incapacities in its own way, as the more robustly party-supporting sides of each approach have given way to hollowing tendencies. Adherents of the accommodationist strand have found no shortage of deals to be struck and palms to be greased, but the open celebration of party as such that had long distinguished this tradition has fallen silent. The anti-party strand runs deep in public consciousness, but with no strong foil against which to make its distinctive claims, its voice has retreated to the soggy ground of neoliberal technocracy. By the same token, times have been good for American business, with myriad points of entry for influence into the political system. But the corporate statesmanship that brings forth the best in the pro-capital strand has been in shorter supply. As the vision of programmatic party renewal faded, proponents of the policy-reform strand have instead searched for political salvation via good policy alone. Actors toiling at the leftward margins within the radical strand have mounted a surprising return as factional battlers in the Democratic fold—but with a vision of party that remains ambivalent. And, perhaps most important of all, the populist strand has gained a new potency—in culture-war flash fires, in the prospect of strong-man demagoguery, and in an anti-system politics that looks to blood-and-soil nationalism.

Our Approach

Readers should get from this book a new way of thinking about present-day political problems—our concept of party hollowness—and a new way of thinking about how parties have shaped and been shaped by history—our framework of party strands. But understanding what these ideas mean in practice requires digging into the actual particulars of party politics. And so the bulk of the pages in this book are devoted to a new historical narrative of American politics, one told through its parties.

We seek to understand parties as party actors have seen them. At the core of this book is close, sustained engagement with the words and actions of elite political figures grappling with the challenges of their historical experiences. We scour diverse evidence, piecing together our account from a mixture of periodicals, monographs, and, wherever possible, archives. At the same time, we bring divergent party projects together in a common framework.

Our goal is a kind of arbitrage, both opening up the study of American parties to broader perspectives and bringing party to bear on conversations where it has been too often absent. We treat the back-and-forth between social forces and political change as the very heart of party politics. This attention to social structure departs somewhat from the emphasis on formal and informal organization dominant in political science. If, in some sense, ours is an old-fashioned work, it is also one that looks far beyond the confines of the convention hall.

On the one side, we attend to parties' particular stamp on social change.[62] We stress the ways that nuts-and-bolts party maneuvering affects big transformations, from patronage in the Civil War–era Republican Party to Chicago mayor Richard J. Daley's calculations when the Democratic National Convention met in his city in 1968. In contrast to much recent work in political history that dwells on the social and political constellations surrounding parties, we bring the parties back in, put them center stage, and shine the klieg lights on them. In particular, we push forward a growing line of scholarship on the links between social movements and political parties by emphasizing dynamics inside the parties themselves.[63]

On the other side, we see parties as essential players on a larger terrain of struggle, embedded in social systems shaped by class, race, gender, and nationality.[64] Any interpretation of American party conflict must confront those systems foursquare, rather than treating them as background to party machinations. The Jacksonian Democratic Party, for instance, created the spoils system—and the Trail of Tears. Yet a book about political parties such as this one necessarily focuses on those included in or on the edges of formal politics, rather than seeking out the political expression of those excluded. And so, especially in earlier chapters, this story is predominantly male and white.

We work inside three intellectual traditions: scholarship on American political parties, on American political development (APD), and on American political history. From scholars of party, we take our core focus on what parties have done and how they have done it; from scholars of APD, we take our multivalent approach to political development; and from historians, we take our concern to understand party actors in the full context of their lives and times. For an extended discussion of how we build on, and also critique, the scholarship in each of these traditions, see appendix 2.

Where We Stand

Part of being fair means being open about where we come from. We write about American political parties because we care about them. We are partisans of parties. Democracy, we believe, is not only "unthinkable save in terms of the parties" but best served by being largely organized and enacted *by* those parties.[65] Nevertheless, our vision for civic reinvention transcends any by-the-numbers checklist. Party forms have always varied along with party projects. As we explore possibilities taken and forgone, we seek not to retreat into bygone glories but to open up new vistas.

We are proud and loyal, albeit often-disillusioned, capital-*D* Democrats. Our politics are broadly left-liberal. Since the New Deal, the Democratic Party's finest moments, in our judgment, have come when it forthrightly stood up for principles and advanced a universalistic and solidaristic politics. While many American liberals look to technocratic solutions, claims of a unitary public interest often deny the realities of social conflict. As for the radical tradition, it too often fails to face head-on the problem of building majority coalitions in the American electoral system. At a critical hour, we write to put contemporary concerns in historical context.

Coming Attractions

Proceeding largely chronologically, the pages that follow flesh out these themes. Chapter 2 explores the uneven rise of party politics emerging out of the fluid factionalism of the Early Republic. In the 1830s, Jacksonian

Democrats brought the mass party to fruition. Controlled by men de-voted to the practice of politics and desirous of the fruits of office, the Jacksonian project embodied the core ethos of the accommodationist strand. In turn, their Whig opponents ambivalently combined an abid-ing anti-partyism celebrating moral virtue with frenzied campaigning at election time.

Chapter 3 traces the Republican Party from its founding in 1854 until the Compromise of 1877. In form, the party innovated little. Neverthe-less, as it fought the Civil War, freed the slaves, and remade the Consti-tution, free labor Republicanism pursued a transformative party project without peer, one that deserves pride of place in any reckoning with the possibilities of party in the United States.

Chapter 4 delineates the wide variety of party responses to industri-alism during the Gilded Age and Progressive Era. With Democratic and Republican organizations at full flower, Mugwumps, Populists, and So-cialists all sought alternatives. In their stead, the Progressives recast old anti-party sentiment in a newly plebiscitarian light, aiming to strip away the middlemen and recenter politics on the unmediated relationship between leader and citizen.

Chapter 5 examines three visions of party that emerged amid the break-throughs and contradictions of the New Deal order. Midcentury pragma-tists, most prominent in the cities still under machine rule, held fast to the accommodationist politics of wheedling and dealmaking. Programmatic liberals—their factional opponents across the North—epitomized the policy-reform strand's issue-oriented politics. Finally, the framers of McGovern-Fraser envisioned active parties working alongside social movements, only to find that continual vigilance against capture by en-trenched interests turned procedural reform into an end in itself.

The Long New Right is the subject of chapter 6, which traces conser-vatives' encounter with party from the 1950s to the 1990s. Generations of conservatives, exploiting grievance and mobilizing status resent-ments, broke free from the strictures of the old party politics. Even as the relevant issues and organizations shifted over the years, the Long New Right's commitment to conflict and the ruthless instrumentalism toward institutions remained constants. If readers want evidence that the right broke American party politics, this chapter is where they should turn.

Chapter 7 looks at the Democrats in the decades since Ronald Reagan's inauguration in 1981. Its twin themes are polarization and neoliberalism, and its central story is of a party whose project remained continually out of reach. Even as ideological sorting of the party system removed old-line conservatives from its ranks, an increasingly middle-class party struggled to bring its diverse constituencies and claimants together, or to connect political strategy with the levers of public policy.

Chapter 8 follows the Republican Party from Newt Gingrich to Donald Trump. It portrays a party confident in its use of state power to reward friends and punish enemies—but not to solve public problems. In contrast to portrayals of the GOP that emphasize either its allegedly brutal effectiveness or its ruthless efficiency, our depiction shows a party beset by forces it cannot control and dangerously incapable of policing itself *or* governing the country.

Chapter 9 concludes, offering recommendations both left and right for party renewal that meets the crises of our time. To ground our prescriptions, we travel to Las Vegas to investigate the intertwined successes of the Nevada Democratic Party's "Reid Machine" and of the powerful Culinary Workers Union. We seek vigorous, participatory parties with broad legitimacy across the polity and a deep commitment to enacting their democratic visions. As a scholarly Committee on Party Renewal affirmed in 1977, just on the cusp of our hollowed era, "Without parties, there can be no organized and coherent politics. When politics lacks coherence, there can be no accountable democracy."[66]

2

The Affirmation of Party in Antebellum America

ON THE rain-soaked streets of Columbus in February 1840, the Ohio state convention of the Whig Party took the form of a "monster gathering of the clans," in one veteran's fond reminiscence.[1] Delegates attended to party business, passing resolutions in praise of the party's presidential nominee—Ohio's own war hero and former senator William Henry Harrison—and organizing campaign committees to turn out the vote in November. But, as attendee Aaron Perry chronicled in a report for a Whig newspaper in Boston, the real action was in the streets:

> One delegation came armed with brooms, signifying that the next election shall be made a sweeping operation. . . . Yonder comes a real, bona fide log cabin! See the raccoon-skins hanging upon its sides. Upon the door is written in charcoal, in awkward characters, "Hard Cider." It is filled with men in hunting shirts, eating corn-bread, and as many of the same description as can sit on the roof or hang upon it in any way, are singing rude songs in praise of the "Log Cabin Candidate," "Old Tippecanoe." . . .
>
> But you can no longer think of particulars. All is one dense, enthusiastic mass of human bodies. On either hand, so far as the eye can extend, the streets are filled with flags, pictures, and all sorts of signs and symbols. Still they thicken, still on they come. Windows are all

thrown up and filled with ladies, who join in the excitement and wave their white handkerchiefs to the crowd.[2]

Such scenes occurred all across the country during the Whigs' "Log Cabin" campaign that year (so themed in puckish response to a Democratic jibe about retiring Harrison to a cabin with a pension and a full supply of cider). By 1840, electoral pageantry was old hat for the Whigs' opponents, the Jacksonian Democrats. But it was hardly characteristic of a party known for its more genteel base, its aversion to partisan politicking, and its reverence for individual conscience over mob rule. Perry touched on this seeming incongruity when he invoked a prototypical "businessman, or a scholar . . . he is a Whig—to be sure." Such a man believes that "shouts convince nobody, shouts are not intellectual." But when that same man looks on at the teeming mass in Columbus, "he strains every muscle in shouts." What is more, "Being a man of moral courage," such a gentleman "not only shouts when the rest do, but breaks forth occasionally alone, to show that he does it as a matter of principle."[3] Mass party politics, encompassing spectacle and principle alike, had fully come of age.

This chapter ushers in our developmental account of American parties by tracing political thought and practice from the drafting of the Constitution through the Compromise of 1850. It sketches the emergence of party visions that—brashly in the Democrats' case, more hesitantly in the Whigs'—affirmed the value of popular collective political action. It then follows the unraveling of those visions in the face of the sectional crisis over slavery. Though the Jacksonians were innovators who left an important institutional legacy for mass democracy, we treat their approach as a significant tradition in American party history but not *the* tradition.[4] This chapter, as well as the two that follow, repeatedly draws attention to the sheer variety and scope of party visions in nineteenth-century politics.

The anti-party ethos that had dominated Western thought cast a long shadow on the political life of the Early Republic. By contrast, the Second Party System, scholars' term for the period in electoral politics that ran from the election of 1828 to the prelude to Civil War, represented a

genuine global innovation: an organized system of national party competition centered around the mobilization of mass publics. From federated party organizations to delegate conventions, the rules of the game
set in that moment still structure American politics. The party-
dominated nineteenth century saw neither a golden age nor a forgotten
blueprint but rather the origin of core debates over parties' democratic
purposes that have occupied Americans ever since.[5]

The forces behind Andrew Jackson's candidacy and electoral victory in
1828 brought together in a single national party operation the variegated
building blocks of popular politics that had emerged in the previous
decades. Grounding parties in the civic life of ordinary Americans, the
Jacksonians put locally rooted and participatory organizations in service
of a project for power. They helped drive the wave of state-level legislation
and constitutional revision that eliminated the last property requirements
for white male suffrage and widened the range of elective over appointive
offices at all levels of government.[6] As they pursued these institutional
innovations, the Jacksonians in turn defended party politics itself, carving
out a normative space more expansive than the Founding-era justifications of mere emergency efforts to save the republic from its enemies.[7] In
an 1835 statement of principles, Democrats disavowed "an indiscriminate
anathema against all political parties," arguing instead for parties' "public
utility": "They bring into action the greatest talents. They excite a jealousy
and vigilance which insures fidelity in public functionaries. They check
attempts at the usurpation of power, and thereby preserve the rights of
the People. . . . When parties act on honorable principles, there is no danger from its existence."[8]

The Democrats' project took Jeffersonian tenets of equality and yeoman
republican virtue, newly imbued with a rowdy democratic spirit, and
applied them to a disruptive market society.[9] The result was a racially
exclusive democratic egalitarianism well captured in the phrase "white
man's republic." As doctrine, it took the form of anti-statist opposition to
centralized economic power, political empowerment of white men down
the class ladder, systematic exclusion of African Americans from the
political community, and accelerated westward expansion through
the violent expropriation and removal of Native peoples. The world's

first mass political party thus embodied with potent force the intertwined commitments to equality and exclusion that Aziz Rana has termed "the two faces of American freedom."[10]

A party vision soon arose in opposition to the Jacksonian Democrats, one distinguished by an underlying moralism—and by an ambivalence toward party itself. The Whig Party uneasily melded notions of virtue and self-mastery steeped in the anti-party tradition with a turn to popular politics, epitomized by the spectacle of 1840. The very tension that Whigs embodied, between the old and still-resonant verities of republican statesmanship and a halting embrace of organized democratic combat, was at once a hindrance to the party's effectiveness and a source of its appeal to Americans who shared that ambivalence.

The Democracy, the Jacksonians' collective term for their party, crystallized the accommodationist strand in party politics. Cutting against the prevailing civic-republican grain, Jacksonians rendered as virtues two core challenges of democratic politics: forming coalitions to advance collective interests and subordinating individual action to collective decisions. The very "conflict displacement" that suppressed debate over issues dividing the Democratic coalition—above all slavery—became an ethic of party practice.[11] Democrats venerated party loyalty, taking as their "watchword and motto," in Missouri senator Thomas Hart Benton's words, "everything for the cause, nothing for men."[12] And they honed the talents associated with accommodationists ever since: a sympathy for the problems of the ordinary worker; a sensitivity to ethnic and community patterns, sometimes assuaged and sometimes demagogued; a thirst for campaign cash and an insouciance toward its source; and a flexibility around issues and a practical approach to solving problems.

Not every problem could be accommodated, however. Beginning in the 1840s, southerners' increasing agitation over slavery's political future seemed to transform western expansion from a safeguard of the white man's republic to an intensifying threat to white men's own political liberties. When Democrats found themselves incapable of resolving this contradiction, the cross-sectional Second Party System itself collapsed around them.

Alexis de Tocqueville may have foretold this failure. In *Democracy in America*, written after his visit in 1831 and 1832, the Frenchman distinguished "great parties"—"those more attached to principles than to consequences" and "to ideas rather than to personalities"—from "small ones"—those which, not being "elevated and sustained by lofty purposes," reveal "the selfishness of their character . . . in all their actions."[13] In the spirited but petty politics of the Jacksonian era, Tocqueville's jaundiced eye saw only the hallmarks of squabbling small parties.[14] We depart from his assessment of politics in the Second Party System as so much electoral sound and fury, signifying nothing. But confronting the crisis of slavery head-on would indeed ultimately take a new kind of avowedly great party—namely, the free labor Republicans chronicled in chapter 3.

The Building Blocks of Party in an Anti-party World

Mass democracy, organized by national political parties, was no Promethean invention of 1828.[15] Beginning in the 1790s, partisan combat departed from the "formless politics of individual action and shifting liaisons" that had typified colonial- and Revolutionary-era politics, and took on a new continuity and structure.[16] During the First Party System of the 1790s and early 1800s, legislative politics grew organized around stable and competitive coalitions of Federalists and Democratic Republicans, and that political conflict reached deeper into public life. And yet, with personal reputation still all but inextricable from conflict over public matters, a notably venomous and unbounded quality marked the era's politics.[17] The combatants themselves proceeded without a clear sense of political limits—what later party theorists termed "the discipline of regulated rivalry."[18] Nasty and frenzied in proportion to the perceived stakes of the disputes, the clash of two anti-party parties at times put the survival of the young republic in question. In the 1810s, when those animating passions had simmered down, party politics itself briefly receded.

The Constitution reflected the deep ambivalence toward collective political action at the heart of the anti-party strand. The Framers, led by

James Madison, showed a newfound realism about the inevitability of conflict in government. In the system they designed, separated powers and federalism would together channel and temper clashing interests.[19] Yet even in fragmenting power, the Constitution paradoxically drew from the long tradition of civic republicanism, which aimed the design of government toward divining and serving the common good. The Framers had read and taken to heart Bolingbroke's call in 1738 for a Patriot King who, "instead of putting himself at the head of one party in order to govern his people," would "put himself at the head of his people in order to govern, or more properly to subdue, all parties."[20] (John Adams read Bolingbroke's *The Idea of a Patriot King* five times.)[21]

Famously, the same Framers so averse to the dangers of faction promptly dove headlong into party conflict following ratification. As Madison worked with Thomas Jefferson to organize congressional opposition to Alexander Hamilton's economic program, he began to justify such factional activity publicly. Writing in 1792, he declared that the ill effects of party might be mitigated "by making one party a check on the other, so far as the existence of parties cannot be prevented, nor their views accommodated. If this is not the language of reason, it is that of republicanism."[22] Over the next few years, Democratic-Republican clubs formed across the country to advocate the Jeffersonian line, prompting President Washington to denounce "certain self-created societies" in his message to Congress.[23] The First Party System had arrived.

The anti-party Constitution ironically spurred this arrival. Looking to the Patriot King, the Framers had imagined the president as a fundamentally apolitical figure who would rise above squabbling factions and petty intrigues. The idea that the president would mobilize broad coalitions—a notion of ever-increasing importance across American political history—was unknown to them.[24] But very early on, Hamilton grasped just what control of the executive branch would mean, while his foes saw in turn that they would have to line up against it. As stable alliances supplanted ad hoc factionalism, divisions over one question (Hamilton's fiscal policies) begat the same line of cleavage on others (the French Revolution and American foreign policy.)[25] Those alignments then began to reach down into the electorate, as both presidential selection by a majority of electors and frequent elections set to fixed schedules motivated political actors to sustain coalitions over time and across issues.[26]

Nevertheless, the shared elite political culture of the age constricted party development.[27] The classical inheritance that sent leaders "back to the timeless values and eloquent words of Cicero and Horace, Virgil and Plutarch," still cast a long shadow, and so politicians had to fit new realities around old understandings.[28] Practicing the art of "partisan anti-partisanship," Federalists and Republicans each cast themselves as defenders of the nation against their opponents stirring up conflict.[29] Washington's famous remarks on "the baneful effects of the spirit of party" in his farewell address, written with Hamilton, offered a perfect example: a partisan attack on the Republicans disguised as a condemnation of all partisan attacks.[30] And when leaders did the visible work of party building and combat, they justified it as a temporary expediency, necessary to vanquish the republic's enemies. Writing to his attorney general in 1802, Thomas Jefferson described what he saw as his mandate as president in blunt but typical terms: "to sink federalism into an abyss from which there will be no resurrection of it."[31]

The election of 1800 illustrated at once the promise and the peril of the new party politics. A record-shattering 38 percent of white men cast votes as the Republican Jefferson defeated the Federalist incumbent, John Adams. The peaceful transition of party regimes that followed marked a milestone in democratic political development. But the vitriol and paranoia that attended the contest was evident not merely in mud slung (one Federalist paper accused Thomas Jefferson of sacrificing dogs while depicting the Republican option in the election as a vote "for JEFFERSON—AND NO GOD") but also in credible threats of collective violence and secession on both sides.[32] Party combat in an avowedly anti-party age meant political conflict without forbearance.

Though party politics in the Early Republic largely remained an elite affair, innovations in popular politics and challenges to deferential political norms began to augur change.[33] Republicans moved first, but even the Federalists felt pressure to follow suit. "If Jefferson cannot be ousted but by this sort of cant," John Rutledge wrote a co-partisan in

1803, "we must have recourse to it."[34] In the partisan presses, the pro-liferating political clubs, the party assemblies and local nominating conventions, and the "perpetual fetes" of partisan celebrations and stunts—most iconically, a six-ton "Mammoth Cheese" sent in 1802 from Cheshire, Massachusetts, to President Jefferson in the White House—a new democratic political culture began to materialize.[35] And below the level of national politics, overt electioneering supplanted older patterns reliant on patron-client relationships worked out through leading families.[36]

Yet nowhere did elites and masses bring their work together in an open celebration of party. Pointing up the fragility of the First Party System, the Federalists collapsed as a national force after the War of 1812. Their fall ushered in the aberrant one-party Era of Good Feelings under President James Monroe. Lacing his civic-republican bromide with tri-umphalist complacency, Monroe declared in his inaugural address that "discord does not belong to our system"—and later called parties "the curse of the country."[37] Soon, and for the first time, such anti-party sanc-timony would elicit a sustained challenge.

Van Buren and the Path to 1828

In the rise of mass parties, "the Little Magician" of New York, Martin Van Buren, takes pride of place. He and his Empire State allies together developed a particular party form soon exported across the nation.[38] Van Buren drew on fertile soil. Since colonial days, the Mid-Atlantic states of New York, Pennsylvania, and to a lesser extent New Jersey had been distinguished by ethnic, religious, and social diversity, the absence of a cohesive social elite, and sustained political competition. These factors helped to put those states "at the front ranks of sophistication in politics" in the Early Republic, pioneering fragments of what would ultimately become the Jacksonian Democratic approach to party poli-tics.[39] The Albany Regency, the political organization that Van Buren and his allies built in the 1820s, came close to producing that entire package in microcosm: locally rooted, highly participatory, affirmatively pro-party, and dedicated to the principle of *the party over the man*.

Van Buren and his key Regency compatriots—attorney Silas Wright, state comptroller William Marcy, and editor Edwin Crosswell—came from largely middling backgrounds. Their great antagonist and foil was DeWitt Clinton, who epitomized the factionalism of the patrician families dominant in New York state politics since before the Revolution. In 1813, Van Buren broke definitively with Clinton, who was then mayor of New York City, over his party-scrambling entanglements with current and former Federalists. The Little Magician then took the helm of an existing faction of state Republicans—the Bucktails—and started a newspaper, the *Albany Argus*, to tout orthodox Jeffersonian doctrine and the virtue of party regularity. "*Political consistency*," wrote one Bucktail in the *Argus*, is "as indispensable as any other *moral qualification*."[40] In addition, the Bucktails, over the Clintonites' objections, forced a state constitutional convention in 1821 that scrapped property qualifications for white—but not Black—voters.[41] By the time Van Buren left for Washington as a senator that same year, the Regency had secured control of the state legislature and established a full-fledged operation, promulgating party orders from the capitol all the way to the furthest hamlet.

In Washington, Van Buren quickly applied his political critique to the Era of Good Feelings. He decried Monroe's practice of including former Federalists in governance as an "amalgamation policy" that demoralized Republican spirit and unity.[42] And when Monroe refused to play the role of party leader in directly engaging the question of who should succeed him in 1824, "the Republican party," Van Buren later recalled, "so long in the ascendant, and apparently so omnipotent, was literally shattered into fragments."[43] General Andrew Jackson, hero of the Battle of New Orleans, won the most popular votes, but the House ultimately decided the five-way contest for president after no candidate succeeded in garnering a majority in the Electoral College. The vote permanently discredited the party caucus as a decision-making mechanism for presidential nominations while shackling the eventual victor, John Quincy Adams, with an air of illegitimacy.

Convinced that a broader revival of explicit and structured party conflict in the country was urgently needed, Van Buren set out to forge a state-by-state coalition of Jeffersonians that would harness Andrew

Jackson's public following to reclaim power on clarified doctrinal grounds in 1828. After securing the support of the mercurial John C. Calhoun for this plan in late 1826, he turned his attention to the "Virginia junto" in charge of the commonwealth's Republican committee, led by newspaper editor Thomas Ritchie. In January 1827, Van Buren sent Ritchie one of the most consequential letters in the history of American politics, calling for "the substantial reorganization of the Old Republican Party . . . by combining Genl. Jackson's personal popularity with the portion of old party feeling yet remaining." Front and center in Van Buren's pitch was the coalitionist principle at the heart of his approach, expressed here in sectional terms:

> It would greatly improve the condition of the Republicans of the North & Middle States by substituting *party principle* for *personal preference* as one of the leading points in the contest. . . .
>
> We must always have party distinctions and the old ones are the best of which the nature of the case admits. Political combinations between the inhabitants of the different states are unavoidable & the most natural & beneficial to the country is that between the planters of the South and the plain Republicans of the north. The country has once flourished under a party thus constituted & may again. It would take longer than our lives (even if it were practicable) to create new party feelings to keep those masses together. If the old ones are suppressed, Geographical divisions founded on local interests or, what is worse prejudices between free & slave holding states will inevitably take their place.[44]

Van Buren succeeded in enlisting the Virginia junto in his cause. Soon after, supporters used the thirteenth anniversary of the Battle of New Orleans, on January 8, 1828, to organize party meetings in every state. By the summer and fall, mass rallies, barbecues, and planted hickory trees sprung up around the country.

The November election results marked the first American presidential election to see majority turnout among white men—an outcome aided by the final implementation of New York's 1821 suffrage reforms. The ten thousand visitors streaming into the capital in March for Jackson's inauguration foreshadowed a new era of mass partisanship, one that critics, like Supreme Court Justice Joseph Story, deemed tantamount to "the reign of KING MOB."[45] But Van Buren would have urged such critics, as he later put it, "to deal with the subject of Political Parties in a sincerer and wiser spirit—to recognize their necessity, to give them the credit they deserve, and to devote ourselves to improve and to elevate the principles and objects of our own."[46]

Jacksonian Party-Building: Nominations, Campaigns, Patronage

As Jacksonian Democrats took the Albany Regency model national, they brought together a string of long-lasting innovations. The participatory spirit that the Jacksonians imbued lasted through the nineteenth-century age of mass parties, while many of the institutional forms that they pioneered survive to this day. Look to origin stories in the nuts and bolts of party politics, and the Jacksonian Democracy is rarely far away.

In the most lasting organizational contribution of the Second Party System, delegate conventions replaced legislative caucuses as the core mechanism of party decision-making and candidate selection.[47] The national convention offered, in the words of the Democrats' formal party statement in 1835, "the best manner of concentrating the popular will, and giving it effect."[48] It generated participatory activism down through successive levels of organization while decentralizing power within the national party. And its consensus-building mechanisms, which bound individuals to collective party decisions, touched on the very essence of a party project that extolled the virtues of teamsmanship as a political ethic.

Presidential nominating conventions were not a new idea. Thomas Ritchie had editorialized in 1822 in favor of a national convention of delegates to select a candidate, though to little avail.[49] Following the congressional caucus's death knell in 1824, Van Buren had intended his mobilization of a partisan alliance against John Quincy Adams to culminate in a national convention.[50] But Jackson's runaway popular support in 1828 rendered the need moot. Thus it was that the Anti-Masonic Party, many of whose leaders were nearly as hostile to political parties as they were to the nefarious secret society, ironically assumed the mantle of first holder of a national nominating convention in September 1831.[51] Jackson's National Republican opponents, lacking the numbers in Congress to legitimize a nominating decision made by caucus, followed suit in December with their own delegate convention. Jackson himself, deep into a feud with Calhoun over South Carolina's nullification of federal tariffs, finally heeded his aides' suggestion in calling for a convention in May 1832, where his renomination was a fait accompli and the main task was to secure support for Van Buren as vice president in place of Calhoun.

Even with this late start, over subsequent cycles Democrats became the main innovators in, and justifiers of, the delegate convention as a political instrument.[52] For the 1832 gathering, they employed the unit rule (which bound delegates to the majority decisions of their state delegation) and required a two-thirds vote for nominations, thus ensuring the Jacksonians' dominance and preventing anti–Van Buren forces from sneaking a vice presidential nominee through by simple majority.[53] Twelve years later, the Democratic convention would produce the first dark-horse nominee, when state party leaders mobilized against Van Buren's renomination in the wake of his controversial opposition to the annexation of Texas. James K. Polk's nomination in 1844 proved enduringly significant for American parties writ large, affirming both the national convention's deliberative function as a decision-making mechanism and state parties' status as the real power centers within the national body.

For the Democratic Party in particular, the convention that elevated Polk left a lasting legacy for another reason. Delegates had narrowly, but fatefully, readopted the two-thirds rule in a floor vote thanks to the efforts of anti–Van Buren forces, predominant in the South. Van Buren then won simple majorities in successive ballots for the nomination, only to watch Polk amass two-thirds support and prevail on the ninth ballot. It is no small irony that the two-thirds rule had originated in 1832 as a device to disempower allies of Calhoun and ensure the New Yorker's nomination as vice president, for in 1844, it first demonstrated its enduring utility as an instrument of southern power within the Democratic Party. (Notably, neither Whigs nor, in turn, Republicans ever employed such a mechanism.) As long as southern delegations operated as a bloc, the two-thirds rule gave them veto authority in party decision-making.

This exercise of minority power within the party pointed to the thin line separating the accommodationist principle of coalition from the Calhounian tradition that put section over party. When, at the apex of Franklin Roosevelt's political power in 1936, the Democratic convention at last revoked the two-thirds rule, it harbingered a sea change in the balance of forces within the party.

While the congressional caucus had offered an informal connection between legislative and executive authority,[54] the delegate convention placed presidential politics at the very center of party affairs and crystallized an enduring tension in the relationship between parties and the presidency. Van Buren had identified it back in his 1827 letter to Ritchie, when he framed his proposed new party as, among other things, a means to render Jackson's election a "result of a combined and concerted effort of a political party holding in the main to certain tenets" rather than merely "the result of [Jackson's] military service without reference to party and . . . scarcely to principle."[55] The former approach would reconcile democracy with principled governance. The latter promised instead personalistic rule devoid of collective responsibility. But Jackson, whose outsized personal magnetism came to dominate an entire political age, fit awkwardly at the helm of a political movement that took as a very principle the elevation of party over individuals. In later eras, when the authority and vitality of state and local parties declined and plebiscitary tendencies within both the parties and the presidency exerted new influence, the dangers Van Buren identified would overwhelm the restraints of party.[56]

The Second Party System channeled the spectacle of Jeffersonian popular politics into vastly more sustained electioneering machinery. Political rallies and parades, songs, and a wondrous material culture gave nationalized partisanship a highly localized, often rough-hewn expression.[57] State and local parties, aping the Regency approach, served as nodes in a far-flung network, while auxiliary organizations in communities big and small provided the local voluntary base for campaign activity, starting with the Hickory Clubs dotting the country in 1828.

Partisan newspapers reflected the same duality, serving as both national party operators and deeply rooted community fixtures. The major organs worked as the regional communications agents of the party organizations, launching campaign broadsides with hierarchical coordination—"the regular troops in political warfare," James Buchanan remarked in 1844.[58] For their part, the hundreds of small-town newspapers across the country rendered national politics tangible and intensely local. "AGITATION is what is wanted . . . to secure the democratic cause," George Bancroft's *Bay State Democrat* exhorted in 1839. "Agitation by the press—agitation by Lectures and addresses—agitation by the people at home, and abroad, *among the people*, in conversation in the villages, in the fields and by the road side."[59]

In 1840, the Whigs paid tribute to the rivals whose campaign bacchanalias they had so often condemned by beating the Democrats at their own game. "Keep a constant watch on the doubtful voters," young Abraham Lincoln admonished Illinois county Whig agents in January 1840, "and from time to time have them talked to by those in whom they have the most confidence."[60] Spectacles organized by state parties, bankrolled by eastern merchants and manufacturers, and overseen nationally by the arch-accommodationist Thurlow Weed and a Whig executive committee organized in Congress channeled the revivalist zeal of the party's supporters into effective electoral action.[61] When tens of thousands of Whig young men assembled to march in militia formation on the streets of Baltimore in order to upstage the *Democrats'* own convention, they made plain the full extent of the Jacksonians' contribution to American electoral politics, now come to bite them. The Democrats were left to note ruefully, "We have taught them how to conquer us!"[62]

Campaign hoopla and press broadsides were but tools in service of the ultimate goal: corralling men to the polls on election day to vote the party ticket. As the printed ballot supplanted old practices of voice voting during these years, it transformed the entire electoral system.[63] Parties, not any arm of the state, printed and distributed the ballots, which listed party candidates for every level of office, often accompanied by patriotic motifs.[64] At the frequently raucous polling place, voters took tickets from watchful party agents and then deposited them into the ballot box. This system required vast outlays of labor and resources to ensure that every voter got his ticket. And as a matter of strategy, it pushed parties toward all-out mobilization of loyalists more than candidate- or policy-specific campaigns of persuasion.

Election Day polling places were boisterous and thrumming spaces where the sacred exercise of democratic choice took place under decidedly unidealized circumstances. With party agents plying voters with whisky and groups of partisans free to hoorah and harangue outside the polling window, drunkenness was ubiquitous, brawling common, and violence not infrequent. (The overwhelming maleness of polling places only encouraged behaviors and language that mixed company would have likely discouraged.) In a diary entry, a first-time voter in St. Louis recounted his attempt to cast a Democratic ballot in 1838, only to be mobbed by four Whigs and violently turned away. "I saw the Whigs exulting in what they had done. I was very angry but felt much like a whipped dog. I made some remark on the liberty of suffrage, &c., &c."[65] Here was accommodationism in its starkest form, manifest in Election Day practices that made a mockery of republican notions of virtuous deliberation—"a kind of sorcerer's workshop in which the minions of opposing parties turned money into whisky and whisky into votes."[66]

Even as party organizations and electoral practice began to converge toward a national model, regional differences with roots in the colonial period remained salient.[67] Mid-Atlantic states like Pennsylvania, Delaware, and of course New York (the "graduate school of American politics") elaborated furthest many of the Second Party System's core features: extensive organizational machinery, professional operatives, and high voter turnout.[68] New England, long marked by a political culture emphasizing the protection of ordered liberty, was a stronghold for Whiggery with relatively low turnout. (New Hampshire stood out as a rare Democratic bastion in the region thanks to organizer par excellence Isaac Hill, who ruled from a Concord office nicknamed "the Dictator's Palace.")[69] Most southern states retained older imprints of personalism, localism, and disorganization even as national partisan identities solidified.[70] Out West, population growth and churn across underdeveloped communities slowed the emergence of party organization.[71] And at the intersection of southern and frontier political culture in settler-populated areas like western Georgia, Alabama, and Mississippi, electoral politics retained an informality and rowdiness—replete with "barbecues, gander-pullings, shooting-matches, pole-climbings, and, not infrequently, duels"—much less on display back East.[72]

A party that demanded loyalty had to reward its loyalists. Though the Jacksonians hardly invented patronage—any survey of the colonies' courthouse politics should testify to that—the mass party organization they originated proved to be the perfect accommodationist vehicle for mobilizing activism with material incentives. The Jacksonian era saw a great proliferation of elected offices, which created in turn a vast, new, and continuing need for labor and resources to staff and administer the electoral process at all levels of government.[73] At the federal level, Jackson pursued a policy of rotation in the executive branch more comprehensive and broad-based than that of his predecessors, though far from the revolutionary break from past practice hyperbolized by his opponents.[74]

Formal parties remained underorganized in large cities, dependent instead on the delegated work of fire companies, militias, and gangs to get voters to the polls. (William Tweed was one of many rising urban bosses whose political career began in the firehouse.)[75] Only late in the antebellum period, in the cities most advanced along the processes of industrialization, did systems of patronage achieve sufficient density and monopoly control over municipal government to constitute full-fledged party machines.[76] Those machines, with their working-class (and increasingly immigrant-heavy) constituencies and their aversion to more programmatic laborite appeals, embodied the limits of the class politics at work in Jacksonian Democracy.[77] The new machine bosses "began where the patrician left off," aping the beneficence and republican obligation the eighteenth-century gentry had displayed to their constituents. Only now, leaders came armed not with charity but with "municipal construction, the night watch, and . . . paying jobs in the fire department."[78]

The Whigs sang from the old civic-republican hymnal to condemn the ways that spoils had sullied the body politic, as when Virginia governor James Barbour demanded that Democrats "put down the horrible proscription for opinion's sake, which makes slaves of the thousands in office, and of the tens of thousands aspiring to office, who hope by their greater abasement to expel the incumbents."[79] But patronage proved so central to the workings of nineteenth-century politics writ large that no single party could either claim or disclaim ownership over it. Spoils were the payment for party workers' labor and the binding agent of party operations. In turn, the spoils system encouraged specialty less in substantive issues or venues than in that great passion of the Second Party System: the political game itself.

Class, Market, and Politics

The Jacksonians applied old Jeffersonian precepts to the new realities of a bustling, expanding society. In so doing, they merged opposition to the entanglement of economic and political power with a zeal for democracy among white men. That zeal compelled the party to police, often brutally, the boundary for participation in the new mass democracy. As its first practitioners demonstrated, the accommodationist strand of party politics can entail not only great feats of popular mobilization but also extensive collective violence.

Jacksonians offered a particular response to the spread of capitalist relations and flows of information via print, post, and telegraph—"the rise," in one historian's words, "of heartless markets and heartless men."[80] Together, these transformations served to entrench slave-based plantation agriculture in the South, as soaring international demand secured the reign of King Cotton across the region, while swelling the ranks of urban commercial centers across the American North.[81] Advances in transportation— inland canals in the 1820s, railroads in the 1830s—catalyzed industrial transformations that upended working life. Textiles in southern New England and ironworks in Pennsylvania and Ohio converted rapidly to machine-driven production carried out by proletarianized labor in large factories, while the handicrafts predominant in cities saw more small-scale erosion of traditional master-apprentice relations.[82]

In the face of such transformations, Democrats stood less as anticapitalist opponents of growth than as defenders of the market from the corrupt political control of concentrated elites. They were inheritors of a republican tradition that viewed politics as the shaper of economic and class relations rather than the other way around.[83] Jacksonians thus saw in their opponents' aggressive deployments of government action the tyrannical fusion of political and economic power. Those "systems of corporations and exclusive privileges" and "partial legislation," as they put it in their 1835 party statement, "enable the rich to become richer, and render the poor poorer."[84] Their own party project bootstrapped republican virtue to a new kind of rough-and-tumble democratic populism.

The most galvanizing of the Jacksonians' political-economic projects, one that electrified party cadres at the time and endured as political folklore for generations to come, was the Bank War waged against the Second Bank of the United States, then presided over by Philadelphia patrician Nicholas Biddle. Jackson's momentous 1832 veto message concerning the bank's rechartering framed the dispute as a contest pitting the "the rich . . . and the potent" against "the humble members of society—the farmers, mechanics, and laborers." It also made radical new assertions about presidents' democratic legitimacy. The bank, he said to justify his veto, was not only unconstitutional but contrary to "justice and good policy."[85]

Unspoken but implicit in Jackson's argument was a defense of the mass political party that harnessed his power as president by rendering him the tribune of a national popular majority. Each ensuing battle in the war—Jackson's removal of the bank's deposits in 1833 and Biddle's retaliatory contraction of credit; Jackson's censure by the Senate in 1834; Jackson's executive order in 1836 requiring purchases of government land to be backed by gold and silver; and his successor Van Buren's protracted efforts to establish an "independent treasury" to manage the government's money—took center stage in popular electioneering during campaign season.[86]

Drawing on venerable republican themes of mutuality and equality, a more potent note of class politics than that detected in the Bank War emerged from the burgeoning world of labor radicalism. Mechanics in major urban centers of the North made forays into electoral politics by the dawn of the Jacksonian age.[87] The flash-fire faction-ridden Working Men's Party movements were first sparked in 1829 by recessionary conditions and resistance among journeymen to anticipated lengthening of the workday. Movement ideologists like William Gouge of Philadelphia and Thomas Skidmore of New York merged Jeffersonian bromides with a radical new critique of capitalist labor and property relations.

Labor radicalism, in both doctrine and political practice, was distinct from Jacksonian Democracy.[88] Jacksonians, committed to laissez-faire, generally neglected labor priorities such as the ten-hour day and protections for trade unions. For their part, the radicals, scarred by the factional skullduggery that undermined the Working Men's movements, retained a discomfort with the organizational politics of what a unionist paper denounced as the "wire-pullers who move the juggling machines of 'the party.'"[89]

Nevertheless, the tributaries between laborite politics and Jacksonianism were many and varied, and they lent substance to the Democrats' long-standing reputation as the party of the common man. On monopoly, finance, and currency, the "Workies" took Jacksonian stances to their extremes. The Philadelphia Working Men's Party described paper-money banking as "the foundation of *artificial* inequality of wealth, and, thereby, of *artificial* inequality of power."[90] New York's militant Democratic Locofocos, so named for the torches they lit after their factional opponents killed the gaslights to suppress their insurgency, drew both from the Workies' memberships and from their fusion of class consciousness with classical critiques of privilege. Their hard line on currency and banking matters influenced New York and, via Van Buren, national policy, all the way through the passage of the independent treasury in 1840. That same year, Van Buren issued an executive order mandating the ten-hour workday in all federal public works. By 1842, a meeting of Democratic mechanics could combine an assertion of class conflict with explicit partisanship, declaring that "the best protectors of the laboring classes are the laborers themselves" rather than "the Whig capitalists who volunteer on our behalf."[91]

The White Man's Republic

Even as laborite influences informed Jacksonian Democrats' egalitarian political project for white men, the party consistently reaffirmed and refined strict boundaries of inclusion and exclusion, providing a glimpse of the nascent populist strand in American party politics. Where their Whig opponents more naturally countenanced a range of statuses and ranks populating a mutualistic political community, the Democracy's full-throated rejection of political hierarchy required—absent an acceptance of multiracial democracy—an equally committed exclusion of racial minorities from the community altogether.

Nowhere were Jacksonians' egalitarian and eliminationist impulses more violently yoked than in their commitment of state power on behalf of rapid settler expansion and appropriation of Native lands.[92] In both the substance and vote count, the legislative fight over the Indian Removal Act of 1830 offered a polarized harbinger of the party system in formation.[93] National Republicans offered moral indictments of the legislation's betrayal of federal treaties, asking, "How shall we justify this trespass to ourselves?" while the Jacksonian John Forsyth of Georgia dismissed such carping as the self-interested plea of the "Christian party in politics" looking to stir up sympathy for the Indians as a boon to missionaries.[94] As the removal policy unfolded across the decade as a debacle of state incompetence and brutality, Democratic soldiers like Silas Wright and Isaac Hill continued to denounce the policy's critics as "fanatics."[95] It was Van Buren, not Jackson, who presided over the forced march of the Cherokee in 1838 that killed thousands, while also pushing to expel the Seneca from the state of New York.[96]

As with the Bank War, conflict over Indian removal occasioned new claims by the Jacksonians on behalf of popular constitutionalism in the face of conflict with the Supreme Court. And it cut just as directly to a core substantive tenet of their party project: the depiction of obligations toward outsiders to the political community as an intolerable threat to democracy itself. As Jackson explained in his message to Congress in 1833, the subjects of federal removal "have neither the intelligence, the industry, the moral habits, nor the desire of improvement which are essential to any favorable change in their condition. . . . They must necessarily yield to the force of circumstances and ere long disappear."[97]

The same logic governed the tendency—hardly limited to Jacksonian Democrats but strongly associated with them by the 1840s—to pair democratization for whites with disenfranchisement, repression, and physical exclusion of free African Americans.[98] A Democrat at the new state of Michigan's constitutional convention in 1835 took a typical tack in declaring his opposition to enfranchising any African Americans "until we consent to treat them as equal with us in all respects"—a self-evident nonstarter.[99] That same all-or-nothing argument arose at virtually every state-level debate over the reform of suffrage requirements for Black residents. The herrenvolk tendency likewise permeated laborite politics in antebellum cities, notwithstanding notable exceptions among individual radicals who followed their ideological commitments into antislavery and abolitionist politics.[100] More representative, if atypically colorful, was the political career of the Irish immigrant and roughneck Bowery brawler Mike Walsh, who led a faction of New York City Democrats in the 1840s espousing radical anti-capitalist rhetoric while also denouncing abolitionist "fanatics," Free Soil "traitors," and the "long-heeled Negroes" they duped.[101]

The emerging abolitionist movement not only irritated Democrats' accommodationist tenets with its zealous moralism but raised their suspicions as it took aim at the very idea of cross-sectional coalition. Democrats mobbed and disrupted abolitionist meetings in cities across the North. After a crowd in Charleston invaded a post office in 1835 and, with official approval, set abolitionist mailings on fire, postmaster general Amos Kendall agreed that the U.S. postal service would not forward provocative material anywhere where state law prohibited its dissemination. In Congress a year later, Van Buren would shepherd to passage a resolution barring the discussion of antislavery petitions from the House floor—the so-called gag rule. The party's 1835 manifesto denounced the Whigs' "mischievous and wicked" efforts to fulminate division between North and South while touting united Democratic patriotism as the force "which ties the hands of the abolitionists and fanatics in the north, and scorns their doctrines."[102] Within a decade, those very measures would come to be seen by increasing numbers of northern Democrats not as the coalitional glue securing the protection of the white man's republic but as a threat to white men's own political liberties at the hands of an encroaching Slave Power.

The Ambivalence of Whiggery

Jacksonians provoked a political opposition that became, by the later 1830s, the second mass party in history. A powerful tension ran through it. Even as Whigs threw themselves into electoral combat, they retained a profound ambivalence toward party itself, emphasizing individual virtue more than collective organization as the guarantor of liberty. Whigs saw in the encrustation of party organization a corrupting imposition on republican institutions that shackled individual conscience. "This word 'organization' has a harsh, unpleasant sound," wrote the editor of the *Michigan Whig*. "It calls up to our view free minds bound in fetters, drilled, disciplined, like the foot soldiers of a marching regiment." In this line of thinking, party politics was all but synonymous with "Van Buren politics . . . a gigantic system of slavery and corruption."[103] In combating Van Buren himself in the election of 1836, the party would not overcome their own ambivalence about party to choose a national nominee at a delegate convention, running three regional candidates instead. The Whigs' deep connections to the anti-party strand help to explain their recurring organizational struggles and rapid collapse. "It is no accident that the major party to permanently dissolve," writes the party's leading chronicler, "was the one that set less store by its own existence."[104]

And yet the Whig Party contested competitively for offices at all levels of government, forging popular ties of loyalty and meaning in every region of the country. First taking partisan form in the wake of the Bank War in 1834, the Whigs rode periodic waves of electoral enthusiasm but proved less effective than Democrats at building the party machinery to sustain activity between those surges. The party's close connections to the moral reform movements powering so much extrapartisan and third-party politics in antebellum America rendered it all the less resilient in the face of strain. And so, seemingly as soon as it had organized, the party began to disintegrate.

Though such demographic distinctions were hardly absolute, Whigs compared to Democrats tended to be more rather than less prosperous, pietistic rather than liturgical Protestants or Catholics, of Yankee or

English (or, in smaller numbers, Black) rather than Irish or German stock, and located in commercially integrated rather than frontier or self-sufficient communities.[105] This last distinction applied also to the bases of the two parties in the South during the region's last era of stable two-party competition for over a century.

If all party projects contain contradictions, it might be said distinctively for the Whigs that those contradictions were the very heart of the project. The same impulses accounting for the party's institutional fragility and evanescence also supplied much of its vitality and power. The Whigs' substantive project, drawing on incipient themes that would develop into the pro-capital and policy-reform strands, married positive use of the state to promote commercial development and national integration to belief in man's capacity—nudged, or more, by that same active state—to master his own passions in service of moral virtue. Even as Whigs looked askance at the organizational stuff of party-building, their combination of moral zeal and devotion to the constructive use of public power together portended a future of party politics fueled by cause.[106] But it would not be their own future.

Whigs inherited from the old deferential politics the notion that natural leaders embodied civic-republican virtue. "In the same proportion that party spirit obtains a predominance in any free government, and secures its own steady triumph," wrote Supreme Court justice Joseph Story in an unsigned paean to Daniel Webster, "just in the same proportion it will suppress or dispense with the services of statesmen."[107] As party organization suppressed virtuous leadership, so, too, did partisan spirit turn individuals into prisoners of passion and unreason, every bit as much as liquor or licentiousness did. It was thus no surprise that the campaign that saw the Whigs finally wield electioneering hoopla to victory also occasioned intensive hand-wringing. Noting the "immense assemblages" of the Whigs' campaign events in 1840, with crowds routinely numbering in the tens of thousands, John Quincy Adams saw "a revolution in the habits and manners of the people. Where will it end? . . . Their manifest tendency is to civil war."[108] To reconcile their suspicions of party organization and party spirit with the practical necessity of both, Whigs arrived at a normative distinction that separated parties of substantive principle from parties of mere gamesmanship and patronage, in which "the spoils were the highest stake at risk."[109]

If the Whigs suffered from their own ideological suspicions of party organization, they also drew on the distinct commitments and methods of the reform causes to which the party was so closely linked. The great surge of moral reformism attending the Second Great Awakening was concentrated in areas of eventual electoral strength for the party, comprising what a writer in 1822 termed "the Universal Yankee Nation": New England and areas settled by its emigrants in central and western New York, northwestern Pennsylvania, and northeastern Ohio.[110] The road to eternal salvation, revivalist crusaders preached, lay in moral improvement. And so religious revival paved the way for public campaigns on behalf of anti-Masonry, Indian rights, temperance, Sabbatarianism, prison reform, aid to mental hospitals, the abolition of dueling, and—most explosively and most complicating for the Whigs—antislavery.[111]

The underorganized Whigs made extensive use of the reformers' extrapartisan forms of political advocacy. Reform movements such as temperance capitalized on far-flung distribution networks for religious texts that revivalists had devised.[112] Across the 1830s and 1840s, mass petition campaigns aimed at state and national legislatures drew over 800,000 signatories to memorials beseeching action on behalf of causes that had prominent Whig support.[113] Later, the popular mobilization led by ex-drinkers of the Washingtonian movement saw the development of an array of dry social activities—parades, public festivals, public orations, and theatrical performances—intended to supplant the dram shop while tapping into the same communal experiences that suffused party politics.[114] The Whigs' overlap with moral reformism and their comparative comfort with a gradation of civic statuses also help to explain the notable prominence of women in their campaigns—in roles ranging well beyond the waving of white handkerchiefs, which Aaron Perry had highlighted in Columbus in 1840.[115]

The "moralization of politics" that occasioned the Whigs' national surge in the late 1830s generally helped to bolster loyalty and discipline in a party with feebler organizational means of fostering those qualities.[116]

An intense and infectious revivalist spirit, more so than all the claptrap, was at the heart of what made the 1840 campaign such a source of widespread awe and enduring fascination.[117] And when New York governor William H. Seward publicly took the pledge of abstinence in 1842, around the same time that state representative Abraham Lincoln gave a speech to Washingtonians in Illinois praising their movement, it underlined the typically symbiotic relationship between the Whig Party and the temperance crusade.[118] But moralism could have the opposite effect when the tolls of political expediency grew too steep, engendering the kind of denunciation offered up by the reformer Gerrit Smith when he decried those Whigs who "had become so partyized as to be far more concerned for their party than for Temperance or Freedom."[119]

Substantively, the Whigs' gloss on the shared civic-republican inheritance of the Second Party System was providential and forward-looking, while the Jacksonians stood fast and wary. The Whig economic program followed in a tradition of active state action stretching back to Hamilton's *Report on Manufactures*, the spirit of which found stark expression in President John Quincy Adams's message to Congress in 1825: "Liberty is power."[120] The interlocking policies of Henry Clay's American System, designed to develop the country commercially while integrating it across sections, came to provide something of a party doctrine: a high tariff, revenue sharing with the states, and sustained investment in internal improvements. The Whigs' project contrasted with the Democrats' not only in its unbridled advocacy of commercial development and its national as opposed to local orientation, but also in its belief in the harmony of interests and organic unity of society. At times, anticipating a theme in the pro-capital party strand, Whigs' dismissal of zero-sum social conflict flirted with complacency. According to a party ideologist's brief against class politics, "That policy which destroys the profit of money, destroys the profit of labor. Let government strike at the rich, and the blow falls on the heads of the poor."[121]

The Whigs' insistence on the mutuality of interests ranged beyond questions of class to serve as the underlying outlook of its southern wing. It was not a disposition that could withstand the emergence of virulent southern nationalism.[122] Southern Whiggery had disparate bases: in the ports and cities that had formerly proved hospitable to Federalism, among some of the wealthiest and most commercially integrated of the black-belt planters, in the south Louisiana base of the tariff-loving sugar planters, and among smallholders in the backcountry of western Virginia and North Carolina. These differing actors largely shared support for regional economic development and diversification that would help to foster *national* integration. "I have endeavored to implant in the minds of all the people of Georgia," Senator John MacPherson Berrien told a Boston audience in 1844, "that . . . the whole country is their country, and that they have a great and deep interest in whatever concerns the prosperity of the whole country."[123] But southern Whigs' support for economic modernization was an economic bet that failed to pay off. As the consolidation of King Cotton helped to bolster a far more belligerent southern ideology that put sectional interests foremost and celebrated slavery as a positive good, the Whigs' southern ranks collapsed.

If the back-and-forth between party commitment and movement activism had always proved a double-edged sword for Whiggery, it be-came fatal in the face of the sectional crisis. Henry Clay, the great border-state champion of reconciliation through statesmanship, clung to his plan for African colonization and gradual transition from slavery while denouncing the "wild and ruinous schemes" and "intemperate zeal" of those abolitionists "stirring up strife and agitating the pas-sions."[124] But it was the ambitious new antislavery figures—Thaddeus Stevens, Joshua Giddings, Benjamin Wade—whose politics came to define the party's northern wing. Soon enough, the Whigs' great-party reach exceeded their grasp. In the face of *the* great irrepressible cause of the mid-nineteenth century, their jerry-rigged coalition and moralizing tendencies pulled the party in different directions and destroyed it.[125]

Contradictions of Expansionism

Jacksonians' commitment to rapid westward expansion had long mobi-lized the electoral loyalties of western settlers—along with millions of their countrymen—in the name of a hardy and racially circum-scribed egalitarian project. During the booming 1840s, that Democratic expansionism turned at once more forward-looking and more bel-licose.[126] Conflict over war with Mexico and then over slavery in the territories added in the postwar Mexican Cession began to fissure the alignments and coalitions from the brief stable phase of the Second Party System. In the coming years, politics would drift toward the vortex.[127]

For the doomed Whig Party, the destabilizing effects were straight-forward, as northern Whigs became increasingly antislavery in disposi-tion while their southern counterparts grew cowed and ambivalent. But expansionism also struck at the heart of a distinctly Jacksonian contra-diction. The frontier served as a guarantor of white equality in Democratic ideology, ensuring not just yeomen independence but broad-based property distribution.[128] But with free labor northerners dominating the ranks of those heading west, slave interests began to see expansion as a threat to the peculiar institution's political survival. In turn, their agitated response struck at the very liberties that made the white man's republic *republican*.[129] Expansion politics thus forced a choice— for or against the Slave Power—that could no longer be papered over by the coalitionism the Democrats had practiced so effectively for a generation.

Party machinations kicked off the new politics of expansion. Martin Van Buren's unexpected opposition to annexing Texas doomed his re-nomination prospects in 1844 and set the stage for the elevation of "Young Hickory," James K. Polk. New York's delegation held out the longest for Van Buren at the national convention—but that state's De-mocracy was itself riven by two rival factions, each entangled in com-plicated allegiances with party actors in other states: the conservative "Hunkers" under William Marcy, who sought to hunker down for patron-age and keep up ties with the South, and the radical "Barnburners," loyal to Van Buren and leaning toward antislavery policies for new territories. That schism, as New York politics so often did, would bear national significance soon enough.

In his short yet emboldened presidency, Polk married true-blue Jack-sonianism to a maximalist agenda for continental expansion.[130] His maneuvers triggered war with Mexico in spring 1846. The unexpectedly protracted and bloody conflict unfolded over the next two years, drawing U.S. forces all the way to Mexico City. Opposition to the war, both in and out of formal political settings, homed in on the role of slavery, and disaffected northern and western Democrats followed suit.[131] Senator Thomas Hart Benton of Missouri, a slave owner in his own right and an outspoken advocate of Indian removal and settlers' access to western public lands, abandoned his longtime position as protector of the Democrats' sectional alliance. He had first begun to reconsider in the mid-1830s, when southern politicians moved to suppress the mail and impose the congressional gag rule on discussion of antislavery petitions.[132] By the time of the push for an immediate annexation of Texas in 1844, Benton had come to see the proposed treaty as an unjust bid for war that was also, at the hands of slavers' agents, "artfully contrived to dissolve the Union."[133]

David Wilmot, a junior House member from Pennsylvania rather than a titan of the Senate, took Benton's extension of the Democratic project one step further into antislavery politics, with explosive results. Factionalism and doctrine entwined tightly in nineteenth-century parties: as with Benton, Wilmot's antislavery maneuverings stemmed in part from his allegiance to the Van Burenites and the belief that a direct riposte had become necessary as a way to sanction Polk's southern-dominated administration for ignoring what they deemed "the obligations of party."[134] But he ranged far beyond faction in justifying his proposal, first made in 1846 and known as the Wilmot Proviso, for a ban on slavery in all newly acquired territories. Reminding listeners of his record of battling "time and again against the Abolitionists of the North," Wilmot insisted that he "would preserve to free white labor a fair country, a rich inheritance, where the sons of toil, of my own race and color, can live without the disgrace with which association with negro slavery brings upon free labor."[135] The legislative dynamics presaged the tumultuous 1850s. Wilmot's amendment twice passed the House, with support from northern Democrats and northern Whigs, while stalling both times thanks to bipartisan southern opposition in the Senate. In short order, Wilmot, the defender of the old-time Jacksonian religion, would bolt the Democrats to join the Free Soil Party.

The Fall of the Second Party System

Political antislavery emerged in these years to contest what it saw as the untrammeled reach of the Slave Power.[136] The first antislavery party, known as the Liberty Party, formed in 1839 by abolitionists opposed to William Lloyd Garrison and his "non-voting principle." It met little electoral success, winning seven thousand votes in the 1840 presidential election and sixty-two thousand four years later. Dogmatic sectarianism limited its broader appeal, as did a strong anti-party streak that prohibited any support for members of major parties. The Liberty Party even opposed the 1844 reelection of Joshua Giddings, the most ardent antislavery Whig in the House.[137]

The Free Soil Party of 1848 sought to build a bigger tent for political antislavery. Developments in the New York Democracy led the way. Hunkers dominated patronage under Polk and, with a narrow majority at the state Democratic convention, took every delegate slot for themselves over the Barnburners' strenuous protests. The Barnburners sent their own delegation to the national convention in Baltimore, but they walked out once it was clear that a Hunker-allied candidate, Lewis Cass of Michigan, had the presidential nomination sewn up.[138] It was a dramatic departure from the commandment to put party first—but also a signal to the Hunkers that they had violated the expectations of players in the game, and their behavior had consequences.[139] Northern Whigs found reason for a bolt of their own after Zachary Taylor of Louisiana, a favorite of the party's pro-slavery element who claimed to disavow partisanship, won its nomination.

And so the stage was set. Dissident Democrats and Whigs joined together with the bulk of Liberty Party supporters willing to accept a candidate strongly opposed to the expansion of slavery but not calling for its extinction. The Little Magician, surprisingly, signaled his willingness to run. A series of deals, culminating in a convention twenty thousand strong in Buffalo, gave Van Buren the Free Soil Party's presidential nomination, the impeccably Whiggish Charles Francis Adams of Massachusetts the second spot on the ticket, and Liberty Party loyalists a platform strong enough to accept the nominee. "No more Slave States and no more Slave Territory," it proclaimed. "Let the soil of our extensive domains be kept free for the hardy pioneers of our own land, and the oppressed and banished of other lands, seeking homes of comfort and fields of enterprise in the new world."[140]

The Free Soil campaign was at once strongly ideological and issue oriented—unusually so for the nineteenth century—and ambivalent in its purposes. The bolters' status in their old parties remained ambiguous. Antislavery forces had come together for the first time, forging new bonds with one another regardless of old loyalties and demonstrating the possibilities of joint action. Across the North, a slew of future Republicans cut their teeth in the campaign. Yet the party failed to gather all its potential supporters, ultimately winning 10 percent of the vote and no states. In June 1849, the Barnburners, desirous for patronage and again aiming to take control of the Democracy from within, reunited with the Hunkers.[141]

The last gasp to sustain the conflict displacement over slavery came in what posterity would call the Compromise of 1850. The multi-bill package, devised to resolve the fate of slavery in the Mexican Cession, joined Democratic accommodationism together with Whig statesmanship.[142] After months of stalemate, the moderate coalition supporting the measures finally eked out a series of narrow majorities to secure passage through Congress—while finding itself flanked on both sides by opposition. Those opponents' ranks would swell in the ensuing years as conflicts intensified over the Compromise's own policies, most notably the principle of "popular sovereignty" and the new fugitive slave law. In his last floor speech during debate over the package, the dying Henry Clay called out "the violence and intemperance of party spirit," which he now saw stirring not from the formal party lines but from the sectional divide, and made a last plea for "the spirit of mutual forbearance."[143] But his copartisan William Seward came closer to the tenor of the political moment—and of the spirit that would soon animate a new great party—when he insisted on the Senate floor that "there is a higher law than the Constitution" that must be obeyed.[144]

In 1855, Seward would quite literally march straight from a Whig state convention to a Republican one.[145] It is a telling detail of how the institutions that arose at the dawn of American mass politics would continue to structure political life, in the political convention above all. The chapters to come trace how party actors have interpreted and reinterpreted antebellum parties' contradictory legacies. Two overarching points stand out. First, whatever one's appraisal of the *practice* of party politics, the *public discussion* of party politics has unambiguously declined over time. The nineteenth century's frank appraisals of how parties should be organized, and what small-d democratic and small-r republican purposes they might serve, offer models for our own hollowed age, when forthright defenses of political parties are conspicuous by their absence.[146] Still more important is the bedrock truth that early mass parties, for all their flaws, bequeathed a genuinely popular and participatory politics.[147] The torchlight parade would soon fade away. Its unmet promise still haunts American politics.

3

Free Labor Republicanism as a Party Project

IN A pamphlet written for the 1868 campaign and meant to be read aloud, the Union Republican Congressional Committee explained why newly emancipated and enfranchised freedmen should support the Republican Party. Its succinct framing of the differences between the parties offers a window into the extraordinary social and political transformations that the Republicans had wrought:

> Q. Who abolished slavery in the District of Columbia?
> A. A Republican Congress and Abraham Lincoln, a Republican President.
> Q. Who freed the slaves in the South?
> A. Abraham Lincoln, the Republican President, by a proclamation....
> Q. Who passed the Freedmen's Bureau Bill?
> A. A Republican Congress by more than a two-thirds vote over the veto of Andrew Johnson, the leader of the Democratic or Conservative party.
> Q. Who gave us the Civil Rights Bill?
> A. The same Republican Congress.
> Q. What party gave us the right to vote?
> A. The Republican party....
> Q. Colored men should then vote with the Republican or Radical party?

A. They should, and shun the Democratic party as they would the overseer's lash and the auction block. . . .

Q. To what party do the leading colored men belong?

A. Without exception they belong to the Republican party.

Q. What are the most prominent principles advocated by the Republican party?

A. Equal rights before the law and at the ballot box for all men without regard to race or color.[1]

The transformative Republican project of the 1850s and 1860s brought together patronage politics, industrial might, and revolutionary radicalism. Party politicians, engaging in all the blandishments and inducements of their trade, endeavored to stop the expansion of slavery, to free the slaves, and then to give civil and political rights to African Americans. A political party, indisputably great in the Tocquevillian sense, contested for and seized the reins of power and redeemed the promise of the American republic. At the apex of their ambitions, the Republicans of the Civil War era highlighted both the emancipatory and the violent possibilities of parties as agents of change. But as northern Republicans' commitment to southern Reconstruction waned, the party's life as a self-consciously disruptive vehicle in service of high principles came to a close. This chapter connects the nuts and bolts of party politics with the epochal confrontation over slavery and freedom, all joined together in the grandest and highest-stakes party project in the history of the republic.[2]

During the critical years from the run-up to war through Radical Reconstruction, the various supporters of the free labor project all gathered under a common banner. The hastily assembled Republican Party took a decidedly utilitarian approach to party.[3] It replicated familiar forms and localist orientations developed in the prior generation. Yet at their best, parties go beyond the particulars to offer visions of the good society and connect them to real political alternatives. If the bounds of their partisan loyalties proved fuzzy, in the larger task of public philosophy, Republicans of the founding generation succeeded more completely than any other political formulation before or since.

The goals of the Republican Party and the state blurred. Republicans traced their principles back to the Declaration of Independence and conceived their project in terms broader than party alone. The sentiment captured in one 1862 letter from a supporter—"the Administration party . . . really becomes the nation"—pushes against the venerable boundary that makes party claims partial.[4] The party during the Civil War era that actually conceived of itself *as a party*, that took as its animating purpose the advancement of party principles derived as such and followed the precepts of its forebears, was the Democratic Party—not the Republicans.

A counterpoint political tradition, rooted in the South, also came into its own across the middle of the nineteenth century. This apartisan vision, articulated with unmatched fervor by John C. Calhoun in the prior generation, rejected the coalitional ethos of party politics outright in favor of a bedrock commitment to sectional interests and ideology.[5] For southern elites, the cross-sectional Second Party System had failed to protect their interests—and in its wake a new party drove them to outrage and secession. So they embraced an alternative approach: the wartime Confederacy had no parties and no organized opposition to Jefferson Davis.[6] The South would act as a solvent of national party visions and practices in a similar way well into the following century.

Free labor Republicanism brought diverse party strands together in an often-volatile mix. Politicians across the political spectrum still invoke Lincoln and his party, drawing on the pieces of its legacy closest to their own politics. Yet the divisions then and the appropriations now are far from straightforward. Instead, they reflect the ambivalence of the "last bourgeois revolution."[7]

In line with the distributionist patterns of nineteenth-century politics, the political professionals who ran the party engaged in the endless give-and-take of the accommodationist strand. To a degree that would surprise reformers of later vintage who have found small-party scheming evidence of a politician devoid of principles, radicals played the game every bit as arduously as moderates. Nevertheless, even as it availed itself of accommodationist tactics, free labor Republicanism had far larger goals.

The pro-capital strand has a fine Republican lineage as well.[8] Northern industry, along with laborers desirous of moving up in life, cast their lot with the party. "The prudent, penniless beginner in the world," Lincoln told a crowd at the Wisconsin State Fair in 1859, "labors for wages awhile, saves a surplus with which to buy tools or land, for himself; then labors on his own account another while, and at length hires another new beginner to help him. This, say its advocates, is free labor."[9] Not for nothing was Karl Rove a Lincoln buff.

Further leftward, the Republican program offered the still-incomplete glimmerings of a policy-reform strand. The Civil War Congress passed a burst of legislation, including the Homestead Act, the Morrill Act for land-grant colleges, and an income tax and currency measures to finance the war.[10] But extensive regulation of the economy would have to wait until the Progressive Era, while Reconstruction showed the limits of what attenuated federal power could accomplish to reshape the social relations of the South.

In the radical strand, finally, the horizons of party extend beyond the mere setting of policy.[11] Politicians support and open up space for, more than they ultimately direct, larger transformations of state and society powered by oppressed groups' own struggles. In just this way, Radical Republicans such as Joshua Giddings and Thaddeus Stevens fought a two-front war, battling both militants who favored direct action over the messiness of party politics and cautious politicians unready or unwilling to take risks and seize the moment.[12] As enslaved people rose up for their own liberation, turning the Civil War into a war for freedom, Radical Republicans supported the action on the ground.[13]

By treating free labor Republicanism as a party project and that project as a keystone of the Civil War era, we challenge other scholarly interpretations of party and of the period. A Cold War–era school of historical thought saw the Civil War as a deviation from the more "normal" nineteenth-century politics of give and take, one that left largely undisturbed those dominant patterns of localist, patronage-oriented politics stretching from the Albany Regency to the coming of the Progressives.[14] But such a perspective mistakes party form for content, missing the deeper issues behind all the machinations. From a different vantage point, a generation of social historians disillusioned with electoral politics emphasized the Garrisonian abolitionist tradition of direct action as the engine of change, letting high politics recede from view.[15] But that story leaves too much unanswered about who actually wielded power, especially once Republicans assumed office, and to what ends. Finally, current interpretations emphasize continuities in the long, intertwined history of racial oppression and American capitalism across the country's entire developmental trajectory, rather than a sharp rupture with emancipation.[16] But to see up close just how party politics worked as the agent of historical transformation is to reject such a flattened view that pushes collective struggle off to the side. The free labor Republican project offers a demonstration of the possibilities, for good and ill, of great parties.[17]

The Rise of the Republican Party

Within a mere seven years of its founding in 1854, the Republican Party held the presidency and, after secession, Congress. By so thoroughly redrawing the axes of cleavage dividing the parties, the 1850s mark a textbook case of party realignment.[18] The struggle against slavery traced back to the Revolutionary Era, while the core demand to stop its expansion into the territories came directly from the Free Soil Party. But the Republican Party, drawing in Whigs, Democrats, and dissenters in and around minor parties, was a different and altogether bigger endeavor. The cross-sectional bargain that had kept the union together since the Founding—and had explicitly undergirded the Second Party System since Martin Van Buren's 1827 letter to Thomas Ritchie—fell away, as politics reorganized around the slavery question.

Free labor ideology gave the Republican Party a deep coherence.[19] Republicans' antislavery views emerged from their comparison of the bustling North and its free institutions with the South, its spirit strangled by slavery's malicious influence. In the prosperity of its agriculture as it grew more efficient and in the work of artisans and manufacturers, advocates of free labor claimed, the North demonstrated its harmonious social virtues.[20] A free and broadly equal society honored the workman's toil and offered easy avenues for social advancement. The expansion of slavery into the territories encroached on wide-open lands that would extend that society's promise. But even beyond that, the slave system threatened free labor's most cherished values and so gave its critique a universalistic cast. As the redoubtable Radical Henry Wilson told workers of East Boston in an 1860 speech, "Put the brand of degradation upon the brow of one working man and the toiling millions of the globe share in that degradation."[21]

In the free labor view, the Slave Power threatened the North through its control over the national government—and a new party would break its stranglehold. Thus did social critique lead straight to party politics.[22] If the conspiratorial language was overwrought, southern power was very real.[23] The South dominated the Supreme Court, the Senate with its overrepresentation of slave states, and, via the two-thirds rule for presidential nomination, the Democratic Party. Since the Mexican War, southern leaders had feared the consequences from continued growth in the North and had pushed ever more aggressively to extend the reach of slavery into free states.[24]

The proximate issue for the Republican Party's creation was the Kansas-Nebraska Act of 1854, which repealed the Missouri Compromise and allowed settlers in newly organized territories to decide whether they wished to allow slavery. Members of Congress from the dying Whig Party all opposed the measure, while northern Democrats were divided down the middle. In the second volume of his *History of the Rise and Fall of the Slave Power in America*, published two decades hence while he served as vice president, Henry Wilson offered the Republican view: "A region of virgin soil, of fertility and beauty, consecrated by the solemn compact of the government to freedom and free institutions, was opened wide to dominating masters and cowering slaves. That faithless act was consummated by the servility of Northern men, who, seeing that the Slave Power was supreme, were led to believe that its ascendency would outlast their day; and with that assurance they seemed content to bow to its behests and do its bidding."[25]

With this backdrop, antislavery men began to look for a common political home. The process of party formation resembled that of other antislavery combinations. Mass meetings called for conventions, which then elected party officers and nominated candidates. One such meeting, which has gone down in history as the birth of the Republican Party, took place at a schoolhouse in Ripon, Wisconsin, on March 20, 1854, when the town's Whig and Free Soil Parties voted formally to dissolve themselves and form instead a joint committee.[26]

Initially, it was unclear what political formulations would triumph from the Whigs' collapse. In a swath of northern states, the temperance cause had roiled the parties. Another contender was the Know Nothing movement, which combined anti-Catholicism with an anti-party revulsion at mass politics familiar to conservative Whiggery.[27] Moderate antislavery supporters joined the cause, battling conspiracies of Rome and Slave Power alike. Free Soilers, distrusting nativism and keeping their eyes on the prize, generally steered clear.[28] The novelty of the lodge life that defined the movement soon wore off, and Know Nothing state governments in power practiced the same old politics that they had decried. By the time the Know Nothings formally declared themselves the American Party in 1855, their strength had peaked. Neither as organization nor as ideology could they build an effective political party.[29]

That same year, Republicans grew clearer that theirs would be no flash in the pan, and paid more attention to the mechanics of organizing. In New York, with conservatives having departed to the Know Nothings, the remaining Whigs under William Seward and his wily ally, Thurlow Weed, held their final convention in September 1855. There, they dissolved themselves and marched upstairs to join the Republicans, who had named an identical ticket.[30] In February 1856, after months of complex wrangling, Republicans succeeded in electing one of their number, Nathaniel Banks of Massachusetts, as Speaker of the House, with the support of scattered northern Know Nothings.[31] Still, different labels for antislavery parties persisted, and a common Republican identity formed only with the party's experience in power.

Republicans in this founding generation came to their party from others, and those prior commitments shaped their views of party. The Democracy saw itself as permanent; Republicans had come together for a particular purpose. The antislavery bulwark had already bolted from parties with insincere commitments, and if the need arose, they stood ready to do so again. As Lincoln's old law partner William Herndon warned in December 1860, "I helped to make the Republican party, and if it forsakes its distinctive ideas, I can help to tear it down, and help to erect a new party that shall never cower to any slave driver."[32] Only with such caveats did abolitionists support a Republican Party too reformist for their liking.[33] Ex-Democrats, for their part, extended the critique developed in the 1840s and painted a portrait of their former party's finest traditions cast asunder. When Republicans' plans for Reconstruction grew too expansive, many of those ex-Democrats would again stage a bolt. And the ex-Whigs who made up the majority of the new party often calibrated their appeals to the very ambivalence about party that was their inheritance. As Seward put it, "So long as the republican party shrill be firm and faithful to the constitution, the Union, and the rights of man, I shall serve it with the reservation of that personal independence which is my birthright, but, at the same time, with the zeal and devotion that patriotism allows and enjoins."[34]

The first Republican National Convention met in June 1856 in Philadelphia. A limited platform focused on opposing slavery in the territories and admitting Kansas as a free state.[35] The party's nominee, John Charles Frémont, "Pathfinder of the West," had the advantage of personal charisma and none of the prior ties that would repel potential supporters. (Weed kept Seward in reserve for 1860, when he might win.)[36] Along with violence in Kansas, as settlers fought over dueling pro- and antislavery constitutions, the caning of Massachusetts senator Charles Sumner by a South Carolina Democrat stirred northern passions. Together "Bleeding Kansas" and "Bleeding Sumner" furthered the Republican theme that the Slave Power was coming for free white Northerners. After an enthusiastic campaign, Frémont prevailed in New England, New York, and four states in the upper Midwest full of Yankee stock.[37] Adding Pennsylvania and either Indiana or Illinois to their column next time would give Republicans the presidency.

Ex-Whig voters in the lower North were the party's next logical target. Abraham Lincoln, a Kentucky-born longtime Whig in Illinois with no record of either associations with or attacks on Know Nothings, fit the bill for these voters. Moreover, in the "House Divided" speech of June 1858 and in the seven debates with Stephen Douglas across Illinois that followed, he majestically rose beyond the atrocities in Kansas that had dominated Republican oratory to face the slavery question's full implications. As Lincoln argued:

> I do not expect the Union to be dissolved—I do not expect the house to fall—but I do expect it will cease to be divided. It will become all one thing or all the other. Either the opponents of slavery, will arrest the further spread of it, and place it where the public mind shall rest in the belief that it is in the course of ultimate extinction; or its advocates will push it forward, till it shall become alike lawful in all the States, old as well as new—North as well as South.[38]

With Lincoln's nomination in 1860, the Republican Party came of age. The Seward forces had arrived at the convention in Chicago expecting victory. But Seward was hurt by an overstated radical reputation, along with fears about his anti-nativist stances. Weed's high-flying methods, which worked wonders in Albany, failed to persuade the decisive state delegations, while the Lincoln men carefully peeled off votes.[39] No longer neophytes, Republicans followed a typical nineteenth-century playbook: the leading candidate heading into the convention prevailed if his opponents could not coalesce—and lost if someone stitched them together.

The Republican platform of 1860 expanded its ambit as the party grew to encompass a broader project. Continuing to oppose expansion of slavery into the territories while dropping the language from 1856 calling slavery a "relic of barbarism," the platform added calls for internal improvements, a protective tariff, and a homestead act.[40] The new planks broadly reflected the party's social makeup. Republicans were, like the Whigs before them, largely a Protestant party, strong especially among market-oriented farmers, skilled workers, and manufacturers, and conspicuously weak among the lower classes in the cities. "Who form the strength of this party?" asked a Republican newspaper, in a reflection of the party's image that bore more than a trace of reality. "Those who work with their own hands, who live and act independently, who hold the stakes of home and family, of farm and workshop, of education and freedom—these, as a mass, are enrolled in Republican ranks."[41]

The election of 1860 saw a highly unusual four-way contest.[42] In the North, the Republicans competed with the Democrats' nominee, Stephen Douglas. In the South, breakaway Democrat John Breckenridge, running to throw the election into the House, competed against John Bell of a Constitutional Union Party dominated by conservative ex-Whigs. It was a charged campaign. Republicans recast Lincoln, a prosperous lawyer, in the workingman's image as a rail splitter. Ubiquitous companies of Wide Awakes, young men in military garb, marched in parades to whip up enthusiasm.[43] Despite earning less than 40 percent of the national popular vote, the Republican ticket prevailed in every free state but New Jersey, whose electoral votes split. Through the secession winter, Republicans rejected various last-ditch proposals to mollify the South.[44] "And the war came," and with it the hour when the Republican Party would serve as the agent of historical transformation.[45]

Republicanism and the Union Party

The wartime Republican Party renamed itself the Union Party, a label with a shape-shifting quality whose valence changed as the war progressed. In the border states, where prior Republican organization was nonexistent or at loggerheads, "Unionist" served as a particularly useful descriptor for the administration's allies.[46] But as the war for the union became also a war for freedom, the Union Party became sword as well as shield, not just a label for reluctant allies but the vehicle for a cause larger than party.

It was a vast, bloody, transformative conflict. By the time the Confederate Army surrendered in 1865, more than 600,000 men had lost their lives, 360,000 of them on the Union side. Six million enslaved people won their freedom.[47] Two hundred thousand African Americans wore blue uniforms and fought for the Union cause. A total war laid waste to the southern plantations, as Union soldiers lived off the land and liberated slaves enlisted in the fight for freedom. In 1861, most of this was unthinkable. By 1865, the war for freedom had vanquished the Slave Power.

Radical Republicans led the way in a complicated back-and-forth, with moderates and even conservatives accepting as wartime exigencies policies that Radicals championed on ideological grounds.[48] Though the nettlesome Radicals often exasperated their fellow partisans, not least in their bungling attempts to find another presidential candidate to run in 1864, Lincoln carefully kept up good relations. Despite vast differences in temperament, Charles Sumner of Massachusetts joined the Lincolns several times as their guest at the opera.[49] As Lincoln described the Radicals to his secretary, John Hay, "They are nearer to me than the other side, in thought and sentiment, though bitterly hostile personally. They are utterly lawless—the unhandiest devils in the world to deal with—but after all their faces are set Zionwards."[50]

The Lincoln administration was in many ways a coalition government, designed both to rope in supporters of the union cause wherever they could be found and to carry forth the party principles of the Republican Party.[51] The cabinet included representatives of all leading factions, including several of the president's erstwhile rivals led by William Seward as secretary of state. As a Whig, Lincoln had long valued party loyalty and party principle.[52] He was always careful to place himself at the broad center of his party, and that meant recognizing the growing Radical influence beginning in 1863. But Lincoln in the White House was not the partisan figure he had been either as a Whig lieutenant or as an ambitious Republican ideologue. Few formulations since have improved on the tribute from Massachusetts Radical George S. Boutwell in 1888:

> In prosecuting the war for the Union, in the steps taken for the emancipation of the slaves, Mr. Lincoln appeared to follow rather than to lead the Republican party. But his own views were more advanced usually than those of his party, and he waited patiently and confidently for the healthy movements of public sentiment which he well knew were in the right direction. No man was ever more firmly or consistently the representative of a party than was Mr. Lincoln.[53]

Lincoln's statesmanship, one might say, rested on solid party foundations, even as he far transcended transactional politics.[54]

In the Lincoln administration, personnel was policy. Assuring his renomination in 1864 required rewarding key supporters while balancing across factions within and among states. Appointments down to the fourth-class postmasters in country hamlets had to be approved by either members of the House or local Republican "bosslets." Even as the reach of the federal government remained sharply limited, the spoils system offered the opportunity to staff its still-skeletal apparatus top to bottom. Lincoln had more than 1,500 jobs for political appointees. Notably, the president rewarded newspapermen with dozens of posts, from consuls in Glasgow, Hong Kong, Venice, and Zürich to the inevitable array of postmasterships.[55]

The discourse of unionism opened up space for a renewal of the anti-party strand, now expressed in forward- rather than backward-looking language. By pointing up the Democrats' partisan machinations, Republicans cast aspersions on their patriotism. In the Republican view, small-party politics was less a fall from grace than a kind of clinging to old dogmas at just the moment when the war called for renewal. A key source of wartime Republican—or, perhaps more precisely, anti-Democrat—argumentation was the Loyal Publication Society, funded lavishly by leading New Yorkers.[56] Early in 1863, it began to circulate a blizzard of pamphlets to buoy Northerners for a long struggle to victory.[57] Its most important text was an 1863 pamphlet titled *No Party Now, But All for Our Country*, from the pen of Francis S. Lieber. The well-connected German émigré was an early political scientist who had long written on the role of political parties. In 1839, Lieber had warned, "All parties are exposed to the danger of passing over into factions, which, if carried still farther, may become conspiracies."[58] A quarter century later, he had his case in point. His argument against parties amid war—"a time which asks for things more sterling than names, theories, or platforms"—was aimed squarely at the Democrats, "who allow themselves to be misled by shallow names, and by reminiscences which cling around those names from by-gone days."[59]

Party politics came fully back to life in the 1864 campaign. Early in the year, disaffected Radicals gathered in Cleveland under the banner of Radical Democracy to nominate John C. Frémont. As a gambit to push Republicans leftward, the strategy worked.[60] The 1860 Republican Party platform had pledged only to limit slavery in the territories. The 1864 Union Party platform praised "the Proclamation of Emancipation, and the employment as Union soldiers of men heretofore held in slavery," and called for a constitutional amendment to prohibit the institution.[61] In September, after Lincoln accepted the resignation of conservative Montgomery Blair, the radicals' bête noire, as postmaster general, Frémont exited the race and gave Lincoln his support.

Party machinations also moved in the other direction at the convention in Baltimore. Andrew Johnson of Tennessee, a War Democrat, replaced Hannibal Hamlin of Maine as the vice presidential nominee. Hamlin, close to the Radicals, added little to a party hoping to win in the border states and had lost support even in New England. A leading alternative, Daniel Dickinson, risked compromising Seward's position at the State Department as a second New Yorker in the cabinet, and so Weed maneuvered for Johnson. It was a fateful pick.[62]

Entering the first pure two-party contest in a generation, the Union Party conducted the fall campaign as a referendum on its own vision against that of the Democrats' pro-peace platform. Bolstered by the soldier vote, the Union ticket ultimately prevailed everywhere except in New Jersey, Delaware, and Kentucky. Republican rhetoric had advanced from attacking the Slave Power to attacking slavery itself. As a Union Party pamphlet explained: "We have further seen that slavery, the bone of contention in the present strife, is the foundation, the life, the soul of Southern society; that so long as *it* lives, the real and only cause of war continues. . . . We have also shown that the so-called peace party, the pro-Southern, pro-slavery party, of the North, are working in harmony with the Southern rebels that by giving countenance and hope to traitors, they make them more difficult to conquer, they also make their conquest the more necessary."[63] Update the fusty language, and that paragraph could pass for contemporary Civil War scholarship. But it also contained a note of foreboding about the limits of a party project in the immense task that lay ahead.

Civil War Democrats and the Dark Side of Small-Party Politics

The rump Democrats in the North held a view of party sharply different from that of Republicans.[64] They yoked the protean politics of incrementalism to a vicious racism. The Democratic call for a limited politics buttressed by "the constitution as it was" inevitably meant support for a polity where southern planters had exercised vast power. It was the accommodationist strand at its most cramped. An address at the 1862 Wisconsin state convention made the point: "Almost as old as the Union, the Democratic party has no new principles to enunciate, no new loyalty to pledge. It has always been, as it is, the party of the constitution."[65]

In turn, Democrats deployed the familiar defense of party as an anchor in hostile seas. "The vigilance kept alive by party contest guards against corruption or oppression," Horatio Seymour, the wartime governor of New York, declared in an 1862 campaign speech that went on to excoriate the Emancipation Proclamation as "a proposal for the butchery of women and children, for scenes of lust and rapine, of arson and murder, unparalleled in the history of the world."[66] Northern Democrats differed in their views of the conflict. Historians still debate the relative prevalence of Copperhead "Peace Democrats," who reserved their harshest opprobrium not for the rebels but for the Republicans.[67] In contrast, men like Seymour and the party's 1864 presidential nominee George McClellan supported the war and backed the bonds and taxes to fund it.

Though critical of slavery in general terms, Democrats in the North uniformly resisted the Republican drive to eradicate it and opposed every Republican move toward civil and political rights, from the Emancipation Proclamation down through the Fifteenth Amendment. Their campaign appeals came soaked in an open racism notable even by the standards of nineteenth-century American politics. An 1864 pamphlet from New York in the form of a catechism was typical. "By whom has the Constitution been made obsolete? By Abraham Africanus the First. To what end? That his days may be long in office—and that he may make himself and his people the equal of the negroes."[68]

The Democratic coalition included the bulk of Catholic immigrants, especially Irish Catholics suspicious of Republican moralism and fearful of labor market competition from African Americans. Not only financiers enmeshed in international markets dependent on cotton but unskilled laborers, especially in cities, tended to support Democrats.[69] Yet the positive program for these constituencies was conspicuous by its absence. The admittedly blinkered fight for the common man that marked the antebellum Democrats had fallen away, while rural antimonopolism and urban liberalism awaited in the future. If, in the rebelling South, the Confederacy eviscerated party politics altogether, in the North, Democrats' wartime argument for party fell back on the worst in nineteenth-century mass politics.[70]

The Limits of Reconstruction

After the Confederate surrender at Appomattox came the epochal questions of how the South would be governed, the Union reunited, and freed people allowed to live new lives. Over the next decade, as Reconstruction crashed up against hard limits in American state and society, the great party devoted to "freedom national" became a primarily northern-oriented party, and the broad vision of free labor whittled down into a defense of industrial capital.[71] In its heartlands in the North, to an extreme degree in the readmitted states of the South where it aimed to build support, and in the friction between the appeals it made across sections, the Republican Party faced divides that proved insuperable. The party sought to add a heterogeneous mix of blocs in the South, preponderantly consisting of newly enfranchised former slaves. Stitching together the advanced elements of northern capital with landless agricultural workers would have required the ongoing deployment of federal power and the fundamental transformation of the economy in both the North and the South, far beyond what leading Republicans (including Radicals) and the forces behind them ever would have countenanced. By 1877, the project tracing back to political antislavery had receded from the forefront of party politics.[72]

Congressional Republicans repeatedly strained the bounds of the political system as they pushed to fulfill their vast ambitions. As W. E. B. Du Bois declared in 1935, with a forthrightness missing in later defenses of Radicalism, "Party responsibility in government was absolutely blocked at a time of crisis."[73] And so, in their fights against the recalcitrant Andrew Johnson over Reconstruction policy, Republicans played what scholars now call "hardball."[74] Over the president's veto, they reduced the size of the Supreme Court from ten to seven and enacted the Tenure of Office Act, protecting cabinet officials from presidential interference. It was this bill that provided the fig leaf to impeach Johnson in 1868.[75] The ultimate prize was control over the military, necessary for the success of the Republican program that would reconstruct the South and forever keep the former rebels far from power. More aggressively than at any other point in American history, a determined congressional majority seeking to realize a party project tested the limits in a constitutional system of separated powers.

Yet for all the sweep in Republican hopes for Reconstruction, the role of federal action remained limited given still-regnant doctrinal strictures on the appropriate role of national power. Reconstruction occasioned the most important bout of constitutional politics since the Founding, but the policy-reform strand's carefully designed policies and programs, and the linkage of mass demands with expertise, appeared only in the vaguest outline.[76] The "policy state," to use Karen Orren and Stephen Skowronek's term, lay far in the future.[77] And without it, the radical project to transform power relations found itself hamstrung.

Localistic, patronage-oriented parties could not build a national state capable of transforming the defeated South. The Thirteenth, Fourteenth, and Fifteenth Amendments offered a new basis of citizenship—albeit one limited by Congress and the Supreme Court, and restricted to men.[78] Yet the new federal conception of citizenship did not disturb the localist orientation of politics. As Frederick Douglass warned presciently in 1866, "The arm of the Federal government is long, but it is far too short to protect the rights of individuals in the interior of distant States."[79] The fruits of office came in the distribution of tangible, divisible benefits. Republican politicians had mastered the game and saw no reason to supplant it with nationally directed bureaucracy.[80] The under-capitalized South needed vast investment, but even loyal Radical Republicans (especially in the West) sought to build rivers and harbors at home rather than send the money South.[81] And all the while, the vast private railroad boom of the late 1860s set the stage for the bust that followed.[82]

The social harmony that free labor ideology promised came asunder. The very war to defend the wide-open society of free labor and free men accelerated the corporate capitalism that would vitiate the social conditions of that ideal world. In the North, postwar labor reformers, agitating for an eight-hour day and trade unions, won support from only a few Radical Republicans—notably Stevens, who emphasized the common interests of poor whites and Blacks.[83] In the South, newly enfranchised freedmen demanded land reform and protection against oppressive labor contracts. For wary northern Republicans, however, appeals to the freedmen's economic interests raised the specter of demagoguery and mob rule.[84] Finance capital, less closely tied into the Republican orbit, agitated against ongoing deployment of federal troops; bankers worried that the costs of ongoing military occupation would lead to default. Across the sectional divide, proposals that threatened the right to contract and that impinged on businessmen's room for maneuver found little success in the postwar party.[85]

Republicans organized quickly in the South. The end of the old three-fifths clause meant twenty-five additional House seats for the former slave states.[86] Were the Democrats to sweep the region and join with "the Democrats that will in the best time be elected from the North," warned Thaddeus Stevens, "they will at the very first election take possession of the White House and the halls of Congress. I need not depict the ruin that would follow."[87] That electoral imperative shaped the party's strategy in the region.

The extraordinary mobilization of a recently subjugated people into political life alongside the vanquished men who had owned them as property—an experience the United States shared only with Saint-Domingue[88]—at the same time felt very familiar, with its grounding in associational life, collective pageantry of party, and reliance on the fruits of patronage. Union League clubs, modeled on the Wide Awakes of 1860, mobilized young Black voters and encouraged them to organize their communities. These local clubs worked alongside the pillars of associational life in fraternal orders and churches.[89] Spectacle had a special value. Large gatherings, with plenty of food and speakers (occasionally including Northerners like Henry Wilson, who traveled South to rally the party troops), demonstrated that the newly enfranchised male citizens represented a community whose political interests could not be manipulated. They also offered the protection against violence that came in numbers.[90]

Freedmen went from learning about politics to participating in it, with a wave of pioneering elected officials. Below figures such as Hiram Revels of Mississippi, who held the U.S. Senate seat once occupied by Jefferson Davis, came state legislators and delegates to constitutional conventions, most numerous where white Unionists had not already established themselves at the helm of the Republican operation. And a passel of African Americans assumed the critical patronage positions signifying local prominence: postmasters, lighthouse keepers, bailiffs, election registrars. They hardly received anything like their proportionate share, and Black elites protested bitterly against the continuing dominance of "that class of unrefined and uncultured overseers."[91]

The southern party had to placate a vast array of constituents. It included the full range of Black opinion, from the small urban middle class through the vast newly freed population. The white voters combined prominent ex-Whigs now returned to oppose the Democracy, wartime Unionists, up-country smallholders, and northern carpetbaggers. Many of them held to far less radical economic demands than their Black brethren, who sought not just educational opportunities but land. Factional fights proved more intense than in the North. Relentless violence produced strong incentives for defection, especially among white moderates, while precluding the routinized bargaining at the heart of democratic politics.[92] When different factions occupied the governor's mansion, with its control over the state militia, and the Senate, the linchpin in the distribution of federal rewards, conflict was particularly intractable.[93] Adelbert Ames, the carpetbagger governor of Mississippi, wrote of easing conflicts with "my healing art—patronage," but there was never enough to satisfy all comers.[94]

Above all, successful Black-led and biracial politics invited brutally violent reprisals. The Ku Klux Klan and its episodic terrorism arose in the early postwar period.[95] More dangerous to the project of democracy were the paramilitary White Leagues and Rifle Clubs that operated across the Deep South in the decisive years of 1873 to 1876 as the last Republican governments tottered and fell. "Carry the election peaceably if we can, forcibly if we must," enjoined Mississippi Democrats in 1875.[96] Working in close concert with local Democratic elites, the White Leagues attacked Black elected officials, community gatherings, and polling places. The attacks hit at the entire web connecting voters, civic institutions, and electoral politics. As the Democrats' Redeemer governments tightened control and northern Republicans moved on, southern Republican politics could not recover from the assault.[97]

The ebb and flow of party politics followed from these constraints. While Lincoln had adroitly kept his party together, internal conflict inside the Republican fold dominated national politics under Andrew Johnson. As his battle with the Radicals intensified after he vetoed the Freedmen's Bureau bill in March 1866, Johnson made half-hearted attempts to build a new party of administration supporters that would emulate the accommodationist, cross-sectional parties of the Second Party System. But he was an erratic figure ill-equipped to unite diverse players under a common banner. A National Union convention at Philadelphia in August 1866 brought together conservative Republicans and Democratic Johnson supporters, but they agreed only on their common enemy in Thaddeus Stevens. Any chance for a realignment of the parties, however slender it may have been, soon dissipated.[98]

After Republicans won a sweeping victory in the 1866 midterms, bitter conflict between Congressional Republicans and Johnson collided against complex factional battles inside the swollen Republican majorities.[99] Radical strength soon ebbed, and after Johnson's impeachment, the Senate voted not to remove him from office. Seven Republican senators voted to acquit Johnson and stop the Senate president pro tempore, Benjamin Wade of Ohio—a determined Radical—from occupying the presidency.

(All four political survivors among those seven would endorse the Liberal Republican ticket in 1872.)

Ulysses S. Grant easily won the 1868 nomination and the election with pledges to support congressional Reconstruction, backing from conservative moneyed interests, and a unifying slogan: "Let us have peace." The Grant administration signaled the shift away from great party politics to the classic organizational concerns of the accommodationist strand.[100] Though the charges of corruption leveled against him are overblown, they capture an important storyline of the era he inaugurated: "Corruption had less important consequences than the *corruption issue.*"[101]

The Liberal Republican movement of 1872 put forward a distinctive party vision of its own, drawing on venerable currents in the anti-party strand and new currents in political economy that cast doubts on radicalism and accommodationism alike as contrary to the doctrine of orthodox laissez-faire.[102] Elite northeast liberals, often erstwhile Radicals, had grown disillusioned with the Republican Party. In keeping with the anti-party tradition, they viewed their politics as more high-minded than the mere pursuit of office. The previous crusade, in their eyes, had finished. Now the liberals deemed Grant corrupt, disliked high tariffs and taxes that interfered with pure markets, and worried about politicians, in both the North and South, making dangerous appeals to an illiterate electorate.

Dissident factions met at a Liberal Republican convention in Cincinnati in May 1872 to find a candidate. Like the Free Soil Party of 1848, in which many of them had cut their teeth, the liberals saw their bolt as an emergency measure that responded to major-party failure. But compared to the erstwhile cause of stopping the expansion of slavery, reform was a far more diffuse matter. And even as the unfocused calls for moral purity foreshadowed the Progressives of 1912, no figure could encapsulate them as Theodore Roosevelt would four decades hence. On the sixth ballot, Horace Greeley—the vain, eccentric, once-Radical editor of the *New York Tribune*—finally prevailed, as he was acceptable to delegates across the sectional divide.[103] In short order, Democrats followed suit with a Greeley nomination of their own to complete the fusion ticket under what would prove to be a disastrous candidate. Grant won in a landslide. Greeley died in December 1872, and the Liberal Republican movement, bereft of a standing organization, soon vanished.

In the Republican Party's formative years, Radicalism had given substantive direction to elite desires for civic improvement. As Radicalism now floundered, reform succumbed to elitist tendencies.[104] By 1874, E. L. Godkin—founder of the *Nation* and a leading liberal intellectual enamored with social Darwinism—bemoaned that "socialism in South Carolina," perpetrated by the state's biracial Republican government, had created a new hierarchy "with the rich Congo thief on top and the degraded Anglo-Saxon at the bottom."[105]

Mainstream Republicanism fell back to accommodationism. In an 1872 convention speech, Oliver Morton, an old Radical, stood up for the unfinished work of the Fourteenth and Fifteenth Amendments. But Morton also made a case for party regularity that owed more to the Van Buren than to the Whiggish tradition. "In a Government like ours there are, there must be parties. Men entertaining similar principles must act together; they cannot act together without organization and cooperation, and that makes a party."[106] That creed would define what in short order would term itself the Grand Old Party.

By 1877, the Republican era in the South was over, and Redeemer governments had taken over every state in the former Confederacy. The Compromise of 1877 put Rutherford B. Hayes and his conciliatory southern policy in charge, in exchange for the departure of federal troops. The planter elite would never again dominate national politics, even as the South would long exercise influence from its congressional citadel.[107] Republicans would continue to agitate to secure the vote in the South, with the Federal Elections Bill of 1890–91, a proto–Voting Rights Act killed by a Senate filibuster, marking the last great effort before the curtain of Jim Crow fell.[108] The party still waved the bloody shirt in campaigns. But that electoral approach looked backward. In the words of Michael Les Benedict, "The new Republican strategy converted the living issue of equal rights into the dead one of Democratic perfidy in the Civil War."[109] As Republicans worked to grease the wheels between politics and corporate capitalism, their core appeal came in claims to speak for American prosperity—only a distant echo of free labor and its grand promise.

That precipitous fall should not, however, obscure the grand Republican achievement. From the vantage point of contemporary discussions around democratic backsliding, the story of free labor Republicanism is at once heroic and unavoidably discomfiting. Our polarized era draws attention to the volatile consequences stemming from deep partisan loyalties even as party projects seem incapable of orchestrating mass action.[110] As Republicans marshaled the resources of state and society behind their project, they cast aside long-held rules of the game and cast aspersions on their opponents' regime loyalties. In turn, their Unionist opponents in the North—both Democrats and, much more softly, moderate Republicans—deployed language about the limits of politics that would be familiar to those warning today's insurgents against flying too close to the sun. Likewise, conservative Unionists then, like centrist institutionalists now, touted small-party politics as an antidote to extremism. Such critiques, however cramped, mark out important currents in the realities of a convulsive era. But to those seeking a way out of our present discontents, free labor Republicanism offers something altogether more thrilling, and also more dangerous: the promise of mass democracy as the instrument of human freedom.

4

The Politics of Industrialism and the Progressive Transformation of Party

IN JUNE 1873, a prominent Milwaukee lawyer named Edward Ryan delivered a commencement address to graduates of the University of Wisconsin Law School. "The question will arise," Ryan predicted, "and arise in your day, though perhaps not fully in mine, which shall rule— wealth or man; which shall lead—money or intellect; who shall fill public stations—educated and patriotic freemen, or the feudal serfs of corporate capital."[1] In the audience that day in Madison was eighteen-year-old Robert M. La Follette. The young man, taking Ryan's words as his lifelong credo, would become a leading Progressive and, in 1904, push through Wisconsin's pioneering law for statewide direct primary elections. Yet such capacious questions framed more than a single politician's career. Ryan astutely foreshadowed the intertwined themes that would dominate party politics in a transformed republic: the "social question" of how to respond to the challenges of industrialism,[2] and the moral and institutional question of what qualities should hold sway over civic life.

The Gilded Age and Progressive Era saw the widest range of party visions of any point in American history. Across the whole cacophonous scene, political actors collectively grappled with questions of who should rule and in whose interest. Yet the openings proved wider for reforming politics than for transforming the political economy. Amid the fierce challenges in building alliances across sectional divides, insurgents ultimately failed to instantiate alternatives to industrial capitalism. Instead, their targets came largely inside the political system. Taking aim at corruption, Progressives like La Follette toppled the parties from their pedestal as icons and guarantors of democratic life. Proceeding largely chronologically, this chapter surveys mainstream and insurgent forces alike—in sequence, the Gilded Age major parties, Mugwumps, labor radicals, Socialists, Populists, and finally the transformative Progressives. If we strive, more than in most treatments of party politics, to give the range of visions their due, we recognize, more than many of their dedicated chroniclers, the barriers to their success.

Nowhere else in this book does the theme of multiple traditions in American party politics ring quite so loudly. All six party strands that we have identified came into sharper focus during a period marked by deep contestation over both the means and ends of party politics. With new industrial realities, the contest between corporate capital and its antagonists reshaped the pro-capital and radical strands. The defeat of Populism that cemented Democratic control over the "Solid South" at the same time reframed the lowercase-*p* populist strand around a more exclusionary us-versus-them politics. With the rise of social reformers and experts, often armed with the tools of social science and advocating for an activist state, came the distinct view of party from the policy-reform strand.

Above all, the venerable dialectic between accommodationist and antiparty strands took a new turn. Even as Democrats and Republicans in the Gilded Age battled over the tariff, both parties played the accommodationist game to the hilt, greasing the wheels of vast party organizations funded by moneyed interests and sustained by patronage. The upshot was "a kind of politician's state, an untidy social compromise enervating to both working-class radicalism and to a business-oriented efficiency in government."[3] But though brokerage politics appalled reformers and labor radicals alike, bourgeois elites and toiling workers had very different visions about what might replace it. A newly sectional party system after the election of 1896 offered fertile ground for institutional transformations that catalyzed accommodationism's long slide from dominance. The most durably influential contribution came from Progressives.

Parties simplify politics. The Progressive attack on parties complexified it, splitting apart but not destroying so much of what the Van Buren model had assiduously hitched together. New groups, new rules and procedures, and, most importantly, new conceptions of politics all grew up where the parties used to be. In place of the substantive alternatives that had captivated the prior generation, procedural reform came paramount for Progressives. They built their critique not from the top down, as had so many of their elite progenitors in reform, or from the workingman up, in the way of radical contestants for power, but outward from the broad middle class. A potent dose of anti-partyism suffused all their assaults on existing political organization. As the Progressive writer Walter Weyl put it, the reformer "labors for the democratic control of the party, while simultaneously striving for its abolition."[4]

The old parties and their essential institutions proved resilient. The appeal to party loyalty; the convention as a site for party loyalists to hammer out platforms, assess the strength of factions, and give politicians the once-over; the party organization arrayed at the local, state, and national levels—none of these elements vanished. The sectional System of 1896 lumbered on until the New Deal. Many of the outward forms of traditional political organization, most prominently the urban machine, lingered on even longer. Yet there was no turning back, no putting the genie back in the bottle. No longer would mass partisan mobilization rooted in local communities dominate the nation's civic life. No longer would parties control the machinery of electoral politics or serve as the essential intermediaries between officeholders and citizens. No longer would doctrines of party restrain the ambitions of leaders or the reach of the state. Instead, parties lost ground to voters below, to bureaucracies and presidents above, and to the new groups that emerged as vehicles for citizens' activism.

Party Organization in the Gilded Age

During the Gilded Age, Democrats and Republicans practiced transactional glad-handing accommodationism on a grand scale.[5] The organized armies that went to battle in postbellum politics served also as adjuncts of industrial capital. The fundamental patterns traced back to the Jacksonian era. Parties at multiple levels of government came together at conventions, and the party organizations, led by professionals skilled in the art of cutting deals, did the work of campaigning for nominees up and down the party ticket. At the same time, party politics was far more complicated and internally differentiated in the Gilded Age than it had been in the Second Party System. No longer did newspaper editors, tavern keepers, and country lawyers exercise the same kind of influence. Now the raising and dispensing of political funds at the core of party politics required its own specialized expertise.[6] Both parties shared this common understanding of the political game. Through the voice of the journalist William Riordon, George Washington Plunkitt, a Democratic district leader in New York's Tammany Hall, served as the system's most eloquent exponent. Plunkitt and his Republican opposite number, he explained, "differ on tariffs and currencies and all them things, but we agree on the main proposition that when a man works in politics, he should get something out of it."[7]

More than any individual piece, the sheer scale of the electoral operation bears emphasis. Everybody owed something to somebody else. In the words of George H. Williams, attorney general under Ulysses S. Grant, "The business of politics, including party management, has become both an art and a science of great complexity and difficulty, requiring for its understanding and management, high capacity, reinforced by the training of a life."[8] From the national committees first coming into their own through the state organizations that dominated politics and determined the fate of presidential nominations, to the city bosses now consolidating their control, and all the way down to the ward heelers, parties required vast efforts of time and money to make the system go.

Leaders at the apex of organizations, whether at the state, city, or ward levels, had to balance priorities across multiple constituencies. Calling the operation a machine—the metaphor that its reformist adversaries bestowed—implies moving parts all working seamlessly. But the reality was far messier.[9] Soliciting funds at such a scale, satisfying the armies of party workers, keeping rival factions in line, and balancing claimants across geography and ethnicity all pushed in different directions. Bosses worked inside more than they controlled the webs of power and influence. And though they certainly lined their pockets, the real money in the Gilded Age's vast fortunes lay elsewhere.

Republicans and Democrats quickly adapted to the rise of industrial capitalism, mediating the exchange between business and its desired political outcomes. Businesses paid to maintain the army of patronage workers who carried the party banner. Politicians often invested alongside the new corporate elite in "rings" of well-connected enterprises.[10] Amid widespread labor unrest, the parties allowed business to squelch workingmen's demands, whether through the unregulated private violence of the companies' coal and iron police or through the sweeping power of the labor injunction. Presidents of both parties violently put down railroad strikes in 1877, 1886, and 1894. Above all, the courts served as the great redoubt of business power, dominated by railroad lawyers.

Despite all their commonalities in both form and substance, the two Gilded Age parties remained distinct from one another in battles over tariffs and support for industry.[11] Republicans, reflecting their Whig heritage, took a more sympathetic view of government action. By building up "the home market," protection aided manufacturers and specialized farmers alike against foreign incursions, notably from Great Britain. And by boosting wages, it supported the workingman and his family. As in free labor days, the Republican Party emphasized the superiority of commercial life in the American North as its overarching coalitional glue. But that appeal now had a very different valence.[12]

For their part, Democrats retained, as the 1880 platform put it, "opposition to centralization and to that dangerous spirit of encroachment."[13] That philosophy connected the party's southern supporters, reeling from Reconstruction and seeking to escape from the last remnants of federal interference, with the northern proponents of laissez-faire.[14] In 1887, vetoing a bill to distribute seeds to drought-stricken Texas farmers, Grover Cleveland warned that "the lesson should be constantly enforced that though the people support the Government the Government should not support the people."[15] Likewise on sociocultural issues, Democrats, more sympathetic to immigrants (though less, even in the North, to African Americans), opposed prohibition of alcohol and the amendments to northern state constitutions targeting Catholic schools.[16]

The most elaborate organizations emerged in northern industrial states, where politicians mastered the art of exchange among diverse sources and recipients of political favors.[17] The Republican model reached down from the state level. Bosses aimed to balance the countryside, where the bulk of voters lived, with the cities, whose rich businessmen paid the party's bills. Thomas Platt of New York, the "Easy Boss," who began his career as a minor functionary under Thurlow Weed, and the free-spending Matthew Quay of Pennsylvania served as the paradigmatic examples.[18] For their part, Democratic organizations built outward from their beachheads in immigrant-heavy cities.[19] Whatever their party, urban machines succeeded in consolidating power from neighborhood-level contenders, often termed "rings" or "circles," only when they found allies at the state (and later federal) level. Otherwise, competing cliques continued to battle for dominance.[20] Patterns differed elsewhere. In the post-Reconstruction South, a personalistic factionalism never coalesced into internally organized, coherent parties.[21] And in the unruly West, where the tariff question that organized politics loomed less large, railroads bought politicians directly, without a party to mediate between them.[22]

All the electioneering required massive funds. Parties dunned public employees for funds, whether in annual assessments or special fees for hiring and promotion. That source of cash only began to dry up with the uneven spread of civil service reform. Would-be candidates often had to pay up even to run. Public contractors and well-connected businessmen— bankers, printers, lawyers, saloonkeepers, and especially builders—who gave both in anticipation of and in gratitude for services rendered proved another rich vein to mine.[23] Politicians loved free passes on the railroads, the distribution of which was a particular plum.[24] And above all, political managers solicited funds from corporations with business before the public, a practice vividly termed "frying the fat."

The parties then had to distribute all the funds. Mobilization did not come cheap, nor was it always clean. The ticket system placed a premium on organization top to bottom. Armies of patronage workers dispensed favors all through the year, culminating on Election Day. "Vote-buying was not one of the secrets of Gilded Age politics," a historian writes. "It was done out in the open."[25] It reflected the complex moral economy of partisan loyalty, as parties would often cover lost wages for time spent at the polls. Modern-day judgments tend to condemn all the money but view the mass participatory politics more kindly. Yet the two were completely intertwined. All the cash bought a formidable civic presence at a steep price.

The rah-rah party politics that dated back to the 1830s, organized in particular communities and reinforcing ties of place, began to fade in the 1880s and 1890s. In its stead came blizzards of pamphlets designed to inform voters individually more than to energize them collectively. So, too, national corporations forged new ties with national party committees just as presidents, for their part, finally gained control of those committees.[26] As civil service reform cut into parties' contributions from patronage workers, big business more than took up the slack. Together these developments opened up space for national parties to solicit funds from wealthy donors for written campaign messages they controlled directly. State and local parties began to lose their reach as intermediaries, cutting out a whole stratum of what a leading Republican now dismissed as "mercenary newspapers & greedy speakers."[27]

Party organizations refashioned themselves in the face of challenges from labor radicals and elite reformers alike.[28] Tammany Hall recovered from the extravagant and indiscriminate graft of the Tweed Ring, exposed in 1871, with clear lines of authority established under "Honest John" Kelly and Richard Croker.[29] The distribution of favors had always been at the core of accommodationism, but machines began to make a show of their beneficence. Following the stiff challenge from the labor radical Henry George in the 1886 mayoral campaign, Tammany moved beyond the saloons from which it had long done its work and introduced a network of clubhouses. The clubhouses gave district leaders a permanent venue from which to dispense services, not least in bringing new immigrants round to support the Irish-dominated Tammany Hall,

and offered a hub for all the social activity that made politics fun.[30]
Plunkitt explained his methods:

> I hear of a young feller that's proud of his voice, thinks that he can
> sing fine. I ask him to come around to Washington Hall and join our
> Glee Club. He comes and sings, and he's a follower of Plunkitt for life.
> Another young feller gains a reputation as a baseball player in a va-
> cant lot. I bring him into our baseball club. That fixes him. You'll find
> him workin' for my ticket at the polls next election day. . . . I rope
> them all in by givin' them opportunities to show themselves off.
> I don't trouble them with political arguments.[31]

In truth, the proto-social services represented only a small piece of
political machines' ongoing cross-class accommodationism. The real
plums, directed at core supporters, were municipal contracts—not the
oft-celebrated turkeys at Thanksgiving. Still, as new social reformers,
many of them trained in modern social science, sought to understand
their adversaries, they began to see the limits of their own anti-
partyism. "Indeed, what headway can the notion of civic purity, of hon-
esty of administration, make against this big manifestation of human
friendliness, this stalking survival of village kindness?" asked Jane
Addams of Chicago's Hull House in an 1898 essay pondering "Why the
Ward Boss Rules."[32] The complex and sometimes contradictory answers would define the emergent policy-reform strand as it responded
to both accommodationist and anti-party tendencies through the coming century.

Mugwumps

In the presidential election of 1884, elite reformers deserted Republican James Blaine (who, quipped the Nation's E. L. Godkin, "wallowed
in spoils like a rhinoceros in an African pool") for Grover Cleveland.[33]
The Mugwumps, as they were termed, could hardly be said to have
transformed the practice of party politics. Yet they merit mention as
much because of as despite their lack of impact. No other tendency so
completely captures the essence of the anti-party strand. Their reverence

for principled stands over practical results transcended any particular critiques of bossism and spoils, revealing a profound antipathy to the very idea of politics done together. "When I am in a small minority I believe I am right," said one Boston Mugwump, taking the sentiment to its logical extreme. "When I am in a minority of one, I know I am right."[34]

Appalled at corruption both pecuniary and moral, the Mugwump vision saw only declension, from New England's silvery prime to the sprawling country's degraded present, whose contending forces of capital and labor they held in nearly as low esteem as its conniving politicians. The Mugwumps shared substantial continuities with the Liberal Republicans of 1872, as they bolted from a corrupt Republican Party and called for civil service reform. But the refined Mugwump mind was defined less by tooth-and-claw social Darwinism than by a nostalgia for small homogeneous communities where civic-minded elites could act in the public interest. After the local Knights of Labor pushed through major reforms in 1887, Charles Francis Adams lamented the decline of the town meeting in Quincy, Massachusetts, long his family's seat. He rued the transition from "the few score rustics following the accustomed lead of the parson and squire" to the "heterogeneous mass of men numbering hundreds, jealous, unacquainted, and often in part bent on carrying out some secret arrangement in which private interest overrode all sense of public welfare."[35]

Mugwumps had few institutional solutions to the problems they so eloquently bemoaned. After Cleveland's surprise victory in 1884, attempts to work inside the Democratic Party with the Irish-dominated, patronage-oriented organizations ended in predictable failure.[36] Apart from work on adopting the secret ballot, they played no leading part in the procedural reforms of the following decades. Their influence on the wane, the Mugwumps made a final turn to oppose American imperialism after the Spanish-American War. Again, they saw the finest traditions of the republic's past being sundered.[37] The next generation of reformers would take their anger at party machinations in a direction less concerned with civic virtue and more trusting in the capacities of ordinary citizens and popular majorities.[38]

Laborite Possibilities

From strikes to boycotts to political action, Gilded Age workers acted collectively to challenge the forces upending their lives and reshaping their communities. Their repertoires of contention spanned what we would now term the economic and political realms, targeting employers, the state, and their fellow community members alike. Yet widespread radical sentiment was a very different matter from durable party contestation. The most important organization was the Knights of Labor, the largest labor grouping in the nineteenth century. Its calls for the eight-hour day and defense of workers' craft skills and control over production came wrapped in the venerable idiom of republicanism that workingmen regarded as their birthright.[39] "We complain," wrote George McNeill, a labor intellectual and leading figure in the Knights of Labor, "that our rulers, statesmen and orators have not attempted to engraft republican principles into our industrial system."[40] The Knights' vision was at once backward- and forward-looking. "Each for himself is the bosses' plea / Union for all will set you free" read an 1880 banner from the Detroit Coopers' Union, nicely encapsulating a dense thicket of meanings.[41]

Worker militancy failed to penetrate far into mainstream politics. Early mass suffrage had made workingmen into Democrats and Republicans, and mobilization on the jobsite could not dislodge deep and resonant partisan loyalties. Labor tickets arose in more than two hundred cities large and small. Victory tended to come when the Knights joined together with labor and reform groups in their broad orbit. Independent labor politics peaked in the mid-1880s, as the Knights committed to politics, but soon collapsed. Following the Haymarket affair in Chicago and the Great Southwest railroad strike in spring 1886, the Knights could not sustain their wave of enthusiasm in the face of employer and police repression.[42]

Major parties did respond to threats from laborite demands. For Republicans, leaning in labor's direction generally meant state action toward their priorities. For Democrats, it more often meant giving them associational space and opposing monopoly. Very occasionally, as in

Democrat Carter Harrison's Chicago and Republican Hazen Pingree's Detroit, labor and socialist elements successfully secured a position in reform-minded coalitions. Still, even capacious urban regimes soon faced the hard realities of their place in national politics.[43]

Among American workers' bevy of associations, the American Federation of Labor (AF of L) ended up as the only durable survivor from the crucible of the Gilded Age. Founded in 1881, the AF of L worked with rather than against the dominant patterns of a hostile political economy. The federation represented skilled workers organized in craft unions and emphasized what workers could get by negotiating directly with employers. Eschewing national politics, it picked sides with whatever party held power in a given time and place. Close ties connected craft unions with political machines, especially in the Irish-dominated building trades dependent on public works.[44]

The most prominent labor-reform candidacy was that of the single-tax advocate Henry George, who in 1886 came within six thousand votes of winning election as mayor of New York, running on a United Labor Party ticket.[45] The "New Political Forces," as George's backers referred to themselves, offered less a fully born model of party politics than a stillborn inquiry into unfulfilled possibilities. Like the Mugwumps, George complained about the degraded quality of politics, in which "organizations that call themselves political parties are little better than joint stock companies for assessing candidates and dividing public plunder."[46] But while elite reformers looked askance at spending designed to influence ignorant voters, George aimed at the source of funds. "Public opinion in the class you represent visits its condemnation on the poor man who sells his vote for $2," he told his Tammany-backed Democratic opponent, Abram Hewitt, in an open letter, "but has no condemnation for the rich man who furnishes the $2 with which he is tempted."[47]

The New Political Forces rooted themselves in spaces outside the machine's reach, including labor organizations, ethnic associations, and dissident Catholic parishes. Redirecting the Locofoco-Jacksonian and free labor Republican traditions to new purposes, they defined a battle between "representatives of all classes of men who earn their living by exertion of hand or head," in George's words, and "that class who live by appropriating the proceeds of the toil of others."[48] In the end, the broad laborite vision was not enough. The city's commercial and professional elite looked on Georgism with horror.[49] Reformers like E. L. Godkin backed Hewitt as the lesser evil. (Coming in third, on the Republican ticket, was a young Theodore Roosevelt.)[50] And the organization deployed all its best tactics, fair and foul, to defeat the insurgency.

Yet even had the New Political Forces succeeded and kicked off a wave of victories in city halls, the impact would have remained limited. State governments and courts had all the tools they needed to throttle cities' attempts to chart their own course. And in national politics, urban radical parties with a handful of seats in the House would have had to make alliances outside their core support to win seats in the rural-dominated Senate, still chosen by state legislators, or votes in the Electoral College. The full-fledged party that reflected the cooperative commonwealth, however alluring a possibility, was always a distant dream.[51] But as labor fractured, so did "the moral universality of the working class," in the words of David Montgomery. "No single set of values, no commonly accepted vision of the redemption of the republic, any longer guided the many streams of working-class struggle into a single-minded flood of protest."[52]

These defeats in the 1880s, along with those of Populism in the 1890s, framed the fate of the Socialist Party of America as well.[53] For all its rhetoric about party-building, the Socialist Party failed to make deep inroads into the heart of the working class. Officially formed in 1901, the party's best showing came in 1912, when Eugene Debs polled 6 percent of the vote for president. Its vision of a broad working-class party linked the mass socialist politics of Europe, especially the Social Democratic Party of Germany, with home-grown American celebrations of what Debs termed "that democracy which, in its final interpretation, spells universal brotherhood."[54] Socialists had a strong sense of themselves as an organized party that elevated collective goals over individual politicians' ambitions. Unlike the Democrats and Republicans, they had a dues-paying formal membership, empowered to make decisions in party affairs. "As good a man as Eugene V. Debs is I am not going to vote for him in the sense one is voting for Wilson, Taft or Roosevelt," explained Victor Berger of Milwaukee, a leading figure on the party's right. "With us the Socialist movement and its principles are paramount—not the candidate."[55]

With most workers still loyal to the two major parties and native-born and old-stock skilled crafts workers also represented by the AF of L, the Socialist Party found itself frozen out. It garnered support in isolated pockets, most prominently among Jewish immigrants to New York and disaffected small farmers in the Plains. (Debs's best performance came in Oklahoma, where he won 16 percent of the vote in 1912.) The party also suffered from intense factional division. On the right, Berger and his allies wanted good relations with the AF of L and amassed records in municipal offices that largely resembled those of reformist Progressives. On the left, figures like "Big Bill" Haywood of the syndicalist Industrial Workers of the World saw little point in electoral politics.[56] For all Debs's commitment to an explicitly political radicalism, he stayed aloof from the infighting. Weakened by the Red Scare and divided in their response to revolution abroad, the Socialist Party broke apart in 1919. No explicitly radical party would match its electoral record—but its fate was sealed by forces far larger than its own internal battles.

Populism

The Populist movement of the 1880s and 1890s was the last culminating moment in the long tradition of agrarian radicalism.[57] It faced a vexed transition from social movement to political party. The Farmers' Alliance and other like-minded groups with bases across the South, West, and Midwest joined together into the People's Party in advance of the 1892 election. Overlapping divides crosscut the party as its dream "to restore the government of the Republic to the hands of 'the plain people'" faced its version of the same harsh realities that always confront American third parties.[58] Populist rhetoric soared as it attacked the money power; careful treatments of the means and ends of party politics, by contrast, were conspicuously absent.

American farmers selling into world markets suffered from the long decline in prices following the Panic of 1873. Alliance supporters traveled the countryside in the South and West in the late 1880s urging cooperative action, amplified by networks of newspapers. They sought reflationary approaches to the money supply, including bimetallism, to aid indebted farmers.[59] And their clarion call against the encroachments of monopoly traced back to Locofocoism. Yet Populists embraced solutions that Jacksonians would have abhorred, calling for government control of the railroads and a graduated income tax.[60] The major new contribution was a plan from Charles Macune, a newspaperman who led the Southern Farmers' Alliance: subtreasuries that would store agricultural products amid depressed prices.

The harsh realities of race, class, and section all left little space for the Populists to forge a viable party project. Like the Knights of Labor, the Farmers' Alliance celebrated republicanism against the predations of corporate capitalism, and in towns and small cities, membership overlapped.[61] Yet the Knights' collapse after 1886 denied Populists the organizational partner for a farmer-labor coalition that they so desperately needed. In the South, where Populists squared off against Democrats indifferent to the plight of smallholders Black and white, victory required challenging old loyalties that were often enforced with violence. For many in the Alliance, breaking with the Party of the Fathers and supporting the People's Party was a step too difficult to take, and so the party, as a party, never fully congealed. "'When I joined the Alliance,' one southerner protested, 'I was expressly informed that neither my religious nor political convictions would be interfered with.'"[62] The People's Party's 1892 presidential ticket, led by the former Union general and Greenbacker James Weaver, came in first in five western states but failed to make its hoped-for breakthrough in the South.

The biracial promise of Populism was more incipient than realized. Even when southern leaders of the People's Party recognized that they would need Black votes to win, they rarely allowed substantial (let alone proportionate) Black representation at conventions, admitted Black leaders to their leading councils, or slated Black candidates. Nevertheless, the defeat of Populism sealed the final victory of Jim Crow.[63] While many organizers who stayed in politics went on to the Socialist Party, some of the most colorful southern Populists, most notably Georgia's Tom Watson, threw in their lot with the segregationist Democrats.[64]

The connection between capital-*P* Populism and the us-versus-them populist strand is chiefly one of political style. Populists had a penchant for rhetorical boundary-pushing and a "tendency to rely on scapegoats and panacea."[65] They gravitated to the showmanship and cutting language honed by the traveling speakers who tirelessly promoted the farmers' cause. As an opponent recalled of the particularly orotund James Harvey "Cyclone" Davis—clad in sombrero, Prince Albert coat, and alligator boots, with *The Works of Jefferson* stacked on a chair beside him—"No man is so completely the master of the little arts of turning the laughs on his antagonist and making him feel like six pewter nickels."[66]

In substance, however, the differences were fundamental.[67] Capital-*P* Populism, based in thick associational networks built and maintained by ordinary men and women, never venerated unmediated connections to a strong leader. And notwithstanding its checkered record on race and women's suffrage, the movement was egalitarian at its core. In separating "us" and "them," Populists defined "us" capaciously. That essential thread places them firmly in the venerable tradition of American radicalism. As the People's Party platform of 1892 declared, "We believe that the power of government—in other words, of the people—should be expanded . . . to the end that oppression, injustice and poverty, shall eventually cease in the land."[68]

1896 and the "Battle of the Standards"

As the 1896 election approached, the free coinage of silver, long a piece of Populist monetary policy, rose to the top of the national agenda. Silver mine owners organized in the American Bimetallic League had far more resources to spread their cause than anyone else in the fractious and underfunded People's Party.[69] Among Democrats, disillusioned with the hard-money Grover Cleveland after the Panic of 1893, silver appealed not only to Populist sympathizers but also to many southerners who favored reflation but wanted no part of agrarian radicalism.

At the 1896 Democratic convention, William Jennings Bryan, a young Nebraskan silverite acceptable across sections, electrified the crowd with his "Cross of Gold" speech. With strong support from the South and West and just enough from the Midwest, Bryan secured the requisite two-thirds vote for a surprise nomination on the fifth ballot.[70] The most doctrinaire goldbugs soon left the party. At a rump convention that followed the Democrats' gathering, the People's Party nominated Bryan on a fusion ticket while naming Tom Watson as vice president, rather than acceding to the Democrats' choice of Arthur Sewall, a Maine shipbuilding magnate who happened to support free silver.[71] As he barnstormed the country, Bryan studiously ignored the Populist nomination, even as it offered Republicans a potent line of attack in the "Battle of the Standards."

Bryan's nomination augured a durable shift in the Democracy's long trajectory. He gave the ritual invocation of Andrew Jackson and continued a politics that excoriated urban elites. Yet his openness to an income tax and an expanded regulatory state, both soft echoes of Populism, were decidedly un-Jacksonian and more proximately marked a drastic departure from laissez-faire orthodoxy.[72] Still, the tenets of Jim Crow that his southern brethren espoused and to which Bryan easily acquiesced would long limit the Democrats' egalitarian reach.

Critically, Bryan's appeal, contrasting virtuous smallholders on the periphery (and saying nothing about their landless brethren) with their adversaries in the great cities, offered little materially or emotionally to the urban worker. The "Cross of Gold" speech defined the contrast:

> You come to us and tell us that the great cities are in favor of the gold standard; we reply that the great cities rest upon our broad and fertile prairies. Burn down your cities and leave our farms, and your cities will spring up again as if by magic; but destroy our farms, and the grass will grow in the streets of every city in the country.[73]

The Bryan campaign thus pointed in multiple directions at once.[74] It marked the end of the line for Populism and the dream of the cooperative commonwealth. It reoriented the Democratic Party both sectionally— as Democrats lost ground in the Northeast and Midwest and retreated to the periphery—and ideologically. And it roused the ire of corporate capital, which mobilized to vanquish the silverite threat.

The 1896 Republican nominee, Ohio's William McKinley, represented himself as the personally attractive face of a business-friendly worldview, not just another transactional politician. A campaign slogan depicted McKinley as with "the people against the bosses," principally Platt of New York and Quay of Pennsylvania. The claim was thin; he won the Republican nomination by spending freely to assemble a majority from smaller state organizations.[75] Faced with the choice between McKinley and Bryan, the corporate elite, previously split between two sympathetic but internally divided parties, now stood united against a common threat.[76] Much of the support came from hard-money Gold Democrats appalled by their party's new direction. In what may be the purest-ever instance of the pro-capital strand at work, Mark Hanna, an Ohio businessman who orchestrated McKinley's winning campaign, and James J. Hill, a Gold Democrat who led the Great Northern Railway, rode in a carriage down Wall Street, stopping to solicit from each establishment a precisely calculated sum to pay for the fall McKinley campaign. The vast war chest, its contributions led by Standard Oil and JP Morgan, paid for an avalanche of propaganda warning urban workers against the dangers of silver and the snares of Populism. By the end, McKinley easily dispatched the threat from Bryan.[77]

Progressivism in the System of 1896

McKinley had prevailed, the challenge had been repulsed, and Republicans had won a national majority that would endure until the New Deal. The GOP dominated national politics from a secure base in the North, while Democrats held onto a rump in the Solid South. With most states under the effective control of a single party, voter turnout plummeted, especially in the working class.[78] Section more than ideology, still less an explicit class politics, defined what the political scientist Walter Dean Burnham labeled the System of 1896. Now debates came over how to tame, not whether to accept, industrial capitalism.[79] Theodore Roosevelt, in a book preface in 1913, was blunt: "Frank acceptance of the Progressive doctrine by the men at the top is the only effective way to prevent the woeful damage that would come from the triumph of class consciousness."[80]

Though each party contained conservative and reformist elements, the supporters of Progressivism inside the two parties never came together. This was thanks, above all, to the Solid South, where a commitment to white supremacy united white southerners behind the Democracy. In such an alignment, northern and southern conservatives and progressives could not simply sort. A few keen observers saw the shape of things to come. In a 1904 letter, John Coit Spooner, Robert M. La Follette's great rival in Wisconsin and a Stalwart traditionalist, looked "four years from now for a realignment of parties": "The socialists, populists, the social democrats, the radicals of the democracy and the radicals of the Republican party, will probably be together. The conservatives of the democracy and the conservatives of the republican [sic] party are likely to be together. It is not unlikely in that consummation the South will be found to be no longer solid."[81] He was off only in the timing.[82]

Rather than realigning the parties, Progressives transformed the concept of party. They looked for enlightened leadership to realize an agenda of moral and institutional reform that emphasized the organic unity of the people.[83] In contrast to the Mugwumps, they came from the broad Protestant middle classes and not just the old elites, and from the Midwest and the West and not just New England. Though they liked to cite Washington's farewell address, most Progressives were not simply down-the-line anti-party. Instead, in an important shift for anti-party thought, popular and not elite virtue would serve as the check on party machinations. And so Progressives ascribed to the political party a heroic potential inseparable from their own collective desire to make citizens better. If the party is bound together by "a common attachment to principles and a supreme regard for the national welfare[,] its existence is justified," declared a 1914 textbook. "When it becomes a machine for the dispensation of patronage it is a menace to the state."[84]

Progressivism stimulated challenges, rooted in an active citizenry, "to bridge social chasms by building communities of shared faith that would supplement or replace the old parties."[85] And so came nonpartisan municipal elections and city managers, the initiative and referendum, and, above all, the new pressure politics, designed to influence legislatures and agencies directly. Social reformers turned to the new group politics,[86] celebrating a public-spiritedness that contrasted with petty and dirty party politics. From the Anti-Saloon League to women's clubs to state labor federations to the Chamber of Commerce to the Farmers' Union (putting forth bits of the old Populist program), groups organized, pressed their demands, and then sought to entrench their gains in the state—in Elisabeth Clemens's pithy summary, "organize, politicize, bureaucratize."[87] It would not be until the New Deal, and accelerating in the following decades, that group politics would itself become partisan.

The Progressive embrace of the presidency nationalized and personalized party politics.[88] As they sought to expand the reach and professionalism of the state, Progressives extolled the promise of scientific management.[89] With that shift came support for a strong presidency—and a sharp reversal from the Whig attack on the "Caesarist" Jackson. As the parties nationalized, the presidents who now had control of their machinery would serve as focal points for political combat, unconstrained by the old fetters of decentralized parties. Through their power to control delegates to the national convention, governors and senators had once served as the president's equal. Increasingly, they became supplicants.

The parties did not simply retreat from the high ground they held during the nineteenth century. Rather, the underbrush in an already dense landscape grew even thicker. The story, to use the argot of contemporary social science, contains elements of displacement (as the secret ballot supplanted the party ticket), layering (as the primary did not fully replace the convention and the traditional party machinery), drift (as state-building took place outside the parties and as parties lost their luster), and conversion (as party organizations, notably Democratic machines, figured out how to benefit from the new configuration), but serves as a textbook case of none of them.[90] And so Progressives broke the old system without entirely building a new one.

New Rules of the Game

Enduring reforms made over the electoral process. Henceforth the state controlled the registration of voters, set the polling place, and printed the ballots; gone was the madcap Election Day of the party ticket. In states where the currents of reform ran deep, notably in the West, municipal elections became nonpartisan, and citizens gained the power to vote directly on legislation via the initiative and referendum and, in a few instances, to recall elected officials whom they deemed derelict.[91] The Senate—the engine of intergovernmental party power in the late nineteenth century—transformed, as voters, not state legislators, now chose its members. For state and congressional office, direct primaries rather than conventions of party delegates chose nominees.[92] And though they remained uncommon, the first presidential primaries appeared in 1912. Some of these reforms predated the rise of Progressivism; all became fully entrenched after it.

The Australian ballot—that is, a secret ballot, printed by the state— and the direct primary emerged, in the words of John F. Reynolds, from "the very separate agendas of middle-class reformers and partisan-minded public officials."[93] The party ballot induced cooperation for the collective good of the party only at enormous cost.[94] Armies of party workers, a necessity for handing out tickets at each polling place, had to get patronage, while the party's financial patrons needed goodies of their own. Errant factions could bolt the convention and print their own tickets. Ward bosses had to be monitored, lest they issue substitute tickets failing to list the name of a would-be officeholder from a rival faction. And so when reformers pressed for the Australian ballot, parties quickly acceded. Massachusetts came first, adopting a Mugwump proposal in 1888 and implementing it the following year. By the election of 1892, thirty-three states, including all but two outside the South, had moved to the secret ballot.[95]

The effect of replacing the party ballot is hard to treat in isolation, for the direct primary soon followed, and a logic connected the two reforms. When losing factions at the convention could threaten to print their own tickets at the polls, parties had every incentive to mollify them by presenting names minimally acceptable to all. With the Australian ballot, intraparty losers lost their greatest weapon, which in turn worsened the challenges of corralling all the party's supporters at a convention. It was far easier to battle against rival factions in a primary instead, party organizations generally concluded, by slating the right candidates and turning out loyal voters.[96]

The direct primary developed via institutional adaptation, beginning from various local arrangements involving elections for nomination run by parties rather than by the state. An 1897 account explained that the primaries "usually lack the town-meeting feature of the old New England caucus, namely the discussion in open meeting of the merits of the different persons to be voted for."[97] Following adoption of the Australian ballot, the question arose, as it had not in the days of the party ticket, of who had earned a place on the ballot. State recognition of parties and supervision over their nomination procedures offered an easy answer: the winners of duly elected primary elections.[98] A system of state-regulated ballots for the general election, with requirements for the candidates to appear on them, expanded to nomination. It was a consequential shift. "The direct primary," Theodore Roosevelt declared in 1912, "will give the voters a method ever ready for use, by which the party leader shall be made to obey their command."[99] But the command could also be an echo. Leaders, freed from the fetters of organization, had new suasion over voters.

The Progressive Era formalized parties as creatures of state law— "public utilities" in political scientist Leon Epstein's phrase.[100] The parties' internal operations, down in many instances to the membership and meeting requirements for local committees, became matters for the statute books. Ballot access rules privileged major parties and their duly chosen nominees, banning joint fusion tickets between multiple parties.[101] Making parties public utilities in an age of strong federalism rendered them creatures of state and not federal law. State parties became the permanent custodians of precious ballot lines, thereby creating a complex regulatory patchwork and thwarting any attempts at statutory control of the national conventions at the parties' apex.[102] Even where institutional arrangements from the Progressive Era have proven less sticky, subsequent change has largely followed along the lines that they set. Though the "nation-wide preferential primaries for candidates for the presidency" called for in the Progressive Party platform of 1912 never arrived, debates over nomination politics still take place under the normative logic of a national primary.[103]

Robert M. La Follette, Reform Boss

Robert M. La Follette of Wisconsin spoke with a rare directness about the role of the political party. Yet his rhetoric that "the bosses were not the party," and his actions as a leader of Progressive Republican forces in Wisconsin and then in the Senate, stand in notable tension.[104] For La Follette, the politics of expertise melded with personalism. That paradox of the new reform politics cut to the heart of the Progressive redefinition of the anti-party strand.

After a series of bruising convention fights, La Follette wrested control of his state Republican Party from the Stalwart faction by the turn of the new century. He served as governor from 1901 to 1906 and radically modernized state government. In 1904, the voters ratified his plan for the direct primary, the first such statewide law in the country, and for the direct election of senators. From 1906 until his death in 1925, he led Progressive Republican forces, principally from the West, in the Senate. And in Wisconsin, his political organization reigned supreme until his death. Look for Progressivism as it mattered in the states, in the particular admixture of conflict and compromise that Edward Ryan's 1873 speech prefigured, and one soon finds La Follette.[105]

More than other Republican Progressives, and certainly more than Theodore Roosevelt, with whom he was never close and whom he very conspicuously declined to endorse in 1912,[106] La Follette saw the bosses as the servants of capital. To him, the railroad interests, not the Stalwart politicians they backed, ultimately pulled the strings. Unlike the Socialists in Milwaukee with whom he often tactically cooperated, however, La Follette deemed political reform a worthy project in its own right. He did not view citizens in collective terms, still less in class terms. And so he held a very different understanding of "the people" than did the

Populists or even his own personal friend and occasional political ally William Jennings Bryan: they were individual citizens, to be educated for rule. And in his hours-long addresses, La Follette aimed to offer just that education.

La Follette never attacked party regularity, only the interests and the wire-pullers manipulating the party. Celebrating the direct link between the people and the party, he sought to connect individual citizens with the programs to which leaders bound themselves. That was the logic of the direct primary and also of the initiative, referendum, and recall. All limited the possibility for mischief in implementing the popular will. As he told the Wisconsin legislature during the battle for his primary election law, in language drawing on the eighteenth century while leaving few residues from the mass politics of the nineteenth: "The party promise, therefore, is a covenant with the voter upon which he has staked his faith and his interests. He has given his support; he has invested the party with his authority; he has made it possible for the party to control in government. Upon its promise and his support the party has become the custodian of his political rights as a citizen, of his property right as a man."[107]

For La Follette, the platform was "as binding upon the party conscience as though it were the sealed bond of every individual of the party."[108] There was a happy circularity in all this: La Follette effectively wrote his Wisconsin platform and then faced no trouble when he had to follow it. He never explained why the state platform ought to be the binding one, except that he had control of the state party. Every four years for a generation, allies of La Follette would propose language for the national Republican platform excoriating monopoly—and every four years, the party of big business voted them down.

A biographer described La Follette as "a reform boss."[109] The label is accurate. La Follette ran his organization as a strictly top-down affair with no pretense of internal democracy.[110] More than many other Progressives, La Follette had a notion of what a great party genuinely demanded, with goals to remake the polity and make citizens better, and a project that was substantive as well as procedural. Yet the combination of principle and expediency, as he drew together anti-party, policy-reform, and populist strands, proved unstable. La Follette's concept of party fused the primary and the platform, but in the following century, hustling candidates victorious in the primary would see no need for a grand covenant based around issues.

The Progressive Party of 1912

In 1912, the diverse impulses and factions that made up Progressivism came closest to a single common vision as they stood at Armageddon under the banner of the Bull Moose.[111] For that one year, the Progressive tendency rendered itself into a national political party. The Progressive Party of 1912 was more than Theodore Roosevelt, but it is not simply a point of "great man" history to say that there could have been no party without him.[112] Wrote Harold L. Ickes in 1941, while serving as secretary of the interior, "The Progressive party, in large measure, was the outward expression of the love and the admiration, amounting almost to idolatry, that the overwhelming majority of its members felt for Theodore Roosevelt."[113] Such ardor was deep but constrained by the tenacity of the major parties. In the election of 1912, Roosevelt ultimately won 27 percent of the popular vote—running four points ahead of the incumbent, William Howard Taft—but only six states.

In contrast to the model laid down by Van Buren and exemplified by Lincoln of the politician who put party before self, Roosevelt consistently elevated notions of the state and citizenship above those of party.[114] And in contrast to the Mugwumps, he disdained an ethos of skepticism and restraint. As Roosevelt told readers of the *Atlantic* in 1894, in a statement that explains well both the bolt of 1912 and his decision in 1916 to let the Progressive Party dissolve:

The truth is, simply, that there are times when it may be the duty of a man to break with his party, and there are other times when it may be his duty to stand by his party, even though, on some points, he thinks that party wrong; he must be prepared to leave it when necessary, and he must not sacrifice his influence by leaving it unless it is necessary. If we had no party allegiance, our politics would become mere windy anarchy, and, under present conditions, our government could hardly continue at all. If we had no independence, we should always be running the risk of the most degraded kind of despotism,— the despotism of the party boss and the party machine.[115]

Roosevelt preferred moral exhortation to institutional fetters. He praised the *Federalist Papers* as the political reflections of men who "had struggled against their adversaries and prevailed," ignoring Publius's warnings about the dangers of unchecked power.[116] Unlike La Follette, Roosevelt never claimed that platforms should bind candidates. In this sense, La Follette, though substantively the more radical figure, hewed closer to the old model.

The Progressives who bolted from the GOP in 1912 admired the founders of the Republican Party as men who had also met the central challenge of their age with a new political party.[117] However, where free labor ideology had guided Republicanism, the Progressives of 1912 never quite figured out what distinctive partisan loyalty should cleave the electorate.[118] In a letter ten days after the election, Roosevelt admitted, "We have not clear-cut issues as to which we take one side and our opponents the other side, and as to which the conscience of the people is deeply stirred."[119] Instead, their issues were a grab bag, from political reform to the eight-hour day to stewardship over the trusts.

The Progressive Party's upper ranks divided between the idealists whom Roosevelt called "moonbeamers" and the money men, including Frank Munsey, a press baron, and George W. Perkins, a longtime associate of J. P. Morgan who served as the party's executive secretary.[120] Together, Munsey and Perkins gave the Progressive Party almost half its funds. Conveniently ignoring this fact, the *Progressive Volunteer* touted low-dollar donors: "The significant thing about the Progressive movement is that the average citizen is waking up to the fact that if he wants the corrupt boss put out of business, he has got to help do it."[121]

The Progressive Party acquiesced in the racial hierarchies that structured American life. Theodore Roosevelt, whose mother hailed from Georgia, knew well that to win a majority in the Electoral College he had to get electoral votes from the border states, even if he could not crack the

Solid South. When they attacked corrupt party procedures and ill-informed voters, Progressives pointed to African Americans in the South whom Republicans had once championed. In an open letter to Julian Harris, a white Atlanta editor, Roosevelt bemoaned the "venality . . . of the negro delegates," favoring instead a Progressive Party "appealing to the best white men in the South."[122] Similarly, Walter Weyl brought forward the Liberal Republican fear of mass suffrage. "An added impulse was given to an unthinking party loyalty," he warned, "through the sudden enfranchise-ment of the Negroes, and their admission to the Republican party."[123]

In a critical controversy, the Progressive Party attempted a sectional straddle. The Provisional National Progressive Committee voted on August 5, 1912, over the objections of Jane Addams and other social re-formers, to seat lily-white delegations from across the South despite serious procedural shenanigans. At the same time, Blacks served in del-egations from across the North and held two seats apiece on each of the convention's standing committees. Though it tabled a motion to label the Progressives a "white man's party," the committee adopted resolu-tions allowing state parties to certify their own delegates and praising Roosevelt's letter to Julian Harris. State delegate certification was pre-cisely the issue the Mississippi Freedom Democratic Party would raise in 1964—and the Progressive Party of 1912 took the side that liberal reformers a half century later found so deeply abhorrent.[124]

Social Reform and Women's Suffrage

Women rode the political currents that washed away the old edifices. Nineteenth-century mass politics was a deeply male world. At times, its spaces had opened up to women, whose political activism was strongest in the party-movements that challenged the Democrats and Republi-cans, including the Populists.[125] Still denied the franchise everywhere except in a smattering of states in the West, women in the Progressive Era mobilized in clubs and pressure groups apart from the old parties, with particular influence at the state level.[126] Crucially, with the advent of suffrage, no distinctive vision of party would accompany women's entrance into the electorate or the parties themselves.

Progressives' fitful efforts to marry programmatic responsibility with technocracy owed much to professional women deploying expertise from the emergent social sciences. National policy programs maintained on "lines of principle," declared one Progressive Party initiative, would bring the "political economic thought of the day" together with "the will of the people."[127] Ordinary citizens' preferences and expert knowledge would supplant mass party organizations. If a single figure could be said to epitomize this connection to the policy-reform strand, it would be Jane Addams, who served as a Progressive Party delegate.[128] The 1912 Progressive platform combined support for "the adoption of a system of social insurance adapted to American use" with ambivalence toward unions and a record on race that social workers fought but ultimately accepted.[129] As twentieth-century labor-liberalism emerged with new answers to those three aspects of the "social question," its horizons expanded beyond the left wing of the Progressive Party.

Led by Frances Kellor, an immigration expert and a veteran of Hull House, a short-lived party-funded Progressive National Service aimed to synthesize expert knowledge into partisan priorities. Yet as ever in Progressivism, the calls for principle came louder than the particular principles came clear. A pamphlet listing the service's goals illustrates the problem:

1. To destroy the invisible government
2. To establish politics of social responsibility
3. To maintain party integrity on lines of principle
4. To campaign for political ideals[130]

The Progressive National Service, perpetually underfunded by a hostile George W. Perkins, never figured out how to marry the slow pace and tentative conclusions of social science with rapid-fire electoral combat. A century's worth of consultants and self-anointed messaging experts would emerge instead—though with an important difference. Through the service, the party itself, not any campaign or para-organization, developed policies and fit them to "party integrity." With the notable but short-lived exception of the Democratic Advisory Council in the later 1950s, the latter-day Frances Kellors would serve as campaign advisers or think-tankers rather than workers on the party payroll. Nevertheless, the service's vision of a politics made by experts in service to a common good redounds all the way to today's liberalism, in Obamaesque strivings toward benevolent technocracy and in presumptions that educated professionals' preferred policies are always congruent with the popular will.[131]

As for women's suffrage, the direct impact of Progressivism is often overestimated.[132] The suffragist wave, with support from the northern working class and in the South, began to crest just as the Progressive impulse receded. The strong counterfactual, that women's suffrage could not have coexisted with the old party politics—that elimination of the booze-soaked party tickets, and for that matter the clubby relations between senators and state legislators, was a necessary condition for suffrage—thus seems overstated. Certainly, comparative evidence suggests that women under almost any plausible context would have gained the vote at some point in the first half of the twentieth century. Nonetheless, the new political world ushered in by the Progressives profoundly shaped women's experiences after suffrage. Politics had moved from mass display toward privatized spaces that the women in party politics would have to pry open slowly and painfully.[133]

Beyond the Progressive Era

In 1924, Robert La Follette ran for the presidency on a ballot line that again took the Progressive name. It was a farmer-labor fusion cobbled together by a Committee for Progressive Political Action whose constituent elements disagreed about whether they had actually created a new party at all and did not try to form a full slate beyond the presidency.[134] The Bull Moosers divided in 1924. Those closest to Roosevelt, almost to a one, had returned to the Republican camp. They repudiated his old rival and excoriated his misuse of the Progressive label. As they explained in a statement, Roosevelt had in 1912 "sought the welfare of all the people, not the welfare of class against class." A more eclectic set from the fringes of 1912, including Jane Addams, Harold Ickes, and Herbert Croly, backed La Follette.[135] In the end, he won only his home state and placed second in eleven states west of Wisconsin.

Though Progressivism faded, the Progressive political reforms endured. Warren Harding and Calvin Coolidge, for all their revival of the old ways, embraced the new doctrine that saw the president as leader of his party.[136] Despite minor rear-guard actions in the 1920s, essentially no states reversed course on the direct primary. Tellingly, among ten governors surveyed in 1923, eight preferred primaries that would directly nominate candidates over primaries that would choose delegates to state conventions; only two of nine state party chairs concurred. Yet even as party organizations grumbled, they adapted.[137]

Political bosses continued to play a leading role in big cities and to influence state politics and, especially on the Democratic side, national conventions. Thanks to control over malapportioned state legislatures, a few Republican state organizations survived until the New Deal. They continued their delicate balance between rich financiers in cities and rural bulwarks of electoral support. Republican city machines, even more careful than their Democratic counterparts to keep tax rates low lest business succumb to the siren song of reform, hung on in Detroit, Philadelphia, Pittsburgh, and San Francisco.[138] A few suburban Republican machines lingered on well into the postwar years.[139]

The Democratic machines that endured took their accommodationist heritage in multiple directions.[140] At times, they moved toward a pragmatic pro-worker social reform that served as a key seedbed for the New Deal. As the old goldbugs left the party after 1896, space had opened up for a more capacious approach, one whose vote-getting prowess bosses could grow to appreciate. This tradition was most prominent in New York. The Factory Investigating Commission that followed the Triangle Shirtwaist Factory fire of 1911 inaugurated two decades of policymaking that fruitfully joined middle-class reformers and Tammany politicians, each side teaching the other. Frances Perkins recalled her tutelage of two rising stars, then mere state legislators. She brought Al Smith to see women leaving work on the night shift at the rope walks and made "sure that Robert Wagner personally crawled through the tiny hole in the wall that gave egress to a steep iron ladder covered with ice, which was euphemistically labeled 'Fire Escape' in many factories."[141] For their part, the politicians taught the reformers lessons of their own about the give-and-take of getting things done. Though Democrats would be rent by internecine strife for decades to come, both in the cities and in the countryside, the party had made a decisive shift.

At other times, however, machines aimed simply to direct patronage to their core constituencies. While protecting the tangible divisible benefits that had survived from the prior political order, they tamped down the mass mobilization that had characterized the age of the torchlight parade.[142] The machines that survived the New Deal often applied both models at once: liberalism in national politics and divide and conquer at home. Even when they kept control over city and state organizations and, in turn, their delegations to national conventions, the machines' power in the polity waned as the twentieth century wore on, and with it the force of the accommodationist strand that the Progressives had attacked. The sometimes creaky organizations remained custodians of the old Van Buren model, venerating the principles of loyalty that long defined party regularity. But without the webs of partisan connections that the Progressives had cut asunder, their venerable claims, reasserted at conventions, fell on deaf ears. The community leaders, brokers, opportunists, cranks, and ambitious young people of talent who all once saw their path to influence entirely through the political party scattered. That was the cost as new groups and forms of activism rose alongside the traditional party organizations.

The Progressive Legacy

The Gilded Age offered the widest range of party models of any period in American history, but—even as the inequality of the Second Gilded Age prompts scholars to revisit industrial capitalism's rise[143]—the memory of those political responses remains a niche market. The Progressives, by contrast, have endured as central touchstones for successive generations. Midcentury liberals struggling to make parties responsible at a time when they seemed stalled and blurred sought to harness the nationalizing and programmatic side of Progressivism—to make the parties mean something. Looking back from the 1970s, when fears of dealignment and decline filled the air, Progressivism seemed like a one-way ratchet to break apart the institutions Van Buren and his ilk had built up and, in so doing, destroy the wellsprings of party.

In the following decades, the Progressives loomed large as American liberals, especially those with a communitarian bent, looked to unite energetic government with common purpose.[144] Once upon a time, went their narrative, an efflorescence of civic energy solved long-festering problems, and now, equipped with a more expansive view of American pluralism that overcomes the Progressives' failures on race, it may do so again.[145] With the Republican Party intolerant and intransigent, these thinkers have seen the Democrats as the sole repository for national action. But those sentiments beg to reopen an old question at the intersection of the policy-reform and anti-party strands that the Progressives never resolved: if the Democratic Party serves as the nation's prime repository of shared civic commitments, then what is distinctly *partisan* in its vision?

In an age of hollow parties, the Progressive legacy appears not at a single point on the political spectrum but all across it. Progressivism opened up space for antisystem appeals of every stripe. It corroded party guardrails and, particularly in its personalistic and plebiscitarian tendencies, weakened the restraints against demagogy. Bits of the Progressive vision, glimmers off the kaleidoscope, appear across the contemporary polity. The left-wing activist slamming the Democratic National Committee for its illegitimate machinations, the centrist on the Acela from New York to Washington worrying about all the politicians screwing up sensible good government, and the Trump voter yearning for a savior to clean up the politicians' mess—all three bear a Progressive inheritance. Our hollow parties—unable to police boundaries, sell compromises, or generate good feelings among supporters—do not trace directly back to the Progressive Era. But without the Progressives' legacy, there is no making sense of why, once polarized politics arrived, the parties proved so ill-suited to channel and control all the passions brought to bear upon them.

5

Visions of Party from the New Deal to McGovern-Fraser

"THIS DEMOCRATIC Party is a little bit bigger than the individuals who participate in it." Hubert Humphrey was giving remarks to the New York delegation that would soon head to the Democratic National Convention in Chicago. The date was August 17, 1968. "This party has governed this country a long time," he continued. "And it has given this country the basis of its social policy." The vice president invoked the Democrats' towering legacy to underline how much he shared with his rivals for the party's presidential nomination, Eugene McCarthy and George McGovern (stepping in for the slain Robert Kennedy). As heated as the contest might get, he implied, the candidates were brothers-in-arms with common commitments.[1] Just before leaving the podium, Humphrey looked out into the crowd, and a familiar face prompted a final remark. "You know, my father was a great Democrat before me and he brought me up, as we say, in the faith, and the man who preached the faith to him is Jim Farley. Thank you, Jim."[2]

James A. Farley—"Mr. Democrat," Franklin D. Roosevelt's campaign manager and bridge to the bosses, simultaneous chair of the New York State Democratic Committee and the Democratic National Committee (DNC) and postmaster general from 1933 to 1940, sender of over 200,000 Christmas cards in 1936, signatory of 2,800 letters during a typical day in 1937—had represented New York as a delegate at every Democratic National Convention since 1924.[3] An at-large delegate in 1968, the eighty-year-old master accommodationist acted as "a straw-hatted constant," in one reporter's words, "in a generation of change."[4] The change afoot in 1968, however, had sparked unusually intense conflict within the state party.

New York Democrats' hybrid delegate selection procedures in 1968 were typical of the era's mixed system in presidential nomination. After a primary election chose the bulk of the delegation, the state party committee appointed sixty at-large delegates. McCarthy had won a majority of the committed delegates in the primary, and his campaign argued he deserved at least half of the at-large seats as well. County leaders pushed back, insisting that the seats should go to party regulars as reward for loyal service and financial support. At the New York state committee meeting in June, the regulars prevailed, and the party allocated only fifteen-and-a-half seats to McCarthy backers.[5] Three hundred outraged McCarthy supporters bolted the meeting. The chaotic scene, like others across the country during those months, was ripe with portent of the storm to come in Chicago. Protracted negotiations in the shadow of a threatened credentials challenge eventually gave McCarthy forces more support.[6] But the delegation remained a divided and embittered group.[7]

Opposing procedural views reflected competing party visions. The county chairs and their allies saw threats not only to the prerogatives of party loyalists but also to the incentives that sustained day-to-day party organization. McCarthy supporters, mobilized by opposition to the Vietnam War, held to a plebiscitary conception of intraparty decision-making that looked instead to voters and movement activists. At the national convention, these visions would collide in momentous fashion. And, not for lack of trying, Jim Farley, the twelve-time convention stalwart and living emblem of the era that bequeathed a political order, would never hold a delegate credential at a national convention again.

From the 1930s to the 1970s, decisive battles over the shape of American politics were waged as intraparty family conflicts, quarrels inside the Democrats' big tent. This chapter traces the overlapping work of Democrats pursuing three distinct party projects across what scholars term "the New Deal order": midcentury pragmatists, programmatic liberals, and McGovern-Fraser reformers. Amid the wide ideological vistas of the 1930s, Franklin Roosevelt, master juggler across a vast coalition, opened up new approaches to party politics while resolving none of their tensions. In the postwar era, fights among New Deal adherents would crystallize into distinct visions.[8]

These debates among Democrats produced something close to ideal types of both the accommodationist and the policy-reform strands of party politics. Midcentury pragmatists, defending the venerable prerogatives of local and state organizations, espoused Farley's brand of accommodationism. Across the North and West, they soon found themselves the targets of a rising Democratic cadre: programmatic liberals who championed issue-driven activism over the regulars' parochial transactionalism. The liberals' substantive fervor as they led the intraparty struggle against Dixie over civil rights showed the policy-reform strand at its most potent. But their technocratic bent and softened class appeals augured a liberalism distant from ordinary people's workaday concerns.

The tumult of the 1960s, running from race to Vietnam, brought both party regulars and reform liberals to the crisis point. From the fallout of the 1968 national convention, the McGovern-Fraser Commission fashioned a new party project. It combined the policy-reform strand's programmatic commitments, the radical strand's transformational zeal, and the anti-party strand's aversion to formal hierarchy. The McGovern-Fraser reformers' work upended Democrats' process for selecting presidential nominees. Yet even as they struck decisive blows against old-style accommodationism, they failed in their ultimate goal of building a crusading, permeable movement party.

To see the conflicts "fought out within the house of American liberalism" as a clash of party strands is to grasp the structure of a "house" all too easily obscured in a haze of consensus and consumption-driven growth.[9] In the postwar decades, white Americans rushed to suburbia, where Democratic machines had little imprint. The once-reinforcing ties of ethnicity, union, and party faded.[10] Compromises defined the new mixed economy and regulatory state.[11] With the conservative coalition in control of Congress, national health insurance remained out of reach. The social compact rested instead on a welfare state with a distinct bundle of public and private benefits.[12] As the "warfare state" generated millions of jobs in defense-related industries, an economic strategy of military Keynesianism forged a broad political coalition.[13] All that defense spending helped unite liberals and pragmatists alike in a powerful Cold War consensus. In the teeth of the Second Red Scare, dissenters against that consensus, and with it the radical strand in party politics, vanished from mainstream politics for a generation.[14]

Forces both internal and external to this shaky political order would help bring to a close the era when a Democrat could so easily remark, "This party has governed this country a long time." The catastrophe of Vietnam prompted the reemergence, now under a New Left, of a radical critique not only of America's domestic regime but of its role in the world.[15] No sooner had this challenge helped to drive party fracture and party reform than 1970s stagflation—itself a product of the welfare and warfare states both under strain—ended the shared prosperity that formed the bedrock of Democrats' electoral strength. And the New Deal order came unglued.

With fundamental questions over the future of the American political economy up for contestation in the 1970s, Democrats proved less capable of filling the breach than a resurgent GOP under the firm grip of a distinctly instrumentalist Right. In stressing the latter's decisive impact, we therefore break with assessments that specifically target the McGovern-Fraser reforms and the forces behind them. Political scientists have long pointed to those reforms as weakening the parties and disordering American politics.[16] Historians on both the right and the left, moreover—politically disparate but united in a dislike of contemporary liberalism—have seen the reforms as part and parcel of the Democrats' takeover by educated professionals and willful abandonment of the working class (usually coded as white and male).[17] We see some merit in these lines of critique but also a form of analytical blinders, preventing the analysts from seeing *outside* the house of liberalism. The Right's breakthroughs, the subject of chapter 6, would ultimately undermine the basis of party vitality in the United States far more than anything wrought by McGovern-Fraser.[18]

Still, midcentury Democrats' struggles bring us closer to the dilemmas of our own time. Albeit in somewhat different fashion, both programmatic liberals and McGovern-Fraser reformers believed in making parties vehicles for ideological activism.[19] In time, such activism would help to drive the ideological sorting that would revive partisanship in the electorate and in government. But the liberal forces chronicled here, again in different ways, also believed in making formal parties the focal points of politics—and this aspiration remained unmet. Party sorting after the 1970s took place on less civically rooted ground, carried out by outside actors and groups rather than by the parties themselves. The result would be a party system at once ideologically defined, president-centered, and hollow.

New Deal Legacies

Eclectic in its approach to relief and recovery, the New Deal was no more consistent when it came to party politics. Nonpartisan, bipartisan, organizational partisan, ideological partisan—Franklin Roosevelt adopted and discarded each of these roles as he saw fit. His long tenure pushed forward three related developments: the rise of programmatic partisanship, the nationalization of parties, and the presidentialization of politics. The first two of those reflected developments set in train but not far advanced while Roosevelt still lived. The last bore his distinctive stamp.

The effect of the New Deal on the party organizations was Janus-faced. Roosevelt's reformist posture as state senator and then governor of New York had contributed to the resistance he faced at the 1932 convention from urban bosses still loyal to their fellow Roman Catholic, Al Smith.[20] Jersey City mayor Frank Hague made the howlingly incorrect prediction that Roosevelt "cannot carry a single state east of the Mississippi."[21] But Roosevelt worked hard to sustain cross-sectional support, reasoning that "leadership can be successful only through the greatest amount of party harmony."[22] In his successive pursuit of the First and Second New Deals in Congress, Roosevelt fatefully offered vast legislative deference to the southern barons in Congress while bolstering the fortunes of local party organizations through the resources that new federal programs channeled their way.[23]

Jim Farley, the Irish builder of upstate New York Democratic organization, was central to this work. His biographer evokes the continuity in

technique linking Farley's work in New York to his role in the unprecedented federal apparatus forged in the crucible of the Depression: "His
daily business was largely devoted to keeping and maintaining contact,
whether through face-to-face talks, phonecalls, or correspondence. . . . In
a sense, he merely extended and expanded the political model he had used
in Rockland County during his upstate apprenticeship and applied it to
his new situation, thus making a form of politics originally designed
to serve local needs function on the national stage."[24]

As the Roosevelt administration's approach to building political support for the New Deal took a sharper ideological edge over time, it came
unavoidably into conflict with Farley's jawbone-and-favors Democratic
accommodationism. Progressive Republicans like Harold Ickes and
Henry Wallace took important positions in the administration while
their counterparts in Congress—California's Hiram Johnson, Wisconsin's Robert La Follette Jr., Nebraska's George Norris—were strong
legislative allies. Roosevelt sometimes reciprocated with both electoral
and patronage support for such non-Democrats while shutting out un-
cooperative Democratic organizations, to the latter's vocal consternation.[25] In the next generation, those progressive Republicans' political
descendants would shed their anti-party cloaks and become Democrats
seeking to make the party consistently liberal.

After 1936, Farley drifted gradually into the ranks of alienated insiders,
castigating bureaucratic operators like Harry Hopkins and Ickes, with
whom he fought over patronage and federal largesse, as a "small band of
zealots who mocked . . . party loyalty."[26] Roosevelt's decision to seek a
third term marked the breaking point for Farley, who linked the president's
seeming power madness to his rejection of the prudence and order that
parties bring to the political system. Farley threw his own hat in the 1940
ring, lost badly at the convention, and promptly resigned from the DNC
and the administration, never to speak to Roosevelt again.[27]

Farley's disillusionment did not reflect a broader rupture between the
president and traditional Democratic coalition partners, however. Urban
party organizations not only held on but in many cases thrived with the
advent of the New Deal state.[28] A boom-to-bust pattern characterized
some of the most unreformed machines under the most recalcitrant

bosses, such as Hague of Jersey City and Tom Pendergast of Kansas City. But others grew or emerged anew in the 1930s by adapting to the coalitional and programmatic changes flowing from the national party.

Arthur Schlesinger Jr. described a "new type of boss" capable of putting the traditional machinery of mobilization to work "organizing the CIO, the negroes, and independent liberals behind New Deal social policies."[29] In the flourishing of new machines like those in Chicago under Ed Kelly and in Pittsburgh under David Lawrence, observers saw a novel kind of federally instigated political vehicle for modern liberalism.[30] And indeed, for all the symbolic weight of the second-term schism between FDR and Farley, most bosses sided with the president. (At the 1940 convention, Kelly dispatched Chicago's superintendent of sewers to exploit the hall's public address system for a well-timed pro-Roosevelt chant.)[31]

Outside formal party channels, social groups and interests formed connections both to national political leadership and to the state itself.[32] By 1935 and 1936, New Dealers used federal suasion to foster and channel massive social mobilizations, above all by workers newly organized in the industrial unions of the Congress of Industrial Organizations (CIO).[33] New extra-party campaign vehicles like the Progressive National Committee and Labor's Non-Partisan League tied disparate interest groups into the New Deal project.[34] On the left, the Communist-linked coalitional strategy of the Popular Front provided a context in which administration allies in the labor movement could mobilize leftist activism and channel it away from third parties and into the wide Democratic fold.[35]

Roosevelt pushed both to embed New Deal programs within an administrative presidency and to instantiate a personalistic presidency. The first goal meant insulating new policies from political contestation by substituting federal machinery for the collective authority of the parties.[36] At the same time, Roosevelt strove to embody within his own leadership the agenda and the commitments of his administration and allies.[37] Together these dual transformations set a pattern for executive-centered partisanship that would only strengthen in the decades to come. As partisan identities grew more salient and more national in orientation, the personalism, even more than the strengthened administrative state, would ultimately be the presidency's most important effect on the parties.[38] It would vex every future effort to bolster parties' collective capacities and responsibilities.

Programmatic politics, nationalization, and presidentialism all converged in Roosevelt's attempts to realign the two-party system around the new conflicts over federal policy. Roosevelt came to view the party's conservative southern bloc as a dissident faction to be confronted. In 1936, he pushed through a repeal of the Democrats' century-old two-thirds rule, which had required a delegate supermajority to secure the presidential nomination. For the veteran journalist William Allen White, the move offered a premonition of an "urban" and "Hamiltonian" Democratic Party that would rid itself of its southern flank.[39] Two years later, enraged by the emerging conservative coalition's resistance to his court plan, executive reorganization, and the Fair Labor Standards bill, Roosevelt pursued his infamous purge campaign, intervening in primary elections against leading conservative Democrats in Congress. As "head of the Democratic Party," Roosevelt explained to his radio audience, charged with carrying out "the definitely liberal declaration of principles" in the 1936 platform, he was obligated to intervene in primary contests pitting a liberal against a conservative.[40] The logic recurred in 1944, when, remarking to Harry Hopkins that "we ought to have two real parties—one liberal and the other conservative," the president initiated secret inquiries into forming an alliance with his former opponent Wendell Willkie that would unite Democratic and Republican progressives inside a new party formation.[41]

The ideological realignment went unrealized. The hapless, jerry-rigged purge campaign of 1938 produced but a single scalp, that of Tammany's John O'Connor, leaving the southern contingent of Democratic critics unscathed and emboldened. Global crisis softened Roosevelt's combative posture toward the (disproportionately hawkish) southern barons, while the conservative coalition grew in strength as southern Democrats and northern Republicans joined together in roll calls on labor law and civil rights.[42] Whatever lip service Roosevelt paid to the obligations of party platforms, the crosscutting of programmatic and partisan lines would continue to characterize American politics for decades to come.

The Postwar World

The aftermath of World War II refracted and intensified the contradictions of the New Deal. The United States now held a very different position in the international order, with profound implications for politics at home.[43] National security policy, encompassing the secrets of the atom, rested inside a new executive establishment, built with the unstinting support of southern Democrats and largely hidden from public scrutiny.[44] The political economy of the American imperium severed old republican fetters on permanent military mobilization and executive aggrandizement. And as the scope of state power grew, the ambit of partisan contrast shrank.

The task of navigating these treacherous waters fell to Harry Truman, Roosevelt's successor.[45] A faithful regular of Kansas City's Pendergast machine during his political rise, he owed his vice presidential nomination in 1944 to a coterie of bosses.[46] As Truman maneuvered to limit Soviet influence in Europe, he sought broad domestic political support to respond to the Communist threat.[47] On the left, Henry Wallace, dreaming of a "Century of the Common Man," departed the Truman administration and, in short order, the Democratic Party. In this new configuration, the Cold War provided both binding and stricture for liberal politics.[48] New Dealers had dreamed of a peacetime economy committed to full employment. But the conservative coalition in Congress neutered the Employment Act of 1946, limiting the direct federal role in both planning and jobs provision.[49] After that defeat, full employment in the growing postwar economy came to mean recourse to the vast private-sector production, spread across a multitude of congressional districts, that sustained American military might.

As the ardor for economic transformation receded, Democrats' attention to civil rights sharpened, thanks in no small part to insurgent Black activism. It was a new phase in the "long civil rights movement."[50] During the 1930s, African American organizations ranging from the Communist-backed National Negro Congress to the NAACP and the Urban League had responded favorably to the CIO's concerted efforts at Black outreach and support for civil rights policy. World War II began to bring this labor–civil rights coalition into the very center of the liberal agenda, as the Great Migration swelled African American electoral ranks in the North and leaders like A. Philip Randolph pressed for the Fair Employment Practices Commission and desegregation of the armed forces.[51] Such breakthroughs were not primarily a *party* project aimed at Democratic alliance or reform. Nevertheless, they set the stage for battles that transformed postwar liberalism, with heady implications for Democrats' internal sectional juggling act.

The 1948 presidential contest dramatized the new shape of political conflict over the New Deal, the Cold War, and civil rights. Harry Truman evoked both of the visions taking shape within Cold War liberalism. When it came to foreign policy, he told the Democratic convention, "Partisanship should stop at the water's edge; and I shall continue to preach that through this whole campaign."[52] Domestically, Truman married hard-edged partisanship, as he ripped the "do-nothing" 80th Congress, with a vigorous agenda to carry forth the New Deal.[53]

One of the most famous campaign documents in American political history, drafted by attorney and former FDR aide James Rowe but prepared for the president's eyes in late 1947 by White House counsel Clark Clifford, identified the central coalitional challenges that Truman faced. Southern congressional power threatened electoral support in the North and West; labor, African Americans, and ideological liberals might be tempted by Henry Wallace's third-party bid. The solution lay in dramatizing conflict with the GOP Congress, sharpening an anticommunist critique of Wallace ("identify him and isolate him in the public mind with the Communists"), and mobilizing voter blocs through a full-throated program on labor, agriculture, welfare, and civil rights. The last item "would obviously cause difficulties with our Southern friends, but that is the lesser of two evils." Electoral success now depended on programmatic appeals and an in-house presidential campaign operation more than on the traditional party and its bosses, the Clifford memo asserted. "Better education, the rise of the mass pressure group . . . the growth of government functions: all of these have contributed to the downfall of 'the organization.'"[54]

Yet Truman's own relationship with the regulars belied such sweeping death rites. The new-breed bosses like David Lawrence of Pittsburgh and

Ed Flynn of the Bronx, attentive to their growing African American constituencies, had advocated for Truman in 1944 not merely because of hostility to Henry Wallace's leftism but also out of opposition to his likeliest replacement on the ticket, Jimmy Byrnes of South Carolina.[55] Four years later, they moved to Truman's *left* in directing their delegations to vote for the platform committee minority report on civil rights pushed by Americans for Democratic Action's Andrew Biemiller and Hubert Humphrey.[56] Lawrence, the party regular, issued a welcoming call to "continue the Democratic Party as the nation's party of liberalism." Humphrey, the reformist insurgent, followed with his electrifying demand for the party to "get out of the shadow of states' rights and to walk forthrightly into the bright sunshine of human rights."[57] Though battles with reformers and civil rights activists would reveal the exaggerated quality of his claims, the journalist Irwin Ross was pointing to something real when he noted in 1950 that "machines have become, year by year, as uninhibited in support of the Fair Deal . . . as the most militant brain-trusters in Washington."[58]

The Democrats split three ways in the general election of 1948. In the radical strand's last gasp in mainstream politics for a generation, Wallace's breakaway Progressive Party campaign combined a frontal assault on Jim Crow with a critique of the Cold War that would soon recede to the margins. On a visit to North Carolina, he was greeted with pelted eggs and cries of both "Hey, n——lover" and "Hey, Communist."[59] On the other side, States' Rights Democrats, popularly known as Dixiecrats, nominated Strom Thurmond, the governor of South Carolina, as their presidential candidate. It was a strategy in keeping with the apartisan sectional tradition that traced back to John C. Calhoun. The Dixiecrats intended their third-party move not as a bid to realign the party system but as a one-off gambit to deny any candidate a majority of electoral votes. That would thereby throw the decision to the House of Representatives, where southerners could demand a hefty price. The maneuver, though of limited popularity even among segregationist southern elites, augured the coming rupture over civil rights.[60] Frustrated by the conservative coalition after his victory, Truman would achieve little legislatively during his full term. But his win in 1948 cemented the transformations that had taken Wallace and Thurmond out of the Democratic fold—and set the stage for others to come.

Programmatic Liberals

In the decades after the Second World War, programmatic liberals sought a Democratic Party that would succeed where Roosevelt's purge campaign had failed. Their project connected ideologically oriented politics with party realignment and reform, thus fulfilling the New Deal's incomplete political transformations. The programmatic liberals were party-builders, seeking to marry Progressive concerns for expert-driven policymaking to the energy of civically rooted nineteenth-century parties. They mobilized the support of the rising organized exponents of postwar liberalism: middle-class issue activists, organized labor (especially the legacy CIO unions in what was after 1955 the merged AFL-CIO), and civil rights advocates. And they battled, largely separately, against two sets of factional adversaries inside the party. At the state and local levels, liberals fought with old-line Democratic organizations for control. At the national level, they fused civil rights advocacy with a congressional reform agenda, aiming their fire at southern Democrats who controlled congressional committees and so dominated policymaking.

The liberals' success in showcasing an alternative model of party vitality to the machines rested on solid organizational grounding. Yet theirs was a distinctly middle-class vision of party. James Q. Wilson's study of voluntarist Democratic activism distinguished the outlook of the "amateurs" from that of professionals: "The amateur takes the outcome of politics—the determination of policies and the choice of officials—seriously, in the sense that he feels a direct concern for what he thinks are the ends these policies serve and the qualities these officials possess."[61] With this vision, the policy-reform strand came into its fullest flower.

The programmatic liberals often grounded their arguments about political reform and party practice in a scholarly doctrine with pre–New Deal roots: responsible party government.[62] Parties, the midcentury reformers argued, should mobilize voters and organize governance on the basis of issues and program—not patronage or personality. The programs that would define the national parties and their agendas should concern national issues—not a mishmash of parochial interests. And voters would be provided a meaningful choice and a mechanism for holding officials accountable only if the two parties' programs were distinct—not blurred by crosscutting coalitions and rampant bipartisanship in policymaking.

Hubert Humphrey's push for a strong civil rights plank at the 1948 convention highlighted how opposition to Jim Crow could power a factional bid for party dominance. A strong civil rights plank, Humphrey told a fellow reformer, Connecticut's Chester Bowles, would help to foster "a real, liberal Democratic party . . . not a hodge-podge of sections."[63] Anticommunist labor-liberalism and civil rights advocacy merged as well in the paraparty outfit that Humphrey and Bowles helped to cofound in 1947 amid fierce factionalism on the left: Americans for Democratic Action (ADA).[64]

The nationalizing thrust of New Deal politics and the pressures of domestic anticommunism gave firepower to liberal Democrats when battling against third parties and drawing a cordon sanitaire against the red-tinged Left. In Minnesota, Humphrey's liberals first helped to engineer a merger between the Democrats and the state's Farmer-Labor Party and then, in 1948, pushed the Popular Front faction out of the party.[65] In New York, the bipartisan Wilson-Pakula Act of 1947 gave party leaders the right to strike from their ballot any cross-registered nominee whom they disliked. The bill effectively ended the career of the radical congressman Vito Marcantonio of East Harlem and hastened the death of the American Labor Party (ALP).[66] The Liberal Party of New York that emerged in the ALP's stead remained a lower-tier player—"a tail for someone else's kite," in the reformer Ed Costikyan's words, "as the Democratic Party found itself teeming with noisy, youthful, idealistic reformers."[67]

Organized labor, too, fell into line. In 1946, the CIO had launched an ambitious Operation Dixie to organize the South and build a nationwide majority for its labor-left politics. The effort failed miserably.[68] The following year, after Republicans and southern Democrats joined together to override Truman's veto, the Taft-Hartley Act radically redrew the rules for industrial conflict. The CIO called it "a slave labor law."[69] And in 1949, as the Cold War intensified, the CIO expelled the left-led unions that had failed to back its endorsement of Harry Truman.[70] A harder-edged politics of class, one that chafed against the limits of the New Deal but never quite resolved the complexities of party, went into eclipse. Instead, progressive unions, with the United Auto Workers (UAW) under Walter Reuther at the head of the pack, reinvented themselves as loyal Democratic soldiers, purging Communists while pushing for ideological realignment within the two-party system.[71] A 1959 UAW resolution called for "a clear demarcation" between a liberal and a conservative party and "full assurance that when elected [the liberal] party will carry out its liberal program without qualification, compromise, or delay."[72]

At the grassroots, a generation that had come of age politically in the New Deal now sought to carry out a national party realignment on local turf. The 1952 and 1956 presidential campaigns of "the most beautiful loser," Adlai Stevenson, especially galvanized club organizing by liberal activists. [73] Reformers in states dominated by party regulars established influential beachheads like the Democratic Federation of Illinois and New York's Committee for Democratic Voters. They saw a particular victory when New York City's mayor, Robert F. Wagner Jr., won reelection for a third term in 1961 without the support of the city's Democratic organizations. It drew a curtain on Tammany Hall, for generations a byword for bossism.[74] Wholesale transformations of state parties took place where, as in Minnesota, Michigan, and California, activists could successfully fuse left-of-center forces and take over sclerotic existing party organizations.[75]

All this work yielded an efflorescence of political talent that shaped the scene for decades. Reformist parties provided the springboards for a slew of activist, multiterm governors—Orville Freeman in Minnesota, Mennen "Soapy" Williams in Michigan, Pat Brown in California—and liberal congressional leaders—Hubert Humphrey, Eugene McCarthy, Phil Hart, Phil Burton.[76] The 1958 midterm elections gave programmatic liberals the opportunity to tout their electoral prowess when Democrats picked up forty-nine seats in the House and fifteen in the Senate, with big gains across the North and West.[77] A generation later, James Sundquist would note that for all the commentary about party decline in the states, "you can point to as many state party organizations that were strengthened by being liberated from the tight clique control that was characteristic of the old machines."[78]

Programmatic liberals boasted an avowedly pro-party reform agenda. The California Democratic Council's core reform goal at its founding in 1952, achieved six years later, was the repeal of the state's cross-filing system that allowed candidates to enter both parties' primaries. Minnesota's Democratic-Farmer-Labor Party led a push to end the state's nonpartisan legislature, not achieved until the 1970s. In virtually all reform states, the activists supported (and practiced) pre-primary party endorsements, even as many had to settle for informal versions unreflected on ballots.

Women predominated in the amateur milieus of voluntary, unremunerative party activism, though the continued barriers to assuming major leadership roles that they faced would be torn down only in the wake of McGovern-Fraser and second-wave feminism. Reformist clubs and programmatic parties, drawing on the issue-driven activism that women had pioneered in the Progressive Era, offered more opportunities to women than did the traditional organizations.[79] While the 1950s and early 1960s saw the organizational decline of distinctly women-focused operations within the Democratic National Committee, liberal influence helped enable the leadership of dynamic vice chairs and women's division heads like India Edwards and Margaret Price, along with movement-oriented activists outside formal party offices like Mildred Jeffrey of Michigan and Arvonne Fraser of Minnesota.[80]

As civil rights activists inaugurated a new phase of direct action in the wake of the Supreme Court's 1954 *Brown v. Board of Education* decision, they continued to maintain an arm's-length relationship with the party system. "Nothing could be more disastrous than your being maneuvered into an identification with either party at a time when neither party by deeds has earned, or should have, the support or approval of the Negro movement," wrote the veteran activist and Randolph associate Bayard Rustin to Martin Luther King Jr. in 1957.[81] (Rustin and many others would depart from that position by the mid-1960s.) But even as activists on the ground championed moral commitment over party allegiance, liberals like ADA's Joseph L. Rauh Jr., working alongside the NAACP and other established civil rights groups, pushed hard in Washington. Their signal victory was passage of the Civil Rights Act of 1957, which targeted voting rights. While the law was largely toothless, its passage

marked the first civil rights bill to clear Congress since Reconstruction—
and a massive defeat for the liberals' southern antagonists.[82]

Though they beat the drum for party cohesion, programmatic liberals remained factional players in national politics. They bolstered the
tenures of two DNC chairs, Stephen Mitchell and Paul Butler, who
pursued organizational innovations with the support of an ascendant,
like-minded wing among national committee members.[83] Butler was
influenced by the responsible-party prescriptions found in the 1950 report of the American Political Science Association's Committee on
Political Parties.[84] In 1956 he adopted the report's recommendation
for a national party issues council by creating the high-profile and controversial Democratic Advisory Council. Books from academics and
liberal politicians under their influence decried the entrenchment of
segregationist southern power in Congress through seniority and the
committee system and made the case for party government accountable
to the Democrats' liberal majority.[85] And responsible-party emphases
on party cohesion colored relentless critiques of Democratic leaders'
propensity to bargain across the aisle, during both the Eisenhower years
and John F. Kennedy's frustrating tenure.

Programmatic liberals never adequately deciphered how to nationalize
party politics without aggrandizing presidential power and influence.
The APSA Committee on Political Parties had claimed that strengthening and empowering collectively responsible parties would save the
country from "the danger of overextending the presidency."[86] A decade and
a half later, however, James MacGregor Burns, a leading backer of responsible parties, could conclude his study of politics under presidential
domination by declaring, "The prospects seem good that presidential
government will continue to help broaden equality of opportunity at
the same time that it protects our basic freedoms."[87] Building programmatic parties advanced rather than arrested the presidential takeover of
the party system.

The irony of a political movement that found organizational expression
at the local and state levels while fighting for a politics of *national* programmatic conflict eventually imposed a cost as those local and state parties atrophied. "Since the ideologies to which party workers are loyal are

defined largely in terms of national politics," Frank Sorauf observed in his study of voluntary Wisconsin party committees in the 1950s, "the ideological bond has a paramount disadvantage in distracting the attention of the Wisconsin parties from state issues and government."[88] In this realm, the accommodationist politics of the midcentury pragmatists had the relative virtue of an unimpeded focus on local organizational strength.

The political ethic that James Q. Wilson attributed to the club reformers—"the desire to moralize public life, the effort to rationalize power with law"—often threatened to turn party activism into heedless position-taking and abstract proceduralism.[89] Adlai Stevenson himself mused presciently in 1959 about the club-style politics that emerged in the wake of his candidacy. "What are the effects of an almost exclusively 'ideological' political motivation? Is some degree of instability the likely price of a lack of the restraint of economic interest and of part-time interest in politics?"[90]

The programmatic liberals' hour would soon come to a close. The amateurs' postwar rise reflected the lingering civic inclinations of midcentury cohorts acculturated to participation in mass-membership organizations.[91] For all their middle-class zeal, the amateurs could do effective party work beyond the club networks thanks to cross-class partnerships with strong allies in labor. Purposive party activism could effectively supplant declining patronage politics during a period before new technologies and methods drove up costs and personalized campaigns, and before broader declines in Americans' civic engagement produced new challenges to mobilization. Finally, the new political activism emerging from the tumult of the 1960s would be channeled into civil-society groups and paraparty organizations—not into the venerable tradition of formal party work.

Midcentury Pragmatists

For midcentury exemplars of the accommodationist strand, the prerogatives of the formal party and the principle of regularity always remained foremost, while particular issues and policies came and went. Supportive, if often by default, of the party's programmatic agenda at the national level, the pragmatists engaged centrally in the task of sustaining control over organizations that dispensed favors and wielded clout.[92] And if accommodationism no longer defined national politics as it had in its heyday, city bosses from across the industrial states still controlled blocs of delegates at Democratic conventions under the era's mixed system of presidential nomination.

The midcentury pragmatists were rarely the most vocal advocates for their own outlook. Jim Farley's praise of politicians in a 1940 speech could also serve as an argument for parties' proper role in politics: "It is they who must harmonize conflicting points of view; who must reach compromises, who must always look for the greatest common divisor of public opinion, and give the result form and substance."[93] But Mr. Democrat was an exception.

Absent treatises from practitioners themselves, it was left to scholars and journalists to articulate the core elements of the regulars' vision of parties. The rejoinders to the report of the 1950 APSA Committee on Political Parties took aim at its responsible-party presumptions by defending the American tradition of party federalism and non-ideological bargaining.[94] Ethnographic studies of midcentury urban politics treated the jostling of ethnic and religious groups, interests, and party machines as microcosms of American pluralism that served to integrate diverse participants and to foster stability through steady incrementalist bargaining.[95] At times, depictions of the old organizational politics took on a nostalgic hue.[96] Such fond portraits of ward heelers who solved neighborhood problems and offered Thanksgiving turkeys would later serve rhetorical purposes for opponents of the McGovern-Fraser reforms, who warned of issue-oriented parties exacerbating social conflict.

Yet machine politics rested on creaky foundations. As suburbanization and the Great Migration transformed city demographics in the postwar years, racial conflict belied midcentury pragmatists' claims to being the great conciliators of American politics. Local party leaders drank from the federal spigot, opened with the 1949 Housing Act, to pursue urban renewal projects while deploying public housing in a manner intended to sustain residential segregation and, thus, the machines' continued support from core white ethnic constituencies.[97]

But to stay in power, machines faced an ultimately unsustainable balancing act. On the one side, they had to accommodate white supporters' intransigent opposition to residential integration and ongoing demands for jobs. On the other side, they had to incorporate vast new numbers of African Americans through the traditional incentives of patronage and welfare services.[98] Public safety was a flash point. Urban police forces, ever-more militarized and starting to unionize alongside other public-sector employees, nonetheless remained overwhelmingly white. With the repeal of city residency requirements, many officers lived in suburbs that looked nothing like the neighborhoods they patrolled.[99]

The increasingly obstinate posture of Chicago mayor Richard J. Daley toward Black protest movements for fair housing, school integration, and economic development epitomized the failed bargain.[100] In Daley's judgment, the police responses to Black civil disturbances during the push for open housing in 1965 and 1966, and again in the aftermath of Martin Luther King Jr.'s assassination in the spring of 1968, were insufficiently aggressive. It was an omen of his approach to the Democratic convention later that same year, when the targets would be largely white.[101]

Liberal Limits

Programmatic liberals, heretofore united, found themselves at loggerheads as the 1960s wore on and social conflict accelerated. Lyndon Johnson, whose political genius ran through a personalistic understanding of power rather than any coherent understanding of party, attempted to maneuver through and placate all comers.[102] Yet new demands from social movements soon exceeded the limits in postwar Democratic liberalism.[103] For all of liberals' muscular, "vital center" rhetoric, Cold War–era self-policing of ideological lines and the trappings of institutional and state power had softened their social critique. They would now face powerful challengers telling them just that.

In a recurring problem for the policy-reform strand, liberals' technocratic bent undermined linkages between political strategy and policy savvy. In 1963, Frances Perkins, at the age of eighty-three, gave a lecture looking back to the New Deal in light of present developments. The New Deal, for her, was not a plan but "an attitude that found voice in expressions like 'the people are what matter to government.'" John F. Kennedy's New Frontier, she warned presciently, had confined itself to "economic measures" and forgotten "the humanitarian element."[104] The legislative and administrative politics of the Great Society emerged from just such strictures.[105] It was the creation largely of experts with little sense either of practical implementation, as community action agencies fought with big-city mayors, or of the ways that particular programs connected to structural possibilities.[106]

Programmatic liberals had rarely targeted the mixed convention system; their bête noire in national politics was Congress. The presidential nominating system, however, became the arena in which latent tensions burst into open conflict. The credentials challenge waged by the Mississippi Freedom Democratic Party (MFDP) in 1964 augured the new order. A grassroots endeavor spearheaded by Bob Moses of the Student Nonviolent Coordinating Committee (SNCC), the MFDP organized shadow elections at the precinct, county, district, and state levels and produced an alternative slate of delegates, chaired by the NAACP's Aaron Henry, that traveled to the national convention in Atlantic City. Their aim: to be seated in place of the lily-white, Barry Goldwater–supporting Mississippi regulars.[107]

At the convention, working with northern programmatic liberals like their lawyer, Joe Rauh, the challengers emphasized responsible-party principles related to party loyalty and national party authority as much as they did the brutality of white supremacy in Mississippi. Just as the federal government must intervene in local civil rights disputes, activists stressed, the national party must address local infractions against party policy. "Federal support within the state and the seating of the Freedom Democratic Party at the National Convention are inseparable needs," SNCC chair John Lewis wrote to Lyndon Johnson in the run-up to the convention.[108] The MFDP staked its procedural claim on its substantive and political loyalty to a national party that the regulars spurned. Its legal brief devoted more space to the regulars' record of disloyalty than it did to their record of racial discrimination or to the legality of the MFDP itself.[109] The challenge electrified television audiences and seemed to epitomize the potential for programmatic partisan activism, in alliance with mass social movements, to bring about systemic change and political realignment.

The denouement revealed the limits of that potential, the coming crack-up of postwar liberal politics, and the glimmers of a new party project. Johnson fiercely opposed the challenge as a threat to the massive cross-sectional phalanx of support he sought for a landslide victory in November. His information about the MFDP came largely from FBI reports.[110] Beyond making use of old-line accommodationists like credentials committee chair David Lawrence, Johnson dispatched Hubert Humphrey (assisted by his Minnesota protégé Walter Mondale) and Rauh's own patron, Walter Reuther, to pressure Rauh to rein in his clients. The committee's ultimate compromise offer was a limited one—just two at-large seats, with the lily-white regulars undisturbed, and a reform commission chaired by Lawrence. The MFDP interpreted such an offer as a betrayal and balked.[111] "We didn't come all this way for no two seats 'cause all of us is tired," Fannie Lou Hamer, the MFDP delegation's vice chair, told the cameras.[112]

The MFDP struggle soured activists on political horse-trading. "After that it was never the same," Rauh recalled in an oral history. "It was really back to pushing for things from the outside."[113] It turned some civil rights activists and their New Left collaborators away from mainstream politics and toward direct action.[114] And it compelled many of them to take their substantive commitments further than the programmatic liberals had dared. "We're not here to bring politics to our morality," Bob Moses declared, "but to bring morality to our politics." Stokely Carmichael, on his way to a leading role in Black Power, was blunter still: "That was the flat-out dumbest political miscalculation [the] Democratic Party leadership ever made."[115]

The locus of intraparty conflict moved next to the explosive issue of Vietnam. Plenty of liberals recognized trouble in Johnson's war policy early on. (Humphrey sent the president an unheeded memo in early 1965 warning against escalation.)[116] But it was young radicals in the New Left who connected the war to a broader indictment. Drawing on individualistic currents of American radicalism, the Port Huron Statement, the 1962 manifesto of Students for a Democratic Society (SDS), had affirmed man's "unrealized potential for self-cultivation, self-direction, self-understanding, and creativity."[117] That potential was snuffed out by a liberal establishment that had curdled, in the words of SDS president Carl Oglesby, into a "menacing coalition of industrial and military power."[118] Students organizing in Mississippi through Freedom Summer in 1964 under Bob Moses had watched the MFDP saga and emerged radicalized against Democratic powers that be. They would carry their critique into the New Politics, the New Left, and beyond. One Freedom Summer participant recalled that "I went from being a liberal Peace Corps-like Democrat to a raging, maniacal lefty."[119] As Paul Booth, a key figure in left-liberal circles for a half century, later characterized the SDS outlook: "If everything could be restructured starting from the SNCC project in McComb, Mississippi, then we would have participatory democracy."[120]

The drama over Vietnam—both the establishment doubts and the radical entrées—played out in microcosm within the national board of ADA, long the epitome of anticommunist liberalism.[121] Though the national leadership remained publicly quiet about the war across the mid-1960s, the antiwar movement helped to swell the ranks of local and campus ADA chapters. Allard Lowenstein, bridge-builder (and occasional bridge-burner) between the programmatic liberals and the New Left, worked within ADA and in broader left-liberal networks to foster a "Dump Johnson" movement targeting the 1968 election.[122]

By fall 1967, the likes of Joe Rauh, Harvard economist John Kenneth Galbraith, and historian and Kennedy confidante Arthur Schlesinger Jr. (whose keynote address to the ADA's annual dinner that year asked "Is Liberalism Dead?"), had joined the group's antiwar faction and broken openly with the administration over Vietnam.[123] A minority pro-war contingent, loyal to Johnson, included John Roche (feeding reports of ADA deliberations directly to the president) and Gus Tyler of the International Ladies' Garment Workers' Union. The hawks sought to keep the administration, the AFL-CIO leadership, and the central paraparty voice of liberalism bound tightly together. For Tyler, "The whole problem began when we started having membership chapters. Everything was all right when ADA was a coalition of major unions and prominent individuals. Now these new people have come."[124] The doves, skeptical of the kind of backroom politics that had escalated the war and brought the country into crisis, took the opposite view.[125] Eugene McCarthy entered the race in November 1967, and on February 10, 1968, the ADA national board voted 64–47 to offer the group's endorsement.[126] Roche and several unionists soon resigned in protest.

In important ways the Dump Johnson movement, as it transmuted into the McCarthy campaign, showed continuity with the postwar liberals' issue-driven activism. "We are here today as loyal Democrats," California congressman and ADA member Don Edwards insisted at the antiwar Conference of Concerned Democrats in 1967, "seeking to return our party to the course of Franklin D. Roosevelt, Adlai Stevenson, and John F. Kennedy."[127] But the year to come would reveal the impossibility of such a restoration.

Chicago '68

In the presidential nomination contest of 1968, the party of the regulars united behind Hubert Humphrey, long the tribune of programmatic liberals, and the mixed party nomination system exploded into crisis. The Democratic National Convention in Chicago would bear the crudest marks of a party committed to regularity at all costs. Outside the convention hall, the police forces of the last great machine-organized city proved much more than crude in their bloody engagement with radical protesters. And activists and political entrepreneurs, their ranks enlarged and emboldened by the conflict over Vietnam, emerged eager to challenge not only Cold War shibboleths but also the institutions and arrangements sustaining them—the party system included.

On March 12, 1968, McCarthy came within seven points of defeating Johnson in the New Hampshire primary. On March 31, the incumbent bowed out. Humphrey, buoyed by a cheering crowd in Pittsburgh, hoped to announce just after April 4 but learned the news of Martin Luther King Jr.'s assassination when he landed in Washington. By the time he finally declared on April 28, filing deadlines in all but two primaries, South Dakota and New Jersey, had passed. Riding atop national Gallup polls and content to let McCarthy and Robert Kennedy fight it out in the primaries, Humphrey concentrated on the party-run processes that would get him the delegates to win in Chicago.[128]

"There are three groups of importance in a Democratic convention," the veteran Democratic operator James Rowe counseled Humphrey. "They are the bosses, the liberals, and the Southerners. Any candidate will need 2 out of the 3."[129] With many liberals out of reach, the reformer of 1948 relied on the bosses—and the South. Humphrey accepted the endorsement not only of the pioneering liberal governor Terry Sanford in North Carolina but also of John McKeithan in Louisiana, who in 1964 had stayed neutral between Johnson and Goldwater.[130] "We've changed a lot and he's changed a little," McKeithan told *Life*. "He doesn't treat the South like some stepchild."[131]

It was not the primaries where Humphrey didn't collect delegates but the shenanigans in the states where he did that sealed the mixed system's fate. The grinding state-by-state struggle made the activists who powered McCarthy's and Kennedy's insurgent candidacies ever more sympathetic to radical systemic critique. They repeatedly ran into party procedures they deemed impermeable, capricious, or both: arbitrary actions by local officials, including rampant use of proxy voting; unpublished meeting times; and arbitrary enforcement of quorum requirements. In twenty states, written rules detailing the delegate selection process were either nonexistent or inaccessible to those wishing to participate.[132] But the deepest outrage came from the intrinsically closed nature of many states' processes as they operated *free* of abuse.

McCarthy activists in Connecticut encountered such obstacles and, like their New York counterparts that summer, staged a walkout of the state party convention. They soon put together an ad hoc commission, spearheaded by McCarthy campaign organizers Anne Wexler and Geoffrey Cowan and chaired by Iowa's pro-McCarthy governor Harold Hughes, to catalog inequities and inadequacies in nominating processes.[133] Their hastily compiled report, *The Democratic Choice*, called for aggressive enforcement of new rules on racial nondiscrimination as well as an array of state-level procedural changes for the future, starting with a ban on all methods of delegate selection lacking direct popular participation.

Emphasizing the theme of "clarity of purpose," it advocated that delegates be pledged to support specific candidates at the convention. MFDP's dramatic confrontation loomed over their work. "I would never have thought of the convention's power to enforce fairness and democracy," recounted Cowan, "had it not been for the events in Atlantic City in 1964."[134]

The calls for participatory party reform resonated with McCarthy's own themes. In a speech in June, the senator argued that the Democratic Party "has served the country and prospered politically precisely because it has represented democracy in party procedure as well as in public policy."[135] In this light, the mixed convention system stood out for its anachronistic failure to meet a democratic standard. "As the primaries vindicated a politics of conviction," declared an article in *Commonweal*, "the convention stage of the new politics summons the Democratic delegates to set themselves free from the nineteenth-century provisions of the brokerage convention system."[136]

Beyond the procedural wrangling came glimmers of a substantive party vision for that "New Politics." The moniker referred to left-liberals, often with links to the civil rights or antiwar movements, active in the campaigns of McCarthy, Robert F. Kennedy, and later George McGovern. In contrast to the New Left from which it took much inspiration, New Politics forces sought to work within—while institutionally reforming—the Democratic Party. That party would emerge from a new electoral coalition: "middle-class reformers, enlightened labor unions, students, and the poor," as Christopher Lasch put it, "united behind a program of social change that would substantially alter American institutions while stopping short of revolution."[137] The New Politics coalitional vision would remain consequential long after the delegates and protesters left Chicago.

The 1968 Democratic convention's dual masters of ceremonies, working in concert as like-minded political actors, consisted of President Johnson in absentia and Mayor Daley, seemingly everywhere at once. Johnson worked tirelessly through lieutenants to control committee and floor proceedings at the convention. He particularly wanted to prevent any compromise with McGovern or McCarthy forces that would dilute the party's platform plank on Vietnam. Daley, the living icon of bossism, reflected in some respects the adaptive outlook of the midcentury pragmatists, while in others—especially his response to Black political restiveness—he fatefully lacked the give-and-take that brought out the best in pluralism.

The brutality of the Chicago police's confrontations with demonstrators outside the convention hall overshadowed the proceedings at the time and in subsequent historical memory. City officials' provocative refusal all summer to negotiate permitting requests with the main protest organizers had foreshadowed the conflict to come.[138] Daley's assembled forces—12,000 police officers, 6,000 members of the National Guard, and 7,500 regular army troops—outnumbered the protesters two to one.[139] Each day of the convention was marked by violence, but Wednesday, August 28, in Grant Park was the occasion for what a national investigative panel would famously term a "police riot." "The police went, quite literally, berserk," recounted the reporting team behind the 1968 chronicle *An American Melodrama*. Beholding the tear gas and indiscriminate beatings from his hotel suite, McCarthy marveled, "It's incredible, like a Breughel."[140]

Inside the convention hall, the proceedings featured less violence but comparable acrimony and paranoia. The party regulars, those champions and beneficiaries of the deliberative convention system with its putatively autonomous delegate wheeler-dealers, policed delegates' freedom of movement as the security apparatus wielded unprecedented badge and credential requirements.[141] As one McCarthy-backing delegate from New York cried to the sergeants at arms after two days of harassment and one forced ejection from the hall, "I wasn't sentenced and sent here! I was elected."[142] Fannie Lou Hamer, by 1968 a voting delegate from Mississippi, recounted to the party's reform commission, "We was watched, some of us, like we was criminals."[143]

The climactic moment at the International Amphitheatre came from an unlikely source. Abraham Ribicoff, a mild-mannered senator from Connecticut who had served in John Kennedy's cabinet, gave the nomination speech for his colleague George McGovern. Ribicoff departed from his prepared remarks to declare, "With George McGovern as president of the United States, we wouldn't have to have Gestapo tactics in the streets of Chicago." The whole world was watching, and lip-reading, Daley's unprintable reply, as the mayor roared back from just feet below. "How hard it is," Ribicoff responded, "to accept the truth."[144]

Facing a seemingly insurmountable delegate deficit, Rauh and other insurgents, mostly from the McCarthy camp, launched seventeen credentials challenges, covering fifteen states.[145] While southern states largely faced challenges based on claims of racial discrimination, challenges filed against northern delegations invoked procedural principles more sweeping than any wielded at prior party conventions. They not only cited rampant procedural irregularities and rules violations but questioned the legitimacy of many of the rules themselves.

Washington's challengers objected to the state committee's appointment of ex officio delegates. Pennsylvania's questioned the committee's very power to select at-large delegates. Those from Minnesota and Connecticut made the novel argument that adherence to the Supreme Court's "one-man, one-vote" principle (laid out in *Baker v. Carr*) required proportional allocation of delegates from each state to the national convention. And while Michigan's challengers cited inconsistent caucus-level enforcement of the unit rule binding an entire delegation to the preferences of the majority, those in Texas decried the device itself for its racially discriminatory impact. The appointment of ex officio delegates, delegate selection by state committee, and the unit rule were all practices formally allowed under party rules, which left many northern challenges amounting to, in Theodore H. White's words, "a plea demanding a judgment by principles no man had ever defined."[146]

The McCarthy forces pressing such systemic challenges failed to shift the delegate count appreciably, but they helped set in motion future reforms, sanctioned by reports from the Credentials, Rules, and Special Equal Rights Committees (the last originating in the 1964 MFDP challenge). All called for a party commission to study delegate selection practices and offer recommendations for improvements based on participatory principles. Led by Anne Wexler, reform advocates maneuvered to win a narrow late-night floor vote at the 1968 convention requiring that state parties reform their delegate selection procedures in 1972 to ensure timeliness and participation. It provided a formal charge to the McGovern-Fraser commission—and a basis for its mandate claims.[147]

Hubert Humphrey won the nomination shortly after midnight on August 29. At one point during the balloting, he ducked into a room at the Hilton, alone, to cry.[148] "This moment is one of personal pride and gratification," he said at the start of his acceptance speech the following evening. "Yet one cannot help but reflect the deep sadness we feel over the troubles and violence which have erupted, regrettably and tragically, in the streets of this great city."[149] In a memo three weeks earlier, James Rowe had warned Humphrey, "You must steer a difficult course between the Scylla of Lyndon Johnson and the Charybdis of Gene McCarthy." Twenty years after his convention debut, Humphrey watched as the ship headed to the rocks.[150]

The platform that delegates passed with even more acrimony than that marking Humphrey's nomination reflected the culminating tensions of Cold War liberalism: it combined the stay-the-course Vietnam plank that Johnson had strong-armed Humphrey into backing with soaring calls for "total victory in our wars on ignorance, poverty, and the misery of the ghettos."[151] The Vietnam disaster left a dual legacy for the Democratic Party. It prompted the transformation of party procedures, in reflection of a party vision itself shaped profoundly by the antiwar movement. Of even weightier import, the "guns and butter" fiscal commitments of the Johnson era pushed inflation through the economy. And that inflation contributed to the political-economic crises that would help shatter the New Deal order in the following decade.[152]

McGovern-Fraser and the Regulars

Savvy activism from a cohesive network of reformers and a flat-footed regular-party response ensured the transformative impact of the Commission on Party Structure and Delegate Selection, named in common parlance after its successive chairs, South Dakota senator George McGovern and Minnesota congressman Donald Fraser. The commission established uniform standards for state delegate selection that emphasized openness to "meaningful" popular participation. A practical byproduct of states' implementation of these reforms—unintended by the reformers—was the rapid proliferation of primary systems to select delegates.[153] The reform impetus within the national party continued for a decade after the enactment of the McGovern-Fraser guidelines, as three major successor commissions as well as a party charter-writing process all tinkered with the rules while consolidating McGovern-Fraser's core transformations.

The old regulars kept their distance. To the basic question of how to reconcile the party practices they championed with the legitimacy crisis that followed Chicago '68, the anti-reformers had no answer. In a Rules Committee majority report that was narrowly defeated on the floor in favor of Wexler's reform resolution, Humphrey operatives did manage to muster a defense of the party system's traditional decentralization—one not lacking in irony given their candidate's own bona fides as a programmatic liberal: "Ours is the only major Western democracy whose political parties are organized and controlled from the precincts and wards without central party domination or approval. It should remain so. . . . Our concern should not be the nationalization of the party, but the strength and dynamics of its local institutions."[154]

But such celebrations of party federalism sat awkwardly with discriminatory practices in southern states. More broadly, few regulars explicitly challenged the idea of establishing some basic national standards for state nominating procedures, or of emphasizing democratic participation in such standards. Humphrey endorsed the commission's creation as a means of reconciling with the insurgent candidates' supporters, admitting after the November election that "the winds of change are strong."[155] Indeed, the notably weak resistance offered by state party officials to the McGovern-Fraser guidelines once they were promulgated in the fall of 1969 owed to a combination of strategic miscalculation and organizational decline—and signaled the fading of mid-century pragmatism itself.[156]

More than Democratic regulars themselves, it was the AFL-CIO's majority wing under the crusty plumber George Meany that propounded the anti-reform case in the years after the Chicago convention.[157] They boycotted participation in a commission they thought would only "give attention to those 'New Politics' nuts who helped lose the election for us," as one AFL-CIO source told a reporter.[158] Resistance to McGovern-Fraser would segue into resistance to McGovern's 1972 presidential campaign and, in the aftermath of his landslide loss, renewed party-factional efforts to defeat the New Politics. The AFL-CIO provided an organizational nucleus for the Coalition for a Democratic Majority (CDM), which launched after the 1972 election with full-page newspaper ads under the headline "Come Home, Democrats."[159]

The reform opponents' case blended substance with procedure. These proud Cold Warriors recoiled at the New Left, the counterculture, and Black Power. Patriotic defenders of a male labor aristocracy now solidly in the middle class, they bristled at critiques, wielding the cudgels of race and gender, that seemed to them to undercut the labor movement, the Democratic Party, and even the United States of America.[160] Labor benefited both from the privileged position that Meany's AFL-CIO held in the existing constellation of party authority and from long-standing ties between unions and state and local parties.[161] And so, procedurally, the anti-reformers preached the virtues of accommodationism. Newly banned institutions like ex-officio delegates, one CDM report argued, had given "democratically chosen leaders" a proper role as convention brokers with the skill to manage complex party alliances—"a necessity for coalition politics."[162] Another report stressed the dangers of reforms that "run against the grain of American political tradition and the unique coalitional character of the Democratic Party. . . . We should continue to build along the lines of a federative, pluralistic party."[163]

Over time, the substantive and procedural critiques leveled against the New Politics reformers would diverge. The neoconservative reaction to liberal excess still put blame on the radical-chic sixties, though it said less about the end of the unit rule or the requirement for public delegate selection plans. Meanwhile, the Meanyite case presaged the first wave of highly critical scholarly analyses of the McGovern-Fraser reforms in the 1970s and early 1980s. It would reappear in the arguments of self-proclaimed "new realists" in the twenty-first century who wave the anti-reform banner in resistance to a polarized politics of purity.[164] But these latter-day descendants of midcentury pragmatism look back fondly at their forebears' transactionalism without passing judgment on student radicalism or Vietnam.[165]

The McGovern-Fraser Vision of Party

The work of reformers in the McGovern-Fraser era redounded through the decades, influencing not only the rules and practices of presidential nominations but the principles by which players in the political game assess nominations. More generally, this movement-inflected party project reinforced the centrality of national policy to politics even as it ultimately undermined the parties' claims to legitimacy as the *organizers* of politics.[166]

The youthful New Politics activists at the heart of the reform effort continued to sound themes familiar to midcentury programmatic liberals.[167] Most obvious was the critique of closed bossism that now framed the new reformers' analysis of the arbitrary and impermeable procedures rampant in the mixed presidential nominating system. In keeping with a central tenet of the policy-reform strand, they also pushed to nationalize party power, forcing state parties to adhere to detailed standards for delegate selection. As McGovern-Fraser commission member (and Harvard political scientist) Samuel Beer put it, activists such as those behind the 1968 McCarthy candidacy "see themselves not so much as a faction within a state party as part of a nation-wide combination, and therefore want a system which will register their strength in the nation as a whole. . . . Our politics, in short, is becoming more 'nationalized' and the nomination system should reflect this fact."[168]

McGovern-Fraser reformers also sustained their postwar predecessors' belief in the centrality of programmatic motivations for party activism. The Hughes Commission report from 1968 drew attention to the emergence of "issue-oriented individuals who rank relatively abstract ideological questions high among the criteria by which they approve or disapprove of candidates," and who saw themselves as "outside the tightly-knit groups represented by Democratic party operatives."[169] As George McGovern put it a year later, "The real heart and soul of a political party is its policy, its philosophy, its stand on the great issues of the day. Really the only purpose of party reform is to provide a vehicle through which those policies can be determined by the people rather than by the bosses."[170]

The sweep of that final "the people," however, reflected two key distinctions between midcentury programmatic liberalism and the McGovern-Fraser project. First, the reformers' call for parties that privileged the voice of grassroots activists came just as purposive politics itself beat a rapid and enduring retreat from formal party activism. Studies both of parties and of citizens' political involvement tell the same story of decline.[171] But, in a particular loss for the parties stemming in part from sixties-era disruptions, those citizens who *did* choose to engage now tended to eschew the moribund and embattled formal party organizations in favor of candidate campaigns or direct issue advocacy.[172] New public interest groups like the ones pioneered by Ralph Nader took the fight to courts and agencies and sidestepped political coalition-building.[173] "There are numerous causes going with good political activists working in these causes," Iowa's Harold Hughes remarked when surveying liberal forces in the early 1970s. "But there is no central thrust, no overview to unite them and stir them to concerted action. The amalgam is lacking."[174] Parties had long provided that amalgam. But just as the national issue agenda broadened, their own role receded.[175]

The decline of club politics—the motor that had powered postwar programmatic liberalism—embodied activists' shift away from party organization.[176] After the 1968 election, the New Democratic Coalition (NDC) formed as a national federation encompassing both older clubs and new amateur formations drawing from antiwar and New Politics activism. The NDC soon fell on hard times, however. It cycled through two executive directors in as many years, ran up $20,000 in debt by 1970, and canceled a planned convention in 1971 due to a lack of attendees.[177] A new director's plan, as described by Rhode Island chapter activist R. Bruce Allison, neatly captured liberals' ongoing shift from party to paraparty activism: "His strategy was to reduce the role of the national staff and return to the strength of the grassroots, encouraging and cooperating with local and national interest groups such as the National Welfare Rights Association, the Vietnam Moratorium, the Youth Franchise Coalition, the National Committee for an Effective Congress, SANE, the Mexican American Political Association, the American Indian Movement, and others."[178] In short, ideological activists in the postreform system would, indeed, wield new influence over parties—but from groups organizing outside the parties rather than mobilized members within them.

The nature of that organizing speaks to the second distinction between midcentury liberals and the McGovern-Fraser reformers. The latter emerged from movement cultures that emphasized participation and looked askance at formal organization and the prerogatives of rank.[179] Gone was the relative comfort with organization that both responsible party doctrine and the trade union influence had imparted to the programmatic liberals. Instead, the New Left's participatory and antihierarchical values suffused New Politics reformers' outlook and rhetoric. "Leaders mean organization, organization means hierarchy, and hierarchy is undemocratic," wrote journalists Paul Jacobs and Saul Landau in evoking the ethos of SDS and, before it, SNCC.[180] From that perspective, party renewal required institutional openness to continual, self-generating mobilizations.

Though the reformers were soon saddled with a reputation as antiparty neo-Progressives, in fact the framers of McGovern-Fraser envisioned highly active and institutionalized political parties.[181] They supported, for example, a party charter proposal developed by Donald Fraser in 1972 that called for dues-paying party membership and biennial issue conventions.[182] The latter would become a reality in the form of activist-dominated midterm party conferences in 1974, 1978, and 1982. The conferences served, in the approving words of James MacGregor Burns, as "a transmission belt between movement politics and party politics."[183] Yet open participation hardly implied informality. Clear standards and detailed procedures for inclusion, in line with the broader rights revolution, would keep parties in line.[184] In their concern with what McCarthy had called "democracy in party procedure," the reformers hewed fast to the venerable notion that, suitably updated, all the inherited machinery from Van Buren's day—committees and conventions, delegates and platforms—could still define the essence of the political party.

The parties prophesied by McGovern-Fraser activists would serve as vessels for movement politics, seeded at the grassroots where real democracy was to be found, and would sustain themselves through proper procedures and permanent mobilization. The drafters of the commission's final report, *Mandate for Reform*, brought out an old chestnut to justify their work: "The cure for the ills of democracy is more democracy."[185] Critique and prescription alike were grounded on the principle of democracy and little else. When movement politics simmered down, the pursuit of process itself—the eternal refinement of rules—came to constitute for the reformers an intrinsic value as well as a means to party renewal.[186] Yet as the 1970s wore on, proceduralism offered ever less of an answer to the Democrats' grave challenges.

Struggles for Renewal

The McGovern-Fraser project suffered from an early and durable negative turn in its reputation. An initial cycle of scholarly assessments cast the reforms as misguided interventions that weakened the parties (especially Democrats), fragmented political authority, and hastened the rise of candidate-centered politics. This negative view sells the reformers short as agents of party reconfiguration. Activists did indeed build coalitions along the lines envisioned by the New Politics in a newly permeable party. Nevertheless, the reformers would prove inadequate to the larger task of generating a party project that might counter powerful headwinds from the Right.

The coalitional implications could initially be seen in McGovern-Fraser's first two guidelines to state parties, the instant lightning rods A-1 and A-2, which mandated that convention delegations represent racial minorities, women, and young people in proportion to their presence in the population. The results were striking: Blacks' share of delegates rose from 5.5 percent in 1968 to 15.5 percent in 1972, women's rose from 13 to 40 percent; youth's, from 4 to 21 percent.[187] In the post–McGovern-Fraser world, where convention delegates no longer chose the nominee, those results were also largely symbolic.[188] But women and African Americans soon joined the ranks of Democratic influencers in substantial numbers— and the consequences of *that* far transcended the symbolic.

Taking advantage of the new rules, feminists won important victories inside the Democratic Party in the 1970s just as the rise of antifeminist conservatives hastened the parties' great ideological sorting-out on gender issues.[189] The National Women's Political Caucus (NWPC), a new feminist group led by Representatives Bella Abzug of New York and Patsy Mink of Hawaii, played a central role in strengthening the A-1 and A-2 guidelines.[190] Women's status at all levels of party organization grew in the 1970s, as did the number of women holding office, particularly at the state and local levels.[191] Feminists used the 1978 midterm party conference in Memphis to secure a pledge from the DNC to guarantee full gender balance at the 1980 convention.[192] And at the 1980 convention, feminists secured floor passage of a minority plank calling on the party to "withhold financial support and technical campaign assistance from candidates who do not support the ERA."[193]

Likewise, African Americans' breakthroughs in the wake of the Second Reconstruction reshaped the Democratic Party. Black protest, the historical catalyst of party reform, persisted in diffuse ways in the post-reform party.[194] In 1972, an ailing Fannie Lou Hamer, once again a delegate from Mississippi, rallied for Shirley Chisholm's presidential nomination.[195] That same year, Jesse Jackson co-chaired the rival delegation that, after winning a vote at the Credentials Committee, successful challenged Richard J. Daley and his Cook County regulars and took their places at the national convention.[196] Black office-holding rose sharply after 1965, with growth especially pronounced in but hardly limited to the South.[197] It presaged a far more central, if often contested, role for Black politicians and voters in the decades to follow.

Yet the struggles among new and old party players could obscure the larger context. The crisis facing Democrats in the 1970s was structural—and ultimately more wrenching than the dramas of the prior decade.[198] The postwar order collapsed amid stagflation, never to recover, and the results devastated the Democrats' time-tested political formula.[199] In its presentation to the 1976 Democratic platform committee, the UAW, the organizational linchpin of so much in postwar labor-liberalism, had reiterated calls for national planning and full employment. It also offered a distillation of what a responsible party might have looked like had Democrats found a way to cohere in pursuit of a shared project. The UAW backed a "supreme and preemptive" national platform binding state and local parties as well as candidates, alongside a new requirement for a "Democratic president to report annually, not only to the nation on the state of the union, but to the Democratic Party on the state of the party."[200]

Two years later, UAW president Doug Fraser, a protégé of Walter Reuther now confronting a more hostile age, garnered much more attention when he penned an angrily prescient letter to American business warning of "a one-sided class war."[201] Pushing back simultaneously at the fissiparous tendencies weakening American parties, at his own ambivalent allies in the American labor movement, and, most of all, at the resurgent Right, Fraser dreamed of "the transformation of the Democratic Party into a genuinely progressive people's party."[202] Yet the crisis that Fraser correctly diagnosed would devastate liberals' hopes for social transformation. Trouble hit Fraser's own industry in 1979, as a nearly bankrupt Chrysler survived only with federal loan guarantees and painful wage cuts. The Keynesian growth model seemed to have reached the end of the line. Deindustrialization across the Rust Belt ripped at communities foundational to the New Deal order. Ted Kennedy waved the old banner in his 1980 challenge to Jimmy Carter, but the lackluster campaign never came together. The Progressive Alliance, a new labor-liberal umbrella organization that Fraser chaired, made a final attempt to update the old CIO-ADA formula and build a party response for the post-Fordian age. It failed.[203]

It was the Right that successfully seized the moment, and Democrats would spend decades trying to pick up the pieces. Party vitality at mid-century had emerged from social conditions all in reverse after Ronald Reagan's election: formal parties at the state and local levels atrophied, unions' membership and influence declined, social movements on the left receded. The exodus from formal party activism both presaged and embodied a broader shift from federated mass membership groups to staff-driven letterhead operations, as liberalism oriented itself around professional advocacy.[204] And the Democratic Party became something like the inverse of Hubert Humphrey's description to the New York delegation back in August 1968: more than a bit *smaller* than the men and women who participated in it.

Martin Van Buren, the nattily tailored "Little Magician" of New York, looms large in any account of American parties. Van Buren and his Empire State allies in the Albany Regency created the prototype for the mass party organization that subordinated individual ambition to collective party purpose. As loyal lieutenant and then heir to Andrew Jackson, he took the model national. Lithograph by Charles Fenderich, 1839. Library of Congress.

The Whig campaign of 1840 forged new tactics in mass electioneering with vast popular spectacles. Whigs celebrated the party's nominee, William Henry Harrison, as the "Hero of Tippecanoe"; he had defeated Native forces near the Tippecanoe River in Indiana Territory in 1811. The Whigs' paraphernalia depicted Harrison—the scion of a wealthy planter family—at home in a humble log cabin drinking hard cider. Woodcut, 1840. Library of Congress.

In the 1860 election, companies of Wide Awakes, young men in military garb, marched with torches in support of the Republican Party and its nominee, Abraham Lincoln. This image shows a large gathering in New York in early October 1860. *Harper's Weekly*, October 13, 1860, via HathiTrust. Digitized from University of Michigan.

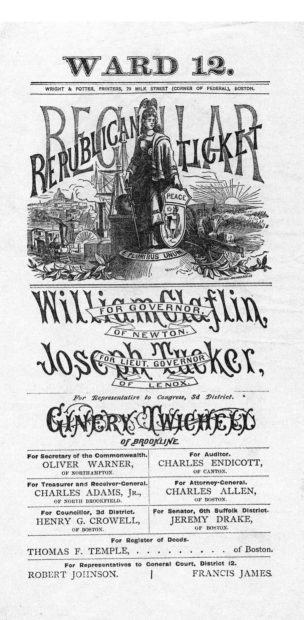

WARD 12.

WRIGHT & POTTER, PRINTERS, 79 MILK STREET (CORNER OF FEDERAL), BOSTON.

REGULAR REPUBLICAN TICKET

PEACE

E PLURIBUS UNUM

FOR GOVERNOR,
William Claflin,
OF NEWTON.

FOR LIEUT. GOVERNOR
Joseph Tucker,
OF LENOX.

For Representative to Congress, 3d District.

GINERY TWICHELL
OF BROOKLINE.

For Secretary of the Commonwealth.	For Auditor.
OLIVER WARNER,	CHARLES ENDICOTT,
OF NORTHAMPTON.	OF CANTON.
For Treasurer and Receiver-General.	**For Attorney-General.**
CHARLES ADAMS, JR.,	CHARLES ALLEN,
OF NORTH BROOKFIELD.	OF BOSTON.
For Councillor, 3d District.	**For Senator, 6th Suffolk District.**
HENRY G. CROWELL,	JEREMY DRAKE,
OF BOSTON.	OF BOSTON.

For Register of Deeds.

THOMAS F. TEMPLE, ... of Boston.

For Representatives to General Court, District 12.

ROBERT JOHNSON. | FRANCIS JAMES.

Before adoption of the secret ballot, parties printed tickets that listed all of the party's nominees for office. Such party ballots also deployed a rich variety of symbolic appeals. Here the Reconstruction-era Republicans show themselves as champions of peace and of progress in industry and agriculture. When the secret ballot replaced the party ticket at the end of the nineteenth century, it eased the way for widespread split-ticket voting. Ward 12 Republican ticket, Boston, 1870. Boston Athenæum.

During Reconstruction, Black legislators served in Congress for the first time, as Republicans representing readmitted southern states. On the far left of this fine lithograph sits Hiram Revels of Mississippi, the first Black member of the U.S. Senate. Currier & Ives lithograph, 1872. Library of Congress.

George Washington Plunkitt, a New York state senator and Tammany district leader, gave a series of informal talks to the journalist William Riordon that constitute the richest record of how political machines in their heyday did their work and thought about their roles. "When a man works in politics," Plunkitt declared, "he should get something out of it." Here he sits at his longtime haunt, a shoeshine stand at the New York County Courthouse. Photo from McClure, Philips, 1905. New York Public Library.

Widespread laborite discontent with the major parties during the Gilded Age never coalesced into a coherent vision offering an alternative to the rise of corporate capital. In 1886, the single tax advocate Henry George came within 6,000 votes of winning election as mayor of New York running on a United Labor Party ticket that sought to unite "representatives of all classes of men who earn their living by exertion of hand or head." *Frank Leslie's Illustrated Newspaper*, October 30, 1886. Internet Archive.

In the Progressive Era, educated women—many of them not yet eligible to vote—applied knowledge from the emerging social sciences to public problems. Frances Kellor led the Progressive National Service, a short-lived effort from Theodore Roosevelt's Progressive Party to apply rigorous policy thinking to party politics. It was a harbinger of a technocratic approach that would grow more prominent later in the century. Photo from Brown Brothers, 1916. Library of Congress.

With his call for the Democratic Party "to walk forthrightly into the bright sunshine of human rights," Minneapolis mayor Hubert Humphrey successfully urged the 1948 convention to adopt a strong minority plank on civil rights. Liberal reformers like Humphrey, eager to remake the party, joined together with northern machines worried about the growing Black vote. Here the exultant Humphrey returns home. Wally Kammann, *Star Tribune*, 1948, via Getty Images.

An integrated delegation from the Mississippi Freedom Democratic Party traveled to the 1964 Democratic convention hoping to be seated in place of the lily-white, Goldwater-supporting official delegation. At Lyndon Johnson's behest, the party turned them down, and the activists in turn rejected an offer of just two at-large seats. Said the delegation's charismatic vice chair Fannie Lou Hamer, "We didn't come all this way for no two seats 'cause all of us is tired." Mississippi, 1960s. Ken Thompson Photo Collection, General Board of Global Ministries of the United Methodist Church.

The disastrous 1968 Democratic convention featured acrimony inside the hall and violence outside it as Chicago mayor Richard J. Daley, the living embodiment of bossism, attempted unsuccessfully to control the proceedings and clamp down on dissent. But if the bosses would never again control presidential nominations, reformers' hopes of a revived, movement-driven party, too, would go unfulfilled. Bettmann, 1968, via Getty Images.

"You Absolutely Sure You're An Elephant?"

In the wake of Barry Goldwater's 1964 defeat, right-wing backers of the Arizona senator formed a series of outside groups, including the American Conservative Union, to advocate for their views outside the formal Republican Party. In the following decades, paraparty groups on the right would do much to hollow out American parties. "You absolutely sure you're an elephant?" Herblock cartoon, July 1, 1965. Herb Block Foundation.

Ray Bliss, the practical-minded, civically rooted chair of the Ohio Republican Party and of the Republican National Committee as it recovered from the Goldwater debacle, emphasized nuts-and-bolts party-building to the exclusion of ideological infighting or explicit comment on policy issues. The goal, he said, was a "government that is alert to the changing times, yet guided by common sense." Bettmann, 1968, via Getty Images.

Richard Viguerie, an important figure on the right from Young Americans for Freedom in the early 1960s through the New Right of the 1970s to the Tea Party of the early 2010s, pioneered the use of direct mail to fundraise on behalf of single-issue groups. Storing his files on reams of magnetic tapes, he could coordinate among disparate entities that collectively sought to play the roles long held by political parties. Wally McNamee/Corbis, 1970s, via Getty Images.

Barry Goldwater and Newt Gingrich would each define conservatism for his generation. Here Goldwater, senator from Arizona and 1964 GOP nominee, campaigns for Gingrich during the latter's unsuccessful 1976 run for Congress. Gingrich would prevail two years later, embolden House Republicans in the minority, and lead them to recapture the chamber in 1994 before serving two tumultuous terms as Speaker. File photo, 1976, Associated Press.

Partners in a high-flying 1980s political consultancy, Paul Manafort (left), Roger Stone (center), and Lee Atwater (right) all got their start in College Republicans in the early 1970s. Atwater, a master of barely coded racial appeals who led the Republican National Committee under George H. W. Bush, died in 1991. Manafort and Stone, the latter a legendary Dirty Trickster, would go on to play major roles in winning Donald Trump the presidency. Harry Naltchayan/ *Washington Post*, 1989, via Getty Images.

Paul Kirk (left) and Tony Coelho (right), who led the Democratic National Committee and the Democratic Congressional Campaign Committee respectively during the 1980s, pushed for Democrats to give up their scruples and fundraise aggressively from business. A Kirk-era "stockholders' report" to members of the DNC's Business Council extolled its members as the "backbone of the Democratic Party's finances." *CQ Roll Call*, 1989, via Getty Images.

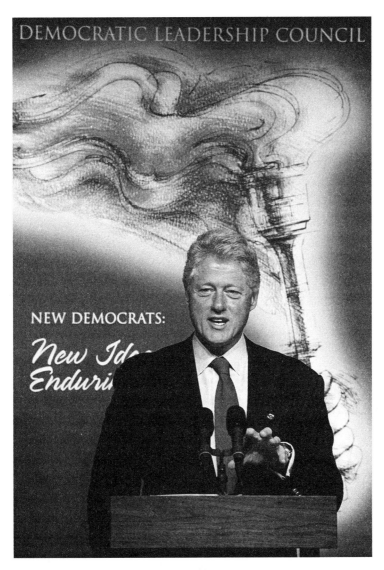

Just before he ran for president in 1992, Bill Clinton chaired the Democratic Leadership Council, a group designed to move Democrats away from liberal political shibboleths dating back to the 1930s and the 1960s and reclaim the center ground. In the 2000s, intraparty battles would begin to move in a different direction, and the DLC shuttered its doors in 2011. Mario Tama/AFP, 2000, via Getty Images.

Heralded first by Howard Dean's presidential run in 2004, the Internet came into its own in Barack Obama's 2008 campaign, which deployed an innovative mix of online savvy and face-to-face engagement. Yet tech's biggest impact ultimately came not via grassroots political renewal, as its loudest enthusiasts had predicted, but through lavishly funded and centrally controlled "big data" operations that transformed campaigning. John Ewing/*Portland Press Herald*, 2008, via Getty Images.

The presidential candidacies of Jesse Jackson, with his pioneering runs in 1984 and 1988, and Bernie Sanders, with the intraparty tides running more in his direction in 2016 and 2020, represent the foremost examples of radical politics in the post-New Deal Democratic Party. Though their styles and coalitions differed, they both aimed less to win than to push party and nation to pay heed to populations long excluded and priorities long forgotten. Anntaninna Biondo/*Grand Rapids Press*, 2020, via Associated Press.

Members of UNITE-HERE Local 226, the Culinary Workers union in Las Vegas, await a visit to their union hall from U.S senator Harry Reid. Together, Local 226 and Reid's Nevada political operation, dubbed the Reid Machine, have produced something uniquely potent in contemporary Democratic politics: a robust political operation with tangible connections to a working-class electoral base. Ethan Miller, 2013, via Getty Images.

As "political entertainment" loomed ever larger in conservative politics from the 1980s onward, Rush Limbaugh proved a master practitioner. On his daily nationwide talk radio show, Limbaugh for decades lambasted liberals' errors and hypocrisies, and leavened the outrage with a bawdy male humor that went for the jugular. When Republican House freshmen assembled in December 1994, they named Limbaugh an honorary member of their class. Ron Galella, 1993, via Getty Images.

Since its launch in 1996, Fox News Channel has served as a central player in the Republican Party firmament—and one with no peer on the Democratic side. Its key players were Roger Ailes (left), a former Nixon aide who served as the channel's chief; and Rupert Murdoch (right), the Australian-born media mogul who led its parent company and influenced conservative politics across the Anglosphere for decades. Allan Tannenbaum, 1996, via Getty Images.

The insurrection of January 6, 2021, laid bare the consequences of a hollow Republican Party determined to hold onto power at all costs. From Trump loyalists in the White House to members of Congress eager to fan the fires of discontent to the rioters who roamed through the ill-defended building for hours, myriad currents on the right joined together with explosive consequences. Spencer Platt, 2021, via Getty Images.

6

The Long New Right and
the World It Made

THE TALK at the second annual Conservative Political Action Conference was all about the Republican Party and whether to junk it. Five hundred conferencegoers had descended on the Mayflower Hotel in Washington, DC, on February 14, 1975. Maryland congressman Robert Bauman, a cofounder of the American Conservative Union, expressed a mercenary outlook on parties that typified activists in his orbit. "Sometimes serving the popular will, sometimes thwarting it," Bauman declared, parties "are no more than instruments, temporary and disposable, by which like-minded citizens can express their views."[1] As the idea of ditching the beleaguered post-Watergate GOP to form a conservative third party took center stage, the conference passed a resolution declaring that "the question of our allegiance to [the two major] political parties is a matter of increasing doubt to conservatives."[2] Even the speakers who cautioned against a splinter effort couched their argument in the ruthless language of corporate warfare. Conservatives were like Arab oil sheiks looking to break into the auto industry, declared Mississippi Republican chair Clark Reed. Why bother trying to start from scratch when you could just "take over General Motors?"[3] The Right's third-party venture went nowhere fast, but its cold-eyed approach to the party form would ultimately transform American politics.

Modern conservatism hollowed out the American party system. That it also polarized the party system captures a central paradox of our times.

This chapter traces how what we term the Long New Right remade the Republican Party in its image and upended American politics in turn.[4] Its approach to politics—centered on conflict, rooted in the relentless pursuit of electoral majority, and marked by an instrumental use of institutions—operated at the convergence of the populist and pro-capital strands of party politics. While the issues in play and even the group identities mobilized changed repeatedly over the years, the lodestar of New Right politics remained the take-no-prisoners exploitation of grievance and status resentments—"knowing who hates who," as Kevin Phillips put it in 1968.[5] In this view, political parties served not as means to cross-cut or tamp down underlying conflict but as instruments of power to extend the domination, or to prevent the domination, of some groups over others.[6] The commitment to conflict and the ruthless instrumentalism toward institutions combined to produce a politics devoid of either internal checks on extremism or—in contrast to traditional understandings of conservatism—a sense of limits, whether tactical or substantive.[7]

The Long New Right took the us-against-them politics of the populist strand so often expressed episodically, gave it a coherent form, and brought it together with a rejuvenated pro-capital strand. The populist notes sound clear: this was an approach with clearly defined friends and enemies. But Long New Right politics also embraced core right-wing tenets to fight labor unions and government bureaucrats and, starting in the pivotal 1970s, to slash taxes. And as a more accommodationist pro-business politics fell away, an authentic convergence that began in the postwar milieus of the Right became a defining theme in national politics. In the Long New Right's enduring project, we see a political economy of resentment that fused class, racial, and often gender politics.

A vision less of party than of partisan majority motivated the Long New Right.[8] The very openness of American parties that to critics made them hopelessly weak gave activist cadres the opportunity to remake them, down to the precinct level.[9] "Conservatism is the wine," William Rusher, longtime publisher of *National Review*, liked to say. "The GOP is the bottle."[10] For Morton Blackwell—a longtime New Right leader and an acknowledged expert on the Republican Party's rules—the great actors in American political history were not party formations but rather electoral coalitions: "To the extent it can be said that our country is governed, decisions are made by an enduring coalition of segments of the population which form a governing majority. The formation, growth, and decline of these coalitions is the real drama of governing America. A party is at most the vehicle through which this drama unfolds."[11] The Republican Party would serve as a continual foil and punching bag ("a social club where the rich people go to pick their noses") even as it provided the New Right its vessel to power.[12]

This approach departed sharply from the respect for party form that had sustained conservative Republicanism down through William Howard and even Robert Taft.[13] Now, as a 1979 memo by Paul Weyrich laid out, both the New Deal coalition that Roosevelt birthed and the parties that served as organizers of conflict seemed to have reached the end of the line: "With the old coalition dead and political parties dying, there is a vacuum." The challenge to fill the vacuum, then, was to "identify the elements of, and form, a new coalition" and to "achieve political power through the coalition."[14]

The 1970s constituted the critical juncture when the movement's actors broke through political fetters and seized the Republican Party's commanding heights. As a continuity of both personnel and political approach, the Long New Right stretched back to the early postwar era. In those decades, however, its reach remained limited. The New Deal order, undergirded by Democrats' dominance at the ballot box and labor's power in the workplace, effectively cabined the Right while buttressing a form of moderate Republicanism.[15] But the very breakdown of those arrangements in the 1970s, instigated in part by the efforts of the Long New Right itself, enabled its ranks to assume a leading role within the GOP—and to defang any forces that might have resisted their further dominance.

This chapter takes a leaf from the Long New Right's own self-chroniclers and tells a generational story.[16] The First Generation's battles over McCarthyism in the early 1950s and Eisenhower's moderation in the later 1950s served as a crucible for its pugilistic style, imbricated by a potent reactionary racial politics. Indeed, the mobilization of racial grievance predated by decades the white "backlash" to civil rights

politics to which analysts have attributed the breakup of the New Deal
order and the subsequent ascendancy of conservatism.[17] The leaders of
the Second Generation, many of them foot soldiers in the Barry Goldwater campaign of 1964, weaponized the politics of resentment in the
1970s. Their substantive themes, again nascent in the postwar Right,
included an emphasis on social conflict and an affective distance from
Big Business, deemed too cozy with the postwar settlement. Paul Weyrich, the quintessential figure of the Second Generation, developed and
applied the strategy to push rightward by mobilizing voter blocs that
could supplant the New Deal coalition. And finally, in the 1980s and
1990s, the young, media-savvy conservatives of the Third Generation
pursued ever-more performative cultural combat through a brand of
smashmouth politics that fused style and substance.

We join a growing body of work that has challenged the allegedly
sharp historical distinction, long touted by the conservative movement's own in-house chroniclers, separating respectable actors from
fringe extremists in their midst.[18] Because we see a rejection of limits as
intrinsic to the Long New Right, we endorse the push to bring the fever
swamps back in, as it were, to the study of the American Right.[19] Less
the resemblance than the *interpenetration* of extremist and mainstream
elements has defined conservative politics across this era. We apply that
analysis directly to party politics. The supplanting of the New Deal
order was not just a matter of mechanically assembling demographic
blocs through electoral addition, proposing new ideas, or contesting
elections. It entailed pursuing an overarching project to bridge power
centers across state and society, deposing old bases of political authority
and breaking through old limits.[20]

This account also cuts somewhat against the grain of an institutional
focus common both to political scientists emphasizing the importance
of particular organizational structures and liberal activists looking to
emulate their opponents' institution-building. Despite being profligate
group-starters, activists of the Long New Right were not, to use Hugh
Heclo's term, "institutionally minded."[21] Most of the organizations they
built—Young Americans for Freedom, the Republican Study Committee, the Committee for the Survival of a Free Congress, *Human Events*,

Conservative Digest, and, looming behind them, the John Birch Society—are either defunct or obsolescent. (The Heritage Foundation and, in the states, the American Legislative Exchange Council are notable exceptions.) Instead, the Long New Right sustained its influence by seizing new opportunities wherever they arose, in settings ranging from the media to the organizational GOP to the courts to Congress to the presidency.[22] Thus in presidential nomination, to reemphasize a central point, we see the Long New Right's breakthrough as neither dependent on nor subsidiary to the party reforms of the 1970s. Though the mixed nomination system proximately met its fate in the wake of the Democrats' McGovern-Fraser reforms, it would not have long survived a rising Long New Right that deemed parties mere expediencies and gained influence through crises far more wrenching than new methods for nomination.

Our narrative of the Long New Right differs somewhat from other chapters in this book. This chapter's protagonists largely stood outside the centers of party power, some far out on the fringe—but they did not stay there. We focus on them, rather than exploring the GOP's leading figures at each election cycle, precisely to convey the central historical dynamic at work: of party capture from without and subsequent hollowing from within. Meanwhile, a potent stylistic streak of gonzo feverishness was central to the Long New Right. To capture that tendency in full, we increase the wattage, so to speak, of our coverage here relative to the usual academic treatment of party politics.[23] The through-line in this chapter is found neither in a specific doctrine nor in an enduring set of organizations but rather in a particular political approach, one that undermined the very means—both institutional and intellectual—to enforce boundaries and set a collective direction.

The Crucible of McCarthyism and the First Generation

If approach more than doctrine defines the Long New Right, the Second Red Scare and the debate over Senator Joe McCarthy stand as crucial, formative conflicts. Right-wing populism and revolts against an overweening state have, of course, a longer history still.[24] But it was in the early Cold War years that factional Republican incentives, a nascent and racialized conservative movement ideology, and a grassroots revanchism nurtured in the postwar boom came together in support of over-the-top grievance politics.

Hallmarks of the Wisconsin demagogue—his fervid demonizing, headlong transgression of institutional and behavioral norms, and suffusion of political debate with potent social grievance—became core elements of a broader, more durable political tendency. Postwar intellectuals like Daniel Bell and Richard Hofstadter later came in for criticism for pathologizing the anticommunist right as a manifestation of status anxiety, and their emphases on insecurities and projection may have missed the mark.[25] But the notes of group resentment were hardly subtle. In McCarthy's infamous, career-making Wheeling, West Virginia, speech in 1950, he revealed the people "who have been selling us out" to be "those who have had all the benefits the wealthiest nation on earth has had to offer—the finest homes, the finest college educations, and the finest jobs in the government that we can give. This is glaringly true in the State Department. There the bright young men who are born with silver spoons in their mouth are the ones who have been worst."[26] Working with his tenacious chief counsel Roy Cohn, the senator pursued targets in the ensuing years meant to stir similar cultural resentments. These ranged from academic China scholars like Owen Lattimore to the shadowy ranks of "communists and queers" in government who, McCarthy alleged, "have the people in a hypnotic trance."[27]

William F. Buckley Jr., still in his twenties, coauthored with L. Brent Bozell a book about McCarthy that epitomized a type of argumentation, soon to be common in the Long New Right, that might be called "anti-anti."[28] Though both authors wrote speeches for the senator, their book, *McCarthy and His Enemies*, offered a more full-throated case against McCarthy's critics than for McCarthy. Distinguishing the flawed man from McCarthy*ism*—the worthy "program of action against those in our land who help the enemy"—they condemned critics for conflating the two while calling on conservatives to "close ranks" lest quibbles over means undermine the cause.[29] The anti-anti-McCarthy argument set Buckley on the path of combative engagement with GOP moderates that he would soon display in *National Review* and the manifesto *Up from Liberalism*. The general posture would endure in Long New Right politics as a reliable tactic to evade or reject policing boundaries against extremism.

The porousness of those boundaries on the right marked the vibrant organizational terrain of the later 1950s and 1960s.[30] The John Birch Society (JBS) was founded in 1958 and, until his death in 1985, dominated by Robert Welch, a former candy manufacturer and National Association of Manufacturers board member. The JBS managed to grow a mass membership in cell-like federated chapters, approaching 100,000 in the mid-1960s by reasonable estimates.[31] It modeled its rigidly hierarchical and secretive internal structure on communist organizing.[32] The eccentric, even megalomaniac Welch ensured that his organization bore the brunt of popular alarm around the conspiracist Right.[33] Dwight Eisenhower was a "dedicated, conscious agent" of international communism, according to Welch, who eventually traced the conspiracy back to the eighteenth-century Bavarian Illuminati.[34]

Yet the paranoid style ranged beyond Robert Welch.[35] Relatively quiescent during the Red Scare's late 1940s and early 1950s heyday, southern anticommunism roared to life in the wake of *Brown v. Board of Education*. Georgia attorney general Eugene Cook worked with House Un-American Activities Committee staffers to reveal what he would later refer to as "the ugly truth about the NAACP" in a 1955 report—namely that it was "part and parcel of the Communist conspiracy to overthrow democratic governments of this nation and its sovereign states."[36] A nationwide right-wing radio infrastructure linked together local anticommunist groups to broadcast the likes of JBS cofounder Clarence Manion, fundamentalist Carl McIntire of the American Council of Christian Churches, and the over-the-top Billy James Hargis of the Christian Crusade.[37] Hargis, a Bircher, promoted protests against UNICEF's Halloween donation drives.[38]

Single-issue-mongering—the politics of the cause célèbre that would come to define New Right campaigns of the 1970s—germinated in ad hoc efforts in the 1950s and 1960s to challenge Cold War consensus politics on foreign policy. Ex-Communists who turned right, such as

James Burnham and Marvin Liebman, brought with them their indefatigable zeal, suspicion of factional opponents, and belief in politics as
a defining struggle. Liebman, who learned to build up single-issue
groups funded by direct mail as a member of the Young Communist
League and would go on to mentor Richard Viguerie, was at the center
of, to give a small sample, the National Committee against the Moscow
Treaty, the Committee of One Million against the Admission of China
to the United Nations, and the Congo- and Rhodesia-focused American-
African Affairs Association.[39]

The "Americanism" espoused by hard-right groups differed only in
tone from the militantly anticommunist conservatism and cheerfully
combative intra-Republican critique emerging from the movement ideologists of *National Review*.[40] And activists and organizations regularly
mingled in person. William F. Buckley appeared at a 1959 panel in Chicago organized by the editors of the ultraright *Independent American* and
featuring Welch and other Birchers.[41] Roger Milliken—textile magnate,
"Daddy Warbucks" to Republican politicians, and *National Review's*
major financial backer—was a Bircher.[42] Annual events like Hargis's
We, the People! meetings; the JBS-backed New England Rally for God,
Family and Country; and *Human Events'* annual Political Action Conference in Washington drew participants that regularly ran the gamut of
mainstream and "ultra" types.

Buckley and his allies, over the objections of *National Review* publisher William Rusher, eventually moved to draw lines of respectability
between their brand of conservatism and the JBS.[43] A series of *National
Review* pieces in 1962 singled out Welch for personal condemnation
while sparing the organization and its members. A more full-throated
attack on the JBS itself followed in 1965.[44] But however mythologized by
movement conservatives since, Buckley's halting project of excommu-
nication was more notable for its tardiness and ultimate ineffectuality than
for its impact in drawing a cordon sanitaire.

The *National Review* crowd itself helped to seed an organization
instrumental in developing the Long New Right style: Young Americans
for Freedom (YAF), formed in September 1960 at Buckley's Connecticut
estate. Built around a core of young veterans from that year's Draft

Goldwater effort, YAF would inject itself into the very center of Republican Party politics by the time Goldwater captured the GOP nomination four years later.[45] More than any other postwar outfit, YAF provided the formative stomping grounds for an entire generation of activists. As the group's chair, James Lacy, observed at the 1980 GOP convention, "The Republican platform reads like a YAF tract from around 1963."[46]

YAF nourished the puckishly aggressive impulses of the postwar Right. The group advised its college chapters to skip the "Libertarian Proposals for Free-Enterprise Lighthouses" and opt instead for programming that would "create controversy and the element of conflict and drama . . . the bigger the controversy, the bigger the crowd."[47] YAF's songbook featured lyrics such as "Deck the halls with Commie corpses," "Adlai the bald-headed Com-Symp," and "We'll follow Bob Welch through thick and thin, / And thank God we have such a captain!!!"[48] The "new maturity of the young Right," the sympathetic young journalist Pat Buchanan wrote in 1966, was evident in the way that YAF eschewed arid "philosophical purity" to pursue "the molding of a political coalition to gain the support of the majority and the levers of democratic power."[49]

Republican Insurgents

No figure did more to put the right at the forefront of popular discussion and anxiety than Arizona senator Barry Goldwater. As he gathered steam in the run-up to 1964, debates over boundary-policing intensified. The general pattern presaged a half century of Republican politics to come. Goldwater rose to national conservative prominence in the 1950s thanks to staunch advocacy of partisanship grounded in principle, along with hearty antagonism of organized labor.[50] Briefly in Goldwater's draft presidential effort in 1960 and again, explosively, in 1964, the extra-party networks of the American Right used him as a vessel for power. During the general election campaign that followed his shocking nomination, and through the aftermath of his overwhelming defeat, Goldwater himself remained a starchy and unyielding proponent of down-the-line conservative doctrine. But he bequeathed to the Long New Right legions of activists who would power conservatism for decades, a principled rejection of policing extremism (no virtue in that, he declared), and fateful early forays into more populist political registers.

Goldwater never blanched at engaging with the networks of the post-war hard Right. His campaign was powered by runaway best-selling tracts like Phyllis Schlafly's *A Choice, Not an Echo*, steeped in the baroquely paranoid style of the JBS and its ilk.[51] A who's who of hard-right organizations and leaders—Billy James Hargis, Carl McIntire, Clarence Manion, the virulent anti-Semite Gerald L. K. Smith—enthusiastically supported his candidacy, and the campaign did little to disavow any of them.[52] Welch deemed Goldwater "a very patriotic American and a very able politician."[53] Goldwater, for his part, had spoken at a We, the People! event in 1959.[54] Echoing the *National Review* crowd, he went as far as to criticize Robert Welch personally—but no further. When Ku Klux Klan chapters in Georgia and Alabama announced their endorsement, Goldwater's aide-turned-RNC-chair Dean Burch told reporters that as long as the KKK is "not in the business of overthrowing the government, we're not in the business of discouraging votes."[55] (Goldwater himself did walk that one back days later.) Even the party establishment that resisted Goldwater's nomination refrained from condemning extremists by name. Pennsylvania governor William Scranton's proposed convention plank denouncing extremism on the left and the right, and naming the JBS explicitly, ran into opposition not only from Goldwaterites but also from Dwight Eisenhower and George Romney.[56]

Sounding a central Long New Right theme, the Goldwater campaign mobilized social conflict as a means to majority. Though Goldwater's constitutionalist objection to the 1964 Civil Rights Act was, by all accounts, sincere, the absorption of anti–civil rights politics by the conservative movement powering his candidacy, and the deep southern inroads that his campaign forged, were hardly lost on anyone. This included the senator himself, who had told an Atlanta audience in 1961 that Republicans were "not going to get the Negro vote as a bloc, so we ought to go hunting where the ducks are."[57] Three years later, racial appeals came couched in a broadening array of social and moral critiques touted by the campaign. The announcer in one television spot intoned, "Graft! Swindle! Juvenile delinquency! Crime! Riots!" before Goldwater appeared to call for a new "standard of responsibility."[58] A minor note in Goldwater's doctrinaire small-government hymnal in 1964, such cultural appeals would grow to a roar over the next decade.

As political activism moved out of formal parties and into the paraparty blobs, a debate over "splinter" organizations forced a reckoning over the relationship between ideological politics and party prerogatives. In the wake of the November debacle, Goldwater supporters moved to sustain their energy through new groups outside the formal Republican umbrella. A particularly important player arrived on the scene when the National Review circle, along with YAF cofounder Robert Bauman and hard-right congressmen John Ashbrook and Donald Bruce, established the American Conservative Union (ACU) in explicit emulation of the liberal Americans for Democratic Action.[59]

Ohio's Ray Bliss, entering the RNC chairmanship following Dean Burch's bitterly contested ouster in 1965, cast a cold eye. "Whenever you have splinter groups, they do not assist in uniting us," he told reporters. "We should present a united front to the opposition. If you believe in a free society, what better way to maintain it than through a strong, two-party system?"[60] Ultimately, party leaders demurred. Bliss, ever mindful of party unity and assured by his finance chair that there was "enough money to go around," declared himself "fed up" with the conflict over outside groups and ready to "live with them and work with them."[61] Bliss and Goldwater issued a joint statement affirming their shared commitment to the party's core goal of winning more elective offices.[62] The fight to legitimize a permanent paraparty role for the right was won.

For their part, formal party leaders could not chart a direction collectively. Though Bliss was a highly efficacious nuts-and-bolts party builder, his refusal to push any kind of party program played indirectly into the Right's hands. At the RNC, Bliss enhanced formal party machinery that conservative forces would ultimately utilize.[63] He worked to rein in the rambunctious national Young Republican National Federation, which came under scrutiny in 1966 for leaked racist and anti-Semitic song parodies—"Riding through the Reich / In my Mercedes-Benz / Shooting all the kikes / Saving all my friends"—written by a radical faction in the New Jersey chapter known as the "Rat Finks."[64] He also managed the fallout over the 1967 election for the National Federation of Republican Women presidency, described by the losing candidate, Phyllis Schlafly, as a purge "pursued by a working alliance between ideological Republican liberals [and] henchmen who are paid or promised favors by the kingmaker clique."[65] Both dust-ups afforded the right-wingers their preferred role of betrayed warriors as well as a new litany of intraparty villains, without actually depleting their factional power.[66]

Meanwhile, the Right's moderate intraparty opponents proved ineffectual factional battlers.[67] As the young moderates of the Ripon Society explained in a postmortem after 1964, "Modern Republicans have not been good political strategists. . . . Their portfolios have come only to include stocks that are on the wane, past their peak."[68] Champions of liberal and moderate Republicanism remained a motley assortment of ambitious politicians—Nelson Rockefeller, Charles Percy, William Scranton, George Romney, John Lindsay—with neither an esprit de corps nor an organized presence at the grassroots. The Stop Goldwater forces knew "for a long time that a hard core of extreme conservatives have been working night and day, year after year, to capture the Grand Old Party," one journalist wrote during the 1964 campaign. But they "sat around and hemmed and hawed and let Barry's supporters get the drop on them."[69] That charge remained potent in the years, then decades, to come.

Indeed, the fact that resistance to the Right was so contingent on individual politicians' short-term incentives pointed to deeper weaknesses. In the unsorted party system of the New Deal order, there were plenty of Republican politicians and voters unsympathetic to the Long New Right vanguard. Most of them practiced a distinctly nonideological politics. It drew on elements of, respectively, the anti-party strand, most visible in colorful figures like Rockefeller and Romney; the pro-capital strand, embodied in the big midcentury corporation; and the accommodationist strand, seen in the efforts of an organization man like Bliss. Moderate Republicans' rolled-sleeve approach to governance as problem-solving and social peace-keeping reflected both the dominant imprint of the New Deal order and the politicians' own embeddedness in local civic networks.[70] As of the 1960s, this disposition rendered moderate

Republicans ill-equipped to mount effective opposition to the Right's party brawlers. And once those New Deal strictures and that community-level civic life both began to disappear, the moderate Republican tradition itself would vanish as well.

Toward Right Populism

The tangle of issues that dominated national politics in the later 1960s were better defined by what they were not—bread-and-butter fights over political economy and the welfare state—than by what, collectively, they shared. Race provided a critical fulcrum. Rising crime, urban riots, and white resistance to integration all deepened fissures within the New Deal order, lending conservative discontents both North and South an increasingly common language.[71] "I think the people of Mississippi ought to come to Chicago to learn how to hate," Martin Luther King Jr. remarked in 1966 following violently contested open housing marches in the city's Gage Park neighborhood. (King himself was struck in the head by a rock.) "While you sit on your butt in Washington," a Chicagoan wrote Democratic senator Paul Douglas a few months before the incumbent lost reelection, "Martin Luther King is violating everything I bought and paid for."[72] As antiwar protests and countercultural currents stoked further resentments, more and more of the vast ranks of what the centrist analysts Richard Scammon and Ben Wattenberg termed the "unyoung, unpoor, and unblack" grew open to new cross-regional political appeals.[73]

In 1968, an avatar of this kind of politics led the most potent third-party presidential challenge since Theodore Roosevelt in 1912. George Corley Wallace grew up lower-middle class in Alabama's Black Belt. A skilled amateur boxer in high school and college, he pursued politics with a pugilistic tenacity in the late 1940s and 1950s. Wallace emulated his liberal-populist mentor Big Jim Folsom and hewed to a moderate line on civil rights in his early years as a state legislator.[74] But in the aftermath of *Brown v. Board of Education*, positions hardened. After losing the 1958 gubernatorial primary, Wallace fatefully vowed never to be "outn——ed" again.[75]

By the time he captured the governorship four years later, Wallace had become the South's most compelling and provocative spokesman for massive resistance, building his persona around a series of set-piece confrontations: with the Kennedy administration over desegregating the University of Alabama; with Martin Luther King Jr. and civil rights demonstrators in Birmingham; and with a federal judge and former law school friend whom, for honoring *Brown*, Wallace deemed a "carpetbagging, scalawagging, integrating, race-mixing, bald-faced liar."[76] His most potent lines, like his inaugural vow of "segregation now, segregation tomorrow, segregation forever," came courtesy of speechwriter Asa Carter, a veteran journalist and Ku Klux Klan organizer. King, who knew talent when he saw it, remarked to Dan Rather in 1962 that Wallace "only gives three, maybe four speeches . . . but he works on them and hones them, so that they are little minor classics."[77]

In the wake of his star-making "stand in the schoolhouse door" in June 1963, Wallace embarked on several northern speaking tours. Right-wing activists in Wisconsin convinced him that a Democratic presidential nominating challenge, starting with the Badger State's open primary contest, would amplify white urban workers' receptivity to his message. Wallace launched his campaign in Joe McCarthy's hometown of Appleton, calling the late senator "just a little ahead of his time," and hit his stride two weeks later at a packed rally at the Serbian Memorial Hall in Milwaukee.[78] Moving smoothly from hits on the Supreme Court atheists who had "outlawed Bible reading in schools" to a lengthy attack on the federal civil rights bill for promising to "destroy the union seniority system and impose racial quotas," Wallace's speech garnered thirty-four ovations in forty-one minutes.[79] In the primary contests the following month, he garnered a third of the vote in Wisconsin and Indiana, and nearly half in Maryland.

His candidacy on the American Independent Party ticket four years later proved no sideshow. In the final stretch of the general election, thanks in part to unions' intensive work to sway wayward members, Wallace's northern support dissipated; in the end, he garnered 8 percent of the popular vote outside the South. But Scammon and Wattenberg extrapolated from the ten million votes he garnered plus the additional numbers who had shown interest in him a portrait of a substantial sub-set of the electorate, between a fifth and a third of the country, that was ripe for a right-wing appeal on "the social issue."[80]

Wallace amplified red-meat appeals on identity and culture while outright rejecting conservative anti-statist orthodoxies. The us-versus-them approach—hard-nosed but lax on policy specifics, with a suspicion of fancy-pants conservative elites to boot—placed him firmly in the populist strand of party politics. Wallace offered a Homeric catalog of the men and women for whom he was standing up: "the bus driver, the truck driver, the beautician, the policeman, and the steelworker, the plumber, and the communications worker, and the little businessman."[81] In a raucous debate on his television program *Firing Line*, William F. Buckley Jr. attacked Wallace from the right, emphasizing his background as "a New Dealer, a person who is intensely concerned to multiply the functions of the state," to which Wallace replied, "Are you against caring for the poor and old? . . . No conservative in this country, who comes out against looking after destitute elderly people, ought to be elected to anything."[82] Survey researchers would eventually confirm that Wallace voters in 1968 were considerably more liberal on economic and role-of-government issues than Nixon voters.[83]

Nevertheless, Wallace's ties to national hard-right networks were extensive. These included the racist and anti-Semitic fringe—the White Citizens' Councils, the Liberty Lobby, the neo-Nazi National States' Rights Party—but were hardly limited to them. The Bircher oil scion Bunker Hunt bankrolled a portion of his 1968 campaign, while the JBS-organized New England Rally for God, Family and Country that year, which Wallace attended, turned into an unofficial rally for his candidacy.[84] When asked about the Birchers in his campaign's ranks, Wallace showed none of the GOP's defensiveness: "I have no quarrel with the John Birch Society."[85]

For the Nixon aide Kevin Phillips, Wallace served as a "way station" for voters on the path to Republicanism.[86] The nascent Second Generation of the Long New Right also saw opportunity in the Wallace constituency but treated it as a core building block worth careful tending, not as a passing phenomenon. Figures ranging from Pat Buchanan to

William Rusher to Paul Weyrich, all of them critical to the Right's future direction, reached out after 1968 to forge ties.[87] The direct-mail fundraiser Richard Viguerie went further, taking Wallace on as a client in 1973 and raising more than $7 million for him over the next three years. Viguerie knew that Wallace had a number of "populist, non-conservative ideas. But he and I agreed on about 80% of the important issues, social issues like busing and law and order, and the need for a strong national defense. So we struck a bargain."[88]

Organizing the Second Generation

For the Long New Right, the Nixon and Ford years were a transitional period. Nixon himself embodied the politics of resentment in myriad ways.[89] Yet he was also comfortable operating within the confines of the very political order that the Long New Right intended to smash.[90] And so his contradictory presidency helped to incubate the core second generation of the Long New Right by mobilizing opposition among its ranks. Activists shifted from an emphasis on doctrinaire party politics— the demand for a choice rather than an echo that defined the Goldwater insurgency—toward a nascent set of extrapartisan tactics and organizational approaches.

An ambitious congressional proposal for a federal childcare system in 1970, supported tentatively by some in the administration, coalesced a conservative revolt that startled the plan's advocates. The single-issue campaign to stop it proved a harbinger of a new kind of politics that would stick.[91] With the encouragement of administration aides like Pat Buchanan, *Human Events* initiated a drumbeat of coverage inveighing against Congress's plan to "Sovietize" America's youth, while the ACU and YAF launched an Emergency Committee for Children to mobilize pressure.[92] The president ultimately vetoed the bill in categorical terms. An official who resigned from his post the following year told the *Washington Post* that "advocates of the day care programs . . . vastly underrated the opposition of conservative opponents who branded a federal day care proposal a Communist scheme to take children away from their parents."[93]

The interlocking entities of the New Right that emerged by the mid-1970s conveyed a sense of momentum and scope beyond the relatively small and tight-knit collection of activists involved, almost to a one veterans of YAF or the College Republicans and now sprinkled across the offices of conservative members of Congress. Beyond Hill staffers, attendees at Weyrich's weekly strategy meetings included the Republican Study Committee (RSC), the National Conservative Political Action Committee (NCPAC), the ACU, the American Legislative Exchange Council (ALEC), Christian Voice (linked to the Unification Church), and the National Association of Manufacturers.[94] During the same period in 1973 that House members formed the RSC, Weyrich used funds from Colorado beer magnate Joseph Coors to organize a conservative think tank, the Heritage Foundation, that would pursue a right-wing program more nimbly and aggressively than the American Enterprise Institute.[95]

The independent expenditure proved the perfect vehicle for the New Right's extra-party style of politics. The 1974 amendments to the Federal Election Campaign Act, which limited individual contributions to parties and candidates, opened up space for political action committees (PACs). With big donations illegal—the work-arounds, aided by the courts, would come later—came the opening for small-dollar donors from direct mail.[96] Weyrich headed the Committee for the Survival of a Free Congress (CSFC) beginning in 1974, while North Carolina senator Jesse Helms was central to the organization of two other major PACs, the Congressional Club and NCPAC.[97] The latter's chair, Terry Dolan, cheerfully prophesied a politics unmoored from the lines of accountability that had long restrained parties and candidates alike. "A group like ours could lie through its teeth," he said in 1980, "and the candidate it helps stays clean."[98]

Jesse Helms and the Full Right Package

Jesse Helms embodied the Long New Right's bridging of organizational and symbolic politics—and of populist and plutocratic commitments—with special southern-accented fervor.[99] He was a Raleigh-based Democratic broadcaster who dominated North Carolina conservatism during the 1960s before switching parties in 1970 and winning a Senate seat two years later. Helms presciently married an unapologetic pugnacity on racial issues with a savvy framing around broader themes of social resentment and anti-liberalism that set him apart from the regional parochialism that George Wallace could never fully shed.

By the time he had become a candidate for public office, Helms was already a fully formed manifestation of the entire modern conservative package, in both substance and tactics. Helms and his closest political ally, Thomas H. Ellis, both cut their political teeth on Willis Smith's racist and red-baiting Senate campaign in 1950. After a stint as a bank lobbyist, Helms turned to broadcasting.[100] In daily five-minute "*Viewpoints*," aired on the WRAL television station starting in 1960, Helms's commentary ran the gamut of proto–culture war crusades—school prayer, law and order, cultural indecency—all while hewing to staunchly right-wing positions on economic policy.

His opposition to civil rights, conflation of civil rights activism with communist subversion, and relentlessly racialized treatment of crime and welfare hardly distinguished him in the South, or in much of the American Right writ large.[101] Rather, Helms in his pre-Senate years presaged a politics of *antics* that would become a New Right calling card. The University of North Carolina was a favorite whipping boy in the 1960s. Helms led the state legislative push for a Speaker Ban law preventing public universities from allowing communists or Fifth-Amendment pleaders to speak.[102] He followed it up with a crusade against a graduate student on trumped-up charges of teaching obscenity.[103] His politics met the moment in 1972, when he defeated liberal congressman Nicholas Galifianakis in a brutal Senate campaign that Ellis managed.

If Helms's PAC work as a senator showed a knack for organizational innovation that supplanted traditional party functions, he also challenged the GOP more directly. Speaking at a dinner honoring Clarence Manion in 1974, Helms asked whether it might be time "to forge new political parties, fashioned along the lines that the people are thinking, not along the existing lines of political power-seeking."[104] Over the next year, Helms discussed the notion of a new party venture with William Rusher, who in turn stirred interest across the ACU and YAF.[105] Realignment around social issues was producing a majority coalition of traditional Republicans and Wallacite populists, Rusher argued in his 1975 book *The Making of the New Majority Party*.[106] What was needed was a partisan vehicle that could organize them free from the incessant interference waged by GOP moderates. The second Conservative Political Action Committee (CPAC), in 1975, featured an array of speakers expressing support for the new-party initiative. But after a meeting with New Right leaders failed to persuade Ronald Reagan to go the third-party route in 1976 rather than pursue a primary challenge to Ford, support for the venture soon melted away.[107]

The New Right took from 1976 the lesson that the Republican Party was more permeable than ever before. At the GOP convention, Ronald Reagan came within 117 delegates of knocking out a sitting president. Helms and Ellis, who had earlier helped to turn Reagan's campaign fortunes around by engineering his victory in the North Carolina primary, now muscled through foreign-policy platform planks with barely veiled criticism of the Nixon-Ford administration.[108] Though the Long New Right never again pursued a third party, it had hardly fallen back in love with the Grand Old Party.

Coalitionism in the Second Generation

The Second Generation aimed to mobilize the resentments of particular voter blocs and build a conservative majority that would supplant the teetering New Deal coalition. The goal to catalyze new electorates dovetailed with a rock-'em, sock-'em approach to politics more performative and combative, and less concerned with doctrinaire "small-government" purity, than that of their forebears. And where parties made commitments to small-*d* democratic and small-*r* republican visions, whether or not honored in the breach, the Long New Right hardly bothered. A 1980 newspaper story explained that though "ethnic and southern accents" were prominent in NCPAC ads, there would be no Black faces. The group's chair, Terry Dolan, was blunt: "Let [Republican National Committee chair Bill] Brock spend the RNC's money to try to get that vote."[109]

Weyrich, ubiquitous and indefatigable, focused the Second Generation on building a majority. "The people in our neighborhood," he said, recalling his upbringing as the son of a furnace stoker in Racine, Wisconsin, in the 1940s and 1950s, "were the real conservatives because they worked hard, brought up their kids right." But "most of the Republicans could have cared less about the so-called wrong side of the tracks."[110] Coalition politics, in Weyrich's central insight, need not mean either compromise politics or party politics. Working together, a range of groups would mobilize voter blocs on the single issues that most mattered to them.

Dense connections bound the New Right together. ALEC, to take one example, emerged from the ACU, and its first board meeting was held alongside the 1975 CPAC.[111] It explicitly took policy direction from the Heritage Foundation and applied to it the states, where it aimed to serve as a counterweight to public-sector unions, and especially teachers' unions.[112] Its executive director, Kathleen Teague, came out of YAF and the Virginia STOP-ERA campaign and had close ties with Weyrich, who served on the board, along with Bob Bauman, Ed Feulner of the Heritage Foundation, and Thomas Winter, editor of *Human Events*. Among its board chairs, Donald "Buz" Lukens of Ohio was a former president of the Young Republicans, a Goldwater veteran, and a chair of Stop the Baby Killers, and Louis "Woody" Jenkins of Louisiana subsequently ran the Council for National Policy.

Where conservatives had once eyed one another with suspicion, they now had a template for cooperation. The Carter-era fight over the Panama Canal Treaties showcased the coalitional single-issue model in action: the Committee to Save the Canal was formally sponsored by eight organizations, most of them Viguerie-funded, including the ACU, NCPAC, the CSFC, Howard Phillips's Conservative Caucus, and the Young Republicans under Roger Stone.[113]

The New Right's most important coalitional move, deeply imbricated with larger stories of race and gender, was to bring white evangelicals, especially in the South, into the conservative and ultimately the GOP fold.[114] The fervid language of sexual morality had long colored conservative politics. Now it came tethered to new issues and networks.

A deacon in the Melkite Greek Catholic Church with its Byzantine liturgical traditions, Weyrich always attached deep importance to abortion and homosexuality—and saw early on how they could bring together Catholics and (white) evangelicals.[115] Eventually, Christian Right pastors would mobilize resentment to build majority in ways very similar to the rest of the Long New Right.[116] "We need an emotionally charged issue to stir people up and get them mad enough to get up from watching TV and do something," Bob Billings of Moral Majority, a Weyrich ally and veteran of the Christian schools movement, explained. "I believe that the homosexual issue is the issue we should use."[117]

As conflict over the family intensified, women's activism broke open the male-dominated confines of right-wing leadership.[118] "A tiny minority of dissatisfied, highly vocal, militant women insist that you are being exploited as a 'domestic drudge' and 'a pretty toy,'" warned Lottie Beth Hobbs of Texas. "And they are determined to 'liberate' you—whether you want it or not!"[119] Phyllis Schlafly, a Roman Catholic, led the successful multifaith coalition behind STOP ERA.[120] Through the Eagle Forum, Schlafly mobilized a massive counter-conference in Houston in 1977 to protest the agenda of the official, feminist-led International Women's Year conclave, chaired by Bella Abzug, just across town. With a far less imperious style, Beverly LaHaye, whose husband Tim was Moral Majority's California chair, founded Concerned Women for America in 1979 as an explicit counter to the National Organization for Women.[121] And inside Weyrich's operation, Connie Coyne Marshner, a veteran of YAF, chaired the Library Court Group, at whose weekly meetings the New Right coordinated its pro-family agenda.[122]

More than old-line conservatives or their liberal counterparts, New Right groups focused on training the young, with robust internship programs designed to groom the next generation of conservative shock troops. No figure in that project looms larger than Morton Blackwell. As a YAFer, he was the youngest delegate to the 1964 convention, then served as executive director of the College Republicans off and on from 1965 to 1970 before editing a Viguerie newsletter and running the youth campaigns for Reagan in 1976 and 1980. Beginning in 1979, he trained thousands of young conservatives through the Leadership Institute, with a special talent for placing them in jobs where they might climb the ladder.[123]

The Long New Right merged the populist and pro-capital strands. If the Second Generation made many of its most important break-throughs on the heated terrain of cultural politics, it nonetheless also embraced core right-wing commitments on labor and taxes.[124] Across milieus and historical eras, the Long New Right stood implacably opposed to union power. The National Right to Work Committee (NRWC) was a key player from the Goldwater era onward, waving a message of "militant patriotism."[125] Its base came in midsize businesses worried that "compulsory unionism" would destroy their cost advantage. Seemingly every coalition or delegation of New Right emissaries included Reed Larson, the NRWC's president, while Stuart Butler of the Heritage Foundation served on the group's board.[126] As public workers sought to unionize in the 1970s, the NRWC responded in kind, both in the courts and at the ballot box.[127] It backed the case against "agency fee" contracts, *Abood v. Detroit Board of Education*, at which the leading academic authority against public-sector unionization, Sylvester Petro, argued for the plaintiff before the Supreme Court in 1976.[128] (From his perch at Wake Forest University, Petro established close ties with Jesse Helms and his network in the 1970s.)[129] And it played a central role in the epochal defeat of labor law reform in 1978.[130]

The 1970s tax revolt also had a deep New Right pedigree. Its emphasis on overtaxed ordinary Americans letting bureaucrats run rampant and welfare programs go unchecked provided a powerful frame for supply-siders to advocate for tax cuts whose direct benefits such Americans would barely notice. On the spending side, moreover, supply-side economics would offer a programmatic answer to any potential tension between traditional conservatives and right-populists by denying the premise of trade-offs altogether. Just as the swashbuckling Second Generation supplanted its dour forebears, a Republican Party that long fretted about deficits enthusiastically embraced tax cuts.

Jack Kemp, a former football star more attuned than others in the New Right orbit to broadening conservatism's appeal, had gotten his start on the 1960s right-wing speaking circuit under the patronage of the Bircher oilman H. L. Hunt.[131] Kemp initially proposed tax cuts on corporations, before the gurus of supply-side economics—Arthur Laffer, an economist at the University of Southern California, and Jude Wanniski, a journalist at the *Wall Street Journal*—converted him to slashing personal income taxes. Fortified by rosy econometric models, the Tax Reduction Act was introduced by Kemp and Senator William Roth in 1977. The shattering of the Keynesian paradigm had met practical politics.[132] As the price for Kemp's endorsement, Ronald Reagan made Kemp-Roth the centerpiece of his economic plan in the fall of 1979.[133]

Another critical link came in June 1978 with California's Proposition 13, which cut and capped property tax rates.[134] Its leader was Howard Jarvis, who had earlier joined tax protests sponsored by the Liberty Lobby.[135] The John Birch Society, for its part, sponsored TRIM (Tax Reform IMmediately) committees in more than three hundred congressional districts.[136] YAF's national director, Randy Goodwin, served as Jarvis's "right-hand man," while his successor, James Lacy, helped to draft Kemp-Roth.[137] In describing his campaign, Jarvis hewed to the classic Long New Right idiom: "Republicans have been trying to reach the other side with reason for 50 years. . . . Finally, we found that Prop 13 will reach the other side because it concerns a very important word to people: M-O-N-E-Y."[138] After Prop 13 gave the imprimatur of popular support for tax reduction, lingering GOP qualms about Kemp-Roth melted away.[139]

The bill set a long-term pattern in which tax cuts served as policy glue for Republicans of all stripes. Even when the Long New Right grumbled about sellouts to fat cats and capitulations to moderates, it never flinched at tax relief for the rich and super-rich. As the mutual accommodation of the Long New Right and orthodox conservatism deepened, any possibility of exit diminished, whether to a genuine economic nationalism that would take the fight to the Rockefellers and the globalists on behalf of the forgotten man, or else to an inclusive free-market conservatism that would reject distinctions based on ascriptive characteristics and put some distance between itself and the fever swamps.

Reagan and the Long New Right

Ronald Reagan was not the Second Generation's initial choice for 1980, and its relationship with the president would often run cool in the years to come.[140] But his Long New Right ties ran deep. The first YAF fundraising appeal under Reagan's name went out in 1962. A famous Reagan metaphor had a New Right pedigree: in 1978, Reagan appeared in a twenty-eight-minute film notably titled *A Shining City on the Hill* and narrated by Jesse Helms that would, Richard Viguerie hoped, "make liberals choke on their popcorn."[141] On the 1980 Reagan campaign, Morton Blackwell ran the youth operation, Roger Stone took charge of the northeastern states, and Bob Billings led outreach to evangelicals.[142]

In the Reagan years, three different understandings of party and leadership brushed up against one another in an unstable equilibrium. Reagan's was an intensely personalistic presidency, and if he defined himself much more than most presidents around a set of core ideological commitments,[143] he and his image makers wrapped them in a gauzy package. At the same time, the institutional Republican Party, building on its work during the previous decade and a half, impressively increased its capacity to raise funds, deploy new technology, train candidates and activists, and build an apparatus to displace long-entrenched Democrats across the land.[144] Neither Reagan's leadership nor Republican partybuilding, however, stood in the way of independent group activism on the right. Far from the flash in the pan predicted by skeptics, the independent groups survived even with a conservative president—and their approach spread.[145]

The episode that opens this book demonstrated the inability of formal parties to dislodge the independent groups. Richard "Dick" Richards, a Utah operative picked by Reagan as RNC chair, resented New Right groups, and particularly NCPAC, for meddling in campaigns with incendiary tactics. Though he claimed no objections to single-issue groups with special sway over their supporters, he opposed multi-issue PACs that arrogated the party's role, deeming them "loose cannonballs on the deck of a ship." After the tense breakfast with New Right leaders in May 1981, Richards attempted to forge a "non-interference agreement" by which NCPAC and others would pledge to stay out of races where Republican candidates or state chairs asked for them to stand aside. NCPAC rejected the request, saying it would run afoul of Federal Election Commission rules against coordination—and adding that it wouldn't want such a deal anyway. And there the matter ended. Richards and his successor, Frank Fahrenkopf, expressed continued irritation with the New Right but shied away from head-on confrontation.[146]

The breakfast meeting had marked a clash between different understandings of political action. Though a conservative, Richards hewed to the classic organizational model, with its lines of accountability and authority, that had defined the political party for a century and a half. "If I'm the chairman of the party and I have responsibility for a campaign in a given area ... I don't want someone else coming in and interfering with my strategy."[147] New Right conservatives identified as conservatives first and Republicans second, if at all. Unlike the Democrats' party reformers, their goal was to supplant the party, not to go through hoops to reorganize and rejuvenate it. Talk like Richards's, they thought, was pure establishment claptrap. "Who do you think the Republican Party is accountable to?" NCPAC chair Dolan asked in 1982. "Do you think it's accountable to registered Republicans? Garbage. They don't give a damn what registered Republicans think. They care about their contributors."[148]

The formal party began to ape the New Right style in the 1980s. Amway's Rich DeVos, a billionaire close to the Christian Right, served as finance chair under Richards. In his year and a half in the role, he brought multilevel marketing tactics to the RNC; ten thousand people paid $10 apiece to watch the speeches and songs at a "shareholders' convention" in Long Beach.[149] Two former Viguerie vice presidents arrived at RNC headquarters to build the party's small-dollar program—while the big donors finally headed to the PACs. After leaving the RNC, DeVos joined the NCPAC policy advisory council.[150] The loser in the new money chase was the old direct-mail king himself. Richard Viguerie was saved from bankruptcy only by a bailout from an arm of the Unification Church and had to sell off *Conservative Digest*.[151]

The Long New Right also suffused and transformed the paraparty network. One particularly influential consultancy—Atwater, Black,

Manafort, and Stone—helps to tell the tale. The men were contemporaries. Lee Atwater managed Karl Rove's successful 1973 campaign for presidency of the College Republicans. Charlie Black, Paul Manafort, and Roger Stone all backed the loser, Terry Dolan. They emerged from just the voter blocs that would power the conservative ascendance. Atwater and Black grew up in the middle-class white South, Manafort and Stone amid Catholic suburbia in the North. Before becoming president of the Young Republicans in 1977, in a campaign managed by Manafort, Stone had worked as a Nixon "dirty trickster," run Reagan's 1976 youth campaign, and served as treasurer of NCPAC.[152] Theirs was the win-at-any-price rather than the doctrinal side of the Long New Right. With their free-flowing mixture of political and lobbying operations—Rupert Murdoch of News Corporation was a notable early client[153]—and devotion to attack politics designed to raise opponents' negatives, the firm took the political style practiced across those early contests and brought it to the center of the resurgent Republican Party.

Weyrich and Stone embodied distinct facets of the politics of resentment. The straitlaced Weyrich, who embraced an alliance with evangelicals to battle abortion and homosexuality, observed in 1982 that "the social issues aren't big in the Country Clubs."[154] Stone, for his part, combined brass-knuckled politics with issue stances that fit with his very public persona as a libertine.[155] (In this combination, he found a kindred spirit in his mentor, Roy Cohn.) He, too, sought a GOP that reached beyond the country club—but, to understand the mindset of swing voters, every week plowed his way through the *National Enquirer*.[156] "It wasn't the evangelical Christian voters that made the difference for Reagan in New York or New Jersey," Stone insisted.[157] Not surprisingly, there was no love lost between the men. "Every meeting I've had with the guy," Weyrich said of Stone, "I wanted to wash my hands three times afterwards."[158]

Though white northern resentment was often ignored in the decades between the ethnic backlash of the 1970s and the pivotal Trump vote in declining industrial cities across the upper Midwest, the Long New Right kept its eye on such sentiments and the politicians who aimed to harness them.[159] At a movement conclave in 1988, a panel discussion on "building a new American majority" featured former Chicago alderman Ed Vrdolyak and former Massachusetts governor Ed King.[160] Both were old-school urban Democrats, their principles formed in Catholic schools. Both cannily practiced the group-oriented politics of mobilizing resentment; a King aide said in 1978, "We created a hate campaign. We put all the hate groups into one big pot and let it boil."[161] Both were known more for scorched-earth battles with leading liberal Democrats—for Vrdolyak, Harold Washington in Chicago; for King, Michael Dukakis in Massachusetts—than for policy achievements of their own. And both conducted their political careers as Democrats and, in defeat, became Republicans.[162]

Extremism Redux

How did conservative activists relate to the extremists in their midst? An extraordinary set of interviews in the *Review of the News*, a weekly JBS front publication, sheds some light. Most weeks, John Rees, a British-born journalist who also ran an extensive operation spying on the campus Left, conducted an interview with a prominent personality, ranging from the Reaganite Right to the fringe. Even as the influence of JBS, rent by infighting and paranoia, had waned, a who's who of the Right in the late 1970s and early 1980s sat down to chat.

It is impossible to know exactly what all the interviewees (or the flaks who arranged the interviews) knew about the *Review of the News*. Though it never identified itself as a Bircher operation, the signs were easy to spot. The *Review of the News* shared its Belmont address with the JBS, and Robert Welch's wife, Marian Probert Welch, appeared on the masthead as assistant editor.[163] Ads regularly promoted JBS speaker series and summer camps. The *Review of the News* was, a JBS official said in 1978, "the most effective door-opener we ever had."[164]

The sweep of the names is telling. From the Reagan camp came campaign aides Richard V. Allen (later the national security adviser) and Richard Wirthlin, and from inside the administration, Jeane Kirkpatrick, Lyn Nofziger, Morton Blackwell, and environmental protection administrator Anne Gorsuch.[165] From Congress came right-wing stalwarts like Larry McDonald of Georgia (a member of the JBS National Council), Jesse Helms of North Carolina, and George Hansen of Idaho, along with a passel of conservatives, including Alan Simpson and Dick Cheney, both of Wyoming; Don Nickles of Oklahoma; Chuck Grassley of Iowa; William Armstrong of Colorado; and, from Texas, Phil Gramm (still a Boll Weevil Democrat).[166] Economic questions rose to the fore for Stuart Butler of the Heritage Foundation, Art Laffer, Jude Wanniski, Howard Jarvis, and, further right, Hans Sennholz and Murray Rothbard.[167] Long New Right figures spanning the generations gave interviews, including M. Stanton Evans, the anti-gay Dallas televangelist James Robison, Jerry Falwell, and Terry Dolan.[168]

The interviews ranged in tone from lovefest to softball. The closer the interviewee to the JBS orbit, the more suggestive the questions and the more expansive the answers. Falwell saw his adversaries as "the same people who attacked Robert Welch and tried to destroy him 20 years ago."[169] The interview with Helms began with a line of questions about his "courageous" battle against the King Day holiday and continued through a long discussion of MLK's communist ties, a Bircher theme for decades.[170] James Robison, in perfect Bircher form, described the Trilateral Commission and the Council on Foreign Relations as "transmission belts for a very dangerous elite."[171] Roy Cohn gave a passionate defense of his mentor, Joe McCarthy.[172] Connie Marshner, Weyrich's close associate, was familiar enough with the *Review* to reference a past interview.[173]

Other interviews made clear their bona fides without veering into the best-known Bircher tropes. Jack Abramoff attacked the "cadre of 12,000 Marxist professors" spouting "the old Big Lie told over and over again."[174] Tom Ellis explained that "in 1982, we saw some good campaigns . . . go down the tubes because the blacks thought Reagan was going to take away all their Welfare programs."[175] With figures known as staunch conservatives but not extreme right-wingers, the questions usually aimed more at programs and priorities, and the answers hardly made news. Still, even there, it is notable just how chummy the Birchers and the mainstream conservatives were. Dick Cheney forthrightly defended U.S. covert action to destabilize Communist governments, adding, "Frankly, I would support similar types of activities in Cuba, as well."[176]

With the borders so porous, who was in or out? An inductive definition of the Long New Right could start with a leaked directory listing members of the Council for National Policy (CNP), formed as an explicit counter to the elite networks centered around the Rockefellers.[177] Since 1981, the CNP has held exclusive, off-the-record meetings three times a year for members across the right-wing firmament to strategize, forge connections, and give candidates and causes the once-over.[178] The Long New Right, the gatherings suggest, is no abstract notion but a label for a political tendency defined by the players themselves. When the CNP voted on whether to admit new members, in a very real sense it defined the contours of the Long New Right.[179]

The idea for the council reportedly originated with Tim LaHaye, a prominent evangelical and author of *The Unhappy Gays*, who called T. Cullen Davis, a Texas oilman (who had been acquitted in separate trials on charges of murder and solicitation of murder), who then called another oilman, Bircher Nelson Bunker Hunt.[180] The CNP's initial thirty-four-member board of governors offers an excellent snapshot of the New Right in the early months of the Reagan era. At its core were the indefatigable institution-builders such as Dolan, Viguerie, and Weyrich. From the Christian Right came Tim and Beverly LaHaye, James Robison, Jerry Falwell, and Pat Robertson, a televangelist (and Falwell rival) just dipping his toes into politics. Other notable names included Joe and Holly Coors, Phyllis Schlafly, Tom Ellis, Reed Larson of the National Right to Work Committee, and Ed Feulner of the Heritage Foundation. Far from facing a cordon sanitaire drawn against them, the Bircher element was represented by Hunt, the Mormon propagandist Cleon Skousen, and Larry McDonald.[181]

After the initial round, the legal conservatives arrived. William Bradford Reynolds, architect of Reagan's civil rights strategy, joined in 1982. John Bolton, a protégé of Jesse Helms who helped to design the elaborate legal structures that sustained the Helms network, was a member in 1987.[182] And though less central to the group itself, other leading figures in the Long New Right made their way through the CNP orbit. Pat Buchanan was elected to the board of governors in October 1982; Newt Gingrich spoke at the August 1984 and November 1988 meetings.[183]

Beyond the big names came the parade of rich conservatives, most from the Sun Belt and disproportionately from extractive industries, who made up the bulk of the CNP membership and whose checkbooks speakers hoped to open. A page from a 1993 program, for instance, lists the head of a waste disposal firm who was involved with Christian Right groups in Colorado, the president of a nationwide Christian radio network, a McDonald's franchisee from Arizona, a homebuilder and "government fee and regulation consultant," a Bible publisher, and an oil distributor.[184]

Another CNP regular in the 1980s was Oliver North, an army colonel detailed to the White House. The Iran Contra scandal that implicated North epitomized the Long New Right's institution-spanning, style-over-substance gonzo politics. North traded on his vast connections across the Right to build a network of conservatives who would send money to and advocate for the Contras in Nicaragua. His allies included Larry McDonald's Western Goals Foundation, the Unification Church–linked CAUSA, and the World Anti-Communist League, led by the far-right general John Singlaub.[185] Starting in 1983, North gave weekly briefings on Central America at the Old Executive Office Building, and Morton Blackwell, who served as Reagan's liaison to conservative groups, described North as "our briefer of choice."[186] While at the White House, North twice addressed Beverly LaHaye's Concerned Women for America.[187] And as congressional investigators and a special prosecutor closed in, North and his allies repeated—with great effectiveness—the venerable right-wing narrative that he had been stabbed in the back.[188]

North's antics offered a glimpse into the hucksterish inner motor powering so much of the Long New Right's endeavors. There is more than a germ of insight in tracing what super-rich donors like Joe and Holly Coors, Bunker Hunt, Richard Mellon Scaife, Rich DeVos, and various right-wing foundations have wrought. But large portions of the Right have run not from their largesse but off the advertising from gold coins and real-estate schemes and the alchemy of direct mail. "For many years," an outfit tracking right-wing activity explained in 1979, in an observation that would hold for many more to come, "there has been an affinity between some right-wingers and various financial experts or enterprisers who deal in gold, investment advice, countering inflation, beating government policies, and surviving financial disaster."[189]

An example brings us back to North's home turf: William Kennedy Jr., "Mr. Platinum"—an affiliate of the Birchers and CSFC who bought *Conservative Digest* from Viguerie—was convicted in 1993 of money laundering for running a Ponzi scheme through which he diverted money from Kuwait to buy the *Digest* and to purchase helicopters for the Contras. Kennedy ran seminars he termed "US Monetary War Colleges" in which right-wing speakers told attendees to buy precious metals as a store of value against a communist takeover. When their prices crashed, the game was up, and Kennedy served a decade behind bars.[190]

The Third Generation

Newt Gingrich, bridging the Long New Right's Second and Third Generations as a bomb-throwing arriviste to Congress in 1979, brought the movement's trademark boundlessness into the federal legislature's inner sanctum with profound long-term consequences.[191] In his youth, he had backed Nelson Rockefeller, never joined YAF, and espoused notions about the "opportunity society" that echoed the moderate Ripon Society. Bits of that early heritage hung on, often melded with his trademark futurism.[192] A portrait of Theodore Roosevelt hung in his House office.[193] But Gingrich saw the error of his Rockefeller-supporting ways early on and tacked rightward.

The New Right groomed Gingrich and shaped his approach. In 1975, Gingrich attended a campaign "school" in Wisconsin run by Weyrich, who immediately spotted talent. Theirs was, as a 1995 profile said, "from the start, a relationship without illusion: a marriage of opportunism."[194] The mentor later declared his pupil "the first conservative I have ever known who knows how to use power."[195] An orientation for new House members put together by eight New Right groups in 1978 included dinner chez Viguerie, while newly hired staffers could spend three days at a Heritage Foundation boot camp.[196]

In a June 1978 speech to the College Republicans, Gingrich made his purpose clear. He had no use for Republican leadership—and skipped entirely past Republican philosophy. Politics was a fight for majority. Party mattered only if it would aid in that essential task:

> You're fighting a war. It is a war for power. . . . But what's the primary purpose of a political leader, above anything else? In this system, it is to build a majority capable of sustaining itself, because if we don't do that, we don't make the laws, we don't write the taxes, we don't decide how to start a war, we don't keep the country strong, we don't do nothing except carve from these people's ability. And in my lifetime, we have not had a single Republican leader capable of doing that.[197]

Weyrich succinctly captured how the Long New Right upended Congress when he noted that Gingrich "is more concerned with achieving certain objectives than in working within the system."[198] For his part, Gingrich reminisced in 2005 that "all of our work was done against the active, continuing opposition of the traditional party."[199]

Outside of government, meanwhile, a Third Generation of conservatives who came of age in the 1980s took to the airwaves and aimed for the jugular, at once responding to and helping to create a media landscape that encouraged performative combativeness and extremism. If the First Generation wielded its pen and the Second Generation organized, for the Third Generation, media was king—and venality its besetting sin. Ratings and profits in organs like talk radio and Fox News became increasingly central, and so, in a theme we take up in chapter 8, the Third Generation arguably had more distance from a purely electoral or majority-building project than their predecessors.

The generational notion came from a regular speaker series at the Heritage Foundation. "The new conservatives appear confident, almost cocky at times," wrote Benjamin Hart, who convened the series.[200] Dinesh D'Souza, the first speaker, set the tone. "I see my role in the movement as helping push intellectual debate farther and farther right," he told the attendees, before they broke to mingle over Coors beer.[201]

As they amplified the New Right rejection of restraint and prudence, which they alleged had kept conservatives happy to lose, the Third Generation also borrowed from the attention-grabbing, antiestablishment antics at the wilder edges of the New Left. In an apologia for Joe McCarthy, Laura Ingraham nicely captured the spirit: "Conservatism errs in failing to go in for the kill. We do not do nearly enough in terms of using the moral and rhetorical weapons available."[202]

The First and Second Generations seeded the Third. The Institute for Educational Affairs (IEA), later known as the Madison Center for Educational Affairs, generously funded and supported the student press as part of its effort to shape "the moral character of the young." Hart, D'Souza, and Ingraham all cut their teeth at the *Dartmouth Review*, one of its grantees.[203] Among other antics, the *Review* controversially "outed" students on campus. Irving Kristol and William E. Simon—Nixon's treasury secretary, president of the John M. Olin Foundation, and a fixture of the rightist economic establishment— co-chaired the IEA's founding board, which at times included Robert Bork and Antonin Scalia. William F. Buckley presided over an annual dinner with student journalists. The highbrow names and corporate money funded a scabrous style that would come to dominate the discourse on the right.[204]

The administration of George H. W. Bush faced rebellion from the right—and though Newt Gingrich and Pat Buchanan pointed in different directions in policy and ideological terms, they played two sides of the same revolt. After Bush, in 1990, made a deal with Democratic leaders in Congress to reduce the deficit by raising taxes and cutting spending, Gingrich led the Republican opposition. He made clear his disagreement not just with the substance but with the president's posture as a statesman above party: "He's head of one of the two teams in the Super Bowl, not commissioner of the National Football League."[205] The following winter, Ed Feulner warned that "if Pat Buchanan's challenge tells the American political establishment anything, it's that conservatives will never again allow themselves to be dragged under by a Republican administration pretending to be conservative."[206]

Pitchfork Prophet

More than any figure in the New Right orbit, Buchanan brought together stylistic and substantive maximalism. His project was never specifically a partisan one. (He even ran, quixotically, for president on the Reform Party line in 2000.) Instead, Buchanan was an ideologist for blood-and-soil nationalism. To Buchanan, Republicans were patsies and wimps afraid to grasp their opportunities because they feared being tarred with extremism or racism. Asked in a 1988 interview to draw the line between the Right and the extreme Right, Buchanan quipped, "It's about two inches off my right shoulder."[207]

Buchanan melded the right-wing Catholic and the neo-Confederate traditions in the Long New Right.[208] Growing up, his family revered Joe McCarthy and Francisco Franco. One of his great-grandfathers died for the Confederacy at Vicksburg; another was captured at the Battle of Jonesboro.[209] After a stint as a journalist, Buchanan served in the Nixon administration, where he honed Spiro Agnew's attacks on liberal elites into barbed language and worked to translate them into policy. A 1970 memo called for "relief for working-class ethnics and Catholics. . . . If we can give 50 Phantoms for the Jews, and a multibillion dollar welfare program for the blacks—neither of whom is going to thank this president— why not help the Catholics save their collapsing school system?"[210]

Buchanan spent the following decades, except for two years as Ronald Reagan's chief speechwriter from 1985 to 1987, as a pundit in print and on television. He said out loud what respectable conservatism would not—and attacked those who blanched at following his lead. A 1988 column left little to the imagination on his core theme: "Nothing so terrifies a moderate Republican as the charge that he is insufficiently progressive on civil rights."[211] While national Republicans distanced themselves from unrepentant former Klansman and Nazi apologist David Duke in his runs for senator and governor of Louisiana in 1990 and 1991, Buchanan skipped the criticism and instead advised Republicans to "look at Duke's portfolio of winning issues, and expropriate those not in conflict with GOP principles. . . . The national press calls these positions 'code words' for racism, but in the hard times of

Louisiana, Duke's message comes across as Middle Class, meritocratic, populist, and nationalist."[212]

One critical dimension made Buchanan anathema and set him apart from many of his successors. Buchanan was a skeptic of Israel and warned the United States to keep its distance from the Jewish state. An infamous comment in 1990 referenced "the Israel Defense Ministry and its amen corner in the United States." Buchanan's bitterest enemies, and not just on Israel, were the once-liberal neoconservatives. He deemed them "ideological vagrants."[213] The neoconservatives, for their part, treated Buchanan as beyond the pale.[214]

In his presidential runs in 1992 and, much more sharply, 1996, Buchanan married that mobilization of grievance, with race at its core, to an economic nationalism hostile to the diktats of globalist orthodoxy. If it was an unapologetically right-wing vision, it was also one willing to part with conservative pieties.[215] In contrast to Bob Dole, "bellhop to the Business Roundtable," Buchanan urged conservatives to worship "at a higher altar than the bottom line."[216] He promised to stop bad trade deals; restore manufacturing; and rein in the bankers, the Trilateral Commission, the United Nations, and the "New World Order."

Though Buchanan gave George H. W. Bush a scare in New Hampshire in 1992 and won the state four years later, he never expanded his support beyond the "peasants with pitchforks" who flocked to his distinctive appeal.[217] If Buchanan was too raw a figure, and the Republican electorate not yet disillusioned enough with mainstream conservatism, for him to prevail at the ballot box, his legacy looms large. In the spring of 1996, a British magazine that monitored the Right predicted "a fight to the finish for control of the conservative movement and the Republican Party: Pat Buchanan's neo-confederates versus William Bennett and Bill Kristol's neo-conservatives. The smart money is on the cavemen."[218]

Making Sense of the Long New Right

By the mid-1990s, with Gingrich in the Speaker's chair, Fox News blaring out the Third Generation, Buchanan articulating a full-throated vision of populist-strand nationalism, and the Oklahoma City bombing auguring a darker version, the Long New Right's legacy for the American party system had fully crystallized.[219] The Republican Party, and the country, would see the results through the coming decades.

Two prescient students of conservatism serve as excellent guides. In May 1995, Kevin Phillips, utterly disillusioned with the grassroots right in which he once saw such promise, looked out over "the map of an ideological fever swamp" and identified the problem of boundary maintenance. "The GOP is failing an old but critical test of U.S. politics: the need for a would-be majority to keep firm control of its fringe groups and radicals. . . . The thrust of the right over the last decade—and especially in the last year—has been to heat up the climate in which these flames have burst forth." Phillips framed his arguments in terms of electoral overreach, but the consequences for democracy were plain to see.[220] That the electoral challenge has, as it played out, proven less daunting than the normative one leads directly to our present discontents.

Writing in 1992, Sam Francis, a neo-Confederate former Heritage Foundation analyst and, until his firing, *National Review* writer, described the same underlying politics of the Republican Party's grassroots with a different gloss: "Reagan conservatism, in its innermost meaning, had little to do with supply-side economics and spreading democracy. It had to do with the awakening of a people who face political, cultural, and economic dispossession."[221] The threat, he said, "is only in part ethnic, but also cultural, economic, and political." His friend Pat Buchanan's presidential bid demonstrated to Francis that "a 'Hard Right' remains politically possible," and that it could overthrow the "Court Conservatives"—"the policy eggheads, direct mail tycoons, 50-year-old youth leaders, and hack journalists who had passed themselves off as the Mainstream Right for the last generation."[222]

Francis was both right and wrong. Donald Trump won by soft-pedaling the Court Conservatives' favorite nostrums while pushing rightward on the very fear of racial and cultural dispossession that Francis identified. Yet apart from a few Never Trumpers, those same Court Conservatives hardly found themselves the losers under his watch. They regrouped and reached an easy accommodation with the tribune of the populist right. This suggests a deeper logic behind the tangled story.

The Court Conservatives and Hard Right shared a common ancestor in root-and-branch attacks on liberals and liberalism emerging in the 1950s and 1960s. As the Court Conservatives gained power, the Republican Party that became their vehicle, though organizationally strengthened, rendered itself vulnerable to a kind of family reunion with the Hard Right. Precisely the desire for power that so motivated the Court Conservatives and that lay at the heart of the Long New Right made that reunion a reality. That desire for power was not a deviation from true principles but the application of a swashbuckling political style to the problematic of partisan majority. The Long New Right hollowed out the Republican Party.

7

The Politics of Listlessness

THE DEMOCRATS SINCE 1981

IN SEPTEMBER 1981, a hundred leading Democratic elected officials from across a beleaguered party convened for a Democratic National Strategy Council, aiming to formulate Democrats' response to Reaganism. Alan Cranston of California, the Senate Democratic whip, chaired "A Conversation among Democrats." The questions prepared for that session could be repeated, nearly verbatim, after every electoral setback for Democrats down through the decades since.

> If our party is a coalition, unlike the Republicans who tend to represent a single group, what are the common denominators, transcending regional differences and local interests, which make us a National Party? . . .
>
> The Republicans cannot, and will not, represent the needs and hopes of middle and lower income Americans, as we are committed to do. Yet numbers of these Americans voted Republican in 1978 and 1980. How have we failed to make clear that the Democratic Party represents the true interests of these and other Americans among our true constituencies?[1]

Inherent in these questions was the goal of a party that would bring together its many constituencies in shared vision and common purpose—but also the recognition of the forces that would militate against that goal.

Cycle after cycle across the decades that followed the crack-up of the New Deal order, Democrats have displayed the politics of listlessness.[2] The ideological sorting of the party system removed many of the fierce internal conflicts that defined the Democratic Party at midcentury, and the party's approach took on a sharper edge over time. Yet in the face of profound electoral headwinds, the candidate-driven and consultant-shaped party repeatedly failed to subordinate particular interests for common purpose or to build public goods that would benefit the party as a whole. Democrats' commitment to inclusiveness proved its own sort of pathology, more often a thin claim to take all comers than a thick vision of universalism. Organizationally, Democrats played the dollar game, often successfully, more than they implanted strong civic roots in a top-heavy party. And credit claiming and blame avoidance, particularly acute problems in the paraparty blob, subverted Democrats' collective task: to forge the partial democratic vision that is the sine qua non of the political party. The goal of mobilizing positive loyalty to an enduring party project remained unmet.[3]

As Democrats after the 1970s maneuvered awkwardly across various party strands, hollowing tendencies came to the fore in each instance. The mix of activity and incapacity that defines our understanding of hollowness more and more directly characterized the party itself. The imperatives of coalition ensured the centrality of the accommodationist strand in Democratic politics. The party's moderates carried forth the grease-the-wheels impulse to raise cash and use it to win elections, but the high-dollar money chase was far more institutionally unmoored than in the machines of yore. Even as mainstream Democrats played hardball more capably than their antagonists charged, they could seem embarrassed about the game itself. Stronger claims for a politics of regularity came from Black leaders eager to defend arrangements that had brought them long-sought seats at the table. And as connections between policymaking elites and mass-membership groups attenuated, the policy-reform strand took on a technocratic hue. Policymaking in the party of the wonk came to elevate technical rigor and consumer choice above practical experience and political know-how,[4] while the good-government ethos at times veered into anti-partyism. Finally, a left-dissident revival in the 2010s blew on the embers of a long-smoldering radical strand. But for all its substantive demands, the left faction had little sense of how to resolve the dilemmas of building a party and winning a majority.

Two intersecting master stories have together shaped the Democrats' political vision. Polarization has divided the parties, while neoliberalism has constricted the space for a traditional center-left politics.[5] The dominant pattern of polarization emerged from largely impersonal processes of ideological sorting, with Democrats serving, especially before the 2000s, as the passive receptacle for the new alignment. Democrats' neoliberal turn, by contrast, emerged from the conscious agency of particular actors who sought to negotiate a new order that was not, in the main, a product of their own design.[6]

Polarization remade the Democratic Party.[7] With the breaking of the Solid South, liberal Republicans and conservative Democrats have vanished from Congress and grown rare in the mass public. As partisan identities became more salient, the courtesies that followed from the old cross-cutting alignment vanished, legislative fights turned bruising, and American politics grew angry.[8] If Republicans, in close alliance with a revanchist conservative movement unbound by the fetters of party, have moved further right than Democrats have moved left, the two have been largely parallel but asymmetric processes.

Yet alongside polarization came neoliberalism. It was a variant on a theme seen across the rich democracies.[9] With the collapse of the postwar political economy, old commitments to what a young Tip O'Neill had encapsulated in 1936 as "work and wages" receded.[10] Questions about the political control of the economy retreated to the background.[11] Steady growth, "easy finance," commercial Keynesianism to balance the business cycle, and the labor power that could keep capital in check had all eased Democrats' paths.[12] Now, amid straitened circumstances, Democrats resisted big-ticket programs in favor of public-private partnerships, incentives delivered through the tax code, and fiscal rectitude to slay the beast of the budget deficit.

Polarization and neoliberalism together made over Democratic moderates in a professional-class mold. White southern Democrats and

old-line urban regulars, the leading voices against responsible-party liberalism at midcentury, fell on hard times. In their stead, first the Atari
Democrats, largely hailing from high-tech, upscale suburbs, and then the
broader "New Democrat" party faction of the later 1980s and 1990s married paeans to the Information Age with small-bore policies.[13] The country crossroads and the clubhouse, each rooted in its particular political
economy of place, were supplanted by the patio at the strip mall.[14]

In the new century, as ideological party sorting rendered the party
less and less of a balky coalition, polarization began to bear constructive
fruit. But a new spirit of aggressive partisanship came without a commitment to party-building. If factionalism from the left and accelerating
class de-alignment marked new departures in the 2010s, the broader
story of a party straining to bring together its panoply of constituencies,
each with its own temperament and priorities, remained the through
line. Democrats labor under this complex inheritance.

"In 1981 the New Deal Doesn't Carry a Lot of Water"

On November 4, 1980, Ronald Reagan defeated Jimmy Carter by a ten-
point popular-vote margin, Democrats lost thirty-one seats in the
House, and Republicans captured a Senate majority through a shocking
twelve-seat gain. If anything, the election tallies undersold the severity
of the Democrats' troubles. The radical legislative breakthroughs of
Reagan's first two years in office came fast before halting just as abruptly.
But they set in profound relief the Democrats' internal factional tensions and programmatic challenges for years to come.

House Speaker Tip O'Neill, the North Cambridge warhorse, channeled the politics-as-brokerage approach of the midcentury Democratic
pragmatists into energetic management of a party in flux. His approach
combined new formal leadership tools—control over committee assignments and floor action, regularized leadership meetings and caucus
outreach—with a recognition of the party's continuing diversity.[15] As
he described his caucus to a reporter, "In another country there would
be five separate parties."[16] In the opening shots of the Reagan Revolution, those "parties" would get the better of him.

The conservative coalition revived for a twilight victory. Following the election, Texan Charles Stenholm invoked Judge Howard Smith's old term for southern dissidents—"boll weevils"—in spearheading the organization of the Conservative Democratic Forum (CDF), all but two of whose forty-seven members hailed from the South. (Another nickname in circulation was the "Redneck Caucus.")[17] By the summer of 1981, House Democrats managed the nearly anomalous historical feat of allowing themselves to be "rolled" in three successive votes on bills constituting the core of the new administration's fiscal agenda.[18] Party leaders sealed their fate from the outset by committing publicly to allowing Reagan's spending and tax proposals to receive consideration on the House floor. But a deeper sense of shock and ideological disarray was also at work. In a letter to his constituents widely circulated in Washington, Les Aspin of Wisconsin invoked history to charge O'Neill with operating "in a fog." "His politics have always been straight New Deal," Aspin wrote. "In 1981 the New Deal doesn't carry a lot of water."[19]

As it happened, the New Deal's patrimony provided the basis for O'Neill's first successful offensive push against the administration, as he pounced on proposed cuts to Social Security benefits for early retirees in the summer of 1981. He made the partisan authorship of the program explicit in a letter to the president in July: "A Democratic Administration created the social security system and as Democratic members of Congress we are committed to protecting the system and preserving the security and dignity of those who depend on it."[20] The administration ultimately abandoned its proposed cuts and agreed to a bipartisan commission to address the program's fiscal imbalances. A year later, in the face of much more massive projected shortfalls in general revenue, Democrats pushed Reagan into a $98 billion partial rollback of the previous year's tax bill.

Reagan never recovered legislatively. The 1982 midterm elections, held amid soaring unemployment wrought by the crushing interest rates imposed by the Federal Reserve under its chair Paul Volcker, expanded Democrats' House majority by twenty-six seats and decisively broke Reagan's legislative coalition in the chamber. With the Boll Weevils' leverage destroyed, leaders used committee assignments to reward loyalists and punish CDF dissidents.[21] Those midterm gains would also provide O'Neill and other leaders with a convenient line: that they had pursued a deliberate rope-a-dope strategy of legislative losses to hang full responsibility for the recession on Republicans.[22] But such rose-tinged retrospectives belied the panic and bungling that produced Democrats' initial humiliations. As majority leader Jim Wright would recall ruefully on those first clashes with Reagan, "That sonofabitch rolled us."[23]

Reforging a Party Base: Feminists, African Americans, Labor

Democrats' challenges in the 1980s emerged not merely from Reagan Republicans and Boll Weevils but from the cross-cutting and competing goals of a variety of liberal and moderate forces, old and new, all jostling in vain to set the party's course. "An American political party resembles a massive geographic formation composed of different strata," wrote Samuel Huntington in 1985, "each representing a constituency or group added to the party in one particular era and then subordinated to new strata produced in subsequent political eras."[24] The fact of such layering was a given, but the contingent arrangement of the layers could either facilitate or impede electoral majority-making.

Feminists secured a presence in Democrats' party affairs that would strengthen even as political fortunes fluctuated. As elsewhere in the party, the story was about institutionalizing power—and about money, with all the limits in class politics that followed. The 1970s heralded these developments, as the McGovern-Fraser reforms opened the party to movement actors,[25] while Carter-era activism on both sides of the Equal Rights Amendment and abortion rights polarized the parties' positioning.[26] The process of party incorporation was evident at the 1982 midterm Democratic conference in Philadelphia, where Queens congresswoman Geraldine Ferraro took the lead in securing the inclusion of language emphasizing women's rights in statements on the economy and Social Security.[27]

When Walter Mondale chose Ferraro as his running mate two years later, the three-term House member's relative obscurity underlined the extent of women's underrepresentation—Democrats counted one female governor and zero senators in 1984. Women seeking public office encountered the highest hurdles in early stages of fundraising, which trapped them in a catch-22 of nonviability. A new venture, targeted at getting donations *from* women *for* Democratic women, aimed to fix the problem. EMILY's List was spearheaded by veteran feminist and IBM heiress Ellen Malcolm (the name is an acronym: "Early money is like yeast," because, Malcolm noted, "it makes the dough rise").[28] The group raised $350,000 for two Senate candidates in the 1986 cycle and soon became one of the largest PACs in the country.[29] At decade's end, Democrats began to outpace Republicans in the percentage of women officeholders in state legislatures and Congress. In 1992, the "Year of the Woman," 25 percent of all nonincumbent Democratic House candidates were women compared with 9 percent for Republicans, while four new Democratic women were elected to the Senate.[30]

For reasons both specific to the women's movement and common to the dynamics of organizational maintenance writ large, the feminist choir in Democratic politics sang with an upper-class accent.[31] To be sure, the leading multi-issue feminist organizations were, as a matter of formal program, down-the-line liberal on not only cultural but also economic issues.[32] The radical critics who ascribed racial and class blinders to such groups identified something real nonetheless. When civic organizations use expressive benefits to induce voluntary contributions, they depend on appeals and approaches that motivate donors. For feminist groups, whatever the litany of formal issue positions they propounded, abortion appeals *produced*; economic campaigns aimed at working-class women did not.[33] Some members of the National Organization for Women (NOW) expressed outright hostility to the notion of providing legal support to welfare recipients. "We stopped doing direct mail on that issue," one official reported in 1996.[34] EMILY's List made abortion its litmus test for candidate support, while other issues were flexible. And so universal childcare, paid family leave, and combating the feminization of poverty remained at the back of the feminist agenda. The limits of Democratic feminism's class politics both befitted and contributed to an era in which the party's economic philosophy, forged for a now-outdated notion of a family led by a male breadwinner, fell into particular confusion and drift.[35]

African Americans' journey "from protest to politics" took them into the citadel of Democratic Party power as its most loyal and cohesive bloc.[36] These erstwhile political outsiders became defenders of an accommodationism that allowed them to work the system. Yet the timing was vexed. Economically, Blacks had finally won their place in the manufacturing industries at the heart of the New Deal social compact, long reserved for white men—just as the jobs disappeared.[37] Politically, Black elected officials ascended to the councils and mayoralties of cities ensnared in crisis and to institutional power in Congress during an era of Republican resurgence.[38]

The rise of Black mayors during the 1970s and 1980s acutely illustrated the problem of timing. Deindustrialization, white flight, fiscal crisis, and Reagan-era federal retrenchment seemed to fulfill scholar H. Paul Friesema's 1969 prediction of the "hollow prize" Black officials would find in their ascension to urban power.[39] Mayors with varying styles—from the pugilism of Detroit's ex-labor radical Coleman Young to the staid coalitionism of Los Angeles's Tom Bradley to the fervent boosterism of Atlanta's Andrew Young—all defaulted to probusiness growth strategies in partnership with private developers. The public sector, and nonprofits dependent on government contracts, built the burgeoning Black middle class from which so many newly elected officials rose. Yet it could not serve as the basis for a revived machine, as mayors contended with concatenated fiscal and economic pressures and the end of traditional patronage channels.[40] Part of their hollow prize were hollowed parties.

In national party politics, too, Black city politicians fell victim to timing. They became a fixture in the Democratic constellation only after local leaders had lost their once-mighty role in party affairs. No group fared worse from the McGovern-Fraser reforms than big-city mayors, stripped of their power to control blocs of delegates at the national convention. Take the most outsized illustration: Harold Washington's untimely demise early in his second term as mayor cut short a powerful political project in Chicago. Nevertheless, for reasons far out of his control, he would never have wielded the clout in Democratic nominating politics once held by Richard J. Daley.

In the U.S. House—the Senate would long remain a much more elusive destination—African Americans pursued dual and at times conflicting imperatives. On the one hand, they sought to institutionalize an independent voice, establishing the Congressional Black Caucus (CBC) in 1971 with an explicit rationale of bloc solidarity. "No permanent friends, no permanent enemies, just permanent interests," Bill Clay of St. Louis said of the new group's outlook.[41] On the other hand, they pursued social welfare and economic policy commitments that, during an era of party sorting, entrenched their position as staunch liberals and Democratic loyalists.[42] As Black representatives climbed committee and party ladders—chairing five standing committees in 1985, assuming the leadership of the House Democratic caucus in 1989, expanding their ranks to thirty-eight in 1993—the balance between independent power-base and coalitional approaches in the caucus's strategic mix shifted irrevocably toward the latter.

Black House members tended toward the hardened pragmatism and skepticism of process reform that are hallmarks of the accommodationist strand.[43] They had fought for the reforms that dethroned white southern committee chairs in the 1970s. But in the ensuing years, such members, typically representing safe seats and blocked from viable paths to statewide office, gained seniority and became defenders of the norm.[44] CBC members likewise resisted good-government reforms targeting money in politics, as its foundation wing swung open the door for corporate donations to underwrite its internship program and lavish annual legislative conferences. (The tobacco industry was a particularly active partner.)[45]

A broader conservatism with respect to party nominations highlighted Black Democrats' links to accommodationist group politics. For those representing districts with enduring machine practices, the lineage was explicit. "I am a product of my club," Shirley Chisholm, then serving her fifth term in the House, told a reporter in 1978 about her Brooklyn political base. "When you understand politics, the cardinal principle is: follow the district leader."[46] Even for others without such organizational ties, and for collective operations like the CBC, the same disposition endured: support for incumbents, hostility to primary challenges, and cautiousness toward insurgent or long-shot candidacies. Black politicians' general coolness toward Jesse Jackson's 1984 presidential bid offered a case in point. (Many of them would endorse him in his second run four years later.) When, in 2018, the Democratic National Committee (DNC) voted to disempower superdelegates in the presidential nominating process, party stalwart Donna Brazile captured the anger that many Black Democratic elites felt at the move: "I earned my place at this table. Hell, I helped build the table."[47]

No account of modern Democratic listlessness can fail to emphasize the fate of the party's venerable partners in organized labor.[48] Under assault from structural dislocations worsened by aggressive antilabor tactics, union membership tumbled from 21.4 percent of the American workforce in 1981 to 10.1 percent in 2022. In the private sector, the rate fell from 18.7 percent to 6.0 percent.[49] On a September afternoon in 1981, the full house of labor summoned a show of force a quarter-million strong on the National Mall: Solidarity Day. Lane Kirkland, the union bureaucrat who had recently succeeded George Meany at the helm of the AFL-CIO, sought to mend fences with potential allies, marching arm in arm with Eleanor Smeal of NOW, Benjamin Hooks of the NAACP, and Coretta Scott King. But Solidarity Day was a swan song. Mere weeks later came Reagan's symbolically momentous firing of striking workers from the Professional Air Traffic Controllers Organization.[50]

Kirkland's strategy was to manage union decline more than counter it.[51] The AFL-CIO worked closely with congressional Democrats, modernizing its lobbying operation and embracing the new PAC game with gusto.[52] Though it held the line after 1981 on hostile legislation from Congress, its substantive agenda was defensive and frequently particularistic. Opposition to trade deals, most prominently the North American Free Trade Agreement (NAFTA), largely came without a broader vision of American workers' role in an interconnected world.

When the Progressive Alliance, the short-lived left-liberal umbrella group founded by United Auto Workers president Doug Fraser and largely underwritten by the union, shuttered in 1981, its dissolution closed any lingering labor push for party responsibility.[53] Progressive unions continued to ally with left-liberal activists—funding, for example, longtime organizer Heather Booth's federated network of public interest and community action groups, Citizen Action.[54] And organized labor and the Democrats sustained their operational partnership. Still, the broader struggle to build an inclusive coalition in lean times advanced only fitfully, as organizational hollowing beset movements and party alike.

Varieties of Moderation:
Southerners, Ataris, New Democrats

Two tributaries, one southern and the other predominantly northern and western, fed into the faction of moderate "New Democrats" that came to prominence during the course of the 1980s. Most of the politicians who founded the Democratic Leadership Council hailed from the South or states with strong influence from Dixie. They saw modernizing the party in a battle against doctrinaire liberals as the way to preserve Democrats' historical strengths amid newly difficult circumstances.[55] Largely eschewing the Boll Weevils' open dissension, white southern moderates sought to sustain the makeshift alliances constructed in post–Jim Crow Democratic politics among ancestral party loyalists, business and civic leaders in the rising Sun Belt, and, as decidedly junior partners, African Americans. This meant a political appeal that resisted the cultural liberalism of Huntington's New Politics stratum and touted "middle-class values" to win back disaffected constituencies.[56] As late as 1986, the *Washington Post*'s David Broder could still report from "rural Democratic courthouses where 'Daddy is sheriff and Bubba is his deputy.'"[57] But in fits and starts, then accelerating from 1994 onward, the tides of demographic party sorting would overwhelm southern Democratic coalitions and party power.[58]

The second moderate tributary emerged from what Huntington termed the Democrats' New Affluent stratum.[59] Hailing from high-tech, upscale suburbs of the North and West, these Democrats championed a new growth politics that forswore the pork barrel. At once evoking and drawing a contrast with neoconservatism, their journalistic guru Charlie Peters propounded the moniker "neoliberals" for them.[60] Also in 1982, Tip O'Neill's quippy aide Chris Matthews coined an alternative label at a DC brunch that spread fast: "Atari Democrats."[61] The neoliberals' generational branding never cohered into an overarching party project. Even Michael Kinsley, a sympathetic journalist, conceded a "rather vacuous blow-dried side to the neolib business."[62] Instead, their close ties to favored sectors and free-floating support for postindustrial policy experiments only encouraged the deeper incorporation of business, including the growing knowledge industries, into the party's inner circle.

Matthews's Atari moniker tweaked the obsession with newness in general and technology in particular that colored the proposals and intraparty critiques of officeholders like Gary Hart and Tim Wirth of Colorado, Michael Dukakis and Paul Tsongas of Massachusetts, and Bill Bradley of New Jersey. Many of them had entered office as "Watergate babies" in the wave election of 1974. Though geographically diverse, their politics reflected a broadly similar suburban and educated voter base, part of the slow shuffling of white partisan alignments underway across the country. "Wirth or Les Aspin could come from a hundred different districts around the country," Matthews remarked to a reporter. "The new-breed guys went away to college. They became unrooted."[63] On cultural and "postmaterialist" issues like ecology and consumer protection, neoliberals took liberal positions. Hart's political genesis as manager of George McGovern's 1972 presidential campaign was no aberration—a strong dose of the New Left and the New Politics suffused the neoliberals' approach. "I had a base among environmentalists and anti-war activists, because I was up front on those issues, as I was on gay rights and women's rights," Tsongas explained. "I had those groups in place, and then I moved on to the business community."[64]

That "business community" was key: it was political economy, not culture, that the neoliberals stressed. They reveled in a rhetoric of hard choices and rejection of "class warfare."[65] Failure to adapt to new economic realities with "tough, fresh policies," Tsongas insisted in 1980, threatened to "reduce liberalism to an interesting dissertation topic for historians."[66] Globalization, in this view, had rendered the New Deal–Keynesian synthesis obsolete. In its stead, neoliberals sought to nurture growth sectors like high-tech while letting aging smokestack industries meet their fate.[67] The debate over a federal bailout of Chrysler in 1979 was a crucible for them. Hart opposed it, while Tsongas and others made their support conditional on labor concessions.[68] It was no coincidence that the very auto-industry bankruptcy in which neoliberals fortified their factional critique also prompted the shuttering of labor-liberalism's Progressive Alliance. To neoliberals' critics on the left, it all confirmed the continuing relevance of Hart's infamous 1974 line about the Watergate babies: "We're not a bunch of little Hubert Humphreys."[69]

In 1985, southern moderates joined with northern Ataris to form the Democratic Leadership Council (DLC).[70] For the next two decades, it would serve as the nerve center for a party faction of self-described New Democrats calling on the party of the people to move "beyond the sterile left-right debate."[71] The DLC's initial leaders were mostly from the South: in the Senate, Lawton Chiles of Florida and Sam Nunn of Georgia and, less centrally, the border-state Joe Biden of Delaware; Governor Chuck Robb of Virginia; and Representative Jim Jones of Oklahoma. But the southerners shared with the Ataris the same essential critique: that the party had become a passive broker for the organized demands of labor, identity groups, and big-government constituencies. "Our party had become the party of caucuses," bemoaned Chiles. "A caucus for every group but Middle America."[72] The DLC simultaneously sought to be that caucus and to transcend the caucuses.[73]

The New Democrats maintained two consistent targets of factional criticism: organized labor and the New Politics.[74] Both camps, in their view, had failed to face hard political facts. (One figure in particular epitomized their antagonisms: Jesse Jackson, whom the DLC pointedly refused to invite to its conventions leading up to the 1992 presidential race.)[75] Labor and its allies provided a foil both as an archaic actor in the political economy, ill-suited for a market-driven era, and as the linchpin of the tired old liberal coalition. The DLC, largely led by politicians from right-to-work states, sought labor-management cooperation in private- and public-sector workplaces alike rather than what it deemed a conflictual model from another age.[76] They applied the same principles to government itself. A leading New Democrat text tellingly ditched the language of citizenship in favor of what it labeled "Consumer-Driven Government."[77]

The second antagonist was more intense but also more amorphous. New Democrats saw coarsened permissiveness and the liberal tendency to explain away antisocial behavior as political legacies of the 1960s that repelled the mainstream. As the DLC put it in its 1990 New Orleans Declaration, "We believe in preventing crime and punishing criminals, not in explaining away their behavior. We believe the purpose of social welfare is to bring the poor into the nation's economic mainstream, not to maintain them in dependence."[78] Democrats across the party and with a range of motivations played a part in the bid-ups in laws, criminal sentences, and prison construction that produced a system of mass incarceration.[79] But it was the DLC in particular that yoked together the pathologies of crime and welfare to tell a narrative of liberals' softness.

After Michael Dukakis's defeat, the DLC established a new think tank: the Progressive Policy Institute. In September 1989 it published the New Democrats' leading call to factional arms: "The Politics of Evasion: Democrats and the Presidency," by William Galston and Elaine Ciulla Kamarck. The authors were both political scientists, Galston a Chicago-trained theorist and Kamarck a student of the anti-reform Nelson Polsby at Berkeley. They had met on Mondale's campaign—but hardly embraced a repeat of his politics. Three successive presidential defeats made the crisis plain, they argued: "The real problem is not insufficient liberalism on the part of the Democratic nominees; it is rather the fact that during the last two decades, most Democratic nominees have come to be seen as unacceptably liberal." Soon, Galston and Kamarck warned their fellow moderates, the "massive political realignment at the top of the ticket will affect races at the bottom of the ticket."[80]

If anything united party moderates in the DLC and beyond, it was concern over deficits, a perennial worry in American politics after the massive 1981 Reagan tax cuts.[81] Moderates came to deficit hawkery from different places, whether fear of liberal profligacy, demonstration of policy seriousness, or fealty to the demands of the bond market.[82] Especially when combined with the tricky politics of revenue, however, all three sentiments ended up in the same place. As deficit hawks precluded New Deal–Keynesians from their old routes to political success via priming the pump and directing spending to favored claimants, Democrats suffered the liabilities of particularistic group-oriented politics while foreclosing its benefits.[83]

Party-Building as a Double-Edged Sword

As factional actors in the 1980s battled over the party's vision, Democrats attempted across several fronts to meet their organizational challenges. "Needless to say," O'Neill aide Kirk O'Donnell wrote in a strategy memo to the DNC in early 1981, "the Democrats are in trouble."[84] On this reality, in the wake of the Carter debacle and the Reagan landslide, all party factions agreed. By decade's end, the party's financial improvements, along with the retreat from programmatic work and factional brokerage, had rendered the national Democratic organization at once busy and hollow—a full-fledged service party, in other words, with donors and their handlers happily exploiting opportunities from the new world of political money.[85]

O'Donnell sought, among other things, to "promote greater participation of Members of Congress, Governors, Mayors and State Legislatures" in party affairs. This impulse propelled the work of the Commission on Presidential Nomination, commonly known as the Hunt Commission after its chair, North Carolina governor Jim Hunt. The latest in the party's long line of presidential nominating reform commissions created, in the face of strikingly little dissent, 550 new unpledged ex officio convention delegates, soon to be known as superdelegates, in time for the 1984 convention.[86] This reversal of a key McGovern-Fraser tenet emerged from multiple sources of dissatisfaction, bringing together both moderates' skepticism of activists in nomination politics and liberals' frustration with pervasive irresponsibility by party actors in Congress. Yet when read from our hollow present, the commission's language is also notable for conveying the sense, long since lost, that the party should serve as a thing greater than the sum of its parts—a source of loyalty from and not just services to the groups and politicians under its banner:

> The commission regards this as an important way to increase the convention's *representativeness* of mainstream Democratic constituencies. It would help restore *peer review* to the process, subjecting candidates to scrutiny by those who know them best. It would put a premium on *coalition-building* within the party prior to nomination, the forming of alliances that would help us govern effectively. It would *strengthen party ties* among officials, giving them a greater sense of identification with the nominee and the platform.[87]

After Democrats spent the 1970s worried about party reform rather than fundraising, the bill had now come due. Nowhere was the sense of crisis wrought by Reagan's election more acutely felt, or were the results more consequential, than in the realm of party finance. In the 1980 cycle, the Republican National Committee (RNC) had raised five times as much money as the DNC. A year later, the DNC would still be paying off the debt accrued *during the 1968 campaign*. In Congress, the disparities approached the comical: the Democratic Congressional Campaign Committee (DCCC) raised just over $2.8 million, and its Senate counterpart $1.6 million in 1980, compared to $20.3 million and $22.3 million, respectively, on the GOP side.[88] Democrats of all stripes grew newly open to crash-financing efforts to close the gap.

The major locus of transformative change in party financing was found in the rejuvenated congressional campaign arms, particularly the DCCC under the leadership of Tony Coelho. The central Californian touted turbocharged fundraising as the answer to Democrats' existential fears after the 1980 election. Key to his strategy was Democrats' retention of House control, and the party's 1982 gains bolstered the force of his pitch: ante up to an incumbent governing party that wasn't going anywhere soon.[89] "Business has to deal with us whether they want to or not," he explained with characteristic bluntness. "I tell them, 'You're going to need to work with us.'"[90] By the 1986 election cycle, House Democrats had come to receive 63 percent of all PAC money, including 48 percent of corporate PAC contributions and 52 percent of those from trade asso-ciation PACs.[91] Though the degree to which the money chase compro-mised governance and party practice can be exaggerated, the blatancy of the new arrangements contributed to a pervasive sense of decadence.[92] "People aren't embarrassed," said one House Democrat. "I'm no Common Causer, but this stuff has really been bothering me."[93]

The DNC followed a similar trajectory. Under Charles Manatt start-ing in 1981, it institutionalized major donors' participation through a Democratic Labor Council and a Democratic Business Council—membership in the latter costing $10,000 in individual contributions or $15,000 from PACs.[94] Manatt's successor, Paul Kirk, offered in 1985 what a conference program dubbed a "stockholders' report" to Democratic Business Council members, extolling the council as the "backbone of the Democratic Party's finances, and its intellectual resources."[95]

Ron Brown's tenure as the DNC's first African American chair, from 1989 to 1993, brought all the pieces together. An Urban League official turned lobbyist at Patton, Boggs and Blow, Brown joined Jesse Jackson's 1988 campaign before launching a race to succeed Kirk at the DNC.[96] The racist opposition he encountered from southern party leaders—Louisiana senator John Breaux's assurance that "you're the wrong man at the wrong time for the job" was one of the more restrained offerings—testified to the party's still-deep divisions.[97] Once in command, Brown took the ethic of inclusivity to a new level, dodging programmatic questions and process reforms alike and showering state parties and candidates with resources.[98] Lavish "finance council weekends" but-tered up the party's donors.[99]

A new political class of "money mechanics," skilled in the task of bun-dling large donations and connecting them to relevant officeholders, grew up to keep the dollars flowing.[100] The party organizations linked office seekers with for-profit suppliers of electoral services, above all television advertising, midwifing the rise of a consultant class and a new preoccupation with messaging.[101] The result was to institutionalize a kind of business accommodationism, one eager to make deals but with-out the machine's old skill in using politics to meet voters on the street corner and solve practical problems of everyday life.

Jesse Jackson

The 1984 and 1988 campaigns of Jesse Jackson stand out sharply against this background of ascendant transactionalism. Jackson ran firmly in the radical tradition, offering a sweeping vision of collective liberation that called Democrats and the country away from selfishness and racism and toward redemption.[102] "The blood at the bottom of the American pool," he warned in 1981, "keeps coming to the surface."[103] Once, when Jackson was called a politician, he snapped back, "I'm not a politician. I'm a public servant, just trying to serve God. Maybe sometimes politics is *a method*, but that's not what I'm driven by."[104]

Jackson, a trained Baptist preacher, began his career as a lieutenant to Martin Luther King Jr. and was with King in Memphis on the night of his assassination. In 1971, Jackson set up shop in Chicago, working through Operation PUSH. He bobbed and weaved politically in the years before his presidential run, even speaking to the RNC at chair Bill Brock's invitation in 1978, where he urged Blacks "to broaden our political options."[105]

The road to Jackson's candidacy went through Chicago. In 1983, Congressman Harold Washington won the city's Democratic mayoral primary in a divided field, with 6 percent of the white vote and 84 percent of the Black vote.[106] After a bitter campaign in which national Democrats stayed loyal to Washington but white ward bosses deserted en masse for the Republican (his slogan: "Before it's too late"), Washington prevailed narrowly.[107] Though Jackson was never close to Washington, Operation PUSH mounted a large voter registration drive before his election.

In the wake of Washington's election, leading African American political figures discussed running a presidential candidate in 1984 to mobilize voters and advance their agenda at the convention. Operation PUSH opened a voter registration drive in the South, and on November 3, 1983, Jackson announced his candidacy, promising to build a Rainbow Coalition. As longtime aide Frank Watkins wrote in a memo, Jackson would run "not as a 'realistic' candidate with a chance to win" but "do to the left what George Wallace and Ronald Reagan did to the right, that is build a potential constituency that must be taken into account."[108] In

1984, Jackson won about three-quarters of the Black vote and only about 5 percent of the white vote. Four years later, he garnered over 90 percent of the Black vote and 12 percent of the white vote.[109] The Black political establishment largely spurned Jackson in his first run, preferring instead to work with Mondale, a long-standing ally. Though they largely came around by 1988, their support remained tepid.

In an important paradox, Jackson the pioneering crusader was also the very last candidate to run with a goal of hammering out an advantageous deal at the national convention. In 1988, Jackson's emissary, Harold M. Ickes—son of Progressive-turned-New Dealer Harold L. Ickes and veteran of convention insurgencies from Eugene McCarthy in 1968 to Ted Kennedy in 1980—garnered a deal for strict proportional representation above a 15 percent district threshold.[110] The rules have remained ever since.[111] It marked the culmination of the long effort, begun with the elimination of the two-thirds rule in 1936 and carried forward by the Mississippi Freedom Democratic Party in 1964, to transform the party of Jim Crow. Twenty years later, having taken advantage of the rules that Ickes (by then a supporter of Hillary Clinton) had crafted, Barack Obama would capture the nomination and the presidency.

Ultimately, the Jackson campaigns cut in two directions. On the one hand, after he pried open the national party citadels, African Americans became loyal institutionalists, eager to harness the power they had struggled so hard to win. Two Jackson aides, Ron Brown and Donna Brazile, later chaired the DNC. On the other hand, Jackson's disdain for mainstream Democrats' transactional politics would, with the 2016 candidacy of his 1988 supporter Bernie Sanders, harden into a call for rejection rather than transformation of the central organs of party.[112] The rising American left began to look back to Jackson's campaigns for a model of multiracial populism.[113] Yet they risked understating just how extraordinary, and how difficult in the American context, was his strategy. As Robert Borosage, Jackson's issues director in 1988, reminisced:

> He was the only civil rights leader trying to make the link between African-Americans and the white working people in the country, whereas most of the civil rights connection had been between the

affluent liberal white community and the impoverished in the black community. . . . But what Jackson did in '88 was reveal people to one another. So they could see themselves in their true strength together, with their shared interests, a much greater strength than they had ever imagined.[114]

Neoliberalism and Polarization in the Clinton Years

In "The Politics of Evasion," Galston and Kamarck had converged on a core prescription: the party should nominate a moderate for the presidency, aiming straight at disillusioned white voters turned off by "racial reductionism" and "the white liberal elites who increasingly dominate national party and presidential politics."[115] Their charge would form the basis for Bill Clinton's candidacy. Clinton served as chair of the DLC in 1990 and 1991, honing the core New Democratic themes of opportunity, responsibility, and community to which he would return time and again through the next decade.[116]

A diffidence toward party-building defined both the New Democrats' factional activity and the formal party's approach during the Clinton years. "We don't care about the party apparatus," the DLC's Al From said in 1992. "What we care about is what this party says, and what its candidates stand for."[117] Though New Democrats had their Tocquevillian streak, they never included parties among the little platoons they wished to empower or treated parties as civic institutions rather than factional battlegrounds.[118] The DLC failed to build its own durable infrastructure in the states; it was, by From's own admission, "more of a grass tops than a grassroots effort"—factional politics for a hollow age.[119]

The DNC, for its part, operated as an adjunct to the Clinton White House.[120] Its unlimited "soft money" went largely to television, under the fig leaf of "issue advocacy" rather than brick-and-mortar party-building.[121] And on the long-simmering questions of party rules, the Clinton years saw no change to the structure of nomination. A president desirous to remake his party left no institutional fingerprints on it.[122] Polarization rather than presidential leadership proved a force for party strengthening during the 1990s. In the blur of prosperity and Clintonian charm, Democratic cohesion, such as it was, emerged as a by-product of Republicans' sustained assaults.

The New Democrats' major policy victories, most notably NAFTA of 1993 and the Personal Responsibility and Work Opportunity Reconciliation Act (welfare reform) of 1996, would come about not by persuading internal adversaries but by making common cause with Republicans.[123] In every case but NAFTA, those successes took place under a divided government, when Democratic congressional leaders had lost their power to stop votes on legislation that would divide the party. Indeed, New Democrats' greatest policy triumphs paradoxically took place after their ranks began to deplete, part of the long process of ideological sorting that pushed the party leftward. The GOP rout of 1994—gaining fifty-four House seats, six Senate seats, and control of both chambers— hit old-line conservative and moderate Democrats who had survived thanks to split-ticket voting.

More than any other episode in the Democrats' decades adrift, welfare reform exposed a clash of dueling worldviews.[124] The administration itself was divided about the bill that Clinton signed. Most of the cabinet (including, interestingly, the influential treasury secretary, Robert Rubin, who had a soft spot for the poor) urged a veto.[125] On the other side, Dick Morris, the president's political strategist, showed Clinton a polling model from Mark Penn, the DLC's preferred pollster, claiming that vetoing welfare reform would turn a fifteen-point win in November into a three-point loss.[126] For New Democrats, the existing Aid to Families with Dependent Children was not just a political millstone but a programmatic disaster.[127] In their drive to "make work pay," New Democrats backed big increases in the Earned Income Tax Credit. But they shared with the Right the same fundamental claim that the welfare mess was rooted in liberalism's excesses.[128]

Liberal and radical critics, by contrast, saw connections across race, class, and gender in the assault on a welfare program associated with the Black underclass.[129] The welfare bill reversed a basic commitment to provide assistance for all eligible beneficiaries made when Title IV of the Social Security Act of 1935 established Aid to Dependent Children.[130]

Now, a block grant to state governments would come with few strings attached. While many feminists steered clear, for those who engaged, the bill's combination of stinginess and moralizing served as only the latest manifestation of the racialized and gendered ways that men in power treated poor women.[131]

In a 1997 poll, Penn divided moderates into two camps. For downscale "Suburban Values Voters," the trick was cutting into Republicans' advantages on issues like welfare and crime. The real growth area, however, came from better-heeled "New Economy Dems."[132] And so, as white southern ranks diminished after 1994 while a long decline in crime rates continued, New Democrats' core concerns moved upscale. A defense of markets familiar to Ataris merged with a politics of finance coming into its own as the stock market, and top-end inequality, soared in the Clinton years. The DLC heralded the party's move out of the Industrial Age—its preferred term for the New Deal era—into the Information Age.[133] In a less factional form than Penn imagined, high-income, high-education voters would prove critical to Democrats' fortunes in the new millennium.

The most important figure from Wall Street in the Clinton administration was Robert Rubin. A banker at Goldman Sachs who rose to co-chair by the time he moved to Washington, he entered Democratic politics when longtime party moneyman Bob Strauss convinced him to chair the DCCC's 1982 banquet.[134] Two years later, Rubin encouraged Walter Mondale's strategy to announce a tax increase in order to attack the deficit.[135] In the Clinton administration, where he chaired the National Economic Council and then served as treasury secretary, Rubin epitomized the new market-friendly orthodoxy. Supporting business confidence came first, which meant reducing the deficit, even if that required paring back on spending for traditional Democratic priorities so as not to crowd out private borrowing. This strategy meshed with the New Democrats' more overtly political goals. For swing voters, Rubin argued, "class conflict is not an effective approach."[136]

The nerve centers of the exchange between New Democrats and finance were the House and Senate Banking Committees, favorite destinations for Democratic members worried about reelection and eager to stockpile a campaign war chest. Many of these members represented the kinds of upscale suburbs that had swung the party's way over the decades and joined the New Democrat Coalition, a business-friendly caucus established in 1997.[137] The Banking Committee moderates tied together four important threads: of a bourgeois suburban party uninterested in a politics of us-and-them, a theme since the Watergate babies; of the unending money chase, back to Tony Coelho, and its implications for Washington work; of the New Democrats as factional players anxious to curb liberals' excesses; and of the rise of finance in the party of the people.

The impeachment of Bill Clinton put an end to the New Democrats' moment in the sun while laying bare the accumulated impact of party polarization. The long-scorned liberals came earliest and loudest to Clinton's defense, as they watched the right-wing attack machine in action. "Now that you've been screwed by your friends," one liberal senator reportedly told Clinton in a phone conversation during the imbroglio, "you may want to talk to some of those you took for granted."[138]

The New Democrats' last great goal for the Clinton years remained unfulfilled. They wanted to add individual private accounts to Social Security, linking risk and reward through the market and thus transforming the program for the Information Age.[139] For liberals, private accounts meant piercing the New Deal's innermost citadel—and after impeachment, they finally had some leverage over Clinton. Amid heightened partisanship, Republicans felt less interested in making small concessions to get a deal. The coalition that had passed welfare reform could not make another go. When privatization again rose to the top of the agenda in 2005, a new House Democratic leader would, as in 1982, rally to the program's defense.[140]

Partisanship without Party-Building in the New Century

The rediscovery of partisanship—as a fact of contemporary politics, a cudgel to wield, and even a normative good—served as the key theme for Democratic actors during George W. Bush's presidency.[141] The protracted denouement of the 2000 election dramatized the problem. As the Gore campaign flailed—hobbled, in the words of analyst Jeffrey Toobin, by "an internal censor so strong that it wiped out not only the killer instinct but also the fighting spirit"—Republicans deployed the procedural ruthlessness at the core of their inheritance from the Long New Right.[142] Democratic partisans frustrated with Gore's weakness found themselves radicalized, at least by the standards of the 1990s, by the militancy of the Republicans' attack. In its wake, Democrats discovered and even embraced polarization's potential. But polarization was no simple antidote to hollowness.

Grassroots outrage at party leaders' hidebound midterm election strategy in 2002 galvanized the new embrace of partisanship. In the first federal elections after the September 11 attacks, carried out amid congressional debate over authorizing invasion of Iraq, Republicans gained two Senate and eight House seats. A morning-after column by Nick Penniman captured how ascendant Democratic activists saw this historically unusual victory for the president's party: "The middle is a byproduct of the tug of war of ideas. Politics has been trending conservative because the right has been tugging harder than the left."[143]

Nowhere was Democratic flailing more evident than on the vexed political terrain of the Afghanistan and Iraq wars on which the 2002 midterms were fought.[144] The overwhelmingly domestic focus of the party's key stakeholders relegated foreign affairs to the purview of technocrats, buttressed by "liberal hawk" intellectuals and translated into action by mercenary consultants looking for a winning campaign message.[145] Even decades after the fall of Saigon, Democrats worried about being seen as tough enough to lead—and blanched at anything that would help opponents portray them as soft. An early 2002 memo to the House Democratic caucus summarizing the work of a "message retreat" for the midterms sounded a typical note: "The public overwhelmingly approves of the President's handling of the war against terrorism, and they want him to succeed," it stated. "Democrats must—and do—wholeheartedly support his efforts abroad." With that, the memo pivoted to Democrats' "message based on shared values."[146]

On the firmer ground of domestic policy, however, congressional Democrats found their sea legs in the Bush years. Most notably, they offered a stand-pat defense of their New Deal birthright that beat back Bush's privatization plan for Social Security in 2005. When a nervous member asked Nancy Pelosi when the party would offer an alternative proposal to Bush's that could be the basis of a compromise, she responded, "Never. Is never good enough for you?"[147]

House leader Pelosi née D'Alesandro, daughter and sister of Baltimore mayors and protégé of legendary San Francisco liberal Phil Burton, embodied in her own biography the key pillars of postwar Democratic politics.[148] She rose through leadership ranks on the strength (and beneficence) of her fundraising prowess and the steady support of liberal factions within the caucus, who outnumbered business-aligned moderates by the new century. Across two decades as leader, Pelosi aggressively influenced committee leadership and, when serving as Speaker, pushed through tough party-line votes on the floor as soon as the whip count assured victory. Her skills at consensus-building and parliamentary combat, however, hardly translated into the construction of an affirmative party project. Her Senate counterpart, Harry Reid, a pro-life Mormon and ex-boxer (journalists never tired of invoking his history of pugilism), epitomized even more clearly the partisan rather than programmatic impetus of congressional Democrats' renewed aggressiveness. A master of parliamentary tactics and a powerful party-builder back home in Nevada, Reid betrayed little of the bipartisan romanticism so common in the chamber. He pushed the procedural envelope, most significantly in 2013 by securing the votes to "nuke" the sixty-vote cloture requirement for confirmation votes on executive and sub-Supreme Court judicial nominations.

Outside Congress, the diagnoses from two sets of rising players—"Netroots" activists and big liberal donors—converged. They emphasized communications, especially political linguistics and framing, rather than party-building or ideological renewal.[149] Emulative awe at the conservative messaging machine, seen as master manipulators of words and images, and confidence in the soundness of an incremental agenda came together in the conviction that "being right is not enough."[150] First came the activists showcasing the Internet's extraordinary potential for political organizing.[151] For all their gate-crashing rhetoric, the Netroots touted their own ideological flexibility and political realism, happy to support moderate candidates in red districts and states.[152] Howard Dean's Netroots-backed presidential campaign in 2004 likewise harnessed outrage at capitulation to Republican misdeeds without advocating a dramatic shift to the left. It was a familiar liberal amateur politics—earnest veering into smug—adapted for the digital age. "The language of paradigm changing and revolutionizing politics," two Dean strategists reminisced, "was deeply felt by those who witnessed the campaign and those who lived it."[153] The changing paradigm was use of the Internet, not anything about the substance of politics.

Big liberal donors spent the 2000s building new paraparty institutions in explicit emulation of the Right and to the exclusion of organizational work inside the formal party. The proximate impetus was a PowerPoint presentation that attorney Rob Stein took on the road in the aftermath of the 2002 midterms titled "The Conservative Message Machine's Money Matrix."[154] The Center for American Progress (CAP), meant as liberals' answer to the Heritage Foundation, the media criticism shop Media Matters, and the short-lived talk-radio venture Air America soon appeared on the scene. Notably, CAP positioned its programmatic work firmly in the mainstream of the Democratic Party even as the Heritage Foundation had long leaned toward the right-wing vanguard. At the same moment in the mid-2000s, MSNBC, seeing a market niche in liberal infotainment, positioned itself as the prime-time vehicle for amorphous center-left politics focused on attacking Republican excesses.[155]

Underlying this approach was a belief in what an influential 2002 book termed *The Emerging Democratic Majority*.[156] The authors, John Judis and Ruy Teixeira, had met three decades prior as joined-up New Leftists in the socialist New American Movement.[157] Now they found themselves firmly in the party's mainstream, trying to bridge the divide between the DLC and its antagonists. Looking back to unmet promises of a majority coalition that would unite college-educated white professionals with minority groups, they argued that new demographic realities amounted to "McGovern's Revenge" and put victory in

Democrats' grasp. But just as critics had warned in the 1970s, without substantial support from the white working class, the new coalition had no chance at victory.[158]

Meanwhile, the party's most important organizational partner grew closer to it, but no stronger at the base. When the left-leaning John Sweeney replaced Lane Kirkland as AFL-CIO president in 1995, hopes abounded that membership would revive and labor would return to the apex of the left-liberal firmament.[159] The first goal failed. After a pause in the late 1990s, membership resumed its decline. Laborite *politics*, by contrast, did revive in fits and starts. Early in the Sweeney years, labor's political operation ramped up, with union professionals parachuted into swing districts to run the "ground game" from which the party organizations had largely retreated.[160] The federation's new leadership, many of whom got their start in the upheavals of the 1960s, worked to heal the breach between the labor movement and the intelligentsia. The AFL-CIO's Union Summer initiative gave college students experience in organizing. A teach-in at Columbia University in 1996 attracted fifteen hundred participants.[161] Yet when the questions of political economy thick in the air at Columbia reached the core of Democratic Party debate in the 2010s, they would do so in the context of an emasculated labor movement struggling to provide the institutional vessel and the political muscle for the ferment.[162]

Party Hollowness in the Obama Years

Barack Obama's 2008 nomination contest with Hillary Clinton unfolded within a party energized by oppositional activism and ideologically cohesive by historical standards, but also unresolved in its sense of a project for power. For all their newfound espousal of partisan combat, Democrats proved more susceptible to the reformist and transpartisan notes sounded by Obama than to Clinton's hard-nosed—to detractors, tawdry—pragmatism. Moreover, the candidates' hazy programmatic agreement reflected no real intraparty consensus on priorities or overall mission.[163] Obama's post-partisan dream quickly came down to earth once he entered office. Intransigent Republican opposition defined both the two climactic years of unified Democratic control and the six long years of trench warfare amid divided government. All the while, the party sorting that squeezed the political middle proceeded apace. When Obama entered office, he could rely on a total of seven Democratic senators in Arkansas, Louisiana, Nebraska, and both Dakotas. By the time he left, there were none.

Disparate and at times contradictory party strands intertwined in Obama's leadership. He entered office with an ambitious agenda that suggested continuities with the policy-reform strand, while his discomfort with small politics and his faith in expertise led back to the Progressives and the anti-party tradition.[164] More proximately, his self-consciously cerebral approach to the political game, not to mention his love affair with the tech industry, linked back to the Ataris. And the personalism intrinsic to Obama's leadership hindered his overall approach to party politics. The financial crisis of 2008 did not break neoliberalism or make Obama the next FDR. But party actors did learn lessons all the same. The rise of a left faction and the party's embrace of a more robust, labor-friendly industrial policy when it next assumed power both emerged from the limits of the Obama moment.[165]

Ideologically, Obama planted himself somewhere between his Democratic predecessor and the party's liberals. The Obama operation disliked carping from what Robert Gibbs, the president's press secretary, in 2010 termed "the professional Left." In an important departure from Franklin Roosevelt and even Lyndon Johnson, it discouraged mass movements on the left that would exert grassroots pressure to push the system.[166] Still, Obama never joined the DLC, and he refrained from the kind of sniping at the party's constituencies that defined the New Democrats. His neoliberalism reflected continuities with Rubinomics, above all in the response to the Great Recession: solicitous of the banks, despite pushing through the Dodd-Frank law in 2010, and limited in its response to the wave of foreclosures and, in an undersized stimulus, the collapse in demand. After flirting early in 2011 with a "Grand Bargain" that might have cut Social Security and Medicare, Obama by year's end returned to Osawatomie, Kansas, site of a famous Teddy Roosevelt speech, to enlist the capital-P Progressive legacy in the cause of fighting inequality.[167]

The multiple iterations of Obama's two-million-strong Obama for America (OFA) volunteer organization dramatized the dilemmas of party hollowness.[168] Obama's 2008 campaign had developed a potent and innovative "blend of community organizing and modern electioneering."[169] After his election, in a move that might have signified a new commitment to formal party-building, Obama folded the organization, now renamed Organizing for America, into the DNC. Under those auspices during his first term, the outfit hewed to the traditional path of presidential party leadership in turning into a one-way mouthpiece for the administration's policy agenda. If, alternatively, Obama and the DNC had empowered OFA chapters, it likely would have prompted conflict with existing local party actors—a fact only underscoring the distance separating a candidate-centered campaign operation, however robustly people-powered, from parties as rooted organizations. By Obama's second term, the DNC experiment was abandoned and OFA— rechristened yet again as Organizing for Action—was spun out as one among countless 501(c) advocacy groups in the paraparty blob.

Collectively, Obama's achievements and failings emerged from decades in which the Democratic Party had failed to develop an effective strategy *as a party*. Obama was too shrewd to think that policy was divorced from politics. His mistake came in the notion that good policy could sell itself, as if political parties' hard tasks of defining alternatives and reaching voters could somehow be short-circuited.[170] More than cultivating constituencies, the Obama operation attended to the president's image, measured by public opinion. When Obama was debating a rescue for the auto industry—a latter-day version of the Chrysler bailout that had so bothered the Ataris—his chief strategist, David Axelrod, did not list the players on each side or remind his boss about the contributions of the UAW to Democratic victories. Instead, he pointed to polling: even in Michigan, respondents told pollsters that they hated bailouts.[171] A decision that reaped political dividends across the Midwest in 2012 came about because Obama overruled his chief strategist.[172]

At the same time, the very technocrats whose legitimacy derived from their claims to speak without fear or favor tailored their advice to what they deemed to be the political winds, lest they lose clout "by appearing naïve or 'unsavvy.'"[173] The American Recovery and Reinvestment Act that Obama signed four weeks into his term amid economic freefall was, in retrospect, too small a stimulus to fill the hole. Though Lawrence Summers, Obama's top adviser on the economy, later claimed the price tag "was as big as the political traffic would bear," the administration never gave a clear estimate of what it thought Congress ought to spend.[174] In a cruel irony, many of the moderate Democrats who, citing the deficit, whittled down the stimulus lost their seats in 2010 as victims of an anemic recovery.

The perverse fate met by such moderates pointed to a fragility, beyond the exigencies of presidential leadership, in Democrats' collective sense of purpose. The Affordable Care Act limped to the finish line as the president's preeminent programmatic achievement after a drawn out and electorally costly legislative process. On the one hand, this sweeping, expensive, highly redistributive fulfillment of a Democratic dream eight decades in the making—in Vice President Joe Biden's piquant phrase, "a big fucking deal"—did, in the end, become law, thanks especially to decisive eleventh-hour commitments by the key principals, Obama, Pelosi, and Reid.[175] On the other hand, it only took one loss in a special Senate election—Democrats' surprise defeat in the race to replace the late Ted Kennedy—to produce a late-stage crisis that nearly killed the bill. The palpable desire by a wide swath of party actors to find a pretext for relinquishing the very power they held in their grasp told the tale of a party still suffused with listlessness, even as decisive leadership ultimately forced their hand.

Even more than Obama, the party politics of Hillary Clinton emerged from the travails of the prior decades—and in few politicians did the twinned, contradictory stories of polarization and neoliberalism run so tightly together. The candidate pilloried for giving speeches to Goldman Sachs also offered, in 2016, the most robustly liberal policy agenda of any nominee in decades.[176] Like so many in her generation, Clinton retained a core of New Politics idealism, determined to use the political system to benefit women and children, even as she made compromises, and got rich, along the way. Her skills combined the technocrat's attention to policy detail, the incrementalist's acceptance of half a loaf, and the modern Democratic institutionalist's realism about the money chase.[177] The result, not for the first time, was a politics smaller than the sum of its parts.

Clinton won support from across the institutional Democratic Party on her road to the 2016 nomination, supplementing her narrow majority among pledged delegates with the overwhelming majority of superdelegates. Yet it was a not entirely requited love affair. The Clinton campaign invested less than the Obama campaigns in building local capacity and ignored warnings about her weakness in the Rust Belt.[178] In the general election, Clinton ran against her opponent's character more than she promoted classic Democratic themes.[179] Her demographic strategy was pure "McGovern's Revenge": win big among college-educated professionals and people of color.[180] With a steep decline in support from white voters without a college education, however, it failed to produce a majority in the Electoral College.[181]

The other important development in 2016 came as mostly young activists rallied to an old candidate and worked to revive the long-dormant radical strand of American party politics. Clinton's opponent for the 2016 nomination, the self-described democratic socialist Bernie Sanders, looked to the class-first themes of the Old Left. For decades—on the fringes in Vermont, as mayor of Burlington, in the House, and in the Senate—he had railed against "millionaires and billionaires" and advocated for big-ticket universal programs paid for with hefty tax increases. Sanders's supporters thrilled to his venerable themes, little changed by the New Politics and resistant to the New Affluent.[182]

But even as Sanders called for a "political revolution," he said little about the mass party apparatus that would bring it about.[183] Instead, he stuck to criticizing insiders and their grubby deals, sounding notes of procedural reformism that ran through McGovern-Fraser back to the Progressives. Though a caucus member and loyal partisan on votes in Congress, Sanders stubbornly refused to call himself a Democrat and barely lifted a finger to reach out to key party stakeholders.[184] He blasted the DNC for a "rigged" process. (The firmest evidence of rigging was that the DNC scheduled debates at unpopular times, like Saturday nights.) In contrast to Jesse Jackson, whom he endorsed in 1988,

Sanders showed little interest, beyond a few platform demands, in affecting the work of the Democratic convention.

Post-election, Democrats reverted to form, pursuing factional rapprochement via a commission to tinker with rules. The results from the revealingly titled Unity Reform Commission testified both to the institutionalists' instinct to accommodate party stakeholders and to the left dissidents' thin sense of party. The long-underlegitimized superdelegates were Sanders supporters' particular bugbear for contingent reasons, but they found ever fewer open defenders by 2017.[185] Significantly, their most vocal proponents were Black officeholders adhering to the party-pragmatic tradition that had secured their seat at the table. "There should be enough room in the process," declared CBC chair Cedric Richmond, "to include the perspective of local party activists and officials, and Members of Congress."[186] This was the closest a Trump-era Democrat might come to evoking the Hunt Commission's original theme of strengthening the party as "a cohesive force" in government and society.[187] In the end, the DNC stripped convention superdelegates of voting privileges on the first presidential ballot if their votes would tip the outcome. The reform formally denied superdelegates a power they had never had the standing to attempt: namely, to block a nominee with a pledged-delegate majority.[188] The clever compromise did nothing to evoke or revive a positive claim for party legitimacy.

The Vast Democratic Party Blob

By the Trump years, the Democratic party blob was collectively better coordinated, more politically focused, and much better funded than ever before.[189] Law, technology, and political polarization all came together to flood progressive politics with cash. Reflecting the general hardening of partisan teamsmanship, many nonprofits traditionally organized as 501(c)(3) "charitable" organizations, from the NAACP to the ACLU, either branched off or fully converted into 501(c)(4)'s, able to engage in open lobbying and electioneering.[190] But the party blob's very growth, encompassing an endless array of entities old and new, worsened, rather than mitigated, Democrats' difficulties in setting priorities, forging cohesive projects, and building meaningful connections with ordinary Americans in their communities.

Democrats' greatest successes came in raising money. Long-standing party disparities in financing disappeared, with Democrats and allied groups jumping ahead of Republicans in online small-donor fundraising after decades of trailing in direct mail. ActBlue, a user-friendly online platform for candidate and group fundraising, raised a total of $600 million between 2004 and 2014 for its clients; hit the $1 billion milestone in early 2016; and then, over the course of the Trump presidency, raised another $6.7 billion.[191] With this abundance, combined with fatalism about the prospects of systemic reform, campaign finance regulation receded as a priority for good-government liberals. Their public financing agenda shifted from restrictionist proposals to "get the money out of politics" to schemes for matching formulas that would ride the tide of small-dollar giving.[192]

For donors ready to do more than just click on a button, new legal instruments and funding strategies awaited, all curated by retinues of courtiers and donor advisers. Big-dollar pass-throughs and mutually contributing Super PACs and dark-money outfits all served to obscure funding sources while showering money on campaigns and consultants. Consider the political giving of just one 501(c)(4) operation, the Berger Action Fund, bankrolled by Swiss billionaire Hansjörg Wyss. As the *New York Times* reported, the fund gives grants "to entities that mostly dispense funds to other groups, and sometimes act as incubators for new outfits."[193] From 2016 to 2020, this included $135 million to the Sixteen Thirty Fund, which in turn donated over $164 million to a wide array of liberal Super PACs in just 2020 alone.[194] Wyss funds also bankrolled an incubator called the Hub Project that spawned a dozen new groups, as well as the New Venture Fund, which, like Sixteen Thirty and a wide array of other dark-money efforts, was managed by the for-profit consulting firm Arabella Advisors.

The vast tech sector grew notably closer to the Democrats in the Obama years even as it hewed to its signature spirit of "disruption."[195] Megadonors brought their professional ethos to the realm of politics, with sometimes rocky results. The volatile Democratic engagement of

LinkedIn founder Reid Hoffman, a well-connected player in Silicon Valley, encapsulated the difficulties. Disengaged from political activism until Trump's rise, Hoffman in short order became a major party donor, then set out to build a data exchange for Democratic-aligned groups and candidates—despite the fact that a partnership between the DNC and the state parties already operated the existing voting file as a cooperative venture.[196] When the party organizations refused to budge, Hoffman shuttered his $35 million project and pivoted to factional politics with a new Super PAC called Mainstream Democrats, which aimed to defeat left candidates in primaries.[197] Meanwhile, a $100 million initiative that Hoffman co-chaired moved away from party entirely: the Institute for Political Innovation sought to apply "industry competitive analysis" to political reform in the service of advocating nonpartisan primaries with ranked choice voting.[198]

Top to bottom, the participants in the contemporary Democratic party blob reflected and in turn reinforced the growing education polarization of the two parties. The thicket of professionalized groups funded by rich liberals assumed an increasingly central role in the extended party network. The "professional Left" that Obama aide Robert Gibbs had dismissed in 2010 (before he took a more classic trip through the revolving door to lead public relations for McDonald's) had, in the ensuing decade, become more professional, more left, and more influential.[199] With few material interests on the line in election outcomes and starkly different incentives from core party actors, it had also become a driver of hollowness.

Philanthropic foundations and the nonprofits they funded operated under long-standing legal limits on financing political activity. A newfound appreciation of edgy and potentially confrontational politics during the era of Donald Trump and George Floyd pushed their funds and energy in the direction of radical-chic advocacy rather than nuts-and-bolts activism.[200] ("Donors must be willing to embrace direct-action tactics such as hunger strikes or civil disobedience," implored an executive at Arabella Advisors tasked with advising super-rich liberals on their giving.)[201] A party blob CEO and former Obama campaign aide, Dan Wagner of Civis Analytics, may have been unintentionally revealing in the way he phrased his plea for progressives to reconnect with the working class: "This is about how we frame the issues we care about for people that look nothing like us."[202]

Beyond Listlessness?

The shock of 2016 occasioned a particularly brutal round of soul-searching, finger-pointing, and grassroots revival.[203] As they called respectively for a big tent to defend democracy or a coalition that would harness leftist energy, two leading tendencies in that revival both looked to the Tea Party as exemplars while drawing different lessons. For the mostly white, female, and college-educated foot soldiers of the Resistance, the answer to Trump was a turn to practical action from the ground up. Groups like Indivisible emulated the Tea Party's attention to the leverage points in the American federal polity and the Civics 101 procedures by which to press them. Green shoots of party revival finally appeared as Resistance groups across the land began to work with and take over local parties, bringing new life to long-moribund operations through old-fashioned, face-to-face organizing.[204] Yet after the successful 2018 midterms, the Resistance faded as a distinctive force as the party's ongoing strategy and messaging assimilated its concerns over a fraying democracy.

The youth-driven left revival of the last decade, for its part, has revealed a notable disposition toward party engagement. In contrast to the protest politics in which so many of the rising leaders got their starts—1990s anti-globalization activism, the 2000 Nader campaign, and the anarchism-inflected Occupy movement of 2011—the resurgent Left signed up as Democrats without the pussyfooting that rubbed so many partisans the wrong way.[205] By their own description, they had an "inside-outside strategy—the blending of protest and electoral politics."[206] That amalgam has a long lineage in movement politics. The rising Left in the Democratic Party took it in a distinctive direction with another Tea Party emulation: the embrace of the ideological primary challenge. Though the Sanders campaign served as its spark, the factional insurgency ranged beyond his class-first themes to embrace the agendas of movements from Black Lives Matter to climate justice. The leading successes came in the House, with a cluster of newly elected members on the party's left, mostly representing urban neighborhoods filled with young adults, that called itself the Squad.[207]

But neither set of actors proved capable of meeting the central challenge that confronted the country's center-left party. Patterns of class dealignment accelerated starting in 2016. The swing toward Donald Trump among voters without college education in the Rust Belt, including plenty of loyal trade unionists, had won him the election. In 2020, that shift extended to Hispanics.[208] Democrats' difficulties connecting with non-college-educated voters' ordinary concerns reflected, among other things, a decline in the party's capacity to speak to a ground-level politics defined by "personal loyalty to family, friends, neighbors, and the local community."[209] With community civic life denuded, the virtues of accommodationism—making things work by greasing the wheels—faded in the shrill din of polarized politics, and Democrats proved unable to renew the kind of political approach that once won it working-class loyalties. If the new drop in support seemed sudden, the roots were deep: both neoliberalism and polarization militated against sustaining just that kind of politics.[210]

On the other side of the divide, survey evidence and maps of the toniest precincts pointed in the same direction: college-educated white voters moved rapidly to the Democrats.[211] The party's increasing support among well-educated professionals was an old story, back to post–New Deal dreams in the incipient McGovern coalition and the Watergate babies. (The exclusionary local politics of housing and education remained a very different matter.) And though most billionaires in the Second Gilded Age long remained quietly Republican, the fundraising circuit well showed that their ranks also included Dems aplenty, accepting somewhat higher taxes than they would pay under the GOP in exchange for what they deemed a sensible, market-friendly pragmatism. Rich Americans had decidedly more liberal preferences on abortion, gay rights, and the environment than on the role of government to help the needy and to stimulate employment. Now the Trumpian GOP repelled them, moving the affluent and the more-than-affluent alike to the Democrats.[212]

Yet worries from leftist critics notwithstanding, a more affluent base hardly crimped Democrats' redistributionist ambitions, at least so far.[213] Instead, it revealed an important divide in the politics of inequality. The Biden administration's proposals in 2021, reflecting broad party consensus, squeezed the very richest Americans, going after tax shelters and imposing myriad taxes and surcharges that hit millionaires hardest. (Proposals for a wealth tax, which attracted less support, followed the same pattern.) Amid fractal inequality, the biggest winners stood in line for the heftiest new tax bills. But Biden dared not cross a bright line: he had promised no tax increases for any filers earning less than $400,000 per year, and no leading voices in the party offered plans to the contrary. The upper reaches of the upper middle class, whose resources would be necessary to implement big universal programs, remained politically inviolable, and not even the party's leftmost voices dared to say otherwise.

Perhaps no one more purely embodied the modern Democratic Party in all its vicissitudes than Joe Biden. For half a century, he had proven happy to zig when the party was zigging and to zag when it was zagging. The Irish Catholic son of Scranton retained a certain midcentury pragmatism. The accommodationist strand still manifest in him, more so than many of his contemporaries, as a specific commitment to soothing the various blocs that made up his party. He credited his 2020 nomination victory, in throwback language, to "hard-working folks, ethnics, and Blacks."[214] Yet he took a haphazard road to victory. After limping along for months, Biden surged to presumptive nominee status when a sudden confluence of endorsers in the three days between the South Carolina primary and Super Tuesday prompted an electoral cascade.[215] In that passive lurch to victory, as much as in the sense of permeability that his campaign touted to actors with clearer goals for power, Biden offered a supremely fitting stand-in for his party.

In office, Biden and congressional leaders genuinely zagged left. Despite a mere four-vote majority in the House and a single-vote majority in the Senate, Democrats in early 2021 harbored high hopes. But with proposals for far-reaching structural reforms like admitting new states going nowhere, the party was left to thread a very thin needle—and scale back its ambitions—to corral unified party-line votes.

Substantively, Democrats aimed for transformation at a scale shocking to veterans of deficit-phobia. They sought to build a care economy with paid leave and generous childcare, in a kind of class-first feminist politics very different from anything on offer in the 1980s, and to combat global warming. The care economy proposals ultimately lacked the votes in the Senate. Krysten Sinema of Arizona, a social liberal once in the Green Party, scotched the tax increases, and Joe Manchin of West Virginia, a more traditional conservative Democrat, was skeptical of giving to the undeserving.

On climate change, the Inflation Reduction Act, passed in the summer of 2022 after seemingly endless negotiations, nicely captured the modern Democratic Party's uneasy entwining of the policy-reform and accommodationist strands. The law harkened back to the Ataris in its embrace of industrial policy—in this case on behalf of green industry—while at the same time rewarding core party team members; labor, for instance, won prevailing-wage rules and apprenticeship provisions for new clean-energy jobs.[216] Above all, the bill encapsulated the Democrats' political and policy bargains as bold big-ticket policy that avoided raising individual tax rates. Biden proved skillful in keeping his party together, but it was a tactical acumen that reflected his old accommodationist roots more than a strategic vision for the Democrats' party project.

Parties need collective capacity the most when they must set priorities together, thinking strategically about a project and the voter blocs to achieve it rather than simply looking out for every tactical advantage. Even as polarization expanded the Democrats' policy ambition, the distinctive combination of activity and incapacity that characterizes hollowness hindered their ability to solve coordination problems, set an agenda, and decide whose ox would get gored. Hopes to end the long cycle augured with the election of Ronald Reagan, to break out of the limits of fifty-fifty politics that requires eking out every vote, and to build a latter-day Rooseveltian majority remained unfulfilled in the Biden years. As the dream receded, the horizon had rarely seemed wider or the road ahead less clear.

8

Politics without Guardrails

THE REPUBLICANS SINCE 1994

ON JANUARY 15, 2021, nine days after the Capitol insurrection during the final, perfervid act of the Trump administration, Mike Lindell, CEO of MyPillow, visited the White House. The company, a manufacturer of pillows and mattress toppers, was wrapped up in the mustachioed image of its CEO, an evangelical recovered crack addict and inveterate pitch-man. "That guy is on television more than anyone I've ever seen, includ-ing me," Trump had observed in 2016. MyPillow had been booted from the Better Business Bureau for deceptive practices.[1] It was also the lead-ing advertiser on the Fox News program of Tucker Carlson, the Trumpian populist, since fired, who deemed white supremacy "a hoax."[2]

The visit was no courtesy call. Despite the best efforts of the insur-rectionists who stormed the Capitol the prior week, Joe Biden had been certified as president-elect. But Lindell still aimed to overturn the result. He had found his way into the Trump orbit, serving as co-chair for the president's reelection campaign in Minnesota and pitching administration insiders on the unproven remedy of oleander oil to defeat COVID-19 as the pandemic raged. Ever since Election Day, Lindell had been whip-ping up enthusiasm to "Stop the Steal." A photograph of his notes for the meeting revealed language suggesting that Trump invoke the Insur-rection Act, a declaration of martial law. After a short chat in the Oval Of-fice with Trump himself, and a visit upstairs with the White House counsel, Lindell pronounced himself displeased. "They are giving the president the wrong advice," he declared outside the White House before flying home to Minnesota on his private jet. Trump did not invoke the Insurrection Act and slunk off to Florida. His presidency ended five days later.[3] An episode in which the specter of democratic backsliding came with a touch of the Marx Brothers' Freedonia well captures the pathologies of a Republican Party careening toward the extreme, at once absurd and deeply dangerous.

This chapter traces the Republican Party from the Republican congressional majority that arrived in 1995 all the way through the aftermath of January 6, 2021.[4] It begins at a time of maximum ambition. Both in Congress, with Tom DeLay as its leading figure in the House, and in the Bush administration, which arrived six years later, Republicans dreamed of generational majorities, but hubris felled their hopes for electoral dominance. Fixated on juicing resentment, talk radio and cable news played an ever more outsized role in the party. Conservative media fed, and in turn benefited from the ratings garnered by, the scorched-earth strategies and bitter intraparty battles of the Tea Party and the House Freedom Caucus in the 2010s. By 2016, it took only Donald Trump's match to ignite the dumpster fire, as party hollowness begat an all-consuming form of grievance politics. Trump's performativity and grift may not have earned him his hoped-for place on Mount Rushmore, but as pure political strategy, it worked better than much of what Republicans had tried.

At the heart of hollowness lies parties' incapacity to meet public challenges. A party often described before 2016 as a well-oiled ideological machine,[5] and more often in recent years as an efficient scam,[6] in this chapter emerges instead as a shambolic, lumbering, and decidedly dangerous mess. Para-organizations with agendas of their own played ever-larger roles in what were once core functions of political parties themselves. In different ways, the Koch network, conservative media, and individual politicians all encroached on the party's turf. The formal party, for its part, expressed activists' passions more than it sought to tame and channel those passions into electoral victory. Republican incapacity became not just the absence of a common public purpose but, more ominously, the inability to control dangerous tendencies located ever more centrally inside the party.

Scholars have repeatedly documented Republicans' move rightward. Taking polarization as an essential backdrop, this chapter focuses instead on its manifestations in institutional breakdown, resentment politics, and recrudescent ethnonationalism. With intensified polarization came not ideological rigor but careening short-termism and irresponsibility. The GOP combined ruthless attention to detail when it came to gaining tactical advantage, a brazenness about extracting favors from the state, and sheer lassitude when it came to fixing public problems. In short, the polarization frame is an essential starting place, but it does not get Mike Lindell into the Oval Office.

Contrary to much commentary, the Trump years hardly occasioned the displacement of business-friendly politics by populism on the right. Since the 1970s, the pro-capital strand and the us-versus-them populist strand have braided tightly together inside the Republican Party. In the making of this "plutopopulism," long-standing patterns have intensified— not transformed.[7] The Republican establishment, epitomized in this century by the Senate Republican leader Mitch McConnell, took from the pro-capital strand a tax-cutting, deregulatory extremism of its own. And even as Republicans retreat from the maximalist attacks on the welfare state that dominated the Obama-era party, they have hardly budged on core priorities to fight taxes, regulations, and unions.[8] In our hollow era, the tradition that has disappeared from the GOP's ranks is that of practical center-right accommodationism.

The plutopopulist synthesis rests on the support of critical elements in American business. In an age when business loyalties vary tremendously by sector, Republican loyalists concentrate in what Godfrey Hodgson termed "Little Big Business"—firms dependent on low-wage labor and centered in manufacturing and extractive industries far from the global cities that prospered in the neoliberal era.[9] Elites tied into the political economy of the South and the nation's interior thus prove key.[10] Charles Koch and his network of fellow super-rich ultra-conservatives come from exactly this milieu. Resistance to taxes and regulations mingle with the same rock-'em, sock-'em style that colors the Right's battles over race, gender, and status.[11] Look at business influence with an eye less to explain discrete policy outcomes than to understand the particular character of the contemporary Republican Party, and these sectoral and geographic influences snap into place.[12]

All the forces that made Republicans so energetic in opposition led them to struggle when Republican politicians actually held the reins of power. (Judges were a different story.) Budget deficits served merely as a cudgel to raise against Democrats rather than a problem to be solved when governing, and tax policy grew into a straightforwardly partisan attempt to reward key constituencies.[13] Even under narrow unified control of government, Republicans failed in their attempts to transform programs like Social Security or to repeal the Affordable Care Act.

If continuity more than change characterizes the GOP since the critical junctures of the 1970s, the party's trajectory since the Contract with America has seen one important shift: Republicans have pursued their project for power increasingly unshackled from a vision of national majority. The Long New Right always sought to wield power wherever in the American political system offered the best opportunities at that moment. But more recently, Republicans have turned to and relied on the features of the complex American political system that frustrate popular majorities: the courts, the malapportioned Senate with its sixty-vote filibuster rule, the gerrymandered U.S. House of Representatives and state legislatures, and a politicized voting process itself. This shift has also opened space for a harder counter-majoritarianism, one whose affronts to core democratic principles lack all subtlety.[14] That variant, whose signal moment was the insurrection of January 6, 2021, steps closer to authoritarianism. It all-but-openly declares that electoral victories by the enemy do not count and countenances extreme measures to stop them. The fundamental criterion of democracy that the losers accept their losses and fight again no longer holds.[15]

Tom DeLay and the Politics of Influence

Congressional Republicans assumed their majorities in January 1995 with high hopes. In the House especially, where forty years in the minority—vastly the longest stretch of single-party control of a chamber in American history—had come to an end, Republicans aimed to overthrow all the powers of entrenched liberalism and dominate national politics. Instead, House Republicans' own dozen years at the helm saw new patterns that fused power in Washington with the political economy of resentment.

Newt Gingrich, masterful in opposition, stumbled in power as he struggled to control his restive caucus and to negotiate against a savvy Democratic president. In 1995 and 1996, Gingrich led the GOP into dramatic confrontations over the federal budget that led to extended federal shutdowns, from which Bill Clinton emerged the popular winner. Inside the caucus, roiling discontent culminated in an abortive coup in the summer of 1997. After the disappointing 1998 midterms, in which Republicans lost seats with the Clinton impeachment looming, Gingrich resigned. "For me to fall into the habits of a machine boss would be an even greater defeat than losing the speakership," Gingrich had written in a mea-culpa-cum-memoir earlier that year.[16] In fact, like machine bosses, Republicans would learn to grease the wheels. But far beyond Gingrich, the accommodationist give-and-take such bosses had perfected would prove impossible for a party weaned on the Long New Right's relentless stoking of controversy.

After Gingrich, House Republicans' attempt to set the agenda in national politics receded, first in the quiet end of the Clinton years and then for six years of executive-centered partisanship under George W. Bush. But by taking the particularism that had long defined Congress and making it explicitly partisan, they forged new ground as party actors nevertheless. The key figure in this development was Tom DeLay, the House Majority Whip from 1995 until 2003 and Majority Leader from 2003 to 2006. A pest exterminator by profession, DeLay entered politics angry at red tape promulgated by the Environmental Protection Agency and retained his passion as he rose in the ranks. He shared this bête noire with Koch Industries and many of the trade associations whose support for the GOP he courted so assiduously. DeLay hated not just the burdensome regulations but the arrogance of the nanny-state regulators. The peroration to a 2003 speech at the deregulatory Competitive Enterprise Institute (CEI) offers a nice glimpse into the DeLay worldview: "Ladies and gentlemen, your support for CEI is support for limited government. It is support for the free market. And most importantly, it is support for a steak dinner in the smoking section of your favorite restaurant."[17]

Nicknamed "the Hammer," DeLay played the inside game shrewdly, rhetorical flourishes notwithstanding. His signature initiative was the K Street Project, which pushed DC's influence peddlers, legendarily located on K Street, into the Republican fold. Seeking to revive the Democratic Party, Tony Coelho in 1981 had told lobbyists and trade associations to donate to the party in power. Now DeLay turned the tables—and upped the stakes.[18] Not only should K Street donate to Republicans, but they should hire Republicans and push Republican priorities. The work began the moment the party took control of Congress, and intensified in 2001 when a Republican president opened up doors across the administrative state.[19]

The approach worked. Sectors from accounting to pharmaceuticals that had divided their giving evenly when Democrats controlled the House shifted rightward; traditional GOP sectors like auto dealers and chemical producers became even more loyal.[20] In 2003, a Republican National Committee (RNC) official noted that thirty-three of thirty-six recently open K Street positions had gone to Republicans, and leading headhunters freely admitted that they always checked with DeLay.[21] That pipeline for former staffers eased a back-and-forth with Congress, extending, as DeLay happily acknowledged, even to the drafting of legislation.[22] For its part, the National Republican Campaign Committee graded every single PAC, sorted by industry, with special marks for giving to freshman Republicans on committees with relevant jurisdiction.[23]

Key allied interest groups served as particularly important allies. At Americans for Tax Reform, Grover Norquist, a joined-up member of the Long New Right—via Young Americans for Freedom, the College Republicans, the National Taxpayers Union, and adventures in the bush fighting communism—used his Taxpayer Protection Pledge, at once gimmicky and powerful, to enforce the orthodoxy.[24] His associates at the Club for Growth, founded in 1999 and particularly influential during the Tea Party era, took a more factional approach, backing aggressive tax cutters in primaries against incumbents who had shown too high a propensity to cut deals.[25] According to Norquist, the strategy to "starve the beast" would inevitably shrink the federal government—but it never happened.

The U.S. Chamber of Commerce, under the leadership beginning in 1997 of the canny former trucking lobbyist Tom Donahue, moved into closer alignment with Republicans. Donahue, a close ally of DeLay, candidly described the Chamber's role as a "reinsurance industry for individual industry associations," which in practice meant carrying water for unpopular industries like tobacco.[26] However tight its embrace of congressional Republicans during its 2000s heyday, the Chamber offered no vision for the pro-capital strand, just ever-more money in an ever-more-wide-open system.[27]

"Many commentators have suggested that the greatest threat to the Republican Party's majority status now is hubris. And they are right," DeLay warned in January 2005.[28] He had written his own epitaph. A Democratic district attorney in Texas indicted him on campaign finance charges stemming from redistricting in Texas.[29] (He was ultimately convicted, and then his conviction was vacated.) Meanwhile, his ally Jack Abramoff, an influential lobbyist who had known Norquist since their College Republican days, pleaded guilty in January 2006 to conspiracy, fraud, and tax evasion, as did two DeLay aides.[30] DeLay left the House in June 2006, five months before the midterms that saw Democrats retake control. Though the GOP after his departure would not rely quite so closely on the circuits of power in DC as a mechanism of exchange, DeLay's brand of smash-and-grab policymaking endured as an alluring template, not least to the Trump administration.

Bush, Rove, and the Last Majoritarian Vision

The presidency of George W. Bush tried to fuse economic, social, and patriotic conservatism together into a generation-long electoral juggernaut.[31] It was a more conscious Republican majority-building project than the helter-skelter mobilization of resentment that had motivated the Long New Right and that would return with a vengeance in the 2010s. In a June 2005 speech, Karl Rove, Bush's top political adviser, offered a sly update to William F. Buckley: "This President and today's conservative movement are shaping history, not trying to stop it."[32] But the revolution from above that Bush and Rove attempted could not contain its own contradictions.[33]

The Bush-Rove strategy emphasized the aggressive use of presidential power to build new constituencies for the Republican Party. Bush lost the popular vote in 2000. After Election Day, ruthless legal skulduggery in the drawn-out Florida recount culminated in the Supreme Court's 5–4 decision in *Bush v. Gore* that finally set the stage for Bush's inauguration. Nevertheless, Bush and Rove were undaunted as the administration fused grand party visions at home with imperial ambitions abroad.[34] The attacks of 9/11 paved the way for the invasion of Iraq, an adventure launched with flimsy intelligence and fatefully undermined by diffidence to the challenges of regime change in a faraway land.[35] The Iraq folly followed a venerable domestic political strategy of handsomely packaged gambits designed to unite Republicans while dividing and demonizing Democrats. ("From a marketing point of view, you don't introduce new products in August," White House chief of staff Andy Card said to explain the war push's fall 2002 rollout.)[36]

The most important architect of this party project was Karl Rove. A political history buff, Rove venerated Abraham Lincoln and William McKinley even as he fatefully lacked their suppleness.[37] Rove the operative's penchant for the nuts and bolts of politics could also at times evoke the 1960s-era RNC chair, Ray Bliss. But nobody would mistake Rove for an accommodationist playing small ball. "To be Rovian," he wrote in his memoir, "a campaign must first be centered on big ideas that reflect the candidate's philosophy and views."[38] That meant sharpening distinctions rather than blurring them. Even closer to the heart of the matter, it also meant dissolving any remaining barriers between campaigning and governing.

Rove cut his teeth in College Republican politics. With help from Lee Atwater, he won a not-all-on-the-up-and-up victory over Terry Dolan for the organization's presidency in 1973.[39] While Atwater took Washington by storm, Rove set up shop in Texas, carving out a niche as the state's preeminent Republican consultant as the old Tory Democrats retreated and the GOP drove toward statewide dominance. His good relations with the Bush family dated back to his College Republican days, when George H. W. Bush was RNC chair, and so Bush the younger's rise to national power proved to be Rove's as well.[40]

Amid nationwide hand-wringing over the decline of social capital, Rove realized how oases of social connection could serve as effective sites to reach voters and would-be voters. He loved to quote Lincoln's advice to Whigs in 1840 to "keep a constant watch on the doubtful voters" and "have them talked to by those in whom they have the most confidence."[41] Picking up a Reagan-era tool, the GOP applied techniques from multilevel marketing that allowed voters to reach out to their personal networks.[42] David Kuo, who led the administration's faith-based initiative, described the strategy that Rove had mapped out: "We held conference after conference in politically important states. An average of 1,500 people per conference received important information, materials, and resources. And those 1,500 people walked away stunned and amazed at how much President Bush and his staff cared about them. . . . They went back to their churches, nonprofit organizations, or places of work, and told everyone else about what they had seen and done."[43]

Rovian party-building catered to the world that the Long New Right had made.[44] In contrast to Dick Richards in 1981, Rove did not try to rein in, or assert the GOP's primacy over, the paraparty groups that largely comprised the polarized Republican Party, but instead worked directly through them. Parties in the hollow era had become vehicles for congeries of engaged activists more than mobilizers in their own right. Rove pushed to rekindle that mobilization in part by festooning the activists with goodies, so that the members of the gun clubs, churches, trade associations, and anti-tax groups would march to the polls as loyal Republicans.[45] The mobilization started from the White House and fanned out from there, both to the RNC and, via Grover Norquist's Wednesday gatherings, to leaders across the conservative firmament.

The Bush approach made policy central to politics, using conservative means to reach out to traditionally Democratic constituencies. Shaped by their experience in Texas, Bush and Rove saw that demographic change, and particularly the rise of Latinos, offered opportunities for the Republican Party.[46] The result would be what Bush called the Ownership

Society, with programs emphasizing consumer choice and individual responsibility. But in place of hard-edged welfare-state retrenchment, Bush espoused a "compassionate conservatism" that was comfortable with a robust role for state action to promote favored claimants.[47] The approach's signal success was the Medicare Modernization Act of 2003, which added a prescription-drug benefit to Medicare on terms friendly to pharmaceutical and insurance companies.[48]

In Bush's second term, it all came crashing down. The failure to privatize Social Security and the inept response to Hurricane Katrina in August 2005 stopped the Ownership Society in its tracks. Bush's short-lived Supreme Court nomination of his White House counsel Harriet Miers, along with his advocacy of comprehensive immigration reform, soured the grassroots right on the president just as the Iraq quagmire depleted Bush's overall standing with the electorate. Richard Viguerie, a figure on the outs in the Bush era, warned that "Big Government Republicans. . . . have spent more time seeking the favors of K Street lobbyists than listening to the conservatives who brought them to power."[49] An approach rooted in Washington depended on the continued benefits of electoral majorities. When that feedback cycle broke, the political approach went down with it. The slashing politics of the jugular that Bush and Rove happily wielded had a long pedigree and a secure future on the right. But the distinctively policy-minded and multicultural version of that politics, never a favorite with the base, had seen its day.

Talk Radio, Fox News, and Beyond

From the 1990s onward, conservative media peddling "political entertainment" for profit grew to take pride of place in the Republican firmament.[50] The trademarks of right-wing media—the cutting insults, the whipped-up controversies, the calls to stop both morally bankrupt liberals and insufficiently zealous Republicans—all emerged in the postwar moment. But talk radio, with Rush Limbaugh its leading figure, and then Fox News, the creation of Rupert Murdoch and Roger Ailes, served up outrage with a pizzazz their predecessors conspicuously lacked. Intensifying trends long in the making, these outlets achieved outsize influence within a hollowed-out GOP during the years in which Bush-era conversative disaffection gave way first to the Tea Party mobilization and then to the relentlessly style-over-substance politics of the Trump era.

Conservative media found its place in the sun precisely because the hollow GOP ceded its own. Had the Republican Party somehow taken a different path as the New Deal order crumbled, then the media would have had less space to peddle outrage. A powerful formal party and networks tightly connected to its leading politicians and interest groups could have performed their roles in selecting candidates and developing policy. A cordon sanitaire could have protected against infiltration from the wilder fringes. Conservative media would have been included in the extended party network—the latest iteration of a story as old as American politics—but would hardly be the definers of the party brand or the enforcers of loyalty to it.

In the 1990s, talk radio was king, and its leading practitioner was Rush Hudson Limbaugh III. Fusing entertainment and politics, Limbaugh puckishly lambasted liberals' errors and hypocrisies as fans, who called themselves "Dittoheads," nodded in approval. A college dropout hailing from a prominent Republican family in Cape Girardeau, Missouri, Limbaugh had bounced around jobs in radio, honed his politics at a station in Sacramento, and made a name for himself as an emcee at roasts for conservative personalities, including Oliver North and Paul Weyrich.[51] He went national, syndicated from New York, in 1988. While the Federal Communications Commission's Fairness Doctrine was always an unenforceable paper tiger, its 1987 repeal, after a generation of conservative agitation, gave stations running room to air a figure like Limbaugh on the AM band.[52]

Limbaugh offered an easy-on-the-ears take on right-wing verities, laced with a bawdy male humor that went for the jugular.[53] Feminists ("feminazis") came in for particular opprobrium. One of his "35 Undeniable Truths of Life" held that "feminism was established as to allow unattractive women easier access to the mainstream of society." Another, even closer to the heart of the Limbaugh appeal, was that "women should not be allowed on a jury if the defendant is a stud."[54] Limbaugh's instinct for scandal and hypocrisy made Bill Clinton his ideal target. When Republican House freshmen assembled in December 1994, they named Limbaugh an honorary member of their class.[55]

In the years that followed, right-wing media's influence proved a double-edged sword in campaigning and a clear hindrance in governing.[56] Limbaugh and a growing brand of imitators mobilized the base and offered GOP politicians a sympathetic microphone. But outrage that played so well on the air often failed to land outside the bubble. Conflict intensified in the 2000s as Limbaugh and his peers hunted for RINOs (Republicans in Name Only) insufficiently committed to the fight. In contrast to the patronage available to the nineteenth-century party press, conservative media gained nothing from the perquisites of office. And so an industry that reveled in attack offered little succor in the messy trade-offs of lawmaking. It was outrage that kept ratings high and dollars flowing.

Limbaugh, who relocated to Palm Beach in 1997, took a two-cheers posture toward his neighbor, Donald Trump. A master of "anti-anti" excoriation, Limbaugh understood the Trump appeal long before many other movement conservatives. His opening monologue on January 20, 2016, explicitly invoked no less than Sam Francis as it homed in on the key element. It was not conservativism that now held Republicans together: "Right now the glue is an absolute opposition to the Democrat Party, to the American left, to the worldwide left, and everything they have done and want to continue doing."[57]

Nevertheless, Limbaugh hewed close to the pre-Trump orthodoxy. The Heritage Foundation had paid him $9.5 million for a five-year sponsorship deal ending in 2014.[58] Though Limbaugh avoided even a hint of Never Trump apostasy—and, terminally ill with cancer, received a Presidential Medal of Freedom in 2020 as a thank-you—he always kept a certain distance. By 2018, *Talkers*, a trade magazine, had put Trump confidant Sean Hannity above Limbaugh at the top of its influence list.[59] Talk radio continued to attract vast audiences; Hannity's fifteen million radio listeners in 2021 dwarfed his three million viewers on Fox News.[60] But as listeners aged and the agenda moved elsewhere, Limbaugh's death in 2021, at seventy, seemed to mark the end of an era. The politics of outrage had reached far beyond the medium that had served as its loudest voice.

Like talk radio, Fox News, which first aired in 1996, came to hold a place in Republican politics that had no equivalent on the Democratic side. Fox News Channel was a partnership between Rupert Murdoch, who ran its parent company, News Corporation, and Roger Ailes, a former Nixon PR man and political consultant who served as the channel's chief from its founding until his departure in 2016 amid myriad allegations of sexual harassment.[61] Starting with its early slogan, "Fair and balanced," Fox poked fun at elite notions of media propriety that Murdoch had long mocked.

For more than half a century and across various media, Murdoch propagated a mix of politics and entertainment derived from the oft-sensational appeals to working-class tastes in the tabloid newspapers he loved. He was never a proper party man, even as his political leanings marched rightward. "I think you prostitute your newspapers once you start joining political parties," he told an interviewer in 1976.[62] He kept up relations with figures on the center-left inclined to reward him for favors rendered—Ed Koch, Bill Clinton, Tony Blair—and voted for Ross Perot in 1992.[63] The signature Murdoch appeal was rooted not in party but in social identity: standing on readers' and viewers' sides against their foes in the cultural elite.

Fueled by debt, the Murdoch empire in print and on television extended from his native Australia to the United Kingdom, where he cheered for Margaret Thatcher and broke the printers' unions, and his adopted United States.[64] In 1976, he made his first major foray into American media by buying the New York Post, then a down-at-the-heels tabloid with a middle-class Jewish readership and liberal politics, and dragging the paper rightward. Eighty Post reporters signed a protest note against the paper's new direction. "It's our newspaper, too," the union shop steward remonstrated. "When you pay the losses, you can say it's your paper too," Murdoch replied. "It's my newspaper. You just work here, and don't you forget it."[65]

Conservatives had dreamed for decades of a television network to call their own. Ailes had participated in an ill-fated effort, the Coors-funded

TVN, in the 1970s. But as cable channels proliferated, interest intensified again in the early 1990s. Paul Weyrich's National Empowerment
Television quickly flopped; his preternatural gifts at organizing did not
extend to making must-watch TV.[66] Fox News was different. It would
rely on advertising—and the patient capital of News Corporation and
its dominant patriarch—rather than on philanthropists' changing
whims.[67] And it was designed foremost *as television*. "The whole day at
Fox is cast by Roger," said Megyn Kelly, an anchor who would later ac-
cuse Ailes of harassment. "There are beautiful blondes, high school
quarterbacks, brainiacs, and the entire spectrum."[68]

Fox's style-as-substance grievance politics and clearly defined villains
borrowed from the Long New Right playbook.[69] The headlines blaring at
the bottom of the screen and, more important, the framing of right-wing
politics as the everyman's pushback against a liberal elite aped tabloid
newspapers.[70] The constant barrage of talk, centered around the host's
carefully constructed persona, drew from soft-focus TV newsmagazines
and talk radio. Sean Hannity and Bill O'Reilly (the network's biggest star
until his departure in 2017 following his own long pattern of sexual harassment) both hailed from the white Irish Catholic suburbs of New York in
Murdoch's sights when he first purchased the *New York Post*.[71]

Fox News helped Republicans win votes.[72] It also appropriated traditional party functions. Ron Johnson of Wisconsin, an executive at a
family-controlled plastics manufacturer, launched his successful 2010
run for Senate after hearing Dick Morris on Fox News describing the
incumbent as vulnerable.[73] Sharron Angle of Nevada, an unsuccessful
candidate the same year, bluntly explained that, unlike other media outlets, Fox News let her flog her website and encourage donations.[74] The
conveyor belt worked in the other direction too, as GOP officials, happily piling on to the latest scandal, seemed to be auditioning for their
next gigs more than using the media to pursue their agendas in power.

Yet for all the power often ascribed to Murdoch and his empire, it
could not buck hard against what its viewers wanted—and what they
wanted was often harder stuff than the network preferred to deliver. In
the summer of 2015, Fox News made its own halting attempts to arrest
the Trump surge through aggressive questioning at debates—and utterly

failed.[75] In the aftermath of the 2020 election, with election conspiracies rampant on the right, Fox indulged its viewers with what it knew to be falsehoods. "Our viewers are good people and they believe it," Tucker Carlson explained in a private text message, later revealed to the world through a lawsuit against the network that would yield one of the largest defamation settlements in American history.[76] For Murdoch, it was all part of doing business.[77] "It's not red or blue, it's green," he explained in his deposition for that same case.[78] A for-profit media firm, whatever its political convictions, had incentives distinct from any party. But like the Republican Party, conservative media often flailed as it sought to channel the all-consuming politics of conspiracy and gonzo.

The Tea Party

The Tea Party—the sprawling, factional mobilization from the right that emerged in the wake of Barack Obama's election in 2008—recast a Republican Party about whose qualities *as a party* it remained profoundly ambivalent.[79] Against the immediate backdrop of the Bush years, the shift was stark. Seen in the longer sweep of the Right's engagement with the populist strand, however, the Tea Party seems altogether more familiar, with its fusion of elite and grassroots protest and of social and economic concerns, all refracted through the prism of race. The Tea Party, and not the party-centered synthesis of the Bush era, represents the continuation of the long-term trajectory on the right.[80]

The Tea Party's label and origin story trace back to an on-air monologue from Rick Santelli, an editor at the business channel CNBC, on February 15, 2009. Santelli called for a Chicago Tea Party to protest against homeowners who had unjustly received money from federal bailouts. In short order, the movement gathered steam. Dramatic confrontations at town hall meetings with Democratic members of Congress over healthcare reform served as rallying points. "You need to rock-the-boat early in the Rep's presentation," advised a widely circulated guide. "Watch for an opportunity to yell out and challenge the Rep's statements."[81]

To Tea Partiers, the vast majority of them older and white, their country seemed to be slipping away. Sharpening the lines between "us" and "them," with elites in both parties always threatening to sell "us" out, they drew deeply from the populist strand in casting opponents as fundamental threats to authentic American values.[82] In turn, Tea Partiers separated their own justified reliance on programs such as Medicare and Social Security from the dangerous dependence of others, especially Blacks, immigrants, and younger cohorts, who had cut the line and broken the rules.[83]

The Tea Party also represented an intraparty reckoning with the Bush legacy that had not taken place in the 2008 cycle. John McCain, the old soldier, won an ill-defined nominating contest that year, steadfastly refused to engage in personal attacks against Barack Obama, and lost badly in November. For the future of the party, he was the less important member of the ticket. McCain picked as his running mate Sarah Palin, the first-term governor of Alaska and a neophyte on the national scene.[84] More than any figure up to that moment, Palin packaged policy-light grievance politics in a way that insouciantly disregarded conventional gatekeeping, with the "lamestream media" a favorite target.[85] After resigning as governor in 2009, she rallied support for Tea Party favorites in contested primaries and appeared regularly on Fox News. Though she soon receded in prominence, Palin marked a genuine shift, one accentuating the reckless rather than the ruthlessly effective side of the Long New Right project.[86]

Tea Partiers practiced the high-octane politics of confrontation that was their inheritance. They depicted Barack Obama as a dangerously un-American figure, shaped by the Third World revolutionary politics that New Left radicals found alluring.[87] At the crude end, "Birtherism," impugning Obama's American citizenship, was a popular trope in Tea Party circles even as conservative elites steered clear.[88] Information and innuendo spread online, whether via Facebook groups through which local Tea Party groups organized, blogs like *RedState*, or forums hosted by national Tea Party federations. Talk radio amplified Tea Party themes; it was an even stronger booster than Fox News. (The conspiracist Glenn Beck, who occupied the 5:00 P.M. slot on Fox, was an exception to that softer line.)[89] James O'Keefe, a veteran of ten trainings at Morton Blackwell's Leadership Institute, produced often-deceptive undercover documentary videos that became staples of the 2010s-era Right.[90]

Institutionally, the Tea Party remained diffuse. It never formed a classic federated membership structure. Instead, state and local groups organized on their own, variously associated with broadly similar national groups—FreedomWorks, Tea Party Express, Tea Party Nation, Tea Party Patriots—that jostled for resources and pride of place.[91] The Koch political operation, centered around Americans for Prosperity (AFP), ramped up at the same time as the Tea Party and supported many of the same candidates. AFP affiliates worked closely with state and local Tea Party groups. But the Kochs kept their distance from the Tea Party label, not least owing to the bad blood between them and Dick Armey of FreedomWorks. And as policy, the drastic cutbacks in Medicare and Social Security favored by the Koch operation found less support among ordinary Tea Partiers.[92]

The Tea Party took the same view of parties espoused by New Right congressman Bob Bauman in 1975: "They are no more than instruments." In a polarized political system, that insight cut differently. Conservative insurgents in the 1970s hoped to orchestrate ad hoc coalitions that would supplant political parties altogether. They viewed primary battles as only one venue among many in the struggle for political influence. By the late 2000s, with party sorting far advanced, the action had shifted entirely inside the GOP. Richard Viguerie, back in his element after decades relegated to the wilderness, summed up the new insurgents' principal insight for achieving influence: "It's the primaries, stupid!"[93] For the Tea Party, nomination fights served as the vortex for determining party priorities, where true conservatives could vanquish squishy RINOs and steer the ship rightward.

Primary challenges from the extremes risk losing seats in November. For Tea Partiers uninterested in the messy work of governing, it was a risk well worth taking. South Carolina senator Jim DeMint, a Tea Party favorite, liked to say that he'd prefer thirty conservative Republicans in the Senate to sixty moderate ones.[94] A primary challenge from the right hung as the sword of Damocles over any elected official who dared to deviate from Tea Partiers' preferences. Amid nationalized politics, victory even in a single primary for Congress could send shock waves. A "Declaration of Tea Party Independence," drafted at a gathering in February 2010, made the case:

> We reject RINO money; we reject RINO "advice"; we reject RINO "professional experience"; we reject RINO "progressivism"; we reject RINO support of Big Government; we reject RINO back room deal making; we reject RINO pork spending; we reject false RINO professions of Conservative views and we reject the RINO's statist subversion of the principles of small government for which the Republican Party is supposed to stand.[95]

In the House of Representatives, Tea Party energy powered the 2010 midterm wave that restored Republicans to the majority. In the Senate, the record was more mixed. In both 2010 and 2012, controversial candidates with penchants for gaffes lost winnable seats.

With all eyes on Republican primaries, the Tea Party largely abandoned the project to assemble a workable conservative majority that would durably supplant the New Deal coalition. The goal instead was to build a pure base from which to obstruct opponents—Obama and his minions and RINOs alike—and win power when they inevitably stumbled. And there the Tea Party more or less stopped. It had political entrepreneurs and tacticians aplenty. But the higher-level strategy to identify the voter blocs, policy programs, and organizational forms that would build long-term party dominance was conspicuous by its absence.

In 2013, Theda Skocpol and Vanessa Williamson wrote that the Tea Party aimed to remake the Republican Party "into a much more uncompromising and ideologically principled force."[96] For Tea Partiers in 2009 and 2010, those two qualities seemed to fit together hand in glove. With time, it was the former characteristic—the rejection of parties' understanding that their visions are necessarily partial—rather than the latter—the down-the-line commitment to conservative bona fides—that marked the Tea Party's lasting legacy. The same restive base, alert to apostasy, would soon aim its fire at politicians they deemed insufficiently Trumpian.

The Kochtopus and the Political Party

In linked but distinct processes, the vacuum at the top of the GOP and the rage at Barack Obama and his administration that propelled the Tea Party also pushed forward the strongest para-organization on the right. Charles Koch, CEO since 1967 of the nation's largest privately held corporation, Koch Industries, Inc., never sought party office. Deep in his ninth decade, he still claimed to be nonpartisan. Yet he was a party actor all the same, at once a fierce ideologue and an assiduous institution-builder. The interlocking entities of the "Kochtopus" yoked the politics of the Long New Right and the carbon economy together with the priorities of the new super-rich and worked through para-organizations that encroached on the core terrain of political parties. The Koch brand of political action, exploiting loose campaign finance rules on independent expenditures, reflects the era of hollow parties. The substantive claim that the lessons of business apply directly to politics is the transhistorical essence of the pro-capital strand. "Capital becomes powerful when it is transformed by ideas," Koch declared in 2016.[97] Whether, in the classic puzzle, his actions ultimately sprang from interests or ideas, he had plenty of both, and they pointed in the same direction.[98]

Koch Industries grew to become the biggest little big business of them all, with its family ownership, deep roots in Wichita, and profits reinvested in growth rather than sloughed off to shareholders. Charles Koch's father, Fred, was a wildcatter who developed new techniques for refining oil, which he deployed in Soviet Russia and Nazi Germany. He was also a prominent member of the John Birch Society. On his death in 1967, his second son, Charles, became CEO of the Rock Island Oil & Refining Company, soon renamed Koch Industries. After bitter infighting among the four Koch brothers, Charles and his younger brother, David—more comfortable in the public limelight but far less influential—assumed control. The key juncture came when Koch Industries took full control over the Pine Bend refinery in Rosemount, Minnesota, and then beat back a strike in 1973 from the militant Oil, Chemical and Atomic Workers Union.[99]

For decades, Charles Koch funded right-libertarian causes with an emphasis on institution-building to propagate ideas. His critique of federal power, including over civil rights, was far more sweeping than most of the other calls to arms during the 1970s business mobilization. As a 1974 speech declared, "We have confiscatory taxation, wage and price controls, commodity allocation programs, trade barriers, restrictions on foreign investments, so-called equal opportunity requirements, safety and health regulations, land use controls, licensing laws, outright government ownership of businesses and industries, and many more interventions. No advocate of free enterprise should confuse all of this with a free, capitalistic economy!"[100]

Koch Industries had battled with the Environmental Protection Agency for decades and sprang into action in 1993 when the Clinton administration proposed an energy tax.[101] In the next Democratic administration, regulation of carbon prices via a cap-and-trade system—the centerpiece of the Obama climate agenda—directly threatened the core Koch businesses, starting with the Pine Bend refinery and rippling through the company.[102] Through AFP, the Koch operation mobilized to stop the plan, using a "No Climate Tax" variant on Grover Norquist's pledge. It worked; after passage in the House, proponents failed to round up the necessary sixty votes to close debate in the Senate.

To leverage its impact, beginning in 2003 the Kochtopus invited allies to help fund its work through donor summits, with a minimum contribution of $100,000 to get in the door. The model—assembling a roomful of donors together with politicians and a few thought leaders for off-the-record talk in a resort-hotel ballroom—borrowed directly from the Council for National Policy, the exclusive Christian Right–linked club started in 1981. But the Seminar Network, as the confabs were called, came with a substantially higher price tag, since the goal was to plow donors' money into Koch causes, not just to pay the group's bills.[103] While more than a third of Koch seminar attendees hailed from the burgeoning FIRE (finance, insurance, real estate) sector, more than 40 percent came from the traditional mining and manufacturing sectors, with their long-standing hostility to taxes, unions, and regulations.[104] Many of their businesses also remained under family control.[105] Beyond the boldest-face names came row after row of business figures from red and purple states unlikely to make headlines in the national press. "I'm proud to be affiliated with the group because it's more about principles," said a metal fabricator from Wisconsin.[106]

The bundled pledges from the summits then moved into various groups under Koch control, which collectively served to re-create the political party under its own roof. Investigative journalists kept busy unraveling the sprawling operations with their anodyne names—American Energy Alliance, Center to Protect Patient Rights, State Policy Network—along with the legal arrangements behind them. But the broader story was straightforward. The Kochtopus would define issues, pick its favored candidates up and down the ballot, and reach out to voters and influencers, both for direct electioneering and for longer-term work to reshape the political terrain.[107] In the past, outside groups had undertaken each of these functions individually. Now a single umbrella actor performed *all* of them. AFP state directors—the key nodes in coordinating various state-level activities—often cycled through jobs that did fundamentally similar work, whether they found themselves employed by AFP, other conservative groups, candidate campaigns, elected officeholders, or the formal Republican Party.[108].

Resentment Policymaking in the 2010s

The influence of the Tea Party and Kochtopus was long-lasting. Though parties have always rewarded favored claimants and punished disfavored ones, they have rarely been as blunt as contemporary Republicans in foregrounding their intention to restructure power relations rather than create resonant loyalties. In Congress, members with Tea Party links, many from deep-red districts, wanted obstruction—and confounded one party leader after another. The first to confront the restive element was John Boehner. Though no moderate, Boehner, more than any other post-1994 Republican leader, had a dealmaking streak in the mold of his fellow Ohioan Ray Bliss. But once he became Speaker in 2011, Boehner found it hard to control his caucus.

In January 2015, the right-wing dissidents in the House of Representatives coalesced as the House Freedom Caucus, an invitation-only grouping that would vote as a bloc to maximize its influence. To an anonymous House aide, it was "the craziest of the crazy."[109] The Freedom Caucus took advantage of narrow majorities to try to force the Republican caucus to adopt hard-right positions even if it meant defeat—or forcing the Speaker to negotiate with Democrats rather than his own rank and file.[110] As a result, the caucus repeatedly pursued the anomalous tactic of obstructing action supported by the majority of the majority while shifting the eventual outcomes *leftward*.[111] This careening quality, maximizing tactical fights with little sense of strategic direction, proved impossible for leaders either to accommodate or, eventually, to survive.

In a 2007 article, journalist Fred Barnes dubbed three rising stars pushing a more doctrinaire conservatism—Eric Cantor of Virginia, Paul Ryan of Wisconsin, and Kevin McCarthy of California—the Young Guns.[112] They positioned themselves to Boehner's right and sought to ride the Tea Party wave. But they found themselves in stormy seas.[113] Cantor, the majority leader, shockingly lost his primary in 2014 to Dave Brat, a political neophyte hitting Cantor hard on immigration. After Boehner, facing a rebellion from the Freedom Caucus, resigned the speakership the following year, Ryan succeeded him. But he, too, struggled with coalition management, both inside his caucus and with Donald Trump, and declined to run for reelection in 2018. Then McCarthy, always the most thoroughly tactical of the Young Guns, had his turn. After initially denouncing the insurrection of January 6, 2021, he soon joined his colleagues in stopping a full investigation. Later, after Republicans narrowly recaptured the House in 2022, the typically routine process to elect a Speaker turned into a weeklong fifteen-ballot saga before McCarthy finally prevailed. Members of the Freedom Caucus extracted their pound of flesh, including rule changes that, among other things, made it easier to trigger a future removal vote.[114] His victory relied on the support of figures such as Marjorie Taylor Greene, previously best known as a fringe adherent of the QAnon conspiracy.[115] After just nine months, McCarthy's rickety Speakership would collapse.

Commitment to all-out grievance politics, not ideology, divided the hard-right faction and leadership, with right-wing media playing a central instigative role in each of the battles.[116] "I knew the crazies in my Conference," Boehner wrote in his memoir. "There was no talking to them. They were being urged on by the talk radio crowd and the cable news know-nothings."[117] His colleagues nicknamed Dave Brat "Bratbart" because he cared so much about his standing at the right-wing site Breitbart.[118]

The old style of Republican policymaking no longer captivated the Republican imagination. One loser was the U.S. Chamber of Commerce, in the Bush-DeLay era the essential DC GOP player. Its buttoned-up approach, focus on free trade, support for immigration reform, and dovish stand toward China put it out of sync with new priorities.[119] "The Chamber left the party a long time ago," said McCarthy in 2022, dismissing leading corporations' "woke" tendencies.[120] But the Chamber had hardly gone soft; it had just shifted venues. In the increasingly friendly confines of the federal courts, it pushed legal arguments, many of them with provenance back to the pre–New Deal *Lochner* era, to defang both the administrative state and organized labor.[121]

The most important bill of the 2010s, the Tax Cuts and Jobs Act of 2017, united the Republican Party in telling fashion. It was policy, all right, but policy from a party whose preeminent goal was sticking it to the libs—and it offered few gestures to those aspiring to the opportunity society. The bill began as a rather technocratic tax reform, but as it edged closer to passage, the politics came to the fore. It rewarded business, permanently slashing the corporate tax rate from 35 to 20 percent while offering incentives for the rich to fiddle around with corporate form in order to avoid paying taxes. The pain went to the upper middle class in blue states, core Trump opponents, who faced harsh new limits on the deductibility of state and local taxes.

Most importantly, the politics of little big business—merging pro-capital and populist commitments—flourished in the states after the critical 2010 midterms, as Republican state legislative majorities slashed taxes, regulations—*and* access to abortion. Knit together by the American Legislative Exchange Council, a business consortium, and the

Koch-linked State Policy Network and Americans for Prosperity, conservatives' shared strategies focused above all on the distribution of power.[122] That meant weakening opponents, especially public employees and their unions, and rewriting the rules of the game itself, including the selection of judges, the drawing of districts, and the regulation of voting.[123] In North Carolina, Art Pope, the megadonor mastermind of the state's right turn, ran a privately held regional discount-store conglomerate that his father had founded; he was also a board member of AFP.[124] In Wisconsin, the strategy sprang from the Lynde and Harry Bradley Foundation, a long-standing conservative funder formed out of an industrial-parts fortune in Milwaukee. (Harry Bradley was a Bircher.) A decade after it bankrolled the campaign to pass Act 10—Wisconsin's 2011 law drastically curtailing the state's public employee unions—Bradley became the leading funder for groups seeking to tighten state election laws across the country.[125]

Donald Trump and the Republican Party

As he stamped personal fealty to himself as the sine qua non of Republican loyalty, Donald Trump pushed the GOP toward the personalism that marks right-populism the world over. In the words of his son-in law and political adviser Jared Kushner, Trump "did a full hostile takeover of the Republican Party."[126] The corporate raider's metaphor is accurate, for rather than reflecting a victory of one well-defined party faction over another, Trump beat *all* the established factions inside the party in 2016.[127] Nevertheless, as this book labors to demonstrate, he emerged from long-standing American currents, most importantly the mobilization of resentment in the Long New Right.

The Trump victory in the 2016 Republican primary was both a genuine shock and a culmination of the GOP's hollowing. A figure straight out of the populist strand, never before elected to office and hardly a loyalist to the party whose banner he carried, easily bested a field of rivals with impeccable Republican credentials.[128] Repeatedly, in the thirteen months from Trump's ride down the escalator at Trump Tower announcing his candidacy to his stage-managed nomination at the

Republican convention in Cleveland, party actors who wanted to stop Trump failed to go beyond vague signaling, put aside immediate squabbles, and unite behind an alternative.[129] The Republicans who might have banded together to stop Trump instead came in dribs and drabs to offer their support.[130]

For models of political parties that emphasize nomination and coordination, the events of 2016 proved particularly climactic. Through informal coordination, leading party actors had largely managed to tame the post-reform presidential nominating system. Trump put an end to all that, laying bare the plebiscitarian tendencies that denied party leaders' legitimate role in the nomination process. But to blame the reforms that followed McGovern-Fraser for the Trump nomination is to mistake form for substance. Trump emerged from tendencies that those very Republican leaders themselves had long indulged, and forces that they themselves had imagined they could control.

Trump instinctively identified and exploited the gap between Republican elites and the Republican voters such elites could not comprehend. (The week before Trump's victory in the New Hampshire primary, John Sununu, a former governor and a party insider for decades, admitted that he and his wife knew no Trump voters whatsoever except for a neighbor down the street.)[131] Trump's rise came at a moment when policy tenets long dear to the pro-capital strand, as epitomized by the likes of Paul Ryan, seemed to occupy the programmatic forefront. The post-election "autopsy" released by the RNC in 2013 had suggested rebranding the Grand Old Party as the "Growth and Opportunity Party."[132] Trump took a different tack. His nomination campaign doubled down on the virulent politics of in-group identity while jettisoning rhetorical or substantive fealty to the most electorally noxious pieces of the conservative catechism, seen above all in forswearing cuts to Medicare and Social Security.

Trump had cut his teeth and made his name amid northern white-ethnic anger at liberalism, forged in the 1970s crucible of outer-boroughs New York. Through his lawyer, former Joseph McCarthy aide Roy Cohn, Trump in 1979 met his longest-serving political advisor, the flamboyant New Right operative Roger Stone.[133] Trump's zero-sum view of politics and human affairs resonated deeply with the Long New Right, and he won by making its long-standing critique, calling out the pieties of a Republican Party too afraid to tell it like it is.[134] Months before her death, Phyllis Schlafly applied the exact same logic she had used for more than half a century when she issued her final presidential primary endorsement. Trump, she said, "is the only hope to defeat the Kingmakers. Because everybody else will fall in line."[135] Another Long New Right player highlighted both the politics of attack at Trump's core and the "anti-anti" logic so long deployed on the right to justify support for dangerous actors. "Trump is not essentially a conservative," Newt Gingrich explained in 2018. "Trump is an anti-liberal. They're not the same phenomenon. But he may be the most effective uprooter of liberalism in my lifetime."[136]

Notwithstanding such deep continuities, Trump spoke in an idiom new to American politics when, having conjured up a nightmare scenario of a nation plunged into chaos and decline, he declared to the 2016 Republican National Convention, "I alone can fix it." The Long New Right had always been institutionally plastic and, in conflicts like Iran-Contra, found little wrong with the freewheeling exercise of executive power. (With Democrats in the White House, of course, the valence shifted.) But its movement culture had tended away from hero-worship, and its longstanding focus on an out-of-touch elite, the stock-in-trade of the populist strand in party politics, did not sync directly with the calls for executive leadership that traced back to the Progressives. With Trump, populism and presidentialism converged, and the United States found its own version of a politics that has manifested itself, in various guises, across the globe.

In such a politics, the leader's legitimacy is rooted in an essential connection with supporters among the people, whom the leader conjures up and for whom the leader alone may speak.[137] Claimants then seek a direct line to the leader and his family, with the spoils flowing through their pockets rather than those of the party organization.[138] Such a neopatrimonial model not only supplants the party as the central principal of political action, as had the Long New Right's push for partisan majority, but vitiates the very space between leaders and ordinary citizens where parties dwell.

Donald Trump's control over the Republican Party was simultaneously total and thin. In one light, the party had transformed into a personal vehicle for Trump's vendettas and fantasies. In another light, the Trump effect was nothing more than smoke and sizzle for a party whose commitments to tax cuts and deregulation remained unchanged. Both stories are true, because Trump demanded so much and yet so little simultaneously.

Presidents since the Gilded Age have quickly seized control over the national party committee. And ever since Eisenhower, Republican presidents have been party builders. Trump followed the pattern—but took it in his own direction.[139] Presidents' political operations long applied the lessons of small-party politics, tamping down controversies and calming fragile egos. By contrast, Trump's interventions in primaries and state party battles promoted figures with a talent for showmanship and, above all, relentless praise for Donald Trump. In the 2018 Florida gubernatorial race, to take one fateful example, Trump endorsed Ron DeSantis, a three-term House member who appeared on Fox News no less than ninety-three times over the course of a year, over the front-runner Adam Putnam, a career politician who warned, "You cannot run Florida from an out-of-state television studio."[140]

For state parties, pressures from above and below pointed in the same direction. Across the country, state organizations mimicked the national party's performative hijinks around culture-war flash points rather than devoting themselves to nuts-and-bolts work in their states.[141] The Trump political team intervened aggressively to find sympathetic chairs who would then promulgate friendly delegate-selection plans for the national convention in 2020.[142] In five states, the 2020 primary was canceled entirely. As that top-down strategy empowered figures in touch with the wilder sentiments at the grassroots, the Right's conspiracism and fixation on high-wattage controversies became ascendant within the formal GOP.[143] All too typically, conspiracy theorist Kelli Ward, having just presided over multiple electoral losses in 2020, won reelection as chair of the Arizona Republican Party at the same January 2021 meeting that passed resolutions censuring Cindy McCain (for endorsing Joe Biden) and the sitting Republican governor (for his pandemic policies)—as well as a resolution standing "firm on the principles of only two genders."[144] It was also of a piece with the diminished role of state parties themselves in the hollow era, valuable now only as custodians of a ballot line and venues to make headlines rather than as sites to hash out partisan priorities.

Trump the lifelong salesman also pushed the limits of the Right's long-standing tendencies toward hucksterism. Under the direction of the for-profit fundraising platform WinRed, Trump's 2020 reelection campaign raked in cash by automatically signing up unsuspecting online contributors for recurring payments, which could only be discontinued manually in a box buried under fine print.[145] Trump-controlled PACs, through relentless appeals to stolen-election conspiracy theories, went on to raise $81 million in the first six months *after* his defeat in November 2020.[146] After a borrowed private jet had to make an emergency landing in 2022, Trump's Save America PAC asked donors to chip in for a "BRAND NEW Trump Force One."[147]

But if domination characterized Trump's approach to the party organization and over-the-top antics his approach to Republican style, the plutopopulist bargain continued to define the party's agenda in power. With the restrictionist turn on trade and immigration a notable exception, Trump largely acceded to long-standing Republican priorities while catering to the Republican base. Even as educated voters continued to shift toward the Democrats, the long-predicted business rebellion against populism again failed to materialize. The Trump administration worked with the Federalist Society to confirm three Supreme Court justices—and as many circuit judges as Obama had in half the time. As governance, the Trump era accomplished little beyond those judges, aggressive deregulation, and the regressive Tax Cuts and Jobs Act of 2017.

That record was more than enough for many donors who had held back in 2016. A fracking executive at a fall 2017 Koch gathering explained that the tax bill "is the crux issue. If you give someone the leadership baton, you expect them to get something done."[148] Alongside such returning players came new, hard-right funders, happy with the party's substantive direction. "When Trump became the nominee, a lot of the

Bush, Romney, and McCain donors simply threw up their hands and left the party," a party strategist told the *Financial Times*, "and a lot of donors who weren't previously engaged stepped up to fill the vacuum."[149] If private equity was one new source of giving, many figures like Richard and Liz Uihlein, hard-right billionaires who parlayed a beer inheritance into a fortune from packaging, followed a more familiar pattern.[150] Leading para-organizations that once served to push the GOP rightward, including the Koch network and the Club for Growth, now stood as defenders of economic conservatism against attempts at populist apostasy.[151] In the modern GOP, the populist and pro-capital strands remained delicately but tightly entwined.

For leading Republicans hoping to stay in Trump's and in turn his supporters' good graces, the trick was fulsome personal support for the president whenever possible, and feigned ignorance of his transgressions when necessary. The formidable anti-anti politics of elite polarization aided the effort. Ben Shapiro, a fast-talking pundit popular with the Kochtopus, justified his vote for Trump in 2020 by saying that Democrats had "lost their fucking minds."[152] The idea, said Senator Lindsey Graham of South Carolina, an early Trump opponent who became a regular golf partner and confidant, was to "harness the magic" of a man he described as a cross of Jesse Helms, Ronald Reagan, and P. T. Barnum.[153]

The bomb throwers in the House Freedom Caucus became Donald Trump's most ardent congressional backers. In the 2016 primaries, members mostly endorsed Ted Cruz and suggested they would defend conservative orthodoxy against a deviationist White House.[154] In short order, however, the group refashioned itself, pushing back against those like Ryan who wanted to sand down Trump's rough edges. The last two White House chiefs of staff under Trump, Mick Mulvaney and Mark Meadows, both came from the Freedom Caucus. In the House, the group's prominent newcomers—Matt Gaetz of Florida, Lauren Boebert of Colorado, Marjorie Taylor Greene of Georgia—presented themselves as controversy-seeking media figures first and legislators passing bills second.

In 2020, the Republican Party used the coronavirus pandemic—about which Trump was otherwise lethally blasé—as an excuse not to write a party platform at all. Instead, the convention passed a resolution that carried over the 2016 platform, dismissed as "political rhetoric" the very institution of party platforms (which the party had adopted without fail every four years since 1856), bashed the media, and proclaimed that "the RNC enthusiastically supports President Trump."[155] It was the perfect marker for both the personalism and the hollowness of the Trump-era GOP. The party, as a party, offered nothing besides praise for its leader.[156]

The Voting Wars, January 6, and Beyond

On January 6, 2021, insurrectionists stormed the U.S. Capitol, forcing both the House and Senate to flee their chambers and disrupting for hours the counting of electoral votes that certified Joe Biden as president-elect. When proceedings resumed, 138 members of the House and 7 members of the Senate, Republicans all, voted to object to certifying election results from Pennsylvania. It was the culmination of two months' effort by Trump and his supporters to "Stop the Steal." The attempts to contaminate election administration—whether by failing to count the votes, having state legislatures unilaterally declare a winner, or allowing Congress to take certification into its own hands—all failed. In the face of pressure to derail the count, Mike Pence did his duty as vice president. But the pin was out of the hand grenade.[157] Stop the Steal's mixture of showmanship and ruthlessly instrumental focus on the rules reflected the Long New Right inheritance. The mass spectacle of disrupting democratic procedure with civic violence raised the specter of fascism.[158] From the White House to the Willard Hotel, where Trump's supporters plotted, to the halls of Congress, where ambitious members aligned themselves with grassroots anger, to the rioters who roamed through the ill-defended building for hours, January 6 joined together myriad currents on the right, with explosive consequences.

Trump had refused to concede defeat in November, instead claiming massive fraud across the states where Biden's narrow wins had decided the contest. Under pandemic conditions, governors, secretaries of state, and judges had expanded absentee and early voting. For Trump, illegal end-runs around state legislatures had irrevocably tainted the election.

As he told the crowd assembled in front of the White House before it marched to the Capitol, "these changes paved a way for fraud on a scale never seen before."[159] Such tainted elections, the argument continued, should not be certified. Courts repeatedly rejected the clownish versions of the arguments that Trump supporters made ex post. But the focus on counts and certifications raised the ominous possibly that, next time, the election subversion would be more sophisticated.

Staring down defamation lawsuits from the makers of voting machines, Fox News finally stopped giving airtime to the most lurid claims of vote fraud peddled by Trump and his associates. Viewers then turned to two tiny right-wing networks making wilder claims: Newsmax, run by Christopher Ruddy, a former *New York Post* reporter; and the even more conspiratorial One America News Network.[160] Beyond them lurked the wild world of disinformation online. In political entertainment, as in so much of the Right, the mainstream and extreme Right had a porous boundary.

The road to January 6 was long. Intense political-legal maneuvering around voting and elections began with the post-election 2000 drama in Florida that culminated in *Bush v. Gore*. The "Brooks Brothers Riot," when a band of Republican staffers coordinated by Roger Stone effectively shuttered the Miami-Dade County vote recount, offered a foretaste of a mob disrupting electoral procedures.[161] As the "voting wars" heated up over the 2000s and 2010s, Republican-controlled states passed increasingly stringent voter ID laws.[162] The stated purpose of the bills was to attack voter fraud, actual evidence of which is vanishingly small. Soon, the Right's prescribed approach moved to encompass counting ballots as well as casting them.[163] In office, Trump created a short-lived Presidential Advisory Commission on Election Integrity led by Kris Kobach, the Kansas secretary of state and a leading figure in those efforts.[164] The impulse, and the rhetoric, only intensified in 2020. As ever, Richard Viguerie got to the heart of the matter. In August 2020, an open letter at his ConservativeHQ site urged action "to forestall the Democrats' planned Election Day chaos and vote fraud" as "preparations necessary to win an existential battle to preserve our country from a Marxist takeover."[165]

Ranging from sophisticated to slapdash, the maneuverings all shared an underlying project: to roll back the federal authority in elections that had been the great state-building achievement of the two Reconstructions.[166] The Supreme Court made an important move in that direction when, in 2013 in *Shelby County v. Holder*, it invalidated preclearance requirements under the Voting Rights Act. Advocates wanted far more. The narrow view of federal power the Right advanced came as part and parcel of its rejoinder to racial liberalism. Racism, this view holds, is a matter of individual treatment. It dismisses comparison across disparate group outcomes as "an unsupportable race-centric legal theory."[167] Thus, long-past discrimination against individuals is no justification for disparate treatment that continually reifies group identity.[168] That approach to federal power has implications beyond race alone. In this view, neither federal courts nor federal bureaucrats have any business constraining states and localities from choosing how they draw districts, set voting rules, count votes, and certify winners.

Conservatives' legal position brought a neat circularity. Gerrymandered state legislatures reliably elect Republican majorities. Those Republican state legislatures are then the only legitimate authorities to set voting rules and certify election winners. Although the legal flash points differ across districting, voting, and election administration, a core logic connects them: states' procedures remain outside scrutiny from federal courts and civil rights bureaucrats. Testifying before Congress in 2021, Hans von Spakovsky, a fellow at the Heritage Foundation who worked on voting issues for the George W. Bush administration, offered a succinct encapsulation: "It is not 1965 and there is no longer any justification for giving the federal government the ability to veto the election laws and regulations that citizens and their elected representatives choose to implement in their respective states."[169]

That statement channeled a very old vision with newfound resonance on the right, one that traces back to John C. Calhoun.[170] In the Calhounian view, the Reconstruction amendments and their progeny fail to justify burdensome intrusion into state legislatures' prerogatives. For Calhoun, as for the southern Democrats who long shielded Jim Crow, institutional bulwarks in the cumbersome American system protect the states, up to and including their antidemocratic practices. Insofar as political parties serve to break down institutional barriers in American politics, the Calhounian impulse pushes back against party power.

But in a polarized and evenly divided party system, that institutional dynamic combines with the partisan view that the other side represents an existential danger. Protecting states' autonomy over voting and elections has thus, for the first time in American history, become a central pillar of a *party* project. Here the paradox wraps around itself: the defense of state legislatures turns into a national priority for the Republican Party. (A photo on January 6 captured an insurrectionist carrying a Confederate flag past a portrait of Charles Sumner.) That claim then fits snugly inside the most fundamental one: that the excesses of liberalism demand maximum response given the existential peril.

Republicans at the Precipice

Once the shock of the insurrection wore off, Trump reasserted control over his party from Palm Beach. The GOP narrative downplayed January 6, or airbrushed it out entirely, and moved to punish dissenters. To the RNC, the insurrection was "legitimate political discourse," while to Georgia congressman Andrew Clyde, it was "a normal tourist visit."[171] The Oregon state party, for its part, took a different tack by declaring it a "'false flag' operation."[172] Wyoming representative Liz Cheney voted to impeach Trump and later worked closely alongside Democrats on the committee investigating January 6. For her troubles, House Republicans removed her as conference chair, the RNC formally censured her, the Wyoming Republican Party voted no longer to recognize her as a Republican, and, by a thirty-seven-point margin, Republican primary voters rejected her renomination.[173]

As Trump continued to fulminate about the "Presidential Election Fraud," the broader Republican universe took a wink-wink line.[174] They decried Democrats' and RINOs' perfidies in 2020 even as they stopped short of saying outright that Trump actually garnered more votes in any of the close-run states. In a line encapsulating how elites pandered to grassroots sentiment on the right as much as they shaped it, the prominent writer Mollie Hemingway reassured readers of her book that "if you believe things went terribly wrong in the 2020 election, well, you're not crazy and you're not alone. But most of all, *you're not wrong*."[175]

For its part, the conservative legal establishment conspicuously failed to dissociate itself from the former law professor John Eastman, who had provided Mike Pence with a full road map for throwing out certification of Biden's election.[176] Instead, Eastman and his colleagues at the Claremont Institute continued the charge.[177] Claremont brought in right-wing sheriffs to study political philosophy in the name of "countering the perversion of the justice system by which the revolutionary Left seeks to advance its totalitarian agenda."[178] Obsessed with enemies and run through with apocalypticism, cadres on the right homed in on the electoral system's soft underbelly, bringing existential risks to American democracy.[179] "Woke elites—increasingly the mainstream left of this country—do not want what we want. What they want is to destroy us," declared Rachel Bovard, a DC think-tank operative who was the breakout star speaker at the National Conservatism Conference in November 2021.[180] The Long New Right's approach and the broader Republican Party's had fully run together.

Yet that same Republican Party, supposedly coming apart at the seams and described by normally even-keeled elites as an outright threat to democracy, remained a viable electoral force. In an important development of the Trump years, Asian American, Black, and, especially, Hispanic voters with low levels of formal education all moved toward the Republican Party, Trump's high-decibel bigotry notwithstanding. Amid the eroding pillars of class, ethnic, and partisan loyalty that had long undergirded Democratic support, Republicans took advantage of new opportunities. Their repertory of appeals, often cheekily deploying in-group idioms, expanded beyond the arid, up-by-the-bootstraps narrative of success that had dominated the party's approach for decades.

The new appeals, in-your-face and at times lurid, produced results. Without any requirement of mutual compatibility, performances of nativism, race, and gender all piled up with appeals to discrete populations in their own networks and information environments.[181] A Hispanic

Republican leader in the Rio Grande Valley of South Texas, for instance, "organized gun groups, Boy and Girl Scout parents, Bible study groups and started College Republicans chapters to run conservative candidates for government."[182] Marco Rubio of Florida, an orthodox Republican in Senate voting behavior who occasionally flirted with new framings for conservatism, spoke with more than a touch of aspiration when he proclaimed after the 2020 election that "the future of the party is based on a multiethnic, multiracial working class coalition." But the line reflected important shifts nonetheless.[183]

Even as their rhetorical embrace cooled, however, the plutopopulist alliance did not break. In March 2021, Rubio ostentatiously opposed Amazon's efforts to stop workers at a plant in Alabama from unionizing. But he had no newfound admiration for trade unionism, declaring that "adversarial labor relations are generally harmful." Rather, he aimed a shot across the bow specifically at "a company whose leadership has decided to wage culture war against working-class values."[184] The rhetoric at the National Conservatism Conference, now concerned with the dangers of woke capitalists and open borders, echoed an earlier generation's obsessions with Rockefellers and Trilateralists. Yet, as ever, the threat to the plutocrats' agenda remained a mirage, as the populists' bark had no genuine anti-capital bite.[185]

On the other side, the mercenary qualities of the pro-capital strand, epitomized by the cold instrumentalism of Mitch McConnell, led its exponents to entente with forces they found distasteful and even dangerous. The desire to hold on to power meant doubling down on advantages in the antimajoritarian parts of the American political system: the Senate, the Electoral College, and the Supreme Court. Republican officialdom was *a*democratic, as it worked alongside party actors who veered toward the *anti*-democratic. In this way, the perils of the Madisonian constitution and the dangers of right populism proved mutually reinforcing.

"While parties at their best are oriented to a conception of the common good," write the political theorists Russell Muirhead and Nancy Rosenblum, "they nonetheless always stand for a part rather than the whole."[186] The Republican Party challenged both elements of that statement, as its substantive agenda appeared cloudy even as the party edged away from accepting its opponents as legitimate political actors.[187] Certainly, events like the National Conservatism Conference paid little heed to policy. As Bovard argued, "Conservatism is not a set of legislative goals."[188] Instead, its project, superior to the available alternatives both as coalitional glue and as electoral appeal, was to own the libs.

The post-policy party hardly left policy alone, to be sure. The Supreme Court's sweeping 2022 decision in *Dobbs v. Jackson Women's Health*—no electoral boon for Republicans—offered a telling example. Even as views on abortion became ever better predictors of voting behavior, the contemporary GOP, with its helter-skelter pugilism, had inched away from the vision of public morality that had animated the pro-life movement's long cross-institutional march toward *Roe*'s defeat. Yet getting *Dobbs* over the finish line required the full suite of Republican maneuvering to achieve their Supreme Court majority. In both 2016 and 2020, with Supreme Court seats on the line after justices' election-year deaths, Senate Republicans led by Mitch McConnell acted ruthlessly to maximize their advantage. Anti-abortion politics, so central to that earlier Republican vision and just a bit askance from the present one, had reaped the downstream rewards of its allied party's institutional hardball.[189]

As for the party's main pursuit, lib-owning as a project meant ratcheting up not just rhetoric but control over the electoral system. With the descent into conspiracism came a rejection of the partiality at the heart of the political party. During the Civil War, the Republicans' forebears had pushed against just that limit in conflating their party's fate with the nation's—but the contrast between free labor's great-party ambitions and those of their twenty-first-century namesakes could not be starker. The Republican Party's vision as a party grew smaller at the very same time that its determination to vanquish what it deemed the mortal threat from the Left made it ever more dangerous. The resolution to that paradox would shape the fate of the American experiment.

9

Toward Party Renewal

THIS BOOK has turned to history as a way to illuminate Americans' contemporary political predicament. Our account should leave readers neither nostalgic for a golden age nor terribly sanguine about the path out of our present discontents. Though we have tempered expectations— more tempered, to be frank, than when we started writing this book in 2016—this chapter nevertheless turns to prescription. Political parties have within them the possibility to serve as democracy's savior or its saboteur. If parties encompassing broad social coalitions and capable of enforcing lines against extremism in their ranks fail to channel political energy and inculcate regime loyalties, more dangerous forces will come into the breach.

Parties play vital ongoing roles in democratic politics: connecting the governed to government, rendering the state accountable, and channeling political conflict into peaceful and meaningful contests for power. Parties can also push against the endemic disorganization, fickleness, and blob-ness that characterize politics in a hollow era. When organizational renewal supports engagement with voters on the ground, parties' dual roles as civic enterprises and organizers of conflict reinforce each other. Party renewal thus offers the promise to inoculate American politics against the distinctive pathologies of Democrats without a collective project and of Republicans without guardrails.

Much of the dysfunction in American governance relates to the poor fit between polarized parliamentary-style parties and Madisonian insti-tutions.[1] Highly disciplined and evenly matched parties pursuing opposed agendas in a fragmented, veto-laden constitutional system typically produce gridlock and brinkmanship. That is a tension we do not claim to know how to resolve—though we suspect that better-grounded and more legitimized parties would mitigate its potential for genuine crisis.

But, in an ironic twist during a global age of disaffection from mainstream parties, the tenacity of the American party duopoly precludes exit as a meaningful option for dissidents. Even as insurgent actors inside America's two parties voice the same kind of dissatisfaction with mainstream party politics as their counterparts elsewhere, the pressures get refracted into internal, asymmetric forms. In multiparty democracies, by contrast, the same tendencies have led to party fragmentation. (To take an extreme example, the 2021 election in the Netherlands gave parliamentary representation to no less than seventeen parties.) In that sense, American-style polarization creates a setting distinctly suited *for parties in particular* to begin building more robust participatory organizations and in turn opens the path to party renewal.

We begin with a straightforward rejection of the venerable anti-party strand and its dismissal of mass politics. In a view prominent today among centrist elites, policy emerges not from conflicts over values and power but from the rational pursuit of "solutions."[2] The soundness of real solutions arrived at through deliberation and compromise—like the objective "public interest" such solutions serve—is self-evident. Whether calling for bipartisanship, a third party, or, to quote one reform group, "America's first Unparty," the anti-party centrists seek end-runs around the barriers to solutionism.[3] Fittingly for an outlook that tends toward savior scenarios during presidential election years, anti-party institutional prescriptions betray a presidentialist streak: fast-track legislative authority, line-item veto power, quick up-or-down votes on appointments. Underlying all these tendencies is the desired evasion of organized, enduring conflict in politics—and thus the escape from party.[4]

On the other end of the reform spectrum, we are sympathetic toward but skeptical of the calls for party strengthening emanating from the loose school of political scientists and lawyers known as "new political realists."[5] The new realists might best be understood as strong proponents of small parties, advocating formal party control over nominations and campaign finance. We share their belief in formal parties steered by electorally oriented politicians as well as their healthy scorn for anti-party cant, but see their prescriptions as myopic. They take from American history less a celebration of parties' possibilities than a nostalgia for bygone accommodationism and an insouciance toward its seamy side. Restoring parties' formal prerogatives—a point where we are notably sympathetic to their prescriptions—and opening the sluice gates to them in the political money game will hardly regain for parties their lost legitimacy or rebuild the frayed ties between insiders and ordinary partisans.[6]

Instead, our approach emphasizes parties' positive civic roles.[7] Since the nineteenth century, political parties have not only organized government but connected ordinary citizens to each other. Parties are at once classic American voluntary associations and uniquely vital "citizen utilities." Yet in our hyperpartisan age, parties as actual organizations have little presence in the lived experience of ordinary Americans. Key to party renewal in the long term is a sustained commitment by party actors, on a continual rather than a quadrennial basis, to robust investment in grassroots outreach.[8]

The obstacles are daunting. The shift in civic advocacy from federated mass membership groups to professionally run operations with checkbook "members" is a half-century-old story.[9] Ideological activism focused largely on national-level issue conflicts has assumed a larger role in party work at the same time that other social institutions, particularly those like unions and civic organizations that built working- or cross-class solidarities, have themselves declined as political actors.[10] All the same, party renewal cannot twiddle its thumbs waiting for a more encompassing civic renewal.[11]

This chapter imagines possibilities for parties to rebuild their organizational and civic capacities. We begin by examining twenty-first-century party renewal on the ground through exploratory fieldwork in the state of Nevada. We then think more systematically about how to address the pathologies of hollowness as we discuss the distinct challenges faced by Democrats and Republicans, respectively. Here

the stakes, and the scale of the challenge, rise to imagining a new balance of social forces that might contain the rising threats to American
democracy.

Renewal in Action: The Case of Nevada Democrats

Up to this point, we have tried to make sense of American parties by
looking to their past, as told through documents and archives. For a
glimpse at party renewal in practice, however, we take a boots-on-the-
ground approach, hearing from some of the people who actually made
it happen. In December 2019, we traveled to Nevada to see for ourselves
how a notable departure from dominant patterns of parties in a hollow
age actually worked. The two core components of Democrats' success
in the Silver State have been, on the one hand, a network of operatives
and staffers initially hired by Senator Harry Reid and dubbed the Reid
Machine and, on the other, UNITE-HERE Local 226, the Culinary
Workers union, in Las Vegas.

The formal Nevada party's largesse and organizational sophistication
and organized labor's grassroots muscle together have produced something uniquely potent in contemporary Democratic politics: a robust
and progressive political operation with tangible connections to ordinary communities and a working-class electoral constituency at its
center. In formal and informal conversations, we sought to find out what
operatives' work looked like in practice, what explained the party renewal evident in Nevada and not elsewhere, and what party-builders in
other states might replicate.[12]

Nevada Democrats' success is undeniable.[13] The Silver State has
overproduced for Democrats relative to what its population mix would
predict, with a string of hard-fought wins in high-stakes races. In 2010,
Harry Reid beat polling expectations to win resounding reelection to the
Senate. In 2016, Nevada Democrats retained his seat while flipping two
U.S. House seats and eking out a win for Hillary Clinton. In 2018, they
won unified control of state government for the first time in a quarter
century. In 2020, following our visit, they garnered a win for Joe Biden.
And in 2022, while losing the governor's mansion, they again prevailed

in a tight Senate race and kept three of four House seats and both legislative chambers.

Political observers unanimously identified a single decisive factor in the Nevada Democratic Party's revival. After state Democrats' major electoral losses during the 2002 cycle, Harry Reid—the state's senior senator and, starting in 2005, the Democratic leader in the Senate—invested in a project to grow and professionalize the formal state party as the central institutional actor in Democratic politics. Reid deployed his own fundraising prowess to keep the money spigot flowing into the organization. He took control of the party apparatus, installing political operative Rebecca Lambe as executive director in 2003 and repeatedly dispatching his aides to state party positions. The party expanded from a permanent staff of two in 2002 to twenty in 2020. Reid and his team aggressively recruited candidates for offices up and down the ticket and, when they deemed it necessary, intervened to discourage weak candidates from running and to prevent contested primaries. Reid's professional diaspora came to dominate state Democratic politics as operatives moved from positions in his Senate office into the state party, then into the extended party network of consultants, advocacy groups, and independent-expenditure operations.

All the components of this approach—the fruits, at least in part, of Reid's enduring financial commitment—bear important lessons. First, a continually well-resourced and well-staffed formal party organization that stays active through off years yields benefits that cannot be realized through paraparty organizations alone. The Nevada party's large permanent staff, including full-time positions in areas like fieldwork and opposition research, enabled party actors to operate with longer time horizons. Meanwhile, keeping major operations in house for tasks like voter registration and the maintenance of a data file skirts the redundancies and coordination problems endemic to the party blobs.

Second, an active formal party attracts and incubates professional talent. "If you have a full-time party operation churning every cycle every year," Lambe told us, "you have a place for good operatives to go. . . . We have an ability to recruit good talented people into Nevada and then we have a place to put them."[14] That emphasis on talent helped to develop an atypical culture of competence and professional ambition that compounds over time. "I didn't think I'd work in a state party," Nevada Democrats' then-executive director, Alana Mounce, told us. A native Oregonian, her political experience prior to taking the job were all outside Nevada. But she cited the "feeling and energy and flow of work" in the Nevada party office and the "growth and development of relationships" that was uniquely available in Nevada Democratic politics.[15] It is worth noting in this context—and, in so doing, endorsing a prescriptive tenet of the new political realists—that Nevada's loose state-level campaign finance laws aided Democrats in making their formal party the central organizational node for revitalized political activity by allowing for unlimited contributions to party committees.

Third, a formal party is also distinctly suited to mobilizing *volunteer* (as opposed to professional) activism. Compared with the party, Lambe said, independent-expenditure operations "aren't as much volunteer-driven. . . . The party really is the apparatus for bringing in that volunteer structure, giving those volunteers a functional activity that's actually going to lead us to winning an election and to using their time well."[16] Amateur clashes with regular party organizations are a recurrent pattern in American politics—one that would come to the Silver State in a major way in 2021. But party professionals' resistance to outside entrants and new sources of activist energy more typically reflects organizational sclerosis than strength, while dynamic party leaders recognize parties' potential as engines of civic engagement.

Finally, a robust party neither neglects the task of candidate recruitment nor shies away from active involvement in the decisions that determine who bears the party's name in contests for office. But crucially, all the *other* tasks the party performs legitimize such interventions. The Reid Machine certainly earned its moniker, as the aggressiveness with which Reid and his team cleared the field in contests for various offices ruffled feathers. But in its heyday, such consternation rarely extended beyond grumbling precisely because of the credibility and goodwill garnered by the party's suite of operations in training, messaging, data analytics, and voter mobilization. Parties' sticks are more effective when deployed after many carrots.

As decisive as Reid's efforts were to Democratic renewal, the emergence of a distinct political force fully outside party auspices arguably proved just as important. The Culinary Workers union, Local 226, runs its own political program and get-out-the-vote operation for its fifty-seven-thousand members every cycle. It points to a path forward for a political party that faces the twin challenges of mobilizing a diverse coalition and forging sustainable cross-class alliances. More generally, it offers a potent model for how rooted and service-oriented organizing can build durable political clout.

Even as they have performed tasks critical to Nevada Democrats' electoral revival in the twenty-first century, Local 226 leaders were quick to disabuse us of the perception that their union's political operation was a kind of subsidiary of the Democratic Party, or even one that should be conceived of as a partner in a shared party project. In the words of D. Taylor, former Local 226 president and current president of its international union, UNITE-HERE, "We're a union that does politics, not a political organization that does union work."[17] Compared to the UAW of midcentury or to the current political operations of the teachers' unions, AFSCME, or SEIU, Local 226 maintains a more arm's-length posture toward the party, guarding its own autonomy and remaining explicitly open to working with sympathetic Republicans. If that approach, along with the union's extensive service provision to its existing membership, echoes narrower business-union traditions in American labor, it coexists with a militant organizing ethic and a broader outlook concerning labor as a social force in American life.[18] The Culinary Workers' political operation began in earnest in the mid-1990s to gain leverage in specific organizing campaigns. The political program grew enormously over the next decade, with Democrats benefiting from the large majority of its efforts. But the union can also sit on its hands to teach a lesson. "When we sat out in 2014," Taylor pointed out, evoking the disastrous midterm cycle during which the union scaled back its electoral program, "Democrats got shellacked."[19]

The exigencies of organizing a transient, multiethnic, multilingual workforce in a right-to-work state demand skills that the union brings to bear on its political work as well. "Every day you come to work, your

priority is organizing," said Local 226's then-secretary-treasurer Geoconda Argüello-Kline, and electoral efforts are "an extension of what we
do every day organizing."[20] The union's membership growth both
tracked and outran the explosion of Vegas's gaming industry and metropolitan population in the 1990s and early 2000s thanks to a series of
protracted, high-profile strike campaigns. Nevada now has the fourth-
highest private-sector unionization rate in the nation.[21] With a current
membership that is majority female and Hispanic, the Culinary Workers emphasize face-to-face engagement by organizers who are rooted in
the same communities and neighborhoods and speak the same native
languages. The union bolsters its community outreach with an array of
practical services, from an industry training academy to assistance in
the naturalization process for immigrants to a first-time homebuyer
program funded through the 2007 collective bargaining agreement.
The dual emphases on acculturation and service provision are likewise central to the union's political program, in which hundreds of
members every cycle receive leaves of absences to pursue full-time electoral organizing.[22]

Reid's operation and Local 226 have together made over Democratic
fortunes in Nevada. But a dramatic coda underscores how party politics
never settles into stable equilibrium. From March 2021 until March 2023,
the Reid machine lost control over the formal Democratic apparatus.
In the wake of a bruising fight over delegate allocation at the 2016 state
party convention, leftist supporters of Bernie Sanders, working via the
Las Vegas Democratic Socialists of America (DSA), had set their sights
on the state Democratic Party. In 2021 they swept the elections for party
officers. In response, the state party's existing staff, from its executive
director on down, quit en masse. In short order, the same actors who
had built up their state's formal party organization maneuvered to work
around it. Using the Washoe County Democratic Party as their vehicle,
Reid operatives formed a new entity called Nevada Democratic Victory
to serve as a conduit for their activities. The new state party chair, Judith
Whitmer, and her team struggled mightily, playing only minor roles
in the 2022 campaign and soon losing the support even of Sanders and
the Las Vegas DSA.[23] In 2023, a new Unity Slate with Reid pedigrees

challenged the erstwhile insurgents, earning the endorsement of Local 226—the first time the union had taken sides in a state party race. After procedural scuffles, challenger Daniele Monroe-Moreno beat Whitmer by a landslide margin of 314 to 99, and the rest of the slate prevailed in turn. The Reid Machine was back in control.[24]

How replicable might the Nevada model be, particularly as private-sector unions struggle to surmount their profound challenges? The growth of the Culinary Workers union is inseparable from the concentration and dynamics of the Vegas gaming industry. But the substance of the union's organizing approach—build durable civic connections to communities on the ground, offer people tangible and valuable services—apply broadly. If not in quite such sweeping terms, something similar could be said about the organizational fruits of Harry Reid's political investment. Nevada's small size makes party–network coordination easier, and the "First in the West" placement in presidential nominating contests that the state has enjoyed since 2008 has provided a unique organizing opportunity. Nevertheless, the decisive factor is transferable: the senator from Searchlight instilled an ethos, propagated by aides in Nevada and beyond, that put formal party capacity at the heart of political strategy. As Lambe recalled of her late mentor, "He instilled that good offense is good defense, to defend every blade of grass, and to be relentless. It doesn't matter where the ball goes on the field, you defend it. And he always believed in playing the long game."[25]

Possibilities for Party Renewal

The lessons from Nevada inform our prescriptions for parties at the local, state, and national levels and for the party blobs all around them. As a first principle, we call on party organizations to hold fast to a core commitment regarding party-building and voter mobilization: show up. Revitalizing parties as civic institutions requires strengthening local parties community by community. Across the country, local parties have tenaciously clung on as organized entities doing discrete tasks.[26] But with few exceptions they are not deeply rooted presences. As of 2016, when he first became interested in participating, a local

Democratic leader in rural Missouri told political scientist Joseph Anthony, "There was no outreach. There was no way for anyone like me to say, 'hey, I just discovered I'm a Democrat. How can I help?'"[27] Where parties' foot soldiers once worked year-round, contacting now comes only when the electoral calendar demands.[28]

Effective local parties keep active year in and year out, through the peaks and valleys of election cycles. Their organizational maintenance complements political work with civic outreach—speaker series, local issue forums, sponsorship of charitable causes—that not only root party activity in community life but make gatherings fun. Local party organizations retain and grow membership by providing people with chances to enjoy the pleasures of fellow-feeling—"solidary incentives" in the academic parlance—and by keeping them active in projects that resonate with their convictions.[29]

When it comes to parties' activities, the past offers not best practices but rather the recurring lesson that parties flourish when their organizational practices resonate with the community life around them.[30] From the boisterous theatrics of the Whigs' 1840 Log Cabin campaign to the Gilded Age's torchlight parades, public spectacle galvanized citizens in the parties' heyday. The block captains of the classic political machines could only perform their electoral role—turning out their voters—thanks to knowledge of their neighbors accrued through regular face-to-face engagement. A single day in the life of Tammany Hall's George Washington Plunkitt involved two funerals, two court visits, a church fair, a wedding, and a 2:00 A.M. trip to the jail to make arrangements for bail.[31]

One step up from the grassroots, state parties have proven the odd men out in a system of nationalized party politics and outside groups' encroachment on party terrain. At their best, state parties serve as the quintessential nodes of the federal American polity.[32] They perform electoral services like voter registration and canvassing. They manage state voter files and control access to their troves of data.[33] They organize state party conventions and oversee the selection of national convention delegates and presidential electors. And they coordinate fundraising to distribute to candidate campaigns and local party committees. But across these roles, state central committees have lost relative influence in the face of legal and institutional strictures and outside groups' unregulated activity.

National party organizations have good reason to invest in local and state party-building. The fruits of twentieth-century efforts in this realm, seen most clearly in sporadic Republican National Committee initiatives to subsidize, support, and train local parties with a view toward building up candidate farm teams, make the case for pursuing such activity as a core party task that sets the path for future success.[34] In the 2000s, Democratic National Committee (DNC) chair Howard Dean's short-lived fifty-state-strategy initiative kicked up an intra-Democratic kerfuffle, but the limited research on its effects, while hardly dispositive, suggests that the presence of DNC field staff under the program helped electorally in ensuing years, particularly in red states.[35] Both parties would do well to commit themselves to new versions of such an approach and to put down roots in rich and barren soil alike.[36]

Robust parties, as the Nevada case demonstrates, deploy both carrots and sticks. We believe that party officials and members should control nomination of candidates, provided that access to participation in party work is permeable and nondiscriminatory. (These conditions were hardly operative, it should be noted, in the pre–McGovern-Fraser era.) And so we oppose calls to "democratize" presidential nomination still further and endorse closed primaries, caucus-convention systems with opportunities for deliberation, institutions like superdelegates that privilege party officials and committed activists, and rejuvenation of the national conventions as deciders of platforms and priorities.[37]

But we also recognize that the parties' legitimacy problems are not airy atmospherics that can be dismissed out of hand. The anti-party strand connecting the Progressives to the McGovern-Fraser reformers lives on in the plebiscitary standard by which reforms get judged and candidates get evaluated. The result is a one-way ratchet toward ever-more direct forms of intraparty "democracy" that not only weakens parties' coordinating capacity but undermines the prospects of real party responsibility.[38] If parties want to advance the idea that they are entitled to a say in deciding who stands for office in their name, then party officers themselves will have to cease speaking out of the sides of their mouths and forthrightly make the case for party itself.

Finally, donors and political professionals have their own roles to play. We indulge no fantasies about escaping the necessity of money, and lots of it, to support robust parties. A strong public campaign financing system substantially run through the parties, our preferred alternative, is not in the cards anytime soon. So we make our recommendation to those who can do something now. The nonprofit wings of the party blobs, often seeking to leverage tax-deductible dollars as nonpartisan voter outreach or to hide their political spending, have crowded onto the parties' terrain. The fact that so much political money currently flows to various 501(c) groups points not only to incentives set by the federal tax code and campaign finance regulations but also to the parties' deep legitimacy problems. To allow parties space to grow, funders should resist giving to groups, often weakly tied into local networks, that impinge on parties' core tasks. And they should recognize the distinct roles of genuine social movements and genuine political parties powered by ordinary citizens working to improve their communities.[39] Hence, here as elsewhere, the challenge of organizational renewal goes hand in hand with the challenge of renewing a positive spirit of party.

Party Renewal in a Shade of Blue

The implications of party renewal differ for the two major parties. Their forms reveal core, asymmetric pathologies—Democratic ineffectuality and Republican extremism. Our prescriptions hardly represent a "view from nowhere" but rather emerge from recognizing this vast asymmetry. For Democrats, we emphasize party-building across multiple dimensions while steering clear of arguments over ideology and coalitional strategy. For Republicans, we likewise eschew substantive commandments, but we are blunt about the necessity of taming pernicious tendencies.

Since midcentury, liberals have been the strongest advocates of government by disciplined parties. For postwar Democrats frustrated at the travails of party factionalism amid constitutional fragmentation, programmatic partisanship signaled a path out of deadlock into the mainstream of democratic welfare capitalism and breakthroughs in civil rights. Over half a century later, the promise of a robust, integrative party likewise provides today's liberals with an answer to the travails of a polarized and plebiscitary national politics. But the path to such a party requires new civic connections and a renewed spirit of party to bolster the collective endeavors of a diverse coalition.

The neglect of party-building is evident not only in the thinned grassroots of local Democratic activity but also in the bloat and drift of national-level party politics dominated by the party blob. The ad makers and consultants who rose to the fore in the more candidate-centered 1980s have been joined by younger staffers in digital campaigning and data analytics cycling through and among formal party organizations and paraparty outfits—the latter groups all too often operating with little accountability to a real membership with concrete political interests. This soup of incentives undermines effectiveness. "Acronym is a perfect example of failing up," Arizona organizer Tomas Robles remarked in 2021, referring to the Democratic dark-money group behind the tech startup Shadow Inc. that we described at the opening of this book. "They completely botched the Iowa caucuses. They still got $90 million to run a digital voter registration campaign."[40]

Key to the listlessness we have diagnosed in the Democrats since the 1970s has been a challenge common to center-left parties across the West, namely the rise of well-educated constituencies in a party with ostensible working-class programmatic commitments.[41] Relative to Democrats' counterparts abroad, the impact of such influence has arguably been sharpened by (while in turn feeding into) America's costlier elections, patchier welfare state, and higher inequality. Party polarization by education during and after the Trump years continued unabated. As Nevada illustrates by way of rare counterexample, the decline of organized labor has left a profound gulf both organizationally and ideologically, unfilled by any other forces. In the New Deal era, the labor movement took advantage of the decline of old party organizations to build its political muscle. Now union decline leaves Democrats without an actor capable of influencing the political economy in ways that would accommodate the party's loftiest programmatic ambitions. Contributing to the revival of labor, across the working class and not just in core strongholds, is not just one party position among many but a matter of existential significance to Democrats.[42]

Rebuilding unions also serves as a counterweight to the influence of groups less in tune with everyday material politics. The nonprofit-industrial complex continues to reproduce the logic of the party blob even in a more progressive party. For all the rhetorical praise given over to movements (and all the repackaging of ordinary politics in the argot of social change), the activists garnering funding have often lacked accountability of their own to a mass base.[43] In this sense, the angst expressed by internal critics during the Trump and Biden years over the place of "woke" rhetoric and cultural politics in the Democratic Party was in part a pointed appraisal of the party's most influential cadres.[44] For their own part, critics from the center worried about a rising left have likewise struggled to bring all the pieces together. The charge, in the words of political scientist Raymond La Raja, "to embrace a pluralism that speaks to different constituencies and is electorally advantageous" awaits a project that meets the challenge.[45]

The recent rise of millionaire and billionaire megadonors bankrolling the thicket of dark money groups and independent expenditure campaigns on the left raises even sharper questions about the potential and limits of the progressive world's material politics. "I think a lot about the role billionaires have to play," mused a leading donor-adviser who assists progressive billionaires with their giving. "Maybe they're part of the problem and part of the solution."[46] Not coincidentally, even as the Democratic blob has lurched left, the politics of work and wages has continued to get short shrift relative to the cultural and political-reform initiatives that capture donors' imaginations.

As the implications of the GOP's anti-democratic turn have become apparent in recent years, progressive political reformers have shifted their energies toward democracy itself. As should be abundantly clear by now, we share the alarm about the condition of American democracy. But Democrats' democracy rap comes in varying flavors, some of which denude rather than bolster their ability to perform the core role of a robust party: to marshal and pursue a project for power. In particular, a fetish for process reforms that prize deliberation and information—often laced with the self-righteous implication that all would be well if only the "correct" facts could flow to the unenlightened—recurs as a special progressive weakness. The tendency connects the smug posturing of Jon Stewart's 2010 "Rally to Restore Sanity and/or Fear" to the Democratic Party blob's Trump-era obsession with battling "misinformation" to the collective failure to set priorities or think strategically about election reform legislation in the Biden years.[47] Whether viewers are watching an ironist's satirical swipes or the earnest declarations of MSNBC's marquee hosts, such democracy talk too often lapses into a kind of politics as performative consumption.[48] It channels the pining for a sanitized politics, long the provenance of the anti-party strand, into symbolic gambits that substitute for real party projects.

We find more merit in a reformist approach, born of polarized conflict with Republicans, that might be termed goo-goo hardball.[49] Across the center-left, thinkers and activists have zeroed in on the structural democratic distortions and impediments to majoritarian progressive politics built into the American constitutional order.[50] Ranging beyond a focus merely on extraconstitutional institutions like the Senate filibuster and political control of redistricting in the states, the public sphere has buzzed in recent years with proposals to end lifetime tenure for Supreme Court justices, pack federal courts, scrap the Electoral College, and admit new states into the union.[51] Ideas to move to proportional representation and to abolish the Senate as a meaningful veto player no longer seem out of place in mainstream discourse.[52] Liberals' attentiveness to the deep linkages between process and power in the American polity is a positive development. But without a commitment to party-building, the new discourse of institutional reform risks lapsing into constitutional cosplay. Parties' core task in winning big majorities comes in identifying voter blocs and going after them. Institutional reforms that allow those majorities to govern effectively, then, serve as complement to, and should not be a substitute for, growing collective capacity from the ground up. As important as the rules are, there's no avoiding the necessity to build power by building party.

A Republican Party Safe for Democracy

Republicans operating under the strictures and pathologies of the Long New Right have a steeper task ahead of them, and a far more dangerous one. The danger stems from a key asymmetry in democratic politics. Though the threat of extremism and the value of parties as temporizers are common to all political persuasions, right parties pose unique system-destabilizing risks. Conservative parties tend both to represent dominant demographic groups primed for status threats and to ally with economic elites who have reason to fear majoritarian politics. As a consequence, should such right parties succumb to extremist influence, democracy finds itself particularly vulnerable. Indeed, the reality that right parties may be civically rooted but also authoritarian makes restraining their dangerous tendencies and ensuring their regime loyalties all the more urgent. As a historical matter, where conservative parties have retained a "capacity to stimulate but subordinate outside groups" so as to balance party activism and forbearance, they have helped to consolidate democracy.[53] Where they have let the fever swamps in, they have hastened democracy's demise.

The trajectories of party strands across American history tell us something about the distinctive dynamics of conservative politics. Political actors close to the interests of capital have pursued three different paths over the centuries. Those who have viewed party politics as a grubby and unscrupulous game, from Liberal Republicans in 1872 to the Progressives to certain high-minded moderate opponents of Barry Goldwater and, in our own time, Donald Trump, have moved toward the anti-party strand, while enduring some cost to their own political durability. Those who, like the Long New Right, have pursued direct conflict with their ideological opponents have drifted toward the pro-capital strand's suppression of popular politics and rapprochement with populist-strand extremists. And finally, those who have granted that politics has its own logic that dictates compromise, from Gilded Age organizations to midcentury exponents of nonideological Republican regularity, have served to synthesize the accommodationist strand with a practical-minded conservatism.

Notwithstanding our general endorsement of Tocquevillian great parties, we cast our lot with a revival of this third, pragmatic tendency. Rebuilding Republican Party organization as a civic force rooted in local communities offers a potential route out of the linked pathologies of rule by donors and rule by demagogues. It is a daunting task, to be sure, far more so now than had Republicans drawn a cordon sanitaire against the most revanchist elements in the Right's revival.

Before divining the means by which to get from here to there, consider first a vision of the end goal—of a reformed, post–Long New Right Republicanism. Such a party would no longer cede its messages to talk radio, Fox News, and YouTube stars. Republican elites would broaden their agenda beyond tax cuts for the super-rich and symbolic fights for the rest, abandon policymaking by litmus test, and argue constructively over whose ox should be gored. The congressional party would have the capacity to meet the challenge of governing. And its party program would emphasize strengthening the frayed bonds of family and civil society and encouraging a patriotism that steers clear of racial and ethnic nationalism.[54] Reflecting the best in conservative parties, such a party would offer avenues of upward mobility and rewards for success to hardworking Americans of all stripes. Above all, it would practice democratic virtues, seeking to persuade voters and not just retreat inside its institutional redoubts, and practicing forbearance when elections go the wrong way.

We have no illusions. The prospects of making even incremental progress in the direction of such a vision appear, for now, dim. Our pessimism stems not only from the behavior of the vast majority of Republican officeholders and voters during the Trump years all the way through January 6, 2021, and beyond but also from some of the leading efforts of Never Trump conservatives. Center-right tracts against Trumpism have appeared by the fistful.[55] Yet for all their righteous anger as they wrestle with the dilemmas of exit and voice, Never Trumpers have yet to identify an alternative political approach grounded in a plausible electoral, activist, and interest-group coalition.[56]

From the young ideologists of 1960s-era moderate Republicanism in the Ripon Society to the more culturally traditionalist 2000s-era

"Reformicons," center-right intellectuals have focused on national politics, emphasized their policy bona fides, eyed the give-and-take of political bargaining warily—and repeatedly foundered.[57] In a similar vein, leaders of the broadly Never Trumpist Niskanen Center claim that "public confidence in government will return only when government demonstrates through successful problem-solving that such confidence is merited."[58] The social basis for such a program, and the organizational forms a party might take to pursue it, fail to enter the discussion.[59]

An alternative moderate tradition can be found in the pragmatic accommodationism of successful Republican politicians in the middle and later twentieth century. Theirs was a rolled-sleeve approach of governance as problem-solving and social peacekeeping, one deeply embedded in community life. Such moderate Republicans, including industrial-state governors like Harold Stassen, Nelson Rockefeller, and George Romney, were hemmed in by the social and institutional alignments of the New Deal state and a still-robust labor movement.[60] But they also expressed an outlook rooted in the social context of their own party's base. The political scientist Clinton Rossiter evoked the "Republican self-image" at midcentury as "men of standing and sobriety . . . sound without being callous." As a journalist put it to him, "The Republicans look to me like Rotarians at the speakers' table, the Democrats like Rotarians at table 16, back near the entrance to the kitchen."[61] Just as important as the class and status politics captured in that quip was its evocation of the civic life in which parties dwelled. A Republican tradition of genteel accommodationist governance thrived in such now-vanished milieus.

Call it Blissism. Ray Bliss, the Akron-raised insurance man and legendary chair of the Ohio Republican Party and then the Republican National Committee in the 1950s and 1960s, earned his reputation as an organizationally focused, "nuts-and-bolts" party-builder par excellence. But he was less a bloodless technician than a distinctly keen organizer of Republican politics in the accommodationist mode. In Ohio, he cross-checked voter registration rolls with membership lists for Kiwanis, country clubs, chambers of commerce, and—yes—Rotarians so as to identify the undermobilized ranks within the civic havens of midcentury

Republicanism.[62] (He also lived the part as a member in good standing of the Kiwanis, the Blue Coats, and the Portage Country Club, the site of his wedding reception.)[63] His famous aversion to ideological in-fighting or even explicit comment on policy issues reflected in part a normative commitment to rendering his own views subservient to the party as a whole. But he never hid his own belief in the avowedly small-party ethos of GOP moderation—of "government which is ef-ficient, yet economical; government that is alert to the changing times, yet guided by common sense; government which is compassionate to the needs of the people, yet wise in the execution of programs to meet those needs."[64]

Blissism's basic acceptance of the New Deal order was, of course, precisely what made the Long New Right despise its adherents. Moder-ate ideologues, for their part, saw in its aversion to explicit discussion of issues a kind of mindless stifling of debate.[65] With hindsight, how-ever, we can recognize in the Bliss approach a viable center-right politics that performed constructive work for the political system—a rooted small-bore pragmatism that at its most vital was a party project unto itself. Just as importantly, Blissism signified perhaps the last significant embodiment of the nineteenth-century notion of vigorous but demar-cated conflict and personal ambition subsumed to the party.

Party renewal as civic renewal invites dangers as much as promise for a party with a petit bourgeois rank and file and super-rich funders, and so this prescription leads to unavoidable tensions. In the current con-text, a vibrant, robust, engaged party politics from the right runs the serious risk of also being an undemocratic politics. Thus we also empha-size making politics about more practical and concrete things. Although one need not go online to get radicalized, social media accelerates gonzo and conspiracist tendencies with long provenance on the right. By con-trast, face-to-face iterated interactions can encourage a politics rooted in real practical needs. Put them together and the door begins to open for a rooted, responsible conservatism.

We dare not propose a full agenda for the country's right-of-center party. Whether it should, say, revive something like the politics of Jack Kemp or, as young intellectuals on the right are urging, depart outright from fusionism is their question, not ours. But rekindling the tradition of rooted small-party Republicanism strikes us as the most plausible potential path out of the democratic crisis that the Long New Right has done so much to provoke.[66] And on the core procedural safeguards in democratic politics, where Republicans have skated on ever-thinner ice, our view is firm: party projects in democracies must be small-*d democratic* projects before they are anything else.

The Way Forward: Grand Coalition or Popular Front?

We are, like many political scientists, pro-party. And we are, like many political scientists, concerned about the trajectory of the present-day Republican Party. Where we differ from many of our peers is to take from those views an emphatic claim about that party's fate at the polls. As a necessary precondition for renewed Republicanism, the Republican Party as it now stands must be defeated electorally.[67] Only *repeated and substantial electoral losses*, in national elections and in closely divided purple states, would provide a sufficiently forceful signal of popular repudiation. Such losses would open up space for internal voices of dissent urging fellow partisans to walk back from the brink, accept the rules of the game, shun all who advocate political violence, and treat their opponents as legitimate political adversaries.[68] Fixing democracy is infinitely easier when all the players remain committed to the game. When that criterion fails to hold, the goal must be to force the losers to regroup. And to bring such pressure to bear, there is no viable democratic alternative to electoral victory.

However unlikely such an achievement might seem, we assert that the alternative strategy of conjuring a top-down grand bipartisan coalition in favor of democracy faces slimmer prospects still.[69] Suspending politics, in the tradition of the anti-party strand, leads into a cul-de-sac. An antiseptic checklist proceduralism is the antithesis of a capacious party project. In practice, most calls for grand coalition also tend to ape the deficit-cutting social liberalism that is the American elite's common ground—and wildly unpopular elsewhere. This is a hard and necessary lesson that center-right democracy funders eager to defend that common ground should take to heart, just as leftists should reckon with the limits of the possible in American politics.

Without lapsing fully into political consultancy, we suggest that the politics necessary for sustained victory would entail meeting voters where they are, with bread-and-butter politics grounded in a substantive vision. The pro-democracy party, in this view, wins less by talking democracy alone than by making appeals that motivate ordinary citizens. Our broad vision, drawing on the accommodationist, policy-reform, and radical strands alike, is less a grand coalition than a popular front.[70] The 2022 midterms provided heartening evidence that election denial is bad politics, as a string of Republican extremists, most badly outspent, went down to defeat. But winning repeated big majorities and reorienting national politics requires more than appealing to the engaged issue public—likely including nearly every reader of this book—who respond when elites wave the banner against democratic backsliding.[71]

A politics that conjures up a decisive electoral majority requires a big tent, with support from diverse backgrounds and up and down the social spectrum.[72] The victories on the scale necessary to force a course correction in the GOP will require more support from the white working class than the Democrats have mustered in the Trump era, along with holding the line among other working-class voters. And achieving *that* will require a disciplined party with the collective capacity to set priorities. Saving American democracy requires not transcending parties but doing party politics better than democracy's adversaries.

Parties without Apology

Party renewal is a tall order. The challenges are legion to making even modest progress in reversing hollowness and restoring some vitality to the parties. Underlying our specific suggestions is a call to cultivate a spirit of party in American politics—to persuade political actors to champion parties openly rather than exploit anti-partyism strategically or erode parties through sheer indifference.[73] Whatever else they may do, parties ought to defend themselves forthrightly. If they won't, who will?

Anti-partyism is a potent and renewable resource in American political culture. When Martin Van Buren insisted in his memoirs that "I never could bring myself for party purposes to deprecate their existence," he set a bar for political behavior that few others have met across American history.[74] "The beneficiaries of the revolution in government wrought by the parties have not generally been grateful," E. E. Schattschneider observed in 1942. "Tories, reactionaries, royalists, and fascists ought to hate parties, but fantastically the parties are treated with contempt by the champions of democratic government."[75] Eight decades later, the contempt has only deepened even as the parties' role in structuring politics has grown more central.

The country's partisan divide is deep, and it is not going anywhere. Better to build robust parties than to leave to hollow shells and unaccountable actors the task of containing the furies of the age. And better to summon the immense collective power of parties to tackle the challenges of our time than to consign ourselves to the drift and rancor of a system in deadlock—or to succumb to demagogy. "Let us concede," Schattschneider wrote, "that the American people will never create a powerful party system unless they want one."[76] If American democracy has a future, the time has come to stand up for the political party.

APPENDIX 1

Facets of Party

POLITICAL PARTIES form out of building blocks that combine and layer in different ways across time. We term these building blocks *facets of party*. They encompass recurring questions about political goals and practice that party actors have faced across American history. We identify eight facets of party: the party's goals in wielding state power; the privileged partisan actors who embody the party's vision and whom it aims to reward; the party's place in the venerable Tocquevillian classification of great and small parties; its orientation to compromise; its funders; its preferred method of nomination; its orientation toward capital; and its views on race.

By design, these facets cover not only parties' mechanics and operations but also parties' place in the power relations that structure social life. Thus, they reflect our view that parties have no one true essence, function, or principal that dictates everything else but rather reflect varied and often uneasy combinations of actors, goals, and organizational approaches. We have arrived at these categories inductively to frame the questions motivating our inquiries, and they are not meant as exhaustive. Tables A.1, A.2, A.3, and A.4 apply these facets to each of the collective party actors we consider. The pithy descriptions in each cell are intended not as canonical statements but, again, as heuristics to ground the narratives in systematic comparison. Beyond this book, these facets invite further comparisons that ask about the place of party across state and society.

Parties seek to control the government, with the chance to mobilize the state to pursue their projects. Table A.1 begins by listing those goals. Some parties may content themselves with the rewards of office or, for the reform-minded, with presiding over an efficient government, while others want vast social transformation. Party actors often define their goals as the defeat of their adversaries: for free labor Republicans, the Slave Power; for Populists, plutocracy; for the Long New Right, the forces of liberalism. This facet comes first because it encapsulates our view of parties as actors with goals in wielding power, goals in turn shaped by the conditions captured in other facets.

Parties privilege certain actors, making them the repositories for the parties' raison d'être. A direct line connects parties' goals in wielding power with the privileged partisan actors who, as ideal types, embody the party's vision and are charged with carrying it out. In political parties, beset with principal-agent problems, exactly who takes orders, or even cues, from whom depends on both doctrine and circumstance. Whether a leader summons up a public, or the voters instruct their leader, and whether the party organization controls or serves the holders of office—such relationships vary across time and setting. From the Jacksonians' celebration of hard-nosed tacticians and the Whigs' veneration of distinguished men to the rise of liberal activists and right populists' privileging of the strong leader, parties have located themselves in different social formulations and reflected different values about party's purposes.

Table A.2 begins by applying the venerable distinction, first made by Tocqueville, between great parties—"those more attached to principles than to consequences, to generalities rather than to particular cases, to ideas rather than to personalities"—and small parties.[1] This distinction has a long provenance. The Progressives, in particular, consciously attacked the smallness of the machine boss but envisioned a future of great principled parties. Though the distinction between great and small parties may seem, to the contemporary eye, fusty or else overly subjective, it captures the connection between parties as historical agents and the possibilities of the political regime to encompass their visions of democracy.

TABLE A.1. Facets of Party—Core Concepts

	Years	Goals in wielding state power	Privileged partisan actors
Jacksonians	1828–1854	Spoils; build the white man's republic	Brokers in each state
Whigs	1840–1854	Internal improvements; moral improvement	Distinguished men
Free Labor Republicans	1854–1877	Vanquish the Slave Power	Partisan loyalists to principle
Gilded Age Organizations	1877–1896	Spoils on a vast scale	Brokers in concert with capital
Mugwumps	1872–1900	Stop wrong element from rule	Distinguished men outside party
Populists	1874–1896	Break banks and railroads	Citizens loyal to principle
Socialist Party	1901–1919	Build the cooperative commonwealth	Partisan loyalists as socialists
Progressives	1900–1916	Procedural reform; build administrative state	Visionary leaders
Midcentury Pragmatists	1932–1968	Balance coalitional interests	Brokers across federalism
Programmatic Liberals	1948–1968	Fulfill the promise of the New Deal	Cross-institutional issue activists
McGovern-Fraserites	1968–1972	Procedural reform; inclusion	Grassroots activists working with movements
Long New Right	1952–1994	Destroy liberalism	Cross-institutional co-belligerents
Left Dissidents	2011–present	Transcend the promise of the New Deal	Grassroots activists
Dem Institutionalists	1981–present	Balance coalitional interests	DC cross-institutional; group/issue activists
Neoliberal Centrists	2001–present	Efficient governance	Elite networks
Reaganite GOP	1981–present	Reward the privileged partisan actors	DC cross-institutional; capital
Right Populists	1992–present	Destroy enemies of leader	Strong leader; media figures

TABLE A.2. Facets of Party—Ambition and Compromise

	Years	Great or small party	Orientation to compromise
Jacksonians	1828–1854	Small	Agreement to disagree
Whigs	1840–1854	Small, sometimes for great purposes	Acceptable if principled
Free Labor Republicans	1854–1877	Great	Varied by faction in diverse party
Gilded Age Organizations	1877–1896	Small	Agreement to disagree
Mugwumps	1872–1900	Anti-small	Against agreement to disagree
Populists	1874–1896	Great but undertheorized	Unacceptable
Socialist Party	1901–1919	Great	Unacceptable
Progressives	1900–1916	Anti-small	Preferable if principled
Midcentury Pragmatists	1932–1968	Small	Acceptable
Programmatic Liberals	1948–1968	Less small	Preferable to have less of it
McGovern-Fraserites	1968–1972	Anti-small	Acceptable if principled
Long New Right	1952–1994	Party as ancillary to power	Unacceptable
Left Dissidents	2011–present	Great but undertheorized	Unacceptable
Dem Institutionalists	1981–present	Small	Rare but not unacceptable
Neoliberal Centrists	2001–present	Party as irrelevant	Preferable
Reaganite GOP	1981–present	Small but radical	Intraparty log rolls acceptable
Right Populists	1992–present	Party as ancillary to power	Unacceptable, even dangerous

The second facet in Table A.2 considers orientation to compromise. Partisanship is a distinctive democratic virtue for recognizing its own partiality. The organization-minded Jacksonians turned coalitional bargaining into a political ethic. By contrast, Whigs, and the reformists following in their wake, emphasized that compromise must emerge from principle rather than pure expediency. A muffled echo of that latter critique reappeared in the Progressive Era. The most notable story since then, as parties became less concerned with form, has been the decline in explicit arguments regarding the necessity of balance between compromise and holding fast. Hollow parties in the new polarized era have no recourse to the language of principled disagreement that their forebears would have found familiar. Meanwhile, even as *intra*party compromise with a rival faction is conceptually distinct from *inter*party compromise across party, the two have always tracked together closely in practice.

Table A.3 moves from questions of who should rule and in whose interest to consider the core, nuts-and-bolts challenges that parties of all stripes face cycle after cycle: how to fund their operations and how to nominate candidates. They make these choices amid the challenges of a changing American political system, as politics has grown nationalized, expensive, and plebiscitarian.

Parties need money—and they have looked to different sources to find it.[2] If parties have no money in their coffers, they have no party campaign. The Populists are a prime case for that harsh reality. The rise and fall of party patronage, the opportunities for influence afforded by corporate capitalism, and the rise, mediated by direct mail and then the Internet, of checkbook activism have all shaped the arc of political finance. Parties have diverged along two central axes. Some have turned to ordinary partisans, while others have looked to the rich. And some have sought funds from those with an interest in the government's work, while the more reform-minded have tried to find sources that they deem to be less corrupting to pay the party's bills.

The rightmost column of Table A.3 asks about preferred methods of nomination. Even as parties' roles go far beyond this task, it is in selecting candidates to carry the party banner that partisans jostle and adjudicate among their visions for the party. Successive historical actors built the American nomination system. The Jacksonians popularized the nominating convention. The Progressives popularized (though it is an overstatement to say that they invented) the direct primary, which quickly became the method to choose nominees for Congress and state-level office. The McGovern-Fraser reformers, albeit not entirely by

TABLE A.3. Facets of Party—Funding and Nomination

	Years	Funders of party	Preferred method of nomination
Jacksonians	1828–1854	Local notables and party workers	Convention
Whigs	1840–1854	Local notables	Convention (reluctantly)
Free Labor Republicans	1854–1877	Local notables and party workers	Convention
Gilded Age Organizations	1877–1896	Big business and party workers	Convention
Mugwumps	1872–1900	Men of means	Bolt from convention
Populists	1874–1896	Silverites (as solution and undoing)	Convention
Socialist Party	1901–1919	Formal membership dues	Convention
Progressives	1900–1916	Citizens in theory, rich patrons in practice	Direct primary
Midcentury Pragmatists	1932–1968	Rich patrons and local notables	Mixed; convention dominated
Programmatic Liberals	1948–1968	Checkbook and party activists	Mixed
McGovern-Fraserites	1968–1972	Checkbook activists	Direct primary or caucus
Long New Right	1952–1994	Rich patrons, checkbook activists, scams	Direct primary
Left Dissidents	2011–present	Low-dollar checkbook activists	Direct primary
Dem Institutionalists	1981–present	Rich patrons, checkbook activists	Mixed; primary dominated
Neoliberal Centrists	2001–present	Rich patrons	Self-nomination by elites
Reaganite GOP	1981–present	Big business and rich patrons	Mixed; primary dominated
Right Populists	1992–present	Anyone they can find	Direct primary

design, made direct primaries the principal method for choosing delegates to presidential nominating conventions. That sequence informs the entire history of preferred methods of nomination, as parties have responded in turn to the convention system, the mixed system, and the primary-dominated system.

Finally, capital and race, the topics of Table A.4, are constitutive subjects in American life. Parties necessarily take sides even when questions of political economy and racial hierarchy fail to dominate campaign rhetoric. Indeed, parties' attempts to wall off politics from the economy or to avoid searing confrontations on race are every bit as much facets of party as are embracing socialism or defending Jim Crow.

Table A.4 first explores the role of capital. The privileged position of business looms large in capitalist democracy. If captains of industry dislike an elected government and its policies, and especially if they fear that they will lose the power to keep workers in line, they can lead a capital strike, crater the economy, and bring down the government. The most significant historical moment for this facet came in the rise of corporate capitalism during the Gilded Age, as party organizations accommodated themselves to the emergence of national-level corporations and Populists and Socialists dreamt of alternatives.

On race, the free labor Republicans stand alone in the nineteenth century for their relatively egalitarian views, while racial conflict returned to party politics in the following century as liberals led and conservative antagonists grappled with the consequences of the Second Reconstruction. Taken together, these two facets of party indicate the increasing correspondence of views on capital and race as both the racial liberalism that emerged with the New Deal and the opposition to it worked their way through the party system. The table also makes clear that the zone of acceptable partisan conflict has varied across time in important ways. To take the most critical example, the Jacksonians did their utmost to keep slavery outside the ambit of party politics. And when the national security state emerged in the early Cold War, the exclusion of party politics was explicit.[3]

TABLE A.4. Facets of Party—Capital and Race

	Years	Orientation toward capital	Views on race
Jacksonians	1828–1854	Municipal-level accommodation	Strongly inegalitarian
Whigs	1840–1854	Ambivalent support	Inegalitarian
Free Labor Republicans	1854–1877	Support free labor	Relatively egalitarian; wide spectrum
Gilded Age Organizations	1877–1896	Accommodation with corporate capitalism	GOP: Halting retreat; Dems: inegalitarian
Mugwumps	1872–1900	Ambivalent support; deemed distasteful	Retreat from egalitarianism
Populists	1874–1896	Opposition to corporate capitalism	Unfulfilled promise in a radical party
Socialist Party	1901–1919	Opposition	Unfulfilled promise in a radical party
Progressives	1900–1916	Support with regulation	Divided; egalitarians lost
Midcentury Pragmatists	1932–1968	Cross-class compromise	Egalitarian nationally, intransigent locally
Programmatic Liberals	1948–1968	Compromise; countervailing power	Egalitarian
McGovern-Fraserites	1968–1972	Drift from political economy	Egalitarian
Long New Right	1952–1994	Support based in "little big business"	Spectrum from color-blind to inegalitarian
Left Dissidents	2011–present	Countervailing power	Egalitarian
Dem Institutionalists	1981–present	Drift from political economy	Egalitarian
Neoliberal Centrists	2001–present	Support; logic of financialization	Individualistic, meritocratic
Reaganite GOP	1981–present	Enthusiastic support	Spectrum from color-blind to inegalitarian
Right Populists	1992–present	Support; noises against "woke capital"	Inegalitarian

Together, these facets of party illuminate the encounter between party politics and broader social forces that is the leitmotif of this book. Parties at once help to shape and are in turn shaped by those social forces. Party projects seek to forge coalitions that will seize and steer the ship of state. Yet as they do so, they engage questions about the means and ends of party politics that have recurred and endured across American history.

Political Parties, American Political Development, Political History

THE HOLLOW PARTIES represents a synthesis—perhaps an idiosyncratic synthesis—of scholarly methodologies and literatures from both history and social science. This appendix spells out our analytical strategy and then proceeds through our engagement with scholarship on party politics, American political development, and political history.

We seek to get inside party actors' heads rather than make inferences from their observed behavior.[1] This approach helps to safeguard against the pitfalls of methodological presentism. We examine historical actors in light of twenty-first-century social science, but we do not force them to speak its language. In turn, our broader goal is to elucidate big, important patterns, not to explain discrete outcomes or to identify causal effects.[2] The concern with preference formation more than causal identification should be familiar to historians and places us slightly upstream from much historical institutionalist scholarship, with its emphasis on precise explanations for cross-institutional change.[3] In line with social science more than history, by contrast, we emphasize common questions, shared across particular party formations, that provide the scaffolding to adduce larger patterns.[4]

This method has limitations. Consistency in intellectual approach across temporal and political settings dictates a somewhat eclectic evidence base. Reformers, for one, have tended to be more loquacious than regulars, who have followed the advice of Boston's Martin Lomasney: "Don't write when you can talk; don't talk when you can nod your head."[5] By the same token, we happily blur boundaries between primary and secondary sources that scholars often seek to keep separate. Party actors often speak in their most expansive register at moments that allow for more rumination than in the day-to-day scrum of events, while academic sources can point the way to new connections when they venture into speculation.[6] Hence, our source material is not amenable to time-series analysis that can be comprehensively searched or coded.[7] We use unvarnished evidence straight from the source, or as close as we can possibly get, and then sift through it to make interpretations outward.

Political scientists who study American parties have offered us a rich legacy. As V. O. Key's tripartite division of party in the electorate, party in government, and party as organization recognized long ago, parties are not a single thing.[8] And so we "take seriously the goal of integrating party theory and probing the relationships between different parts of the party system."[9] Rather than tackle each dimension of party in isolation, we follow parties to wherever the action is: Congress, the county headquarters, the airwaves, the voting booth. By design, the institutional locus jumps around even as the thematic focus remains steady.

Our focus on the variety in party forms and projects takes us in a different direction from most modern party scholars, who typically emphasize similarities in underlying party processes. By contrast, a motivating puzzle for this book is the contemporary parties' basic divergence in their approach to politics and their manifestations of hollowness.[10] "One true essence" theories stumble both in accounting for the contours of historical change and in making sense of such asymmetries across parties. Our central claim, demonstrated across time, is that different logics govern different actors' approaches to party politics.

Prevailing views treat parties chiefly as dependent variables, institutions created in response to needs and preferences derived elsewhere.[11] For candidate-centered analysts of party, parties exist to provide resources to individual office seekers. The parties' basket of services may range from money to electoral information, specialized labor, or association with a party "brand."[12] Because, in this view, the system's central actors want to win elections, changes in a given party's issue positions and ideology emerge from aggregated responses to shifts in the electoral landscape.[13] By contrast, group-centered theorists of party, chief among them a set of collaborators known as the "UCLA school," define parties as long coalitions of "intense policy demanders"—activists, interests, and ideologues all using office seekers as their agents. For group theorists, party positioning comes as jostling alliances vie to distribute society's goodies.[14] When the environment shifts, whether because existing actors change their preferences or because new actors enter the scene, the parties change in turn.[15] Notwithstanding their disagreements, however, for both politician- and group-centric theories, coordination lies at the heart of parties' work. Both theories see parties as agents synchronizing the priorities of underlying claimants. With that analytical view, in turn, comes a focus on party capacities at the nexus of selecting candidates and providing resources for campaigns.[16]

By contrast, we see coordination as a vital part—but only a part—of what parties do, and the ability for actors to coordinate on nominees only one metric—and a historically contingent one—of party power.[17] Cast a long view across American parties, and institutional activity ranges widely, encompassing the control of patronage, fights over platforms, agenda control in Congress, and party leadership by the president.

We treat parties less as battlefields or as sites of struggle than as the battlers and strugglers themselves.[18] As organizers of conflict, parties define and inculcate their visions and set the boundaries of political contestation. As "linkage institutions," they mediate between elites and the mass public, build coalitions of ideas and interests, and mobilize those coalitions on behalf of political projects in power.[19] Without legitimacy, standing, and trust in the eyes of political actors, parties cannot perform these roles effectively. Indeed, precisely because we depart from the shared adherence of both candidate- and group-centered party scholars to a mechanistic conception of party functions, we can connect the dots to identify hollow parties' core failing—namely, their inability to contain the furies of a polarized age. And so, even as we make extensive use of the rich empirical research that both the candidate- and group-centered theories have inspired, our analysis treats coordination as just one facet among many in evaluating parties' work to shape projects and mobilize action.[20]

Because we see parties as operating on multiple dimensions, often with a mix of discipline and vigor in some realms and fragmentation and passivity in others, we likewise eschew the overarching terminology of "weak" and "strong" in evaluating parties.[21] In particular, we reject conflating party unity with party strength. Free labor Republicans pushed forward their world-historical project amid a party rent by factional division. Taking "strong" measures to avoid open party disagreement, on the other hand, can itself be a sign of weakness. Sam Rayburn famously never called a meeting of the Democratic caucus during his decades presiding over a deeply divided party in the House. Again, a wider view of parties leads us to reject such limited view.[22]

As for scholarship in American political development (APD), parties by their nature span the silos that the field seeks to break down: between state and society, between elite and mass politics, and across the fragmented institutions of the state itself. Tracing durable patterns across time with special attention to opportunities taken and forgone, making focused comparisons, emphasizing the interplay between ideas and institutions, interpreting the present in light of the past— these are all hallmarks of APD analysis that we seek to apply.[23] Indeed, the very framework of multiple strands thickening and developing over time emerges from and aims to add to the APD tradition.[24] In particular, we apply Rogers Smith's influential framing of multiple long-running American historical traditions, both liberal and illiberal, to visions of American parties.[25]

Finally, we take from political historians our use of narrative, our concern with precise temporal contexts, and our emphasis on interweaving party politics with the myriad social forces that shaped them and that they shaped in turn.[26] For the last half century, historians have stressed the capacious boundaries of the political, reaching deep into everyday lives.[27] Political historians have also expanded their ambit to encompass voices across the ideological spectrum long important in American history, even if excluded from formal representation in the halls of power.[28]

As for parties themselves, however, their workings frequently remain murky in scholarly historical narratives, especially of twentieth-century politics. Historians lose sight of what matters about parties when they render them as superstructure, ignoring both their internal dynamics and their interactions with other institutions.[29] In attending to those, our approach sharpens the treatment of party in contemporary political history. And we hark back to, even as we seek to provide a more systematic framework for, older historical traditions that plumbed the workings of electoral politics, emphasized the ensuing political conflict, and told the stories of party leaders.[30]

The result of our synthetic approach, then, is a book more attuned to social structure than is most scholarship in party politics and APD, and more tied to high politics than is most political history. We hope that bringing these three intellectual traditions together will offer scholars new points of connection to learn from one another.

ACKNOWLEDGMENTS

WE DECIDED to write this book during a car ride on Saturday, October 29, 2016. We had presented a paper on parties at a conference at Princeton University whose theme was "Can America Govern Itself?" (At coffee breaks, the just-released Comey letter dominated the chatter.) After the conference, Rosenfeld drove Schlozman to Cornell University, where he was to speak on a pre-election panel. In the course of the trip from Princeton to Ithaca, we decided that we worked well together, that we had things to say to the world, and that we'd quickly write a short book. The first point remains true; the second is for readers to judge; and as for the third—well, it's taken much more time and many more words than we imagined, which makes it a particular pleasure that we now get to thank those who have helped us along the way.

We begin with Frances Lee and Nolan McCarty, who solicited our original conference paper and then encouraged us to take things further. Since then, we have received invaluable feedback at too many panels, speaker series, and workshops to count, and in all sorts of coffee shops and Zoom meetings. We particularly appreciate the assistance of Julia Azari, David Bateman, Jeff Broxmeyer, Devin Caughey, the late Joe Cooper, Adam Hilton, David Karol, Matt Karp, Kate Krimmel, Rob Mickey, Sid Milkis, Lara Putnam, Kay Schlozman, Adam Sheingate, Adam Slez, Sid Tarrow, Mason Williams, Vanessa Williamson, and Matthew Yglesias. As both talented historian and incisive editor, Tim Shenk offered suggestions and encouragement at a crucial moment. Lily Geismer, Michael Kazin, and series editor Eric Schickler, all of whom revealed themselves to us, provided extraordinarily generous and generative comments on the entire manuscript during the review process at Princeton University Press. We have had fun strolling down the byways of

American politics past and present with these fellow scholars and writers. More important, they have, to a one, pushed us to go beyond that and to think about why American party politics matters.

Both separately and together, we have tried out ideas that appear in these pages in various articles and reviews. Among the fine editors who have sharpened our thoughts, we want to single out Mark Krotov at *n+1*, who has a knack both for asking smart questions and for knocking prose into shape. We thank Luke Albert, Dimitrios Halikias, Nick Jacobson, Tristan Klingelhöfer, Katy Li, Simon Messineo, and Noah Nardone for excellent research assistance, and want to give special thanks to Jacob Osborne for his work on graphics. Deep thanks go as well to those who shared their time and thoughts with us to make our research trip to Nevada so fruitful: Geoconda Argüello-Kline, Scott Cooper, Molly Forgey, Harry Grill, Adam Jentleson, Megan Jones, Bethany Khan, Rebecca Lambe, Alana Mounce, and D. Taylor. We also appreciate the extraordinary and unheralded work of the many archivists and librarians who have cheerfully accommodated our often hefty requests. We especially thank the Interlibrary Loan departments at Eisenhower Library, Johns Hopkins, and Case-Geyer Library, Colgate. They even laughed at our jokes that we'd earned ILL super-elite frequent-flier status. Our Hopkins and Colgate students have asked good questions and happily acted as guinea pigs for draft chapters. More generally, we appreciate the generosity of our home institutions, whose support for faculty research allowed us the time and resources to write this book without any outside funding.

At Princeton University Press, Bridget Flannery-McCoy has been wonderfully supportive and helpful as that miracle of miracles, an academic-press editor who actually edits. Alena Chekanov, Erin Davis, Elizabeth Byrd, Jamie Thaman, and Fred Kameny ably brought the book into print. Danny thanks family and friends in Baltimore, Chilmark, and beyond, both for regularly chewing the political fat and for all-important reminders of life beyond party politics. Sam thanks his brother Jake Rosenfeld for reliable counsel and ribbing; his children, Henry and Frankie, for being their amazing selves; and his wife, Erica De Bruin—ever the rock, the fire, and the light of his life. And finally, with love and gratitude, we dedicate this book to our parents.

NOTES

Chapter One: The Problem of Hollow Parties

1. "Attendees at the Dick Richards Breakfast" and memo from Morton Blackwell to Elizabeth Dole, May 20, 1981, NCPAC folder 1, box 14, papers of Morton Blackwell, Ronald Reagan Presidential Library (Simi Valley, CA); Richard Richards, *Climbing the Political Ladder One Rung at a Time* (Ogden, UT: Weber State University Press, 2006), 227.

2. Shane Goldmacher and Nick Corasaniti, "How Caucuses Sank into a 'Disaster,'" *New York Times*, February 5, 2020, A1; Matthew Rosenberg, Nick Corasaniti, Sheera Frenkel and Nicole Perlroth, "Key to Democrats' Digital Push: Untested and Hastily Built App," *New York Times*, February 5, 2020, A1; Emily Stewart, "Acronym, the Dark Money Group behind the Iowa Caucuses App Meltdown, Explained," *Vox*, February 5, 2020, https://www.vox.com/recode/2020/2/5/21123009/acronym-tara-mcgowan-shadow-app-iowa-caucus-results; Isaac Stanley-Becker, "Iowa Caucuses Crashed Down under DNC's Watchful Eye," *Washington Post*, February 16, 2020, A1; Tyler Pager, "Iowa Autopsy Report: DNC Meddling Led to Caucus Debacle," *Politico*, December 12, 2020, https://www.politico.com/news/2020/12/12/iowa-caucus-dnc-report-444649.

3. See, for example, Mickey Edwards, "How to Turn Republicans and Democrats into Americans," *Atlantic*, July/August 2011, 102–6; Frances Rosenbluth and Ian Shapiro, "Political Partisanship Is Vicious. That's Because Parties Are Too Weak," *Washington Post*, November 28, 2018, https://www.washingtonpost.com/outlook/2018/11/28/political-partisanship-is-vicious-thats-because-political-parties-are-too-weak/.

4. Steven W. Webster, *American Rage: How Anger Shapes Our Politics* (New York: Cambridge University Press, 2020).

5. On the nationalization of mass partisanship and political behavior, see Steven Rogers, "National Forces in State Legislative Elections," *Annals of the American Academy of Political and Social Science* 667 (2016): 207–25; Daniel J. Hopkins, *The Increasingly United States: How and Why American Political Behavior Nationalized* (Chicago: University of Chicago Press, 2018).

6. Former Obama aide Ben Rhodes has used the same term to describe the bipartisan foreign-policy establishment; his blob overlaps but is hardly coterminous with ours. See David Samuels, "The Storyteller and the President" *New York Times Magazine*, May 8, 2016, 44–54.

7. The scholarship on party networks challenges arbitrary categorical distinctions between formal and informal party entities, defining parties themselves as webs of official and satellite organizations that coordinate within and across political domains. The structural looseness of contemporary parties makes network analysis a particularly appealing strategy, but our conception of the party blob departs from it precisely at the assumption of a common set of goals among all the participants. See Gregory Koger, Seth Masket, and Hans Noel, "Partisan Webs: Information Exchange and Party Networks," *British Journal of Political Science* 39 (2009): 633–53; Gregory Koger, Seth Masket, and Hans Noel, "No Disciplined Army: American Political Parties as Networks," in

The Oxford Handbook of Political Networks, ed. Jennifer Victor, Alexander Montgomery, and Mark Lubell (New York: Oxford University Press, 2017), 453–66. As a good example of clashing incentives, while ideological media serve as critical nodes of forming and disseminating messages, their fortunes tend to rise in opposition. The left-wing publisher Victor Navasky once quipped that "Ronald Reagan is bad for the country but good for *The Nation*." See Elizabeth Mehren, "A Journalistic Love-In for *The Nation* Magazine," *Los Angeles Times*, March 20, 1986, 1.

8. Kay Lawson, "How State Laws Undermine Parties," in *Elections American Style*, ed. A. James Reichley (Washington, DC: Brookings Institution, 1987), 242.

9. Steve Fraser and Gary Gerstle, eds., *The Rise and Fall of the New Deal Order, 1930–1980* (Princeton, NJ: Princeton University Press, 1989).

10. Judith Stein *Pivotal Decade: How the United States Traded Factories for Finance in the 1970s* (New Haven, CT: Yale University Press, 2010). Scholars across disciplines see in the 1970s a turning point. See, for example, Mark Blyth, *Great Transformations: Economic Ideas and Institutional Change* (New York: Cambridge University Press, 2002), 126–250; Greta Krippner, *Capitalizing on Crisis: The Political Origins of the Rise of Finance* (Cambridge, MA: Harvard University Press, 2011); Paul Pierson and Theda Skocpol, eds., *The Transformation of American Politics: Activist Government and the Rise of Conservatism* (Princeton, NJ: Princeton University Press, 2007); Jefferson Cowie, *Stayin' Alive: The 1970s and the Last Days of the Working Class* (New York: New Press, 2010); Laura Kalman, *Right Star Rising: A New Politics, 1974–1980* (New York: W. W. Norton, 2010); Bruce J. Schulman and Julian E. Zelizer, eds., *Rightward Bound: Making America Conservative in the 1970s* (Cambridge, MA: Harvard University Press, 2008); Daniel T. Rodgers, *Age of Fracture* (Cambridge, MA: Belknap Press of Harvard University Press, 2011). Our emphasis on social changes and developments inside institutions explains why we date the critical junctures to the 1970s rather than to the 1990s, when the system-level manifestations of polarization appeared, as in Paul Pierson and Eric Schickler, "Madison's Constitution under Stress: A Developmental Analysis of Political Polarization," *Annual Review of Political Science* 23 (2020): 37–58; Nicole Hemmer, *Partisans: The Conservative Revolutionaries Who Remade American Politics in the 1990s* (New York: Basic Books, 2022).

11. Neoliberalism has many dimensions. We lean on William Davies, who treats neoliberalism as "an attempt to replace political judgment with economic evaluation, including, but not exclusively, the evaluation of markets." See William Davies, *The Limits of Neoliberalism: Authority, Sovereignty, and the Logic of Competition* (London: Sage, 2015), 5–6. For helpful guides, see Peter B. Evans and William H. Sewell Jr., "Neoliberalism: Policy Regimes, International Regimes, and Social Effects," in *Social Resilience in the Neoliberal Era*, ed. Peter A. Hall and Michèle Lamont (New York: Cambridge University Press, 2013); Angus Burgin, "The Neoliberal Turn," typescript, 2019. For historical reflections focusing on the United States, see Kim Phillips-Fein, "The History of Neoliberalism," in *Shaped by the State: Toward a New Political History of the Twentieth Century*, ed. Brent Cebul, Lily Geismer, and Mason B. Williams (Chicago: University of Chicago Press, 2019), 347–62; Gary Gerstle, *The Rise and Fall of the Neoliberal Order: America and the Free World in the Free Market Era* (New York: Oxford University Press, 2022).

12. See the essays in *Beyond the New Deal Order: U.S. Politics from the Great Depression to the Great Recession*, ed. Gary Gerstle, Nelson Lichtenstein, and Alice O'Connor (Philadelphia: University of Pennsylvania Press, 2019), esp. 143–278.

13. Jeffrey M. Berry and Clyde Wilcox, *The Interest Group Society*, 6th ed. (New York: Routledge, 2018), 19–43.

14. John H. Aldrich, "Presidential Campaigns in Party- and Candidate-Centered Eras," in *Under the Watchful Eye: Managing Presidential Campaigns in the Presidential Era*, ed. Mathew D. McCubbins, (Washington, DC: CQ Press, 1992), 59–82. See also Robin Kolodny and David A. Dulio, "Political Party Adaptation in Congressional Campaigns: Why Political Parties Use

Coordinated Expenditures to Hire Political Consultants," *Party Politics* 9 (2003): 729–46; Brendan Nyhan and Jacob M. Montgomery, "Connecting the Candidates: Consultant Networks and the Diffusion of Campaign Strategy in American Congressional Elections," *American Journal of Political Science* 59 (2015): 292–308.

15. For key contributions to the literature on service parties, see Cornelius B. Cotter and John S. Bibby, "Institutional Development of Parties and the Thesis of Party Decline," *Political Science Quarterly* 95 (1980): 1–27; M. Margaret Conway, "Republican Political Party Nationalization, Campaign Activities, and Their Implications for the Party System," *Publius* 13 (1983): 1–17; Paul Herrnson, *Party Campaigning in the 1980s* (New York: Cambridge University Press, 1988). For an early dissent that anticipates many of our themes, see John J. Coleman, "Resurgent or Just Busy? Party Organizations in Contemporary America," in *The State of the Parties: The Changing Role of Contemporary American Parties*, 2nd ed., ed. Daniel M. Shea and John C. Green (Lanham, MD: Rowman & Littlefield, 1996), 367–84.

16. Seth Masket and Hans Noel, *Political Parties* (New York: W. W. Norton, 2021), 176–77.

17. For an interpretation that emphasizes these shifts, see Samuel L. Popkin, *Crackup: The Republican Implosion and the Future of Presidential Politics* (New York: Oxford University Press, 2021).

18. Robert Bauman, CPAC speech, February 17, 1975, box 3, folder 27, American Conservative Union (ACU) Papers, Brigham Young University, Provo, Utah.

19. Jacob Hacker and Paul Pierson, *Let Them Eat Tweets: How the Right Rules in an Age of Extreme Inequality* (New York: Liveright, 2020).

20. Conservative parties' decisive role during the rise of mass democracy in western Europe weighs heavily on our focus on the particular danger they can pose. Daniel Ziblatt, *Conservative Parties and the Birth of Democracy* (New York: Cambridge University Press, 2017).

21. For an echo of the early McGovern-Fraser critiques, see Jonathan Rauch and Ray La Raja, "Too Much Democracy Is Bad for Democracy," *Atlantic*, December 2019, 62–68.

22. Thomas E. Mann and Norman J. Ornstein, *It's Even Worse Than It Looks: How the American Constitutional System Collided with the New Politics of Extremism*, rev. ed. (New York: Basic Books, 2016); Pierson and Schickler, "Madison's Constitution under Stress"; synthesizing a vast literature, Nolan McCarty, *Polarization: What Everyone Needs to Know* (New York: Oxford University Press, 2019).

23. Lilliana Mason, *Uncivil Agreement: How Politics Became Our Identity* (Chicago: University of Chicago Press, 2018); Shanto Iyengar, Yphtach Lelkes, Matthew Levendusky, Neil Malhotra, and Sean J. Westwood, "The Origins and Consequences of Affective Polarization in the United States," *Annual Review of Political Science* 22 (2019): 129–46; Webster, *American Rage*. But see also Amber Hye-Yon Lee, Yphtach Lelkes, Carlee B. Hawkins, and Alexander G. Theodoridis, "Negative Partisanship Is Not More Prevalent Than Positive Partisanship," *Nature Human Behaviour* 6 (2022): 951–63. The topic of voters' positive loyalties to and beliefs in the capacities of political parties deserves more scholarly attention.

24. Suzanne Mettler and Robert Lieberman, *Four Threats: The Recurring Crises of American Democracy* (New York: St. Martin's Press, 2020); James A. Morone, *Republic of Wrath: How American Politics Turned Tribal, from George Washington to Donald Trump* (New York: Basic Books, 2020).

25. "The current Republican Party," Seth Masket and Hans Noel write, "is diverging from our conception of parties." "Writing about a Party System under Duress and in Dispute," *PS: Political Science & Politics* 55 (2022): 641–42. Though we root the critical junctures somewhat earlier and deeper in social structure, we build on the admirable Mann and Ornstein, *It's Even Worse Than It Looks*; see also E. J. Dionne Jr., Norman J. Ornstein, and Thomas E. Mann, *One Nation after Trump: A Guide for the Perplexed, the Disillusioned, the Desperate, and the Not-Yet Deported* (New York: St. Martin's Press, 2017).

26. The most comprehensive treatments placing U.S. democratic backsliding in comparative perspective come from Steven Levitsky and Daniel Ziblatt. Steven Levitsky and Daniel Ziblatt, *How Democracies Die* (New York: Crown, 2018); Steven Levitsky and Daniel Ziblatt, *Tyranny of the Minority: Why American Democracy Reached the Breaking Point* (New York: Crown, 2023).

27. Peter Mair, *Ruling the Void: The Hollowing of Western Democracy* (London: Verso, 2013), 16.

28. See Richard S. Katz, "European and American Political Parties: Becoming More Similar?," *Journal of Elections, Public Opinion and Parties* 29 (2019): 427–47; Nicol C. Rae, "The Diminishing Oddness of American Political Parties," in *The Parties Respond: Changes in American Parties and Campaigns*, 5th ed., ed. Mark D. Brewer and L. Sandy Maisel (Boulder: Westview Press, 2013), 25–46.

29. For a good discussion, see E. J. Dionne Jr., "The Biden Victory and the Future of the Centre-Left," *Social Europe*, December 4, 2020, https://socialeurope.eu/the-biden-victory-and -the-future-of-the-centre-left. On social democracy more generally, see Giacomo Benedetto, Simon Hix, and Nicola Mastrorocco, "The Rise and Fall of Social Democracy, 1918–2017," *American Political Science Review* 114 (2020): 928–39; Adam Przeworski, "From Revolution to Reformism," *Boston Review*, January 28, 2021, https://bostonreview.net/politics/adam-przeworski-revolution -reformism; Amory Gethin, Clara Martínez-Toledano, and Thomas Piketty, "Brahmin Left versus Merchant Right: Political Cleavages in 21 Western Democracies, 1948–2020," *Quarterly Journal of Economics* 137 (2022): 1–48; Daniel Oesch and Line Rennwald, "Electoral Competition in Europe's New Tripolar Political Space: Class voting for the Left, Centre-Right and Radical Right," *European Journal of Political Research* 57 (2018): 783–809; Tarik Abou-Chadi and Simon Hix, "Brahmin Left versus Merchant Right? Education, Class, Multiparty Competition, and Redistribution in Western Europe," *British Journal of Sociology* 72 (2021): 79–92.

30. On different approaches to defining populism, see Bart Bonikowski and Noam Gidron, "Multiple Traditions in Populism Research: Toward a Theoretical Synthesis," *Comparative Politics Newsletter*, Fall 2016, 7–14. See also Peter Mair, "Populist Democracy vs. Party Democracy," in *Democracies and the Populist Challenge*, ed. Yves Mény and Yves Surel (Houndsmills, Basingstoke: Palgrave, 2002), 81–98.

31. Kenneth M. Roberts, "Parties, Populism, and Democratic Decay: A Comparative Perspective on Political Polarization in the United States," in *When Democracy Trumps Populism: European and Latin American Lessons for the United States*, ed. Kurt Weyland and Raúl L. Madrid (New York: Cambridge University Press, 2019); Kenneth M. Roberts, "Left, Right, and the Populist Structuring of Political Competition," in *Routledge Handbook of Global Populism*, ed. Carlos de la Torre (Milton Park, Abingdon: Routledge, 2019); Noam Gidron and Daniel Ziblatt, "Center-Right Political Parties in Advanced Democracies," *Annual Review of Political Science* 22 (2019): 17–35.

32. Phrase from Martin Wolf, "Donald Trump's Pluto-populism Laid Bare," *Financial Times*, May 2, 2017.

33. "Historical comparison," Samuel Beer once wrote, "reveals not only what is new but what is old." Samuel H. Beer, *Modern British Politics: Parties and Pressure Groups in the Collectivist Age* (New York: W. W. Norton, 1982 [1965]), xii.

34. Rogers M. Smith, "Beyond Tocqueville, Myrdal, and Hartz: The Multiple Traditions in America," *American Political Science Review* 87 (1993): 558. We thus endorse Eric Schickler's characterization of parties as "historical composites shaped by multiple logics," in *Racial Realignment: The Transformation of American Liberalism, 1936–1965* (Princeton, NJ: Princeton University Press, 2016), 11–12.

35. E. E. Schattschneider, *Party Government* (New York: Rinehart 1942), ix.

36. Legal scholarship on parties starts from this essential distinction. See, for example, Joseph Fishkin and Heather K. Gerken, "The Party's Over: McCutcheon, Shadow Parties, and

the Future of the Party System," *Supreme Court Review* 2014, 175–214; Samuel Issacharoff, "Outsourcing Politics: The Hostile Takeover of Our Hollowed-Out Political Parties," *Houston Law Review* 54 (2017): 845–80; and, with an associational view close to ours, Tabatha Abu El-Haj, "Networking the Party: First Amendment Rights and the Pursuit of Responsive Party Government," *Columbia Law Review* 118 (2018): 1282–301.

37. For important efforts emphasizing party form, see Austin Ranney, *Curing the Mischiefs of Faction: Party Reform in America* (Berkeley: University of California Press, 1975); James W. Ceaser, *Presidential Selection: Theory and Development* (Princeton, NJ: Princeton University Press, 1979); Leon D. Epstein, *Political Parties in the American Mold* (Madison: University of Wisconsin Press, 1986); John H. Aldrich, *Why Parties? A Second Look* (Chicago: University of Chicago Press, 2011); Kathleen Bawn, Marty Cohen, David Karol, Seth Masket, Hans Noel, and John Zaller, "A Theory of Parties: Groups, Policy Demands, and Nominations in American Politics," *Perspectives on Politics* 10 (2012): 571–97.

38. We take this phrase from Stanley Lieberson, *A Piece of the Pie: Blacks and White Immigrants since 1880* (Berkeley: University of California Press, 1981), 382.

39. Our view is thus sympathetic to but more expansive than Jacob Hacker and Paul Pierson, "After the Master Theory: Downs, Schattschneider, and the Rebirth of Policy-Focused Analysis," *Perspectives on Politics* 12 (2014): 643–62. On the sublimation of questions of state and society into those of policy, see the discussion of "policy-mindedness" in Hugh Heclo, "Sixties Civics," in *The Great Society and the High Tide of Liberalism*, ed. Sidney M. Milkis and Jerome M. Mileur (Amherst: University of Massachusetts Press, 2005), 60–63, 70–75.

40. By the same token, many collective party actors have been political entrepreneurs, developing innovations and shaping lasting change, but others have not. See Adam D. Sheingate, "Political Entrepreneurship, Institutional Change, and American Political Development," *Studies in American Political Development* 17 (2003): 185–203.

41. For analyses of parties' worldviews that treat entire parties, see John Gerring, *Party Ideologies in America, 1828–1996* (New York: Cambridge University Press, 1998); Matt Grossmann and David A. Hopkins, *Asymmetric Politics: Ideological Republicans and Group Interest Democrats* (New York: Oxford University Press, 2016); on factions, see Daniel DiSalvo, *Engines of Change: Party Factions in American Politics, 1868–2010* (New York: Oxford University Press, 2012); Rachel M. Blum, *How the Tea Party Captured the GOP: Insurgent Factions in American Politics* (Chicago: University of Chicago Press, 2020).

42. We thus largely sidestep the engagement with individual agency at the heart of biography. For a book whose themes resonate strongly with ours but that is organized around particular individuals confronting the task of building majority coalitions, see Timothy Shenk, *Realigners: Partisan Hacks, Political Visionaries, and the Struggle to Rule American Democracy* (New York: Farrar, Straus & Giroux, 2022).

43. On the matter of party projects we might have included, DiSalvo, *Engines of Change*, discusses five party-factions not treated separately here. The Stalwarts and Half-Breeds in the post–Civil War Republican Party were factions inside Gilded Age organizations. Old Guard Republicans during the Progressive Era, and especially Southern Democrats and Liberal Republicans during the mid-twentieth century, all rooted themselves in particular institutional configurations without making substantial public claims about the place of party. By the same token, we exclude or treat only in passing the individualistic insurgents and their "personalist pseudomovements" in and out of third parties that have proliferated during the last century. See Andrew E. Busch, *Outsiders and Openness in the Presidential Nominating System* (Pittsburgh: University of Pittsburgh Press, 1997), 171.

44. While our interest in parties as agents of historical change resonates powerfully with the realignment tradition, our approach differs. As realignment theory homes in on how majority

coalitions get made and broken, it emphasizes the discontinuities in successive party systems. By contrast, we trace changing and recurrent patterns over time more than we seek to explain why particular forces dominate at any given moment. For preliminary and culminating soundings in the realignment tradition, see, respectively, Arthur M. Schlesinger Sr., *Paths to the Present* (New York: Macmillan, 1949); James L. Sundquist, *Dynamics of the Party System: Alignment and Realignment of Political Parties in the United States*, rev. ed. (Washington, DC: Brookings Institution, 1983). In a more materialist strain, see Walter Dean Burnham, *Critical Elections and the Mainsprings of American Politics* (New York: W. W. Norton, 1970); Thomas Ferguson, *Golden Rule: The Investment Theory of Party Competition and the Logic of Money-Driven Political Systems* (Chicago: University of Chicago Press, 1995). The emphasis on majority building reappears in Shenk, *Realigners*.

45. Our understanding of accommodationism encompasses, but is broader than, the specific forms of clientelism explored in Susan C. Stokes, Thad Dunning, Marcelo Nazareno, and Valeria Brusco, *Brokers, Voters, and Clientelism: The Puzzle of Distributive Politics* (New York: Cambridge University Press, 2013). For a good earlier attempt to link U.S. machines with comparative patterns, see James C. Scott, "Corruption, Machine Politics, and Political Change," *American Political Science Review* 63 (1969): 1142–58.

46. Harold F. Gosnell, "The Political Party versus the Political Machine," *Annals of the American Academy of Political and Social Science* 169 (1933): 21–28.

47. Milton Rakove, *Don't Make No Waves . . . Don't Back No Losers: An Insider's Analysis of the Daley Machine* (Bloomington: Indiana University Press, 1975), 121.

48. On anti-party thought, see Nancy L. Rosenblum, *On the Side of the Angels: An Appreciation of Parties and Partisanship* (Princeton, NJ: Princeton University Press, 2008).

49. Gil Troy, *See How They Ran: The Changing Role of the Presidential Candidate* (New York: Free Press, 1991), 162.

50. For a shining rhetorical example, see Lawrence B. Glickman, *Free Enterprise: An American History* (New Haven, CT: Yale University Press, 2019).

51. Beyond these alignments stands the structural position of business in capitalist society. Michel Kalecki, "Political Aspects of Full Employment," *Political Quarterly* 14 (1943): 322–30; Charles E. Lindblom, *Politics and Markets: The World's Political Economic Systems* (New York: Basic Books, 1977).

52. Beardian and Marxist analyses that emphasize the material interests of powerful elites have struggled to capture how American parties aggregate diverse interests and constituencies. But such analyses offer powerful insight into the pro-capital strand. See Ferguson, *Golden Rule*.

53. For a narrative that covers this broad ground, see Michael Kazin, *American Dreamers: How the Left Changed a Nation* (New York: Alfred A. Knopf, 2011). For a twentieth-century account sensitive to party politics, see James N. Gregory, "Remapping the American Left: A History of Radical Discontinuity," *Labor: Studies in Working-Class History* 17 (2020): 11–45. Reflecting the diverse manifestations of American radicalism, their formulations, and ours, deliberately go beyond explicitly socialist politics.

54. Richard Oestreicher, "Urban Working-Class Political Behavior and Theories of American Electoral Politics, 1870–1940," *Journal of American History* 74 (1988): 1257–86.

55. For a recent meditation on these themes, see Jedediah Purdy, *Two Cheers for Politics: Why Democracy Is Flawed, Frightening—and Our Best Hope* (New York: Basic Books, 2022).

56. Jan-Werner Müller, *What Is Populism?* (Philadelphia: University of Pennsylvania Press, 2017).

57. Aziz Rana, *The Two Faces of American Freedom* (Cambridge, MA: Harvard University Press, 2010).

58. To be clear, we treat populism here in its American context. While we find some resonances between Populism in the 1880s and 1890s and contemporary American right-populism, and stronger resonances between contemporary American right-populism and its counterparts

overseas, the transitive property does not hold: the farmers in the South and West angry at depressed agricultural prices in the 1880s have little in common with Viktor Orbán or Jair Bolsonaro. See Charles Postel, "Populism as a Concept and the Challenge of U.S. History," *Idées d'Amériques* 14 (2019), http://journals.openedition.org/ideas/6472.

59. The classic account of these links is Michael Kazin, *The Populist Persuasion: An American History* (New York: Basic Books, 1995). As Kazin makes clear and as chapter 4 explains, the connection between this approach to politics and capital-*P* Populism is complex.

60. V. O. Key Jr., *Southern Politics in State and Nation* (Knoxville: University of Tennessee Press, 1984 [1949]), 315.

61. On the continuities in this reactionary lineage, see Jeffrey K. Tulis and Nicole Mellow, *Legacies of Losing in American Politics* (Chicago: University of Chicago Press, 2018); Heather Cox Richardson, *How the South Won the Civil War: Oligarchy, Democracy, and the Continuing Fight for the Soul of America* (New York: Oxford University Press, 2020). On the regional dimensions, see Key, *Southern Politics in State and Nation*; Michael Perman, *The Southern Political Tradition* (Baton Rouge: Louisiana State University Press, 2012); David A. Bateman, Ira Katznelson, and John S. Lapinski, *Southern Nation: Congress and White Supremacy after Reconstruction* (Princeton, NJ: Princeton University Press, 2018). Compare Devin Caughey, *The Unsolid South: Mass Politics and National Representation in a One-Party Enclave* (Princeton, NJ: Princeton University Press, 2018).

62. For an excellent example of how internal Republican Party politics—including Benjamin Harrison's shaky prospects of renomination—shaped a deadly confrontation, see Heather Cox Richardson, *Wounded Knee: Party Politics and the Road to an American Massacre* (New York: Basic Books, 2010).

63. Doug McAdam and Karina Kloos, *Deeply Divided: Racial Politics and Social Movements in Postwar America* (New York: Oxford University Press, 2014); Daniel Schlozman, *When Movements Anchor Parties: Electoral Alignments in American History* (Princeton, NJ: Princeton University Press, 2015); Sidney Tarrow, *Movements and Parties: Critical Connections in American Political Development* (New York: Cambridge University Press, 2021); and, mediated through the presidency, Sidney M. Milkis and Daniel J. Tichenor, *Rivalry and Reform: Presidents, Social Movements, and the Transformation of American Politics* (Chicago: University of Chicago Press, 2019).

64. For a recent synthesis that marries social history with high politics, see Michael Kazin, *What It Took to Win: A History of the Democratic Party* (New York: Farrar, Straus & Giroux, 2022).

65. The quote, famous to political scientists, is from Schattschneider, *Party Government*, 1.

66. "Professional Notes," *PS: Political Science & Politics* 10 (1977): 144.

Chapter Two: The Affirmation of Party in Antebellum America

1. Anthony Banning Norton, *The Great Revolution of 1840: Reminiscences of the Log Cabin and Hard Cider Campaign* (Cleveland: Arthur H. Clark, 1888), 44.

2. The account was published on February 24, 1840, in the *Boston Atlas*, reprinted in Norton, *Great Revolution of 1840*, 54–56.

3. Norton, *Great Revolution of 1840*, 57.

4. We thus break from a tendency within political science to portray Martin Van Buren's work leading up to the 1828 election as some wholesale invention of mass parties. For a sophisticated theoretical rendering of that story, see John Aldrich, *Why Parties? A Second Look* (Chicago: University of Chicago Press, 2011), 102–29.

5. The strongest corrective to nostalgia—too strong, in our view—comes from Glenn C. Altschuler and Stuart M. Blumin, *Rude Republic: Americans and Their Politics in the Nineteenth Century* (Princeton, NJ: Princeton University Press, 2000). The reality that many local party

organizations effectively operated as closed cliques and that popular partisan commitments were often shallow hardly undermines the distinctive roles of nineteenth-century parties. For historiographical overviews, see Joel H. Silbey, *The Partisan Imperative: The Dynamics of American Politics before the Civil War* (New York: Oxford University Press, 1985); Richard L. McCormick, *The Party Period and Public Policy: American Politics from the Age of Jackson to the Progressive Era* (New York: Oxford University Press, 1986); Michael F. Holt, *Political Parties and American Political Development from the Age of Jackson to the Age of Lincoln* (Baton Rouge: Louisiana State University Press, 1992); Ronald P. Formisano, "The 'Party Period' Revisited," *Journal of American History* 86 (1999): 93–120.

6. On the culmination of universal white manhood suffrage, see Alexander Keyssar, *The Right to Vote: The Contested History of Democracy in the United States* (New York: Basic Books, 2000), 26–52.

7. The acceptance of regular party competition was a long process, to be sure, and older habits that dismissed opponents as minoritarian conspirators endured long after 1828. Compare Richard Hofstadter, *The Idea of a Party System: The Rise of Legitimate Opposition in the United States, 1780–1840* (Berkeley: University of California Press, 1970), 212–71. On the endurance of anti-partyism through the Second Party System and beyond, see Altschuler and Blumin, *Rude Republic*, esp. 105–83; Mark Voss-Hubbard, *Beyond Party: Cultures of Antipartisanship in Northern Politics before the Civil War* (Baltimore: Johns Hopkins University Press, 2002).

8. "Statement by the Democratic Republicans of the United States," July 31, 1835, in *History of American Presidential Elections, 1789–1968*, ed. Arthur M. Schlesinger Jr. (New York: Chelsea House, 1971), 1:621, 622.

9. The significance of republicanism to Jacksonian thought is a central theme of Marvin Meyers, *The Jacksonian Persuasion: Politics and Belief* (Stanford, CA: Stanford University Press, 1957). On republicanism's historiography, see Daniel T. Rodgers, "Republicanism: The Career of a Concept," *Journal of American History* 79 (1992): 11–38. Integrating scholarship on civic republicanism, the market revolution, and the organizational mechanics of the Second Party System, Harry L. Watson's *Liberty and Power: The Politics of Jacksonian America* (New York: Hill and Wang, 1990) set an interpretive template for the period that has endured. It is visible both in Sean Wilentz's Jacksonophilic *The Rise of American Democracy: Jefferson to Lincoln* (New York: W. W. Norton, 2005) and in the less sympathetic portrayals of the Jacksonians in Daniel Walker Howe, *What Hath God Wrought: The Transformation of America, 1815–1848* (New York: Oxford University Press, 2007).

10. Aziz Rana, *The Two Faces of American Freedom* (Cambridge, MA: Harvard University Press, 2010). The dyad recurs as a long historiographic preoccupation, from Edmund S. Morgan, *American Slavery, American Freedom: The Ordeal of Colonial Virginia* (New York: W. W. Norton, 1975) to Joshua A. Lynn, *Preserving the White Man's Republic: Jacksonian Democracy, Race, and the Transformation of American Conservatism* (Charlottesville: University of Virginia Press, 2019). A belated reckoning with it drives contemporary Democrats' disavowal of any Jacksonian philosophical inheritance. See Jonathan Martin, "Democrats Sever Ties to Founders of Party," *New York Times*, August 12, 2015, A12.

11. E. E. Schattschneider, *The Semisovereign People: A Realist's View of Democracy in America* (New York: Holt, Rinehart and Winston, 1960), 62–77.

12. Thomas Hart Benton to Alfred Ward Grayson Davis, December 16, 1834, Papers of Martin Van Buren [digital edition], ed. Mark R. Cheathem et al., https://vanburenpapers.org/document-mvb01739.

13. Alexis de Tocqueville, *Democracy in America*, ed. J. P. Mayer, trans. George Lawrence (New York: Harper & Row, 1966), 175.

14. This depiction has lived on in historical interpretations that see few substantive stakes in the Second Party System's elaborate electoral competition. For canonical portrayals of

Jacksonians as liberal capitalists just like their opponents, see Richard Hofstadter, *The American Political Tradition and the Men Who Made It* (New York: Vintage Books, 1948), 57–86; Louis Hartz, *The Liberal Tradition in America: An Interpretation of American Political Thought since the Revolution* (New York: Harcourt, Brace, and World, 1955), 89–144. Hofstadter offered his portrayal as a rejoinder to Arthur M. Schlesinger Jr.'s influential depiction of Jacksonian politics as class-driven and ideological in *The Age of Jackson* (Boston: Little, Brown, 1945). The "ethnocultural school" of historians, in emphasizing the demographic determinants of voting behavior, reinforced the notion that consensus more than conflict defined the material politics of the period. See Lee Benson, *The Concept of Jacksonian Democracy: New York as a Test Case* (Princeton, NJ: Princeton University Press, 1961); Ronald P. Formisano, *The Birth of Mass Political Parties in Michigan, 1827–1861* (Princeton, NJ: Princeton University Press, 1971).

15. Our approach draws on scholarship that challenges an earlier, starkly delineated model positing Andrew Jackson's election in 1828 as a sharp break from what preceded it. For overviews of the new work, see Daniel Peart and Adam I. P. Smith, introduction to *Practicing Democracy: Popular Politics in the United States from the Constitution to the Civil War*, ed. Daniel Peart and Adam I. P. Smith (Charlottesville: University of Virginia Press, 2015), 1–20; Reeve Huston, "Rethinking the Origins of Partisan Democracy in the United States, 1795–1840," in Peart and Smith, *Practicing Democracy*, 47–71. For a recent account that emphasizes early partisan strength and its implications for transcending the Van Buren model in scholarly understandings of party, see Jeffrey L. Pasley, *The First Presidential Contest: 1796 and the Founding of American Democracy* (Lawrence: University Press of Kansas, 2013).

16. William Nisbet Chambers, *Political Parties in a New Nation: The American Experience, 1776–1809* (New York: Oxford University Press, 1963), 72.

17. Joanne B. Freeman, *Affairs of Honor: National Politics in the New Republic* (New Haven, CT: Yale University Press, 2001).

18. Russell Muirhead and Nancy L. Rosenblum, "Speaking Truth to Conspiracy: Partisanship and Trust," *Critical Review* 28 (2016): 86.

19. See Gordon S. Wood, *The Creation of the American Republic, 1776–1787* (Chapel Hill: University of North Carolina Press, 1969), 391–564; Gerald Leonard and Saul Cornell, *The Partisan Republic: Democracy, Exclusion, and the Fall of the Founders' Constitution, 1780s–1830s* (New York: Cambridge University Press, 2019), 1–83.

20. Henry Saint-John, Viscount Bolingbroke, "The Patriot King and Parties," in *Perspectives on Political Parties: Classic Readings*, ed. Susan E. Scarrow (New York: Palgrave Macmillan, 2002), 30. For context, see Max Skjönsberg, *The Persistence of Party: Ideas of Harmonious Discord in Eighteenth-Century Britain* (New York: Cambridge University Press, 2021).

21. Pasley, *The First Presidential Contest*, 2.

22. Quoted in Stanley Elkins and Eric McKitrick, *The Age of Federalism: The Early American Republic, 1788–1800* (New York: Oxford University Press, 1993), 267.

23. George Washington, "Sixth Annual Address to Congress," November 19, 1794, American Presidency Project, https://www.presidency.ucsb.edu/documents/sixth-annual-address-congress.

24. Jack Rakove, *Original Meanings: Politics and Ideas in the Making of the Constitution* (New York: Alfred A. Knopf, 1997), 268.

25. For evidence of growing party discipline in Congress across the 1790s, see John F. Hoadley, "The Emergence of Political Parties in Congress, 1789–1803," *American Political Science Review* 74 (1980): 757–79; on the early parties' impact on procedural changes in Congress, see Sarah A. Binder, "Partisanship and Procedural Choice: Institutional Change in the Early Congress, 1789–1823," *Journal of Politics* 57 (1995): 1093–1118.

26. Morton Keller, *America's Three Regimes: A New Political History* (New York: Oxford University Press, 2007), 48.

27. Hofstadter, *Idea of a Party System*; Ralph Ketcham, *Presidents above Party: The First American Presidency, 1789–1829* (Chapel Hill: University of North Carolina Press, 1984). See also, with an emphasis on the Revolution's contribution to anti-party culture, Ronald P. Formisano, *The Transformation of Political Culture: Massachusetts Parties, 1790s–1840s* (New York: Oxford University Press, 1983), esp. 57–106.

28. Quoted line from Ketcham, *Presidents above Party*, 208.

29. David Waldstreicher, *In the Midst of Perpetual Fetes: The Making of American Nationalism, 1776–1820* (Chapel Hill: University of North Carolina Press, 1998), 201–16.

30. George Washington, "Farewell Address," September 17, 1796, American Presidency Project, https://www.presidency.ucsb.edu/documents/farewell-address.

31. Keller, *America's Three Regimes*, 60.

32. John Ferling, *Adams vs. Jefferson: The Tumultuous Election of 1800* (New York: Oxford University Press, 2004), 135; Robert C. Lieberman and Suzanne Mettler, *Four Threats: The Recurring Crises of American Democracy* (New York: St. Martin's Press, 2020), 29–50.

33. Our empirical understanding of early American voting behavior owes much to Philip J. Lampi's research, now available through the A New Nation Votes collection at Tufts University: http://elections.lib.tufts.edu. See the special issue dedicated to findings from the initiative in the *Journal of the Early Republic* 33 (2013): 183–334.

34. Rutledge to Harrison Gray Otis, quoted in David Hackett Fischer, *The Revolution of American Conservatism: The Federalist Party in the Era of Jeffersonian Democracy* (New York: Harper & Row, 1965), 140.

35. Waldstreicher, *In the Midst of Perpetual Fetes*; Jeffrey L. Pasley, "The Cheese and the Words: Popular Political Culture and Participatory Democracy in the Early American Republic," in *Beyond the Founders: New Approaches to the Political History of the Early American Republic*, ed. Jeffrey L. Pasley, Andrew W. Robertson, and David Waldstreicher (Chapel Hill: University of North Carolina Press, 2004), 31–56. On popular political activity outside party channels, see Daniel Peart, *Era of Experimentation: American Political Practices in the Early Republic* (Charlottesville: University of Virginia Press, 2014).

36. Alan Taylor "'The Art of Hook & Snivey': Political Culture in Upstate New York during the 1790s," *Journal of American History* 79 (1993): 1371–96.

37. Hofstadter, *Idea of a Party System*, 197, 200.

38. On the ideational story, see Michael Wallace, "Changing Concepts of Party in the United States: New York, 1815–1828," *American Historical Review* 74 (1968): 453–91.

39. Chambers, *Political Parties in a New Nation*, 70. See also Roy F. Nichols, *The Invention of the American Political Parties* (New York: Macmillan, 1967), 80–85; Patricia U. Bonomi, *A Factious People: Politics and Society in Colonial New York* (New York: Columbia University Press, 1971); Alan Tully, *Forming American Politics: Ideals, Interests, and Institutions in Colonial New York and Pennsylvania* (Baltimore: Johns Hopkins University Press, 1994).

40. Ketcham, *Presidents above Party*, 143. Italics original.

41. Nichols, *Invention of the American Political Parties*, 251; Leonard and Cornell, *Partisan Republic*, 166–75.

42. Martin Van Buren, *Autobiography of Martin Van Buren*, ed. John Fitzpatrick, vol. 2 of *Annual Report of the American Historical Association for the Year 1918* (Washington, DC: Government Printing Office, 1920), 124, 303; Robert V. Remini, *Martin Van Buren and the Making of the Democratic Party* (New York: Columbia University Press, 1959), 18–23.

43. Martin Van Buren, *Inquiry into the Origin and Course of Political Parties in the United States* (New York: Hurd and Houghton, 1867), 3.

44. Martin Van Buren to Thomas Ritchie, January 13, 1827, Papers of Martin Van Buren [digital edition], http://vanburenpapers.org/document-mvb00528. On the Democrats' conflict

displacement as a mechanism for limiting the potential for violence, see Jeffrey Selinger, *Embracing Dissent: Political Violence and Party Development in the United States* (Philadelphia: University of Pennsylvania Press, 2016), 83–108.

45. Wilentz, *Rise of American Democracy*, 312.

46. Van Buren, *Autobiography*, 125.

47. James S. Chase, *Emergence of the Presidential Nominating Convention, 1789–1832* (Urbana: University of Illinois Press, 1973), 3–66; James W. Davis, *National Conventions in an Age of Party Reform* (Westport, CT: Greenwood Press, 1983), 26–27.

48. "Statement by the Democratic Republicans of the United States," July 31, 1835, in Schlesinger, *History of American Presidential Elections*, 1:616, 620, 621.

49. Nichols, *Invention of the American Political Parties*, 264.

50. Chase, *Emergence of the Presidential Nominating Convention*, 101–3.

51. Chase, *Emergence of the Presidential Nominating Convention*, 121–81. Notwithstanding their aversion to party-building, the evangelicals who predominated within the Anti-Masons' ranks had experience in organizing national conventions of their benevolent societies. Ronald P. Formisano, "Political Character, Anti-Partyism, and the Second Party System," *American Quarterly* 21 (1969): 696–97.

52. Richard P. McCormick, *The Presidential Game: The Origins of American Presidential Politics* (New York: Oxford University Press, 1982), 164–206.

53. Nichols, *Invention of the American Political Parties*, 310.

54. E. E. Schattschneider, *Party Government* (New York: Farrar and Rinehart, 1942), 151–58; Theodore J. Lowi, "Party, Policy, and Constitution in America," in *The American Party Systems: Stages of Political Development*, ed. William Nisbet Chambers and Walter Dean Burnham, 2nd ed. (New York: Oxford University Press, 1975), esp. 245–49.

55. Van Buren to Ritchie, January 13, 1827, Papers of Martin Van Buren, http://vanburenpapers .org/document-mvb00528.

56. James W. Ceaser, *Presidential Selection: Theory and Development* (Princeton, NJ: Princeton University Press, 1979), esp. 146–49, 166–69. See also Robert A. Dahl, "Myth of the Presidential Mandate," *Political Science Quarterly* 105 (1990): 355–72.

57. Roger A. Fischer, *Tippecanoe and Trinkets Too: The Material Culture of American Presidential Campaigns, 1828–1984* (Urbana: University of Illinois Press, 1988), 29–70.

58. Quoted in Charles Sellers, "Election of 1844," in Schlesinger, *History of American Presidential Elections*, 1:750.

59. Quoted in Formisano, *Transformation of Political Culture*, 306. Italics original.

60. Campaign circular from Whig Committee, January 1840, in *The Collected Works of Abraham Lincoln*, vol. 1, ed. Roy P. Basler (New Brunswick, NJ: Rutgers University Press, 1953), 202, https://quod.lib.umich.edu/l/lincoln/.

61. William Nisbet Chambers, "Election of 1840," in Schlesinger, *History of American Presidential Elections*, 1:673.

62. "The War of the Five Campaigns," *United States Magazine and Democratic Review*, June 1840, 486.

63. Erik J. Engstrom and Samuel Kernell, *Party Ballots, Reform, and the Transformation of America's Electoral System* (New York: Cambridge University Press, 2014), 35. The last holdouts, Virginia, Oregon, and Kentucky, would not abandon oral voting until after the Civil War. See Richard Franklin Bensel, *The American Ballot Box in the Mid-Nineteenth Century* (New York: Cambridge University Press, 2004), 54.

64. For illustrations, see (from the collection of James Michael Curley, no less) "Nineteenth-Century Political Ballots," Boston Athenæum Digital Collection, https://cdm.bostonathenaeum .org/digital/collection/p16057coll29.

65. Henry B. Miller, quoted in Robert J. Dinkin, *Election Day: A Documentary History* (Westport, CT: Greenwood Press, 2002), 69–70.

66. Bensel, *American Ballot Box in the Mid-Nineteenth Century*, 295.

67. On Jacksonian-era developments in campaign practices, see Mark R. Cheathem, *The Coming of Democracy: Presidential Campaigning in the Age of Jackson* (Baltimore: Johns Hopkins University, 2018). The essential state-by-state account remains Richard P. McCormick, *The Second American Party System: Party Formation in the Jacksonian Era* (Chapel Hill: University of North Carolina Press, 1966); later scholarship is ably synthesized in Huston, "Rethinking the Origins of Partisan Democracy in the United States," 55–62.

68. The quoted phrase is from Nichols, *Invention of American Political Parties*, 264.

69. Donald B. Cole, *Jacksonian Democracy in New Hampshire* (Cambridge, MA: Harvard University Press, 1970), 167.

70. Kentucky, North Carolina, and especially Virginia had largely shed such imprints by 1840; William G. Shade, *Democratizing the Old Dominion: Virginia and the Second Party System, 1824–1861* (Charlottesville: University of Virginia Press, 1996).

71. Formisano, *Birth of Mass Political Parties*, 15–30, 81–101; Kenneth J. Winkle, *The Politics of Community: Migration and Politics in Antebellum Ohio* (New York: Cambridge University Press, 1988).

72. McCormick, *Second American Party System*, 238.

73. For an excellent recent synthesis, see Gary Gerstle, *Liberty and Coercion: The Paradox of American Government from the Founding to the Present* (Princeton, NJ: Princeton University Press, 2016), 149–73.

74. Leonard White, *The Jacksonians: A Study in Administrative History* (New York: Macmillan, 1954).

75. Amy Bridges, *A City in the Republic: Antebellum New York and the Origins of Machine Politics* (New York: Cambridge University Press, 1984), 74–75.

76. White, *Jacksonians*, 340–41.

77. Martin Shefter, *Political Parties and the State: The American Historical Experience* (Princeton, NJ: Princeton University Press, 1994), 61–71.

78. Bridges, *City in the Republic*, 74.

79. James Barbour address to the Whig National Convention, Harrisburg, Pennsylvania, December 4, 1839, in Schlesinger, *History of American Presidential Elections*, 1:703.

80. John Lauritz Larson, *The Market Revolution in America: Liberty, Ambition, and the Eclipse of the Common Good* (New York: Cambridge University Press, 2010), 98.

81. On the transformative impact of markets in antebellum America, see Watson, *Liberty and Power*, esp. 17–72; Charles Sellers, *The Market Revolution: Jacksonian America, 1815–1846* (New York: Oxford University Press, 1991). See also Christopher Clark, *The Roots of Rural Capitalism: Western Massachusetts, 1780–1860* (Ithaca, NY: Cornell University Press, 1990). Early criticism of the "market revolution" concept as imprecise and normatively loaded can be found in Daniel Feller, "The Market Revolution Ate My Homework," *Reviews in American History* 25 (1997): 408–15. Howe gives that critique full narrative expression in *What Hath God Wrought*.

82. Our understanding of early industrialization and antebellum free labor continues to rest on the wave of local studies carried out by "new labor historians" taking inspiration from E. P. Thompson and, closer to home, Herbert Gutman. See especially Alan Dawley, *Class and Community: The Industrial Revolution in Lynn* (Cambridge, MA: Harvard University Press, 1976); Bruce Laurie, *Working People of Philadelphia, 1800–1850* (Philadelphia: Temple University Press, 1980); Sean Wilentz, *Chants Democratic: New York City and the Rise of the American Working Class, 1788–1850* (New York: Oxford University Press, 1983).

83. Wilentz, *Rise of American Democracy*, xxi.

84. "Statement by the Democratic Republicans of the United States," July 31, 1835, in Schlesinger, *History of American Presidential Elections*, 1:619.

85. Andrew Jackson, "Veto Message," July 10, 1832, American Presidency Project, https://www.presidency.ucsb.edu/documents/veto-message-the-re-authorization-bank-the-united-states.

86. James Roger Sharp, *The Jacksonians versus the Banks: Politics in the States after the Panic of 1837* (New York: Columbia University Press, 1970).

87. On artisan republicanism as both the framework for laborers' response to industrialization and itself an ideology undergoing transformation, see Wilentz, *Chants Democratic*, 61–103; Bruce Laurie, *Artisans into Workers: Labor in Nineteenth-Century America* (New York: Hill and Wang, 1989), 47–73.

88. The relationship between the two, and the broader question of the significance of class politics to the Second Party System, have served as recurring subjects of historical debate. Arthur M. Schlesinger's depiction of urban, eastern, and working-class hard-money doctrine as the north star of Democratic politics after 1833 reads into the Jacksonian project a programmatic policy commitment to working-class interests that the party's record cannot support. Schlesinger, *Age of Jackson*, esp. 115–31. But an alternative historical tendency has the effect of underplaying the political significance of labor radicalism. See, for example, Howe, *What Hath God Wrought*, 532–52. On the distinctive radical labor tradition in antebellum politics, see Edward Pessen, *Most Uncommon Jacksonians: The Radical Leaders of the Early Labor Movement* (Albany: State University of New York Press, 1967); Wilentz, *Chants Democratic*. For persuasive accounts of the laborite influence on Democratic politics, see Watson, *Liberty and Power*, 191–95; Wilentz, *Rise of American Democracy*, esp. 457–65.

89. Wilentz, *Chants Democratic*, 236.

90. Quoted in Wilentz, *Rise of American Democracy*, 357.

91. Bridges, *City in the Republic*, 27.

92. On Jacksonians' pursuit of expansion through state and national policy, see Paul Frymer, *Building an American Empire: The Era of Territorial and Political Expansion* (Princeton, NJ: Princeton University Press, 2017), 128–219.

93. Fred S. Rolater, "The American Indian and the Origin of the Second Party System," *Wisconsin Magazine of History* 76 (1993): 180–203.

94. Anthony F. C. Wallace, *The Long, Bitter Trail: Andrew Jackson and the Indians* (New York: Hill and Wang, 1993), 69.

95. Donald B. Cole, *Martin Van Buren and the American Political System* (Princeton, NJ: Princeton University Press, 1984), 270.

96. He defended Indian removal at length in his memoirs. Van Buren, *Autobiography*, 275–94.

97. Andrew Jackson, "Fifth Annual Message to Congress," December 3, 1833, Miller Center, University of Virginia, https://millercenter.org/the-presidency/presidential-speeches/december-3-1833-fifth-annual-message-congress.

98. For useful recent treatments, see Christopher Malone, *Between Freedom and Bondage: Race, Party, and Voting Rights in the Antebellum North* (New York: Routledge, 2008); David A. Bateman, *Disenfranchising Democracy: Constructing the Electorate in the United States, the United Kingdom, and France* (New York: Cambridge University Press, 2018), 136–200; Leonard and Cornell, *Partisan Republic*, 146–77.

99. Wilentz, *Rise of American Democracy*, 513.

100. For varying perspectives, see David Roediger, *The Wages of Whiteness: Race and the Making of the American Working Class* (New York: Verso, 1991); Eric Arnesen, "Whiteness and the Historians' Imagination," *International Labor and Working-Class History* 60 (2001): 3–42;

Bruce Laurie, "Workers, Abolitionists, and the Historians: A Historiographical Perspective," *Labor* 5 (2008): 17–55.

101. Robert Ernst, "The One and Only Mike Walsh," *New-York Historical Society Quarterly* 36 (1952): 61; see also Wilentz, *Chants Democratic*, 326–35.

102. "Statement by the Democratic Republicans of the United States," July 31, 1835, in Schlesinger, *History of American Presidential Elections*, 1:623, 626.

103. George Corselius, quoted in Formisano, "Political Character, Antipartyism, and the Second Party System," 702.

104. Daniel Walker Howe, *The Political Culture of the American Whigs* (Chicago: University of Chicago Press, 1979), 280.

105. Persuasive syntheses of a contentious body of scholarship can be found in Watson, *Liberty and Power*, 234–37; Michael F. Holt, *The Rise and Fall of the American Whig Party: Jacksonian Politics and the Onset of the Civil War* (New York: Oxford University Press, 1999), 113–21; Howe, *What Hath God Wrought*, 579–83.

106. In addition to Howe, *Political Culture of the American Whigs*, see John Ashworth, *"Agrarians" and "Aristocrats": Party-Political Ideology in the United States, 1837–1846* (New York: Cambridge University Press, 1983); Thomas Brown, *Politics and Statesmanship: Essays on the American Whig Party* (New York: Columbia University Press, 1985); Joseph W. Pearson, *The Whigs' America: Middle-Class Political Thought in the Age of Jackson and Clay* (Lexington: University Press of Kentucky, 2020).

107. Daniel Webster, "Statesmen—Their Rareness and Importance," *New-England Magazine*, August 1834, reprinted in *New-England Magazine*, vol. 7, *From July to December Inclusive, 1834* (Boston: J. T. Buckingham, 1834), 94–95.

108. *Memoirs of John Quincy Adams: Comprising Portions of His Diary from 1795 to 1848*, vol. 10, ed. Charles Francis Adams (Philadelphia: J. B. Lippincott, 1876), 352. On Adams, see Howe, *Political Culture of the American Whigs*, 43–68.

109. "The Result of the Election," *American Review* 1, no. 2 (February 1845): 113, 115.

110. Robert Walsh coined the term in the *Philadelphia National Gazette*; quoted in Donald J. Radcliffe, "Antimasonry and Partisanship in Greater New England, 1826–1836," *Journal of the Early Republic* 15 (1995): 202.

111. Ronald G. Walters, *American Reformers, 1815–1860* (New York: Hill and Wang, 1978); Paul E. Johnson, *A Shopkeeper's Millennium: Society and Revivals in Rochester, New York, 1815–1837* (New York: Hill and Wang, 1978); Nancy A. Hewitt, *Women's Activism and Social Change: Rochester, New York, 1822–1872* (Ithaca, NY: Cornell University Press, 1984); Mark A. Noll, *America's God: From Jonathan Edwards to Abraham Lincoln* (New York: Oxford University Press, 2002), 161–224.

112. Ian R. Tyrrell, *Sobering Up: From Temperance to Prohibition in Antebellum America, 1800–1860* (Westport, CT: Greenwood Press, 1979), 63–65.

113. Daniel Carpenter, *Democracy by Petition: Popular Politics in Transformation, 1790–1870* (Cambridge, MA: Harvard University Press, 2021), 37. Whigs' own formation as a party to supplant the crumbling National Republican edifice owed much to mass petition campaigns in 1833 and 1834. Carpenter, *Democracy by Petition*, 275–93; Daniel Carpenter and Benjamin Schneer, "Party Formation through Petition: The Whigs and the Bank War of 1832–1834," *Studies in American Political Development* 29 (2015): 213–34.

114. Tyrrell, *Sobering Up*, 177–79; Walters, *American Reformers*, 137–38.

115. Elizabeth R. Varon, *We Mean to Be Counted: White Women and Politics in Antebellum Virginia* (Chapel Hill: University of North Carolina Press, 1998), esp. 71–102; Ronald Zboray and Mary Zboray, "Whig Women, Politics, and Culture in the Campaign of 1840," *Journal of the Early Republic* 17 (1997): 277–315.

116. Formisano, *Birth of Mass Political Parties*, 128–36.

117. Ronald P. Formisano, "The New Political History and the Election of 1840," *Journal of Interdisciplinary History* 23 (1993): esp. 678–82; Richard Carwardine, "Evangelicals, Whigs, and the Election of William Henry Harrison," *Journal of American Studies* 17 (1983): 47–75.

118. Glyndon G. Van Deusen, *William Henry Seward* (New York: Oxford University Press, 1967), 64.

119. Quoted in Tyrrell, *Sobering Up*, 263.

120. John Quincy Adams, "First Annual Message to Congress," December 6, 1825, American Presidency Project, https://www.presidency.ucsb.edu/documents/first-annual-message-2.

121. Calvin Colton, "Labor and Capital," *The Junius Tracts*, no. 7 (March 1844), 8–9.

122. Howe, *Political Culture of the American Whigs*, 238–62; Brown, *Politics and Statesmanship*, 154–188; Shade, *Democratizing the Old Dominion*, 78–157, 191–224; Michael Perman, *Search for Unity: A Political History of the American South* (Chapel Hill: University of North Carolina Press, 2010), 38–59.

123. Quoted in Brown, *Politics and Statesmanship*, 175.

124. *Speech of the Hon. Henry Clay, in the Senate of the United States, on the Subject of Abolition Petitions, February 7, 1839* (Boston: James Munroe, 1839), 41; Henry Clay to Jacob Gibson, July 25, 1842, in *The Papers of Henry Clay*, vol. 9, *The Whig Leader, January 1, 1837–December 31, 1843* (Lexington: University Press of Kentucky, 1988), 746.

125. For both international and temporal comparisons, see Holt, *Political Parties and American Political Development*, 237–64.

126. Charles Sellers, *James K. Polk: Continentalist, 1843–1846* (Princeton, NJ: Princeton University Press, 1966); Yonatan Eyal, *The Young America Movement and the Transformation of the Democratic Party, 1828–1861* (New York: Cambridge University Press, 2007).

127. For extended statements on the endurance of party politics along traditional Jackson-era lines of cleavage into the 1850s, see Silbey, *Partisan Imperative*, 33–68; Holt, *Political Parties and American Political Development*, 290–302. For treatments of the political struggles over expansion framed as prelude to eventual civil war, see James M. McPherson, *Battle Cry of Freedom: The Civil War Era* (New York: Oxford University Press, 1988), 47–77; William Freehling, *The Road to Disunion*, vol. 1, *Secessionists at Bay, 1776–1854* (New York: Oxford University Press, 1990), 353–510; Gary J. Kornblith, "Rethinking the Coming of the Civil War: A Counterfactual Exercise," *Journal of American History* 90 (2003): 76–105.

128. Even scholars who disagree about the relative centrality of white supremacy to Jacksonian ideology agree on this particular function of expansion in that ideology. See Andrew Saxton, *The Rise and Fall of the White Republic: Class Politics and Mass Culture in Nineteenth-Century America* (New York: Verso, 1990), 127–62; Jonathan H. Earle, *Jacksonian Antislavery and the Politics of Free Soil, 1824–1854* (Chapel Hill: University of North Carolina Press, 2004).

129. As Timothy Shenk puts it, maintaining democracy, sustaining the union, and continuing expansion thus became "the great trilemma of antebellum politics. . . . Americans would have to choose two out of three." Timothy Shenk, *Realigners: Partisan Hacks, Political Visionaries, and the Struggle to Rule American Democracy* (New York: Farrar, Straus & Giroux, 2022), 68.

130. On Polk's relation to Jackson, see Stephen Skowronek, *The Politics Presidents Make: Leadership from John Adams to Bill Clinton*, rev. ed. (Cambridge, MA: Belknap Press of Harvard University Press, 1997), 155–76.

131. On opposition to the war in party politics, popular culture, and grassroots social movements, see Amy S. Greenberg, *A Wicked War: Polk, Clay, Lincoln, and the 1846 U.S. Invasion of Mexico* (New York: Alfred A. Knopf, 2012), esp. 113–99; John J. Schroeder, *Mr. Polk's War: American Opposition and Dissent, 1846–1848* (Madison: University of Wisconsin Press, 1973).

132. Ken S. Mueller, *Senator Benton and the People: Master Race Democracy on the Early American Frontiers* (DeKalb: Northern Illinois University Press, 2014), 192–93.

133. *Washington Globe*, August 29, 1844, quoted in Sellers, *James K. Polk*, 128.

134. Joel Silbey, *Storm over Texas: The Annexation Controversy and the Road to Civil War* (New York: Oxford University Press, 2005), 123.

135. Watson, *Liberty and Power*, 243.

136. On antislavery politics, see Corey M. Brooks, *Liberty Power: Antislavery Third Parties and the Transformation of American Politics* (Chicago: University of Chicago Press, 2016); Richard H. Sewell, *Ballots for Freedom: Antislavery Politics in the United States, 1837–1860* (New York: Oxford University Press, 1976); Frederick J. Blue, *No Taint of Compromise: Crusaders in Antislavery Politics* (Baton Rouge: Louisiana State University Press, 2005). On abolition, see Manisha Sinha, *The Slave's Cause: A History of Abolition* (New Haven, CT: Yale University Press, 2016); Stanley Harrold, *American Abolitionism: Its Direct Political Impact from Colonial Times into Reconstruction* (Charlottesville: University of Virginia Press, 2019).

137. James Brewer Stewart, *Joshua R. Giddings and the Tactics of Radical Politics* (Cleveland: Press of Case Western Reserve University, 1970), 95–98.

138. The best guide to the factional machinations is Joseph G. Rayback, *Free Soil: The Election of 1848* (Lexington: University Press of Kentucky, 1970). On their relation to national developments, see Joseph T. Murphy, "Neither a Slave nor a King: The Antislavery Project and the Origins of the American Sectional Crisis, 1820–1848" (PhD diss., City University of New York, 2016), 352–507.

139. Nichols, *Invention of American Political Parties*, 370. See also Joel H. Silbey, *Party over Section: The Rough and Ready Presidential Election of 1848* (Lawrence: University Press of Kansas, 2009), 53.

140. "Free Soil Platform of 1848," American Presidency Project, https://www.presidency.ucsb.edu/documents/free-soil-party-platform-1848/.

141. Sewell, *Ballots for Freedom*, 223–29.

142. David M. Potter, *The Impending Crisis, 1848–1861*, comp. and ed. Don E. Fehrenbacher (New York: Harper & Row, 1976), 90–120.

143. Henry Clay to Senate, February 5–6, 1850, in *History of U.S. Political Parties*, ed. Arthur M. Schlesinger Jr., vol. 1, *1789–1860: From Factions to Parties* (New York: Chelsea House, 1973), 447, 449.

144. William H. Seward to Senate, "Freedom in the New Territories," March 11, 1850, http://www.senate.gov/artandhistory/history/resources/pdf/SewardNewTerritories.pdf.

145. Hendrik Booraem V, *The Formation of the Republican Party in New York: Politics and Conscience in the Antebellum North* (New York: New York University Press, 1983), 7–13.

146. We follow James W. Ceaser in making this point. See Ceaser, *Presidential Selection*; Ceaser, "The Presidential Nomination Mess," *Claremont Review of Books*, Fall 2008, 21–25.

147. See especially Michael McGerr, *The Decline of Popular Politics: The American North, 1865–1928* (New York: Oxford University Press, 1986).

Chapter Three: Free Labor Republicanism as a Party Project

1. *The Position of the Republican and Democratic Parties: A Dialogue between a White Republican and a Colored Citizen* (Washington, DC: Union Republican Congressional Committee, 1868), 2–3.

2. We take a "fundamentalist" rather than a "revisionist" view of the Civil War, emphasizing the underlying conflict of interests and worldviews rather than the decisions of political elites. At the same time, the practical stuff of politics in an intensely political age is what translated structural parameters into real-world conflict and particular, contingent outcomes. For fundamentalist views that attend to party, see Eric Foner, *Free Soil, Free Labor, Free Men: The Ideology*

of the Republican Party before the Civil War, rev. ed. (1970; repr. with new intro., New York: Oxford University Press, 1995); John Ashworth, *Slavery, Capitalism, and Politics in the Antebellum Republic*, vol. 2, *The Coming of the Civil War, 1850–1861* (New York: Cambridge University Press, 2007); James Oakes, *Freedom National: The Destruction of Slavery in the United States* (New York: W. W. Norton, 2013); James Oakes, *The Scorpion's Sting: Antislavery and the Coming of the Civil War* (New York: W. W. Norton, 2014); Matthew Karp, "The People's Revolution of 1856: Antislavery Populism, National Politics, and the Emergence of the Republican Party," *Journal of the Civil War Era* 9 (2019): 524–45. For revisionist views, see William E. Gienapp, *The Origins of the Republican Party, 1852–1856* (New York: Oxford University Press, 1986); Michael F. Holt, *The Political Crisis of the 1850s* (New York: John Wiley, 1978); Daniel W. Crofts, *Lincoln and the Politics of Slavery: The Other Thirteenth Amendment and the Struggle to Save the Union* (Chapel Hill: University of North Carolina Press, 2016). For literature reviews, see Frank Towers, "Party Politics and the Sectional Crisis: A Twenty-Year Renaissance in the Study of Antebellum Political History," in *The Routledge History of Nineteenth-Century America*, ed. Jonathan David Wells (New York: Routledge, 2018), 109–30, and, particularly valuable for spanning the Civil War, Rachel A. Shelden, "The Politics of Continuity and Change in the Long Civil War Era," *Civil War History* 65 (2019): 319–41.

3. Mark E. Neely Jr., *Lincoln and the Democrats: The Politics of Opposition in the Civil War* (New York: Cambridge University Press, 2017), 74.

4. William Claflin, quoted in Adam I. P. Smith, *No Party Now: Politics in the Civil War North* (Oxford: Oxford University Press, 2006), 5.

5. Michael Perman, *The Southern Political Tradition* (Baton Rouge: Louisiana State University Press, 2012). For an intellectual history, see Lacy K. Ford Jr., "Inventing the Concurrent Majority: Madison, Calhoun, and the Problem of Majoritarianism in American Political Thought," *Journal of Southern History* 60 (1994): 19–58.

6. On the Confederacy, see Michael Perman, *Search for Unity: A Political History of the American South* (Chapel Hill: University of North Carolina Press, 2010), 97–113; George C. Rable, *The Confederate Republic: A Revolution against Politics* (Chapel Hill: University of North Carolina Press, 1994).

7. Barrington Moore, *Social Origins of Dictatorship and Democracy: Lord and Peasant in the Making of the Modern World* (Boston: Beacon Press, 1966), 111–55.

8. Gabor S. Boritt, *Lincoln and the Economics of the American Dream* (Urbana: University of Illinois Press, 1978); Allen C. Guelzo, "The Bicentennial Lincolns," *Claremont Review of Books*, Winter 2010, 39–65.

9. Abraham Lincoln, "Address before the Wisconsin State Agricultural Society," September 30, 1859, https://www.abrahamlincolnonline.org/lincoln/speeches/fair.htm.

10. Heather Cox Richardson, *The Greatest Nation of the Earth: Republican Economic Policies during the Civil War* (Cambridge, MA: Harvard University Press, 1997).

11. In recent years, a rising left searching for American models of mass politics has looked to free labor Republicans. See Matt Karp, "The Mass Politics of Antislavery," *Catalyst* 3 (2019): 131–78.

12. This is an important theme in Richard H. Sewell, *Ballots for Freedom: Antislavery Politics in the United States, 1837–1860* (New York: Oxford University Press, 1976).

13. The original statement is W. E. B. Du Bois, *Black Reconstruction in America: Toward a History of the Part Which Black Folk Played in the Attempt to Reconstruct Democracy in America, 1860–1880* (New York: Russell & Russell, 1935), 49–75. For a more recent argument for "self-emancipation," see Ira Berlin, Barbara J. Fields, Steven F. Miller, Joseph P. Reidy, and Leslie R. Rowland, *Slaves No More: Three Essays on Emancipation and the Civil War* (New York: Cambridge University Press, 1992), 1–76.

14. For good presentations of this view, see Morton Keller, *America's Three Regimes: A New Political History* (New York: Oxford University Press, 2007), 105–32, and, more generally, Joel H. Silbey, *The American Political Nation, 1838–1893* (Stanford, CA: Stanford University Press, 1991). Though framed differently, an emphasis on continuity and deemphasis on the Republicans' revolutionary character also marks Adam I. P. Smith, *The Stormy Present: Conservatism and the Problem of Slavery in Northern Politics, 1846–1865* (Chapel Hill: University of North Carolina Press, 2017).

15. See, for example, Henry Mayer, *All on Fire: William Lloyd Garrison and the Abolition of Slavery* (New York: St. Martin's Press, 1998).

16. See, for example, Sven Beckert, *Empire of Cotton: A Global History* (New York: Alfred A. Knopf, 2014). For an extreme popularized version of the thesis, see Mathew Desmond, "Capitalism," in *The 1619 Project: A New Origin Story*, ed. Nikole Hannah-Jones, Caitlin Roper, Ilena Silverman, and Jake Silverstein (New York: One World, 2021). We agree with the political thrust of James Oakes, "Capitalism and Slavery and the Civil War," *International Labor and Working-Class History* 89 (2016): 195–220.

17. Thus, we agree with the central contention of Karp, "Mass Politics of Antislavery," even as we see implications and legacies beyond the Left. For a similar invocation of Radical Republicanism to ours, see Joseph Fishkin and William E. Forbath, *The Anti-Oligarchy Constitution: Reconstructing the Economic Foundations of American Democracy* (Cambridge, MA: Harvard University Press, 2022), 109–37.

18. For a fine presentation, see James L. Sundquist, *Dynamics of the Party System: Alignment and Realignment of Political Parties in the United States*, rev. ed. (Washington, DC: Brookings Institution, 1983), 74–105.

19. The best treatment is still Foner, *Free Soil, Free Labor, Free Men*.

20. On agriculture, see Ariel Ron, *Grassroots Leviathan: Agricultural Reform and the Rural North in the Slaveholding Republic* (Baltimore: Johns Hopkins University Press, 2020).

21. Henry Wilson, *How Ought Workingmen to Vote in the Coming Election?* (Boston: Wright & Potter, 1860), 2. On Wilson, see Richard Abbott, *Cobbler in Congress: The Life of Henry Wilson, 1812–1875* (Lexington: University Press of Kentucky, 1972).

22. Corey M. Brooks, *Liberty Power: Antislavery Third Parties and the Transformation of American Politics* (Chicago: University of Chicago Press, 2016). This claim remains central even if one sees the conflict with the Slave Power as ultimately rooted in incompatible economic systems. See the discussion in Ashworth, *Slavery, Capitalism, and Politics in the Antebellum Republic*, 2:244–64, 333–34.

23. Leonard L. Richards, *The Slave Power: The Free North and Southern Domination, 1780–1860* (Baton Rouge: Louisiana State University Press, 2000).

24. On this vision, see Carl Lawrence Paulus, *The Slaveholding Crisis: Fear of Insurrection and the Coming of the Civil War* (Baton Rouge: Louisiana State University Press, 2017).

25. Henry Wilson, *History of the Rise and Fall of the Slave Power in America*, vol. 2 (Boston: James R. Osgood, 1874), 404–5.

26. Wilson, *Rise and Fall of the Slave Power*, 2:410; Francis Curtis, *The Republican Party: A History of Its Fifty Years' Existence and a Record of Its Measures and Leaders, 1854–1904* (New York: G. P. Putnam's Sons, 1904), 172–94.

27. Mark Voss-Hubbard, *Beyond Party: Cultures of Antipartisanship in Northern Politics before the Civil War* (Baltimore: Johns Hopkins University Press, 2002), 104–37; Ashworth, *Slavery, Capitalism, and Politics in the Antebellum Republic*, 2:521–39.

28. Sewell, *Ballots for Freedom*, 265–77; Foner, *Free Soil, Free Labor, Free Men*, 232–47; Tyler Anbinder, *Nativism and Slavery: The Northern Know Nothings and the Politics of the 1850s* (New York: Oxford University Press, 1992), 162–219.

29. Anbinder, *Nativism and Slavery*. On relations between Know Nothings and Republicans, see Gienapp, *Origins of the Republican Party*, though he sees more contingency in the overall trajectory than we do.

30. Hendrik Booraem V, *The Formation of the Republican Party in New York: Politics and Conscience in the Antebellum North* (New York: New York University Press, 1983), 7–13.

31. Jeffrey A. Jenkins and Charles Stewart III, *Fighting for the Speakership: The House and the Rise of Party Government* (Princeton, NJ: Princeton University Press, 2013); 177–208; Brooks, *Liberty Power*, 207–11.

32. Quoted in J. G. Randall and David Donald, *The Civil War and Reconstruction*, 2nd ed. (Boston: D. C. Heath, 1961), 172.

33. Oakes, *Scorpion's Sting*; Kenneth M. Stampp, *America in 1857: A Nation on the Brink* (New York: Oxford University Press, 1990), 126–30.

34. William H. Seward, "The Advent of the Republican Party," in *The Works of William H. Seward*, ed. George E. Baker, vol. 4 (Cambridge: Riverside Press, 1884), 240.

35. "Republican Party Platform of 1856," June 18, 1856, American Presidency Project, https:// www.presidency.ucsb.edu/documents/republican-party-platform-1856.

36. Glyndon G. Van Deusen, *Thurlow Weed: Wizard of the Lobby* (Boston: Little, Brown, 1947), 208–11.

37. Compare Holt, *Political Crisis of the 1850s*, 194–197; Karp, "People's Revolution of 1856." For an account of the campaign, see David M. Potter, *The Impending Crisis, 1848–1861*, comp. and ed. Don E. Fehrenbacher (New York: Harper & Row, 1976), 249–65.

38. Abraham Lincoln, "House Divided Speech," June 16, 1858, https://www.abrahamlincoln online.org/lincoln/speeches/house.htm. For deeper reflections, compare Harry Jaffa, *Crisis of the House Divided: An Interpretation of the Issues in the Lincoln-Douglas Debates* (Garden City, NY: Doubleday, 1959); J. David Greenstone, *The Lincoln Persuasion: Remaking American Liberalism* (Princeton, NJ: Princeton University Press, 1993), esp. 24–34.

39. Reinhard H. Luthin, *The First Lincoln Campaign* (Cambridge, MA: Harvard University Press, 1944), 167. See also Van Deusen, *Thurlow Weed*, 249–54.

40. "Republican Party Platform of 1860," May 17, 1860, American Presidency Project, https:// www.presidency.ucsb.edu/documents/republican-party-platform-1860. On the new planks, see James L. Huston, "A Political Response to Industrialism: The Republican Embrace of Protectionist Labor Doctrines," *Journal of American History* 70 (1983): 35–53.

41. Quoted in William E. Gienapp, "Who Voted for Lincoln?," in *Abraham Lincoln and the American Political Tradition*, ed. John L. Thomas (Amherst: University of Massachusetts Press, 1986), 70.

42. Luthin, *First Lincoln Campaign*; Michael S. Green, "The Political Organizer: Abraham Lincoln's 1860 Campaign," in *The Election of 1860 Reconsidered*, ed. A. James Fuller (Kent, OH: Kent State University Press, 2013), 7–27. For an overview, see Potter, *Impending Crisis*, 405–47.

43. Jon Grinspan, "'Young Men for War': The Wide Awakes and Lincoln's 1860 Presidential Campaign," *Journal of American History* 96 (2009): 357–78.

44. David M. Potter, *Lincoln and His Party in the Secession Crisis*, rev. ed. (1942; repr. with new preface, New Haven, CT: Yale University Press, 1962).

45. Abraham Lincoln, "Second Inaugural Address," March 4, 1865, https://www .abrahamlincolnonline.org/lincoln/speeches/inaug2.htm.

46. William E. Gienapp, "Abraham Lincoln and the Border States," *Journal of the Abraham Lincoln Association* 13 (1992): 13–46.

47. The classic modern synthesis is James M. McPherson, *Battle Cry of Freedom: The Civil War Era* (New York: Oxford University Press, 1988) (numbers on p. 854).

48. Philip Shaw Paludan, *"A People's Contest": The Union and Civil War* (Lawrence: University Press of Kansas, 1988), 255–59; Herman Belz, *Emancipation and Equal Rights: Politics and Constitutionalism in the Civil War Era* (New York: W. W. Norton, 1978), 23–46.

49. David Donald, *Charles Sumner and the Rights of Man* (New York: Alfred A. Knopf, 1970), 168.

50. John Hay, *Lincoln and the Civil War in the Diaries and Letters of John Hay*, ed. Tyler Dennett (New York: Dodd Mead, 1939), 108.

51. On Lincoln, see Richard Carwardine, "'A Party Man Who Did Not Believe in Any Man Who Was Not': Abraham Lincoln, the Republican Party, and the Union," in *In the Cause of Liberty: How the Civil War Redefined American Ideals*, ed. William J. Cooper Jr. and John M. McCardell Jr. (Baton Rouge: Louisiana State University Press, 2009), 40–62. On the party, see Michael S. Green, *Freedom, Union, and Power: Lincoln and His Party during the Civil War* (New York: Fordham University Press, 2004); Philip Shaw Paludan, "War Is the Health of the Party: Republicans in the American Civil War," in *The Birth of the Grand Old Party: The Republicans' First Generation*, ed. Robert F. Engs and Randall M. Miller (Philadelphia: University of Pennsylvania Press, 2002), 60–80.

52. See Richard Hofstadter, *The American Political Tradition*, 92–134; Joel H. Silbey, "'Always a Whig in Politics': The Partisan Life of Abraham Lincoln," *Journal of the Abraham Lincoln Association* 8 (1986): 21–42.

53. Quoted in *Reminiscences of Abraham Lincoln by Distinguished Men of His Time*, ed. Allen Thorndike Rice, 7th ed. (New York: North American Review, 1888), 154.

54. See broadly Greenstone, *Lincoln Persuasion*, 244–85.

55. Harry J. Carman and Reinhard H. Luthin, *Lincoln and the Patronage* (New York: Columbia University Press, 1943), 59–78, 126–28.

56. Paul Taylor, *"The Most Complete Political Machine Ever Known": The North's Union Leagues in the American Civil War* (Kent, OH: Kent State University Press, 2018), 102–3, 222–24.

57. Charles J. Stillé, *How a Free People Conduct a Long War*, no. 13 (New York: Loyal Publication Society, 1863).

58. Francis Lieber, *Manual of Political Ethics Designed Chiefly for the Use of Colleges and Students at Law*, vol. 2 (Boston: Little, Brown, 1839), 413.

59. Francis Lieber, *No Party Now, But All for Our Country*, no. 16 (New York: Loyal Publication Society, 1863), 2.

60. For slightly different interpretations, compare Paludan, *"A People's Contest,"* 255–59; Michael Vorenberg, *Final Freedom: The Civil War, the Abolition of Slavery, and the Thirteenth Amendment* (New York: Cambridge University Press, 2001), 121–27; James Oakes, *The Radical and the Republican: Frederick Douglass, Abraham Lincoln, and the Triumph of Antislavery Politics* (New York: W. W. Norton, 2007), 225–29.

61. "Republican Party Platform of 1860"; "Republican Party Platform of 1864," June 7, 1864, American Presidency Project, https://www.presidency.ucsb.edu/documents/republican-party -platform-1864.

62. According to the most comprehensive treatment, the evidence that Lincoln affirmatively favored Johnson is weak, based entirely on retrospective narratives written in the 1890s. Don E. Fehrenbacher, "The Making of a Myth: Lincoln and the Vice-Presidential Nomination in 1864," *Civil War History* 41 (1995): 273–90.

63. Union Congressional Committee, *Peace, to be Enduring, Must Be Conquered* (Washington, DC: Union Congressional Committee, 1864), 6.

64. See J. Matthew Gallman, *The Cacophony of Politics: Northern Democrats and the American Civil War* (Charlottesville: University of Virginia Press, 2021); Adam I. P. Smith, "Northern Democrats," in *The Cambridge History of the American Civil War*, ed. Aaron Sheehan-Dean, vol. 2,

Affairs of the State (Cambridge: Cambridge University Press, 2019), 394–413; Joel H. Silbey, *A Respectable Minority: the Democratic Party in the Civil War Era, 1860–1868* (New York: W. W. Norton, 1977); Jean Baker, *Affairs of Party: The Political Culture of Northern Democrats in the Mid-Nineteenth Century* (New York: Fordham University Press, 1998).

65. Edward George Ryan, *Address to the People by the Democracy of Wisconsin: Adopted in State Convention at Milwaukee, Sept. 3rd, 1862* (Madison: Patriot Office Print, 1862), 1.

66. Horatio Seymour, "Mr. Seymour at the Democratic State Convention, Albany, September 10, 1862, on Receiving the Nomination of Governor," in *Public Record: Including Speeches, Messages, Proclamations, Official Correspondence, and Other Public Utterances of Horatio Seymour; from the Campaign of 1856 to the Present Time*, comp. and ed. Thomas W. Cook and Thomas W. Knox (New York: I.W. England, 1868), 50, 54.

67. Compare Jennifer Weber, *Copperheads: The Rise and Fall of Lincoln's Opponents in the North* (New York: Oxford University Press, 2008); Neely, *Lincoln and the Democrats*.

68. "The Lincoln Catechism," in *History of American Presidential Elections, 1789–1968*, ed. Arthur M. Schlesinger Jr. (New York: Chelsea House, 1971), 2:1214.

69. New York was an important but atypical city. On elite Democrats, see Irving Katz, *August Belmont: A Political Biography* (New York: Columbia University Press, 1968); Sven Beckert, *The Monied Metropolis: New York City and the Consolidation of the American Bourgeoise, 1850–1896* (New York: Cambridge University Press, 2001), 111–44. On the relationship between social and political cleavages, see Iver Bernstein, *The New York City Draft Riots: Their Significance for American Society and Politics in the Age of the Civil War* (New York: Oxford University Press, 1990).

70. For the suggestion that party politics aided the Union war effort, see Eric L. McKitrick, "Party Politics and the Union and Confederate War Efforts," in *The American Party Systems: Stages of Political Development*, ed. William Nisbet Chambers and Walter Dean Burnham, 2nd ed. (New York: Oxford University Press, 1975), 117–51. For a skeptical view, see Mark E. Neely Jr., *The Union Divided: Party Conflict in the Civil War North* (Cambridge, MA: Harvard University Press, 2002).

71. The classic synthesis is Eric Foner, *Reconstruction: America's Unfinished Revolution, 1863–1877* (New York: Harper & Row, 1988). It builds on Du Bois, *Black Reconstruction in America*. For an account that ties Reconstruction together with the machinations of Gilded Age politics, see Mark Wahlgren Summers, *The Ordeal of the Reunion: A New History of Reconstruction* (Chapel Hill: University of North Carolina Press, 2014). For literature reviews, see Michael Perman, "The Politics of Reconstruction," in *A Companion to the Civil War and Reconstruction*, ed. Lacy K. Ford (Malden, MA: Blackwell, 2005), 323–41; Thomas C. Holt, "Political History," *Journal of the Civil War Era*, March 2017, https://www.journalofthecivilwarera.org/forum-the-future-of-reconstruction-studies/political-history/.

72. For recent overviews, see Brooks Simpson, "Consider the Alternatives: Reassessing Republican Reconstruction," in *A Political Nation: New Directions in Mid-Nineteenth-Century American Political History*, ed. Gary W. Gallagher and Rachel A. Shelden (Charlottesville: University of Virginia Press, 2012), 214–30; Michael Green, "Reconstructing the Nation, Reconstructing the Party: Postwar Republicans and the Evolution of a Party," in *The Great Task Remaining Before Us: Reconstruction as America's Continuing Civil War*, ed. Paul A. Cimbala and Randall M. Miller (New York: Fordham University Press, 2010), 183–203. From more traditional political history, see Morton Keller, *Affairs of State: Public Life in Nineteenth Century America* (Cambridge, MA: Belknap Press of Harvard University Press, 1977), 238–83.

73. Du Bois, *Black Reconstruction in America*, 343.

74. Thomas M. Keck, "Court-Packing and Democratic Erosion," in *Democratic Resilience: Can the United States Withstand Rising Polarization?*, ed. Robert C. Lieberman, Suzanne Mettler, and Kenneth M. Roberts (New York: Cambridge University Press, 2022), 152–53.

75. Michael Les Benedict, *A Compromise of Principle: Congressional Republicans and Reconstruction, 1863–1869* (New York: W.W. Norton, 1974), 276–94.

76. William Shade, "'Revolutions May Go Backwards': The American Civil War and the Problem of Political Development," *Social Science Quarterly* 55 (1974): 753–67.

77. Karen Orren and Stephen Skowronek, *The Policy State: An American Predicament* (Cambridge, MA: Harvard University Press, 2017).

78. Jean H. Baker, "Defining Postwar Republicanism: Congressional Republicans and the Boundaries of Citizenship," in Engs and Miller, *Birth of the Grand Old Party*, 128–47; Faye E. Dudden, *Fighting Chance: The Struggle over Woman Suffrage and Black Suffrage in Reconstruction America* (New York: Oxford University Press, 2011).

79. Frederick Douglass, "Reconstruction," in *Reconstruction: Voices from America's First Great Struggle for Racial Equality*, ed. Brooks D. Simpson (New York: Library of America, 2018), 295.

80. Keller, *Affairs of State*, 85–127.

81. Terry Seip, *The South Returns to Congress: Men, Economic, Measures, and Intersectional Relationships, 1868–1879* (Baton Rouge: Louisiana State University Press, 1983).

82. Mark W. Summers, *Railroads, Reconstruction, and the Gospel of Prosperity: Aid under the Radical Republicans, 1865–1877* (Princeton, NJ: Princeton University Press, 1984).

83. David Montgomery, *Beyond Equality: Labor and the Radical Republicans, 1862–1872* (New York: Alfred A. Knopf, 1967); Eric Foner, *Politics and Ideology in the Age of the Civil War* (New York: Oxford University Press, 1980), 128–49; Hans Trefousse, *Thaddeus Stevens: Nineteenth-Century Egalitarian* (Chapel Hill: University of North Carolina Press, 1997), 210–11.

84. Heather Cox Richardson, *The Death of Reconstruction: Race, Labor, and Politics in the Post–Civil War North* (Cambridge, MA: Harvard University Press, 2001), 63.

85. Montgomery, *Beyond Equality*, esp. 335–86; Richard Franklin Bensel, *Yankee Leviathan: The Origins of Central State Authority in America* (New York: Cambridge University Press, 1990), 303–415; Foner, *Reconstruction*, 309–13.

86. Lawrence Powell, "Centralization and Its Discontents in Reconstruction Louisiana," *Studies in American Political Development* 20 (2006): 106.

87. Quoted in Richard M. Valelly, *The Two Reconstructions: The Struggle for Black Enfranchisement* (Chicago: University of Chicago Press, 2004), 29.

88. Steven Hahn, "Class and State in Postemancipation Societies: Southern Planters in Comparative Perspective, *American Historical Review* 95 (1990): 84.

89. Elsa Barkley Brown, "Negotiating and Transforming the Public Sphere: African American Political Life in the Transition from Slavery to Freedom," in *Jumpin' Jim Crow: Southern Politics from Civil War to Civil Rights*, ed. Jane Dailey, Glenda Elizabeth Gilmore, and Bryant Simon (Princeton, NJ: Princeton University Press, 2001), 28–66.

90. Michael Fitzgerald, *The Union League Movement in the Deep South: Politics and Agricultural Change during Reconstruction* (Baton Rouge: Louisiana State University Press, 1989), esp. 113–35; Steven Hahn, *A Nation under Our Feet: Black Political Struggles in the Rural South from Slavery to the Great Migration* (Cambridge, MA: Belknap Press of Harvard University Press, 2003), 163–313 (description of Wilson visit on p. 201).

91. Hahn, *Nation under Our Feet*, 239.

92. Our explanation, then, is both somewhat more structural in orientation and somewhat earlier in timing than the more fully institutionalist one in Valelly, *Two Reconstructions*.

93. For overviews, see Michael Perman, *The Road to Redemption: Southern Politics, 1869–1879* (Chapel Hill: University of North Carolina Press, 1984); Carl H. Moneyhon, "The Failure of Southern Republicanism, 1867–1876," in *The Facts of Reconstruction: Essays in Honor of John Hope Franklin*, ed. Eric Anderson and Alfred A. Moss Jr. (Baton Rouge: Louisiana State University

Press, 1991), 99–119. On native white Republicans, see Carl Degler, *The Other South: Southern Dissenters in the Nineteenth Century* (New York: Harper & Row, 1974), 191–229. On carpetbaggers, see Lawrence N. Powell, "The Politics of Livelihood: Carpetbaggers in the Deep South," in *Region, Race, and Reconstruction: Essays in Honor of C. Vann Woodward*, ed. J. Morgan Kousser and James M. McPherson (New York: Oxford University Press, 1982), 315–47.

94. Quoted in Justin Behrend, *Reconstructing Democracy: Grassroots Black Politics in the Deep South after the Civil War* (Athens: University of Georgia Press, 2015), 167.

95. Gregory P. Downs, *After Appomattox: Military Occupation and the Ends of War* (Cambridge, MA: Harvard University Press, 2015).

96. Michael Perman, "Counter Reconstruction: The Role of Violence in Southern Redemption," in Anderson and Moss, *Facts of Reconstruction*, 132. See also Perman, *Road to Redemption*, 149–77.

97. Behrend, *Reconstructing Democracy*, 207–34. For an analytical framework, see J. Morgan Kousser, "The Voting Rights Act and the Two Reconstructions," in *Colorblind Injustice: Minority Voting Rights and the Undoing of the Second Reconstruction* (Chapel Hill: University of North Carolina Press, 1999), 14–37.

98. Thomas Wagstaff, "The Arm-in-Arm Convention," *Civil War History* 14 (1968): 101–19; Thurlow Weed Barnes, *Memoir of Thurlow Weed* (Cambridge: Riverside Press, 1884), 452. Text of resolutions in "Restoration and Peace," *New York Times*, August 17, 1866, 1.

99. Benedict, *Compromise of Principle*, 21–69. For a more general treatment of factions, see Michael Les Benedict, *Preserving the Constitution: Essays on Politics and the Constitution in the Reconstruction Era* (New York: Fordham University Press, 2006), 67–89.

100. For a political history, see Charles W. Calhoun, *The Presidency of Ulysses S. Grant* (Lawrence: University Press of Kansas, 2017).

101. Mark Wahlgren Summers, *The Era of Good Stealings* (New York: Oxford University Press, 1993), x.

102. John G. Sproat, *"The Best Men": Liberal Reformers in the Gilded Age* (New York: Oxford University Press, 1968); Wilbert H. Ahern, "Laissez Faire vs. Equal Rights: Liberal Republicans and Limits to Reconstruction," *Phylon* 40 (1979): 52–65; Nancy L. Cohen, *The Reconstruction of American Liberalism, 1865–1914* (Chapel Hill: University of North Carolina Press, 2002).

103. William Gillette, "Election of 1872," in Schlesinger, *History of American Presidential Elections*, 2:1303–30; Matthew T. Downey, "Horace Greeley and the Politicians: The Liberal Republican Convention in 1872," *Journal of American History* 53 (1967): 727–50.

104. This interpretation follows Benedict, *Preserving the Constitution*, 168–85.

105. "Socialism in South Carolina," *Nation*, April 23, 1874, 247–48. On South Carolina, see Thomas Holt, *Black over White: Negro Political Leadership in South Carolina during Reconstruction* (Urbana: University of Illinois Press, 1977).

106. *Official Proceedings of the National Republican Conventions of 1868, 1872, 1876 and 1880* (Minneapolis: Charles W. Johnson, 1903), 131.

107. Steven Hahn, "What Sort of World Did the Civil War Make?," in *The World the Civil War Made*, ed. Kate Masur and Gregory P. Downs (Chapel Hill: University of North Carolina Press, 2015), 337–56; McPherson, *Battle Cry of Freedom*, 859–62; David A. Bateman, Ira Katznelson, and John S. Lapinski, *Southern Nation: Congress and White Supremacy after Reconstruction* (Princeton, NJ: Princeton University Press, 2018).

108. Charles W. Calhoun, *Conceiving a New Republic: The Republican Party and the Southern Question, 1869–1900* (Lawrence: University Press of Kansas, 2006); Xi Wang, *The Trial of Democracy: Black Suffrage and Northern Republicans, 1860–1910* (Athens: University of Georgia Press, 2012).

109. Benedict, *Preserving the Constitution*, 128. For a speech from 1876 with this framing, see Robert G. Ingersoll, "Speech at Indianapolis," in Simpson, ed., *Reconstruction: Voices from America's First Great Struggle for Racial Equality*, 626–31.

110. This is the backdrop for Nathan P. Kalmoe, *With Ballots and Bullets: Partisanship and Violence in the American Civil War* (New York: Cambridge University Press, 2020).

Chapter Four: The Politics of Industrialism and the Progressive Transformation of Party

1. Edward G. Ryan, *An Address Delivered before the Law School Class of the University of Wisconsin, June 16, 1873* (Madison: Democrat Company Book and Job Printers, 1873), 25. On the irascible Irish-born Ryan, who would go on to serve as chief justice of the Wisconsin Supreme Court, see Alfons J. Beitzinger, *Edward G. Ryan: Lion of the Law* (Madison: State Historical Society of Wisconsin, 1960).

2. Holly Case, "The 'Social Question,' 1820–1920," *Modern Intellectual History* 13 (2016): 747–75.

3. Leon Fink, *Workingmen's Democracy: The Knights of Labor and American Politics* (Urbana: University of Illinois Press, 1983), 227.

4. Walter E. Weyl, *The New Democracy: An Essay on Certain Political and Economic Tendencies in the United States* (New York: Macmillan, 1912), 305.

5. For overviews, see H. Wayne Morgan, *From Hayes to McKinley: National Party Politics, 1877–1896* (Syracuse, NY: Syracuse University Press, 1969); Robert D. Marcus, *Grand Old Party: Political Structure in the Gilded Age, 1880–1896* (New York: Oxford University Press, 1971); Morton Keller, *Affairs of State: Public Life in Late Nineteenth Century America* (Cambridge, MA: Belknap Press of Harvard University Press, 1977); Charles W. Calhoun, "The Political Culture: Public Life and the Conduct of Politics," in *The Gilded Age: Perspectives on the Origins of Modern America*, ed. Charles W. Calhoun, 2nd ed. (Lanham, MD: Rowman & Littlefield, 2007), 239–64.

6. Mark Wahlgren Summers, *Party Games: Getting, Keeping, and Using Power in Gilded Age Politics* (Chapel Hill: University of North Carolina Press, 2004); C. K. Yearley, *The Money Machines: The Breakdown and Reform of Governmental and Party Finance in the North, 1860–1920* (Albany: State University of New York Press, 1970); Gary Gerstle, *Liberty and Coercion: The Paradox of American Government from the Founding to the Present* (Princeton, NJ: Princeton University Press, 2015), 149–81; Paula Baker, "Campaigns and Potato Chips; or Some Causes and Consequences of Political Spending," *Journal of Policy History* 14 (2002): 4–29.

7. George Washington Plunkitt, *Plunkitt of Tammany Hall: A Series of Very Plain Talks on Very Practical Politics*, ed. William L. Riordon (New York: McClure, Phillips, 1905; New York: E. P. Dutton, 1963), 38. Citations refer to the Dutton edition.

8. Quoted in Keller, *Affairs of State*, 274.

9. James J. Connolly, *An Elusive Unity: Urban Democracy and Machine Politics in Industrializing America* (Ithaca, NY: Cornell University Press, 2010), 65.

10. Jeffrey D. Broxmeyer, *Electoral Capitalism: The Party System in New York's Gilded Age* (Philadelphia: University of Pennsylvania Press, 2020).

11. Richard Franklin Bensel, *The Political Economy of American Industrialization, 1877–1900* (New York: Cambridge University Press, 2000).

12. Charles W. Calhoun, "Political Economy in the Gilded Age: The Republican Party's Industrial Policy," *Journal of Policy History* 8 (1996): 291–309; Lewis L. Gould, *The Republicans: A History of the Grand Old Party* (New York: Oxford University Press, 2014), 61–87. For an account that accentuates continuities, see George S. Boutwell, *I Am a Republican: A History of the*

Republican Party, a Defense of Its Policies, and the Reasons Which Justify Its Continuance in Power (Hartford, CT: William J. Betts, 1884).

13. "1880 Democratic Platform," June 22, 1880, American Presidency Project, https://www .presidency.ucsb.edu/documents/1880-democratic-party-platform.

14. R. Hal Williams, "'Dry Bones and Dead Language': The Democratic Party," in *The Gilded Age*, ed. H. Wayne Morgan, rev. ed. (Syracuse: Syracuse University Press, 1969), 129–48.

15. Grover Cleveland, "Veto Message," February 17, 1887, American Presidency Project, https://www.presidency.ucsb.edu/documents/veto-message-237.

16. On ethnocultural politics, see Paul Kleppner, *The Third Electoral System, 1853–1892: Parties, Voters, and Political Cultures* (Chapel Hill: University of North Carolina Press, 1979).

17. John M. Allswang, *Bosses, Machines, and Urban Voters*, rev. ed. (Baltimore: Johns Hopkins University Press, 1986); Harold Zink, *City Bosses in the United States: A Study of Twenty Municipal Bosses* (Durham, NC: Duke University Press, 1930).

18. Harold S. Gosnell, "Thomas C. Platt—Political Manager," *Political Science Quarterly* 38 (1923): 443–69; Richard L. McCormick, *From Realignment to Reform: Political Change in New York State, 1893–1910* (Ithaca, NY: Cornell University Press, 1981), 69–103; James A. Kehl, *Boss Rule in the Gilded Age: Matt Quay of Pennsylvania* (Pittsburgh: University of Pittsburgh Press, 1981). In the bitter but often obscure fight between Stalwarts and Half-Breeds that divided Republicans in the 1870s and 1880s, the machines were Stalwarts, insistent on regularity to defeat a rising Democracy in their states. See Allan Peskin, "Who Were the Stalwarts? Who Were Their Rivals? Republican Factions in the Gilded Age," *Political Science Quarterly* 99 (1984): 703–16.

19. Steven P. Erie, *Rainbow's End: Irish-Americans and the Dilemmas of Urban Machine Politics, 1840–1985* (Berkeley: University of California Press, 1987), 67–106.

20. Alan DiGaetano, "The Rise and Development of Urban Political Machines: An Alternative to Merton's Functionalist Analysis," *Urban Affairs Quarterly* 24 (1988): 242–67. On patterns in urban government, see Jon C. Teaford, *The Unheralded Triumph: City Government in America, 1870–1900* (Baltimore: Johns Hopkins University Press, 1984).

21. Contrast the portraits of Tammany Democrats in New York and Redeemer Democrats in South Carolina in Michael Kazin, *What It Took to Win: A History of the Democratic Party* (New York: Farrar, Straus & Giroux, 2022), 83–115.

22. Martin Shefter, *Political Parties and the State* (Princeton, NJ: Princeton University Press, 1994), 177.

23. For a detailed accounting, see William M. Ivins, *Machine Politics and Money in Politics in New York City* (New York: Harper & Brothers, 1887).

24. Richard White, *Railroaded: The Transcontinentals and the Making of Modern America* (New York: W. W. Norton, 2011), 119.

25. Summers, *Party Games*, 93.

26. Daniel Klinghard, *The Nationalization of American Political Parties, 1880–1896* (New York: Cambridge University Press, 2010).

27. Michael McGerr, *The Decline of Popular Politics: The American North, 1865–1928* (New York: Oxford University Press, 1986), 42–106; quote from Alexander S. Clarkson on p. 83.

28. Connolly, *Elusive Unity*, 135–88.

29. M. R. Werner, *Tammany Hall* (Garden City, NY: Doubleday Doran, 1928; repr., New York: Greenwood Press, 1968), 276–481; Martin Shefter, "The Electoral Foundations of the Political Machine: New York City, 1884–1897," in *The History of American Electoral Behavior*, ed. Allan G. Bogue and Joel H. Silbey (Princeton, NJ: Princeton University Press, 1978), 263–98; Terry Golway, *Machine Made: Tammany Hall and the Creation of Modern American Politics* (New York: Liveright, 2014), 105–77.

30. Golway, *Machine Made*, 153–56. For a fine tour, see Roy V. Peel, *The Political Clubs of New York City* (New York: G. P. Putnam's Sons, 1935).

31. Plunkitt, *Plunkitt of Tammany Hall*, 25–26.

32. Jane Addams, "Why the Ward Boss Rules," *Outlook*, April 2, 1898, 880.

33. Robert L. Beisner, *Twelve against Empire: The Anti-Imperialists, 1888–1900* (Chicago: University of Chicago Press, 1968), 13. The name Mugwumps came from an Algonquin word meaning "great chief." Wags joked that they had their "mugs" on one side of the fence and their "wumps" on the other.

34. William Everett, quoted in Geoffrey Blodgett, *The Gentle Reformers: Massachusetts Democrats in the Cleveland Era* (Cambridge, MA: Harvard University Press, 1966), 42. See also the speeches and tracts collected in Raymond L. Bridgman, ed., *The Independents of Massachusetts in 1884* (Boston: Cupples, Upham, 1885).

35. Charles Francis Adams, *Three Episodes of Massachusetts History*, vol. 2 (Boston: Houghton Mifflin, 1892), 965–66.

36. Blodgett, *Gentle Reformers*; Gordon S. Wood, "The Massachusetts Mugwumps," *New England Quarterly* 33 (1960): 435–51.

37. Beisner, *Twelve against Empire*.

38. On Mugwumps' views of Progressivism, see Gerald W. McFarland, *Mugwumps, Morals & Politics, 1884–1920* (Amherst: University of Massachusetts Press, 1975), 125–48.

39. Leon Fink, "The New Labor History and the Powers of Historical Pessimism: Consensus, Hegemony, and the Case of the Knights of Labor," *Journal of American History* 75 (1988): 115–36; Fink, *Workingmen's Democracy*, esp. 3–35; Richard Oestreicher, "Terence Powderly, The Knights of Labor, and Artisanal Republicanism," in *Labor Leaders in America*, ed. Melvyn Dubofsky and Warren Van Tine (Urbana: University of Illinois Press, 1983), 30–61; Richard Schneirov, *Labor and Urban Politics: Class Conflict and the Origins of Modern Liberalism in Chicago, 1864–97* (Urbana: University of Illinois Press, 1998); Alan Dawley and Paul Faler, "Working-Class Culture and Politics in the Industrial Revolution: Sources of Loyalism and Rebellion," *Journal of Social History* 9 (1976): 466–80. For a theoretical perspective, see Alex Gourevitch, *From Slavery to the Cooperative Commonwealth: Labor and Republican Liberty in the Nineteenth Century* (New York: Cambridge University Press, 2015).

40. George McNeill, *The Labor Movement: The Problem of To-Day* (New York: M. W. Hazen, 1891), 455.

41. Richard Jules Oestreicher, *Solidarity and Fragmentation: Working People and Class Consciousness in Detroit, 1875–1900* (Urbana: University of Illinois Press, 1989), 60.

42. David Montgomery, *Citizen Worker: The Experience of Workers in the United States with Democracy and the Free Market during the Nineteenth Century* (New York: Cambridge University Press, 1993), 154–155; James Green, *Death in the Haymarket: A Story of Chicago, the First Labor Movement and the Bombing That Divided Gilded Age America* (New York: Pantheon Books, 2006).

43. Melvin G. Holli, *Reform in Detroit: Hazen S. Pingree and Urban Politics* (New York: Oxford University Press, 1969); Schneirov, *Labor and Urban Politics*; Richard Schneirov, "Urban Regimes and the Policing of Strikes in Two Gilded Age Cities: New York and Chicago," *Studies in American Political Development* 33 (2019): 258–74; Gerald Friedman, "Success and Failure in Third-Party Politics: The Knights of Labor and the Union Labor Coalition in Massachusetts, 1884–1888," *International Labor and Working-Class History* 62 (2002): 164–88.

44. Shefter, *Political Parties and the State*, 101–68; Philip Taft, *The A.F. of L. in the Time of Gompers* (New York: Harper & Brothers, 1957), 1–122; Michael Rogin, "Voluntarism: The Political Functions of an Antipolitical Doctrine," *ILR Review* 15 (1962): 521–35.

45. The best guide to the campaign's political possibilities is David Scobey, "Boycotting the Politics Factory: Labor Radicalism and the New York City Mayoral Election of 1886," *Radical*

History Review 28 (1984): 280–325. See also Edward T. O'Donnell, *Henry George and the Crisis of Inequality: Progress and Poverty in the Gilded Age* (New York: Columbia University Press, 2015). For a wider view, see Christopher William England, *Land and Liberty: Henry George and the Crafting of Modern Liberalism* (Baltimore: Johns Hopkins University Press, 2023).

46. Louis F. Post and Fred C. Leubuscher, *Henry George's 1886 Campaign: An Account of the George-Hewitt Campaign in the New York Municipal Election of 1886* (John W. Lovell, 1887; repr. New York: Henry George School, 1961), 9, 112. Citations refer to the Henry George School edition.

47. Post and Leubuscher, *Henry George's 1886 Campaign*, 60.

48. Post and Leubuscher, *Henry George's 1886 Campaign*, 48.

49. Sven Beckert, *The Monied Metropolis: New York City and the Consolidation of the American Bourgeoise, 1850–1896* (New York: Cambridge University Press, 2001), 277–79.

50. Theodore Roosevelt, "Machine Politics in New York," *Century*, November 1886, 74–82.

51. Richard Oestreicher, "Urban Working-Class Political Behavior and Theories of American Electoral Politics, 1870–1940," *Journal of American History* 74 (1988): 1257–86; Victoria Hattam, "Economic Visions and Political Strategies: American Labor and the State, 1865–1896," *Studies in American Political Development* 4 (1990): 82–129.

52. David Montgomery, "Labor and the Republic in Industrial America: 1860–1920," *Le Mouvement Social* 111 (1980): 211; see also David Montgomery, *The Fall of the House of Labor: The Workplace, the State, and American Labor Activism, 1865–1925* (New York: Cambridge University Press, 1987).

53. For the political blow-by-blow, see Ira Kipnis, *The American Socialist Movement, 1897–1912* (New York: Columbia University Press, 1952); David A. Shannon, *The Socialist Party of America, A History* (New York: Macmillan, 1955); Jack Ross, *The Socialist Party of America: A Complete History* (Lincoln: University of Nebraska Press, 2015). For good thematic treatments from leading chroniclers, best read side by side, see Irving Howe, *Socialism and America* (San Diego: Harcourt Brace Jovanovich, 1985), 3–48; Mike Davis, *Prisoners of the American Dream: Politics and Economy in the History of the US Working Class* (London: Verso, 1986), 40–51; Michael Kazin, *American Dreamers: How the Left Changed a Nation* (New York: Alfred A. Knopf, 2011), 109–54.

54. Eugene V. Debs, "Why You Should Vote for Socialism," *Appeal to Reason*, August 31, 1912, 1.

55. Victor L. Berger, "Socialism, the Logical Outcome of Progressivism," *American Magazine*, November 1912, 19.

56. Melvyn Dubofsky, *We Shall Be All: A History of the Industrial Workers of the World* (Chicago: Quadrangle Books, 1969), 146–70.

57. The most comprehensive party-political account of Populism is still John D. Hicks, *The Populist Revolt: A History of the Farmers' Alliance and the People's Party* (Minneapolis: University of Minnesota Press, 1931). For important treatments, see Lawrence Goodwyn, *Democratic Promise: The Populist Moment in America* (New York: Oxford University Press, 1976); Robert C. McMath, *American Populism: A Social History, 1877–1898* (New York: Hill and Wang, 1993); Elizabeth Sanders, *The Roots of Reform: Farmers, Workers, and the American State, 1877–1917* (Chicago: University of Chicago Press, 1999), 101–47; Charles Postel, *The Populist Vision* (New York: Oxford University Press, 2007).

58. "Populist Party Platform of 1892," July 4, 1892, American Presidency Project. https://www .presidency.ucsb.edu/documents/populist-party-platform-1892.

59. Gretchen Ritter, *Goldbugs and Greenbacks: The Antimonopoly Tradition and the Politics of Finance in America* (New York: Cambridge University Press, 1997).

60. Thomas Goebel, "The Political Economy of Populism from Jackson to the New Deal," *Studies in American Political Development* 11 (1997): 109–48.

61. Matthew Hild, *Greenbackers, Knights of Labor, and Populists: Farmer-Labor Insurgency in the Late-Nineteenth-Century South* (Athens: University of Georgia Press, 2007).

62. Hicks, *Populist Revolt*, 269. See also William Ivy Hair, *Bourbonism and Agrarian Protest: Louisiana Politics, 1877–1900* (Baton Rouge: Louisiana State University Press, 1969), 198–279.

63. For a party-focused treatment, see Gerald H. Gaither, *Blacks and the Populist Movement: Ballots and Bigotry in the New South*, rev. ed. (Tuscaloosa: University of Alabama Press, 2005). See also Omar H. Ali, *In the Lion's Mouth: Black Populism in the New South, 1886–1900* (Jackson: University Press of Mississippi, 2013); Edward L. Ayers, *Southern Crossing: A History of the American South, 1877–1906* (New York: Oxford University Press, 1995), 111–78; Postel, *The Populist Vision*, 173–204.

64. See, respectively, James C. Green, *Grass-Roots Socialism: Radical Movements in the Southwest, 1895–1943* (Baton Rouge: Louisiana State University Press, 1978); C. Vann Woodward, *Tom Watson: Agrarian Rebel* (New York: Macmillan, 1938).

65. James Turner, "Understanding the Populists," *Journal of American History* 67 (1980): 369.

66. Goodwyn, *Democratic Promise*, 374.

67. See Michael Kazin, *The Populist Persuasion: An American History* (New York: Basic Books, 1995), 37–46.

68. "Populist Party Platform of 1892."

69. On this process as a "shadow movement," see Goodwyn, *Democratic Promise*, 387–469.

70. Richard Bensel, *Passion and Preferences: William Jennings Bryan and the 1896 Democratic Convention* (New York: Cambridge University Press, 2008). The book offers a fine guide to the workings of national conventions in their heyday.

71. Robert F. Durden, *The Climax of Populism: The Election of 1896* (Lexington: University Press of Kentucky, 1965), esp. 23–44; Henry Demarest Lloyd, "The Populists at St. Louis," *Review of Reviews* 14 (1896): 298–303.

72. William Jennings Bryan, *The First Battle: A Story of the Campaign of 1896* (Chicago: W. B. Conkey, 1896), 446.

73. Bryan, *First Battle*, 205.

74. Michael Kazin, *A Godly Hero: The Life of William Jennings Bryan* (New York: Alfred A. Knopf, 2006), esp. 45–79; Kazin, *What It Took to Win*, 116–21.

75. Marcus, *Grand Old Party*, 195–228; R. Hal Williams, *Realigning America: McKinley, Bryan, and the Remarkable Election of 1896* (Lawrence: University Press of Kansas, 2010), 46–66.

76. For a good overview, see David Nasaw, "Gilded Age Gospels," in *Ruling America: A History of Wealth and Power in a Democracy*, ed. Steve Fraser and Gary Gerstle (Cambridge, MA: Harvard University Press, 2005), 123–48.

77. Herbert Croly, *Marcus Alonzo Hanna: His Life and Work* (New York: Macmillan, 1912), 220; Marcus, *Grand Old Party*, 239–50; Morgan, *From Hayes to McKinley*, 482–524; Williams, *Realigning America*, 137. To be read as both a primary and a secondary source, see also Karl Rove, *The Triumph of William McKinley: Why the Election of 1896 Still Matters* (New York: Simon & Schuster, 2015).

78. Walter Dean Burnham, "The System of 1896: An Analysis," in *The Evolution of American Electoral Systems*, ed. Paul Kleppner (Westport, CT: Greenwood, 1981), 147–202; Oestreicher, "Urban Working-Class Political Behavior."

79. On Progressivism's hostility to radicalism, see David Huyssen, *Progressive Inequality: Rich and Poor in New York, 1890–1920* (Cambridge, MA: Harvard University Press, 2014); Jacob A. C. Remes, *Disaster Citizenship: Survivors, Solidarity, and Power in the Progressive Era* (Urbana: University of Illinois Press, 2016); from the New Left, Gabriel Kolko, *The Triumph of Conservatism: A Reinterpretation of American History, 1900–1916* (New York: Free Press, 1963).

80. Theodore Roosevelt, introduction to *The Progressive Movement: Its Principles and Its Programme*, by S. J. Duncan-Clark (Boston: Small, Maynard, 1913), xvi–xvii.

81. John Coit Spooner to J. Hicks, November 11, 1904, box 180, John Coit Spooner Papers, Library of Congress, Washington, DC.

82. The same applied for a magazine story—"fanfic" as it would later be termed—that imagined a 1912 election with a Conservative and a Radical party. Samuel G. Blythe, "How the Big Split Came," *McClure's*, June 1912, 205–14, 68, 70.

83. On Progressive historiography, see the classic Peter G. Filene, "An Obituary for the Progressive Movement," *American Quarterly* 22 (1970): 20–34; Daniel T. Rodgers, "In Search of Progressivism," *Reviews in American History* 10 (1982): 113–32. For an intellectual history, see James Kloppenberg, *Uncertain Victory: Social Democracy and Progressivism in European and American Thought, 1870–1920* (New York: Oxford University Press, 1986). For syntheses, see Michael McGerr, *A Fierce Discontent: The Rise and Fall of the Progressive Movement in America, 1870–1920* (New York: Oxford University Press, 2005); Maureen A. Flanagan, *Progressives and Progressivisms, 1890s–1920s* (New York: Oxford University Press, 2007). For a still-useful topic-by-topic survey, see Benjamin Parke De Witt, *The Progressive Movement: A Non-partisan, Comprehensive Discussion of Current Tendencies in American Politics* (New York: Macmillan, 1915). Though our perspective on parties' place in Progressivism differs from his, Robert D. Johnston has made impressive efforts to historicize the movement and its memory. From his oeuvre, see "Re-Democratizing the Progressive Era: The Politics of Progressive Era Political Historiography," *Journal of the Gilded Age and Progressive Era* 1 (2002): 68–92; "Long Live Teddy/Death to Woodrow: The Polarized Politics of the Progressive Era in the 2012 Election," *Journal of the Gilded Age and Progressive Era* 13 (2014): 411–43.

84. James Albert Woodburn, *Political Parties and Party Problems in the United States*, 2nd ed. (New York: G. P. Putnam's Sons, 1914), 471.

85. Rebecca Edwards, *Angels in the Machinery: Gender in American Party Politics from the Civil War to the Progressive Era* (New York: Oxford University Press, 1997), 162.

86. Ellen Fitzpatrick, *Endless Crusade: Women Social Scientists and Progressive Reform* (New York: Oxford University Press, 1994); Daniel T. Rodgers, *Atlantic Crossings: Social Politics in a Progressive Age* (Cambridge, MA: Belknap Press of Harvard University Press, 1998).

87. Elisabeth S. Clemens, *The People's Lobby: Organizational Innovation and the Rise of Interest Group Politics in the United States* (Chicago: University of Chicago Press, 1997), 276.

88. Jeffrey K. Tulis, *The Rhetorical Presidency* (Princeton, NJ: Princeton University Press, 1987); Sidney M. Milkis, *Theodore Roosevelt, the Progressive Party, and the Transformation of American Democracy* (Lawrence: University Press of Kansas, 2009); Joseph Cooper, "The Balance of Power between Congress and the President: Issues and Dilemmas," in *Congress Reconsidered*, ed. Lawrence C. Dodd and Bruce I. Oppenheimer, 11th ed. (Thousand Oaks, CA: Sage, 2017), 357–98.

89. Stephen Skowronek, *Building a New American State: The Expansion of National Administrative Capacity, 1877–1920* (New York: Cambridge University Press, 1982).

90. Categories taken from James Mahoney and Kathleen Thelen, "A Theory of Gradual Institutional Change," in *Explaining Institutional Change: Ambiguity, Agency, and Power*, ed. James Mahoney and Kathleen Thelen (New York: Cambridge University Press, 2010), 15–18. The same central point is made in Morton Keller, *Regulating a New Economy: Public Policy and Economic Change in America, 1900–1933* (Cambridge, MA: Harvard University Press, 1990), 3.

91. Shefter, *Political Parties and the State*, 169–90; Amy Bridges, *Morning Glories: Municipal Reform in the Southwest* (Princeton, NJ: Princeton University Press, 1997).

92. Alan M. Ware, *The American Direct Primary: Party Institutionalization and Transformation in the North* (Cambridge: Cambridge University Press, 2002); John F. Reynolds, *Testing*

Democracy: Electoral Behavior and Progressive Reform in New Jersey, 1880–1920 (Chapel Hill: University of North Carolina Press, 1988); John F. Reynolds, *Demise of the American Convention System, 1880–1911* (New York: Cambridge University Press, 2006), 231.

93. Reynolds, *Testing Democracy*, 168.

94. Erik J. Engstrom and Samuel Kernell, *Party Ballots, Reform, and the Transformation of America's Electoral System* (New York: Cambridge University Press, 2014), 186.

95. Joseph B. Bishop, "The Secret Ballot in Thirty-Three States," *Forum*, January 1892, 589–94; Eldon Cobb Evans, *A History of the Australian Ballot System in the United States* (Chicago: University of Chicago Press, 1917). On Massachusetts, see the reminiscences in Richard Henry Dana, "Sir William Vernon Harcourt and the Australian Ballot Law," *Proceedings of the Massachusetts Historical Society* 58 (1925): 401–18.

96. Critically, the severe malapportionment of delegate allotments to state conventions benefited rural areas with weaker organizations. In primaries, the urban vote could effectively secure the nomination for a machine favorite. The same logic explains the machines' support for direct election of senators, which increased the power of urban voters given the rural bias of state legislative malapportionment.

97. Frederick W. Dallinger, *Nominations for Elective Office in the United States* (New York: Longmans, 1897), 56.

98. Charles Edward Merriam and Louise Overacker, *Primary Elections* (Chicago: University of Chicago Press, 1928), 24–25. For the logic, see "Address by Prof. John R. Commons," *National Conference on Practical Reform of Primary Elections Held at the Rooms of the New York Board of Trade and Transportation: New York City, Thursday and Friday, January 20 and 21, 1898* (Chicago: W. C. Hollister, 1898), 22; "Direct Primaries," *Outlook*, May 1, 1897, 9.

99. Theodore Roosevelt, "The Right of the People to Rule," March 20, 1912, p. 7, folder 164, Progressive Party Papers, Houghton Library, Harvard University, Cambridge, MA. For a view from a framer of the Democrats' McGovern-Fraser reforms, see Geoffrey Cowan, *Let the People Rule: Theodore Roosevelt and the Birth of the Presidential Primary* (New York: W. W. Norton, 2016). See also Daniel Tichenor and Daniel Fuerstman, "Insurgency Campaigns and the Quest for Popular Democracy: Theodore Roosevelt, Eugene McCarthy, and Party Monopolies," *Polity* 40 (2008): 49–69.

100. Leon D. Epstein, *Political Parties in the American Mold* (Madison: University of Wisconsin Press, 1986), 155–99. This logic, of course, hardly applied nationally. Not until *Smith v. Allwright* in 1944 did the Supreme Court, with enormous consequences, strike down the white primary in the South. See Michael J. Klarman, "The White Primary Rulings: A Case Study in the Consequences of Supreme Court Decisionmaking," *Florida State University Law Review* 29 (2001): 55–107; Robert W. Mickey, "The Beginning of the End for Authoritarian Rule in America: *Smith v. Allwright* and the Abolition of the White Primary in the Deep South, 1944–1948," *Studies in American Political Development* 22 (2008): 143–82.

101. Peter H. Argersinger, "'A Place on the Ballot': Fusion Politics and Antifusion Laws," *American Historical Review* 85 (1980): 287–306. See also Lisa Jane Disch, *The Tyranny of the Two-Party System* (New York: Columbia University Press, 2002).

102. On parties and the law, see Samuel Issacharoff, Pamela S. Karlan, and Richard Pildes, *The Law of Democracy: Legal Structure of the Political Process*, 4th ed. (New York: Foundation Press, 2012), 214–331.

103. "First National Convention of the Progressive Party," August 7, 1912, 245, Theodore Roosevelt Center, https://www.theodorerooseveltcenter.org/Research/Digital-Library/Record?libID=o284845.

104. Robert M. La Follette, *La Follette's Autobiography: A Personal Narrative of Political Experiences*, 5th ed. (Madison: Robert M. La Follette, 1913), 195.

105. For a synthesis, see John D. Buenker, "Robert M. La Follette's Progressive Odyssey," *Wisconsin Magazine of History* 82 (1998): 2–31.

106. "The New Party," *La Follette's Weekly Magazine*, July 13, 1912, 1.

107. Robert M. La Follette, *The Political Philosophy of Robert M. La Follette: As Revealed in His Speeches and Writings*, comp. Ellen Torelle (Madison: Robert M. La Follete, 1920), 14. Similarly, *La Follette's Autobiography*, 203.

108. La Follette, *Political Philosophy of Robert M. La Follette*, 22, 23.

109. Robert S. Maxwell, *La Follette and the Rise of the Progressives in Wisconsin* (Madison: State Historical Society of Wisconsin, 1956), 58.

110. David P. Thelen, *Robert M. La Follette and the Insurgent Spirit* (Boston: Little Brown, 1976), 34.

111. By contrast, Democrats' ambitious plans had little connection with Woodrow Wilson's own views of party leadership. On the former, see Sanders, *Roots of Reform*, 179–386. On the latter, compare James W. Ceaser, *Presidential Selection: Theory and Development* (Princeton, NJ: Princeton University Press, 1979), 170–212; Daniel D. Stid, *The President as Statesman: Woodrow Wilson and the Constitution* (Lawrence: University Press of Kansas, 1998), 172–78; John A. Dearborn, "The 'Two Mr. Wilsons': Party Government, Personal Leadership, and Woodrow Wilson's Political Thought," *Congress & the Presidency* 47 (2020): 32–61.

112. Milkis, *Theodore Roosevelt*; George E. Mowry, *Theodore Roosevelt and the Progressive Movement* (Madison: University of Wisconsin Press, 1946); John Allen Gable, *The Bull Moose Years: Theodore Roosevelt and the Progressive Party* (Port Washington, NY: Kennikat Press, 1978).

113. Harold L. Ickes, "Who Killed the Progressive Party?" *American Historical Review* 46 (1941): 329.

114. See Eldon Eisenach, "A Progressive Conundrum: Federal Constitution, National State, and Popular Sovereignty," in *The Progressives' Century: Political Reform, Constitutional Government, and the Modern American State*, ed. Stephen Skowronek, Stephen M. Engel, and Bruce Ackerman (New Haven, CT: Yale University Press, 2016). See also Eldon J. Eisenach, *The Lost Promise of Progressivism* (Lawrence: University Press of Kansas, 1994), 120–22.

115. Theodore Roosevelt, "The College Graduate and Public Life," *Atlantic Monthly*, August 1894, 260; similarly, see Theodore Roosevelt, "The Manly Virtues and Practical Politics," *Forum*, July 1894, 551–57.

116. Jean Yarbrough, *Theodore Roosevelt and the American Political Tradition* (Lawrence: University Press of Kansas, 2012), 85. For a more positive conservative appraisal (from a future U.S. senator), see Joshua David Hawley, *Theodore Roosevelt: Preacher of Righteousness* (New Haven, CT: Yale University Press, 2008).

117. In a private letter in January 1913, Roosevelt praised Lincoln for distancing himself in the 1864 campaign from "well-meaning extremists" such as Benjamin Wade. Amos R. E. Pinchot, *History of the Progressive Party 1912–1916*, ed. Helene Maxwell Hooker (New York: New York University Press, 1958), 199. Taft, by contrast, he deemed "the spiritual heir of the cotton whigs." See James MacGregor Burns and Susan Dunn, *The Three Roosevelts: Patrician Leaders Who Transformed America* (New York: Atlantic Monthly Press, 2001), 131.

118. This reading owes much to Nancy L. Rosenblum, *On the Side of the Angels: An Appreciation of Parties and Partisanship* (Princeton, NJ: Princeton University Press, 2008), 186–209.

119. TR to Gifford Pinchot, November 15, 1912, box 12, George W. Perkins Papers, Special Collections, Columbia University, New York.

120. Mowry, *Theodore Roosevelt*, 225. On Perkins, see John A. Garraty, *Right-Hand Man: The Life of George W. Perkins* (New York: Harper, 1960); Jonathan Levy, *Freaks of Fortune: The Emerging World of Capitalism and Risk in America* (Cambridge, MA: Harvard University Press, 2014), 264–307. For financial records, see folder 340, Progressive Party Papers.

121. *Progressive Volunteer*, April 1914, p. 1, folder 340, Progressive Party Papers.

122. Arthur S. Link, ed., "Correspondence Relating to the Progressive Party's 'Lily White' Policy in 1912," *Journal of Southern History* 10 (1940): 487.

123. Weyl, *New Democracy*, 60.

124. "Proceedings of the Provisional National Progressive Committee," August 5, 1912, Theodore Roosevelt Center, http://www.theodorerooseveltcenter.org/Research/Digital-Library/Record/PrintFull?libID=o284844.

125. Paula Baker, "The Domestication of Politics: Women and American Political Society, 1780–1920," *American Historical Review* 89 (1984): 620–47; Edwards, *Angels in the Machinery*; Melanie Susan Gustafson, *Women and the Republican Party, 1854–1924* (Urbana: University of Illinois Press, 2001).

126. Clemens, *People's Lobby*; Theda Skocpol, *Protecting Soldiers and Mothers: The Political Origins of Social Policy in the United States* (Cambridge, MA: Belknap Press of Harvard University Press, 1992). Such voluntary activity continued long after suffrage, in ways that a focus on party politics necessarily obscures. On this point, see Nancy F. Cott, *The Grounding of Modern Feminism* (New Haven, CT: Yale University Press, 1987), 85.

127. "The Progressive National Service," folder 164, Progressive Party Papers.

128. Jane Addams, "Pragmatism in Politics," *Survey*, October 5, 1912, 11–12; Jane Addams, "My Service as a Progressive Delegate," *McClure's*, November 1912, 12–14.

129. "Progressive Party Platform of 1912." The Progressive platform drew from a comprehensive report issued by a who's-who of reformers. See *Social Standards for Industry: A Platform* (New York: Committee on Standards of Living and Labor, 1912). On race, see Jane Addams, "The Progressive Party and the Negro," *Crisis*, November 1912, 30–31.

130. "The Progressive National Service." On similar themes, see Frances A. Kellor, "A New Spirit in Party Organization," *North American Review* 199 (1914): 879–92; Jane Addams, "Social Justice through National Action," in Progressive National Committee, ed., *Nationalism: Its Need in Our Social, Industrial and Political Growth* (New York: Progressive National Committee, 1914), 6–9. The best account of the Progressive National Service is Fitzpatrick, *Endless Crusade*, 149–57.

131. James T. Kloppenberg, "Barack Obama and the Traditions of Progressive Reform," in Skowronek, Engel, and Ackerman, *Progressives' Century*, 431–52.

132. Eleanor Flexner and Ellen Fitzpatrick, *Century of Struggle: The Woman's Rights Movement in the United States*, enlarged ed. (Cambridge, MA: Belknap Press of Harvard University Press, 1995), 255. See also Corrine M. McConnaughy, *The Woman Suffrage Movement in America: A Reassessment* (New York: Cambridge University Press, 2013); Alexander Keyssar, *The Right to Vote: The Contested History of Democracy in the United States*, rev. ed. (New York: Basic Books, 2009), 139–78; and, for a male Progressive view, S. J. Duncan-Clark, *Progressive Movement* (Boston: Small, Maynard, 1913), 90–108.

133. Jo Freeman, *A Room at a Time: How Women Entered Party Politics* (Lanham, MD: Rowman & Littlefield, 2000); Kristi Andersen, *After Suffrage: Women in Partisan and Electoral Politics before the New Deal* (Chicago: University of Chicago, 1996); Anna L. Harvey, *Votes without Leverage: Women in American Electoral Politics, 1920–1970* (New York: Cambridge University Press, 1998). From party women themselves, see Frances Kellor, "Women in British and American Politics," *Current History*, February 1, 1923, 831–35; Eleanor Roosevelt, "Women Must Learn to Play the Game as Men Do," *Red Book*, April 1928, 78–79, 141–42; Emily Newell Blair, "Women in the Political Parties," *Annals of the American Academy of Political and Social Science* 143 (1929): 217–29.

134. Charles Merz, "Progressivism—1912 and 1924," *New Republic*, August 13, 1924, 312–14; Kenneth Campbell MacKay, *The Progressive Movement of 1924* (New York: Columbia University Press, 1947).

135. See the dueling statements and their signers: "48 Roosevelt Aids Repudiate 3d Party," *New York Times*, September 15, 1924, 3; "42 Bull Moosers for La Follette," *New York Times*, October 24, 1924, 3. For more on the story, see Otis L. Graham, *An Encore for Reform: The Old Progressives and the New Deal* (New York: Oxford University Press, 1967).

136. Robert James Maddox, "Keeping Cool with Coolidge," *Journal of American History* 53 (1967): 772–80.

137. Ware, *American Direct Primary*, 228–29; Merriam and Overacker, *Primary Elections*; William E. Hannan, "Opinions of Public Men on the Value of the Direct Primary," *Annals of the American Academy of Political and Social Science* 106 (1923): 59. On long-run effects, see Shigeo Hirano and James M. Snyder Jr., *Primary Elections in the United States* (New York: Cambridge University Press, 2019).

138. See, notably, Peter McCaffery, *When Bosses Ruled Philadelphia: The Emergence of the Republican Machine, 1867–1933* (University Park: Pennsylvania State University Press, 1993).

139. John Morrison McLarnon III, *Ruling Suburbia: John J. McClure and the Republican Machine in Delaware County, Pennsylvania* (Newark: University of Delaware Press, 2003); Marjorie Freeman Harrison, "Machine Politics Suburban Style: J. Russel Sprague and the Nassau County (N.Y.) Republican Party at Midcentury" (PhD diss., Columbia University, 2005).

140. John D. Buenker, *Urban Liberalism and Progressive Reform* (New York: W. W. Norton, 1973), 162; see also J. Joseph Huthmacher, "Urban Liberalism and the Age of Reform," *Mississippi Valley Historical Review* 49 (1962): 231–41. A similar argument grounded in historical-institutionalist logic appears in Kenneth Finegold, *Experts and Politicians: Reform Challenges to Machine Politics in New York, Cleveland, and Chicago* (Princeton, NJ: Princeton University Press, 1995).

141. Frances Perkins, *The Roosevelt I Knew* (New York: Viking Press, 1946), 22. See also Richard A. Greenwald, *The Triangle Fire, the Protocols of Peace, and Industrial Democracy* (Philadelphia: Temple University Press, 2005), 154–213.

142. Erie, *Rainbow's End*.

143. Richard White, "Gilded Ages," *Journal of the Gilded Age and Progressive Era* 19 (2020): 314–20.

144. E. J. Dionne Jr., *They Only Look Dead: Why Progressives Will Dominate the Next Political Era* (New York: Simon & Schuster, 1996); Robert D. Putnam, *Bowling Alone: The Collapse and Revival of American Community* (New York: Simon & Schuster, 2000); Robert D. Putnam with Shaylyn Romney Garrett, *The Upswing: How America Came Together a Century Ago and How We Can Do It Again* (New York: Simon & Schuster, 2020); John Podesta, *The Power of Progress: How America's Progressives Can (Once Again) Save Our Economy, Our Climate, and Our Country* (New York: Crown, 2008); K. Sabeel Rahman, *Democracy against Domination* (New York: Oxford University Press, 2017); Ganesh Sitaraman, *The Crisis of the Middle-Class Constitution: Why Economic Inequality Threatens Our Republic* (New York: Alfred A. Knopf, 2017). On the limits of such a politics, see Sanders, *Roots of Reform*, esp. 387–89; Linda Gordon, "If the Progressives Were Advising Us Today, Should We Listen?" *Journal of the Gilded Age and Progressive Era* 1 (2002): 109–21.

145. For a perceptive reading, see James T. Kloppenberg, *Reading Obama: Dreams, Hope, and the American Political Tradition* (Princeton, NJ: Princeton University Press, 2012).

Chapter Five: Visions of Party from the New Deal to McGovern-Fraser

1. On common commitments, see a Humphrey aide's compendium of party Jefferson-Jackson dinners. Ronald F. Stinnett, *Democrats, Dinners, & Dollars: A History of the Democratic Party, Its Dinners, Its Rituals* (Ames: Iowa State University Press, 1967).

2. Hubert Humphrey address to New York State Democratic Delegates, August 17, 1968, Hubert H. Humphrey Papers, Minnesota Historical Society, http://www2.mnhs.org/library/findaids/00442/pdfa/00442-02676.pdf. On Humphrey's relationships with his two rivals, see, respectively, Albert Eisele, *Almost to the Presidency: A Biography of Two American Politicians* (Blue Earth, MN: Piper, 1972); Bruce Miroff, "From Friends to Foes: George McGovern, Hubert Humphrey, and the Fracture in American Liberalism," in *Making Sense of American Liberalism*, ed. Jonathan Bell and Timothy Stanley (Urbana: University of Illinois Press, 2012), 90–109.

3. On Farley's letter-signing, see Daniel Scroop, *Mr. Democrat: Jim Farley, the New Deal, and the Making of Modern American Politics* (Ann Arbor: University of Michigan Press, 2006), 162.

4. R. W. Apple Jr., "Delegate Reforms Bring New Types to the Convention," *New York Times*, July 9, 1972, 1.

5. Thomas Ronan, "Burns Seeks Accord on Slate of Delegates for Democratic Convention," *New York Times*, June 27, 1968, 25; Thomas Ronan, "O'Connor Hoping for Party Unity," *New York Times*, June 30, 1968, 44; Lewis Chester, Godfrey Hodgson, and Bruce Page, *An American Melodrama: The Presidential Campaign of 1968* (New York: Viking Press, 1969), 409.

6. *The Presidential Nominating Conventions, 1968* (Washington, DC: Congressional Quarterly, 1968), 88.

7. The delegation's divides worsened in Chicago. See, from a McCarthy delegate, Murray Kempton, "The Decline and Fall of the Democratic Party," *Saturday Evening Post*, November 2, 1968, 19–20, 66–79.

8. On periodizing the era, see, among others, Steve Fraser and Gary Gerstle, eds., *The Rise and Fall of the New Deal Order, 1930–1980* (Princeton, NJ: Princeton University Press, 1989); David Plotke, *Building a Democratic Political Order: Reshaping American Liberalism in the 1930s and 1940s* (New York: Cambridge University Press, 1996); Jefferson Cowie, *The Great Exception: The New Deal and the Limits of American Politics* (Princeton, NJ: Princeton University Press, 2016); Gary Gerstle, Nelson Lichtenstein, and Alice O'Connor, eds., *Beyond the New Deal Order: U.S. Politics from the Great Depression to the Great Recession* (Philadelphia: University of Pennsylvania Press, 2019).

9. The quoted line is from Nelson Lichtenstein, *The Most Dangerous Man in Detroit: Walter Reuther and the Fate of American Labor* (New York: Basic Books, 1995), 425. For useful synthetic statements on postwar liberalism, see Steve Fraser and Gary Gerstle, introduction to *Rise and Fall of the New Deal Order*, ed. Fraser and Gerstle, ix–xxv; Meg Jacobs, "The Uncertain Future of American Politics, 1940–1973," in *American History Now*, ed. Eric Foner and Lisa McGirr (Philadelphia: Temple University Press, 2011), 151–74.

10. Richard Oestreicher, "The Rules of the Game: Class Politics in Twentieth-Century America," in *Organized Labor and American Politics, 1894–1994: The Labor-Liberal Alliance*, ed. Kevin Boyle (Albany: State University of New York Press, 1998), esp. 40–43. For classic readings on race and space in the postwar era, see Thomas J. Sugrue, *The Origins of the Urban Crisis: Race and Inequality in Postwar Detroit* (Princeton: Princeton University Press, 1996); Lizabeth Cohen, *A Consumers' Republic: The Politics of Mass Consumption in Postwar America* (New York: Alfred A. Knopf, 2003), esp. 194–256.

11. Alan Brinkley, *The End of Reform: New Deal Liberalism in Recession and War* (New York: Vintage Books, 1995). For a comparative account, see Isser Woloch, *The Postwar Moment: Progressive Forces in Britain, France, and the United States after World War II* (New Haven, CT: Yale University Press, 2019).

12. Jacob S. Hacker, *The Divided Welfare State: The Battle over Public and Private Social Benefits in the United States* (New York: Cambridge University Press, 2002); Jennifer Klein, *For All These Rights: Business, Labor, and the Shaping of America's Public-Private Welfare State* (Princeton, NJ: Princeton University Press, 2003).

13. Ann Markusen, Peter Hall, Scott Campbell, and Sabina Deitrick, *The Rise of the Gunbelt: The Military Remapping of Industrial America* (New York: Oxford University Press, 1991); Rebecca Thorpe, *The American Warfare State: The Domestic Politics of Military Spending* (Chicago: University of Chicago Press, 2014); Michael Brenes, *For Might and Right: Cold War Defense Spending and the Remaking of American Democracy* (Amherst: University of Massachusetts Press, 2020).

14. Ellen Schrecker, *Many Are the Crimes: McCarthyism in America* (New York: Little, Brown, 1998), 359–416; Landon R. Y. Storrs, *The Second Red Scare and the Unmaking of the New Deal Left* (Princeton, NJ: Princeton University Press, 2012).

15. On the lineages and the distinctions between the Old Left and the New Left, see Maurice Isserman, *If I Had a Hammer . . . : The Death of the Old Left and the Birth of the New* (New York: Basic Books, 1987). For a good capsule summary, see Van Gosse, *Rethinking the New Left: An Interpretive History* (New York: Palgrave Macmillan, 2005), 29.

16. Jeane Kirkpatrick, *Dismantling the Parties: Reflections on Party Reform and Party Decomposition* (Washington, DC: American Enterprise Institute, 1978); Nelson W. Polsby, *Consequences of Party Reform* (New York: Oxford University Press, 1983); Byron E. Shafer, *Quiet Revolution: The Struggle for the Democratic Party and the Shaping of Post-Reform Politics* (New York: Russell Sage Foundation, 1983). Recent assertions of McGovern-Fraser's significance include Frances McCall Rosenbluth and Ian Shapiro, *Responsible Parties: Saving Democracy from Itself* (New Haven, CT: Yale University Press, 2018); Lawrence R. Jacobs, *Democracy under Fire: Donald Trump and the Breaking of American History* (New York: Oxford University Press, 2022); Nicholas F. Jacobs and Sidney M. Milkis, *Whatever Happened to the Vital Center? Presidentialism, Populist Revolt, and the Fracturing of America* (New York: Oxford University Press, 2022).

17. Ronald Radosh, *Divided They Fell: The Demise of the Democratic Party, 1964–1996* (New York: Free Press, 1996); Jeffrey Bloodworth, *Losing the Center: The Decline of American Liberalism, 1968–1992* (Lexington: University Press of Kentucky, 2013; David Paul Kuhn, *The Hardhat Riot: Nixon, New York City, and the Dawn of the White Working-Class Revolution* (New York: Oxford University Press, 2020). The crowning left-wing version of this critique is Judith Stein, *Pivotal Decade: How the United States Traded Factories for Finance in the Seventies* (New Haven, CT: Yale University Press, 2010).

18. Sam Rosenfeld and Daniel Schlozman, "Did the Democrats Fuck It Up?," *n+1*, May 19, 2022, https://www.nplusonemag.com/online-only/online-only/did-the-democrats-fuck-it-up/.

19. For resonant assessments, see David Plotke, "Party Reform as Failed Democratic Renewal in the United States, 1968–1972," *Studies in American Political Development* 10 (1996): 223–88; Adam Hilton, *True Blues: The Contentious Transformation of the Democratic Party* (Philadelphia: University of Pennsylvania Press, 2021).

20. Sean D. Savage, *Roosevelt: The Party Leader, 1932–1945* (Lexington: University Press of Kentucky, 1991), 51–53.

21. "Mayor Hague Holds Roosevelt 'Weak,'" *New York Times*, June 24, 1932, 12.

22. Susan Dunn, *Roosevelt's Purge: How FDR Fought to Change the Democratic Party* (Cambridge, MA: Harvard University Press, 2010), 36.

23. On the South, see Ira Katznelson, *Fear Itself: The New Deal and the Origins of Our Time* (New York: W. W. Norton, 2013), 133–222.

24. Scroop, *Mr. Democrat*, 103.

25. Anthony J. Badger, "The New Deal and the Localities," in *The Growth of Federal Power in American History*, ed. Rhodri Jeffreys-Jones and Bruce Collins (DeKalb: Northern Illinois University Press, 1983), 108–9.

26. James A. Farley, *Jim Farley's Story: The Roosevelt Years* (New York: Whittlesey House, 1948), 68.

27. Donna Gill, "Mr. Democrat Retains Love for Politics," *Chicago Tribune*, August 26, 1968, 9.

28. For a balanced overview, see Savage, *Roosevelt*, 48–79.

29. Arthur M. Schlesinger Jr., *The Age of Roosevelt: The Politics of Upheaval, 1935–1936* (Boston: Houghton Mifflin, 1960), 442.

30. Roger Biles, *Big City Boss in Depression and War: Mayor Edward J. Kelly of Chicago* (DeKalb: Northern Illinois University Press, 1984); Bruce M. Stave, *The New Deal and the Last Hurrah: Pittsburgh Machine Politics* (Pittsburgh: University of Pittsburgh Press, 1970); Michael Weber, *Don't Call Me Boss: David L. Lawrence, Pittsburgh's Renaissance Mayor* (Pittsburgh: University of Pittsburgh Press, 1988). Machine leaders replaced Kelly in 1947 following his embrace of citywide open housing, after which point the Cook County Democratic organization grew considerably less amenable to ideological politics. See Arnold R. Hirsch, "Chicago: The Cook County Democratic Organization and the Dilemma of Race, 1931–1987," in *Snowbelt Cities: Metropolitan Politics in the Northeast and Midwest since World War II*, ed. Richard M. Bernard (Bloomington: Indiana University Press, 1990), 63–90; J. David Greenstone, *Labor in American Politics* (New York: Alfred A. Knopf, 1969), 81–109; Richard Allan Anderson, "The City That Worked: Machine Politics and Urban Liberalism in Chicago, 1945–1963" (PhD diss., Princeton University, 2018).

31. "'Voice' Tells How He Made Stampede," *New York Times*, July 18, 1940, 2.

32. William E. Leuchtenburg, *Franklin D. Roosevelt and the New Deal, 1932–1940* (New York: Harper & Row, 1963), 85–89; Plotke, *Building a Democratic Political Order*, 77–161.

33. Irving Bernstein, *The Turbulent Years: A History of the American Worker, 1933–1940* (Boston: Houghton Mifflin, 1969); Lizabeth Cohen, *Making a New Deal: Industrial Workers in Chicago, 1919–1939* (New York: Cambridge University Press, 1990), 251–360.

34. Savage, *Roosevelt*, 80–127; Scroop, *Mr. Democrat*, 99–122; James MacGregor Burns, *Roosevelt: The Lion and the Fox* (New York: Harcourt Brace, 1956), 278–88; Daniel Schlozman, *When Movements Anchor Parties: Electoral Alignments in American History* (Princeton, NJ: Princeton University Press, 2015), 61–68.

35. Steven Fraser, *Labor Will Rule: Sidney Hillman and the Rise of American Labor* (New York: Free Press, 1991), 352–72.

36. Clinton Rossiter, *The American Presidency* (New York: Harcourt, Brace & World, 1956), 95–127; Sidney M. Milkis, *The President and the Parties: The Transformation of the American Party System since the New Deal* (New York: Oxford University Press, 1993), 98–146; Matthew J. Dickinson, *Bitter Harvest: FDR, Presidential Power, and the Growth of the Presidential Branch* (New York: Cambridge University Press, 1996).

37. Leuchtenburg, *Franklin D. Roosevelt and the New Deal*, 330–32.

38. For a somewhat different gloss, see Milkis, *President and the Parties*, 300–307.

39. William Allen White, *What It's All About: Being a Reporter's Story of the Early Campaign of 1936* (New York: Macmillan, 1936), 67, 75.

40. Franklin D. Roosevelt, "Fireside Chat," June 28, 1938, American Presidency Project, https://www.presidency.ucsb.edu/node/208978.

41. Dunn, *Roosevelt's Purge*, 231.

42. Dunn, *Roosevelt's Purge*, 217–23; James T. Patterson, *Congressional Conservatism and the New Deal: The Growth of the Conservative Coalition in Congress, 1933–1939* (Lexington: University of Kentucky Press, 1967), 288–324; Sean Farhang and Ira Katznelson, "The Southern Imposition: Congress and Labor in the New Deal and Fair Deal," *Studies in American Political Development* 19 (2005): 1–30.

43. Melvyn P. Leffler, *A Preponderance of Power: National Security, the Truman Administration, and the Cold War* (Stanford, CA: Stanford University Press, 1992); Michael J. Hogan, *A Cross of Iron: Harry S. Truman and the Origins of the National Security State, 1945–1954* (New York: Cambridge University Press, 2007); Aaron L. Friedberg, *In the Shadow of the Garrison State: America's Anti-statism and Its Cold War Grand Strategy* (Princeton, NJ: Princeton University Press, 2000).

44. On the role of the South, see Katznelson, *Fear Itself*, 403–66; Jeff Woods, *Richard B. Russell: Southern Nationalism and American Foreign Policy* (Lanham, MD: Rowman & Littlefield, 2007).

45. Alonzo Hamby, *Beyond the New Deal: Harry S. Truman and American Liberalism* (New York: Columbia University Press, 1973); William E. Leuchtenburg, *In the Shadow of FDR: From Harry Truman to Barack Obama* (Ithaca, NY: Cornell University Press, 2009), 1–40.

46. On Pendergast-era Missouri as an underappreciated harbinger of Truman-era liberalism, see Jeffrey L. Pasley, "Big Deal in Little Tammany: Kansas City, the Pendergast Machine, and the Liberal Transformation of the Democratic Party," in *Wide Open Town: Kansas City in the Pendergast Era*, ed. Diane Mutti Burke, Jason Roe, and John Herron (Lawrence: University Press of Kansas, 2018), 32–56.

47. Richard M. Freeland, *The Truman Doctrine and the Origins of McCarthyism: Foreign Policy, Domestic Politics, and Internal Security, 1946–1948* (New York: Alfred A. Knopf, 1971); Jonathan Bell, *The Liberal State on Trial: The Cold War and American Politics in the Truman Years* (New York: Columbia University Press, 2004).

48. On the Cold War's benefits to liberalism, see Jennifer Delton, *Rethinking the 1950s: How Anticommunism and the Cold War Made America Liberal* (New York: Cambridge University Press, 2013). On the Cold War's conservative impact, see, from a vast literature, Schrecker, *Many Are the Crimes*, esp. 369–416; Bell, *Liberal State on Trial*. On the Cold War's relation to civil rights, see Mary Dudziak, *Cold War Civil Rights: Race and the Image of American Democracy* (Princeton, NJ: Princeton University Press, 2000).

49. Margaret Weir, *Politics and Jobs: The Boundaries of Employment Policy in the United States* (Princeton, NJ: Princeton University Press, 1992), 27–61; Brinkley, *End of Reform*, 227–64.

50. Jacquelyn Dowd Hall, "The Long Civil Rights Movement and the Political Uses of the Past," *Journal of American History* 91 (2005): 1233–63.

51. Nancy Weiss, *Farewell to the Party of Lincoln: Black Politics in the Age of F.D.R.* (Princeton, NJ: Princeton University Press, 1983), 62–119, 180–208; Thomas J. Sugrue, *Sweet Land of Liberty: The Forgotten Struggle for Civil Rights in the North* (New York: Random House, 2008), 32–129; Eric Schickler, *Racial Realignment: The Transformation of American Liberalism, 1932–1965* (Princeton, NJ: Princeton University Press, 2016), 58–68, 81–97; Keneshia Grant, *The Great Migration and the Democratic Party: Black Voters and the Realignment of American Politics in the 20th Century* (Philadelphia: Temple University Press, 2020).

52. Harry S. Truman, "Address in Philadelphia upon Accepting the Nomination of the Democratic National Convention," July 15, 1948, American Presidency Project, https://www.presidency.ucsb.edu/documents/address-philadelphia-upon-accepting-the-nomination-the-democratic-national-convention.

53. Zachary Karabell, *The Last Campaign: How Harry Truman Won the 1948 Election* (New York: Alfred A. Knopf, 2001).

54. See Clark Clifford memo to Harry S. Truman, November 14, 1947, https://www.trumanlibrary.gov/sites/default/files/1948Campaign_CliffordMemo.pdf. On its provenance, see John Acacia, *Clark Clifford: The Wise Man of Washington* (Lexington: University Press of Kentucky, 2009), 119–50. For the Rowe memo, see "The Politics of 1948," box 87, folder "Clifford Memo," James H. Rowe, Jr. Papers, Franklin D. Roosevelt Presidential Library, Hyde Park, NY.

55. Robert H. Ferrell, *Choosing Truman: The Democratic Convention of 1944* (Columbia: University of Missouri Press, 1994).

56. Sean D. Savage, *Truman and the Democratic Party* (Lexington: University Press of Kentucky, 1997), 135; Samuel G. Freedman, *Into the Bright Sunshine: Young Hubert Humphrey and the Fight for Civil Rights* (New York: Oxford University Press, 2023), 330–82. For an interpretation of the 1948 convention that de-emphasizes party, see Christopher Baylor, *First to the Party: The*

Group Origins of Political Transformation (Philadelphia: University of Pennsylvania Press, 2018), 77–85.

57. "Welcome Speech by Lawrence," *Philadelphia Inquirer*, July 13, 1948; Hubert H. Humphrey address, July 14, 1948, http://www.americanrhetoric.com/speeches/huberthumphey 1948dnc.html.

58. Irwin Ross, "Big City Machines and Liberal Voters," *Commentary*, October 1950, 305.

59. John N. Popham, "Wallace Pelted with Eggs, Fists Bang His Car in South," *New York Times*, August 31, 1948, 1.

60. Charles Wallace Collins, *Whither Solid South? A Study in Politics and Race Relations* (New Orleans: Pelican, 1947); Kari Frederickson, *The Dixiecrat Revolt and the End of the Solid South, 1932–1968* (Chapel Hill: University of North Carolina Press, 2001).

61. James Q. Wilson, *The Amateur Democrat: Club Politics in Three Cities* (Chicago: University of Chicago Press, 1962), 3.

62. Austin Ranney, *The Doctrine of Responsible Party Government: Its Origins and Present State* (Urbana: University of Illinois Press, 1954), 25–110; John Kenneth White and Jerome M. Mileur, "In the Spirit of Their Times: 'Toward a More Responsible Two-Party System' and Party Politics," in *Responsible Partisanship? The Evolution of American Political Parties Since 1950*, ed. John C. Green and Paul S. Herrnson (Lawrence: University Press of Kansas, 2000), 13–35; Sam Rosenfeld, *The Polarizers: Postwar Architects of Our Partisan Era* (Chicago: University of Chicago Press, 2018), 23–54.

63. Jennifer A. Delton, *Making Minnesota Liberal: Civil Rights and the Transformation of the Democratic Party* (Minneapolis: University of Minnesota Press, 2002), 120, 150.

64. Steven M. Gillon, *Politics and Vision: The ADA and American Liberalism, 1947–1985* (New York: Oxford University Press, 1987).

65. John Earl Haynes, *Dubious Alliance: The Making of Minnesota's DFL Party* (Minneapolis: University of Minnesota Press, 1984), 106–210; Delton, *Making Minnesota Liberal*, 1–39.

66. Martin Shefter, *Political Parties and the State: The American Historical Experience* (Princeton, NJ: Princeton University Press, 1994), 197–232.

67. Edward N. Costikyan, *Behind Closed Doors: Politics in the Public Interest* (New York: Harcourt, Brace & World, 1966), 45. See also Daniel Soyer, *Left in the Center: The Liberal Party of New York and the Rise and Fall of American Social Democracy* (Ithaca, NY: Cornell University Press, 2022).

68. Barbara S. Griffith, *The Crisis of American Labor: Operation Dixie and the Defeat of the CIO* (Philadelphia: Temple University Press, 1988); Michael Goldfield, *The Southern Key: Class, Race, and Radicalism in the 1930s and 1940s* (New York: Oxford University Press, 2020), esp. 289–330.

69. Nelson Lichtenstein, "Taft-Hartley: A Slave-Labor Law?" *Catholic University Law Review* 47 (1998): 763–89.

70. Robert H. Zieger, *The CIO, 1935–1955* (Chapel Hill: University of North Carolina Press, 1995), 253–93.

71. Schlozman, *When Movements Anchor Parties*, 132–47, 155–56; Stephen Amberg, "The CIO Political Strategy in Historical Perspective: Creating a High-Road Economy in the Postwar Era," in Boyle, *Organized Labor and American Politics*, 169–73; Lichtenstein, *Most Dangerous Man in Detroit*, 299–326; Martin Halpern, *UAW Politics in the Cold War Era* (Albany: State University of New York Press, 1988).

72. Partial Report of the Resolutions Committee, 17th Constitutional Convention of the United Auto Workers, October 1959, box 446, folder "Chairman's Files, 1960—Chapin, Arthur," Democratic National Committee Records, John F. Kennedy Presidential Library, Boston, MA.

73. Quote from Hendrik Hertzberg, "Concession Stand," *New Yorker*, November 11, 1996, 35.

74. Theodore J. Lowi, *At the Pleasure of the Mayor: Patronage and Power in New York City, 1898–1958* (New York: Free Press, 1964); Warren Moscow, *The Last of the Big-Time Bosses: The Life and Times of Carmine DeSapio and the Decline and Fall of Tammany Hall* (New York: Stein and Day, 1971), esp. 139–86.

75. James L. Sundquist, *Dynamics of the Party System: Alignment and Realignment of Political Parties in the United States*, rev. ed. (Washington: Brookings Institution, 1983), 264.

76. Delton, *Making Minnesota Liberal*; Dudley W. Buffa, *Union Power and American Democracy: The UAW and the Democratic Party, 1935–1972* (Ann Arbor: University of Michigan Press, 1984); Jonathan Bell, *California Crucible: The Forging of Modern Liberalism* (Philadelphia: University of Pennsylvania Press, 2012).

77. On the downstream significance of 1958 for civil rights, see Edward G. Carmines and James A. Stimson, *Issue Evolution: Race and the Transformation of American Politics* (Princeton, NJ: Princeton University Press, 1989), 70–71.

78. "Discussion of the Thelen Essay," in *The American Constitutional System under Strong and Weak Parties*, ed. Patricia Bonomi, James MacGregor Burns, and Austin Ranney (New York: Praeger, 1981), 77–78.

79. Jo Freeman, *A Room at a Time: How Women Entered Party Politics* (New York: Rowman & Littlefield, 2000), 176–80. See also Alan Ware, *Breakdown of Democratic Party Organization: The Breakdown of Democratic Party Organization, 1940–1980* (New York: Oxford University Press, 1985), 76–79. Frances H. Costikyan offers a rich depiction of the work of a district captain in 1960s Manhattan in Costikyan, *Behind Closed Doors*, 57–84.

80. Kimberly Brodkin, "'We Are Neither Male nor Female Democrats': Gender Difference and Women's Integration within the Democratic Party," *Journal of Women's History* 19 (2007): 111–37. See also, more generally, Kimberly Brodkin, "For the Good of the Party: Gender, Partisanship, and American Political Culture from Suffrage to the 1960s" (PhD diss., Rutgers University, 2001). For a revealing memoir from a longtime Democratic National Committee member, see Betty Taymor, *Running against the Wind: The Struggle of Women in Massachusetts Politics* (Boston: Northeastern University Press, 2000).

81. Bayard Rustin letter to Martin Luther King Jr., June 1957, in Rustin, *I Must Resist: Bayard Rustin's Life in Letters*, ed. Michael G. Long (San Francisco: City Light Books, 2012), 198. In the following decade, Rustin would change his position on party coalitionism. Bayard Rustin, "From Protest to Politics," *Commentary*, February 1965, 25–31.

82. Robert A. Caro, *Master of the Senate* (New York: Vintage Books, 2002), 831–1012; Denton L. Watson, *Lion in the Lobby: Clarence Mitchell, Jr.'s Struggle for the Passage of Civil Rights Laws* (New York: William Morrow and Company, 1990), 319–99.

83. Ralph M. Goldman, *The National Party Chairmen and Committees: Factionalism at the Top* (New York: M.E. Sharpe, 1990); Philip Klinkner, *The Losing Parties: Out-Party National Committees, 1956–1993* (New Haven, CT: Yale University Press, 1994), 12–40. For Mitchell's thoughts on political clubs, see Stephen A. Mitchell, *Elm Street Politics* (New York: Oceana, 1959).

84. *Toward a More Responsible Two-Party System: A Report of the Committee on Political Parties*, supplement, *American Political Science Review* 44, no. 3 (1950).

85. James MacGregor Burns, *The Deadlock of Democracy: Four-Party Politics in America* (New York: Prentice-Hall, 1963); Joseph S. Clark, *Congress: The Sapless Branch* (New York: Harper & Row, 1964); Richard Bolling, *House Out of Order* (New York: E. P. Dutton, 1965). See also Julian E. Zelizer, *On Capitol Hill: The Struggle to Reform Congress and Its Consequences, 1945–2000* (New York: Cambridge University Press, 2004), 39–44.

86. *Toward a More Responsible Two-Party System*, 14.

87. James MacGregor Burns, *Presidential Government: The Crucible of Leadership* (Boston: Houghton Mifflin, 1965), 330.

88. Frank J. Sorauf, "Extra-Legal Political Parties in Wisconsin," *American Political Science Review* 48 (1954): 703.

89. Wilson, *Amateur Democrat*, 9, borrowing "Yankee political ethic" from Richard Hofstadter, *The Age of Reform* (New York: Vintage Books, 1960), 9.

90. Adlai Stevenson, "So You Want to Be in Politics?," *New York Times*, April 12, 1959, BR1.

91. Robert D. Putnam, *Bowling Alone: The Collapse and Revival of American Community* (New York: Simon & Schuster, 2000), 38–40.

92. We use "pragmatism" in the sense of the first definition in *Merriam-Webster's Collegiate Dictionary*, "a practical approach to problems and affairs," rather than to link to the intellectual tradition of William James and John Dewey.

93. Scroop, *Mr. Democrat*, 187.

94. Julius Turner, "Responsible Parties: A Dissent from the Floor," *American Political Science Review* 45 (1951): 143–52; Austin Ranney and Willmoore Kendall, *Democracy and the American Party System* (New York: Harcourt, Brace, 1956). For more general versions of the critique, see Edward C. Banfield, "In Defense of the American Party System," in *Political Parties, U.S.A.*, ed. Robert A. Goldwin (Chicago: Rand McNally, 1965), 21–39; Nelson W. Polsby and Aaron B. Wildavsky, *Presidential Elections: Strategies of American Electoral Politics*, 3rd ed. (New York: Charles Scribner's Sons, 1971), 223–92.

95. Robert Dahl, *Who Governs? Democracy and Power in an American City* (New Haven, CT: Yale University Press, 1961); Edward C. Banfield and James Q. Wilson, *City Politics* (Cambridge, MA: Harvard University Press, 1963); Daniel Patrick Moynihan and James Q. Wilson, "Patronage in New York State, 1955–1959," *American Political Science Review* 58 (1964): 286–301. For a rejoinder, see Steven P. Erie, *Rainbow's End: Irish Americans and the Dilemmas of Urban Machine Politics, 1840–1985* (Berkeley: University of California Press, 1988).

96. Robert Merton, *Social Theory and Social Structure*, rev. ed. (Glencoe, IL: Free Press, 1957), 71–82; Oscar Handlin, *The Uprooted: The Epic Story of the Great Migrations That Made the American People* (New York: Grosset & Dunlap, 1951). The tendency is particularly strong in the fictional portrayal of Frank Skeffington, a thinly disguised James Michael Curley of Boston, in Edwin O'Connor, *The Last Hurrah* (Boston: Little, Brown, 1956). On this intellectual trajectory, see Alan Lessoff and James J. Connolly, "From Political Insult to Political Theory: The Boss, the Machine, and the Pluralist City," *Journal of Policy History* 25 (2013): 139–72.

97. Erie, *Rainbow's End*, 145–50; Arnold R. Hirsch, *Making the Second Ghetto: Race and Housing in Chicago, 1940–1960* (Chicago: University of Chicago Press, 1998).

98. By emphasizing the dual specters of anti-machine rebellion from African Americans and from white ethnics trending rightward, Hirsch, "Chicago," treats together phenomena usually explored separately. See also Sugrue, *Sweet Land of Liberty*; Jason Sokol, *All Eyes Are upon Us: Race and Politics from Boston to Brooklyn* (New York: Basic Books, 2014); and, on the implications for congressional politics, Thomas K. Ogorzalek, *The Cities on the Hill: How Urban Institutions Transformed National Politics* (New York: Oxford University Press, 2018).

99. Robert M. Fogelson, *Big-City Police* (Cambridge, MA: Harvard University Press, 1977), esp. 245–68.

100. Mike Royko, *Boss: Richard J. Daley of Chicago* (New York: E. P. Dutton, 1971), esp. 131–57; Hirsch, "Chicago"; Roger Biles, *Richard J. Daley: Politics, Race, and the Governing of Chicago* (DeKalb: Northern Illinois University Press, 1995), 84–138; Simon Balto, *Occupied Territory: Policing Black Chicago from Red Summer to Black Power* (Chapel Hill: University of North Carolina Press, 2019).

101. David Farber, *Chicago '68* (Chicago: University of Chicago Press, 1988), 124–45.

102. Caro, *Master of the Senate*; Doris Kearns, *Lyndon Johnson and the American Dream* (New York: Harper & Row, 1976), 152–59; Milkis, *President and the Parties*, 178–210.

103. From the eve of change, see Meg Greenfield, "LBJ and the Democrats," *Reporter*, May 22, 1966, 8–13.

104. Frances Perkins, "Labor under the New Deal and the New Frontier," in *Two Views of American Labor* (Los Angeles: Institute of International Relations, 1965), 2, 18.

105. James L. Sundquist, *Politics and Policy: The Eisenhower, Kennedy, and Johnson Years* (Washington, DC: Brookings Institution, 1968), 389–415; Michael K. Brown, *Race, Money, and the American Welfare State* (Ithaca, NY: Cornell University Press, 1999), 203–92; Julian E. Zelizer, *The Fierce Urgency of Now: Lyndon Johnson, Congress, and the Battle for the Great Society* (New York: Penguin, 2015), 11–60, 163–223.

106. On these themes, see Brown, *Race, Money, and the American Welfare State*; Michael B. Katz, *The Undeserving Poor: America's Enduring Confrontation with Poverty*, 2nd ed. (New York: Oxford University Press, 2013), 102–55; Alice O'Connor, *Poverty Knowledge: Social Science, Social Policy, and the Poor in Twentieth-Century U.S. History* (Princeton, NJ: Princeton University Press, 2001).

107. John Dittmer, *Local People: The Struggle for Civil Rights in Mississippi* (Urbana: University of Illinois Press, 1994), esp. 272–302; Charles M. Payne, *I've Got the Light of Freedom: The Organizing Tradition and the Mississippi Freedom Struggle* (Berkeley: University of California Press, 1995). On the MFDP itself, the best source is Michael Paul Sistrom, "'Authors of the Liberation': The Mississippi Freedom Democrats and the Redefinition of Politics" (PhD diss., University of North Carolina at Chapel Hill, 2002).

108. John L. Lewis to Lyndon Johnson, August 19, 1964, box 27, folder "Hu 2 / ST 24–7/17/64–11/30/64," WHCF–Human Rights, Lyndon Baines Johnson Presidential Library, Austin, Texas.

109. "Brief Submitted by the Mississippi Freedom Democratic Party," pp. 21–52, box 86, folder "LEGAL FILE—Mississippi Freedom Democratic Party briefs, 1964, 1965," Joseph L. Rauh, Jr., Papers, Library of Congress, Washington, DC.

110. Robert Dallek, *Flawed Giant: Lyndon Johnson and His Times, 1961–1973* (New York: Oxford University Press, 1998), 162–64; Beverly Gage, *G-Man: J. Edgar Hoover and the Making of the American Century* (New York: Viking, 2022), 597–99.

111. From the Humphrey-Reuther vantage point, see John Frederick Martin, *Civil Rights and the Crisis of Liberalism, 1945–1976* (Boulder: Westview Press, 1979), 208–12. From the MFDP vantage point, see Sistrom, "'Authors of the Liberation,'" 156–96; Kate Clifford Larson, *Walk with Me: A Biography of Fannie Lou Hamer* (New York: Oxford University Press, 2021), 166–85.

112. Kay Mills, *This Little Light of Mine: The Life of Fannie Lou Hamer* (New York: Plume, 1994), 5.

113. Quoted in Mark Stern, *Calculating Visions: Kennedy, Johnson, and Civil Rights* (New Brunswick, NJ: Rutgers University Press, 1992), 209.

114. For an illustration of the radicalizing effect of such an interpretation, see Stokely Carmichael [Kwame Ture] and Charles V. Hamilton, *Black Power: The Politics of Liberation* (New York: Random House, 1967), 86–97.

115. Both quotes in Thomas C. Holt, *The Civil Rights Movement: A Very Short Introduction* (New York: Oxford University Press, 2023), 85–86.

116. Hubert Humphrey to Lyndon Johnson, February 17, 1965, in *Foreign Relations of the United States, 1964–1968*, vol. 2, *Vietnam, January–June 1965*, ed. David C. Humphrey, Ronald D, Landa, and Loyis J. Smith, https://history.state.gov/historicaldocuments/frus1964-68v02/d134.

117. Students for a Democratic Society, Port Huron Statement, June 1962, http://www2.iath.virginia.edu/sixties/HTML_docs/Resources/Primary/Manifestos/SDS_Port_Huron.html.

118. Carl Oglesby, "Liberalism and the Corporate State," speech delivered at the March on Washington, November 27, 1965, in *The New Radicals: A Report with Document*, ed. Paul Jacobs and Saul Landau (New York: Vintage Books, 1966), 258.

119. Doug McAdam, *Freedom Summer* (New York: Oxford University Press, 1988), 127.

120. James Miller, *Democracy Is in the Streets: From Port Huron to the Siege of Chicago* (Cambridge, MA: Harvard University Press, 1987, 1994), 144.

121. See Gillon, *Politics and Vision*, 177–224.

122. Allard K. Lowenstein and Arnold S. Kaufman, "The Case for Opposing Johnson's Renomination," *War/Peace Report*, November 1967, 12–13; William H. Chafe, *Never Stop Running: Allard Lowenstein and the Struggle to Save American Liberalism* (New York: Basic Books, 1993), 262–75.

123. Program for ADA National Roosevelt Day Dinner, January 31, 1967, box 151, folder "Politics," Rowe Papers. See the testy exchange in Gus Tyler, "The Liberal Crisis," *New Leader*, October 23, 1967, 3–6; Joseph L. Rauh Jr., "The Liberal Crisis II," *New Leader*, November 20, 1967, 10–11; Gus Tyler, "In Reply to Rauh," *New Leader*, November 20, 1967, 11–12. Tyler, taking the argument to the extreme, argued that "Peace in Vietnam is not apt to reverse or check racial conflict. Indeed, quite the opposite is probable" given that war's end would mean "demobilization of Negro soldiers, fewer job openings, [and] a higher rate of Negro joblessness." Tyler, "The Liberal Crisis," 3–4.

124. John Quirk, "ADA and LBJ," *Commonweal*, March 1, 1968, 643.

125. Schlozman, *When Movements Anchor Parties*, 119–21.

126. Quirk, "ADA and LBJ."

127. Donald Edwards address to the Conference of Concerned Democrats, December 2, 1967, box 54, folder 2113, Allard K. Lowenstein Papers, Louis Round Wilson Special Collections Library, University of North Carolina, Chapel Hill, NC.

128. Carl Solberg, *Hubert Humphrey: A Biography* (New York: W. W. Norton, 1984), 327–28.

129. Undated letter from Rowe to Humphrey, early June 1965, box 98, folder "Humphrey, Hubert, 1964–65," Rowe Papers.

130. Timothy N. Thurber, *The Politics of Equality: Hubert H. Humphrey and the African American Freedom Struggle* (New York: Columbia University Press, 1999), 203; "The Once and Future Humphrey," *Time*, May 3, 1968, 15–23.

131. Susanna McBee, "How He Plans to Get the Boss's Job," *Life*, May 3, 1968, 32B.

132. The Commission on Party Structure and Delegate Selection, *Mandate for Reform* (Washington, DC: Democratic National Committee, 1970), 21.

133. Commission on the Democratic Selection of Presidential Nominees, *The Democratic Choice* (New York, 1968).

134. Quoted in Michael Schudson, *The Good Citizen: A History of American Civic Life* (New York: Free Press, 1998), 272.

135. Eugene McCarthy speech, Des Moines Iowa, June 29, 1968, text in authors' possession.

136. John J. Quirk, "McCarthy Fights for an Open Convention," *Commonweal*, August 9, 1968.

137. Christopher Lasch, "The New Politics: 1968 and After," *New York Review of Books*, July 11, 1968. Three post-1968 works sympathetic to the New Politics would offer up variants on this vision: Frederick G. Dutton, *Changing Sources of Power: American Politics in the 1970s* (New York: McGraw-Hill, 1971); Lanny J. Davis, *The Emerging Democratic Majority: Lessons and Legacies from the New Politics* (New York: Stein and Day, 1974); Stephen C. Schlesinger, *The New Reformers: Forces for Change in American Politics* (Boston: Houghton Mifflin, 1975).

138. Farber, *Chicago '68*, 42–55, 101–14.

139. Michael Kazin, *What It Took to Win: A History of the Democratic Party* (New York: Farrar, Straus & Giroux, 2022), 240.

140. Chester, Hodgson, and Page, *American Melodrama*, 582–83. See also John Schultz, *No One Was Killed: The Democratic National Convention, August 1968*, rev. ed. (1969; repr., Chicago: University of Chicago Press, 2009).

141. Polsby, *Consequences of Party Reform*, 29–30.

142. Chester, Hodgson, and Page, *American Melodrama*, 541.

143. Fannie Lou Hamer, "Testimony Before the Democratic Reform Committee, Jackson, Mississippi, May 22, 1969," in *The Speeches of Fannie Lou Hamer: To Tell It Like It Is*, ed. Maegan Parker Brooks and Davis W. Houck (Jackson: University Press of Mississippi, 2011), 96.

144. Abraham Ribicoff, "Speech Nominating George McGovern for the U.S. Presidency," delivered August 28, 1968, https://www.americanrhetoric.com/speeches/abrahamribicoff1968dnc.htm. Video, the best way to appreciate the searing moment, is available online at https://www.youtube.com/watch?v=Gj9TkjL87Rk. Ribicoff, a nondelegate, had to borrow a credential in order to get to the podium. The following day, the representative who lent it denounced Ribicoff as "contemptible" and added, "I hope they Mace you." See Peggy McCarthy, "Ribicoff and Daley Head to Head," *New York Times*, August 25, 1996, CN13.

145. All challenges chronicled in *The Presidential Nominating Conventions, 1968*, 101–23.

146. Clarence Cannon, *The Official Manual for the Democratic National Convention of 1968* (Washington, DC: Democratic National Committee, 1968), 22–23, 50–52; Theodore H. White, *The Making of the President, 1968* (New York: Atheneum, 1969), 274.

147. Shafer, *Quiet Revolution*, 34–38.

148. Kazin, *What It Took to Win*, 241.

149. Hubert Humphrey, "Address Accepting the Presidential Nomination at the Democratic National Convention in Chicago," August 29, 1968, American Presidency Project, https://www.presidency.ucsb.edu/documents/address-accepting-the-presidential-nomination-the-democratic-national-convention-chicago-2.

150. Rowe to Humphrey, August 7, 1968, box 152, folder "Vice President II," Rowe Papers.

151. "1968 Democratic Party Platform," August 26, 1968, American Presidency Project, https://www.presidency.ucsb.edu/documents/1968-democratic-party-platform.

152. Irving Bernstein, *Guns or Butter: The Presidency of Lyndon Johnson* (New York: Oxford University Press, 1995), 358–78.

153. The titular Donald Fraser, who defended the participatory thrust of the reforms and worked to protect them from rollback, nonetheless did not hesitate to call primaries "awful things" in 1979. "Discussion of the Ladd Essay," in Bonomi, Burns, and Ranney, *American Constitutional System*, 99.

154. Text of the majority report is in box 44, folder "1968 Democratic National Convention Credentials Committee," James O'Hara Papers, Bentley Historical Library, University of Michigan, Ann Arbor.

155. William J. Crotty, *Decision for the Democrats: Reforming the Party Structure* (Baltimore: Johns Hopkins University Press, 1978), 29.

156. For contrasting views, see Plotke, "Party Reform as Failed Democratic Renewal"; Shafer, *Quiet Revolution*, esp. 156–57, 223–25, 358–62, 527–29.

157. Taylor E. Dark, *The Unions and the Democrats: An Enduring Alliance* (Ithaca, NY: Cornell University Press, 1999), 77–92.

158. "Labor Boycotting McGovern Reforms," *Washington Post*, September 21, 1969, 1.

159. Jules Witcover, "Democratic Coalition Formed to Curb 'New Politics' Wing," *International Herald Tribune*, December 8, 1972.

160. Ben Wattenberg, *Fighting Words: A Tale of How Liberals Created Neo-Conservatism* (New York: St. Martin's Press, 2008), 135–51; Bloodworth, *Losing the Center*, 131–54. For a trenchant

critique of backlash narratives, see Felicia A. Kornbluh, "Political Arithmetic and Racial Division in the Democratic Party," *Social Policy* 22 (1996): 49–63.

161. Greenstone, *Labor in American Politics.*

162. CDM Task Force on Democratic Party Rules and Structure, *Toward Fairness and Unity for '76,* pp. 1 and 26, April 1973, Series RG9-003, box 42, folder 9, George Meany Memorial Archives, Silver Spring, MD.

163. Coalition for a Democratic Majority, "Unity out of Diversity: A Draft Position Paper on a New Charter for the Democratic Party of the United States," July 1973, Series RG9-003, box 42, folder 9, Meany Archives. See also Penn Kemble and Josh Muravchik, "The New Politics and the Democrats," *Commentary,* December 1, 1972, 78–84.

164. We discuss the "new political realism" in chapter 9. For a journalistic synthesis, see Jonathan Rauch, *Political Realism: How Hacks, Machines, Big Money, and Back-Room Deals Can Strengthen American Democracy* (Washington, DC: Brookings Institution, 2015).

165. As both a leading McGovern-Fraser critic and the mentor to many future exponents of New Realism, Nelson Polsby embodied the anti-reformist lineage across the decades. See the collected essays in a special tribute issue of the *Forum* 5, no. 1 (March 2007).

166. On the role of policy, see Hugh Heclo, "Sixties Civics," in *The Great Society and the High Tide of Liberalism,* ed. Sidney M. Milkis and Jerome M. Mileur (Amherst: University of Massachusetts Press, 2005), 53–82.

167. On the overlap between programmatic liberals and the early New Left, including their views on party realignment, see Nelson Lichtenstein, "A Moment of Convergence," in *The Port Huron Statement: Sources and Legacies of the New Left's Founding Manifesto,* ed. Richard Flacks and Nelson Lichtenstein (Philadelphia: University of Pennsylvania, 2015), 95–106.

168. Beer to McGovern, November 4, 1969, box 18, folder "Responses to the Guidelines II," Democratic National Committee (DNC) Records, National Archives, Washington, DC.

169. Commission on the Democratic Selection of Presidential Nominees, *The Democratic Choice,* 14.

170. Transcript of the proceedings, Commission on Party Structure and Delegate Selection hearing, New York, NY, May 3, 1969, box 22, folder "3A New York Hearing," DNC Records.

171. On parties, see Ware, *Breakdown of Democratic Party Organization*; David Mayhew, *Placing Parties in American Politics: Organization, Electoral Settings, and Government Activity in the Twentieth Century* (Princeton, NJ: Princeton University Press, 1986); and for evidence from the mass public, Martin Wattenberg, *The Decline of American Political Parties, 1952–1980* (Cambridge, MA: Harvard University Press, 1984). On civic decline, see Putnam, *Bowling Alone,* 31–47.

172. Jeffrey M. Berry, *Lobbying for the People: The Political Behavior of Public Interest Groups* (Princeton, NJ: Princeton University Press, 1977), 288–89; Alan Ware, "Why Amateur Politics Has Withered Away: The Club Movement, Party Reform, and the Decline of American Party Organizations," *European Journal of Political Research* 9 (1981): 232–33.

173. Michael Pertschuk, *Giant Killers* (New York: W. W. Norton, 1986), 229–42; Paul Sabin, *Public Citizens: The Attack on Big Government and the Remaking of American Liberalism* (New York: W. W. Norton, 2021).

174. John S. Saloma III and Frederick H. Sontag, *Parties: The Real Opportunity for Effective Citizen Politics* (New York: Alfred A. Knopf, 1972), 229.

175. Bryan D. Jones, Sean M. Theriault, and Michelle Whyman, *The Great Broadening: How the Vast Expansion of the Policymaking Agenda Transformed American Politics* (Chicago: University of Chicago Press, 2019).

176. Scholarship here is sparse. The best efforts remain Ware, "Why Amateur Politics Has Withered Away"; Ware, *Breakdown of Democratic Party Organization,* 75–79, 91–103.

177. Saloma and Sontag, *Parties*, 226; R. Bruce Allison, *Democrats in Exile, 1968–1972: The Political Confessions of a New England Liberal* (Hinsdale: Sol Press, 1974), 88. See also Paul R. Wieck, "What Happened to the New Politics?," *New Republic*, February 28, 1970, 12.

178. Allison, *Democrats in Exile*, 30.

179. Jo Freeman, "The Tyranny of Structurelessness," *Ms. Magazine*, July 1973, 76–78, 86–89.

180. Jacobs and Landau, *New Radicals*, 33.

181. Hilton, *True Blues*, 66–109; Jaime Sánchez Jr., "Revisiting McGovern-Fraser: Party Nationalization and the Rhetoric of Reform," *Journal of Policy History* 32 (2020): 1–24. Jeane Kirkpatrick placed the McGovern-Fraser reformers in "the anti-party tradition that views party organizations as an obstacle to popular government and seeks through such mechanisms as the direct primary and the 'open' party to bypass an 'entrenched' party leadership." Jeane Kirkpatrick, *The New Presidential Elite: Men and Women in National Politics* (New York: Russell Sage Foundation, 1976), 355. See also James W. Ceaser, "Direct Participation in Politics," *Proceedings of the Academy of Political Science* 34 (1981): 121–37.

182. "A New Charter for the Democratic Party of the United States: A Draft Proposal," March 24, 1972, box 44, folder "Democratic Party, O'Hara Rules Commission, Charter Proposal 2," O'Hara Papers.

183. Thomas E. Cronin, "On the American Presidency: A Conversation with James MacGregor Burns," *Political Science Quarterly* 16 (1986): 536. For a more caustic appraisal, see Nelson W. Polsby and Aaron B. Wildavsky, *Presidential Elections: Strategies of American Electoral Politics*, 6th ed. (New York: Charles Scribner's Sons, 1984), 241.

184. John D. Skrentny, *The Minority Rights Revolution* (Cambridge, MA: Harvard University Press, 2002).

185. Commission on Party Structure and Delegate Selection, *Mandate for Reform*, 14. The line traces back to Jane Addams, *Democracy and Social Ethics* (New York: Macmillan, 1905), 11–12.

186. Crotty, *Decision for the Democrats*, 222–53; Klinkner, *Losing Parties*, 105–32.

187. Crotty, *Decision for the Democrats*, 72–79.

188. After all the successor commissions had their say, the provisions on gender emerged even stronger, and those on race survived; the mandate for youth delegates, however, did not. At no time, to take one of the critics' points, did the party ever reserve delegate slots on the basis of class.

189. Christina Wolbrecht, *The Politics of Women's Rights: Parties, Positions, and Change* (Princeton, NJ: Princeton University Press, 2000); Marjorie J. Spruill, *Divided We Stand: The Battle over Women's Rights and Family Values That Polarized American Politics* (New York: Bloomsbury, 2017). On both the limits and the strengths of professional feminist advocacy, see Kristin A. Goss, *The Paradox of Gender Equality: How American Women's Groups Gained and Lost Their Public Voice* (Ann Arbor: University of Michigan Press, 2012).

190. On the NWPC and McGovern-Fraser, see Bruce Miroff, "Movement Activists and Partisan Insurgents," *Studies in American Political Development* 21 (2007): 92–109. On the transition from movement activism to party politics, see Jo Freeman, *The Politics of Women's Liberation: A Case Study of an Emerging Social Movement and Its Relation to the Policy Process* (New York: McKay, 1975); Jo Freeman, "Something DID Happen at the Democratic Convention," *Ms.*, October 1976, 74–76, 113–15.

191. M. Kent Jennings and Barbara G. Farah, "Social Roles and Political Resources: An Over-Time Study of Men and Women in Party Elites," *American Journal of Political Science* 25 (1981): 462–82; Susan M. Hartmann, *From Margin to Mainstream: American Women and Politics since 1960* (Philadelphia: Temple University Press, 1989), 84–96.

192. Alan Ehrenhalt, "The Democratic Left Faces a Dilemma," *Congressional Quarterly*, December 16, 1978, 3431–2.

193. "1980 Democratic Party Platform," August 11, 1980, American Presidency Project, https://www.presidency.ucsb.edu/node/273253.

194. Stephen Tuck, "'We Are Taking Up Where the Movement of the 1960s Left Off': The Proliferation and Power of African-American Protest during the 1970s," *Journal of Contemporary History* 43 (2008): 637–54. On connections with McGovern-Fraser, see Robert Mickey, *Paths out of Dixie: The Democratization of Authoritarian Enclaves in America's Deep South, 1944–1972* (Princeton, NJ: Princeton University Press, 2015), 277–80.

195. Hartmann, *From Margin to Mainstream*, 81. At Chisholm's behest, Hamer publicly seconded the nomination of Sissy Farenthold for vice president; see "Seconding Speech for the Nomination of Frances Farenthold, Delivered at the 1972 Democratic National Convention, Miami Beach, Florida, July 13, 1972," in Brooks and Houck, *Speeches of Fannie Lou Hamer*, 145–46.

196. William Crotty, "Anatomy of a Challenge: The Chicago Delegation to the Democratic National Convention," in *Cases in American Politics*, ed. Robert L. Peabody (New York: Praeger, 1984), 111–58.

197. Steven F. Lawson, *In Pursuit of Power: Southern Blacks and Electoral Politics, 1965–1982* (New York: Columbia University Press, 1982), 191–303; Richard M. Valelly, *The Two Reconstructions: The Struggle for Black Enfranchisement* (Chicago: University of Chicago Press, 2004), 173–223.

198. For this perspective writ broad, see Charles S. Maier, "'Malaise': The Crisis of Capitalism in the 1970s," in *The Shock of the Global: The 1970s in Perspective*, ed. Niall Ferguson, Charles S. Maier, Erez Manela, and Daniel J. Sargent (Cambridge, MA: Harvard University Press, 2010), 25–48. For our views on counterfactual possibilities, see Rosenfeld and Schlozman, "Did the Democrats Fuck It Up?"

199. See, among many, Jefferson Cowie, *Stayin' Alive: The 1970s and the Last Days of the Working Class* (New York: New Press, 2010); Stein, *Pivotal Decade*.

200. "America's Unfinished Agenda: The Statements of Leonard Woodcock, President, United Automobile, Aerospace, and Agricultural Implement Workers of America (UAW) to the Democratic Platform Committee 1976," in box 377, folder "National Convention/Campaign: Democratic National Conventions: Labor Union Platforms/Biographies," Thomas P. O'Neill Papers, John J. Burns Library, Boston College, Boston, MA.

201. Jefferson Cowie, "'A One-Sided Class War': Rethinking Doug Fraser's 1978 Resignation from the Labor-Management Group," *Labor History* 44 (2003): 312.

202. Quoted in David S. Broder, "Fraser's Strategy," *Washington Post*, October 15, 1978, C7.

203. Andrew Battista, *The Revival of Labor Liberalism* (Urbana: University of Illinois Press, 2008), 83–102; Rosenfeld, *Polarizers*, 242–63.

204. Jeffrey M. Berry, *The New Liberalism: The Rising Power of Citizen Groups* (Washington, DC: Brookings Institution Press, 1999); Theda Skocpol, *Diminished Democracy: From Membership to Management in American Civic Life* (Norman: University of Oklahoma Press, 2003), 127–220.

Chapter Six: The Long New Right and the World It Made

1. Robert Bauman, CPAC speech, February 17, 1975, box 3, folder 27, American Conservative Union (ACU) Papers, Harold B. Lee Library, Brigham Young University, Provo, UT.

2. Text of CPAC resolution, February 16, 1975, box 3, folder 26, ACU Papers.

3. R. W. Apple Jr., "Conservative Parley Taken Up with Talk of 3rd Party," *New York Times*, February 15, 1975, 13.

4. We borrow from historians the practice of revision via re-periodization. The tactic elongates or constricts either calendar periods or conceptual phenomena as a way of delineating key themes. See, for example, Eric Hobsbawm's introduction of the term "long nineteenth century" in *The Age of Empire: 1875–1914* (New York: Random House, 1987); Jacquelyn Dowd Hall, "The Long Civil Rights Movement and the Political Uses of the Past," *Journal of American History* 91 (2005): 1233–63; and, with themes resonant with our own, both Laura Kalman's political history of "the short 1970s," *Right Star Rising: A New Politics, 1974–1980* (New York: W. W. Norton, 2010); and Angie Maxwell and Todd Shields, *The Long Southern Strategy: How Chasing White Voters in the South Changed American Politics* (New York: Oxford University Press: 2019).

5. Reported by Garry Wills in *Nixon Agonistes: The Crisis of the Self-Made Man*, rev. ed. (Houghton Mifflin, 1970; repr. Boston: Mariner Books, 2002), 265.

6. Though we do we not root our analysis in his Marxisant idiom, we end up in a similar place as Walter Dean Burnham's analysis of Reaganism in 1982: "Right-wing thought and practice accepts the reality of major conflicts among classes over the social product, but provides its own characteristic justifications in terms of a general and national interest." Walter Dean Burnham, "The Eclipse of the Democratic Party," *Democracy*, July 1982, 17.

7. This is the key point of departure from the work of Matt Grossmann and David A. Hopkins, notwithstanding our agreement on the deep asymmetry of American party politics. To us, the Right's specific approach to a politics of conflict, rather than a commitment to an ideology, accounts for its distinct partisan manifestation. Grossmann and Hopkins, *Asymmetric Politics: Ideological Republicans and Group Interest Democrats* (New York: Oxford University Press, 2016).

8. On the pursuit of majority as the defining frame for intra-GOP politics during the New Deal order, and conservatives' advantage in those debates by the 1970s, see Robert Mason, *The Republican Party and American Politics from Hoover to Reagan* (New York: Cambridge University Press, 2012), esp. 216–81.

9. See, generally, Richard S. Katz and Robin Kolodny, "Party Organization as an Empty Vessel: Parties in American Politics," in *How Parties Organize: Change and Adaptation in Party Organizations in Western Democracies*, ed. Richard S. Katz and Peter Mair (London: Sage, 1994), 23–50.

10. Quoted in Jay Nordlinger, "#ExGOP," *National Review*, June 7, 2016, https://www.nationalreview.com/2016/06/exgop-shock-disaffiliation-leaving-gop/.

11. Morton Blackwell, "Building a Conservative Governing Majority," in *Steering the Elephant: How Washington Works*, ed. Robert Rector and Michael Sanera (New York: Universe, 1987), 29.

12. The line is from the National Conservative Political Action Committee's Terry Dolan. See Myra MacPherson, "The New Right Brigade," *Washington Post*, August 10, 1980, F1. "The New Right," as a phrase to describe the 1970s right-wing orbit, originated with Kevin Phillips, and no single definition, let alone a common program, applies to the full constellation of figures associated with it. Many initially dissociated themselves from the term. Soon, however, Richard Viguerie embraced the label, jauntily titling his 1981 book *The New Right: We're Ready to Lead* (Falls Church, VA: Viguerie, 1981).

13. Michael J. Korzi, "Our Chief Magistrate: A Reconsideration of William Howard Taft's 'Whig' Theory of Presidential Leadership," *Presidential Studies Quarterly* 33 (2003): 305–24; Robert A. Taft, "The Republican Party," *Fortune*, April 1949, 108–18.

14. "The Moral Majority: (An Answer to the Challenge?)," unprocessed accretion of September 1986, Paul M. Weyrich Papers, American Heritage Center, Laramie, WY. (The Weyrich Papers were fully cataloged between our visits, so the box numbers do not match.) The memo references a journalistic analysis of party decline and the limits of the formal GOP. Rhodes Cook, "Bill Brock Concentrates on the Grass Roots, but Conservatives Are Critical," *CQ Weekly Report*, April 28, 1979, 775–79.

15. Kristoffer Smemo, "A 'New Dealized' Grand Old Party: Labor and the Emergence of Liberal Republicanism in Minneapolis, 1937–1939," *Labor* 11 (2014): 35–59; Smemo, "The Little People's Century: Industrial Pluralism, Economic Development, and the Emergence of Liberal Republicanism in California, 1942–1946," *Journal of American History* 101 (2015): 1166–89. For more general reflections, see Gary Gerstle, *The Rise and Fall of the Neoliberal Order: America and the World in the Free Market Era* (New York: Oxford University Press, 2022), 38–47.

16. Benjamin C. Hart, ed., *The Third Generation: Young Conservatives Look to the Future* (Washington, DC: Regnery, 1987).

17. A classic statement of the backlash thesis is Thomas Byrne Edsall and Mary D. Edsall, *Chain Reaction: The Impact of Race, Rights, and Taxes on American Politics* (New York: Norton, 1991).

18. From movement conservatism's resident historian, see Lee Edwards, *The Conservative Revolution: The Movement That Remade America* (New York: Free Press, 1999). The classic account stressing ideas is George H. Nash, *The Conservative Intellectual Movement in America* (New York: Basic Books, 1976). For a reinterpretation, see Joshua Albury Tait, "Making Conservatism: Conservative Intellectuals and the American Political Tradition" (PhD diss., University of North Carolina at Chapel Hill, 2020). On the threads connecting conservative reaction across changing historical and ideological contexts, see Corey Robin, *The Reactionary Mind: Conservatism from Edmund Burke to Donald Trump*, 2nd ed. (New York: Oxford University Press, 2018).

19. See, among others, Jonathan Schoenwald, *A Time for Choosing: The Rise of Modern American Conservatism* (New York: Oxford University Press, 2001); Michele Nickerson, *Mothers of Conservatism: Women of the Postwar Right* (Princeton, NJ: Princeton University Press, 2012); Edward H. Miller, *Nut Country: Right-Wing Dallas and the Birth of the Southern Strategy* (Chicago: University of Chicago Press, 2015); Nicole Hemmer, *Messengers of the Right: Conservative Media and the Transformation of American Politics* (Philadelphia: University of Pennsylvania Press, 2015); David Austin Walsh, "The Right-Wing Popular Front: The Far Right and American Conservatism in the 1950s," *Journal of American History* 107 (2020): 411–32; John S. Huntington, *Far-Right Vanguard: The Radical Roots of Modern Conservatism* (Philadelphia: University of Pennsylvania Press, 2021); Edward H. Miller, *A Conspiratorial Life: Robert Welch, the John Birch Society, and the Revolution of American Conservatism* (Chicago: University of Chicago Press, 2021); Rick Perlstein, "The Corrections," *New York Times Magazine*, April 11, 2017, 36–41. Kim Phillips-Fein similarly calls for renewed attention to the extreme Right in "Conservatism: A State of the Field," *Journal of American History* 98 (2011): 723–43. By contrast, Matthew Dallek, *Birchers: How the John Birch Society Radicalized the American Right* (New York: Basic Books, 2022), preserves more of the distinction between the mainstream and fringe Right.

20. In this way, our view differs from Mark D. Brewer and Jeffrey M. Stonecash, *Dynamics of American Political Parties* (New York: Cambridge University Press, 2009).

21. Hugh Heclo, *On Thinking Institutionally* (New York: Oxford University Press, 2011), esp. 81–128.

22. For an understanding of the Right resonant with ours, see Jean Hardisty and Deepak Bhargava, "Wrong about the Right," *Nation*, November 7, 2005, 22–26. See also Jean Hardisty, *Mobilizing Resentment: Conservative Resurgence from the John Birch Society to the Promise Keepers* (Boston: Beacon Press, 1999). Hardisty spent decades at Political Research Associates (PRA) compiling information about the Right, and we take advantage of PRA's extensive files at Tufts University.

23. We thus attempt to synthesize the emphasis on the gonzo politics of resentment in Rick Perlstein, *The Invisible Bridge: The Fall of Nixon and the Rise of Reagan* (New York: Simon & Schuster, 2014), and the rebuke not to let flash and sizzle distract from political economy in Judith Stein, "The Rise of Reagan's America," *Dissent*, Fall 2014, 123–26.

24. On the prior decades, see George Wolfskill, *The Revolt of the Conservatives: A History of the American Liberty League, 1934–1940* (Boston: Houghton Mifflin, 1962); Alan Brinkley, *Voices of Protest: Huey Long, Father Coughlin, and the Great Depression* (New York: Vintage Books, 1982); Leo Ribuffo, *The Old Religious Right: The Protestant Far Right from the Great Depression to the Cold War* (Philadelphia: Temple University Press, 1983); Kathryn S. Olmsted, *Right Out of California: The 1930s and the Big Business Roots of Modern Conservatism* (New York: New Press, 2015); Lawrence B. Glickman, *Free Enterprise: An American History* (New Haven, CT: Yale University Press, 2019).

25. The initial diagnosis is found in Daniel Bell, ed., *The New American Right* (New York: Criterion Books, 1955); it was updated at a moment of peak public interest in the John Birch Society and other hard Right groups in Daniel Bell, ed., *The Radical Right* (Garden City, NJ: Doubleday, 1963). See also Arnold Forster and Benjamin Epstein, *Danger on the Right* (New York: Random House, 1964). Michael Paul Rogin offered an early rejoinder in *The Intellectuals and McCarthy: The Radical Specter* (Cambridge, MA: MIT Press, 1967). Later, Alan Brinkley and Lisa McGirr offered representative historiographical critiques of the status-anxiety thesis in respectively, "The Problem of American Conservatism," *American Historical Review* 99 (1994): 411–12, and *Suburban Warriors: The Origins of the New American Right* (Princeton, NJ: Princeton University Press, 2001), 6–11.

26. Joseph McCarthy, speech, Wheeling, WV, February 9, 1950, http://historymatters.gmu .edu/d/6456. See also Seymour Martin Lipset, "The Sources of the 'Radical Right,'" in Bell, *The New American Right*, 210–14.

27. Ellen Schrecker, *Many Are the Crimes: McCarthyism in America* (Boston: Little, Brown, 1998), 250–58; Thomas C. Reeves, *The Life and Times of Joe McCarthy: A Biography* (New York: Stein & Day, 1982), 278. See also, more broadly, David K. Johnson, *The Lavender Scare: The Cold War Prosecution of Gays and Lesbians in the Federal Government* (Chicago: University of Chicago Press, 2004).

28. See, for instance, Sam Francis's argument that "Joe McCarthy tore a mask from the face of liberalism." Samuel T. Francis, *Beautiful Losers: Essays on the Failure of American Conservatism* (Columbia: University of Missouri Press, 1993), 151. The John Birch Society offered more straightforward appreciation. See, for example, James J. Drummey, "McCarthy: The Truth, the Smear, and the Lesson," *American Opinion*, May 1964, 1–10.

29. L. Brent Bozell Jr. and William F. Buckley Jr., *McCarthy and His Enemies: The Record and Its Meaning* (New York: Regnery, 1954), 329, 335. See also Nash, *Conservative Intellectual Movement in America*, 84–130.

30. The alarm—and no small amount of paranoid overreach—that early 1960s conservative activism kindled among liberal politicians and analysts also instigated a long-running feat of sustained documentation that serves as an archival bedrock to this chapter. Group Research, Inc., was a tiny operation that, by subscribing to publications and monitoring mailings, amassed a vast storehouse of knowledge on the intricacies of the American Right, which it disseminated in monthly reports to subscribers. Its sole editor, Wesley McCune, worked as an aide in Truman's agriculture department and ran public relations for the National Farmers Union before starting Group Research in 1962. Assisted only by Gladys Segal, he ran it on a shoestring for thirty-four years until he finally retired at eighty. See Niel M. Johnson, "Oral History Interview with Wesley McCune," September 15–16, 1988, Harry S. Truman Library and Museum, https:// www.trumanlibrary.org/oralhist/mccunew.htm; Lloyd Grove, "The Liberal Watch at 25," *Washington Post*, April 16, 1987, C1.

31. D. J. Mulloy, *The World of the John Birch Society: Conspiracy, Conservatism, and the Cold War* (Nashville: Vanderbilt University Press, 2014), 2, 75, 213n9.

32. "Leaders' Manual," box 15, folder 33, John Birch Society (JBS) Papers, John Hay Library, Brown University, Providence, RI.

33. According to a JBS recruitment pamphlet, Welch worked on Fermat's Last Theorem, played chess masters to a draw, "read all of Goethe in German, and, even now, can quote many of La Fontaine's *Fables* in French." "Mr. Robert Welch," box 27, folder 20, JBS Papers.

34. Robert Welch, *The Politician* (Belmont, MA: privately printed, 1963); *Seventeen Eighty Nine: An Unfinished Manuscript Which Explores the Early History of the Communist Conspiracy* (Belmont, MA: American Opinion, 1968).

35. Phrase from Richard Hofstadter, "The Paranoid Style in American Politics," *Harper's*, November 1964, 77–86.

36. M. J. Heale, *McCarthy's Americans: Red Scare Politics in State and Nation, 1935–1965* (Athens: University of Georgia Press, 1998), 251–52, 260–62; Jeff Woods, *Black Struggle, Red Scare* (Baton Rouge: Louisiana State University Press, 2003), 85–111; Eugene Cook, *The Ugly Truth about the NAACP: An Address by Attorney General Eugene Cook of Georgia Before the 55th Annual Convention of the Peace Officers Association of Georgia* (Jacksonville, FL: Bostwick & Bostwick, ca. 1955).

37. Heather Hendershot, *What's Fair on the Air? Cold War Right-Wing Broadcasting and the Public Interest* (Chicago: University of Chicago Press, 2011); Hemmer, *Messengers of the Right*; Darren Dochuk, *From Bible Belt to Sunbelt: Plain-Folk Religion, Grassroots Politics, and the Rise of Evangelical Conservatism* (New York: W. W. Norton, 2011), esp. 141–95.

38. *Group Research Report*, October 19, 1962, 3. The complete series run can be found in Group Research, Inc. Records, box 425, Rare Book and Manuscript Library, Columbia University, New York, NY.

39. *Group Research Report*, August 26, 1963, 62; *Group Research Report*, February 26, 1966, 15; *Group Research Report*, December 19, 1966, 89. See also Marvin Liebman, *Coming Out Conservative: An Autobiography* (San Francisco: Chronicle Books, 1992); Takahito Moriyama, *Empire of Direct Mail: How Conservative Marketing Persuaded Voters and Transformed the Grassroots* (Lawrence: University Press of Kansas, 2022), 35–55.

40. Samuel Brenner, "Fellow Travelers: Overlap between 'Mainstream' and 'Extremist' Conservatives in the Early 1960s," in *The Right Side of the Sixties: Reexamining Conservatism's Decade of Transformation*, ed. Laura Jane Gifford and Daniel K. Williams (New York: Palgrave Macmillan, 2012), 83–100; Mulloy, *World of the John Birch Society*, 172–82.

41. Brenner, "Fellow Travelers," 92.

42. John B. Judis, *William F. Buckley, Jr.: Patron Saint of the Conservatives* (New York: Simon & Schuster, 1998), 194.

43. Judis, *William F. Buckley*, 247.

44. William F. Buckley Jr., "The Uproar," *National Review*, April 22, 1961, 241–43; William F. Buckley Jr., "The Question of Robert Welch," *National Review*, February 13, 1962, 83–88; "The John Birch Society and the Conservative Movement: The Background," *National Review*, October 19, 1965, 914–15; Frank S. Meyer, "The Birch Malady," *National Review*, October 19, 1965, 919–24; James Burnham, "The Third World War: Get US Out!," *National Review*, October 19, 1965, 925–26. See also Miller, *Conspiratorial Life*, esp. 254–59.

45. See John A. Andrew III, *The Other Side of the Sixties: Young Americans for Freedom and the Rise of Conservative Politics* (New Brunswick, NJ: Rutgers University Press, 1997); Wayne Thorburn, *A Generation Awakes: Young Americans for Freedom and the Creation of the Conservative Movement* (Ottawa, IL: Jameson Books, 2010).

46. *Group Research Report*, July/August 1980, 26.

47. Jerry Norton to college chairmen, November 20, 1968, box 25, folder 5, Young Americans for Freedom (YAF) Papers, Hoover Institution Library and Archives, Stanford, CA.

48. "Glory Be, There Goes Another! Songs of the Militant Extreme," Weyrich Papers, unprocessed accretion of April 1988. The song can also be found in box 27, folder 20, JBS Papers.

49. Patrick Buchanan, "What Happened to the Student Right?," *Washington World*, January 1966, p. 24, box 5, folder 10, YAF Papers. On conservative countermobilizations against the student Left in ensuing years, see Lauren Lassabe Shepherd, *Resistance from the Right: Conservatives and the Campus Wars in Modern America* (Chapel Hill: University of North Carolina Press, 2023).

50. Elizabeth Tandy Shermer, "Origins of the Conservative Ascendancy: Barry Goldwater's Early Senate Career and the De-legitimization of Organized Labor," *Journal of American History* 95 (2008): 678–709.

51. Schlafly long denied membership in JBS. Researcher Ernie Lazar, who has collected documents on the radical Right via Freedom of Information Act requests for three decades, acquired letters by Schlafly and Welch from 1959 and 1964, respectively, confirming that Schlafly had been a member until the success of *A Choice, Not an Echo* prompted her to resign, so as to avoid associating Goldwater with the JBS. Ronald Radosh, "Phyllis Schlafly, 'Mrs. America,' Was a Secret Member of the John Birch Society," *Daily Beast*, April 20, 2020, https://www.thedailybeast.com/phyllis-schlafly-mrs-america-was-a-secret-member-of-the-john-birch-society.

52. *Group Research Report*, June 12, 1964, 41–42; *Group Research Report*, August 15, 1964, 58–59. See also Rick Perlstein, *Before the Storm: Barry Goldwater and the Unmaking of the American Consensus* (New York: Hill and Wang, 2001), 427–28.

53. Robert Welch, "About Senator Barry Goldwater," July 10, 1963, box 24, folder 3, JBS Papers.

54. *Group Research Report*, October 15, 1964, 73.

55. Associated Press, "G.O.P. Welcomes Votes of Ku Klux Klan Members," *Bakersfield Californian*, August 4, 1964.

56. Tom Wicker, "Platform Voted," *New York Times*, July 15, 1964, 1.

57. Jack Bass and Walter De Vries, *The Transformation of Southern Politics: Social Change and Political Consequence since 1945* (New York: Basic Books, 1976), 26.

58. Andrew E. Busch, "The Goldwater Myth," *Claremont Review of Books*, Winter 2005/6, 10–12.

59. "Confidential Preliminary Report," undated, box 131, folder 8, William Rusher Papers, Library of Congress, Washington, DC.

60. "Goldwater Calls Bliss 'Mistaken,'" *New York Times*, June 20, 1965, 48.

61. David S. Broder, "Splinters Vying for G.O.P. Funds," *New York Times*, August 22, 1965, 62; Robert S. Boyd, "The Republican Family Keeps Growing," *Chicago Daily News*, September 7, 1965; *Group Research Report*, April 14, 1966, 25–26.

62. Russell Freeburg, "Bliss, Goldwater Talk of Splinter Groups," *Chicago Tribune*, September 1, 1965, A7.

63. Brian Conley, "The Politics of Party Renewal: The 'Service Party' and the Origins of the Post-Goldwater Republican Right," *Studies in American Political Development* 27 (2013): 51–67.

64. "Songs of the Rat Finks," *ADL Bulletin*, May 1966.

65. Phyllis Schlafly, *Safe—Not Sorry* (Alton, IL: Pere Marquette Press, 1967), 149. See also Donald Critchlow, *Phyllis Schlafly and Grassroots Conservatism: A Woman's Crusade* (Princeton, NJ: Princeton University Press, 2005), 137–62.

66. See, respectively, William Rusher, "The Plot to Steal the GOP," *National Review*, July 12, 1966, 668–71; Marie Smith, "Mrs. Schlafly Charges 'Purge,'" *Washington Post*, March 9, 1967, B1.

67. Nicol Rae, *The Decline and Fall of the Liberal Republicans from 1952 to the Present* (New York: Oxford University Press, 1989), 59–121; Geoffrey Kabaservice, *Rule and Ruin: The Downfall of Moderation and the Destruction of the Republican Party, from Eisenhower to the Tea Party* (New York: Oxford University Press, 2012).

68. Ripon Society, *From Disaster to Distinction: A Republican Rebirth* (New York: Pocket Books, 1966), 113.

69. The journalist was Leverett Chapin of the *Denver Post*, quoted in *Group Research Report*, July 15, 1964, 50.

70. Josh Pacewicz, *Partisans and Partners: The Politics of the Post-Keynesian Society* (Chicago: University of Chicago Press, 2016), 31–108.

71. From a vast scholarly literature, see Jonathan Rieder, *Canarsie: The Jews and Italians of Brooklyn against Liberalism* (Cambridge, MA: Harvard University Press, 1985); Matthew D. Lassiter, *The Silent Majority: Suburban Politics in the Sunbelt South* (Princeton, NJ: Princeton University Press, 2006), 225–75; Thomas J. Sugrue and John D. Skrentny, "The White Ethnic Strategy," in *Rightward Bound: Making America Conservative in the 1970s*, ed. Bruce J. Schulman and Julian E. Zelizer (Cambridge, MA: Harvard University Press, 2008), 171–92; Michael Flamm, *Law and Order: Street Crime, Civil Unrest, and the Crisis of Liberalism in the 1960s* (New York: Columbia University Press, 2005); Vesla Weaver, "Frontlash: Race and the Development of Punitive Crime Policy," *Studies in American Political Development* 21 (2007) 230–65; Aaron Thomas Bekemeyer, "The Labor of Law and Order: How Police Unions Transformed Policing and Politics in the United States, 1939–1985" (PhD diss., Harvard University, 2021), 142–78.

72. Rick Perlstein, *Nixonland: The Rise of a President and the Fracturing of America* (New York: Scribner, 2008), 126.

73. Richard M. Scammon and Ben J. Wattenberg, *The Real Majority: An Extraordinary Examination of the American Electorate* (New York: Coward-McCann, 1970), 45.

74. Dan T. Carter, *The Politics of Rage: George Wallace, the Origins of the New Conservatism, and the Transformation of American Politics* (New York: Simon & Schuster, 1995), 84–86.

75. The infamous line appeared first in Marshall Frady, *Wallace* (New York: Dutton, 1968), 127. Its veracity has long been a subject of controversy, though Carter offers additional supporting interviews in *Politics of Rage*, 96. Other versions report Wallace saying "outsegged." See, for example, Harold H. Martin, "The Race of a Thousand Clowns," *Saturday Evening Post*, May 7, 1966, 26. To the end of his career, Wallace vehemently denied using either term. See special section, "George C. Wallace," *Montgomery Advertiser*, January 11, 1987, 16.

76. Michael Kazin, *The Populist Persuasion: An American History* (New York: Basic Books, 1995), 231.

77. Dan Rather with Mickey Herskowitz, *The Camera Never Blinks: Adventures of a TV Journalist* (New York: William Morrow, 1977), 100.

78. Carter, *Politics of Rage*, 204.

79. Carter, *Politics of Rage*, 207. See also Richard C. Haney, "Wallace in Wisconsin: The Presidential Primary of 1964," *Wisconsin Magazine of History* 61 (1978): 259–78.

80. Scammon and Wattenberg, *Real Majority*, 197.

81. Kazin, *Populist Persuasion*, 234–35.

82. Transcript to *Firing Line*, January 4, 1968, Firing Line Broadcast Records, Hoover Institution Library and Archives, https://digitalcollections.hoover.org/images/Collections/80040/80040_088_trans.pdf.

83. Scammon and Wattenberg, *Real Majority*, 194–95.

84. Carter, *Politics of Rage*, 335–37; *Group Research Report*, July 15, 1968, 49.

85. *Group Research Report*, September 17, 1968, 70; see also Harry S. Dent, *The Prodigal South Returns to Power* (New York: John Wiley and Sons, 1978), 160.

86. Kevin P. Phillips, *The Emerging Republican Majority* (New York: Anchor Books, 1970), 463.

87. Carter, *Politics of Rage*, 396; Patrick Buchanan, "Wallace, One of a Kind in a Full House," *New York Daily News*, February 26, 1976.

88. Viguerie, *New Right*, 33.

89. Nixon's politics of resentment is the master theme of Perlstein, *Nixonland*, esp. 20–43.

90. Sarah Katherine Mergel, *Conservative Intellectuals and Richard Nixon: Rethinking the Rise of the Right* (New York: Palgrave Macmillan, 2010).

91. Jill Quadagno, *The Color of Welfare: How Racism Undermined the War on Poverty* (New York: Oxford University Press, 1994), 117–54; Kimberly J. Morgan, "A Child of the Sixties: The Great Society, the New Right, and the Politics of Federal Child Care," *Journal of Policy History* 13 (2001): 215–50.

92. "Big Brother Wants Your Children," *Human Events*, September 18, 1971, 4–5; "Nixon Must Veto Child Control Law," *Human Events*, October 9, 1971, 1; James J. Kilpatrick, "'Child Development Act' Called Scheme to Sovietize U.S. Youth," *Spokane Daily Chronicle*, October 25, 1971; *Group Research Report*, December 21, 1971, 57.

93. Nick Kotz, "Nixon's Child Care Expert Resigns," *Washington Post*, July 15, 1972, A2.

94. *Group Research Report*, July/August 1977, 25; *Group Research Report*, February 28, 1979, 6.

95. On the RSC, see Edwin J. Feulner Jr., *Conservatives Stalk the House: The Republican Study Committee, 1970–1982* (Ottawa, IL: Green Hill, 1983). On Heritage, see Lee Edwards, *The Power of Ideas: The Heritage Foundation at 25 Years* (Ottawa, IL: Jameson Books, 1997), 6–11; Jason Stahl, *Right Moves: The Conservative Think Tank in American Political Culture since 1945* (Chapel Hill: University of North Carolina Press, 2016), 70–80.

96. Paul M. Weyrich, "The New Right: PACs and Coalition Politics," in *Parties, Interest Groups, and Campaign Finance Law*, ed. Michael J. Malbin (Washington, DC: American Enterprise Institute, 1980), 68–81; Larry Sabato, *PAC Power: Inside the World of Political Action Committees* (New York: W. W. Norton, 1984).

97. *Group Research Report*, April 28, 1975, 15. On the legal structures, see Irwin B. Arieff, Nadine Cohodas, and Richard Whittle, "Sen. Helms Builds a Machine of Interlinked Organizations to Shape Both Politics, Policy," *CQ Weekly Report*, March 6, 1982, 499–505.

98. MacPherson, "The New Right Brigade." For a good account of Dolan's work, see Marc C. Johnson, *Tuesday Night Massacre: Four Senate Elections and the Radicalization of the Republican Party* (Norman: University of Oklahoma Press, 2021).

99. Elizabeth Drew, "A Reporter at Large: Jesse Helms," *New Yorker*, July 20, 1981, 78–95; William A. Link, *Righteous Warrior: Jesse Helms and the Rise of Modern Conservatism* (New York: St. Martin's Press, 2008); William A. Link, "Time Is an Elusive Companion: Jesse Helms, Barry Goldwater, and the Dynamic of Modern Conservatism," in *Barry Goldwater and the Remaking of the American Political Landscape*, ed. Elizabeth Tandy Shermer (Tucson: University of Arizona Press, 2013), 238–58.

100. See Bryan Hardin Thrift, *Conservative Bias: How Jesse Helms Pioneered the Rise of Right-Wing Media and Realigned the Republican Party* (Gainesville: University Press of Florida, 2014).

101. His research files for *Viewpoint* editorials on subjects like civil rights, Martin Luther King Jr., and busing offer a cross-section of such positions and their evolution from the 1960s to the 1970s. See, for example, series RG-1, box 5, folders 97, 101, 113, Jesse Helms Papers, Jesse Helms Center, Wingate, NC.

102. Jesse Helms, "Communists DO Try to Indoctrinate at Colleges," *Human Events*, May 4, 1963; Jesse Helms, *Viewpoint*, editorial, WRAL-TV, May 11, 1965, series RG-1, box 8, folder 142, Helms Papers.

103. Link, *Righteous Warrior*, 89–98.

104. Jesse Helms, "American Parties: A Time for Choosing," *New Guard*, December 1974, 6–9. Speech originally delivered May 15, 1974.

105. Jesse Helms to William Rusher, May 28, 1974, box 39, folder 1, Rusher Papers; minutes of the ACU board meeting, September 22, 1974, box 21, folder 10, and December 15, 1974, box 21, folder 11, both in ACU Papers.

106. William Rusher, *The Making of the New Majority Party* (New York: Sheed and Ward, 1975).

107. See, for example, ACU board minutes, September 27, 1975, box 21, folder 14, ACU Papers.

108. Sam Rosenfeld, *The Polarizers: Postwar Architects of Our Partisan Era* (Chicago: University of Chicago Press, 2018), 197–198.

109. MacPherson, "The New Right Brigade." On Brock's approach, modeled on that of Ray Bliss, see Cook, "Bill Brock Concentrates on the Grass Roots."

110. Frederick K. Berns, "State Man Leads with His Right," *Kenosha News*, October 28, 1980, 4.

111. In the late 1980s, ALEC shifted strategy away from the New Right and toward closer ties with corporate America. See Alexander Hertel-Fernandez, *State Capture: How Conservative Activists, Big Businesses, and Wealthy Donors Reshaped the American States—and the Nation* (New York: Oxford University Press, 2019); and, from ALEC's executive director, Samuel Brunelli, "State Legislatures: The Next Conservative Battleground" (Washington, DC: Heritage Foundation, 1990).

112. Joanne Omang, "'New Right' Figure Sees McCarthyism in NEA's Conference," *Washington Post*, February 24, 1979, A2.

113. *Group Research Report*, January 31, 1978, 1. See also Adam Clymer, *Drawing the Line at the Big Ditch: The Panama Canal Treaties and the Rise of the Right* (Lawrence: University Press of Kansas, 2008).

114. The best history of the Christian Right is William Martin, *With God on Our Side: The Rise of the Religious Right in America*, rev. ed. (New York: Broadway Books, 2005). See also Daniel K. Williams, *God's Own Party: The Making of the Christian Right* (New York: Oxford University Press, 2010); Daniel Schlozman, *When Movements Anchor Parties: Electoral Alignments in American History* (Princeton, NJ: Princeton University Press, 2015), 77–107, 198–222.

115. Paul M. Weyrich, "Coalition-Building and the Pro-Life Movement," in *To Rescue the Future: The Pro-Life Movement in the 1980s*, ed. Dave Andrusko (Toronto: Life Cycle Books, 1983).

116. For a comparative view of the connection between cultural and social resentments and Protestant politics, see Steve Bruce, *Conservative Protestant Politics* (Oxford: Oxford University Press, 1998), 21–23.

117. *Group Research Report*, October 30, 1981, 34.

118. Kristin Luker, *Abortion and the Politics of Motherhood* (Berkeley: University of California Press, 1984); Rebecca E. Klatch, *Women of the New Right* (Philadelphia: Temple University Press, 1987); Robert O. Self, *All in the Family: The Realignment of American Democracy since the 1960s* (New York: Hill and Wang, 2012); Mary Ziegler, *Dollars for Life: The Anti-Abortion Movement and the Fall of the Republican Establishment* (New Haven, CT: Yale University Press, 2022).

119. Quoted in Marjorie J. Spruill, *Divided We Stand: The Battle over Women's Rights and Family Values That Polarized American Politics* (New York: Bloomsbury, 2017), 101.

120. Critchlow, *Phyllis Schlafly and Grassroots Conservatism*, 212–69; Jane J. Mansbridge, *Why We Lost the ERA* (Chicago: University of Chicago Press, 1986), esp. 90–117.

121. See Beverly LaHaye, *The New Spirit-Controlled Woman* (Eugene, OR: Harvest House, 2005); Ronnee Schreiber, *Righting Feminism: Conservative Women and American Politics* (New York: Oxford University Press, 2008). On the differences between Schlafly and LaHaye, see Hardisty, *Mobilizing Resentment*, 73–84.

122. Connaught Coyne Marshner, *The New Traditional Woman* (Washington, DC: Free Congress Research & Education Foundation, 1982).

123. Morton C. Blackwell, "Staffing the Conservative Movement," *Conservative Digest*, April 1979, 4.

124. See Kim Phillips-Fein, *Invisible Hands: The Businessmen's Crusade Against the New Deal* (New York: Norton, 2010).

125. Roscoe Born, "Right-to-Work Drive, Left for Dead in '58, Aims for a Comeback," *Wall Street Journal*, April 19, 1961, 1.

126. *Group Research Report*, July/August, 1981, 27.

127. Joseph A. McCartin, "'A Wagner Act for Public Employees': Labor's Deferred Dream and the Rise of Conservatism, 1970–1976," *Journal of American History* 95 (2005): 123–48; Sophia Z. Lee, "Whose Rights? Litigating the Right to Work, 1940–1980," in *The Right and Labor in America: Politics, Ideology, and Imagination*, ed. Nelson Lichtenstein and Elizabeth Tandy Shermer (Philadelphia: University of Pennsylvania Press, 2012), 161–80.

128. Jon Shelton, "'Compulsory Unionism' and Its Critics: The National Right to Work Committee, Teachers Unions, and the Defeat of Labor Law Reform in 1978," *Journal of Policy History* 29 (2017): 388.

129. Sylvester Petro, "Sovereignty and Compulsory Public-Sector Bargaining," *Wake Forest Law Review* 25 (1974): 25–165; Jesse Helms, foreword to *Let Our Cities Burn*, by Ralph de Toledano (New Rochelle, NY: Arlington House, 1975).

130. Jerry Flint, "Reed Larson vs. the Union Shop," *New York Times*, December 4, 1977, 145; Juan Cameron, "Small Business Trips Big Labor," *Fortune*, July 31, 1978, 80–82; Thomas Ferguson and Joel Rogers, "Labor Law Reform and Its Enemies," *Nation*, January 6, 1979, 1, 17–20.

131. Irwin Ross, "Jack Kemp Wants to Cut Your Taxes—a Lot," *Fortune*, April 10, 1978, 36–40; Adam Clymer, "Quarterbacking for the GOP," *Atlantic Monthly*, December 1978, 14–21; *Group Research Report*, February 28, 1978, 6.

132. Robert M. Collins, *More: The Politics of Economic Growth in Postwar America* (New York: Oxford University Press, 2000), esp. 174–79. See also Sidney Blumenthal, *The Rise of the Counter-Establishment: From Conservative Ideology to Political Power* (New York: Times Books, 1986), 166–209; Godfrey Hodgson, *The World Turned Right Side Up: A History of the Conservative Ascendancy in America* (New York: Houghton Mifflin, 1996), 186–216.

133. Martin Anderson, *Revolution: The Reagan Legacy* (Harcourt Brace Jovanovich, 1988; repr. Stanford, CA: Hoover Institution Press 1990), 161–63.

134. David O. Sears and Jack Citrin, *Tax Revolt: Something for Nothing in California* (Cambridge, MA: Harvard University Press, 1982); Clarence Y. H. Lo, *Small Property versus Big Government: Social Origins of the Property Tax Revolt* (Berkeley: University of California Press, 1990); Isaac William Martin, *The Permanent Tax Revolt: How the Property Tax Transformed American Politics* (Stanford, CA: Stanford University Press, 2008), 98–125. Though Kemp cheered Prop 13's passage, he made clear his preference for slashing income taxes ahead of property taxes. Jack Kemp, "Prop 13 Fever," *New York Daily News*, July 23, 1978, 40.

135. *Group Research Report*, May 30, 1978, 18.

136. Hodgson, *World Turned Right Side Up*, 209; box 22, folder 31, and box 27, folder 60, JBS Papers.

137. *Group Research Report*, October 31, 1978, 34.

138. "Howard Jarvis and Gary Allen Discuss Your Taxes," *Review of the News*, April 11, 1979, 41.

139. Bruce Bartlett, "The Revolution of 1978," *National Review*, October 27, 1978, 1333–36; Robert Kuttner, *Revolt of the Haves: Tax Rebellions and Hard Times* (New York: Simon & Schuster, 1980). For a synoptic view, see Alan Brinkley, "Reagan's Revenge: As Invented by Howard Jarvis," *New York Times Magazine*, June 19, 1994, 36–37.

140. On the seesaw dynamics of social conservatives' engagement with the Reagan administration, see Self, *All in the Family*, 367–98.

141. *Group Research Report*, February 28, 1978, 6.

142. *Group Research Report*, September 29, 1980, 29.

143. Hugh Heclo, "Ronald Reagan and the American Public Philosophy," in *The Reagan Presidency: Pragmatic Conservatism and Its Legacies*, ed. W. Elliot Brownlee and Hugh Davis Graham (Lawrence: University Press of Kansas, 2003), 17–39.

144. Daniel J. Galvin, *Presidential Party Building: Dwight D. Eisenhower to George W. Bush* (Princeton, NJ: Princeton University Press, 2010), 120–42. From the RNC, see, for example, "Achieving Majority Status," *First Monday*, August 1981, 12–14; S. J. Masty, "Republican Party Strives for Majority Status—'84 and Beyond," *First Monday*, November 1983, 17–18. On the South, see Lee Atwater to Elizabeth Dole, "Dole Memo," May 31, 1981, OA2903, Lee Atwater Papers, Ronald Reagan Presidential Library (RRPL), Simi Valley, CA.

145. Arguably, the most influential outside groups were those behind the long project to remake the courts. See Steven M. Teles, *The Rise of the Conservative Legal Movement: The Battle for Control of the Law* (Princeton, NJ: Princeton University Press, 2008); Amanda Hollis-Brusky, *Ideas with Consequences: The Federalist Society and the Conservative Counterrevolution* (New York: Oxford University Press, 2015). For an account sympathetic to ours that pushes the story back, see Calvin TerBeek, "'Clocks Must Always Be Turned Back': *Brown v. Board of Education* and the Racial Origins of Constitutional Originalism," *American Political Science Review* 115 (2021): 821–34.

146. "Attendees at the Dick Richards Breakfast" and memo, Morton Blackwell to Elizabeth Dole, May 20, 1981, NCPAC folder 1, box 14, papers of Morton Blackwell, RRPL; Adam Clymer, "New G.O.P. Chairman Criticizes Party's Right Wing," *New York Times*, January 18, 1981, 18; "GOP National Chairman Angers Conservatives," *Human Events*, May 9, 1981; Bill Peterson, "GOP 'Peace Mission' Becomes Stormy," *Washington Post*, May 20, 1981, A2; Edward Walsh, "GOP-NCPAC Marriage of Convenience Fails," *Washington Post*, June 27, 1981, A4; Frank J. Fahrenkopf Jr., "Reagan as Political Leader," in *Leadership in the Reagan Presidency: Seven Intimate Perspectives*, ed. Kenneth W. Thompson (Lanham, MD: University Press of America, 1992).

147. "GOP National Chairman Angers Conservatives," 6.

148. Robert Trimberg, "The Political Money Machines: Fat, Fancy, Free of Curbs," *Baltimore Sun*, July 11, 1982, A10.

149. Lou Cannon, "Mike Curb Will Replace Richard DeVos at RNC," *Washington Post*, August 14, 1982, A4; Bill Peterson, "Reagan Aide Warns GOP on Economy," *Washington Post*, June 9, 1982, A3; Adam Clymer, "G.O.P. Money Doesn't Buy Harmony," *New York Times*, October 9, 1981, A24.

150. Thomas B. Edsall, "Money, Technology Revive GOP Force," *Washington Post*, June 17, 1984, A1.

151. David Brooks, "Please, Mr. Postman: The Travails of Richard Viguerie," *National Review*, June 20, 1986, 28–32; Lloyd Grove, "The Graying of Richard Viguerie," *Washington Post* June 29, 1989, D1.

152. Thomas B. Edsall, "Partners in Political PR Firm Typify Republican New Breed," *Washington Post*, April 7, 1985.

153. Roger Stone to Ronald Reagan, September 8, 1980, box 249, Ronald Reagan 1980 Presidential Campaign Papers, RRPL.

154. John Judis, "Will Real Conservatives Step Forward?," *In These Times*, March 10, 1982, 3.

155. Roger Stone, *Stone's Rules: How to Win at Politics, Business, and Style* (New York: Skyhorse, 2018).

156. Jacob Weisberg, "State-of-the-Art Sleazeball," *New Republic*, December 5, 1985, 21.

157. Judis, "Will Real Conservatives Step Forward?"

158. Stephanie Mansfield, "The Rise and Gall of Roger Stone," *Washington Post*, June 16, 1986, C1.

159. See, on these themes, Timothy J. Lombardo, *Blue-Collar Conservatism: Frank Rizzo's Philadelphia and Populist Politics* (Philadelphia: University of Pennsylvania Press, 2018). For an

early New Right presentation, see Daniel J. Rea Jr., "Democratic Support for a New Party," in *Which Way for Conservatives?*, ed. Wayne J. Thorburn (Baltimore: Publications Press, 1975), 95–101.

160. "Council for National Policy; August 12 & 13 1988," series 3, box 19, folder "Council for National Policy," Political Research Associates (PRA) Papers, Tufts University, Medford, MA. King also spoke, during his term as governor, to the 1981 YAF convention in Boston. "YAF," OA2906, Lee Atwater Papers, RRPL.

161. Nick King, "King—Simple, Direct Campaign Issues," *Boston Evening Globe*, September 20, 1978, 13.

162. Gary Rivlin, *Fire on the Prairie: Harold Washington, Chicago Politics, and the Roots of the Obama Presidency*, rev. ed. (Philadelphia: Temple University Press, 2012), 246; Mark Feeney and Brian MacQuarrie, "Edward King, Hard-Charging Governor, Dies," *Boston Globe*, September 19, 2006, A1.

163. *Review of the News*, January 2, 1980, 1.

164. Minutes of JBS Council meeting, June 15, 1978, box 9, folder 19, JBS Papers.

165. John Rees, "Foreign Policy Analyst Richard V. Allen," *Review of the News*, May 21, 1980, 39–52; John Rees, "The 1980 Presidential Campaign as Seen by Richard Wirthlin," *Review of the News*, September 10, 1980, 39–52; John Rees, "Ronald Reagan Chooses Conservative Democrat, Georgetown Professor Dr. Jeane J. Kirkpatrick," *Review of the News*, January 14, 1981, 31–42; John Rees, "Lyn Nofziger," *Review of the News*, March 10, 1982, 39–48; John Rees, "Conservative Advocate Morton C. Blackwell," *Review of the News*, April 28, 1982, 39–54; John Rees, "The Amazing Anne M. Gorsuch," *Review of the News*, June 16, 1982, 39–50.

166. John Rees, "Congressman Lawrence Patton McDonald," *Review of the News*, November 11, 1981, 47–58; John Rees, "U.S. Senator Jesse Helms," *Review of the News*, November 30, 1983, 39–50; John Rees, "Conservative Congressman George Hansen," *Review of the News*, January 7, 1981, 39–52; John Rees, "U.S. Senator Alan K. Simpson," *Review of the News*, April 30, 1980, 39–48; John Rees, "Conservative Congressman Dick Cheney," *Review of the News*, December 14, 1983, 31–38; John Rees, "U.S. Senator Donald Nickles," *Review of the News*, February 4, 1981, 39–48; John Rees, "U.S. Senator Charles Grassley," *Review of the News*, March 18, 1981, 39–48; John Rees, "U.S. Senator William L. Armstrong," *Review of the News*, December 15, 1982, 31–40; John Rees, "Phil Gramm," *Review of the News*, March 25, 1981, 39–52.

167. John Rees, "Heritage Foundation's Stuart Butler," *Review of the News*, March 4, 1981, 39–50; John Rees, "Supply-Side Economist Arthur Laffer," *Review of the News*, June 11, 1980, 39–54; John Rees, "Supply-Side Economist Jude Wanniski," *Review of the News*, May 12, 1982, 39–50; "Howard Jarvis and Gary Allen Discuss Your Taxes," *Review of the News*, April 11, 1979, 31–46; John Rees, "Economist Hans F. Sennholz," *Review of the News*, January 9, 1980, 39–50; John Rees, "Economist for the Free Market Murray N. Rothbard," *Review of the News*, February 2, 1983, 39–50.

168. John Rees, "Moral Majority Conservative Jerry Falwell," *Review of the News*, May 6, 1981, 39–52; John Rees, "Conservative Evangelist James Robison," *Review of the News*, July 1, 1981, 39–48; John Rees, "Author and Columnist Stanton Evans," *Review of the News*, April 23, 1980, 39–52; John Rees, "Leader of the National Conservative Political Action Committee Is Terry Dolan," *Review of the News*, September 22, 1982, 31–38.

169. Rees, "Moral Majority Conservative Jerry Falwell," 45.

170. Rees, "U.S. Senator Jesse Helms." For the JBS view, see Alan Stang, *It's Very Simple: The True Story of Civil Rights* (Belmont, MA: Western Islands, 1965), 118–28, 157–59.

171. John Rees, "Conservative Evangelist James Robison," 47.

172. John Rees, "Conservative Champion Roy Cohn," *Review of the News*, September 16, 1981, 39–54.

173. John Rees, "Pro-Family Leader Connie Marshner," *Review of the News*, January 21, 1981, 45. Minutes of JBS Council meetings, June 10, 1978, and June 9, 1980, box 9, folder 19, JBS Papers; Paul M. Weyrich, "The White House, the 1982 Elections, and the Right," *American Opinion*, April 1982, 7–10, 67–76; Paul M. Weyrich, "Congress vs. the Courts," *American Opinion*, May 1982, 43–54. Weyrich, who spoke at JBS meetings in 1978 and 1980, contributed columns to the *Review of the News* and the flagship JBS periodical, *American Opinion*.

174. John Rees, "Collegiate Conservative Jack A. Abramoff," *Review of the News*, September 8, 1982, 50.

175. John Rees, "North Carolina Conservative Tom Ellis," *Review of the News*, January 5, 1983, 33.

176. Rees, "Conservative Congressman Dick Cheney," 38.

177. See the membership lists and conference programs in "Council for National Policy," box 6, Blackwell Papers; "Council for National Policy," series 3, box 19, PRA Papers; and "Council for National Policy," unprocessed accretion of April 1988, Weyrich Papers. All references from PRA papers unless otherwise noted.

178. "The media," Morton Blackwell, then the group's executive director, warned members in 1993, "should not know when or where we meet or who takes part in our programs." Chip Berlet, "Festive CNP Conclave in St Louis," *CovertAction*, Spring 1994, 50. A barebones website now includes audio recordings from some speakers; see cfnp.org.

179. See the membership votes in CNP Executive Committee minutes, April 5, 1989, in PRA Papers.

180. Tim LaHaye, *The Unhappy Gays: What Everyone Should Know about Homosexuality* (Wheaton, IL: Tyndale House, 1978); *Group Research Report*, June 26, 1981, 21; Gary Cartwright, "How Cullen Davis Beat the Rap," *Texas Monthly*, May 1979, https://www.texasmonthly.com/articles/how-cullen-davis-beat-the-rap-2/. On Hunt's Birch ties, see Miller, *Conspiratorial Life*, 333–40.

181. Member list in Weyrich Papers.

182. See Sidney Blumenthal, "The Enemy Within," *Guardian*, March 9, 2005, https://www.theguardian.com/world/2005/mar/10/usa.comment.

183. See Weyrich Papers.

184. Program, October 1993 meeting, St. Louis, in PRA Papers.

185. Louis Trager, "Evidence Points toward North Tie to Rev. Moon," *San Francisco Examiner*, July 20, 1987, A-4; Jack Colhoun, "A Cut-Off by Congress Won't Stop Contra Funding," *Guardian*, March 13, 1985, series 3, box 70, folder "Unification Church," PRA Papers; Robert Reinhold, "General Aiding Contras Hints at a Broader Role," *New York Times*, October 14, 1986, A6; "Singlaub. John" and "Singlaub Freedom Foundation," series 3 folders, box 67, PRA Papers; *Frontline*, "The Resurrection of Reverend Moon" transcript, 9 series 3, box 70, folder "Unification Church," PRA Papers.

186. *Group Research Report*, December 1986, 37.

187. *Group Research Report*, December 1986, 38; Kyle Burke, *Revolutionaries for the Right: Anticommunist Internationalism and Paramilitary Warfare in the Cold War* (Chapel Hill: University of North Carolina Press, 2018), 118–54.

188. Sidney Blumenthal, "North the Charge of the Right Brigade," *Washington Post*, August 5, 1987, C1.

189. *Group Research Report*, March 23, 1979, 11.

190. *Group Research Report*, July/August 1985, 25; Greg Johnson and James Bornemeier, "The Downfall of Conservative 'Mover and Shaker,'" *Los Angeles Times*, July 20, 1992; "Investor Fraud Conviction," *New York Times*, September 22, 1993, D13.

191. Sean M. Theriault, *The Gingrich Senators: The Roots of Partisan Warfare in Congress* (New York: Oxford University Press, 2013); Julian E. Zelizer, *Burning Down the House: Newt Gingrich,*

the Fall of a Speaker, and the Rise of the New Republican Party (New York: Penguin, 2020); Matthew N. Green and Jeffrey Crouch, *Newt Gingrich: The Rise and Fall of a Party Entrepreneur* (Lawrence: University Press of Kansas, 2022).

192. John R. Pitney Jr., "Understanding Newt Gingrich" (paper presented at the 1996 meetings of the American Political Science Association). See also the testy exchanges with paleoconservative John Lofton in "A Philosophical Exchange with Newt Gingrich," *Human Events*, December 30, 1989, 1064–65.

193. Steven K. Beckner, "Rep. Newt Gingrich: A New Conservative Leader for the '80s," *Conservative Digest*, May 1982, 9.

194. Connie Bruck, "The Politics of Perception," *New Yorker*, October 9, 1995, 55.

195. Bruck, "The Politics of Perception," 70. See also (in the official Bircher journal) Weyrich, "The White House, the 1982 Elections, and the Right," 75–76; Weyrich, interview for a 1996 *Frontline* documentary, https://www.pbs.org/wgbh/pages/frontline/newt/newtintwshtml/weyrich.html.

196. *Group Research Report*, January 29, 1979, 1.

197. "1978 Speech by Gingrich," June 24, 1978, https://www.pbs.org/wgbh/pages/frontline/newt/newt78speech.html.

198. Beckner, "Rep. Newt Gingrich," 11. See also Paul M. Weyrich, "Conservatives Must Prepare to Govern," *Conservative Digest*, April 1980, 4.

199. Newt Gingrich, "The GOP Revolution Holds Powerful Lessons for Changing Washington," in *The Republican Revolution Ten Years Later: Smaller Government or Business as Usual?*, ed. Chris Edwards and John Samples (Washington, DC: Cato Institute, 2005), 2.

200. Hart, *Third Generation*, 21–22.

201. Hart, *Third Generation*, 12.

202. Hart, *Third Generation*, 75.

203. *Group Research Report*, April 20, 1979, 13; Dudley Clendinen, "Conservative Paper Stirs Dartmouth," *New York Times*, October 13, 1981, A18.

204. *Group Research Report*, Spring 1991, 3.

205. Adam Meyerson, "Miracle Whip," *Policy Review*, Winter 1991, 16.

206. *Group Research Report*, Spring 1992, 5.

207. D. C. Denison, "Patrick Buchanan: The Interview," *Boston Globe Magazine*, June 12, 1988, series 3, box 9, folder "Buchanan, Patrick," PRA Papers.

208. The one full-length biography is Timothy Stanley, *The Crusader: The Life and Tumultuous Times of Pat Buchanan* (New York: St. Martin's Press, 2012). See also Martin Durham, *The Christian Right, the Far Right, and the Boundaries of American Conservatism* (Manchester: Manchester University Press, 2000), 147–67; Nicole Hemmer, *Partisans: The Conservative Revolutionaries Who Remade American Politics in the 1990s* (New York: Basic Books, 2022), 209–29.

209. Ben Smith III, "Buchanan Invokes Confederate Forebears in Bid for South's Votes," *Atlanta Journal-Constitution*, February 26, 1992, A5.

210. John Aloysius Farrell, "Files Reveal Buchanan Views in '70s," *Boston Globe*, January 4, 1992, A1, series 3, box 9, folder "Buchanan, Patrick," PRA Papers. Buchanan referred to the 1968 sale of fifty F-4 Phantom aircraft to Israel; see David Rodman, "Phantom Fracas: The 1968 American Sale of F-4 Aircraft to Israel," *Middle Eastern Studies* 40 (2004): 131–44.

211. Patrick J. Buchanan, "Ambush Lurking in New Rights Act?" *Washington Times*, March 9, 1988, box 79, folder 5, People for the American Way Papers, Bancroft Library, University of California, Berkeley.

212. Patrick Buchanan, "Challenge to Right: Win Back Duke Backers," undated column, box 67, folder 3, Louisiana Coalition against Racism and Nazism Papers, Amistad Research Center, New Orleans, LA.

213. Quoted in *Group Research Report*, May/June 1991, 10.

214. See Joshua Muravchik, "Patrick J. Buchanan and the Jews," *Commentary*, January 1991, 29–36; David Frum, "The Conservative Bully Boy," *American Spectator*, July 1991, 12–14.

215. David Frum, "Patrick J. Buchanan, Left-Winger," *Weekly Standard*, November 27, 1995.

216. Quotes from respectively James Bennet, "Buchanan Attacking on All Fronts," *New York Times*, February 29, 1996, B8; James Bennet, "Buchanan, in Unfamiliar Role, Is under Fire as a Left-Winger," *New York Times*, December 31, 1995, 1.

217. Tom Raum, "Buchanan: Leading a Revolution of 'Peasants with Pitchforks,'" Associated Press, February 18, 1996, https://apnews.com/article/720fec7aefc16463dfdef6b32cdd5926. On the campaign, see, Thomas B. Edsall and Richard Morin, "Angry, White, Working Class Voters Come to the Fore," *Washington Post*, February 21, 1996, A14; Thomas B. Edsall, "After Luring Disaffected, GOP Elite Is Uneasy," *Washington Post*, February 22, 1996, A12; Adam Nagourney, "At Rallies for Buchanan, Fervent Supporters Are Part of the Show, Too," *New York Times*, February 26, 1996, B6.

218. "Pat Buchanan's Real Agenda," *Searchlight*, April 1996, 22.

219. On the far right in these decades, see Kathleen Belew, *Bring the War Home: The White Power Movement and Paramilitary America* (Cambridge, MA: Harvard University Press, 2018).

220. Kevin Phillips, "Friendly Fire," *Los Angeles Times*, May 7, 1995, 1.

221. Samuel Francis, "The Education of David Duke," *Chronicles*, February 1992, 7–9. On Francis's significance, see Michael Brendan Dougherty, "The Castaway," *America's Future*, January 14, 2007, https://americasfuture.org/the-castaway/; Timothy Shenk, "The Dark History of Donald Trump's Rightwing Revolt," *Guardian*, August 16, 2016, https://www.theguardian.com/news/2016/aug/16/secret-history-trumpism-donald-trump; and John Ganz, "The Year the Clock Broke," *Baffler*, November 7, 2018, https://thebaffler.com/salvos/the-year-the-clock-broke-ganz.

222. Samuel Francis, "Buchanan II," *Chronicles*, August 1992, 10–11. Buchanan eulogized Francis in 2005; see Patrick J. Buchanan, "Sam Francis: Obdurate for Truth," *WorldNetDaily*, March 7, 2005, https://www.wnd.com/2005/03/29236/. Note the laudatory block quote from Francis in Michael Anton, *The Stakes: America at the Point of No Return* (Washington, DC: Regnery, 2020), 399–400.

Chapter Seven: The Politics of Listlessness

1. "A Conversation among Democrats—Chaired by Sen. Alan Cranston," Kirk O'Donnell files, box 23, "Strategy Council Meeting, 1981," Thomas P. O'Neill, Jr., Papers, Burns Library, Boston College, Chestnut Hill, MA.

2. Though this view of the Democrats shares much with Matt Grossmann and David A. Hopkins, *Asymmetric Politics: Ideological Republicans and Group Interest Democrats* (New York: Oxford University Press, 2016), we do not treat group interests as determinative but instead emphasize the ways that groups do or do not render themselves into a larger party project.

3. For an incisive account that treats many of the same episodes covered in this chapter from a factionally left vantage point, see Ed Burmila, *Chaotic Neutral: How the Democrats Lost Their Soul in the Center* (New York: Bold Type Books, 2022).

4. Binyamin Appelbaum, *The Economists' Hour: False Prophets, Free Markets, and the Fracture of Society* (New York: Little, Brown, 2019); Elizabeth Popp Berman, *Thinking Like an Economist: How Efficiency Replaced Equality in U.S. Public Policy* (Princeton, NJ: Princeton University Press, 2022), esp. 181–200.

5. The two themes have received bifurcated treatment across the disciplines. Political scientists emphasize polarization, while sociologists and historians excavate a neoliberal

"neo-consensus." On post-1960s historiography, see Bruce J. Schulman, "Post-1968 History: Neo-consensus History for the Age of Polarization," *Reviews in American History* 47 (2019): 479–49. For historical critiques of the polarization framework, see Matthew D. Lassiter, "Political History beyond the Red-Blue Divide," *Journal of American History* 98 (2011): 760–64; Brent Cebul, Lily Geismer, and Mason B. Williams, "Beyond Red and Blue: Crisis and Continuity in Twentieth-Century U.S. Political History," in *Shaped by the State: Toward a New Political History of the Twentieth Century*, ed. Brent Cebul, Lily Geismer, and Mason B. Williams (Chicago: University of Chicago Press, 2019), 3–23. For a historical synthesis instead framed around division and polarization, see Kevin M. Kruse and Julian E. Zelizer, *Fault Lines: A History of the United States Since 1974* (New York: W. W. Norton, 2019).

6. For a contrary argument to the last claim, see Thomas Frank, *Listen, Liberal; or, What Ever Happened to the Party of the People?* (New York: Henry Holt, 2016).

7. For a recent synthesis of a vast literature, see Nolan McCarty, *Polarization: What Everyone Needs to Know* (New York: Oxford University Press, 2019).

8. Lilliana Mason, *Uncivil Agreement: How Politics Became Our Identity* (Chicago: University of Chicago Press, 2018); Barbara Sinclair, *Party Wars: Polarization and the Politics of National Policy Making* (Norman: University of Oklahoma Press, 2006); Frances Lee, *Insecure Majorities: Congress and the Perpetual Campaign* (Chicago: University of Chicago Press, 2016); Steven W. Webster, *American Rage: How Anger Shapes Our Politics* (New York: Cambridge University Press, 2020).

9. Stephanie Mudge, *Leftism Reinvented: Western Parties from Socialism to Neoliberalism* (Cambridge, MA: Harvard University Press, 2018). For broader perspective on what he terms the "non-left left," see Charles S. Maier, *The Project-State and Its Rivals: A New History of the Twentieth and Twenty-First Centuries* (Cambridge, MA: Harvard University Press, 2023), 297–303, 325-333, 358; phrase at p. 301.

10. Thomas P. O'Neill Jr., *Man of the House: The Life and Political Memoirs of Speaker Tip O'Neill*, with William Novak (New York: Random House, 1987), 376.

11. Greta R. Krippner, *Capitalizing on Crisis: The Political Origins of the Rise of Finance* (Cambridge, MA: Harvard University Press, 2011).

12. "Easy finance" comes from W. Elliot Brownlee, *Federal Taxation in America* (New York: Cambridge University Press, 2016), 149.

13. Lily Geismer, *Left Behind: The Democrats' Failed Attempt to Solve Inequality* (New York: Public Affairs, 2022).

14. By attending to the politics of polarization and noting the differences between national politics and the conflicts over schools and housing as they played out in subnational contexts, we offer a somewhat different emphasis from Lily Geismer and Matthew D. Lassiter, "Turning Affluent Suburbs Blue Isn't Worth the Cost," *New York Times*, June 10, 2018, SR7. See also William Marble and Clayton Nall, "Where Self-Interest Trumps Ideology: Liberal Homeowners and Local Opposition to Housing Development," *Journal of Politics* 83 (2021): 1747–63.

15. On leadership tactics, see Barbara Sinclair, *Majority Leadership in the U.S. House* (Baltimore: Johns Hopkins University Press, 1983), 53, 66–67.

16. Robert Healey, "It's Time for Round 2 and Things Are Looking Up, *Boston Globe*, May 15, 1981, 1.

17. Viveka Novak, "After the Boll Weevils," *National Journal*, June 26, 1993, 1630–34.

18. Gary W. Cox and Mathew D. McCubbins, *Setting the Agenda: Responsible Party Government in the U.S. House of Representatives* (New York: Cambridge University Press, 2005), 117.

19. Les Aspin to constituents, undated, box 25, folder "Kirk O'Donnell Files: 1981 Budget—Memos, Statements, Analysis, March 5–July 11," O'Neill Papers.

20. Tip O'Neill to Ronald Reagan, July 20, 1981, box 20, folder "Press Assistant Files—Social Security, 1981–1985," O'Neill Papers.

21. Steven V. Roberts, "The Democrats Get Even," *New York Times*, January 8, 1983, WR1.

22. This story was previewed in Margot Hornblower, "'Horatio' at the Bridge: O'Neill Fought Back, Feels Like a Winner," *Washington Post*, October 10, 1982, A1.

23. John A. Farrell, *Tip O'Neill and the Democratic Century* (Boston: Little, Brown, 2001), 547.

24. Samuel P. Huntington, "The Visions of the Democratic Party," *Public Interest* 79 (Spring 1985): 64.

25. Denise L. Baer, "Political Parties: The Missing Variable in Women and Politics Research," *Political Research Quarterly* 46 (1993): 547–76; Jo Freeman, "Whom You Know versus Whom You Represent: Feminist Influence in the Democratic and Republican Parties," in *The Women's Movements of the United States and Western Europe: Consciousness, Political Opportunity, and Public Policy*, ed. Mary F. Katzenstein and Carol McClurg Mueller (Philadelphia: Temple University Press, 1987), 215–44.

26. Christina Wolbrecht, *The Politics of Women's Rights: Parties, Positions, and Change* (Princeton, NJ: Princeton University Press, 2000); Marjorie Spruill, *Divided We Stand: The Battle over Women's Rights and Family Values That Polarized American Politics* (New York: Bloomsbury, 2017).

27. Frank Lynn, "Women's Issues Given Strong Support by Democrats in Philadelphia," *New York Times*, June 28, 1982, B7.

28. Harriett Woods, *Stepping Up to Power: The Political Journey of American Women* (Boulder: Westview Press, 2000), 99; Ellen Malcolm, *When Women Win: EMILY's List and the Rise of Women in American Politics*, with Craig Unger (Boston: Houghton Mifflin, 2016), 38–41; Amanda Spake, "Women Can Be Power Brokers, Too," *Washington Post*, June 5, 1988, 35, 50.

29. Wolbrecht, *Politics of Women's Rights*, 62.

30. Kira Sanbonmatsu, *Democrats, Republicans, and the Politics of Women's Place* (Ann Arbor: University of Michigan Press, 2002), 45–48.

31. For an important critical analysis of class dynamics in feminist activism, see Jane Mansbridge, *Why We Lost the ERA* (Chicago: University of Chicago Press, 1986).

32. For evidence from Congress, see Anne Costain and Heather Fraizer, "Congress and the Transformation of the Women's Movement," in *Women Transforming Congress*, ed. Cindy Simon Rosenthal (Norman: University of Oklahoma Press, 2002), esp. 79–84.

33. On the particular salience of abortion, see Sanbonmatsu, *Democrats, Republicans, and the Politics of Women's Place*, 98–111, 173–215.

34. Felicia Kornbluh, "Feminists and the Welfare Debate: Too Little? Too Late?" *Dollars & Sense*, November–December 1996, 24–27.

35. Ann Shola Orloff, "Transforming Gendered Labor Policies in Sweden and the United States, 1960s–2000s," in *Democracy and the Welfare State: The Two Wests in the Age of Austerity*, ed. Alice Kessler-Harris and Mauricio Vaudagna (New York: Columbia University Press, 2018), 249–72. On breadwinner liberalism, see Robert O. Self, *All in the Family: The Realignment of American Democracy Since the 1960s* (New York: Hill & Wang, 2012), esp. 17–46.

36. Patricia Gurin, Shirly Hatchett, and James S. Jackson, *Hope and Independence: Blacks' Response to Electoral and Party Politics* (New York: Russell Sage Foundation, 1989); Michael C. Dawson, *Behind the Mule: Race and Class in African-American Politics* (Princeton, NJ: Princeton University Press, 1994); Ismail K. White and Chryl N. Laird, *Steadfast Democrats: How Social Forces Shape Political Behavior* (Princeton, NJ: Princeton University Press, 2020). The quote references Bayard Rustin, "From Protest to Politics: The Future of the Civil Rights Movement," *Commentary*, February 1965, 25–31.

37. William Julius Wilson, *The Declining Significance of Race: Blacks and Changing American Institutions* (Chicago: University of Chicago Press, 1978).

38. On Republicans' fitful outreach, see Leah Wright Rigueur, *The Loneliness of the Black Republican: Pragmatic Politics and the Pursuit of Power* (Princeton, NJ: Princeton University Press, 2016).

39. H. Paul Friesama, "Black Control of Central Cities: The Hollow Prize," *American Institution of Planners Journal* 35 (1969): 75–79; Neil Kraus and Todd Swanstrom, "Minority Mayors and the Hollow-Prize Problem," *PS: Political Science & Politics* 34 (2001): 99–105.

40. Charles V. Hamilton, "The Patron-Recipient Relationship and Minority Politics in New York City," *Political Science Quarterly* 94 (1979): 211–27; Peter Eisinger, "Black Mayors and the Politics of Racial Economic Advancement," in *Culture, Ethnicity, and Identity: Current Issues in Research*, ed. William C. McCready (New York: Academic Press, 1983), 95–108; Adolph Reed Jr., "The Black Urban Regime: Structural Origins & Constraints," in *Comparative Urban and Community Research*, vol. 1, *Power, Community and the City*, ed. Michael Peter Smith (New Brunswick, NJ: Transaction Books, 1988), 138–89. For recent evidence, see Daniel J. Hopkins and Katherine T. McCabe, "After It's Too Late: Estimating the Policy Impacts of Black Mayoralties in U.S. Cities," *American Politics Research* 40 (2012): 665–700.

41. Paul Delaney, "Blacks in House Seeking Negro Leadership Nationally," *New York Times*, March 29, 1971, 19. On internal dynamics, see Alex Poinsett, "The Black Caucus: Five Years Later," *Ebony*, June 1973, 64–73.

42. Note both trends and enduring differences. While the CBC became less liberal and non-CBC House Democrats more liberal over time, the CBC remains substantially more liberal than the House Democratic median. For data, see Katherine Tate, *Concordance: Black Lawmaking in the U.S. Congress from Carter to Obama* (Ann Arbor: University of Michigan Press, 2014), 165.

43. On the broader historical debate over solidaristic versus coalitional strategies in Black politics, see Fredrick C. Harris, *The Price of the Ticket: Barack Obama and the Rise and Decline of Black Politics* (New York: Oxford University Press, 2012).

44. Alan Gerber, "African Americans' Congressional Careers and the Democratic House Delegation," *Journal of Politics* 58 (1996): 831–45. See also Robert Singh, *The Congressional Black Caucus: Racial Politics in the U.S. Congress* (Thousand Oaks, CA: SAGE, 1998), 114–22, 159–60.

45. Myron Levin, "Women, Blacks Courted: Big Tobacco Buying New Friendships," *Los Angeles Times*, May 22, 1988, 1; Eric Lipton and Eric Lichtblau, "In Black Caucus, a Fund-Raising Powerhouse," *New York Times*, February 14, 2010, A1; Myron Levin, "Big Tobacco's Big Race Play," *Salon*, November 27, 2015, https://www.salon.com/2015/11/26/big_tobaccos_unsavory_racial_politics_philip_morris_the_naacp_and_the_future_of_menthol_cigarettes_partner/.

46. Charlie Cooper with Wayne Barrett, "Chisholm's Compromise," *Village Voice*, October 30, 1978, 37.

47. Donna Brazile, "Democrats Stripped My Superpowers. Now I'm a Notch above a Coin Toss," *USA Today*, August 31, 2018, https://www.usatoday.com/story/opinion/voices/2018/08/31/democratic-national-committee-weakened-superdelegates-like-me-party-faithful-column/1135303002/.

48. For general histories, see Nelson Lichtenstein, *The State of the Union: A Century of American Labor*, rev. ed. (Princeton, NJ: Princeton University Press: 2013), 141–296; Timothy J. Minchin, *Labor under Fire: A History of the AFL-CIO since 1979* (Chapel Hill: University of North Carolina Press, 2017). On the labor-Democratic partnership, see Taylor E. Dark, *The Unions and the Democrats: An Enduring Alliance* (Ithaca, NY: ILR Press, 1999); Daniel Schlozman, *When Movements Anchor Parties: Electoral Alignments in American History* (Princeton, NJ: Princeton University Press, 2015), esp. 172–97, 242–56.

49. "Union Membership, Coverage, and Earnings from the CPS, 2022," March 22, 2023, unionstats.com.

50. Joseph A. McCartin, *Collision Course: Ronald Reagan, the Air Traffic Controllers, and the Strike That Changed America* (New York: Oxford University Press, 2011).

51. For a good statement of his worldview, see Lane Kirkland, "'It Has All Been Said Before . . . ,'" in *Unions in Transition: Entering the Second Century,* ed. Seymour Martin Lipset (San Francisco: Institute for Contemporary Studies Press, 1986), 393–404.

52. Dark, *Unions and the Democrats,* 141–57.

53. Jack W. Germond and Jules Witcover, "Liberal Alliance Falls Apart at Strange Time," *Washington Star,* March 23, 1981, 3.

54. Harry C. Boyte, Heather Booth, and Steve Max, *Citizen Action and the New American Populism* (Philadelphia: Temple University Press, 1986).

55. Bruce J. Schulman, *From Cotton Belt to Sunbelt: Federal Policy, Economic Development, and the Transformation of the South, 1938–1980* (New York: Oxford University Press, 1991).

56. Al From, "Democrats in the Center," *Louisville Courier-Journal,* November 3, 1996.

57. David S. Broder, "Republicans Gain Strength in Region's Political Cauldron," *Washington Post,* May 18, 1986, A1.

58. Compare Earl Black and Merle Black, *The Rise of Southern Republicans* (Cambridge, MA: Belknap Press of Harvard University Press, 2005); and James M. Glaser, *The Hand of the Past in Contemporary Southern Politics* (New Haven, CT: Yale University Press, 2005).

59. Huntington, "Visions of the Democratic Party."

60. See Charles Peters, "A Neo-liberal's Manifesto," *Washington Post,* September 5, 1982, C1. Though the substantive overlap is clear, Peters's time-bound meaning of the term should be distinguished from the broader transnational concept.

61. Randall Rothenberg, *The Neoliberals: Creating the New American Politics* (New York: Simon & Schuster, 1984), 79. See also John B. Judis, "Neoliberals: High-Tech Politics for the '80s?," *Progressive,* October 1982, 27–32; Patrick Andelic, *Donkey Work: Congressional Democrats in Conservative America, 1974–1994* (Lawrence: University Press of Kansas, 2019), 150–80.

62. Walter Goodman, "As Neoliberals Search for Closest Fit, Hart Is Often Mentioned," *New York Times,* May 15, 1984, A24.

63. Hedrick Smith, *The Power Game: How Washington Works* (New York: Random House, 1988), 135.

64. William Schneider, "JFK's Children: The Class of '74," *Atlantic,* March 1989, 46. See also E. J. Dionne, "Greening of Democrats: An 80's Mix of Idealism and Shrewd Politics," *New York Times,* June 14, 1989, A23.

65. Les AuCoin of Oregon, quoted in Schneider, "JFK's Children," 42.

66. Paul E. Tsongas, "Update Liberalism, or It's a 60's Relic," *New York Times,* June 30, 1980, A19.

67. Brent Cebul, "Supply-Side Liberalism: Fiscal Crisis, Post-Industrial Policy, and the Rise of the New Democrats," *Modern American History* 2 (2019): 139–64; Nicholas Short, "The Politics of the American Knowledge Economy," *Studies in American Political Development* 36 (2022): 41–60; Lily Geismer, *Don't Blame Us: Suburban Liberals and the Transformation of the Democratic Party* (Princeton, NJ: Princeton University Press, 2015), 251–79.

68. Robert Reich and John D. Donahue, *New Deals: The Chrysler Revival and the American System* (New York: Random House, 1985), 268–97. On the rise of industrial policy as a topic of Democratic debate, see Otis L. Graham Jr., *Losing Time: The Industrial Policy Debate* (Cambridge, MA: Harvard University Press, 1992), 59–74.

69. Quoted in Schneider, "JFK's Children," 35.

70. Kenneth Baer, *Reinventing Democrats: The Politics of Liberalism from Reagan to Clinton* (Lawrence: University Press of Kansas, 2000); Curtis Atkins, "Forging a New Democratic Party: The Politics of the Third Way from Clinton to Obama" (PhD diss., York University, 2015);

Mudge, *Leftism Reinvented*, 260–303; Geismer, *Left Behind*, esp. 120–29; Al From, *The New Democrats and the Return to Power* (New York: St. Martin's Press, 2013).

71. Quote from "The New Progressive Declaration: A Political Philosophy for the Information Age," Progressive Policy Institute, July 10, 1996, http://web.archive.org/web/20020116151449/http://www.ndol.org/print.cfm?contentid=839.

72. Janet Hook, "Officials Seek Moderation in Party's Image," *CQ Weekly Report*, March 9, 1985, 457.

73. Metaphor taken from Richard E. Cohen, "Democratic Leadership Council Sees Party Void and Is Ready to Fill It," *National Journal*, February 1, 1986, 267–70.

74. The DLC shared the second critique but not the first with the hawkish regulars of the Coalition for a Democratic Majority. Justin Vaïsse, *Neoconservatism: The Biography of a Movement*, trans. Arthur Goldhammer (Cambridge, MA: Harvard University Press, 2011), 208–17. For the CDM perspective, see Joshua Muravchik, "Why the Democrats Lost Again," *Commentary*, February 1989, 13–22.

75. Robert A. Jordan, "DLC Gets Jesse Jackson's Dander Up," *Boston Globe*, May 5, 1991, 87. Jackson returned fire, excoriating "Democrats for the Leisure Class . . . who didn't march in the sixties and won't stand up in the eighties." Jack W. Germond and Jules Witcover, *Whose Broad Stripes and Bright Stars: The Trivial Pursuit of the Presidency 1988* (New York: Warner Books, 1989), 44–45.

76. For the factional debate, see Jeff Faux, "The Myth of the New Democrats," *American Prospect*, Fall 1993; Will Marshall, "Friend or Faux," *American Prospect*, Winter 1994.

77. David Osborne and Ted Gaebler, *Reinventing Government: How the Entrepreneurial Spirit Is Transforming the Public Sector* (New York: Plume, 1992), 166. For background, see Reuel Schiller, "Regulation and the Collapse of the New Deal Order, or How I Learned to Stop Worrying and Love the Market," in *Beyond the New Deal Order: U.S. Politics from the Great Depression to the Great Recession*, ed. Gary Gerstle, Nelson Lichtenstein, and Alice O'Connor (Philadelphia: University of Pennsylvania Press, 2019), 168–85.

78. "The New Orleans Declaration: Statement Endorsed at the Fourth Annual DLC Conference," Democratic Leadership Council, March 1990, http://web.archive.org/web/20030526020448/http://www.ndol.org/print.cfm?contentid=878.

79. Naomi Murakawa, *The First Civil Right: How Liberals Built Prison America* (New York: Oxford University Press, 2014), 113–47; Elizabeth Hinton, *From the War on Poverty to the War on Crime: The Making of Mass Incarceration in America* (Cambridge, MA: Harvard University Press, 2016); James Forman Jr., *Locking Up Our Own: Crime and Punishment in Black America* (New York: Farrar, Straus & Giroux, 2017).

80. William Galston and Elaine Ciulla Kamarck, "The Politics of Evasion: Democrats and the Presidency," Progressive Policy Institute, 1989, 3, 14, https://www.progressivepolicy.org/wp-content/uploads/2013/03/Politics_of_Evasion.pdf.

81. Iwan Morgan, *The Age of Deficits: Presidents and Unbalanced Budgets from Jimmy Carter to George W. Bush* (Lawrence: University Press of Kansas, 2009); Paul Pierson, "The Deficit and the Politics of Domestic Reform," in *The Social Divide: Political Parties and the Future of Activist Government*, ed. Margaret Weir (Washington, DC: Brookings Institution Press, 1998), 126–78.

82. Novak, "After the Boll Weevils."

83. Robert Kuttner, "Reaganism, Liberalism, and the Democrats," in *The Reagan Legacy*, ed. Sidney Blumenthal and Thomas Byrne Edsall (New York: Random House, 1988), 99–133.

84. Kirk O'Donnell to Al Barkan, Dick Moe, and Paul Kirk, undated, box 22, folder "KOD: DNC Information, 1980–1981," O'Neill Papers.

85. Paul S. Herrnson, *Party Campaigning in the 1980s* (Cambridge, MA: Harvard University Press, 1988); David Menefee-Libey, *The Triumph of Campaign-Centered Politics* (New York: Chatham House, 2000).

86. The same reassertion of elected officials' clout over intraparty activists extended to curtailing the 1982 midterm convention and scrapping such events altogether by 1986. See memo by Ann Lewis, April 11, 1981, and "Recommendations from Mid-Term Task Force to Chairman Manatt," undated, both in box 1043, Democratic National Committee (DNC) Records, National Archives, Washington, DC. (This collection is unprocessed; folders are unlabeled.)

87. *The Report of the Commission on Presidential Nomination*, p. 16, box 1073, folder "Hunt Commission," DNC Records.

88. Timothy Clark, "The RNC Prospers, the DNC Struggles as They Face the 1980 Election," *National Journal*, September 27, 1980, 1617–21; remarks by Peter Kelly, Executive Committee meeting, May 8, 1981, box 1043, DNC Records; Herrnson, *Party Campaigning in the 1980s*, 33.

89. Brooks Jackson, *Honest Graft: Big Money and the American Political Process* (New York: Alfred A. Knopf, 1988), 77.

90. Robert Kuttner, "Ass Backwards," *New Republic*, April 22, 1985, 21.

91. Jackson, *Honest Graft*, 93.

92. Compare Philip A. Klinkner, *The Losing Parties: Out-Party National Committees, 1956–1993* (New Haven, CT: Yale University Press, 1994), 168–71; Thomas Ferguson and Joel Rogers, *Right Turn: The Decline of the Democrats and the Future of American Politics* (New York: Hill and Wang, 1986), 141–45.

93. Elizabeth Drew, "Politics and Money—I," *New Yorker*, December 6, 1982, 96.

94. Manatt got rich exploiting the intricacies of banking law and continued to derive income from his law firm's corporate lobbying while he chaired the DNC. Phil Gailey and Warren Weaver Jr., "Briefing," *New York Times*, June 14, 1982, B8; Jonathan Alter, "With Friends Like These . . . ," *Washington Monthly*, January 1983, 12–22.

95. Brooks Jackson, "Democrats Court Small Band of Business Donors Who Contribute Advice Along with Needed Cash," *Wall Street Journal*, August 15, 1985, 54.

96. Robert Shogan, "New Democratic Chief Ron Brown," *Los Angeles Times*, February 9, 1989, 1.

97. Tracey L. Brown, *The Life and Times of Ron Brown: A Memoir by His Daughter* (New York: William Morrow, 1998), 181–83.

98. Menefee-Libey, *Triumph of Campaign-Centered Politics*, 108–10; Anthony Corrado, "The Politics of Cohesion: The Role of the National Party Committees in the 1992 Election," in *The State of the Parties*, ed. John C. Green and Daniel Shea (Lanham, MD: Rowman & Littlefield, 1994), esp. 66–71.

99. Remarks by Bob Farmer, Executive Committee meeting, May 1, 1989, box 187, DNC Records.

100. Quote from Kuttner, "Ass Backwards."

101. Larry Sabato, *The Rise of Political Consultants: New Ways of Winning Elections* (New York: Basic Books, 1983); John H. Aldrich, "Presidential Campaigns in Party- and Candidate-Centered Eras," in *Under the Watchful Eye: Managing Presidential Campaigns in the Television Era*, ed. Mathew D. McCubbins (Washington: CQ Press, 1992), 59–82; Robin Kolodny, "Electoral Partnerships: Political Consultants and Political Parties," in *Campaign Warriors: Political Consultants in Elections*, ed. James A. Thurber and Candice J. Nelson (Washington, DC: Brookings Institution Press, 2000), 110–33. For the longer arc, see Adam Sheingate, *Building a Business of Politics: The Rise of Political Consulting and the Transformation of American Democracy* (New York: Oxford University Press, 2016).

102. On these themes, see Allen D. Hertzke, *Echoes of Discontent: Jesse Jackson, Pat Robertson, and the Resurgence of Populism* (Washington, DC: CQ Press, 1993), 58–80, 260–65. This interpretation is largely compatible with the leading critical treatment, Adolph L. Reed Jr., *The Jesse Jackson Phenomenon: The Crisis of Purpose in Afro-American Politics* (New Haven, CT: Yale University Press, 1986).

103. Jesse L. Jackson, *Straight from the Heart*, ed. Roger D. Hatch and Frank E. Watkins (Philadelphia: Fortress Press, 1987), 49. This speech, "Liberation and Justice: A Call for Redefinition, Refocus, and Rededication," is an excellent distillation of Jackson's worldview.

104. Marshall Frady, *Jesse: The Life and Pilgrimage of Jesse Jackson* (New York: Random House, 1996), 501.

105. Jackson, *Straight from the Heart*, 35.

106. Paul Kleppner, *Chicago Divided: The Making of a Black Mayor* (DeKalb: Northern Illinois University Press, 1985), 166.

107. See Kleppner, *Chicago Divided*; William J. Grimshaw, *Bitter Fruit: Black Politics and the Chicago Machine, 1931–1991* (Chicago: University of Chicago Press, 1992), 143–224; Gordon K. Mantler, *The Multiracial Promise: Harold Washington's Chicago and the Democratic Struggle in Reagan's America* (Chapel Hill: University of North Carolina Press, 2023); and, as a sample of his coverage, David Axelrod, "'The Party's Over—Again—for Chicago's Political Machine," *Chicago Tribune*, April 17, 1983, M1.

108. Frady, *Jesse*, 304. On the contours of the Jackson coalition, see Manning Marable, *Black American Politics: From the Washington Marches to Jesse Jackson* (London: Verso, 1985), 254–82.

109. E. J. Dionne Jr., "Jackson's Share of Votes by Whites Triples in '88," *New York Times*, June 13, 1988, B7.

110. Larry Eichel, "Jackson Gets Rule Change on Delegates," *Philadelphia Inquirer*, June 26, 1988, A1. For longer context, see Elaine Kamarck, *Primary Politics: Everything You Need to Know about How America Nominates Its Presidential Candidates*, 3rd ed. (Washington, DC: Brookings Institution Press, 2018), 87–124.

111. Although the deal Ickes struck had eliminated members of the DNC as superdelegates, the DNC restored its own votes the following year. Thomas B. Edsall, "Democrats Avoid Fight on Rules," *Washington Post*, June 18, 1989, A11.

112. "In Vermont, Jackson and Dukakis Virtually Tie in Delegate Contests," *New York Times*, April 21, 1988, D26.

113. Jamelle Bouie, "Keep Hope Alive," *Slate*, November 27, 2016, http://www.slate.com /articles/news_and_politics/cover_story/2016/11/jesse_jackson_s_presidential_campaigns _offer_a_road_map_for_democrats_in.html; Ryan Grim, *We've Got People: From Jesse Jackson to Alexandria Ocasio-Cortez, the End of Big Money and the Rise of a Movement* (Washington, DC: Strong Arm Press, 2019).

114. Frady, *Jesse*, 383.

115. Galston and Kamarck, "Politics of Evasion," 14, 17.

116. Bill Clinton, "Keynote Address of Gov. Bill Clinton to the DLC's Cleveland Convention," May 6, 1991, http://web.archive.org/web/20010513055339/http://www.ndol.org/print .cfm?contentid=3166. See also the "New American Choice Resolution" adopted at the convention, https://web.archive.org/web/20040313082824/http://www.ndol.org/documents /cleveland_proclamation.pdf; Baer, *Reinventing Democrats*, 163–92; From, *New Democrats and the Return to Power*, 131–59.

117. Lloyd Grove, "Al From, the Life of the Party," *Washington Post*, July 24, 1992, D1.

118. Among the DLC's various manifestoes, the New Democrat Credo well captures this communitarian impulse. "The New Democrat Credo," Democratic Leadership Council,

May 1998, http://web.archive.org/web/20010528150505/http://ndol.org/print.cfm?contentid =533.

119. From, *New Democrats and the Return to Power*, 139. See also Rob Gurwitt, "Go Past the Beltway and Turn Right," *Governing*, April 1991.

120. Daniel Galvin, *Presidential Party Building: Dwight D. Eisenhower to George W. Bush* (Princeton, NJ: Princeton University Press, 2010), 225–46.

121. Anthony Corrado, "Party Soft Money," in *Campaign Finance Reform: A Sourcebook*, ed. Anthony Corrado (Washington, DC: Brookings Institution, 1996), 169.

122. See Sidney M. Milkis, "Bill Clinton and the Politics of Divided Democracy," in *Seeking the Center: Politics and Policymaking at the New Century*, ed. Martin A. Levin, Marc K. Landy, and Martin Shapiro (Washington, DC: Georgetown University Press, 2001), 350–80; Stephen Skowronek, *The Politics Presidents Make: Leadership from John Adams to Bill Clinton*, 2nd ed. (Cambridge, MA: Belknap Press of Harvard University Press, 1997), 447–63. For a trenchant liberal critique, see James MacGregor Burns and Georgia J. Sorenson, *Dead Center: Clinton-Gore Leadership and the Perils of Moderation*, with Robin Gerber and Scott W. Webster (New York: Scribner, 1999), 343.

123. In 1996 alone, this description applies not only to the Personal Responsibility and Work Opportunity Act but also to the Prison Litigation Reform Act, the Illegal Immigration Reform and Immigration Responsibility Act, the Antiterrorism and Effective Death Penalty Act, and the Defense of Marriage Act.

124. Gwendolyn Mink, *Welfare's End* (Ithaca, NY: Cornell University Press, 1998), 33–68; R. Kent Weaver, *Ending Welfare as We Know It* (Washington, DC: Brookings Institution Press, 2000).

125. Joe Klein, *The Natural: The Misunderstood Presidency of Bill Clinton* (New York: Doubleday, 2002), 153.

126. Dick Morris, *Behind the Oval Office: Winning the Presidency in the Nineties* (New York: Random House, 1997), 300. On Penn's tricks to produce such results, see William Saletan, "Centrists vs. Progressives," *Slate*, April 22, 1997, https://slate.com/news-and-politics/1997/08/centrists-vs-progressives.html.

127. See Will Marshall and Elaine Ciulla Kamarck, "Replacing Welfare with Work," in *Mandate for Change*, ed. Will Marshall and Martin Schram (New York: Berkley Books, 1993), 217–36.

128. Michael Katz, *The Undeserving Poor: America's Enduring Confrontation with Poverty* (New York: Oxford University Press, 2013), 156–203.

129. Martin Gilens, *Why Americans Hate Welfare: Race, Media, and the Politics of Antipoverty Policy* (Chicago: University of Chicago Press, 1999).

130. Michael K. Brown, "Ghettoes, Fiscal Federalism, and Welfare Reform," in *Race and the Politics of Welfare Reform*, ed. Sanford F. Schram, Joe Soss, and Richard C. Fording (Ann Arbor: University of Michigan Press, 2003), 47–71.

131. Felicia Kornbluh and Gwendolyn Mink, *Ensuring Poverty: Welfare Reform in Feminist Perspective* (Philadelphia: University of Pennsylvania Press, 2018).

132. Peter Grier, "Democrats' Values Moving to Suburbs," *Christian Science Monitor*, August 27, 1997, 1. See also Geismer, *Left Behind*, 233–61.

133. See, for example, Al From, "The New Democratic Platform," *New Democrat*, September/October 1996, 12–14. For a critical take on this iteration of the DLC, see Robert Dreyfuss, "How the DLC Does It," *American Prospect*, April 23, 2001, 20–25.

134. Robert E. Rubin and Jacob Weisberg, *In an Uncertain World: Tough Choices from Wall Street to Washington* (New York: Random House, 2003), 93.

135. Susan Dentzer, "Walter Mondale Learns a Lesson," *Newsweek*, October 22, 1984, 77.

136. Rubin and Weisberg, *In an Uncertain World*, 353. See also Laura Tyson, "A Squandered Legacy," *Prospect*, March 25, 2004.

137. Juliet Eilperin, "House's New Democrats at Center of Influence," *Washington Post*, May 29, 2000, A1.

138. Jackie Calmes, "Fast Friends: Clinton's Best Allies Now Are the Liberals He Spurned in the Past," *Wall Street Journal*, October 9, 1998, A1.

139. Robert J. Shapiro, "A New Deal on Social Security," in *Building the Bridge: 10 Big Ideas to Transform America*, ed. Will Marshall (Lanham, MD: Rowman & Littlefield, 1997), 39–56.

140. Steven M. Teles and Martha Derthick, "Social Security from 1980 to the Present: From Third Rail to Presidential Commitment—and Back?" in *Conservatism and American Political Development*, ed. Brian J. Glenn and Steven M. Teles (New York: Oxford University Press, 2009), 261–90.

141. Michael Tomasky, "Dems' Fightin' Words," *American Prospect*, August 26, 2002, 22–26.

142. Jeffrey Toobin, *Too Close to Call: The Thirty-Six-Day Battle to Decide the 2000 Election* (New York: Random House, 2001), 276.

143. Nick Penniman, "Goodbye to All That," *American Prospect*, November 7, 2002, https://prospect.org/article/goodbye/.

144. Spencer Ackerman, *Reign of Terror: How the 9/11 Era Destabilized America and Produced Trump* (New York: Viking, 2021), 87–154, 187–220.

145. Joseph Stieb, "The Vital Center Reborn: Redefining Liberalism between 9/11 and the Iraq War," *Modern American History* 4 (2021): 285–304; Matthew Yglesias, *Heads in the Sand: How the Republicans Screw Up Foreign Policy and Foreign Policy Screws Up the Democrats* (Hoboken, NJ: John Wiley & Sons, 2008), 53–126; Michael T. Heaney and Fabio Rojas, *Party in the Street: The Antiwar Movement and the Democratic Party after 9/11* (New York: Cambridge University Press, 2015), 173–204.

146. Memo from Rosa DeLauro and Frank Pallone to Democratic Colleagues, January 27, 2002, box 449, folder 1, Richard A. Gephardt Congressional Papers, Missouri Historical Society, St. Louis.

147. Perry Bacon Jr., "Anybody Knows Not to Mess with Me," *Time*, September 4, 2006, 30–32.

148. Ronald M. Peters Jr. and Cindy Simon Rosenthal, *Speaker Nancy Pelosi and the New American Politics* (New York: Oxford University Press, 2010), 3–4, 29–62. On her father's battles in factionalized Baltimore, see Matthew A. Crenson, *Baltimore: A Political History* (Baltimore: Johns Hopkins University Press, 2017), esp. 412–31.

149. George Lakoff, *Moral Politics: How Liberals and Conservatives Think*, 2nd ed. (Chicago: University of Chicago Press, 2002); George Lakoff, *Don't Think of an Elephant! Know Your Values and Frame the Debate: The Essential Guide for Progressives* (White River Junction, VT: Chelsea Green, 2004). The emphasis on framing and language as a way out of thorny problems would endure as the party moved leftward. For example, it can be seen in the "Race-Class Narrative" designed to offer a progressive message showing the connections across race and economic pain. See Ian Haney López, *Merge Left: Fusing Race and Class, Winning Elections, and Saving America* (New York: New Press, 2019).

150. Paul Waldman, *Being Right Is Not Enough: What Progressives Can Learn from Conservative Success* (New York: Wiley, 2006).

151. David Karpf, *The MoveOn Effect: The Unexpected Transformation of American Political Advocacy* (New York: Oxford University Press, 2012).

152. Jerome Armstrong and Markos Moulitsas Zuniga, *Crashing the Gate: Netroots, Grassroots, and the Rise of People-Powered Politics* (White River Junction, VT: Chelsea Green, 2006);

Daniel Kreiss, *Taking Our Country Back: The Crafting of Networked Politics from Howard Dean to Barack Obama* (New York: Oxford University Press, 2012), 61–86.

153. Zephyr Teachout and Thomas Streeter, "The Legacies of Dean's Internet Campaign," in *Mousepads, Shoe Leather, and Hope: Lessons from the Howard Dean Campaign for the Future of American Politics* (Boulder, CO: Paradigm, 2008), 233.

154. Matt Bai, *The Argument: Billionaires, Bloggers, and the Battle to Remake the Democratic Party* (New York: Penguin Press, 2007), 23–48. For a write-up based on the Stein presentation, see "The Conservative Infrastructure," in *The Practical Progressive: How to Build a Twenty-first Century Political Movement*, ed. Erica Payne (New York: PublicAffairs, 2008), 31–40.

155. Jacques Steinberg, "Cable Channel Nods to Ratings and Leans Left," *New York Times*, November 6, 2007, A1.

156. John B. Judis and Ruy Teixeira, *The Emerging Democratic Majority* (New York: Scribner, 2002), esp. 37–68. For a critique, see Benjamin Ross, "The New McGovernites," *Dissent*, Spring 2003, 7–10.

157. John Judis, "Why the Left Will (Eventually) Triumph: An Interview with Ruy Teixeira," *Talking Points Memo*, April 28, 2017, https://talkingpointsmemo.com/cafe/why-left-will-eventually-win-ruy-teixeira/.

158. Teixeira himself had emphasized this point in previous work. Ruy Teixeira and Joel Rogers, *America's Forgotten Majority: Why the White Working-Class Still Matters* (New York: Basic Books, 2000). By the Biden years, he would sound this theme anew while taking a distinctly centrist line in intraparty disputes. Ruy Teixeira, "How Not to Build a Coalition," *Liberal Patriot*, January 20, 2022, https://theliberalpatriot.substack.com/p/how-not-to-build-a-coalition.

159. Harold Meyerson, "Mother Jones Returns," *LA Weekly*, November 3, 1995, 18–23; Julie Kosterlitz, "Laboring Uphill," *National Journal*, March 2, 1996, 474–79.

160. James A. Barnes and Richard E. Cohen, "Divided Democrats," *National Journal*, November 15, 1997, 2304–7; Steven Greenhouse, "Despite Defeat on China Bill, Labor Is on Rise," *New York Times*, May 30, 2000, A1; Gary C. Jacobson, "The Effect of the AFL-CIO's 'Voter Education' Campaigns on the 1996 House Elections," *Journal of Politics* 61 (1999): 185–94.

161. Steven Fraser and Joshua B. Freeman, eds., *Audacious Democracy: Labor, Intellectuals, and the Social Reconstruction of America* (Boston: Houghton Mifflin, 1997).

162. Steve Fraser and Joshua Freeman, "Hope for Labor at the End of History," *Dissent*, Fall 2021, 111–24.

163. On Obama and party politics, see Sidney M. Milkis, Jesse H. Rhodes, and Emily J. Charnock, "What Happened to Post-Partisanship? Barack Obama and the New American Party System," *Perspectives on Politics* 10 (2012): 57–76; Julia R. Azari, "Party Foul: How Obama Made Partisan, Not Party, Politics in a Polarized Environment," in *The Obama Legacy*, ed. Bert A. Rockman and Andrew Rudalevige (Lawrence: University Press of Kansas, 2019), 44–70.

164. For varying perspectives, see James T. Kloppenberg, *Reading Obama: Dreams, Hope, and the American Political Tradition* (Princeton, NJ: Princeton University Press, 2012); Charles Kesler, *I Am the Change: Barack Obama and the Crisis of Liberalism* (New York: Broadside Books, 2012); Timothy Shenk, *Realigners: Partisan Hacks, Political Visionaries, and the Struggle to Rule American Democracy* (New York: Farrar, Straus & Giroux, 2022), 295–339.

165. On the latter, see Jake Sullivan, "Remarks by National Security Advisor Jake Sullivan on Renewing American Economic Leadership at the Brookings Institution," April 27, 2023, https://www.whitehouse.gov/briefing-room/speeches-remarks/2023/04/27/remarks-by-national-security-advisor-jake-sullivan-on-renewing-american-economic-leadership-at-the-brookings-institution/.

166. Sam Stein, "Robert Gibbs Clarifies 'Professional Left' Criticism, Calls Initial Comments Inartful," *Huffington Post*, August 10, 2010, https://www.huffpost.com/entry/robert-gibbs-clarifies-pr_n_676934.

167. Barack Obama, "Remarks at Osawatomie High School in Osawatomie, Kansas," December 6, 2011, American Presidency Project, https://www.presidency.ucsb.edu/documents/remarks-osawatomie-high-school-osawatomie-kansas.

168. Sidney M. Milkis and John Warren York, "Barack Obama, Organizing for Action, and Executive-Centered Partisanship," *Studies in American Political Development* 31 (2017): 1–23. See also Charles Homans, "The Party of Obama," *Washington Monthly*, January–February 2010, 19–20, 37–40; Sam Graham-Felsen, "Has Obama Forgotten His Roots?" *Washington Post*, December 17, 2010, A33.

169. Elizabeth McKenna and Hahrie Han, *Groundbreakers: How Obama's 2.2 Million Volunteers Transformed Campaigning in America* (New York: Oxford University Press, 2015), 184.

170. Daniel Galvin and Chloe Thurston, "The Democrats' Misplaced Faith in Policy Feedback," *Forum* 15 (2017): 333–43.

171. Reed Hundt, *A Crisis Wasted: Barack Obama's Defining Decisions* (New York: Rosetta Books, 2019), 307–8.

172. Alec MacGillis, "How Obama Won Ohio," *New Republic*, November 7, 2012, https://newrepublic.com/article/109821/obama-campaign-made-2012-election-all-about-ohio-start-heres-how-they-won-it.

173. Adam Tooze, *Crashed: How a Decade of Financial Crises Changed the World* (New York: Viking, 2018), 281.

174. Quoted in Hundt, *Crisis Wasted*, 321.

175. Jonathan Cohn, "How They Did It," *New Republic*, June 10, 2010, 14–25; John E. McDonough, *Inside National Health Reform* (Berkeley: University of California Press, 2011).

176. Paul Starr, "What Is Hillary Clinton's Agenda," *American Prospect*, Summer 2016, 18–23.

177. See Ezra Klein, "Hillary Clinton and the Audacity of Political Realism," *Vox*, January 28, 2016, https://www.vox.com/2016/1/28/10858464/hillary-clinton-bernie-sanders-political-realism; Ezra Klein, "Understanding Hillary," *Vox*, July 11, 2016, https://www.vox.com/a/hillary-clinton-interview/the-gap-listener-leadership-quality.

178. Edward-Isaac Dovere, "How Clinton Lost Michigan—and Blew the Election," *Politico*, December 14, 2016, https://www.politico.com/story/2016/12/michigan-hillary-clinton-trump-232547; Daniel Schlozman, "The Lists Told Us Otherwise," *n+1*, December 24, 2016, https://nplusonemag.com/online-only/online-only/the-lists-told-us-otherwise/.

179. John Sides, Michael Tesler, and Lynn Vavreck, *Identity Crisis: The 2016 Campaign and the Battle for the Meaning of America* (Princeton, NJ: Princeton University Press, 2018), 130–53.

180. See, for example, Jim Geraghty, "Chuck Schumer: Democrats Will Lose Blue-Collar Whites but Gain in the Suburbs," *National Review*, July 28, 2016, https://www.nationalreview.com/corner/chuck-schumer-democrats-will-lose-blue-collar-whites-gain-suburbs/.

181. Brian F. Schaffner, Matthew MacWilliams, and Tatishe Nteta, "Understanding White Polarization in the 2016 Vote for President: The Sobering Role of Racism and Sexism," *Political Science Quarterly* 133 (2018): 9–34.

182. On the historical roots of Sanders's politics, see Daniel Schlozman, "The Sanders Phenomenon," *n+1*, October 13, 2015, https://nplusonemag.com/online-only/online-only/the-sanders-phenomenon/; Matthew Karp, "The Long Shot," *Nation*, May 20, 2019, 27–31. Sanders voters hardly shared all the candidate's views; see Christopher H. Achen and Larry M. Bartels, "Do Sanders's Supporters Favor His Policies?" *New York Times*, May 23, 2016.

183. For good examples of the Left's critique of the Democrats, see "Autopsy: The Democratic Party in Crisis," Action for a Progressive Future, October 30, 2017, https://democraticautopsy.org/wp-content/uploads/Autopsy-The-Democratic-Party-In-Crisis.pdf; Brendan O'Connor, "When the Party's Over," *Baffler*, May 2021, https://thebaffler.com/salvos/when-the-partys-over -oconnor. For a more synoptic view, see Burmila, *Chaotic Neutral*.

184. See, for example, Alexander Burns and Jonathan Martin, "Mistakes and Internal Strife Hobbled Sanders Campaign," *New York Times*, March 22, 2020, A1.

185. "Democrats Want to Change the Party. They Just Disagree on How," *Politico*, December 7, 2017, https://www.politico.com/magazine/story/2017/12/07/democrats-want-to -change-the-democratic-party-they-just-disagree-on-how-216055.

186. David Siders, "Black Caucus Chairman Opposes DNC Plan to Weaken Superdelegate Influence," *Politico*, August 14, 2018, https://www.politico.com/story/2018/08/14/dnc-super -delegates-cedric-richmond-776345.

187. *Report of the Commission on Presidential Nomination*, p. 2, box 1073, folder "Hunt Commission," DNC Records.

188. On the final deliberations inside the DNC, see David Weigel, "Democrats Weaken 'Superdelegates' in Effort to Avoid Repeat of Bitter Primaries," *Washington Post*, August 26, 2018, A2; Alex Seitz-Wald, "Democrats Strip Superdelegates of Power and Reform Caucuses in 'Historic' Move," NBC News, August 25, 2018, https://www.nbcnews.com/storyline/democrats-vs-trump /democrats-strip-super-delegates-power-reform-caucuses-historic-move-n903866. For rules, see "Call for the 2020 Democratic National Convention," 16, https://democrats.org/wp-content /uploads/sites/2/2019/07/2020-Call-for-Convention-WITH-Attachments-2.26.19.pdf.

189. For an illustration of how much changed in the first two decades of the twenty-first century, compare Jeffrey Berry, "Nonprofit Organizations as Interest Groups: The Politics of Passivity," in *Interest Group Politics*, ed. Allan J. Cigler and Burdett A. Loomis, 7th ed. (Washington, DC: CQ Press, 2007), 235–55; Jeffrey Berry, "Interest Groups and Elections," in *The Oxford Handbook of Electoral Persuasion*, ed. Elizabeth Suhay, Bernard Grofman, and Alexander H. Trechsel (New York: Oxford University Press, 2020), 340–57.

190. Rachel Cohen, "The Democratic Dilemma on Dark Money," *American Prospect*, December 2, 2021, https://prospect.org/power/democratic-dilemma-on-dark-money/.

191. Derek Willis, "How ActBlue Became a Powerful Force in Fundraising," *New York Times*, October 9, 2014, https://www.nytimes.com/2014/10/09/upshot/how-actblue-became-a -powerful-force-in-fund-raising.html; Erin Hill, "One. Billion. Dollars," *ActBlue* (blog), March 7, 2016, https://blog.actblue.com/2016/03/07/one-billion-dollars/; Sarah Potter, "2020 Election Cycle Recap," *ActBlue* (blog), December 3, 2020, https://blog.actblue.com/2020/12/03/2020 -election-cycle-recap/. It would not be until 2019 that the GOP finally launched an answer to the platform on the right: WinRed.

192. Robert Boatright, "The End of the Reform Era? Campaign Finance Retrenchment in the United States and Canada," *Forum* 10 (2012), https://doi.org/10.1515/1540-8884.1440; Adam Skaggs and Fred Wertheimer, "Empowering Small Donors in Federal Elections," Brennan Center for Justice, 2012, https://www.brennancenter.org/sites/default/files/2019-08/Report _Empowering_Small_Donors_Federal_Elections.pdf.

193. Kenneth P. Vogel, "A Swiss Billionaire Becomes a Democratic Force," *New York Times*, May 4, 2021, A1.

194. Theodore Schleifer, "Inside the Dems' Dark Money Machine," *Puck*, November 30, 2021. https://puck.news/inside-the-dems-dark-money-machine/.

195. The full political economy merits far more scholarly scrutiny. See David E. Broockman, Gregory Ferenstein, and Neil Malhotra, "Predispositions and the Political Behavior of American Economic Elites: Evidence from Technology Entrepreneurs," *American Journal of Political*

Science 63 (2019): 212–33. For background, see Margaret O'Mara, *The Code: Silicon Valley and the Remaking of America* (New York: Penguin Press, 2019).

196. Theodore Schleifer, "This Billionaire Built a Big-Money Machine to Oust Trump. Why Do Some Democrats Hate Him?," *Recode*, September 23, 2020, https://www.vox.com/recode /21451481/linkedin-reid-hoffman-billionaire-democratic-party-tension-silicon-valley; Issie Lapowsky, "Alloy Promised Democrats a Data Edge over Trump. The DNC Didn't Buy It. Now What?," *Protocol*, October 22, 2020, https://www.protocol.com/reid-hoffman-alloy-political -data-dnc; Theodore Schleifer, "Inside the Implosion of the $35 Million Startup Meant to Fix the Democratic Party," *Recode*, December 15, 2020, https://www.vox.com/recode/22175186 /alloy-drama-reid-hoffman-democratic-data-startup.

197. Ryan Grim, "Silicon Valley Billionaire Storms into Texas to Bail Out Abortion Foe Henry Cuellar," *Intercept*, May 24, 2022, https://theintercept.com/2022/05/24/henry-cuellar -reid-hoffman-primary/. See also an interview with Hoffman's political consigliere, Micah Sifry, "Special Bonus Edition: The Changing Politics of Abortion," *Connector*, May 5, 2022, https:// theconnector.substack.com/p/special-bonus-edition-the-changing.

198. Theodore Schleifer, "The $100 Million Plan to Completely Fix Washington," *Puck*, October 20, 2021, https://puck.news/silicon-valleys-100-million-plan-to-completely-fix -washington/.

199. Hiroko Tabuchi, "A Former Top Spokesman for the Obama White House Heads to the Golden Arches," *New York Times*, June 10, 2015, B2.

200. From the president of the Ford Foundation, see Darren Walker, *From Generosity to Justice: A New Gospel of Wealth* (New York: Ford Foundation, 2019).

201. Loren McArthur, "From Crisis to Opportunity: How Philanthropy Can Help Secure the Future," *Medium*, April 20, 2022, https://medium.com/@lorenmcarthur/from-crisis-to -opportunity-how-philanthropy-can-help-secure-the-future-719d933ac2fb.

202. Michael Scherer, "Democrats See Grim Prospects in Final Election Results," *Washington Post*, December 27, 2020, A10.

203. For a similar but more glass-half-full interpretation, see E. J. Dionne Jr., *Code Red: How Progressives and Moderates Can Unite to Save Our Country* (New York: St. Martin's Press, 2020). For a good tour d'horizon, see Robert Kuttner, "The Movement, the Party, and the President," *American Prospect*, January 2021, 16–25.

204. Lara Putnam, "Middle America Reboots Democracy: The Emergence and Rapid Electoral Turn of the New Grassroots," in *Upending American Politics: Polarizing Parties, Ideological Elites, and Citizen Activists from the Tea Party to the Anti-Trump Resistance*, ed. Theda Skocpol and Caroline Tervo (New York: Oxford University Press, 2020), 175–90; Leah E. Gose, Theda Skocpol, and Vanessa Williamson, "Saving America Once Again, from the Tea Party to the Anti-Trump Resistance," in Skocpol and Tervo, *Upending American Politics*, 191–212.

205. Emily Stewart, "We Are (Still) the 99 Percent," *Vox*, April 30, 2019, https://www.vox .com/the-highlight/2019/4/23/18284303/occupy-wall-street-bernie-sanders-dsa-socialism.

206. Alexandra Rojas and Waleed Shahid, "From Protest to Primaries: The Movement in the Democratic Party," in *Winning the Green New Deal: Why We Must, How We Can*, ed. Varshini Prakash and Guido Girgenti (New York: Simon & Schuster, 2020), 245. See also Mark Engler and Paul Engler, "Can You Plan a Realignment?" *Dissent*, April 2, 2021, https://www .dissentmagazine.org/online_articles/can-you-plan-a-realignment.

207. David Freedlander, *The AOC Generation: How Millennials Are Seizing Power and Rewriting the Rules of American Politics* (Boston: Beacon Press, 2021); Andrew Marantz, "The Left Turn," *New Yorker*, May 31, 2021, 30–39.

208. For helpful data, see Equis Research, "2020 Post Mortem, Part One: Portrait of a Persuadable Latino," April 1, 2021, https://downloads.ctfassets.net/ms6ec8hcu35u/5BR9iHBhsy

QtqUU1gNgfaR/b0f4d0be5f55297c627a3f2373fb11b8/Equis_Post-Mortem_Part_One.pdf; Equis Research, "2020 Post Mortem, Part Two: The American Dream Voter," December 14, 2021, https://assets.ctfassets.net/ms6ec8hcu35u/4E5a5nNoWi9JNFqeAylkmS/bf542d82f90 0dbfb62cc6e6d7253a24a/Post-Mortem_Part_Two_FINAL_Dec_14.pdf.

209. Stephanie Muravchik and Jon A. Shields, *Trump's Democrats* (Washington, DC: Brookings Institution Press, 2020), 88.

210. Josh Pacewicz, *Partisans and Partners: The Politics of the Post-Keynesian Society* (Chicago: University of Chicago Press, 2016).

211. Compare Larry M. Bartels, "What's the Matter with *What's the Matter with Kansas?*," *Quarterly Journal of Political Science* 1 (2006): 201–26; and Sam Zacher, "Polarization of the Rich: The New Democratic Allegiance of Affluent Americans and the Politics of Redistribution," *Perspectives on Politics*, February 8, 2023, https://doi.org/10.1017/S1537592722003310.

212. On the views of the rich, see Benjamin I. Page, Jason Seawright, and Matthew J. Lacombe, *Billionaires and Stealth Politics* (Chicago: University of Chicago Press, 2019); Benjamin I. Page, Larry M. Bartels, and Jason Seawright, "Democracy and the Policy Preferences of Wealthy Americans," *Perspectives on Politics* 11 (2013): 51–73. Their data predate Trump and we lack good individual-level evidence, let alone panel data, to explain recent shifts.

213. From the left, see, for example, Matthew Karp, "Party and Class in American Politics, *New Left Review*, January–February 2023, 131–44. Left critics focusing on class dealignment have been astute in showing descriptive patterns but less persuasive in offering full explanations for them. For a range of views among political scientists on the parties' shifting class bases, see Thomas B. Edsall, "It's Not Your Father's Democratic Party. But Whose Party Is it?," *New York Times*, August 16, 2023, https://www.nytimes.com/2023/08/16/opinion/democrats -republicans-2024.html.

214. Edward-Isaac Dovere, *Battle for the Soul: Inside the Democrats' Campaigns to Defeat Trump* (New York: Viking, 2021), 491.

215. The best treatment of the Democrats' primary contest in 2020 comes from Seth Masket, though he rates party influence more highly than we do. Masket, *Learning from Loss: The Democrats, 2016–2020* (New York: Cambridge University Press, 2020), 207–32.

216. See the essays in Roosevelt Institute, "Industrial Policy Synergies: Reflections from Biden Administration Alumni," April 25, 2023, https://rooseveltinstitute.org/wp-content /uploads/2023/04/RI_Industrial-Policy-Synergies-Reflections-from-Biden-Administration -Alumni_Report_202304.pdf.

Chapter Eight: Politics without Guardrails

1. Jane Wells, "How This Entrepreneur Went from a Crack Addict to a Self-Made Multimillionaire," CNBC, September 4, 2017, https://www.cnbc.com/2017/09/20/how-mypillow -founder-went-from-crack-addict-to-self-made-millionaire.html; Mary Bowerman, "Here's Why the BBB Revoked MyPillow's Accreditation," *USA Today*, January 4, 2017, https://www .usatoday.com/story/money/nation-now/2017/01/04/why-bbb-revoked-mypillows -accreditation/96160874/; Annie Karni, "Who Is MyPillow C.E.O. Mike Lindell, One of Trump's Last Remaining Supporters from Corporate America?" *New York Times*, January 16, 2021, https://www.nytimes.com/2021/01/16/us/politics/mypillow-notes-lindell-trump.html.

2. Lyz Lenz, "The Mystery of Tucker Carlson," *Columbia Journalism Review*, September 5, 2018, https://www.cjr.org/the_profile/tucker-carlson.php; Emily S. Rueb and Derrick Bryson Taylor, "Making False Claims about Hateful Doctrine," *New York Times*, August 9, 2019, A12; Philip Bump, "Tucker Carlson Is Telling His Viewers That Democrats See Them as Terrorists,"

Washington Post, January 28, 2021, https://www.washingtonpost.com/politics/2021/01/28/tucker-carlson-is-telling-his-viewers-that-democrats-see-them-terrorists/.

3. Ben Terris, "All the President's Guys," *Washington Post*, November 20, 2020, C1; Philip Rucker, Josh Dawsey, and Ashley Parker, "A Warm Welcome for President's Next Act," *Washington Post*, January 17, 2021, A1.

4. For synthetic accounts of Republicans and conservatism that, with varying emphases, treat recent decades up through the 2010s, see E. J. Dionne Jr., *Why the Right Went Wrong: Conservatism from Goldwater to the Tea Party and Beyond* (New York: Simon & Schuster, 2016); Jacob S. Hacker and Paul Pierson, *Let Them Eat Tweets: How the Right Rules in an Age of Inequality* (New York: Liveright, 2020); Nicole Hemmer, *Partisans: The Conservative Revolutionaries Who Remade American Politics in the 1990s* (New York: Basic Books, 2022); Matthew Continetti, *The Right: The Hundred-Year War for American Conservatism* (New York: Basic Books, 2022); Julian E. Zelizer, "Reckoning with the Trumpian GOP," in *The Presidency of Donald J. Trump: A First Historical Assessment*, ed. Julian E. Zelizer (Princeton, NJ: Princeton University Press, 2022), 27–48; Richard A. Viguerie, *Takeover: The 100-Year War for the Soul of the GOP and How Conservatives Can Finally Win It* (Washington: WND Books, 2014). For a thoughtful view from slightly earlier, see George H. Nash, "The Uneasy Future of American Conservatism," in *The Future of Conservatism: Conflict and Consensus in the Post-Reagan Era*, ed. Charles W. Dunn (Wilmington, DE: ISI Books, 2007), 1–19.

5. See, for example, Thomas B. Edsall, *Building Red America: The New Conservative Coalition and the Drive for Permanent Power* (New York: Basic Books, 2006).

6. See, for example, Hacker and Pierson, *Let Them Eat Tweets*.

7. Martin Wolf, "Donald Trump's Pluto-Populism Laid Bare," *Financial Times*, May 2, 2017.

8. Because we emphasize the ways that patterns came bundled together as part of a project for power, our account takes a different tone from the policy-forward essays, designed to draw out lessons for liberals, in the special edition on "New Policies, New Politics? Policy Feedback, Power-Building, and American Governance," *Annals of the American Academy of Political and Social Science* 691 (2019).

9. Godfrey Hodgson, *The World Turned Right Side Up* (Boston: Houghton Mifflin, 1996), 210.

10. Here as elsewhere, the emphasis on social context reflects the influence of the New History of Capitalism. See Shane Hamilton, *Trucking Country: The Road to America's Wal-Mart Economy* (Princeton, NJ: Princeton University Press, 2008); Bethany Moreton, *To Serve God and Wal-Mart: The Making of Christian Free Enterprise* (Cambridge, MA: Harvard University Press, 2010); Kim Phillips-Fein and Julian Zelizer, eds. *What's Good for Business: Business and American Politics since WWII* (New York: Oxford University Press, 2012). There is enormous opportunity for synthesis between the history of capitalism and the approaches drawn from comparative political economy in Kathleen Thelen, Jacob S. Hacker, Alexander Hertel-Fernandez, and Paul Pierson, eds., *American Political Economy: Institutions, Interests, and Inequalities* (New York: Cambridge University Press, 2021). For an impressive overall sketch, see Ruth Berins Collier and Jake Grumbach, "The Deep Structure of Democratic Crisis," *Boston Review*, January 6, 2022, https://bostonreview.net/articles/the-deep-structure-of-democratic-crisis/. See also, anecdotally, Patrick Wyman, "American Gentry," *Atlantic*, September 23, 2021, https://www.theatlantic.com/ideas/archive/2021/09/trump-american-gentry-wyman-elites/620151/.

11. Jeremy W. Peters, "An Outlet for the Outrage against Trump's Enemies," *New York Times*, August 4, 2020, A18; Derek Robertson, "How 'Owning the Libs' Became the GOP's Core Belief," *Politico*, March 21, 2021, https://www.politico.com/news/magazine/2021/03/21/owning-the-libs-history-trump-politics-pop-culture-477203.

12. The literature in political science tends to emphasize the back-and-forth between inequality and policy more than the social location of the new rich. See Larry M. Bartels, *Unequal Democracy: The Political Economy of the New Gilded Age*, 2nd ed. (New York: Russell Sage Foundation; Princeton, NJ: Princeton University Press, 2016); Benjamin I. Page, Jason Seawright, and Matthew J. Lacombe, *Billionaires and Stealth Politics* (Chicago: University of Chicago Press, 2019); Adam Bonica, Nolan McCarty, Keith T. Poole, Howard Rosenthal, "Why Hasn't Democracy Slowed Rising Inequality?" *Journal of Economic Perspectives* 27 (2013): 103–24. For very different explorations into the Democratic and Republican rich, see Alexander Hertel-Fernandez, Theda Skocpol, and Jason Sclar, "When Political Mega-Donors Join Forces: How the Koch Network and the Democracy Alliance Influence Organized U.S. Politics on the Right and Left," *Studies in American Political Development* 32 (2018): 127–65; Thomas Ferguson, Paul Jorgensen, and Jie Chen "Industrial Structure and Political Outcomes: The Case of the 2016 US Presidential Election," in *The Palgrave Handbook of Political Economy*, ed. Ivano Cardinale and Roberto Scazzieri (London: Palgrave Macmillan, 2018), 333–440. For a view resonant with ours, see Paul Heideman, "Behind the Republican Party Crack-Up," *Catalyst*, Summer 2021, 45–101.

13. John Cassidy, "Tax Code," *New Yorker*, September 6, 2004, 70–76; Jacob S. Hacker and Paul Pierson, "Tax Politics and the Struggle over Activist Government," in *The Transformation of American Politics: Activist Government and the Rise of Conservatism*, ed. Paul Pierson and Theda Skocpol (Princeton, NJ: Princeton University Press, 2007), 256–80; Iwan Morgan, *The Age of Deficits: Presidents and Unbalanced Budgets from Jimmy Carter to George W. Bush* (Lawrence: University Press of Kansas, 2009).

14. The connection between these two kinds of counter-majoritarian politics is the central theme of Steven Levitsky and Daniel Ziblatt, *Tyranny of the Minority: Why American Democracy Reached the Breaking Point* (New York: Crown, 2023).

15. Adam Przeworski, *Democracy and the Market: Political and Economic Reforms in Eastern Europe and Latin America* (New York: Cambridge University Press, 1991); for an interview with Przeworski, see Henry Farrell, "Trump's Refusal to Respect the Vote Shatters 'All the Historically Ingrained Expectations' about American Democracy," *Washington Post* Monkey Cage, September 27, 2020, https://www.washingtonpost.com/politics/2020/09/27/trump-wont-commit-respecting-vote-no-one-knows-what-will-happen-next-few-months/.

16. Newt Gingrich, *Lessons Learned the Hard Way: A Personal Report* (New York: Harper Collins, 1998), 169. See also Matthew N. Green and Jeffrey Crouch, *Newt Gingrich: The Rise and Fall of a Party Entrepreneur* (Lawrence: University Press of Kansas, 2022), 116–64.

17. "Remarks to the Competitive Enterprise Institute's Annual Dinner," May 20, 2003, in "The Collected Speeches of Tom DeLay," box 80, folder 21, Tom DeLay Papers, University of Houston, Houston, TX. Similarly, see "Remarks by Representative Tom DeLay at the American Legislative Exchange Council," December 11, 1992, "Former Speeches," box 102, folder 43, DeLay Papers. Resistance to EPA regulations is a key theme on the right that deserves more scholarly scrutiny.

18. This lineage is not obscure. Americans for Tax Reform maintained a website tracking K Street hires and donations, which prominently mentioned a tell-all book about Coelho. "The True K Street Project Revealed," https://web.archive.org/web/20060217082538/http://www.kstreetproject.com/index.php?content=KSTProject. The book was Brooks Jackson, *Honest Graft: Big Money and the American Political Process* (New York: Alfred A. Knopf, 1988).

19. For an overview, see Nicholas Confessore, "Welcome to the Machine," *Washington Monthly*, July/August 2003, 30–37. See also Tom DeLay with Stephen Mansfield, *No Retreat, No Surrender: One American's Fight* (New York: Sentinel, 2007), 141–44.

20. Thomas B. Edsall, "Big Business's Funding Shift Boosts GOP," *Washington Post*, November 27, 2002, A1.

21. Jim VandeHei and Juliet Eilperin, "Targeting Lobbyists Pays Off for GOP," *Washington Post*, June 26, 2003, A1; Louis Jacobson, "The DeLay Factor on K Street," *National Journal*, January 4, 2003, 44–46.

22. John B. Judis, "Tammany Fall," *New Republic*, June 20, 2005, 21; Michael Weisskopf and David Maraniss, "Forging an Alliance for Deregulation," *Washington Post*, March 12, 1995, A1.

23. "The NRCC Tactical PAC Project," box 98, folder 1, DeLay Papers.

24. *Group Research Report*, September 30, 1982, 31; Nina Easton, *Gang of Five: Leaders at the Center of the Conservative Ascendancy* (New York: Touchstone, 2000), 278; John Cassidy, "The Ringleader," *New Yorker*, August 1, 2005, 42–53; Thomas Medvetz, "The Strength of Weekly Ties: Relations of Material and Symbolic Exchange in the Conservative Movement," *Politics & Society* 34 (2006): 343–68; Grover Norquist, *A U-Turn on the Road to Serfdom* (London: Institute of Economic Affairs, 2014). The federal pledge commits the signer to "ONE, oppose any and all efforts to increase the marginal income tax rates for individuals and/or businesses; and TWO, oppose any net reduction or elimination of deductions and credits, unless matched dollar for dollar by further reducing tax rates." Americans for Tax Reform, https://www.atr.org/sites/default/files/assets/2020PledgeFederal.pdf.

25. Eliza Newlin Carney, "Right on the Money," *National Journal*, October 26, 2002, 3128–32; Josh Kraushaar and Matt Vasilogambros, "Club for Growth Fueling, and Fueled by, GOP's Rightward Shift, *National Journal*, September 17, 2011, 2.

26. James Verini, "Show Him the Money," *Washington Monthly*, July–August 2010, 13.

27. Jim VandeHei, "Major Business Lobby Wins Back Its Clout by Dispensing Favors," *Wall Street Journal*, September 11, 2001, A1; Carol D. Leonnig, "Corporate Donors Fuel Chamber of Commerce's Political Power, but Secrecy Remains," *Washington Post*, October 19, 2012, A9; Peter Hamby, "Company Men," CNN, 2014, https://www.cnn.com/interactive/2014/politics/hamby-midterms-chamber-tea-party/; Danny Hakim, "Big Tobacco's Powerful Friend in Washington, *New York Times*, October 10, 2015, A1.

28. "1994 Class Retreat," January 7, 2005, "The Quotable," box 100, folder 21, DeLay Papers.

29. The redistricting saga brought Karl Rove and DeLay together and offered a preview of political hardball around voting. See Steve Bickerstaff, *Lines in the Sand: Congressional Redistricting in Texas and the Downfall of Tom DeLay* (Austin: University of Texas Press, 2007), esp. 285–313.

30. David E. Rosenbaum, "At $500 an Hour, Lobbyist's Influence Rises with G.O.P.," *New York Times*, April 3, 2002, A1; Susan Schmidt and James V. Grimaldi, "The Fast Rise and Steep Fall of Jack Abramoff," *Washington Post*, December 29, 2005, A1; Matthew Continetti, *The K Street Gang: The Rise and Fall of the Republican Machine* (New York: Doubleday, 2006).

31. Sidney M. Milkis and Jesse H. Rhodes, "George W. Bush, the Republican Party, and the 'New' American Party System," *Perspectives on Politics* 5 (2007): 461–88; more generally, see Nicholas F. Jacobs, Desmond King, and Sidney M. Milkis, "Building a Conservative State: Partisan Polarization and the Redeployment of Administrative Power," *Perspectives on Politics* 17 (2019): 453–69; Richard M. Skinner, "George W. Bush and the Partisan Presidency," *Political Science Quarterly* 123 (2008): 605–62; Daniel J. Galvin, *Presidential Party Building: Dwight D. Eisenhower to George W. Bush* (Princeton, NJ: Princeton University Press, 2010), 255–59.

32. Quoted in Naftali Bendavid, *The Thumpin': How Rahm Emanuel and the Democrats Learned to Be Ruthless and Ended the Republican Revolution* (New York: Doubleday, 2010), 10.

33. This interpretation draws on that of E. J. Dionne Jr. in *Why the Right Went Wrong*, 180–81. The best guide to the Bush-Rove vision for the GOP is Edsall, *Building Red America*. On the strategy in practice, see Tom Hamburger and Peter Wallsten, *One Party Country: The Republican Plan for Dominance in the 21st Century* (Hoboken, NJ: John Wiley and Sons, 2006). For a negative overall assessment, see William G. Mayer, *The Uses and Misuses of Politics: Karl Rove and the Bush Presidency* (Lawrence: University Press of Kansas, 2021).

34. Charlie Savage, *Takeover: The Return of the Imperial Presidency* (New York: Back Bay Books, 2007).

35. On the freighted question of how politics shaped the decision to invade Iraq, see James Mann, *The Rise of the Vulcans: The History of Bush's War Cabinet* (New York: Viking, 2004); Robert Draper, *To Start a War: How the Bush Administration Took the U.S. into Iraq* (New York: Penguin Books, 2020). On the consequences, see Spencer Ackerman, *Reign of Terror: How the 9/11 Era Destabilized America and Produced Trump* (New York: Viking, 2021).

36. Elisabeth Bumiller, "Bush Aides Set Strategy to Sell Policy on Iraq," *New York Times,* September 7, 2002, A1.

37. Karl Rove, *The Triumph of William McKinley: Why the Election of 1896 Still Matters* (New York: Simon & Schuster, 2015).

38. Karl Rove, *Courage and Consequence: My Life as a Conservative in the Fight* (New York: Threshold, 2010), 65.

39. John Saar, "GOP Probes Official as Teacher of 'Tricks,'" *Washington Post,* August 10, 1973, A4.

40. James Moore and Wayne Slater, *Bush's Brain: How Karl Rove Made George W. Bush Presidential* (Hoboken, NJ: John Wiley and Sons, 2003), esp. 111–54. See also interview with Wayne Slater for *Frontline*, "Karl Rove: The Architect," March 2, 2005, https://www.pbs.org/wgbh/pages/frontline/shows/architect/interviews/slater.html.

41. Michael Gerson, "What History Taught Karl Rove," *Washington Post,* August 17, 2007, 23.

42. Matt Bai, "The Multilevel Marketing of the Presidency," *New York Times Magazine,* April 25, 2004.

43. David Kuo, *Tempting Faith: An Inside Story of Political Seduction* (New York: Free Press, 2006), 230–31. See also Thomas B. Edsall and Alan Cooperman, "GOP Using Faith Initiative to Woo Voters, *Washington Post,* September 15, 2002, A5.

44. Note Rove's generally dim assessments of Bush-era RNC chairs in his oral history. "Karl Rove Oral History," part 2, Miller Center, University of Virginia, interview conducted November 8, 2013, https://millercenter.org/the-presidency/presidential-oral-histories/karl-rove-oral-history-part-ii.

45. See Nicholas Lemann, "The Controller," *New Yorker,* May 12, 2003, 68–83; more generally, see Edsall, *Building Red America*, 40–49.

46. Gary Gerstle, "Minorities, Multiculturalism, and the Presidency of George W. Bush," in *The Presidency of George W. Bush: A First Historical Assessment*, ed. Julian E. Zelizer (Princeton, NJ: Princeton University Press, 2010), 280; Geraldo Cadava, *The Hispanic Republican: The Shaping of an American Political Identity from Nixon to Trump* (New York: HarperCollins, 2020), 267–93.

47. Marvin Olasky, *Compassionate Conservatism: What It Is and How It Can Transform America* (New York: Free Press, 2000). For context, see Gary Gerstle, *The Rise and Fall of the Neoliberal Order: America and the World in the Free Market Era* (New York: Oxford University Press, 2022), 205–17. For a critique, see Ramesh Ponnuru, "Swallowed by Leviathan," *National Review*, September 29, 2003, 31–33. This line of argument would become key to conservative disaffection after 2006. See Viguerie, *Takeover*.

48. Kimberly J. Morgan and Andrea Louise Campbell, *The Delegated Welfare State: Medicare, Markets, and the Governance of Social Policy* (New York: Oxford University Press, 2011).

49. Richard A. Viguerie, "The Show Must Not Go On," *Washington Monthly*, October 2006, 42.

50. The phrase is from Hemmer, *Partisans*, 96. See Jeffrey M. Berry and Sarah Sobieraj, *The Outrage Industry: Political Opinion Media and the New Incivility* (New York: Oxford University Press, 2014); Hemmer, *Partisans*, 93–111, 187–208; Dannagal Goldthwaite Young, *Irony and*

Outrage: The Polarized Landscape of Rage, Fear, and Laughter in the United States (New York: Oxford University Press, 2020); Nicole Hemmer, *Messengers of the Right: Conservative Media and the Transformation of American Politics* (Philadelphia: University of Pennsylvania Press, 2016), 253–76; Jackie Calmes, "'They Don't Give a Damn about Governing': Conservative Media's Influence on the Republican Party," Shorenstein Center on Media, Politics and Public Policy Discussion Paper Series #D-96, Harvard Kennedy School, 2015.

51. "Conservative Forum," *Human Events*, April 7, 1990, 19; "Conservative Forum," *Human Events*, March 23, 1991, 18.

52. Brian Rosenwald, *Talk Radio's America: How an Industry Took Over a Political Party That Took Over the United States* (Cambridge, MA: Harvard University Press, 2019), 15–17.

53. For a clarifying audio discussion from the left, see "The Rush Limbaugh Show (w/ Nicole Hemmer)," March 9, 2021, *Know Your Enemy*, podcast, https://know-your-enemy-1682b684 .simplecast.com/episodes/rush-limbaughs-america-w-nicole-hemmer.

54. Zev Chafets, *Rush Limbaugh: An Army of One* (New York: Sentinel, 2010), 72–73.

55. Katherine Q. Seelye, "Republicans Get a Pep Talk from Rush Limbaugh," *New York Times*, December 12, 1994, A16.

56. This is the main theme of Rosenwald, *Talk Radio's America*.

57. Rush Limbaugh, "Understanding Trump's Appeal," *The Rush Limbaugh Show*, January 20, 2016, https://www.rushlimbaugh.com/daily/2016/01/20/understanding_trump_s_appeal-2/.

58. Kenneth P. Vogel and Mackenzie Weinger, "The Tea Party Radio Network," *Politico*, April 17, 2014, https://www.politico.com/story/2014/04/tea-party-radio-network-105774.

59. Jason Schwartz, "Rush Limbaugh Roars Back," *Politico*, December 21, 2018, https://www .politico.com/story/2018/12/21/rush-limbaugh-trump-comeback-1073726.

60. Jennifer Harper, "Reality Check: Talk Radio Dominates the Media," *Washington Times*, January 3, 2020, A2; "FOX News Channel Reclaims Lead Sweeping Total Day and Primetime Viewers and Demo for the Month of March," *Business Wire*, March 30, 2021, https://www .businesswire.com/news/home/20210330005946/en/FOX-News-Channel-Reclaims-Lead -Sweeping-Total-Day-and-Primetime-Viewers-and-Demo-for-the-Month-of-March.

61. In 2013, after a corporate split, Fox News became part of the Fox Corporation, still under Murdoch family control.

62. Alexander Cockburn, "Rupert Murdoch Tells All," *Village Voice*, November 29, 1976, 17.

63. Gabriel Sherman, *The Loudest Voice in the Room: How the Brilliant, Bombastic Roger Ailes Built Fox News—and Divided a Country* (New York: Random House, 2014), 175.

64. On the Wapping dispute of 1986, an important moment in British labor relations and an essential part of the Murdoch story, see Linda Melvern, *The End of the Street* (London: Methuen, 1986), esp. 1–22, 119–60; William Shawcross, *Murdoch* (New York: Simon & Schuster, 1992), 256–75; Rupert Murdoch, "The War on Technology," *City Journal*, Autumn 1990.

65. Michael Leapman, *Barefaced Cheek: The Apotheosis of Rupert Murdoch* (London: Hodder and Stoughton, 1983), 110. See also Rinker Buck, "Can the 'Post' Survive Rupert Murdoch?" *More*, November 1977, 11–23.

66. Sherman, *Loudest Voice in the Room*, 98–107; Reece Peck, *Fox Populism: Branding Conservatism as Working Class* (New York: Cambridge University Press, 2019), 27–29.

67. News Corp invested, by some estimates, $500 million in Fox News during its first half-dozen years. Its profit margins by 2020 hovered above 50 percent. Alex Barker, Anna Nicolaou, and James Fontanella-Khan, "Succession and One Last 'Big Play,'" *Financial Times*, March 2, 2021, 19.

68. Quoted in Zev Chafets, *Roger Ailes: Off Camera* (New York: Sentinel, 2013), 174.

69. On patterns in the choice of villains, see Jeffrey M. Berry, James M. Glaser and Deborah J. Schildkraut, "Race and Gender on Fox and MSNBC," *Forum* 18 (2020): 297–317.

70. On Fox News' tabloid style, see, evocatively, Charles P. Pierce, "Fox Populi," *Salon*, August 22, 2002, https://www.salon.com/2002/08/22/fox_19/.

71. In much this spirit, Ailes claimed that O'Reilly "is closer to an old blue-collar Democrat than even a Republican." Marvin Kitman, *The Man Who Would Not Shut Up: The Rise of Bill O'Reilly* (New York: St. Martin's Press, 2007), 228.

72. See Gregory J. Martin and Ali Yurukoglu, "Bias in Cable News: Persuasion and Polarization," *American Economic Review* 107 (2017): 2565–99; Elliott Ash, Sergio Galletta, Matteo Pinna, and Christopher Warshaw, "The Effect of Fox News Channel on U.S. Elections: 2000–2020," typescript, 2021, https://papers.ssrn.com/sol3/papers.cfm?abstract_id=3837457.

73. Eric Hananoki, "GOP Candidate: I'm Running because of Dick Morris' Solicitation on Fox News," *Media Matters for America*, May 18, 2010, https://www.mediamatters.org/fox-news/gop-candidate-im-running-because-of-dick-morris-solicitation-fox-news. The anecdote comports perfectly with Kevin Arceneaux, Johanna Dunaway, Martin Johnson, and Ryan J. Vander Wielen, "Strategic Candidate Entry and Congressional Elections in the Era of Fox News," *American Journal of Political Science* 64 (2020): 398–415.

74. Eric Hananoki, "Sharron Angle Suggests She Prefers to Appear on Fox Because They Let Her Raise Money," *Media Matters for America*, July 14, 2010, https://www.mediamatters.org/fox-news/sharron-angle-suggests-she-prefers-appear-fox-because-they-let-her-raise-money.

75. See Callum Borchers, "The Long, Strange History of the Donald Trump–Megyn Kelly Feud," *Washington Post*, January 27, 2016, https://www.washingtonpost.com/news/the-fix/wp/2016/01/27/the-long-strange-history-of-the-donald-trump-megyn-kelly-feud/.

76. Jeremy W. Peters and Katie Robertson, "Fox Stars Voiced Voter Fraud Doubts," *New York Times*, February 17, 2023, B1.

77. Jack Shafer, "Rupert Wins Again," *Politico*, April 18, 2023, https://www.politico.com/news/magazine/2023/04/18/rupert-murdoch-dominion-settlement-00092694.

78. Anna Nicolaou, "Lawsuit Reveals How Murdochs Agonised over Trump's Claims," *Financial Times*, March 6, 2023, 10.

79. See Rachel M. Blum, *How the Tea Party Captured the GOP: Insurgent Factions in American Politics* (Chicago: University of Chicago Press, 2020), 5, describing the Tea Party as an "insurgent faction" inside the GOP.

80. This view matches Hemmer, *Partisans*, 285–98.

81. Bob MacGuffie, "Rocking the Town Halls—Best Practices," *Right Principles*, August 6, 2009, https://web.archive.org/web/20091009003426/http://www.rightprinciples.com/memo.html.

82. For a thoughtful conservative view, see Zachary Courser, "The Tea 'Party' as a Conservative Social Movement," *Society* 49 (2012): 43–53.

83. These themes make up the core claims, respectively, of Christopher S. Parker and Matt Barreto, *Change They Can't Believe In: The Tea Party and Reactionary Politics in America* (Princeton, NJ: Princeton University Press, 2013); Theda Skocpol and Vanessa Williamson, *The Tea Party and the Remaking of Republican Conservatism* (New York: Oxford University Press, 2012).

84. Jane Mayer, "The Insiders," *New Yorker*, October 27, 2008, 38–42.

85. Andy Barr, "Palin Trashes 'Lamestream Media,'" *Politico*, November 18, 2009, https://www.politico.com/story/2009/11/palin-trashes-lamestream-media-029693. Criticism of the media is a dominant theme in her memoir: Sarah Palin, *Going Rogue: An American Life* (New York: HarperCollins, 2009).

86. For an insider account, see John Heilemann and Mark Halperin, *Game Change: Obama and the Clintons, McCain and Palin, and the Race of a Lifetime* (New York: HarperCollins, 2010), 353–76, 395–416. For a defense of Palin in the populist tradition, see Matthew Continetti, "The Palin Persuasion," *Weekly Standard*, November 16, 2009, 16–23. For a look back, see

Katie Couric and Brian Goldsmith, "What Palin Saw Clearly," *Atlantic*, October 6, 2018, https://www.theatlantic.com/ideas/archive/2018/10/what-sarah-palin-understood-about-politics/572389/.

87. See, from a Third Generation conservative who moved toward the fever swamps, Dinesh D'Souza, *The Roots of Obama's Rage* (Washington, DC: Regnery, 2010).

88. Parker and Barreto, *Change They Can't Believe In*, 197–200. For the argument, see Jerome Corsi, *Where's the Birth Certificate? The Case That Barack Obama Is Not Eligible to Be President* (New York: WND Books, 2011).

89. Berry and Sobieraj, *Outrage Industry*, 164–67; Rosenwald, *Talk Radio's America*, 184–99.

90. Jerry Markon, "'Wired' Conservatives Get the Message Out," *Washington Post*, February 1, 2010, A1.

91. Chris Good, "A Guide to the Six Major Tea Party Groups," *National Journal*, September 11, 2010, 12; Matt Bai, "The Tea Party's Not-So-Civil War," *New York Times Magazine*, January 15, 2012, 44.

92. Heath Brown, *The Tea Party Divided: The Hidden Diversity of a Maturing Movement* (Santa Barbara, CA: ABC-CLIO, 2015), 70–77; Kenneth P. Vogel, "Tea Party's Growing Money Problem," *Politico*, August 9, 2010, https://www.politico.com/story/2010/08/tea-partys-growing-money-problem-040800.

93. Viguerie, *Takeover*, 246. See also Richard Viguerie, "Tips for a Proper Tea Party," *Dallas Morning News*, May 6, 2010, https://www.dallasnews.com/opinion/commentary/2010/05/06/richard-viguerie-tips-for-a-proper-tea-party/.

94. Tim Alberta, *American Carnage: On the Front Lines of the Republican Civil War and the Rise of President Trump* (New York: HarperCollins, 2019), 76. In a sign of the incentives on the right, DeMint left the Senate in 2013 for what turned out to be an unsuccessful stint at the helm of the Heritage Foundation.

95. "Declaration of Tea Party Principles," February 24, 2010, https://nassautea.wordpress.com/2010/02/24/declaration-of-tea-party-independence/.

96. Skocpol and Williamson, *Tea Party and the Remaking of Republican Conservatism*, 155.

97. Charles Koch, "Perspective," *Discovery: The Quarterly Newsletter of Koch Companies*, October 2016, 8.

98. See Jane Mayer, "Covert Operations," *New Yorker*, August 30, 2010, 44–55; Jane Mayer, *Dark Money: The Hidden History of the Billionaires behind the Rise of the Radical Right* (New York: Doubleday, 2016); Jane Mayer, "One Koch Brother Forces the Other out of the Family Business," *New Yorker*, June 7, 2018, https://www.newyorker.com/news/news-desk/the-meaning-of-a-koch-brothers-retirement; Theda Skocpol and Alexander Hertel-Fernandez, "The Koch Network and Republican Party Extremism," *Perspectives on Politics* 14 (2016): 681–99; Hertel-Fernandez, Skocpol, and Sclar, "When Political Mega-Donors Join Forces"; Christopher Leonard, *Kochland: The Secret History of Koch Industries and Corporate Power in America* (New York: Simon & Schuster, 2019); Leah Cardamore Stokes, *Short-Circuiting Policy: Interest Groups and the Battle over Climate Policy in the American States* (New York: Oxford University Press, 2020); and, as a rejoinder, Matthew Continetti, "The Paranoid Style in Liberal Politics," *Weekly Standard*, April 4, 2011, 20–33.

99. Leonard, *Kochland*, 53–79.

100. Charles G. Koch, *Anti-Capitalism and Business* (Menlo Park, CA: Institute for Humane Studies, 1974); see also "Koch Industries, Inc. Sons make a global business flower in Kansas," *Nation's Business*, February 1970, 48–53.

101. Guy Boulton, "Politics That Can't Be Pigeonholed," *Wichita Eagle*, June 26, 1994, 12A; W. John Moore, "Wichita Pipeline," *National Journal*, May 16, 1992, 1168.

102. Leonard, *Kochland*, esp. 392–461; David Sassoon, "Koch Brothers' Political Activism Protects Their 50-Year Stake in Canadian Heavy Oils," *Inside Climate News*, May 10, 2012, https://insideclimatenews.org/news/10052012/koch-industries-brothers-tar-sands-bitumen-heavy-oil-flint-pipelines-refinery-alberta-canada/. See also Tom Hamburger, Kathleen Hennessey, Kathleen, and Neela Banerjee, "Conservative Duo Reach Seat of Power," *Los Angeles Times*, February 6, 2011, A1; Coral Davenport and Eric Lipton, "How G.O.P. Shifted on Climate Science," *New York Times*, June 4, 2017, A1. For the Koch Industries view, see "Going to Extremes," *Discovery*, July 2009, 4–5; "What's the Best Energy Policy?," *Discovery*, May 2013, 4–5.

103. Despite his libertarian streak, the CNP had awarded Charles Koch its Richard DeVos Free Enterprise Award in 1999. Anne Nelson, *Shadow Network: Media, Money, and the Secret Hub of the Radical Right* (New York: Bloomsbury, 2019), 127.

104. Hertel-Fernandez, Skocpol, and Sclar, "When Political Mega-Donors Join Forces," 139.

105. See, suggestively, Melinda Cooper, "Family Capitalism and the Small Business Insurrection," *Dissent*, Winter 2022, 97–106, and the reply from Paul Heideman, "Focus on the Family?," *Dissent*, February 9, 2022, https://www.dissentmagazine.org/online_articles/focus-on-the-family.

106. Patrick O'Connor, "Donors Who Fund Koch Brothers' Causes Say They're Tired of Being 'Demonized,'" *Wall Street Journal*, August 3, 2015. See also Daniel Schulman and Andy Kroll, "The Koch Brothers Left a Confidential Document at Their Donor Conference," *Mother Jones*, February 5, 2014, https://www.motherjones.com/politics/2014/02/koch-brothers-palm-springs-donor-list/.

107. See, among many, Mike Allen and Jim VandeHei, "The Koch Brothers' Secret Bank," *Politico*, September 11, 2013, https://www.politico.com/story/2013/09/behind-the-curtain-exclusive-the-koch-brothers-secret-bank-096669; Matea Gold, "A Koch-Tied Labyrinth of Political Spending," *Washington Post*, January 6, 2014, A1; Kenneth P. Vogel, "How the Koch Network Rivals the GOP," *Politico*, December 30, 2015, https://www.politico.com/story/2015/12/koch-brothers-network-gop-david-charles-217124; Catherine Ho, "How Americans for Prosperity Gets Out the Vote," *Washington Post*, June 3, 2016, https://www.washingtonpost.com/news/powerpost/wp/2016/06/03/how-americans-for-prosperity-gets-out-the-vote/; Ashley Parker, "Effort by Kochs Seeks to Attract Hispanic Voters," *New York Times*, November 27, 2017, A1.

108. Skocpol and Hertel-Fernandez, "Koch Network and Republican Party Extremism," 687–92.

109. Quoted in Matt Fuller, "House Freedom Caucus Looks to Be a Force—in Leadership and Lawmaking," *Roll Call*, February 4, 2015, https://www.rollcall.com/2015/02/04/house-freedom-caucus-looks-to-be-a-force-in-leadership-and-lawmaking-2/.

110. David M. Herszenhorn, "Conservatives Want to Change More Than Speaker," *New York Times*, October 8, 2015, A20; Ryan Lizza, "A House Divided," *New Yorker*, December 14, 2015, 30–37.

111. Matthew N. Green, *Legislative Hardball: The House Freedom Caucus and the Power of Threat-Making in Congress* (New York: Cambridge University Press, 2019); Ruth Bloch Rubin, "Organizing at the Extreme: Hardline Strategy and Institutional Design," *Congress & the Presidency* 49 (2022): 1–30.

112. Fred Barnes, "Young Guns of the House GOP," *Weekly Standard*, October 1, 2007, 10–15; Eric Cantor, Paul Ryan, and Kevin McCarthy, *Young Guns: A New Generation of Conservative Leaders* (New York: Threshold, 2010).

113. See, for example, Jennifer Steinhauer, "Ryan Now Faces Tea Party Forces He Helped Unleash," *New York Times*, March 3, 2016, A16.

114. Stephen Collinson, "McCarthy Is Speaker, but the Extremists Hold the Power," CNN, January 9, 2023, https://www.cnn.com/2023/01/09/politics/kevin-mccarthy-house-speaker-test/index.html.

115. Catie Edmondson, "Speaker's Union with Firebrand May Shape G.O.P.," *New York Times*, January 23, 2023, A1.

116. Bryan T. Gervais and Irwin L. Morris, *Reactionary Republicanism: How the Tea Party in the House Paved the Way for Trump's Victory* (New York: Oxford University Press, 2019).

117. John Boehner, *On the House: A Washington Memoir* (New York: Macmillan, 2021), 172.

118. Alberta, *American Carnage*, 417.

119. Brody Mullins and Alex Leary, "Washington's Biggest Lobbyist Gets Shut Out," *Wall Street Journal*, May 3, 2019, A1.

120. Matthew Boyle, "Exclusive—Kevin McCarthy: Chamber of Commerce 'Left' Republican Party 'a Long Time Ago,' Not Welcome Back, *Breitbart*, January 11, 2022, https://www.breitbart.com/politics/2022/01/11/exclusive-kevin-mccarthy-the-chamber-of-commerce-left-republican-party-a-long-time-ago-not-welcome-back/.

121. Compare the Chamber's self-presentation of its work with that of its adversaries at the left-leaning Constitutional Accountability Center. "U.S. Chamber of Commerce Litigation Center," https://www.chamberlitigation.com/; Brian R. Frazelle, "A Quiet Year for Business at the Supreme Court, with One Huge Exception: 2021–2022 Term," Constitutional Accountability Center, July 11, 2022, https://www.theusconstitution.org/think_tank/a-quiet-year-for-business-at-the-supreme-court-with-one-huge-exception-2021-2022-term/. For more general implications, see Nikolas Bowie, "Antidemocracy," *Harvard Law Review* 160 (2021): 160–219.

122. On policy change and its limits, compare Jacob M. Grumbach, *Laboratories against Democracy: How National Parties Transformed State Politics* (Princeton, NJ: Princeton University Press, 2022); Matt Grossmann, *Red State Blues: How the Conservative Revolution Stalled in the States* (New York: Cambridge University Press, 2019). On the contours of power, see Alexander Hertel-Fernandez, *State Capture: How Conservative Activists, Big Businesses, and Wealthy Donors Reshaped the American States—and the Nation* (New York: Oxford University Press, 2019).

123. David Daley, "How to Get Away with Gerrymandering," *Slate*, October 2, 2019, https://slate.com/news-and-politics/2019/10/alec-meeting-gerrymandering-audio-recording.html.

124. Jane Mayer, "State for Sale," *New Yorker*, October 10, 2011, 90–103; Matea Gold, "Magnate Now the Official State Money Man," *Washington Post*, July 20, 2014, A1.

125. On unions, the key document was a blueprint from a Bradley-funded think tank. Brian Fraley, "The Time Is Now to Reform Labor Laws Which Threaten Our State's Future," MacIver Institute, November 24, 2010, https://www.maciverinstitute.com/2010/11/the-time-is-now-to-reform-labor-laws-which-threaten-our-states-future/. See also Daniel Bice, Bill Glauber, and Ben Poston, "Conservative Empire Grew from Local Roots," *Milwaukee Journal-Sentinel*, November 20, 2011, A1. On Bradley's election funding, see Jane Mayer, "The Big Money behind the Big Lie," *New Yorker*, August 9, 2021, 30–41.

126. Bob Woodward, *Rage* (New York: Simon & Schuster, 2020), 264.

127. For a contrasting view, see Marty Cohen, David Karol, Hans Noel, and John Zaller, "Party versus Faction in the Reformed Presidential Nominating System, *PS: Political Science & Politics* 49 (2016): 701–8; Hans Noel, "Ideological Factions in the Republican and Democratic Parties," *Annals of the American Academy of Political and Social Science* 667 (2016): 166–88.

128. See Michael Kazin, "Trump and American Populism," *Foreign Affairs*, November 2016, 17–24.

129. As a proximate matter, the last man standing as an alternative in the field was Senator Ted Cruz of Texas, who had few friends at the top of the GOP. And the Republicans'

winner-take-all rules benefited Trump in ways that the Democrats' strict proportional allocation and superdelegates would not have. But hanging too much on such contingencies, and on the mechanics of coordination more generally, risks missing the forest for the trees. See William G. Mayer, "Was the Process to Blame? Why Hillary Clinton and Donald Trump Won Their Parties' Presidential Nominations," *New York University Law Review* 93 (2018): 759–85; Jonathan Woon, Sean Craig, Amanda Leifson, and Matthew Tarpey, "Trump Is Not a (Condorcet) Loser! Primary Voters' Preferences and the 2016 Republican Presidential Nomination," *PS: Political Science & Politics* 53 (2020): 407–12.

130. On the timing of endorsements, see Zachary Albert and David J. Barney, "The Party Reacts: The Strategic Nature of Endorsements of Donald Trump," *American Politics Research* 47 (2019): 1239–1358.

131. Byron York, "GOP Fear and Loathing in New Hampshire," *Washington Examiner*, January 25, 2016, https://www.washingtonexaminer.com/byron-york-gop-fear-and-loathing-in-new-hampshire/article/2581329.

132. Republican National Committee, "Growth & Opportunity Project," March 18, 2013, https://s3.documentcloud.org/documents/624293/republican-national-committees-growth-and.pdf.

133. Roger Stone, *The Making of the President 2016: How Donald Trump Orchestrated a Revolution* (New York: Skyhorse Publishing, 2017), xi–xiii. For a classic ethnography of a neighborhood where Fred Trump owned apartment buildings, see Jonathan Rieder, *Canarsie: The Jews and Italians of Brooklyn against Liberalism* (Cambridge, MA: Harvard University Press, 1985).

134. For a similar observation from a movement conservative, see Continetti, *The Right*, 368.

135. Julia Hahn, "Phyllis Schlafly Makes the Case for President Trump," *Breitbart*, January 10, 2016, https://www.breitbart.com/big-government/2016/01/10/phyllis-schlafly-makes-the-case-for-president-trump/.

136. Meena Venkataramanan, "Trump Is the 'Most Effective Uprooter of Liberalism,'" ABC News, June 27, 2018: https://abcnews.go.com/Politics/trump-effective-uprooter-liberalism-newt-gingrich-talks-gop/story?id=56200932.

137. Jan-Werner Müller, *What Is Populism?* (Philadelphia: University of Pennsylvania Press, 2016); Federico Finchelstein, *From Fascism to Populism in History* (Berkeley: University of California Press, 2017).

138. See Jeffrey D. Broxmeyer, "A Political Machine for the 21st Century," *Public Seminar*, August 22, 2019, https://publicseminar.org/essays/political-machine-of-the-21st-century/.

139. Daniel J. Galvin, "Party Domination and Base Mobilization: Donald Trump and Republican Party Building in a Polarized Era," *Forum* 18 (2020): 135–68.

140. Janet Hook, "The 'Era of Trump' Remakes the GOP," *Wall Street Journal*, August 28, 2018, A1; Jonathan Martin, "At State Level, Just One Issue Counts: Trump," *New York Times*, July 31, 2018, A1.

141. Aaron Blake, "As Trump Departs, His Extremes Live on in State GOPs," *Washington Post*, January 25, 2021, https://www.washingtonpost.com/politics/2021/01/25/trump-departs-his-extremes-live-state-gops/.

142. Galvin, "Party Domination and Base Mobilization," esp. 153–55. For details, see Maggie Haberman and Annie Karni, "Trump Tightens His Hold on the G.O.P. Convention to Stifle Dissent," *New York Times*, October 3, 2019, A15; Jonathan Swan and Margaret Talev, "How Trump Wins in 2020," *Axios*, December 14, 2019, https://www.axios.com/how-trump-wins-in-2020-68c9a4de-1274-418c-8115-7e031e17e83c.html.

143. See, generally, Perry Bacon Jr., "The Trumpiest Republicans Are at the State and Local Levels—Not in D.C.," *FiveThirtyEight*, February 16, 2021, https://fivethirtyeight.com/features/the-trumpiest-republicans-are-at-the-state-and-local-levels-not-in-d-c/. For particulars, see Elaina Plott, "The After Party" *New York Times Magazine*, May 9, 2021; Jason Silverstein, "Michigan GOP

Chair Seen on Video Calling State's Female Leaders 'Witches' and Joking about Assassinating Republicans Who Voted for Trump Impeachment," CBS News, March 27, 2021, https://www.cbsnews.com/news/ron-weiser-michgan-republican-party-chair-comments-video/.

144. Hank Stephenson and Jennifer Medina, "Arizona G.O.P. Rebukes 3 Influential Figures," *New York Times*, January 24, 2021, A15.

145. Shane Goldmacher, "Trump Steered Supporters into Unwitting Donations," *New York Times*, April 4, 2021, A1.

146. Alex Isenstadt and Meridith McGraw, "Trump Political Groups Have over $100 Million in the Bank," *Politico*, July 31, 2021, https://www.politico.com/news/2021/07/31/trump-political-groups-82-million-501958.

147. Sarakshi Rai, "Trump Asking Supporters to Fund New Plane after Emergency Landing," *The Hill*, March 10, 2022, https://thehill.com/homenews/administration/597673-trump-asking-supporters-to-fund-new-plane-after-emergency-landing.

148. Annie Linskey, "The Koch Brothers (and Their Friends) Want President Trump's Tax Cut. Very Badly," *Boston Globe*, October 14, 2017, A1.

149. Courtney Weaver and Sam Lerner, "New Donors Boost Hardline Republicans," *Financial Times*, March 6, 2023, 4.

150. Stephanie Saul and Danny Hakim, "Power Couple Pumps Millions to the Hard Right," *New York Times*, June 8, 2018, A1.

151. The Koch network has made moves to soften its image in recent years, even predating Trump's election. The ultimate impact of the new approach remains unclear. See Mayer, *Dark Money*, 357–61; Charles Koch, *Believe in People: Bottom-Up Solutions for a Top-Down World*, with Brian Hooks (New York: St. Martin's Press, 2020), 204–32. For a critique from a former staffer, see Adam Kissel, "New Koch," *American Mind*, April 26, 2023, https://americanmind.org/features/new-koch/.

152. Yael Halon, "Ben Shapiro Explains Why He'll Vote for Trump This Time Around," Fox News, October 20, 2020, https://www.foxnews.com/media/ben-shapiro-why-voting-trump-in-2020.

153. Jonathan Swan, "Graham Deals with Trump 'Dark Side' to 'Harness the Magic,'" *Axios*, March 7, 2021, https://www.axios.com/lindsey-graham-trump-destroy-republican-party-613ce2af-8914-4764-9492-80a8424c628c.html.

154. Jim Jordan and Mark Meadows, "No More Excuses, Republicans," *The Hill*, January 11, 2017, https://thehill.com/blogs/congress-blog/politics/313781-no-more-excuses-republicans.

155. "Resolution Regarding the Republican Party Platform," Republican National Committee, August 24, 2020, https://www.presidency.ucsb.edu/documents/resolution-regarding-the-republican-party-platform.

156. See Annie Lowrey, "The Party of No Content," *Atlantic*, August 24, 2020, https://www.theatlantic.com/ideas/archive/2020/08/party-no-content/615607/.

157. Richard L. Hasen, *Election Meltdown: Dirty Tricks, Distrust, and the Threat to American Democracy* (New Haven, CT: Yale University Press, 2020); Richard L. Hasen, "Identifying and Minimizing the Risk of Election Subversion and Stolen Elections in the Contemporary United States," *Harvard Law Review Forum* 135 (2022): 265–301.

158. Compare, from eminent historians, Robert O. Paxton, "I've Hesitated to Call Donald Trump a Fascist. Until Now," *Newsweek*, January 11, 2021, https://www.newsweek.com/robert-paxton-trump-fascist-1560652; Richard J. Evans, "Demons of the Present," *New Statesman*, January 15, 2021, 33–35.

159. "Transcript of Trump's Speech at Rally before US Capitol Riot," Associated Press, January 13, 2021, https://apnews.com/article/election-2020-joe-biden-donald-trump-capitol-siege-media-e79eb5164613d6718e9f4502eb471f27.

160. Michael M. Grynbaum and John Koblin, "Newsmax Rises Out of Obscurity After Refusing to Call Election," *New York Times*, November 23, 2020, B1; Rachel Abrams, "It's One America News, but It Acts Like Trump TV," *New York Times*, April 20, 2021, B1.

161. Dana Canedy and Dexter Filkins, "A Wild Day in Miami, with an End to Recounting, and Democrats' Going to Court," *New York Times*, November 23, 2000, A31; Jake Tapper, *Down and Dirty: The Plot to Steal the Presidency* (Boston: Little, Brown, 2001), 254–81; Jeffrey Toobin, "The Dirty Trickster," *New Yorker*, June 2, 2008, 54–63.

162. For voting rules by state, see National Conference of State Legislatures, "Voter ID Laws," https://www.ncsl.org/research/elections-and-campaigns/voter-id.aspx. See also Keith G. Bentele and Erin E. O'Brien, "Jim Crow 2.0? Why States Consider and Adopt Restrictive Voter Access Policies," *Perspectives on Politics* 11 (2013): 1088–1116; William D. Hicks, Seth C. McKee, Mitchell D. Sellers, and Daniel A. Smith, "A Principle or a Strategy? Voter Identification Laws and Partisan Competition in the American States," *Political Research Quarterly* 68 (2015): 18–33. Voter ID laws, whatever their effects on the margin, have not led to large-scale declines in voter turnout. See Justin Grimmer, Eitan Hersh, Marc Meredith, Jonathan Mummolo, and Clayton Nall, "Obstacles to Estimating Voter ID Laws' Effect on Turnout," *Journal of Politics* 80 (2018): 1045–51. On reconciling these findings with concerns about voter suppression, see Emily Rong Zhang, "Questioning Questions in the Law of Democracy: What the Debate over Voter ID Laws' Effects Teaches about Asking the Right Questions," *UCLA Law Review* 69 (2022): 1028–74. For historical context, see David A. Bateman, "Race, Party, and American Voting Rights," *Forum* 14 (2016): 39–65.

163. For examples, see John Fund and Hans von Spakovsky, *Who's Counting: How Fraudsters and Bureaucrats Put Your Vote at Risk* (New York: Encounter Books, 2012); John Fund and Hans von Spakovsky, *Our Broken Elections: How the Left Changed the Way You Vote* (New York: Encounter Books, 2021); "Stealing Your Vote," Fox News, April 22, 2012, https://www.youtube.com/watch?v=03helhoBVMk; Republican National Lawyers Association, "Vote Fraud Survey," https://web.archive.org/web/20121116022658/http://www.rnla.org/survey.asp. For critiques, see Lorraine C. Minnite, *The Myth of Voter Fraud* (Ithaca, NY: Cornell University Press, 2010); Richard L. Hasen: *The Voting Wars: From Florida 2000 to the Next Election Meltdown* (New Haven, CT: Yale University Press, 2012), 41–73.

164. In the face of multiple legal challenges, Trump shuttered the panel six months after its first meeting. Hasen, *Election Meltdown*, 15–46.

165. "Urgent Letter to President Trump—Chaos and Fraud Central Elements of Biden-Harris Campaign," ConservativeHQ, August 17, 2020, http://www.conservativehq.com/article/33097-urgent-letter-president-trump-chaos-and-fraud-central-elements-biden-harris-campaign/.

166. Richard M. Valelly, *The Two Reconstructions: The Struggle for Black Enfranchisement* (Chicago: University of Chicago Press, 2004).

167. John Fund and Hans von Spakovsky, *Obama's Enforcer: Eric Holder's Justice Department* (New York: Broadside Books, 2014), 72.

168. Abigail Thernstrom, *Voting Rights—and Wrongs: The Elusive Quest for Racially Fair Elections* (Washington, DC: AEI Press, 2009).

169. Hans von Spakovsky, "Debunking the Left's Propaganda on Voting," *Daily Signal*, September 30, 2021, https://www.dailysignal.com/2021/09/30/debunking-the-lefts-propaganda-on-voting/.

170. Jamelle Bouie, "Politics," in *The 1619 Project: A New Origin Story*, ed. Nikole Hannah-Jones, Caitlin Roper, Ilena Silverman, and Jake Silverstein (New York: One World, 2021), 195–210.

171. Jonathan Weisman and Reid J. Epstein, "G.O.P. Calls Riot 'Legitimate Political Discourse,'" *New York Times*, February 5, 2022, A1; Holmes Lybrand and Tara Subramaniam, "Fact Check: Republicans Continue to Push False Narratives about January 6," CNN, May 12, 2021,

https://www.cnn.com/2021/05/12/politics/republican-falsehoods-january-6-insurrection
-fact-check/index.html.

172. Oregon GOP tweet, January 19, 2021, https://twitter.com/Oregon_GOP/status
/1351656484392759297/photo/1.

173. Aaron Blake, "Liz Cheney's Historic Margin of Defeat," *Washington Post*, August 17, 2022,
https://www.washingtonpost.com/politics/2022/08/17/liz-cheney-historic-defeat/.

174. Josh Dawsey and Michael Scherer, "Trump Asserts Dominance in GOP, Presses 2020
Focus," *Washington Post*, October 15, 2021, A4.

175. Mollie Hemingway, *Rigged: How the Media, Big Tech, and the Democrats Seized Our Elections* (Washington, DC: Regnery, 2021), xv. Similarly, see Fund and von Spakovsky, *Our Broken
Elections*.

176. Eastman memo at https://cdn.cnn.com/cnn/2021/images/09/20/eastman.memo.pdf
. See also Richard L. Hasen, "The Legal Minds Who Tried to Overturn the Election for Trump
Are Being Welcomed Back into Polite Society," *Slate*, September 1, 2021, https://slate.com/news
-and-politics/2021/09/trump-john-eastman-2020-election-law.html; J. Christian Adams, "The
Mob Attacking Trump's Lawyer Is More Dangerous Than Anything John Eastman Is Accused
of Doing," *PJ Media*, October 6, 2021, https://pjmedia.com/jchristianadams/2021/10/06
/trump-derangement-syndrome-endangers-the-right-to-counsel-n1522281. For a back-and-
forth between a more traditional conservative and Eastman, see Joseph M. Bessette, "A Critique
of the Eastman Memos," *Claremont Review of Books*, Fall 2021, 16–26; John C. Eastman, "Constitutional Statesmanship," *Claremont Review of Books*, Fall 2021, 27–35.

177. On Claremont, founded by Lincoln scholar and Goldwater speechwriter Harry Jaffa,
and its move to the extreme, see Laura K. Field, "The Decay at the Claremont Institute Continues," *Bulwark*, April 21, 2022, https://www.thebulwark.com/the-decay-at-the-claremont
-institute-continues/; Marc Fisher and Isaac Stanley-Becker, "Think Tank Is Facing Blowback
over Jan. 6," *Washington Post*, July 25, 2022, A1. On its worldview, see Publius Decius Mus
[Michael Anton], "The Flight 93 Election, *Claremont Review of Books*, September 5, 2016, http://
www.claremont.org/crb/basicpage/the-flight-93-election/; Michael Anton, *The Stakes: America
at the Point of No Return* (Washington, DC: Regnery, 2020); Glenn Elmers, "'Conservatism' Is
No Longer Enough," *American Mind*, March 24, 2021, https://americanmind.org/salvo/why
-the-claremont-institute-is-not-conservative-and-you-shouldnt-be-either. For a broad view
with slightly less heated rhetoric, see Charles Kesler, *Crisis of the Two Constitutions: The Rise,
Decline, and Recovery of American Greatness* (New York: Encounter Books, 2021).

178. Jessica Pishko, "Here's the Secret 'Sheriff Fellowship' Curriculum from the Country's
Most Prominent MAGA Think Tank," *Slate*, September 21, 2022, https://slate.com/news-and
-politics/2022/09/claremont-institute-secret-sheriff-fellowship-curriculum-revealed.html.

179. For a vivid example, see the wargame simulated by the Claremont Institute and the
Texas Public Policy Foundation, "79 Days to Inauguration Taskforce Report," October 20, 2020,
https://www.claremont.org/79daysreport.pdf.

180. Rachel Bovard, "What the New Right Must Do Next Time It Earns Power," *Federalist*,
November 4, 2021, https://thefederalist.com/2021/11/04/national-conservatism-must-prioritize
-fights-over-american-values-not-just-legislation/. For reportage, see David Brooks, "The Ter-
rifying Future of the American Right," *Atlantic*, November 18, 2021, https://www.theatlantic.com
/ideas/archive/2021/11/scary-future-american-right-national-conservatism-conference
/620746/; Sam Adler-Bell, "The Other Radical Youth," *New Republic*, December 2021, 38–45.
For a broadly integralist appraisal, see Gladden Pappin, "From Conservatism to Postliberalism:
The Right after 2020," *American Affairs*, Fall 2020, 174–90.

181. See, suggestively, Daniel Martinez HoSang and Joseph E. Lowndes, *Producers, Parasites,
Patriots: Race and the New Right-Wing Politics of Precarity* (Minneapolis: University of

Minnesota Press, 2019); Gabriel Winant, "We Live in a Society," *n+1*, December 12, 2020, http:// nplusonemag.com/online-only/online-only/we-live-in-a-society/.

182. Quoted in Winant, "We Live in a Society." Original source is Arelis R. Hernández and Brittney Martin, "In Texas's Overwhelmingly Latino Rio Grande Valley, a Shift toward Trump," *Washington Post*, November 10, 2020, A16. See also Jennifer Medina, "Trump-Style Grievance Lures Hispanic Voters," *New York Times*, March 1, 2022, A17. For background, see Cadava, *Hispanic Republican*.

183. Alayna Treene, "Rubio Says the GOP Needs to Reset after 2020," *Axios*, November 11, 2020, https://www.axios.com/rubio-gop-reset-trump-872340a7-4c75-4c2b-9261-9612c 590ee14.html.

184. Marco Rubio, "I Support Union Drive at Amazon," *USA Today*, March 15, 2021, A7. The five House Republicans who voted for the Democrats' big pro-labor bill in 2021 were all moderates with vestigial ties to the building trades, not coalition-brokers for a new workers' bloc. Roll call on passage of Protecting the Right to Organize Act, March 9, 2021, https://clerk.house.gov /Votes/202170.

185. Compare Park MacDougald, "The New American Millennial Right," *Tablet*, February 5, 2020, https://www.tabletmag.com/sections/news/articles/the-new-millennial-american -right; Daniel Luban, "The Not-So-Strange Death of Right Populism," *Dissent*, Winter 2021, 45–49.

186. Russell Muirhead and Nancy L. Rosenblum, *A Lot of People Are Saying: The New Conspiracism and the Assault on Democracy* (Princeton, NJ: Princeton University Press, 2019), 87. For meditations on this theme from a leading Straussian, see Harvey C. Mansfield, "Parties vs. Factions in America," Hoover Institution, September 21, 2017, https://www.hoover.org /research/parties-vs-factions-america.

187. On the lack of a policy agenda, see Jeff Stein and Yeganeh Torbati, "Heritage Foundation Adjusts to Keep Up in Age of Trump," *Washington Post*, February 8, 2022, A14.

188. Bovard, "What the New Right Must Do Next Time It Earns Power."

189. On similar themes, see Mary Ziegler, *Dollars for Life: The Anti-Abortion Movement and the Fall of the Republican Establishment* (New Haven, CT: Yale University Press, 2022).

Chapter Nine: Toward Party Renewal

1. Daryl J. Levinson and Richard H. Pildes, "Separation of Parties, Not Powers," *Harvard Law Review* 119 (2006): 2311–86.

2. According to Harvard Business School professor Michael Porter and Centrist Project board member Katherine Gehl, "Solutions are policies that address important problems or expand opportunities for citizens. A solution is a policy that actually works and makes things better in practice." Katherine M. Gehl and Michael E. Porter, *The Politics Industry: How Political Innovation Can Break Partisan Gridlock and Save Our Democracy* (Boston: Harvard Business Review Press, 2020), 83.

3. This tendency manifests itself in the output of elite commentators as well as splashy efforts like Americans Elect and No Labels. Thomas Friedman, "Third Party Rising," *New York Times*, October 3, 2010, WK8; Jim VandeHei, "Bring on a Third Party Candidate," *Wall Street Journal*, April 26, 2016, A13.

4. Contemporary anti-party advocates celebrate ranked-choice voting. Though Lee Drutman endorses the reform and attacks the two-party duopoly, his call for *more* rather than *no* parties and insistence that "the anti-party tradition belongs in the dustbin of history" place him squarely outside the anti-party strand. Lee Drutman, *Breaking the Two-Party Doom Loop: The Case for Multiparty Democracy in America* (New York: Oxford University Press, 2020), 14.

5. Richard H. Pildes, "Romanticizing Democracy, Political Fragmentation, and the Decline of Government," *Yale Law Journal* 124 (2014): 804–52; Nathaniel Persily, "Stronger Parties as a Solution to Polarization," in *Solutions to Political Polarization in America*, ed. Nathaniel Persily (New York: Cambridge University Press, 2015), 123–35; Jonathan Rauch, *Political Realism: How Hacks, Machines, Big Money, and Back-Room Deals Can Strengthen American Democracy* (Washington, DC: Brookings Institution, 2015); Raymond J. La Raja and Bryan F. Schaffner, *Campaign Finance and Political Polarization: When Purists Prevail* (Ann Arbor: University of Michigan Press, 2015).

6. Mark Schmitt, "Democratic Romanticism and Its Critics," *Democracy: A Journal of Ideas*, Spring 2015, https://democracyjournal.org/magazine/36/democratic-romanticism-and-its-critics/.

7. On parties' civic functions, see Sidney M. Milkis, *Political Parties and Constitutional Government: Remaking American Democracy* (Baltimore: Johns Hopkins University Press, 1999), esp. 13–41; Nancy L. Rosenblum, *On the Side of the Angels: An Appreciation of Parties and Partisanship* (Princeton, NJ: Princeton University Press, 2008); Russell Muirhead, *The Promise of Party in a Polarized Age* (Cambridge, MA: Harvard University Press, 2014).

8. For a notably similar set of prescriptions, see Tabatha Abu El-Haj and Didi Kuo, "Associational Party-Building: A Path to Rebuilding Democracy," *Columbia Law Review* 122 (2022): 127–76.

9. Theda Skocpol, *Diminished Democracy: From Membership to Management in American Civic Life* (Norman: University of Oklahoma Press, 2003), 36–40, 254–94; Robert D. Putnam, *Bowling Alone: The Collapse and Revival of American Community* (New York: Simon & Schuster, 2000); Margaret Weir and Marshall Ganz, "Reconnecting People and Politics," in *The New Majority: Toward a Popular Progressive Politics*, ed. Stanley B. Greenberg and Theda Skocpol (New Haven, CT: Yale University Press, 2008), 149–71; Anton Jäger, "From Bowling Alone to Posting Alone," *Jacobin*, Fall 2022, 48–61.

10. Josh Pacewicz, *Partisans and Partners: The Politics of the Post-Keynesian Society* (Chicago: University of Chicago Press, 2016); Lainey Newman and Theda Skocpol, *Rust Belt Union Blues: Why Working-Class Voters Are Turning Away from the Democratic Party* (New York: Columbia University Press, 2023); Stephanie Ternullo, *Becoming Partisans: How Place Makes Politics in the American Heartland* (Princeton, NJ: Princeton University Press, 2024).

11. For a series of case studies of effective community-level political organizing, see Hahrie Han, Elizabeth McKenna, and Michelle Oyakawa, *Prisms of the People: Power & Organizing in Twenty-First Century America* (Chicago: University of Chicago Press, 2021).

12. For a sampling of media coverage, see David McGrath Schwartz, "Rebecca Lambe: The Force behind Democrats' State Success," *Las Vegas Sun*, August 9, 2009, https://lasvegassun.com/news/2009/aug/09/rebecca-lambe-force-behind-state-democrats-success/; Molly Ball, "Comeback: How Did Reid Do It?," *Politico*, November 4, 2010, https://www.politico.com/story/2010/11/comeback-how-did-reid-do-it-044714; Ella Nilsen, "Harry Reid Is Still a Democratic Kingmaker," *Vox*, October 11, 2018, https://www.vox.com/policy-and-politics/2018/10/11/17864706/harry-reid-jacky-rosen-dean-heller-nevada; Michelle L. Price and Nicholas Riccardi, "Reid Machine Keeps Humming in Nevada, Even in His Retirement," Associated Press, November 18, 2018, https://apnews.com/9e580a5d4c274084afa36bf39795d8e4.

13. For a contrasting report on the notably dysfunctional New York Democratic Party, see Ross Barkan, "'What the Hell Are We Even Doing?,'" *New York Times Magazine*, February 26, 2023.

14. Rebecca Lambe, interview by authors, Las Vegas, Nevada, December 11, 2019.

15. Alana Mounce, telephone interview by author, December 16, 2019.

16. Lambe, interview by authors.

17. D. Taylor, interview by authors, Las Vegas, Nevada, December 10, 2019.

18. Ruben J. Garcia, "Politically Engaged Unionism: The Culinary Workers in Las Vegas," in *The Cambridge Handbook of U.S. Labor Law for the Twenty-First Century*, ed. Richard Bales and Charlotte Garden (New York: Cambridge University Press, 2020), 373–80. See also Steven Greenhouse, *Beaten Down, Worked Up: The Past, Present, and Future of American Labor* (New York: Alfred A. Knopf, 2019), 33–45; Hamilton Nolan, "How the Mighty Culinary Union Survived the Apocalypse," *In These Times*, December 15, 2021, https://inthesetimes.com/article/vegas-culinary-union-pandemic-shutdown-workers. On immigration and ethnicity in a fast-growing city, see Jerry L. Simich and Thomas C. Wright, eds., *The Peoples of Las Vegas: One City, Many Faces* (Reno: University of Nevada Press, 2005); Jerry L. Simich and Thomas C. Wright, eds., *More Peoples of Las Vegas: One City, Many Faces* (Reno: University of Nevada Press, 2010).

19. Taylor, interview by authors.

20. Geoconda Argüello-Kline, interview by authors, Las Vegas, Nevada, December 11, 2019.

21. Garcia, "Politically Engaged Unionism," 373.

22. Tim Murphy, "What the Democratic Party Can Learn from Nevada Casino Workers, Cooks, and Housekeepers," *Mother Jones*, Nov./Dec. 2018, https://www.motherjones.com/politics/2018/10/what-the-democratic-party-can-learn-from-nevada-casino-workers-cooks-and-housekeepers/.

23. Holly Otterbein, "Sanders Supporters Took Over the Nevada Democratic Party. It's Not Going Well." *Politico*, February 25, 2023, https://www.politico.com/news/2023/02/25/bernie-world-nevada-democratic-party-00084426; Las Vegas Democratic Socialists of America, "LVDSA Statement on Nevada State Democratic Party Election," February 13, 2023, https://lvdsa.org/2023/02/13/dempartyelection/.

24. Jacob Solis, "Assemblywoman Announces 'Unity' Bid to Lead Divided State Democratic Party," *Nevada Independent*, February 7, 2023, https://thenevadaindependent.com/article/assemblywoman-announces-unity-bid-to-lead-divided-state-democratic-party; Gabby Birenbaum and Jacob Solis, "Ahead of 2024 Election, NV Dems Leadership Race Heightens Tension between Establishment, Progressives," *Nevada Independent*, March 3, 2023, https://thenevadaindependent.com/article/ahead-of-2024-election-nv-dems-leadership-race-heightens-tension-between-establishment-progressives; Jacob Solis, "Monroe-Moreno Elected NV Dems Chair, Ousts Democratic Socialist Incumbent," *Nevada Independent*, March 4, 2023, https://thenevadaindependent.com/article/monroe-moreno-elected-nv-dems-chair-ousts-democratic-socialist-incumbent.

25. Carl Hulse, "'The Reid Machine' Rolls On," *New York Times*, January 25, 2023, A12.

26. Douglas D. Roscoe and Shannon Jenkins, *Local Party Organizations in the Twenty-First Century* (Albany: State University of New York Press, 2016); David Doherty, Conor M. Dowling, and Michael G. Miller, *Small Power: How Local Parties Shape Elections* (New York: Oxford University Press, 2022).

27. Joseph Anthony, "Party Blight in Rural Missouri: Causes and Consequences of Organizational Decline" (PhD diss., University of Missouri–St. Louis, 2019), 119.

28. On "field" in political campaigns, see Rasmus Kleis Nielsen, *Ground Wars: Personalized Communication in Political Campaigns* (Princeton, NJ: Princeton University Press, 2012); Joshua P. Darr and Matthew S. Levendusky, "Relying on the Ground Game: The Placement and Effect of Campaign Field Offices," *American Politics Research* 42 (2014): 529–48.

29. See Kenneth T. Andrews, Hahrie Han, Alexander Hertel-Fernandez, Sarah James, Lara Putnam, Daniel Schlozman, Theda Skocpol, Caroline Tervo, Vanessa Williamson, and Michael Zoorob, "How to Revitalize America's Local Political Parties," Scholars Strategy Network, January 30, 2019, https://scholars.org/contribution/how-revitalize-americas-local-political-parties;

Lara Putnam, Daniel Schlozman, Tabatha Abu El-Haj, Joseph Anthony, Jacob M. Grumbach, Alexander Hertel-Fernandez, Adam Seth Levine, and Caroline Tervo, "Local Political Parties as Networks: A Guide to Self-Assessment," Scholars Strategy Network, May 19, 2020, https://scholars.org/contribution/local-political-parties-guide; Abu El-Haj and Kuo, "Associational Party-Building," 151–55; and, generally, Eitan Hersh, *Politics Is for Power: How to Move Beyond Political Hobbyism, Take Action, and Make Real Change* (New York: Scribner, 2020).

30. Even in an age of party-organizational sclerosis at the local level, active counterexamples do exist. Eitan Hersh highlights one such case, a "neighborhood leader" program initiated by the Washington County Democrats in Oregon starting in 2006. Hersh, *Politics Is for Power*, 147–50. For the type of community-oriented activity that parties might undertake, see Donald P. Green and Oliver McClellan, "The Effects of Election Festivals on Voter Turnout: A Field Experiment Conducted During a Presidential Election," July 17, 2017, https://papers.ssrn.com/sol3/papers.cfm?abstract_id=2999305.

31. George Washington Plunkitt, *Plunkitt of Tammany Hall: A Series of Very Plain Talks on Very Practical Politics*, ed. William L. Riordon (New York: McClure, Phillips, 1905; New York: E. P. Dutton, 1963), 91–93.

32. On state parties' integrative role, see Raymond J. La Raja and Jonathan Rauch, "The State of State Parties—and How Strengthening Them Can Improve Our Politics," Brookings Institution, March 2016, 2–5.

33. As an operative observed of state Democratic parties, "The reason presidential candidates show up to their Jefferson-Jackson dinner is because of the voter file." Kevin Robillard and Daniel Marans, "Here's What the Big Fight over the DNC's Data Is Really About," *Huffington Post*, December 18, 2018, https://www.huffpost.com/entry/heres-what-the-big-fight-over-the-dncs-data-is-really-about_n_5c184f03e4b0432554c36e42.

34. Daniel Galvin, *Presidential Party Building: Dwight D. Eisenhower to George W. Bush* (Princeton, NJ: Princeton University Press, 2010); Brian Conley, "The Politics of Party Renewal: The 'Service Party' and the Origins of the Post-Goldwater Republican Right," *Studies in American Political Development* 27 (2013): 51–67.

35. Elaine Kamarck, "Assessing Howard Dean's Fifty State Strategy and the 2006 Midterm Elections," *Forum* 4, no. 3 (December 2006); Louis Jacobson, "Looking Back at Howard Dean's 50-State Strategy," *Governing*, May 6, 2013, https://www.governing.com/topics/politics/gov-democrat-howard-deans-fifty-state-strategy.html.

36. The DNC renewed a formal commitment to Dean's initiative in 2017 and again, with expanded funds, in 2021, though in practice it revived the monthly grants to state party organizations but not the deployment of paid staffers. Bill Barrow, "Dems Reach New Fundraising Deal, with BOOST for GOP States," Associated Press, May 12, 2021, https://apnews.com/article/jaime-harrison-joe-biden-campaigns-campaign-finance-donald-trump-ebe3ca311ebee0f002c471aa885efa13.

37. For calls to de-democratize candidate selection, see Seth Masket, "How to Improve the Primary Process? Make It Less Democratic," *Pacific Standard*, August 11, 2017, https://psmag.com/magazine/how-to-improve-the-primary-process; Elaine C. Kamarck, "Returning Peer Review to the Presidential Nomination Process," *New York University Law Review* 93 (2018): 709–27; Jonathan Rauch and Ray La Raja, "Too Much Democracy Is Bad for Democracy," *Atlantic*, December 2019, 62–68; Lawrence R. Jacobs, *Democracy under Fire: Donald Trump and the Breaking of American History* (New York: Oxford University Press, 2022), 163–88.

38. For a statement on parties' coordinating functions in candidate selection, see Julia Azari, "Kamala Harris Is Out. What Have We Learned about Party Politics?," *Mischiefs of Faction* (blog), December 3, 2019, https://www.mischiefsoffaction.com/post/kamala-harris-is-out-what-have-we-learned-about-party-politics.

39. Sam Adler-Bell, "The Democratic Party Is Wasting Its Grassroots Energy," *New York*, April 24, 2022, https://nymag.com/intelligencer/2022/04/the-democratic-party-is-wasting-its -grassroots-energy.html.

40. Angela Lang, Doran Schrantz, Gara LaMarche, and Tomas Robles, "Organizing Philanthropy," *The Forge*, June 17, 2021, https://forgeorganizing.org/article/organizing-philanthropy.

41. On the dynamics of education polarization, see Joshua N. Zingher, "Diploma Divide: Educational Attainment and the Realignment of the American Electorate," *Political Research Quarterly* 75 (2022): 263–77. For a longer view, see Herbert P. Kitschelt and Philipp Rehm, "Secular Partisan Realignment in the United States: The Socioeconomic Reconfiguration of White Partisan Support since the New Deal Era," *Politics & Society* 47 (2019): 425–79.

42. See, from somewhat different vantage points, Rich Yeselson, "Union Power after the Election," *Dissent*, November 25, 2020, https://www.dissentmagazine.org/online_articles /union-power-after-the-election; Gabriel Winant, "We Live in a Society," *n+1*, December 12, 2020, https://nplusonemag.com/online-only/online-only/we-live-in-a-society/; Harold Meyerson, "In 2023, Everyone Who Can Go Union Is Doing Just That," *American Prospect*, May 1, 2023, https://prospect.org/labor/05-01-2023-starbucks-amazon-teamsters-uaw-union-movement/; Newman and Skocpol, *Rust Belt Union Blues*.

43. On progressive groups' continued disinclination to fund sustained grassroots organizing, see a special issue of *The Forge*, edited (with much self-criticism) by outgoing Democracy Alliance president Gara LaMarche. "Philanthropy and Organizing," *The Forge*, July 17, 2021, https:// forgeorganizing.org/issues/philanthropy-organizing.

44. See, for example, Ezra Klein, "Can Democrats Find a Winning Message?," *New York Times*, October 10, 2021, SR4; Ian Ward, "The Democrats' Privileged College-Kid Problem," *Politico*, October 9, 2021, https://www.politico.com/news/magazine/2021/10/09/david-shor -democrats-privileged-college-kid-problem-514992. More than these critics, we emphasize the accommodationist virtues rather than the merits or demerits of public opinion polls in determining party positioning.

45. Raymond La Raja, "Democratic Party's Pluralism Is Both a Strength and Weakness," *The Conversation*, April 20, 2018, https://theconversation.com/democratic-partys-pluralism-is-both -a-strength-and-weakness-92649.

46. Sampriti Ganguli of Arabella Advisors, quoted in Emma Green, "The Massive Progressive Dark-Money Group You've Never Heard Of," *Atlantic*, November 2, 2021, https://www .theatlantic.com/politics/archive/2021/11/arabella-advisors-money-democrats/620553/.

47. Alex Shephard, "*The Daily Show*'s Rally to Restore Sanity Predicted a Decade of Liberal Futility," *New Republic*, December 27, 2019, https://newrepublic.com/article/155928/daily -shows-rally-restore-sanity-predicted-decade-liberal-futility; Dannagal Goldthwaite Young, *Irony and Outrage: The Polarized Landscape of Rage, Fear, and Laughter in the United States* (New York: Oxford University Press, 2019); Joseph Bernstein, "Bad News," *Harper's*, September 2021, 25–31; Theodore Schleifer, "Silicon Valley's Doomed Pursuit of D.C. Nirvana," *Puck*, January 18, 2022, https://puck.news/silicon-valleys-manchin-sinema-voting-rights-campaign/. For a good study that emphasizes "the highly asymmetric pattern of susceptibility to and diffusion of propaganda and bullshit in the American media ecosystem," see Yochai Benkler, Robert Faris, and Hal Roberts, *Network Propaganda: Manipulation, Disinformation, and Radicalization in American Politics* (New York: Oxford University Press, 2018).

48. Hersh, *Politics Is for Power*.

49. *Bush v. Gore* marked an inflection point. See, from a law professor who went on to the House of Representatives, where he served as an impeachment manager against Donald Trump in February 2021, Jamin B. Raskin, "Bandits in Black Robes," *Washington Monthly*, March 2001, 25–28.

50. On the accelerating exercise of politics via procedure, see Mark Tushnet, "Constitutional Hardball," *John Marshall Law Review* 32 (2004): 523–53; Joseph Fishkin and David E. Pozen, "Asymmetric Constitutional Hardball," *Columbia Law Review* 118 (2018): 915–82. A starting point for the new skepticism of the Constitution is Robert A. Dahl, *How Democratic Is the American Constitution?*, 2nd ed. (New Haven, CT: Yale University Press, 2003).

51. The maximalist version of this tendency is laid out in David Faris, *It's Time to Fight Dirty: How Democrats Can Build a Lasting Majority in American Politics* (New York: Melville House, 2018). See also Leah Greenberg and Ezra Levin, *We Are Indivisible: A Blueprint for Democracy after Trump* (New York: Atria/One Signal Publishers, 2019), 233–307, and unsigned note "Pack the Union: A Proposal to Admit New States for the Purpose of Amending the Constitution to Ensure Equal Representation," *Harvard Law Review* 133 (2020): 1049–70.

52. Drutman, *Breaking the Two-Party Doom Loop*; Garrett Epps, "How to Fix the Senate by Essentially—Though Not Quite—Abolishing It," *Washington Monthly*, January 3, 2022, https://washingtonmonthly.com/2022/01/03/how-to-fix-the-senate-by-essentially-though-not-quite-abolishing-it/.

53. Daniel Ziblatt, *Conservative Parties and the Birth of Democracy* (New York: Cambridge University Press, 2017), 49. On the contingent dynamics of conservatives' turn to parliamentarism in western Europe, see Noel D. Cary, *The Path to Christian Democracy: German Catholics and the Party System from Windthorst to Adenauer* (Cambridge, MA: Harvard University Press, 1996); Stathis N. Kalyvas, *The Rise of Christian Democracy in Europe* (Ithaca, NY: Cornell University Press, 1996).

54. See, for a bird's-eye sketch, Steven Levitsky and Daniel Ziblatt, *How Democracies Die* (New York: Crown, 2018), 206–8, 222–26.

55. For samplings, see Jeff Flake, *Conscience of a Conservative: A Rejection of Destructive Politics and a Return to Principle* (New York: Random House, 2017); Charles J. Sykes, *How the Right Lost Its Mind* (New York: St. Martin's Press, 2017); Max Boot, *The Corrosion of Conservatism: Why I Left the Right* (New York: Liveright, 2018); Stuart Stevens, *It Was All a Lie: How the Republican Party Became Donald Trump* (New York: Alfred A. Knopf, 2020). With a comparative lens, see Anne Applebaum, *Twilight of Democracy: The Seductive Lure of Authoritarianism* (New York: Doubleday, 2020). For a sympathetic study, see Robert P. Saldin and Steven M. Teles, *Never Trump: The Revolt of the Conservative Elites* (New York: Oxford University Press, 2020).

56. Steven Teles and Robert Saldin emphasize the importance of building up the organizational capacity of moderate party factions, though they leave unclear what should distinguish moderate Republicans from moderate Democrats. Steven Teles and Robert Saldin, "The Future Is Faction," Niskanen Center, November 25, 2019, https://www.niskanencenter.org/the-future-is-faction/.

57. Ripon Society, *From Disaster to Distinction: The Rebirth of the Republican Party* (New York: Pocket Books, 1966); Ross Douthat and Reihan Salam, *Grand New Party: How Republicans Can Win the Working Class and Save the American Dream* (New York: Doubleday, 2008).

58. Brink Lindsay, Steve Teles, Will Wilkinson, and Samuel Hammond, "The Center Can Hold: Public Policy for an Age of Extremes," Niskanen Center, December 2018, https://www.niskanencenter.org/wp-content/uploads/old_uploads/2018/12/Niskanen-vision-paper-final-PDF.pdf, 2.

59. The unrootedness of this ideological tradition is a major theme in Geoffrey Kabaservice, *Rule and Ruin: The Downfall of Moderation and the Destruction of the Republican Party, from Eisenhower to the Tea Party* (New York: Oxford University Press, 2012); Nicol C. Rae, *The Decline and Fall of the Liberal Republicans from 1952 to the Present* (New York: Oxford University Press, 1989).

60. Kristoffer Smemo, "The Making of "Liberal" Republicans during the New Deal Order," in *Beyond the New Deal Order: U.S. Politics from the Great Depression to the Great Recession,*

ed. Gary Gerstle, Nelson Lichtenstein and Alice O'Connor (Philadelphia: University of Pennsylvania Press, 2019), 54–70.

61. Clinton Rossiter, *Parties and Politics in America* (Ithaca, NY: Cornell University Press, 1960), 115, 118.

62. William L. Hershey and John C. Green, *Mr. Chairman: The Life and Times of Ray C. Bliss* (Akron: University of Akron Press, 2017), 61–62; Kabaservice, *Rule and Ruin*, 134.

63. Hershey and Green, *Mr. Chairman*, 52, 110.

64. Ray C. Bliss, "The Role of the State Chairman," in *Politics U.S.A.: A Practical Guide to the Winning of Public Office*, ed. James M. Cannon (Garden City, NY: Doubleday, 1960), 160.

65. Ripon Society, *From Disaster to Distinction*, 79–94.

66. There are sporadic examples at the state level of Blissist Republican forces emerging in the aftermath of particularly destructive rule by Long New Right exponents. See, for example, Eric Levitz, "Kansas Just Proved That a Better GOP Is Possible, *New York*, January 9, 2020, https://nymag.com/intelligencer/2020/01/kansas-medicaid-expansion-plan-republican-party.html.

67. We offer no specific recommendations concerning the complex question of tactical voting among residents of Republican strongholds who seek to strengthen democracy. And while we oppose intervening in opposing parties' nomination fights against those who robustly defend democracy—as when the Democratic Congressional Campaign Committee sought to defeat Peter Meijer, a Michigan Republican who voted to impeach Donald Trump, in favor of a Trump-backed candidate in 2022—not every case is as clear-cut. Sarah Ferris and Ally Mutnick, "House Dems Berate Campaign Arm for 'Very Dangerous' GOP Primary Scheme," *Politico*, July 27, 2022, https://www.politico.com/news/2022/07/27/meijer-dccc-trump-primaries-00048104.

68. Lee Drutman argues that the transformation of the political system into a proportional multiparty system—while admittedly a tall order—offers a more plausible solution than realignment to the current democratic crisis. While we take no position on the merits of his prescription, our read of the long historical saga of moderate Republicanism suggests that rule changes alone, however sweeping, are insufficient to empower a center-right that will abandon the extremes and protect democracy. Lee Drutman, "Moderation, Realignment, or Transformation? Evaluating Three Approaches to America's Crisis of Democracy," *Annals of the American Academy of Political and Social Science* 699 (2022): 158–74.

69. See David Leonhardt, "Republicans for Democracy," *New York Times*, January 6, 2022, https://www.nytimes.com/2022/01/06/briefing/republicans-democracy-capitol-attack.html. Our view echoes David A. Bateman, "Elections, Polarization, and Democratic Resilience," in *Democratic Resilience: Can the United States Withstand Rising Polarization*, ed. Robert C. Lieberman, Suzanne Mettler, and Kenneth M. Roberts (New York: Cambridge University Press, 2022), esp. 366–68.

70. This language is deliberately meant to evoke the broad coalition against fascism. On affinities between the vision of the contemporary American Right and classical fascism, see John Ganz, "From Gods to Monsters," *New Statesman*, June 9, 2022, https://www.newstatesman.com/ideas/2022/06/the-new-nationalism-of-the-us-right. See, more generally, Geoff Eley, "What Is Fascism and Where Does It Come From?" *History Workshop Journal* 91 (2021): 1–28.

71. For thinking along notably similar lines to ours from a leading New Democrat, see Simon Rosenberg, "Memo: Get to 55, Expanding Our Coalition, The Youth Opportunity," *Hopium Chronicles*, March 9, 2023, https://simonwdc.substack.com/p/memo-get-to-55-expanding-our-coalition.

72. This emphasis on majority-making resonates with the concerns of Timothy Shenk, *Realigners: Partisan Hacks, Political Visionaries, and the Struggle to Rule American Democracy* (New York: Farrar, Straus & Giroux, 2022).

73. Muirhead, *Promise of Party in a Polarized Age.*

74. Martin Van Buren, *The Autobiography of Martin Van Buren*, vol. 2 (Washington, DC: Government Printing Office, 1918), 125.

75. E. E. Schattschneider, *Party Government* (New York: Farrar & Rhinehart, 1942), 3, 4.

76. E. E. Schattschneider, *The Struggle for Party Government* (College Park: University of Maryland Press, 1948), 12.

Appendix One

1. Alexis de Tocqueville, *Democracy in America*, ed. J. P. Mayer, trans. George Lawrence (New York: Harper & Row, 1966), 175.

2. This facet of party concerns itself with how parties seek to raise money rather than how they spend it, where parties are hemmed in by changing legal rules, communications technologies, and decisions by outside groups. For a nice framework, see David C. W. Parker and John J. Coleman, "Pay to Play: Parties, Interests, and Money in Federal Elections," in *The Medium and the Message: Television Advertising and American Elections*, ed. Kenneth M. Goldstein and Patricia Strach (Upper Saddle River, NJ: Prentice Hall, 2004), 126–54.

3. Though we do not list immigration—primarily a state issue in the nineteenth century and one whose salience has been episodic—as a core party facet, the same story of increasing correspondence across issue dimensions holds there as well. See James A. Morone, *Republic of Wrath: How American Politics Turned Tribal, from George Washington to Donald Trump* (New York: Basic Books, 2020). On immigration politics over time, see Daniel Tichenor, *Dividing Lines: The Politics of Immigration Control over Time* (Princeton, NJ: Princeton University Press, 2002). Similarly, the sharp divides between pre- and post-suffrage gender politics limit comparison across time.

Appendix Two

1. For an excellent account that takes the latter tack, thus offering a useful analytical contrast, see David A. Bateman, *Disenfranchising Democracy: Constructing the Electorate in the United States, United Kingdom, and France* (New York: Cambridge University Press, 2018).

2. We proceed in a very different direction from the ones suggested by the essays in Jeffery A. Jenkins, Nolan McCarty, and Charles Stewart III, eds., "Causal Inference and American Political Development," special issue, *Public Choice* 185, no. 3–4 (2020): 245–511. The idea, if the academic division of labor works correctly, is that our admittedly messy attempts to make sense of complex historical developments should offer readers jumping-off points for thinking about explicit hypothesis-testing.

3. See Adam Sheingate, "Institutional Dynamics and American Political Development," *Annual Review of Political Science* 17 (2014): 461–77; Kathleen Thelen and James Conran, "Institutional Change," in *The Oxford Handbook of Historical Institutionalism*, ed. Orfeo Fioretos, Tulia G. Falleti, and Adam Sheingate (New York: Oxford University Press, 2016), 51–70. In addition, our attention to actors' *interests* more than *identities* distinguishes us from the tradition represented in, for example, Daniel Martinez HoSang and Joseph E. Lowndes, *Producers, Parasites, Patriots: Race and the New Right-Wing Politics of Precarity* (Minneapolis: University of Minnesota Press, 2019).

4. Although we do not follow their rational-choice methodology, our approach owes much to Robert H. Bates, Avner Greif, Margaret Levi, Jean-Laurent Rosenthal, and Barry R. Weingast, *Analytic Narratives* (Princeton, NJ: Princeton University Press, 1998).

5. Quoted in Thomas H. O'Connor, *The Boston Irish: A Political History* (Boston: Back Bay Books, 1995), xviii.

6. Indeed, sources that we reject as scholarly interpretation can illuminate actors' world-views. For instance, while Ronald Radosh, *Divided They Fell: The Decline of the Democratic Party* (New York: Free Press, 1996) strikes us as tendentious, it helpfully distills the viewpoint of traditionalist Democrats unhappy with the transformations of the 1960s.

7. This approach has been used repeatedly and impressively by David Mayhew, along with many of his students. On party politics, see, for example, David Mayhew, *Placing Parties in American Politics: Organization, Electoral Settings, and Government Activity in the Twentieth Century* (Princeton, NJ: Princeton University Press, 1986); Philip A. Klinkner, *The Losing Parties: Out-Party National Committees, 1956–1993* (New Haven, CT: Yale University Press, 1994); John Gerring, *Party Ideologies in America, 1828–1996* (New York: Cambridge University Press, 1998); Daniel J. Galvin, *Presidential Party Building: Dwight D. Eisenhower to George W. Bush* (Princeton, NJ: Princeton University Press, 2010); Daniel DiSalvo, *Engines of Change: Party Factions in American Politics, 1868–2010* (New York: Oxford University Press, 2012). By the same token, given our close textual analysis, we do not employ "big data," though large-N studies of speeches, pamphlets, and platforms across American political history offer ample opportunity to advance many of the themes discussed here. See, for example, Daniel J. Hopkins, Eric Schickler, and David L. Azizi, "From Many Divides, One? The Polarization and Nationalization of American State Party Platforms, 1918–2017," *Studies in American Political Development* 36 (2022): 1–20.

8. V. O. Key Jr., *Politics, Parties and Pressure Groups*, 5th ed. (New York: Crowell, 1964).

9. John J. Coleman, "Resurgent or Just Busy? Party Organizations in Contemporary America," in *The State of the Parties: The Changing Role of Contemporary American Parties*, ed. Daniel M. Shea and John C. Green, 2nd ed. (Lanham, MD: Rowman & Littlefield, 1996), 380.

10. Similarly, see Matt Grossmann and David A. Hopkins, *Asymmetric Politics: Ideological Republicans and Group Interest Democrats* (New York: Oxford University Press, 2016), though we do not see Republicans as simply motivated by ideology and Democrats by group loyalty.

11. John H. Aldrich, *Why Parties? A Second Look* (Chicago: University of Chicago Press, 2011); Marty Cohen, David Karol, Hans Noel, and John Zaller, *The Party Decides: Presidential Nominations before and after Reform* (Chicago: University of Chicago Press, 2008); Kathleen Bawn, Marty Cohen, David Karol, Seth Masket, Hans Noel, and John Zaller, "A Theory of Parties: Groups, Policy Demands, and Nominations in American Politics," *Perspectives on Politics* 10 (2012): 571–97. In their review, Nolan McCarty and Eric Schickler emphasize the "distinctive roles and capacities of office holders and voters in shaping the party." "On the Theory of Parties," *Annual Review of Political Science* 21 (2018): 177.

12. Paul Herrnson, "The Roles of Party Organizations, Party-Connected Committees, and Party Allies in Elections," *Journal of Politics* 71 (2009): 1207–24. On party brands, see Boris Heersink, *National Party Organizations and Party Brands in American Politics: The Democratic and Republican National Committees, 1912–2016* (New York: Oxford University Press, 2023).

13. To be sure, many analysts interpreting partisan change over time chiefly in terms of parties' responses to social and electoral shifts leave analytical space for motivations other than vote seeking to drive developments, particularly through struggles between party factions. Mark D. Brewer and Jeffrey M. Stonecash, *Dynamics of American Political Parties* (New York: Cambridge University Press, 2009); Robert Mason, *The Republican Party and American Politics from Hoover to Reagan* (New York: Cambridge University Press, 2011).

14. Once formally nominated and elected by duped and distracted voters, the group theorists argue, engaged elites pursue relatively extreme agendas in office, which helps explain the sustained absence of convergence to the median voter in American elections. It is a testament to the cold-eyed, disillusioned bent of the UCLA school's work that the authors' normative

conclusions have ranged from ambivalence to cautious endorsement of this very system and the structuring role that parties play in it. See Cohen, Karol, Noel, and Zaller, *Party Decides*, 360–63; Bawn, Cohen, Karol, Masket, Noel, and Zaller, "A Theory of Parties," 589–91; Marty Cohen, David Karol, Hans Noel, and John Zaller, "Party versus Faction in the Reformed Presidential Nominating System, *PS: Political Science & Politics* 49 (2016): 707–8. For a good overview of what a group-oriented view means in practice, see David Karol, "Party Activists, Interests Groups, and Polarization in American Politics," in *American Gridlock: The Sources, Character, and Impact of Political Polarization*, ed. James A. Thurber and Antoine Yashinaka (New York: Cambridge University Press, 2015), 68–85.

15. David Karol, *Party Position Change in American Politics: Coalition Management* (New York: Cambridge University Press, 2009); Hans Noel, *Political Ideologies and Political Parties in America* (New York: Cambridge University Press, 2013).

16. The emphasis on nomination traces back at least to Nelson W. Polsby, *Consequences of Party Reform* (New York: Oxford University Press, 1983). See also David A. Hopkins, "This 37-Year-Old Book Helps the Long Democratic Primary Make Sense," Monkey Cage, *Washington Post*, March 21, 2020, https://www.washingtonpost.com/politics/2020/03/21/this-37-year-old -book-helps-long-democratic-primary-make-sense/. For a good recent application using nominations as a framework, see Hans J. G. Hassell, *The Party's Primary: Control of Congressional Nominations* (New York: Cambridge University Press, 2018).

17. Coordination looms larger for some party formulations than for others. It is essential, for example, to understand the traditional political organizations in what we term the accommodationist strand but far less important to understand the populist and radical strands on the extremes.

18. In this sense, we broadly follow in the tradition of responsible party government that Schattschneider and others propounded at midcentury, most famously in the 1950 report of the American Political Science Association's Committee on Political Parties. For assessments, at times mechanistic, of contemporary party practices and their relationship to specific midcentury responsible-party prescriptions, see John Kenneth White and Jerome M. Mileur, eds., *Challenges to Party Government* (Carbondale: Southern Illinois University Press, 1992); John C. Green and Paul S. Herrnson, eds., *Responsible Partisanship? The Evolution of American Political Parties since 1950* (Lawrence: University Press of Kansas, 2002). On the 1950 report, see Mark Wickham-Jones, *Whatever Happened to Party Government: Controversies in American Political Science* (Ann Arbor: University of Michigan Press, 2018). For a recent revival of the doctrine's Westminster-philia and celebration of internally disciplined parties, see Frances McCall Rosenbluth and Ian Shapiro, *Responsible Parties: Saving Democracy from Itself* (New Haven, CT: Yale University Press, 2018).

19. Russell J. Dalton, David M. Farrell, and Ian McAllister, "Parties and Representative Government," in *Political Parties and Democratic Linkage: How Parties Organize Democracy*, ed. Russell J. Dalton, David M. Farrell, and Ian McAllister (New York: Oxford University Press, 2011), 3–27.

20. In particular, the UCLA approach and ours share a deep similarity in treating party politics as the work of contending actors wanting things from the state. But we go beyond the overarching category of "intense policy demanders" to explore the players' internal dynamics, asking what particular actors want given their historical circumstances. And we look outward to parties' roles, expressed differently across time and space, in shaping state and society. We, too, see politics as group conflict, but like E. E. Schattschneider we emphasize the distinctive qualities of party in mediating that conflict—and add to Schattschneider a close attention to the variance across parties' goals and relations to their claimants. Rather than explicitly going against or adding to the UCLA approach, then, this book largely accepts its central premises— but then proceeds in very different directions.

21. Self-identified "new realist" scholars, emphasizing parties' roles as gatekeepers, are starkest in their characterization of today's parties as weak; see, for example, Nathaniel Persily, ed., *Solutions to Political Polarization in America* (New York: Cambridge University Press, 2015). In a series of writings, Julia Azari has dichotomized weak parties and strong partisanship and explored the combination of the two; see Julia Azari, "Weak Parties and Strong Partisanship Are a Bad Combination," *Vox*, November 3, 2016, https://www.vox.com/mischiefs-of-faction/2016/11/3/13512362/weak-parties-strong-partisanship-bad-combination.

22. Our concern with the relationship between social structure and parties, and our attention to the porous boundaries between movement and party politics, also place us in dialogue with sociologists who study parties. For a review, see Stephanie L. Mudge and Anthony S. Chen, "Political Parties and the Sociological Imagination: Past, Present, and Future Directions," *Annual Review of Sociology* 40 (2014): 305–30. For a recent example in this tradition, see Adam Slez, *The Making of the Populist Movement: State, Market, and Party on the Western Frontier* (New York: Oxford University Press, 2020). For a neo-Gramscian view, see Cedric de Leon, Manali Desai, and Cihan Tugal, eds., *Building Blocs: How Parties Organize Society* (Stanford, CA: Stanford University Press, 2015).

23. See Suzanne Mettler and Richard Valelly, "Introduction: The Distinctiveness and Necessity of American Political Development," in *The Oxford Handbook of American Political Development*, ed. Richard Valelly, Suzanne Mettler, and Robert Lieberman (New York: Oxford University Press, 2016). For three earlier books in the APD tradition that we take as models and that also speak directly to political parties and political history, see Steven P. Erie, *Rainbow's End: Irish-Americans and the Dilemmas of Urban Machine Politics, 1840–1985* (Berkeley: University of California Press, 1987); Richard M. Valelly, *Radicalism in the States: The Minnesota Farmer-Labor Party and the American Political Economy* (Chicago: University of Chicago Press, 1989); Martin Shefter, *Political Parties and the State* (Princeton, NJ: Princeton University Press, 1994).

24. Karen Orren and Stephen Skowronek, *The Search for American Political Development* (New York: Cambridge University Press, 2004).

25. Rogers M. Smith, "Beyond Tocqueville, Myrdal, and Hartz: The Multiple Traditions in America," *American Political Science Review* 87 (1993): 549–66.

26. On disciplinary differences, see Richard John, "American Political Development and Political History," in Valelly, Mettler, and Lieberman, *The Oxford Handbook of American Political Development*; Ira Katznelson, "On (Lost and Found) Analytical History in Political Science," in *History in the Humanities and Social Sciences*, ed. Richard Bourke and Quentin Skinner (Cambridge: Cambridge University Press, 2023), 260–85.

27. The rise of social and then cultural history generally, and the revolution in labor history spurred by E. P. Thompson and others in the 1960s more specifically, prompted this turn to the politics of the everyday. E. P. Thompson, *The Making of the English Working Class* (London: Victor Gollancz, 1963). For an account of the scholarly turn, see Daniel T. Rodgers, *Age of Fracture* (Cambridge, MA: Belknap Press of Harvard University Press, 2011), 77–110.

28. Notable examples include Alan Brinkley, *Voices of Protest: Huey Long, Father Coughlin, and the Great Depression* (New York: Alfred A. Knopf, 1982); Robin D. G. Kelley, *Hammer and Hoe: Alabama Communists during the Great Depression* (Chapel Hill: University of North Carolina Press, 1990); Lisa McGirr, *Suburban Warriors: The Origins of the New American Right* (Princeton, NJ: Princeton University Press, 2001).

29. Similarly, the burgeoning, and invaluable, literature on the history of American capitalism has generally paid insufficient heed to specifically political questions, still less to the intricacies of party politics. The task of bringing together insights from American political development and political history with those from the history of capitalism ought to engage future scholars from varying perspectives and paradigms. For overviews, see Sven Beckert, "History of

American Capitalism," in *American History Now*, ed. Eric Foner and Lisa McGirr (Philadelphia: Temple University Press, 2011), 314–45; Sven Beckert and Christine Desan, introduction to *American Capitalism: New Histories*, ed. Beckert and Desan (New York: Columbia University Press, 2019), 1–32. For a synthetic history, see Jonathan Levy, *Ages of American Capitalism: A History of the United States* (New York: Random House, 2021).

30. The essays in Paula Baker and Donald T. Critchlow, eds., *The Oxford Handbook of American Political History* (New York: Oxford University Press, 2020), attest to the continuing vitality of this tradition.

INDEX

abolitionism, 23, 45, 48–54; free labor Republicanism and, 57, 60, 61–62
Abood v. Detroit Board of Education (1977), 166
abortion, 165, 170, 187, 188, 217, 255
Abramoff, Jack, 172, 226
Abzug, Bella, 143, 165
accommodationist strand, 14–15; coalition-building central to, 19, 28; decline of, 20, 217; in Democratic politics, 69, 111, 114, 125–26, 138, 183, 189, 190, 213, 218, 219; disruption and violence linked to, 39, 41; during Gilded Age, 79, 80; Jacksonian version of, 23, 28, 40; machine politics linked to, 19, 38, 84, 85, 106, 127; under New Deal order, 23; nostalgia for, 258; policy-reform strand and, 17; postbellum, 74, 75; pro-capitalist strand distinguished from, 10; Progressive attacks on, 107; in Republican politics, 58, 75, 76, 146, 156, 167, 222, 224, 273; slavery and, 54
ActBlue (fundraising platform), 214
Adams, Charles Francis, 53, 86
Adams, Henry, 13
Adams, John, 30, 31
Adams, John Quincy, 13, 33, 35, 47, 49
Addams, Jane, 84, 103, 104, 105
Affordable Care Act (2010), 211, 223
Afghanistan War, 205
African Americans, 44–45, 72–74, 103, 117, 126–27, 142, 143, 189–91, 192, 201; in elected office, 73, 143, 190, 213
Agnew, Spiro, 178
Aid to Families with Dependent Children (AFDC), 202

Ailes, Roger, 229, 232–33
Air America (radio network), 207
Albany Argus (newspaper), 33
Albany Regency, 32–33, 35, 37, 59
Allen, Richard V., 171
Allison, R. Bruce, 140
Amazon (corporation), 254
American Bimetallic League, 92
American Civil Liberties Union (ACLU), 213
American Conservative Union (ACU), 155, 160, 161, 162, 164
American Council of Christian Churches, 151
American Energy Alliance, 240
American Enterprise Institute, 161
American Federation of Labor (AF of L), 88, 90
American Federation of Labor-Congress of Industrial Organizations (AFL-CIO), 120, 130, 137–38, 191, 208
American Federation of State, County and Municipal Employees (AFSCME), 262
American Indian Movement, 140
American Labor Party (ALP), 121
American Legislative Exchange Council (ALEC), 149, 161, 164, 242–43
American Party (Know Nothings), 62
American political development (APD), 21–22, 292
American Political Science Association (APSA), 124, 126
American Recovery and Reinvestment Act (2009), 211
Americans for Democratic Action (ADA), 119, 121, 130

397

PRINCETON STUDIES IN AMERICAN POLITICS

Historical, International, and Comparative Perspectives

*Paul Frymer, Suzanne Mettler, and
Eric Schickler, Series Editors*

*Ira Katznelson, Theda Skocpol, Martin Shefter,
Founding Series Editors*